Under the General Editorship of

GORDON N. RAY

The University of Illinois

The English Novel

A PANORAMA

Lionel Stevenson

DUKE UNIVERSITY

HOUGHTON MIFFLIN COMPANY · BOSTON

𝔗𝔥𝔢 ℜ𝔦𝔳𝔢𝔯𝔰𝔦𝔡𝔢 𝔓𝔯𝔢𝔰𝔰 ℭ𝔞𝔪𝔟𝔯𝔦𝔡𝔤𝔢

The Riverside Press
Cambridge, Massachusetts
Printed in the U.S.A.

Contents

Contents

INTRODUCTION

What Is a Novel ?

THE TELLING OF STORIES is the oldest of all the arts. And ever since its earliest stage it must have taken two forms. One is the brief narrative that can be recounted on a single occasion. Thence emerged the fairy tale, the folk ballad, and eventually what is now called the short story. The other form is longer and more complex, requiring a series of sessions for its delivery. From it descended the saga, the epic, and finally the novel.

When a primitive man told a story, it could have no permanent survival in its original form. If it was effective enough to be remembered beyond the first utterance, the gist of it would have to be put into new words each time it was repeated, whether by its originator or by a hearer. With the development of poetic forms, however, the memory was aided by various devices — rhythm, tune, and such patterning of words as rhyme and alliteration; and thus a story could be transmitted with little alteration from place to place and from one generation to another. Hence the only "literature" that acquired permanence was embodied in verse. For centuries narrative poetry was the basic form of literary art.

The invention of writing at last made possible the perpetuating of extensive compositions in prose; but as long as this vehicle remained restricted to a scholarly minority, the material that was written in prose was mainly of an intellectual nature — history, philosophy, oratory, and so forth. The stories that gave pleasure to the masses of people, on all social levels, were still recited and listened to, and therefore continued to be in verse.

In addition to the monotonous recitation of a single entertainer, however, a more complex process emerged — the drama. When city life developed, so that large groups could easily and frequently assemble, the drama evolved as a vehicle that made stories more vivid than straight narration could. In ancient Greece and Rome, and again in western Europe during the Renaissance, the stage became the medium by which the greatest creative authors presented their stories to the largest number with the maximum of effect. The audience, by responding emotionally to the physical presence of the actors, entered into the reality of the events.

Nevertheless, drama had limitations. Because of its ritualistic origins, it only gradually freed itself from traditions of formality and dignity. Not until the late sixteenth century did English drama begin to present stories with anything approaching resemblance to real human experience. And other, more insuperable handicaps remained. Only certain types of situation could be shown upon the stage, owing to its physical limitations of space, the restricted personnel of a theatrical company, and the brief time in which the whole plot must be deployed. Its expensive, immovable mechanism meant that the theater could be enjoyed only by the relatively few people who were in the right place at the right time to attend a performance.

The drama, therefore, though it achieved an immense improvement over other forms of narrative in structure and characterization, could not deal with the wide range of time and place, and the complicated relationship of events, which are often essential for the presentation of a story. The dramatists of the Elizabethan age struggled valiantly against these restrictions, but could not vanquish them; and by the time the theaters were closed by the Puritans in 1642, the great creative age of English drama was already at an end because there was nothing new for a playwright to accomplish.

There remained the need for a form of narration that could encompass all sorts of action with a maximum of vividness, so as to rival the drama in its illusion of reality, and yet be available to every person everywhere. After the invention of printing this was gradually made possible by the large-scale distribution of books and the concurrent extension of literacy. A story could now have wide circulation and popular appeal when embodied in prose. For purposes of listening, verse had been easier than prose; but on the printed page its patterns distracted the reader's attention, and verse came to be regarded as an artificial and difficult form of communication.

The adoption of prose, in turn, produced a change in the handling of narrative material. Familiar details could be included, and the natural phrases and rhythms of everyday speech could be reproduced. Prose began to perform the same function in promoting the illusion of reality that had been contributed to drama by the physical presence of the actor, his gestures and inflections, and the costumes and stage settings. Prose narrative moved out of the realm of historical exposition, which it had held from the time of Herodotus to that of Clarendon, and started to talk to readers about themselves and their surroundings. It is more than a coincidence that the history of the English novel begins at the same time as the history of journalism.

I have been discussing "story-telling" without mentioning the word "fiction." The discrimination of fact from invention is a comparatively recent idea. No matter how much of the supernatural or the incredible occurred in his tale, every early story-teller claimed to be reporting only the truth. Probably each story did originate in an actual event, but in the course of transmission it became expanded and exaggerated by superstition, confusion of memory, and the sheer artistic instinct to make a good story better. Honestly convinced that he was repeating the tale essentially as he first heard it, the narrator would nevertheless contribute his share of elaboration and distortion. Yet Homer and Virgil were accepted as strict historians, Sir Thomas Malory cited sources for his tales, the compiler of travelers' yarns who called himself Sir John Mandeville insisted that he was soberly reporting his own observation. "The old chronicles tell us" or "I found it in an ancient book" was the conventional opening for a story and sanctioned any sort of fantastic episode. Even

Shakespeare and his fellow-dramatists set no store by "originality"; the author would feel flattered rather than embarrassed if he could see modern editions of his plays which demonstrate how faithfully *Richard III* followed Holinshed, or *Julius Caesar* followed Plutarch, or *Romeo and Juliet* followed Brooke (who followed Bandello).

The theory that a story-teller should invent his own plot and characters is an outgrowth of the past two or three centuries. Previously, though it was in days when popular stories were at the furthest remove from probability and familiar experience, the gravest insult to a story-teller would be the accusation of inventing his tale: this would imply that he had run out of material and was too ignorant to find more. Nowadays, though the objective of almost every author is to achieve "realism" by any possible device, the unforgivable affront is to charge him with lack of originality. No matter how often a standard plot has been used, each author must pretend that it is altogether his own. The concept of "fiction," then, is essentially a modern development.

The foregoing discussion provides the elements for a definition of what is ordinarily understood to be "a novel," namely, that it is a long, fictitious, prose narrative. The word "long" is necessarily relative. As a pragmatic distinction, a "short story" can be heard or read at a single sitting, whereas a "novel" extends through an indefinite number of sessions. This original difference came to be reinforced by later influences: a short story is usually one of several items in a magazine, which satisfies its customers by providing as much diversity as possible, whereas a novel has to be long enough to make a volume by itself, of sufficient bulk to justify its cost. Through these external pressures, two clearly unlike techniques were developed: the short story has a single action, with unity of mood and strict limitation of characters; the novel is expected to have a slower tempo, a wider range of character and scene, and a more complex action. In practice, the maximum length of a short story is perhaps 10,000 words; the minimum length of a novel, perhaps 70,000. Various authors have experimented with works in the intervening area, and some of these have proved to be excellent achievements; but they are so few in proportion to the other two types, and their media of publication are so restricted, that not even a satisfactory name for such stories has been accepted. The term "novelette" has acquired a contemptuous connotation, and "long short story" is absurd.

The inclusion of the word "prose" in our definition of the novel is also pragmatic. Some historians of fiction insist that Chaucer displayed all the talents and techniques of the novelist and that his *Troilus and Criseyde* should be termed the first English novel. In the past century a few competent writers have produced what they described as "novels in verse," some of which enjoyed temporary success, such as Elizabeth Barrett Browning's *Aurora Leigh* and Owen Meredith's *Lucile*. But, in the long run, the assumption that a novel is an imitation of experience is incompatible with the formalities of phrase and patterning that are inherent in verse. At its best, a novel in verse is unconvincing; when not at its best, it is ludicrous. With the sole exception of *Don Juan*, it must be regarded as a bastard genre inheriting the worst traits of both parents.

The description of a novel as "a long, fictitious, prose narrative" is adequate for the purposes of a publisher classifying his trade list, a bookseller arranging his counter, a librarian assigning shelf numbers. In terms of literary history and critical evaluation, however, further criteria have emerged. These can be understood only by tracing the process of their development, as will be done in the subsequent pages of this book.

The essential quality for an acceptable novel is the illusion of reality. This does not mean the exclusion of everything fantastic or supernatural; when such elements are present, the author merely faces a severer test of his ability to induce the "willing suspension of disbelief." Acceptance of the requirement does demand, however, the subordination of ulterior purposes. If a work of fiction is obviously intended primarily for didactic or satiric ends, the author does not want his reader's attention misled by too much illusion of reality. *Gulliver's Travels* and *Erewhon*, though among the masterpieces of prose fiction, are not novels. None the less, a writer's creative imagination sometimes takes hold so tyrannically that in something intended for parody, such as *Don Quixote*, or for moral instruction, such as *The Pilgrim's Progress*, the original purpose is almost obliterated by the sheer plausibility of the events. This plausibility in its turn depends upon the portrayal of character. No matter how believable the action may be in itself, it does not win the reader's full credulity unless it is performed by distinct individuals who are recognizable in terms of our experience. Conversely, he will believe in action that is inherently impossible, so long as the participants behave in a natural manner. The supremacy of characterization had long been recognized in drama before novelists discovered that they could handle it more effectively because they were not confined to external manifestations only and to a few brief disconnected scenes.

Considered as a work of art, a piece of fiction cannot be regarded as a novel unless it has unity of structure. Many stories that possess lifelike characterization are invalidated by being a series of episodes, each virtually complete in itself, which could be rearranged in any order without diminishing the effect. Here again the novel learned from its predecessors, for not only the drama but also the epic had achieved structural unity long before, and from Aristotle onward the critics had talked about conflict, suspense, and climax. When the writers of fiction became aware of these principles they ceased to string together picaresque adventures and began to build the vast and complex fabric of the novel with architectural proportions.

When these specifications of structural unity, individualized characters, and the pre-eminent illusion of reality are added to the basic traits of long, fictitious, prose narrative, we realize that the novel cannot be considered a distinctive literary genre until the eighteenth century. There still remains the question why it immediately became — and has continued for two hundred years to be — the most appropriate vehicle for giving artistic expression to human experience.

Several reasons combine to explain this phenomenon. For one thing, a large new reading public came into existence as the middle class increased in numbers, education, and leisure. These were mainly literal-minded people with neither the scholarly background nor the imaginative responsiveness needed for appreciating poetry with its ornate style and oblique allusions. Practical men and women preferred to read something that was easy to understand both because it used simple language and because it dealt with material that was familiar to them. They were less interested in the heroic exploits of antique nobles than in the difficulties of people with whom they could identify themselves — a working girl such as Pamela or a well-meaning blunderer such as Tom Jones. They were particularly gratified when the story ended with the obtaining of wealth and domestic happiness, which were their own major goals in life. It is not an overstatement to say that the novel is primarily the literary medium of a bourgeois culture.

Secondly, the range of everyday experience was growing wider. The growth of cities, the improvement of travel facilities, the establishing of newspapers, and many other factors resulted in a more complex pattern of life. The average man or woman encountered a greater variety of people and faced a greater assortment of problems than ever before. A picture of contemporary life was no longer recognizable unless it embraced a throng of diversified characters and events, conveyed in the language of ordinary speech. In this sense, the novel can be described as the literary manifestation of modern urbanized relationships and social complexity.

A third reason for its emergence was implicit in the intellectual climate of the eighteenth century. The rationalistic, inductive methods of Bacon had eventuated not only in the various physical sciences but also in a scientific attitude of inquiry toward the workings of the mind and the structure of society. John Locke had promulgated his pragmatic theory of the human understanding, and Thomas Hobbes had analyzed politics and government as an anatomist would dissect a laboratory specimen. People thus became adjusted to the scientific procedures of diligent observation and precise records. This is just what Richardson or Fielding was doing when he accumulated an enormous hoard of details, many of them seemingly trivial, which added up into a revealing investigation of human nature and of the whole social system. The novel is thus the literary counterpart of the scientific rationalism that has dominated the thought of the modern era.

Paradoxically, then, whilst story-telling is the most ancient form of literary art, the novel is a very recent one. Until the invention of cinema, radio, and television, it was the most recent. They, in their turn, are now in the process of detaching themselves from the novel and other earlier forms of narration. It is one of the most interesting aspects of the history of the novel that we can observe the whole process of its evolution, instead of having to infer early stages for which no evidence survives. The first three chapters of the present study will scrutinize the varieties of long prose fiction in English prior to 1740, with a view to identifying the separate elements that gradually coalesced into what can properly be termed the novel.

A backward view over any historical process is bound to be distorted. Knowing the later developments, we select arbitrarily the beginnings and the influences that proved significant; and we sometimes perhaps become impatient with the slow and awkward functioning of the trial-and-error method by which the new form shapes itself. But the vitality of the novel derived chiefly from the fact that it was evolved by many authors of utterly different personalities and purposes, and that they were not handicapped by any prescribed critical canon. We should not make the mistake of beginning with a rigid present-day definition of the novel, by which we would measure all earlier works of prose fiction. Instead of the deductive fallacy, which adopts an absolute prototype and accepts or rejects every specimen on the basis of its conformity thereto, we must try to use the inductive approach; by examining the phenomena we can hope to arrive at a valid grasp of the general principle.

I

Pastoral and Picaresque

(to 1600)

PROBABLY THE MOST SUCCESSFUL of the books printed by William
Caxton in the closing years of the fifteenth century was Sir
Thomas Malory's *Morte Darthur.* This fact substantiates the
hypothesis that the preliminary conditions for the development
of prose fiction in England came into existence with the introduction of the printed book. Though Malory may have been merely
a conscientious historian, compiling material from the huge mass
of Arthurian romances, he seems to have worked rather in the
manner of a modern historical novelist, following his sources as
far as they were available and effective, but feeling free to invent details and to elaborate characters in order to give artistic
as well as factual validity.

Another popular work of prose narrative at the end of the
middle ages was *The Travels of Sir John Mandeville.* This
purported to be the actual experiences of an English knight who
ranged over most of Europe and Asia in the middle of the
fourteenth century. It was first written in Norman-French, supposedly in 1356, and the authorship remains uncertain. It was

11

translated into English about the beginning of the fifteenth century, and the first printed English edition was in 1496. Like Malory, the author derived most of his information from earlier sources — in this case, from travel narratives of varying degrees of authenticity; but there can be little doubt that he was consciously writing fiction, in his creation of the hero-narrator and in his invention of further adventures. The author's skill lay in his use of plausible detail to support even his most fantastic episodes.

It must be remembered that until recent times both Malory and Mandeville were read as genuine records of history and travel, in just the same way as John Froissart's *Chronicle* and other books of authentic history, all of which served to foster the taste for vigorous narrative of action and adventure.

Better recognized as artistic creation was the prose fiction written by Italian authors who were addressing themselves to cultivated audiences. The term "novella" to describe a prose story was in use early in the thirteenth century. The word is equivalent to the modern English "news" and the stories were not unlike the sensational items in a present-day newspaper, recounting concisely and impassively some shocking crime or some scandalous intrigue. Whether or not the early examples are indeed reports of actual occurrences, they are at any rate told in the matter-of-fact manner of a reporter. But before long the creative imagination entered into the grouping and linking of the stories and probably also into the invention of plots. Of the many such collections the most famous is Boccaccio's *Decameron*, written about 1350. Dealing with contemporary life, the stories departed from the flowery style and idealized plots of medieval romance, but their realism was limited by the artificial conventions of the courtly society they depicted. Stories of this type were known to Chaucer, providing him both with plots and with techniques; but he was not influenced by them to the extent of using prose for his narratives. The *novelle* cannot be regarded as closely akin to the novel of later centuries; because of their brevity and their simplicity of structure, they can be better classified as short stories.

With the coming of the Renaissance the writing of prose fiction on the Continent rose to greater prominence. The *Novelle* of Matteo Bandello were published in 1554; the *Heca-*

tommithi of Giraldi Cinthio in 1565; and the *Heptameron* of
the French queen Marguerite of Navarre (probably assisted by
men of letters at her court) was written before 1550 and printed
in 1558. One hundred and one tales from these sources were
brought out in English by William Painter in his *Palace of
Pleasure* (1566–67). The success of this book led to others:
Tragical Discourses, by Geoffrey Fenton (1567), contained thirteen tales from Bandello; *A Petite Palace of Pettie his Pleasure*,
by George Pettie (1576), derived its twelve tales from classical
myths but portrayed the gods and goddesses in a Renaissance
court atmosphere.

The stories were erotic and sadistic, full of violent crime and
abnormal passion. Such themes have universal appeal, especially
when they are provided with sophisticated, aristocratic characters
and a picturesque, exotic setting. The compilers, to be sure,
claimed the worthiest objectives. Fenton interlarded his lewd
passages with puritanical commendations of chastity, and Painter
said in his preface that

> the contents of these novels . . . offer rules for avoiding of vice
> and imitation of virtue to all estates. This book is a very court
> and palace for all sorts to fix their eyes therein, to view the devoirs
> of the noblest, the virtues of the gentlest, and the duties of the
> meanest.

In spite of such protestations, the popular response evoked a
startled protest from the serious-minded. Roger Ascham, Professor of Greek at Cambridge and tutor of Queen Elizabeth in
her girlhood, wrote bitterly in *The Schoolmaster* (1570):

> These be the enchantments of Circe, brought out of Italy to mar
> men's manners in England; much by example of ill life, but more
> by precepts of fond books, of late translated out of Italian into
> English, sold in every shop in London, commended by honest titles
> the sooner to corrupt honest manners, dedicated over boldly to
> virtuous and honorable personages, the easilier to beguile simple
> and innocent wits. Ten sermons at Paul's Cross do not so much
> good for moving men to true doctrine as one of those books do
> harm with enticing men to ill living.

Such condemnations probably did more to arouse interest in
the "fond books" than to suppress it. The vogue for these
stories is illustrated by what happened to George Gascoigne, a

dissipated Cambridge graduate, soldier, and duelist, whose writings were remarkably original and diversified. One of them was a short and witty novel, *The Adventures of Master F. J.* (1573), influenced by the Italian *novelle* but with a realistic setting in the north of England and a convincing fidelity to everyday life. The torrid love story would have been acceptable enough if presented with an Italian background, but the shock of its sudden localization was more than the reading public could stand. Gascoigne was obliged to rewrite the story as *The Pleasant Fable of Ferdinando Jeronimi and Leonora de Valasco,* "translated out of the Italian riding tales of Bartello."

Prose fiction, it is apparent, was not yet naturalized in England. Its arrival happened to coincide with the flowering of the drama, and therefore the Italian stories were used as sources of plots for plays rather than as models for imitation. The theater could reach a far wider audience than the printed page, and a successful playwright could expect more direct financial profits than a published author. Hence the most creative minds of the Elizabethan age devoted themselves to writing drama, whether or not their natural talent was particularly suited to that form of expression. The insatiable demand for new plays led them to ransack all available narratives and borrow from them the episodes and characters best suited for the stage.

As the Italian *novelle* have to be regarded as short stories, a different model can be identified as leading to the writing of long works of prose fiction. This was the leisurely and fanciful pastoral romance, which came into England from two sources. One was the Greek writers of the second century A.D. and their Latin imitators: *The Golden Ass,* by Apuleius (translated in 1556), *An Ethiopian History,* by Heliodorus (1569), and *Daphnis and Chloe,* by Longus (1587). The other source, a conventionalized outgrowth of the romances of chivalry, was the work of Italian and Hispanic authors of the sixteenth century. The best known of these books, *Arcadia,* by Jacopo Sannazaro, and *Diana Enamorada,* by Jorge de Montemayor, were familiar to many cultivated Englishmen before they were translated into English.

The outcome of these influences was a group of long prose stories that can be regarded as precursors of the novel. The earliest was *The Golden Aphrodite,* by John Grange, a law student, published in 1577. The scene is ancient Greece, and the deities of Olympus mingle with the wooings and duels of mortals; but the characters and their manners are recognizably English and Elizabethan. The style of writing is ornate and learned.

A more pretentious book was published the next year. This was *Euphues, or The Anatomy of Wit,* by John Lyly. The author was a good specimen of the new type of clever young man produced by the universities: well-read, confident in his literary ingenuity, and eager to win advancement through authorship. He had fixed his ambition upon the post of master of the revels, a court appointment that was gaining in importance with the burgeoning popularity of the drama. Undoubtedly his chief motive in writing *Euphues* was to call attention to his originality and brilliance, and in this he thoroughly succeeded. The subtitle of the book could be rephrased in modern parlance as "How to be Clever." Ostensibly, however, his purpose was to study human psychology and to set up models for the improvement of both manners and morals. In his dedicatory epistle he announced his intention of being sternly realistic:

> In all perfect works as well the fault as the face is shown. The fairest leopard is set down with his spots, the sweetest rose with his prickles, the finest velvet with his brack. Seeing then that in every counterfeit as well the blemish as the beauty is colored I hope I shall not incur the displeasure of the wise in that in the discourse of Euphues I have as well touched the vanities of his love as the virtues of his life. . . . For as every painter that shadoweth a man in all parts giveth every piece his just proportion, so he that deciphereth the qualities of the mind ought as well to show every humour in his kind as the other doth every part in his color.

The plot of the story is a simple triangle situation, and there is some evidence that it was based on an occurrence in Lyly's life at Oxford. Two friends fall in love with the same girl and go through much heart-searching before she solves their problem by marrying someone else. But this plot is a mere thread on which hang interminable conversations and letters on love, friendship, conduct, education, and religion. The author inveighs against drunkenness, atheism, sexual incontinence, and other immoralities. The characters are little more than mouthpieces for Lyly's ideas; there is no effort to give them individuality. The setting is equally vague. It is nominally Naples, and the hero is a Greek who is visiting Italy; but most of the names are Greek, in Latinized forms, and the locality is seldom described. To complicate the matter, part of the author's intention was to criticize contemporary English life, and so Naples was to be equated with London, and Athens with Oxford. It is not surprising that a modern reader is baffled in the effort to visualize either the places or the persons.

The success of *Euphues* was due partly to its being based on the "courtesy books" of Italian origin that were in great demand because the English were modeling themselves on the Continental ideal of the gentleman. Lyly was one of the first writers to realize that fiction can exert a social influence because it illustrates precepts in action instead of merely stating them in general terms. Specific proof is the vogue aroused by Lyly's artificial style. To display his cleverness he frolicked spectacularly with vocabulary, syntax, and metaphor. Almost every sentence was built upon antithesis or parallelism and adorned with similes or analogies. This florid, redundant style appealed so strongly to the Elizabethan love of color and extravagance that "Euphuism" became a fad among courtiers and their imitators.

In fact, the author discovered that his book was being enjoyed as an entertaining pastime rather than as a moral treatise. The mannerisms and the sentimental theme outweighed the self-proclaimed didacticism. On the other hand, the unfavorable reflections upon contemporary behavior aroused some annoyance. Lyly hastened to adjust himself to both reactions. Within two years he brought out a sequel, *Euphues and his England*, which was more romantic than moralistic and in which the praise of everything English was fulsome. In particular, Lyly had come to realize that an important segment of his public was feminine. Fifty years later Edward Blount wrote that "all our ladies were then his scholars, and that beauty in court who could not parley Euphuism was as little regarded as she which now there speaks not French." The second book, therefore, retained no trace of the diatribes against women that had been prominent in the first. Instead, Lyly addressed a special preface to "the Ladies and Gentlewomen of England," assuring them that it resteth, Ladies, that you take the pains to read it, but at such times as you spend in playing with your little dogs. And yet will I not pinch you of that pastime. For I am content that your dogs lie in your laps, so Euphues be in your hands. . . . Euphues had rather be shut in a lady's casket than open in a scholar's study.

Another change was an increased attention to plot. In the early part the interweaving of several strands is awkward; but for a while in the middle of the story some scenes between Philautus and the coquettish Camilla are in the true vein of drawing-room comedy. The general effect, however, is no more realistic than before. The supposedly English characters have classical names — Fidus, Surius, Martius, Camilla — and even an old Kentish beekeeper philosophizes on love and politics in the purest Euphuistic rhetoric.

In spite of the success of his two volumes, Lyly found himself no nearer to the hoped-for court preferment, and so he deserted fiction for playwriting, which was beginning to give promise as a professional career. It is pleasant to know that before the end of his life he served four terms as a Member of Parliament. The composing of prose romance passed into the hands of others, who avoided his egregious mannerisms of style but otherwise remained as remote from any sense of coherent structure or portrayal of actuality.

In the year when the second part of *Euphues* was published, an episode that might have figured in its pages was being enacted in real life by Philip Sidney. The most brilliant and versatile of the gifted young men surrounding the queen, Sidney fell into disfavor by objecting to her project of marrying a French prince, and by quarreling in public with one of her favorite councilors during a tennis match. Refusing to apologize, he withdrew temporarily to the country estate of his sister, the Countess of Pembroke; and bored by the rural quietness, he occupied some weeks in writing a long story for the amusement of his sister and her lady friends.

Sidney was a very different sort of person from Lyly. Though only twenty-six, and not yet knighted, he had served on foreign embassies and had become the admired friend of leading authors of the day. Secure in his kinship with influential noble families, he had no need to seek fame through publication. Besides, being a serious poet and critic, he regarded the story as a frivolous pastime that would impair his reputation. In his letter transmitting the manuscript to his sister he wrote disparagingly:

> I could well find in my heart to cast out, in some desert of forgetfulness, this child, which I am loth to father. . . . Now, it is done only for you, only to you; if you keep it to yourself, or commend it to such friends who will weigh errors in the balance of goodwill, I hope, for the father's sake, it will be pardoned, perchance made much of, though in itself it have deformities. For indeed, for severer eyes it is not, being but a trifle, and that triflingly handled. Your dear self can best witness the manner, being done in loose sheets of paper, most of it in your presence; the rest by sheets sent unto you, as fast as they were done.

In accordance with this wish, the story was circulated only in manuscript among his eminent friends; and not until 1590, four years after his death, did it appear in print, under the title of *The Countess of Pembroke's Arcadia.* The printed version, however, differs extensively from the surviving manuscripts; Sidney had begun to rewrite the book about 1582, but had not been able to complete the revision before his premature death. It was this version, extending about half way through, that was printed in 1590. A second edition (1593) added the final half as it had been in the original form.

Evidently, after he finished the first writing of the novel, Sidney began to realize that it was not such a "trifle" as he had thought. It insisted on remaining in his mind. His experience was the converse of Lyly's: Lyly offered his book to serious masculine readers, and then wrote the sequel for a more congenial audience of frivolous ladies; Sidney wrote his book for frivolous ladies, and then revised it to make it more acceptable to serious gentlemen.

His changes show two main intentions: to add touches of psychological subtlety in the characterization, and to elaborate the plot and style according to the accepted rules for the heroic poem. Statements in his *Apology for Poetry,* which he wrote about the same time, show that in his mind there was no essential distinction between prose and verse; and the revised *Arcadia* has much in common with the great poem that was subsequently written by his friend Edmund Spenser. As late as 1649 John Milton, in his *Eikonoklastes*, spoke of "the vain amatorious poem of Sir Philip Sidney's *Arcadia*."

Sidney's original version, though slow-moving and digressive, had a fairly well unified plot, and closely resembled the classical pastoral fiction and such recent imitations as Montemayor's *Diana*. The heroines of those tales had been intelligent and energetic girls, refreshingly different from the conventional ladies of chivalry, and Sidney must have pleased his sister and her friends by the independence of spirit that his feminine characters displayed. His setting was the traditional Greek province, which the poets had converted into a sort of wonderland where shepherds sang songs of their own composition to graceful damsels amid perpetual blossoms. Unlike *Euphues*, which was supposedly laid in contemporary Europe but contained little description of scenes, the *Arcadia* is full of long lyrical portrayals of its imaginary landscape.

In the revised version, this idyllic simplicity of the classical pastoral is subordinated to material more akin to the romances of chivalry. The additions extended it to such length that the central story almost vanishes. The eighty-eight characters, though varied as types of human personality and studied with some attention to psychological analysis, are still so little differentiated by individual detail that a modern reader has trouble in keeping the names attached to the proper persons. It has not lacked admirers, however, even at the present day. "In the *Arcadia*," said Virginia Woolf, "as in some luminous globe, all the seeds of English fiction lie latent."

Whereas the plot of *Euphues* was almost static, that of the *Arcadia* is overcrowded with violent action. It is full of disguises, battles, disappearances, dangerous accidents, cross-purposes, coincidental meetings; and it is retarded by accounts of masques, tournaments, and hunts. The main theme, of course, is a protracted series of love-makings. The happy ending comes arbitrarily as though the author had finally felt impelled to bring the intricate tale to a positive stop. As in *The Faerie Queene*, the reader can enjoy it best if he allows himself to become lost in its enchanted mazes without looking for coherent structure.

Although allegory is not emphasized as strongly as in Spenser's poem, Sidney was a zealous Protestant and a dedicated Platonist, and both creeds obliged him to consider the deeper meanings of human experience. The gist of his *Apology for Poetry* was that the objective of all literature must be "virtuous action," and that poetry (i.e., epic and drama) is the highest form of literature, "for whatsoever the philosopher saith should be done, [the poet] giveth a perfect picture of it in some one, by whom he presupposeth it was done." In his "poem," the *Arcadia*, he bodied forth his ideals of loyalty, constant love, and courageous action. Some critics find also in the book a connection with Elizabethan politics, and certain episodes may be based on actual occurrences in Sidney's own life and the lives of his close relations.

The style is less mechanical than Lyly's perpetual antithesis and analogy, but it is almost as remote from natural speech. If Lyly's style is excessively rhetorical, Sidney's is excessively poetical. The sentences move rhythmically under a load of metaphors, personifications, and "conceits"; and Sidney loved to juggle with a word through all its possible meanings and paradoxes so that it produced a pattern as formal as rhyme. Extended narrative fiction was making a tentative transition from verse to prose, but had not yet recognized this new form as a separate genre.

Though neither Lyly nor Sidney continued the writing of prose fiction, there was the usual contingent of professional authors ready to profit by the success of someone else's experiment. They were brazen in their efforts to float their imitations upon the wave of the two best sellers. In the very year of Lyly's second *Euphues*, Anthony Munday published *Zelauto: The Fountain of Fame*, "given for a friendly entertainment to Euphues at his late arrival into England." *Don Simonides*, by Barnabe Rich (1581–84), followed the plot scheme of *Euphues and his England* and introduced Euphues' friend Philautus as an incidental character. Written about 1586, though not printed until 1590, was Thomas Lodge's *Rosalynde*, "Euphues' golden legacy, found after his death in his cell at Silexedra." Robert Greene followed in 1589 with *Menaphon*, subtitled "Camilla's alarm to slumbering Euphues in his melancholy cell at Silexedra." And as evidence of impartiality, Greene changed the affiliation of his novel in later editions by dropping the subtitle and renaming the book *Greene's Arcadia, or Menaphon*. This was nearer the truth, as the story was closely modeled on Sidney's

Arcadia, which Greene must have read in manuscript. The vogue of Lyly, however, was not yet ended; as late as 1594 John Dickenson brought out *Arisbas: Euphues amidst his Slumbers.*

Other novels of the group, while not so openly claiming descent from Lyly or Sidney, were even closer in their affinity. Greene's first novel, *Mamillia: A Looking Glass for the Ladies of England* (1583), took the plot of *Euphues* and reversed it by depicting a man making love to two women at once. During the next few years Greene wrote *Gwydonius: The Card of Fancy* and *Arbasto: The Anatomy of Fortune,* revealing a gradual transfer of allegiance from Lyly's type of story to Sidney's, a process that culminated in *Pandosto: The Triumph of Time* and *Menaphon.* He also published half-a-dozen books in which pastoral romance formed a framework for short stories.

Thomas Lodge's first romance was a short tale, *Forbonius and Prisceria* (1584), written in Euphuistic style but dedicated to Sidney and resembling Sidney's work in its adherence to Greek pastoral tradition. His *Rosalynde,* which is better handled, is also a combination of Lyly's style with Sidney's pastoralism. Relatively short, with an uncomplicated plot and a charming open-air atmosphere, *Rosalynde* was widely popular in its day and remains the most readable example of its genre. Lodge's final novel, *A Margarite of America,* is long but fairly well constructed, and is unique among the pastoral romances in having a tragic ending.

By the end of the century the writing of heroic romance had degenerated into hack-work. Cultured taste had moved on to other interests, but the ever-growing middle class was avid for these tales of high nobility. An industrious professional named Emanuel Forde used all the established formulas and wrote in a flat style with little literary pretension. His *Parismus, the Renowned Prince of Bohemia,* published in 1598, went through countless editions and was finally condensed into a chapbook for sale to the semi-literate. Forde ground out other potboilers, which delighted his undiscriminating audience well into the seventeenth century.

It is ironical that most of these authors led lives more eventful than the stories they wrote. Anthony Munday began as an actor, became an apprentice stationer, traveled to Paris and Rome in disguise to spy on the activities of English Catholic refugees,

and returned to England to spend five more years on the stage
before being appointed a royal messenger as a reward for his
anti-Catholic propaganda. Robert Greene was a dissolute university graduate who traveled as far as Spain, Denmark, and Poland,
consorted with the rascals of the London slums, deserted his
wife and child and lived in sin with the sister of a notorious
thief. Thomas Lodge, son of a Lord Mayor of London, gave
up the study of law in favor of dissipation, and then went to
sea with freebooting expeditions. His *Rosalynde* was actually
written during a voyage to the Canary and Azores Islands, and
his *Margarite of America* during a dangerous venture as far
as Brazil and the Straits of Magellan. If these authors could have
conceived the possibility of making fiction out of the real hardships, intrigues, and excesses of their own experience, they would
have produced something totally unlike the elegant courtships
and high-souled heroism that formed their stock in trade.

This is not to be taken to mean that all Elizabethan fiction
ignored the cruder side of real life. During the years when the
heroic romance was flourishing, another type of narrative
emerged, utterly different in subject and style. Some Elizabe-
thans were fascinated with the violence, the ingenious trickery,
and the salty speech of the contemporary underworld. Several
authors compiled handbooks of thieves' slang. Others wrote
pamphlets on the art of "cony-catching" — the underworld term
for confidence tricks. Greene was one of those who drew from
their intimate experience to expound the knavery of the cony-
catchers.

Even more successful were the jest books, which had begun
with *A Hundred Merry Tales* in 1525. Later these collections
of rowdy anecdotes were sometimes given a semblance of unity
by being attributed to some popular buffoon, such as John
Scoggin or Richard Tarlton. They were the unpolished reader's
equivalent for Painter's *Palace of Pleasure* and the other elegant
story anthologies that pleased the genteel class.

The jest books were related to the mass of chapbook literature, the only reading matter which both in price and in simplicity of style was within the reach of people on a minimum
level of literacy. Most of the chapbooks offered vulgarizations
of the romances of chivalry, like *Palmerin of England* and
Guy of Warwick, or tissues of supernatural marvels, like *Mother*

Shipton. The naïve outlook and elementary style of these brochures made them precursors of children's literature: such nursery favorites as Tom Thumb and Jack the Giant Killer and Dick Whittington originated thus. Some of the chapbooks, however, were comic and realistic, appealing to the universal love of laughter and even implying a sort of primitive social criticism in the zest with which they recounted successful defiances of law and order.

While the upper-class stories came into England from the Renaissance culture of Italy and France, some of the most popular chapbooks were adapted from the earthy low-life reading matter of Germany. A favorite comic book of this type was based on the story of *Til Eulenspiegel,* widely circulated in several European languages at the beginning of the sixteenth century. The English version was printed before 1550 as *A Merry Jest of a Man who was Called Howleglass.* The unscrupulous peasant hero cheated and played pranks on respectable people of all ranks from innkeepers all the way up to princes. The humor was scurrilous and sometimes obscene.

Something of the same spirit permeates the greatest work of prose fiction written on the Continent during the Renaissance, *Gargantua and Pantagruel,* by François Rabelais, published in 1533–35. This cannot be regarded as coming within our definition of the novel: it is episodic and digressive; it is a fantasy as regards plot and is equally fantastic in its exaggerated style, precluding any illusion of reality; and it is obviously controlled by its ulterior purpose of attacking scholasticism and asceticism. On the other hand, by introducing lusty humor and earthy satire into a long prose narrative, it exerted a lasting influence on novels of later centuries.

As well as the chapbooks, another type of literature also set an example for the portrayal of the characters and speech of common people. Early in the sixteenth century the interlude had developed as an effective stage vehicle for gaining comic effect from anecdotes of everyday life. Such interludes as *The Four PP* not only led naturally into the vulgar farce of *Gammer Gurton's Needle* but also improved upon the use of similar material in the jest books. An interesting specimen intermediate between drama and fiction is *A Dialogue Against the Fever Pestilence,* by William Bullein (1564), a grimly comic adaptation of Boccaccio's device. In this short book a rich Londoner and his wife, fleeing from the plague, are entertained with folk tales by their manservant and with wild travel yarns by chance acquaintances. The typographical arrangement makes it look like an interlude, but it was manifestly not intended for the stage.

In addition to native interludes and jest books, and translated chapbook tales, another foreign model had an immediate effect in lending prestige to the comic portrayal of low life. *Lazarillo de Tormes,* published in Spain in 1554 and translated into English in 1576, established a type that came to be known as the *novella picaresca* (rogue novel). A kind of burlesque of the romance of chivalry, it was a farcical and disillusioned tale of a social outcast and his disreputable devices for making a living. Though not much more than a series of episodes, it derived a sort of unity from the personality of the central character, as in the modern comic strip. So many books of this sort followed the lead of *Lazarillo* that the term "picaresque novel" gradually acquired a definite connotation, implying not only a cynical narrative about amusing scoundrels but also a loose, episodic type of structure, usually based on the hero's wanderings over a wide territory.

One of the cleverest critics and most facile writers among the "university wits" was Thomas Nashe, who earned a precarious living among the London pamphleteers and playwrights. Opinionated and combative, he plunged into the paper wars over religion and literature; one of the plays that he helped to write was so seditious and scurrilous that the authorities closed the theater and imprisoned some of the collaborators, and his verbal battle with a distinguished family of scholars incurred the intervention of the Archbishop of Canterbury. In books like *The Anatomy of Absurdity* and *Pierce Penniless* he attacked with humorous bitterness the social follies and intellectual fads of the time.

Naturally, with his robust common sense, he had nothing but scorn for the writers of sentimental romance, declaring that they were trying to revive

> that forgotten legendary licence of lying, to imitate afresh the fantastical dreams of those exiled abbey-lubbers, from whose idle

pens proceeded those worn-out impressions of the famed nowhere acts of Arthur of the Round Table, Arthur of Little Britain, Sir Tristram, Huon of Bordeaux, the Squire of Low Degree, the Four Sons of Aymon, with infinite others.

This appeal to current prejudice by associating the romances with the hated Catholics represents a method of controversy that still survives.

When Nashe turned to fictitious narrative, his contempt for the romances impelled him to write in the vein of the picaresque novel. In *The Unfortunate Traveller, or The Life of Jack Wilton* (1594), he proved that the sordid occurrences of real life could yield as much of adventurous excitement as the most fanciful exploits of traditional princes and knights. He used the most potent device for making his story vivid and plausible — the first-personal point of view. The book purported to be the autobiography of a scapegrace English page with an insatiable love of practical jokes. For some reason Nashe chose to set it in the reign of Henry VIII, eighty years before the date of writing, and he took some pains to consult authentic sources in order to connect his hero's fictitious feats with the events of that era, thus enhancing the illusion of reality. To this extent the book can be classified as the first historical novel.

Beginning at the siege of Tournay in France, where Jack indulges in hoaxes at the expense of sundry officers and camp followers, the story comes back to England at a time of epidemic, and then goes abroad again for the battle of Marignano and a religious massacre in Germany. Taking service under a real historical celebrity, the Earl of Surrey, Jack wanders with him over much of Europe, meeting Sir Thomas More, Erasmus, Luther, and Pietro Aretino. They have adventures with a German magician and a Venetian courtesan; in Florence, Surrey organizes a tournament which is described with outrageous burlesque; later, amid the horrors of the plague in Rome, Jack becomes involved in the melodramatic atrocities of various Italian scoundrels. The unflagging gusto and frank sensationalism of the whole story are not handicapped by any trace of sensitive squeamishness or moral judgment.

While Nashe was thus exploiting the picaresque novel as an antidote to sentimental romanticism, another kind of realism

also made its appearance in prose fiction. The tradesmen and
their apprentices in London and other towns were gaining self-
respect as they became an important element in society, and
had acquired a degree of literacy that enabled them to delight
in stories glorifying their own virtues. Toward the end of the
sixteenth century they were flocking to the theaters to see plays
celebrating the deeds of people representing their class.

This new theme was injected into prose fiction by Thomas
Deloney, a silk weaver from Norwich who had followed his
trade in various towns before setting up as a ballad-writer in
Cripplegate, a poor part of London. Unlike such brilliant young
university men as Greene and Nashe, he had always known the
seamy side of life and so he took it for granted. In their books
the sordid material was in violent contrast with their elaborate
style and intellectual complexity. Deloney, on the other hand,
presents the life of humble people with good-natured sympathy
and humor; and the harsher elements, when they occur, are
accepted as a matter of course. His vocabulary is simple and the
dialogue rings true to everyday speech, sometimes lapsing into
local dialect.

Deloney laid the scene of most of his stories in the past, but
his motive was different from Nashe's. He chose traditional
heroes, in the spirit of the chapbooks; he did not consult reference works, and the locating of a story in an earlier century
merely gave the sanction of time to the significance of the
achievements. Whatever the nominal date of the action might
be, the way of life depicted was that of the Cheapside shops
among which Deloney and his readers plied their callings.

This points to another difference between his realism and
Nashe's. Nashe was striving for the shock effect that results
when gruesome or violent actions are invested with the illusion
that such things may be going on around the reader without his
knowing it. Deloney, on the contrary, exploited the appeal of
recognition. He offered his readers their own environment,
slightly idealized, and they enjoyed it because they could participate in the story with a minimum of imaginative effort.

Deloney seems to have made the shift from ballad mongering
to prose narrative for the purpose of propaganda. The textile
trade was suffering from a depression, and the workers blamed
certain government restraints that survived from the old guild

system. Strikes and unemployment were prevalent, and a food shortage aggravated the crisis. It has been suggested that Deloney was subsidized by the cloth manufacturers to write his first book in order to present their case to the public.

The Pleasant History of John Winchcomb, in his Younger Years Called Jack of Newbury was published in 1597, and told the life story of a real man who had lived a century before. It used one of the eternally popular plots — the poor youth's rise to wealth. Jack begins as a hard-working prentice, honest but actuated by strictly practical self-interest. His master's widow falls in love with him and marries him, and he ends as a powerful industrialist. His character is clearly drawn, and the story moves through a series of both comic and pathetic episodes. Jack's wealthy wife proves intractable and gives him much discomfort before she dies and leaves him free to marry a pretty country lass. In the later part of the book, after Jack is established as a magnate, the author throws in a series of broadly comic occurrences in his household, contributing nothing to the story of his career. The influence that Jack gains with Henry VIII, and his successful opposition to Cardinal Wolsey's legal restraints of trade, were not introduced merely to prove how great a man he had become, but were intended to warn the government of Deloney's own day that it must recognize the significance of English industry.

Thus established as the spokesman of business, Deloney turned from the clothiers to the shoemakers. His next book, however, must be classified as a collection of short stories: *The Gentle Craft* reviews the history of cordwainers from the days of their patron saints down to recent times, in a series of comic incidents intermingled with sentimental love intrigues. In a third book, *Thomas of Reading*, Deloney returned to the cloth-workers and to their troubles with the authorities, setting his time as far back as the reign of Henry I, and interspersing two or three genuinely tragic episodes among the hearty humorous scenes.

Deloney was not the only writer catering to the new self-conscious bourgeois customers. Writing the same sort of fictionized history, but with little of Deloney's humor or power of characterization, were Richard Johnson, author of *The Nine Worthies of London* and *The Pleasant Conceits of Old Hobson*, and Henry Roberts, author of *Haigh for Devonshire* and other commonplace tales. Many books, such as *The Pinner of Wake-field*, were anonymous. One feature of all these books, as indicated often in the titles, was the plentiful local color. The readers must have enjoyed identifying the very streets and buildings that were mentioned.

Within a scant period of twenty years, the last two decades of the sixteenth century, prose fiction not only had come into existence in England but also had developed the several distinct species that were to prevail until the present day. These may be regarded in two main classifications, best labeled as the "masculine novel" and the "feminine novel." The masculine novel is tough-minded, pragmatic, ribald in its humor and grim in its frank presentation of sordidness and cruelty. The feminine novel is tender-minded, idealistic, and inclined to be didactic. Within each category can be seen various subtypes, and also a wide range of artistic merit, depending both on the abilities of the authors and on the sort of reader for whom the book was intended. At its best the feminine novel is a moving presentation of the highest visions the human mind can conceive and of the noblest conduct that men and women are capable of achieving. It can be graceful, witty, and poetical. At its worst the feminine novel is sentimental, wordy, and shallow, distorting the actualities of life to arouse easy sympathy or to force a happy ending. The masculine novel at its best is a sturdy acceptance of man's destiny, seeing deeply into the truths of experience and recording factual observation with an accompaniment of tolerant humor or of ruthless satire. At its worst it is rowdy and violent, seeking to shock the sensibility of respectable readers or to titillate the sadism of impressionable ones. In sum, the new literary genre of prose fiction took its place in the permanent tradition of literature by aligning itself with both the fundamental philosophical attitudes — the idealistic line that extends back through St. Augustine to Plato and the rationalistic line extending through Thomas Aquinas to Aristotle.

I I

Romance, Allegory, and Scandal

(1600 – 1700)

THE LARGE OUTPUT of prose fiction between 1580 and 1600 did not establish the novel as a literary type. After the turn of the century several forces militated against it. For one thing, the theater was still flourishing and monopolized the best writers and the best plots. The Arcadian fiction of Sidney and Lodge was absorbed into the tragicomedies of Beaumont and Fletcher, the realism of Nashe and Deloney into the bourgeois comedies of Thomas Dekker and the satirical plays of Ben Jonson. A few years later, the growing power of puritanism opposed not only the drama, but fiction also, as mere worldly frivolity and lies. Thus a large proportion of the middle-class audience was discouraged from reading for entertainment.

On a higher level of education, another type of serious-mindedness was equally inimical to fiction. As the scientific rationalism of Bacon gained currency, intelligent minds could no longer find satisfaction in the idealistic dream-world of Lyly and Sidney. Factual observation and analysis won the day.

Nevertheless, the apparent interruption proved in the long run

29

to have a vital influence on the development of the novel. The new inductive methods were applied not only in the physical sciences but also in the realm of human behavior. Attempts to classify people according to types, and to determine the principles governing their relationships, were essentially concerned with the materials out of which fiction is made. Robert Burton's *Anatomy of Melancholy* was a treatise on psychology that probed almost clinically into one special form of aberration. The collections of short "characters," notably *Characters of Virtues and Vices*, by Joseph Hall, *Witty Characters and Conceited News*, by Sir Thomas Overbury and his friends, *Microcosmography*, by John Earle, and *The Holy State and the Profane State*, by Thomas Fuller, were brief sketches of varied human types, classified sometimes by vocation, sometimes by psychological traits. Though modeled on the work of the Greek moralist Theophrastus, whose essays were intended to teach lessons in ethics, these studies of behavior were much influenced by the scientific theories of personality which also affected Jonson's characterization by "humours"; and they had something in common with the realistic pamphlets on criminals and their victims by Greene, Nashe, and Dekker. Even within this limited genre the two basic attitudes of the novel can be detected: Hall's *Characters* are solemn and moralistic, Overbury's are satirically humorous.

After the middle of the century the writers of biography and history furthered the trend toward psychological analysis. Thomas Fuller's *Worthies of England* and Izaak Walton's *Lives* showed real insight into human nature and recognized the value of trivial details in building up a portrait. The Earl of Clarendon filled his *History of the Rebellion and the Civil Wars* with incisive character sketches of the public men of his time.

If these books can be regarded as being ancillary to the novel by their attention to individual psychology, another type of seventeenth-century prose used some techniques of fiction for exploring the structure of society. A series of "utopian" treatises, following the example set by Sir Thomas More a century earlier, invented imaginary countries to illustrate their sociological theories. Francis Bacon's unfinished *New Atlantis* included a circumstantial narrative of the adventurous voyage of his travelers. Subsequent books of the same sort, some of them more concerned with satirizing contemporary society than with proposing reforms, were *The Man in the Moon*, by Francis Godwin, *The Commonwealth of Oceana*, by James Harrington, and many others. In all these books, however, the narrative and descriptive elements are merely a frame for the expository discussion, and therefore none of them can be included within our definition of the novel.

During those years the most notable developments in prose fiction were taking place outside of England. In Spain the new rationalistic spirit found utterance in the masterpiece of Miguel de Cervantes. Earlier in his career he had written a pastoral romance, *Galatea* (1585); but in the next twenty years his financial troubles, including terms in jail, made him all too familiar with the unpleasant realities of life, and he set out to prove the absurdity of the romances of chivalry by means of a parody. Apparently he started *Don Quixote* with the intention of writing only a short story; but soon the central characters took on such living reality that he could not dismiss them. The imaginative knight of La Mancha grew into something more than a grotesque old man who had gone crazy with too much reading of chivalric fiction. He became an embodiment of all the impractical ideals and noble visions that have inspired and frustrated mankind, while his servant Sancho was the very essence of blunt common sense. For many readers the book is merely a series of riotously comic predicaments. For others it is an ironical analysis of the social conflicts of Renaissance Spain. Others read it as a spiritual autobiography. It can also be viewed as a symbolic picture of man's eternal dilemma between idealism and pragmatism, with passages that are profoundly serious probings of the nature of reality.

The story had unmistakable affinities with the picaresque novel, in its gallery of rogues and vagabonds and also in its loose episodic structure. Its string of incidents might be rearranged in almost any order without damage to the book's continuity, and the climax is not clearly prepared for. Therefore, in spite of its immense influence on subsequent fiction, *Don Quixote* cannot be classified as a novel. It lacks not only a unified plot but also a primary purpose of creating an illusion of reality. The reader can seldom forget the author's intention of ridiculing the old romances, because to produce this effect the events are usually exaggerated beyond the bounds of probability. Cervantes' great contribution was the creation of two central characters endowed with the vividness and consistency that make them "round" rather than "flat" characters, and the exploration of their minds through dialogue.

Though *Don Quixote* was soon being read in many parts of Europe, it did not strike a death-blow to fanciful romance. In France, particularly, the romance was blossoming into fresh vitality. A French-born Scotsman named John Barclay, whose life was divided between Paris and London, wrote *Argenis* in Latin and published it in Paris in 1621. Following the Lyly-Sidney tradition, this long story had a conventional Arcadian setting and a solemn moral purpose of condemning political intrigue. Prominent people of the time could be identified as originals of the characters. The book was immensely popular, as was *Astrée*, by Honoré d'Urfé, which appeared at intervals between 1610 and 1627. The type became standardized in *Polexendre*, by Marin le Roy de Gomberville (1632), who discarded pastoral settings and supernatural characters such as giants and enchanters, replacing them with pseudo-historical events in remote times and nations, in imitation of the epic. This new species is known as the "heroic romance."

A strong vogue for everything French prevailed at the court of Charles I through his marriage to the French princess Henrietta Maria. The fashionable world flaunted its ability to read French fluently, and the new heroic romances proved to be the French books most enjoyable to read. Through the middle years of the century, while the English courtiers were living in exile at Versailles, more of the interminable stories were being written by Gauthier de la Calprenède (*Cassandre, Cléopâtre, Faramond*), by Georges and Madeleine de Scudéry (*Le Grand Cyrus, Clélie, Ibrahim*), and by many others. Often extending to ten volumes, they came to be known as *romans à longue haleine* — "long-winded novels." The settings were in ancient Greece or Rome or in Asiatic countries, but there was no attempt at historical accuracy, and usually the characters were unmistakable portraits of individual contemporaries. Their behavior was invariably noble and they indulged in endless debate on moral problems. In spite of the high-flown sentiment and allegory, however, violent action burst in at frequent intervals — battles, shipwrecks, capture by pirates, recognition of disguised princes. The exotic settings were described with florid baroque decoration. Dozens of complete short stories, or "histories," were inserted, by the simple device of having each character recount his past adventures or those of his friends. The discussions of abstract topics often reached the dimensions of separate essays embedded in the narrative. Long letters also occurred frequently. The feminine characters were intellectual and formidably modest — an idealized version of the *précieuses* of the salons where this cult of Platonic love and playful conversation flourished. The real merit of the books was in this polished dialogue, which approximated the talk of cultivated people of the time. With ample leisure on their hands, the ladies of society and many of their gentleman friends were not appalled by the vastitude of the witty and subtle conversations.

The absence of the court from England did not halt the vogue of these books. The royalist families used them as a sort of symbolic cult to maintain aristocratic values in the midst of defeat. It is true that the bluestocking Duchess of Newcastle had no use for them:

> I never read a Romancy Book throughout in all my life, I mean such as I take to be Romances, wherein little is writ which ought to be practiced, but rather shunned as foolish amorosities, and desperate follies, not noble love's discreet virtues, and true valor.

But when James Philips and his wife Katherine established a royalist salon at their country house in Wales, they and their friends adopted pseudonyms from the romances — "Orinda," "Antenor," "Poliarchus." The witty Dorothy Osborne devoured the French books and forwarded them volume by volume to her eminent friend Sir William Temple:

> Have you read *Cléopâtre?* I have six tomes on't here that I can lend you if you have not; there are some stories in't you will like, I believe. But what an ass I am to think you can be idle enough at London to read romance. . . . If you have done with the first part of *Cyrus*, I should be glad Mr Hollingsworth had it, because I mentioned some such thing in my last to my Lady. . . . To encourage you, let me assure you that the more you read of them you will like them still better.

Mrs. Samuel Pepys was equally addicted to the romances, though her husband made it plain in his diary that he had no use for them. One Sunday, it is true, weakened by an upset stomach, he wasted his time with some of her books: "Took physic all day, and, God forgive me, did spend it in reading of some little French romances." But this was the only time he lapsed. When she was devouring *Le Grand Cyrus* until midnight one night, he remained immersed in Fuller's *Church History;* and he bought her a copy of *Ibrahim* only because he was in the bookshop to have a learned work rebound. He once reduced her to tears by "checking her in the coach in her long stories out of Grand Cyrus, which she would tell, though nothing to the purpose, nor in any good manner." The romances, in fact, were the only subject on which Mrs. Pepys could rank as a scholarly expert; at a new play by Dryden she recognized it as based on an episode in *Ibrahim,* and she proved the point to her husband next day by reading him the source passage.

Being French, Mrs. Pepys presumably read the romances in the original language; but most of her neighbors lacked this aristocratic accomplishment, and so during the Commonwealth many of the romances were translated into English, thus becoming available to middle-class women. Miss Osborne was scornful:

> I have no patience either for these translations of romances. I met with *Polexendre* and *L'Illustre Bassa* both so disguised that I, who am their old acquaintance, hardly knew them; besides that, they were still so much French in words and phrases that 'twas impossible for one that understands not French to make anything of them.

Feeble though the translations were, they could not destroy the appetite for such fascinating fare. A natural outcome was the writing of original fiction in imitation of the French model. The earliest was the anonymous *Cloria and Narcissus, or The Royal Romance,* "written by a person of honor," of which the first volume came out in 1653. The preface explained that the actual theme was the current state of international politics, and that identification of the real people, places, and events should offer no difficulty to "any who have been but indifferently versed in the affairs of Europe; and for others of the more vulgar sort, a bare romance of love and chivalry, such as this may be esteemed to be at the worst, will provide entertainment enough for their leisure." Similarly the history of England from Elizabeth to the death of Cromwell was fictionized in 1659 in another "royal romance," *Panthalia*, probably by Richard Brathwait.

In 1654, by issuing the first three volumes of his *Parthenissa*, Roger Boyle, Lord Broghill (later Earl of Orrery), showed that it was not beneath the dignity of an aristocrat to write a romance. Dorothy Osborne was not overenthusiastic:

> 'Tis handsome language; you would know it to be writ by a person of good quality though you were not told it; but, on the whole, I am not very much taken with it. All the stories have too near a resemblance with those of other romances, there is nothing new or *surprenant* in them; the ladies are all so kind they make no sport, and I met only with one that took me by doing a handsome thing of the kind. . . . And though he makes his people say fine handsome things to one another, yet they are not easy and *naïve* like the French, and there is a little harshness in most of the discourse that one would take to be the fault of a translator rather than that of an author.

The mania for romances was intensified when Charles II was restored to the throne in 1660 and his courtiers brought French tastes back from their exile. Not only did the romances lead to a new type of drama — the heroic plays of Dryden and Howard — but during the next quarter-century ponderous volumes of this prose fiction were written by a lawyer, a clergyman, even a scientist, as well as by the inevitable professionals. And yet, as the acute Dorothy Osborne had perceived, the English writers never felt wholly confident in practicing the imported genre. A lingering trace of puritan conscience nagged them with doubt as to the value of the romance, no matter how noble its sentiments; and most of them prefaced their books with profuse explanations or apologies.

George Mackenzie, a law student, gave his *Aretina* (1660) a subtitle, "The Serious Romance." "I am confident," he protested in the preface, "that where romances are written by excellent wits, and perused by intelligent readers, that the judgment may pick more sound information from them, than from history." The modern reader can scarcely believe his eyes when he finds Mackenzie justifying his novel by boasting that it is *not* like real life: "Whereas romances present to us virtue in its holy-day robes, history presents her only to us in these ordinary and spotted suits which she wears whilst she is busied in her servile and lucrative employments." Mackenzie quickly became absorbed in the "servile and lucrative employments" of his own career, in which he enforced the royal authority over the Scottish Covenanters so rigorously that he earned a knighthood and the nickname of "Bloody Mackenzie." He never found time for composing the subsequent volumes that would have brought *Aretina* to the proper bulk.

The Reverend Nathaniel Ingelo, D.D., was definitely offering a religious allegory in his romance, *Bentivolio and Urania* (1660–64), and a superlatively tedious romance it was. With many scholarly citations, his preface dealt with "the writing and reading of romances" as one of "the impertinencies of mankind." After condemning Homer and other ancients because they "made the fabulous rind so thick that few can see through it into the useful sense," he went on to assert that some romances of a later date are

> most to be blamed because . . . their chief design is to put fleshly lust into long stories, and sometimes not without very unhandsome mixtures, tending only to the service of brutish concupiscence, the nourishment of dishonorable affections, and by exciting in the readers muddy fancies, to indispose them for their attendance upon God by their better part.

The professional authors followed the trend set by such amateurs as Mackenzie and Ingelo. John Bulteel's *Birinthia* (1664), which was composed, he explained, "in my greener youth, and most of it during the intervals of a sharp distemper," laid strong claim to realism:

> Such as can relish no romance that is not forced with extravagant impossibilities (no less ridiculous than improbable) will find little gusto and cold entertainment here . . . for I have endued my heroes with no greater strength or courage than may reside in generous persons; nor do I fill their veins with streams of blood greater than those small channels should contain. . . . This is a romance accommodated to history, to whose text I have added those auxiliary embellishments rather to illustrate than disguise or corrupt it.

Lord Broghill, too, when he resumed his *Parthenissa* after a ten-year interval, insisted that the value of his book lay in its inclusion of historical material, which might tempt some readers into studying the subject:

I may say that this way of writing romances is less ill than any I have yet seen originally in our language; for all that have been presented to the world first in English have been purely fabulous.

Though *Parthenissa* was never completed, because Broghill worked on it only when attacks of gout interrupted his social and political career, it was the only English romance that came anywhere near the French models in length, complexity, ornate settings, and number of persons — 143 who play individual roles in the action.

Lord Broghill's brother, the Hon. Robert Boyle, the eminent physicist, also had succumbed to the temptation of romance-writing. When his *Theodora and Didymus* was published in 1687, many years after its composition, he explained lengthily that

the nature of the subject refused me most of those embellishments which in other themes, where young gallants and fair ladies are the chief actors, are wont to supply the deficiencies of the matter. Besides, my task was not near so easy as it would have been, if I had been only to recite the intrigues of an amour, with the liberty to feign surprising adventures, to adorn the historical part of the account, and to make a lover speak as passionately as I could, and his mistress as kindly as the indulgent laws of decency would permit. But I was to introduce a Christian and pious lover, who was to contain the expressions of his flame within the narrow bounds of his religion; and a virgin, who, being as modest and discreet as handsome, and as devout as either, was to own an high esteem for an excellent lover, and an uncommon gratitude to a transcendent benefactor, without entrenching either upon her virtue or her reservedness.

Boyle's short book is a precursor of the historical novel, for he used the recorded facts as far as available, and then added "such supplements of circumstances, as were not improbable in the nature of the thing, and were little less than necessary to the clearness and entireness of the story, and the decent connection of the parts it should consist of."

It will be seen that these writers were wrestling with a contradiction. On the one hand, they were insisting that, whereas previous romances had dealt with impossibilities, theirs presented strict truth; on the other hand, they were equally positive that their books would not cater to sensuality by portraying human nature in any of its lower manifestations. Nor was their difficulty confined to the dilemma of entertainment *vs.* morality; they were bothered also with problems of style. While they all paid tribute to Sidney as their great progenitor, they were aware that his florid figures of speech and long rambling sentences were no longer usable. In their day English prose was undergoing a transformation. The need for precise expression of scientific thinking impelled the newly founded Royal Society to recommend a simplified kind of expository writing, "a close, naked, natural way of speaking; positive expressions, clear senses, a native easiness, . . . and preferring the language of artisans, countrymen, and merchants before that of wits and scholars."

Besides, the clarity and elegance of French prose made Elizabethan English seem intolerably old-fashioned; in Mackenzie's preface to *Aretina* he found fault with "the first writers of romance" not only because "they stuffed their books with things impracticable," but also for

> the style, which because of its soaring pitch was inimitable. Wherefore the famous Scudery has written so as that his invention may suit well with our practice, and his style with our discourse, and especially in his *Clelia*, wherein he professes that he hath adapted all to the present converse of the French nation, and that is really the mould wherein all our romances should be casten.

Similarly, John Crowne's preface to his *Pandion and Amphigenia* (1665) declared that an author should not "bolster up a crooked invention with fungous words" and that a romance should not be "an hospital of lame conceits" — precepts that were violated throughout the book. In diction, therefore, as well as in purpose, the English heroic romances were uncomfortably stranded between past and present, between elaborate rhetoric and conversational ease.

The justifications and compromises so profusely offered by the writers indicate an awareness that they were shaping a new literary medium, but at the same time they were unable to break away from the dominance of a moribund genre, the heroic poem. Sir William Temple in 1691 remarked that "the last kind of poetry in prose is that which in later ages has overrun the world under the name of Romances." A viable art of prose fiction could not emerge so long as the authors were seeking to serve two masters. Therefore the vogue of the heroic romance lasted barely twenty years, exactly coeval with that of its dramatic equivalent, the heroic play.

It remained for an author who was totally ignorant of literary tradition, who had never read Aristotle or Julius Caesar Scaliger, to use prose for a kind of fiction that told its story bluntly and colloquially and therefore achieved a full illusion of reality in spite of a burden of moral preachment. While the elite of England were absorbed in the refinements of French romances, they were oblivious to the momentous development that was obscurely occurring at the other extreme of the social scale.

John Bunyan was the son of a tinker in a village near Bedford, and he received only a rudimentary schooling. In his young days he delighted in the popular chapbooks, such as *The Seven Champions of Christendom* and *Bevis of Hampton*, which he later condemned as "beastly romances, and books full of ribaldry, even such as immediately tended to set all fleshly lusts on fire." A vivid imagination tormented him with dreams of fiends trying to kidnap him, and even in childhood he was afflicted by fits of remorse and despair. At sixteen he was conscripted as a trooper in the Parliamentary army, in which he served for more than two years. When he was twenty he married an earnestly religious woman, whose only dowry was two pious treatises, and she took pains to improve his conduct. After an agonizing period of doubt and mental torture he was converted to religious devotion, and before he was thirty he became an itinerant preacher for one of the innumerable little evangelical sects of the time. Soon he gained such a reputation that crowds flocked to listen to him. Using simple words that were within the comprehension of his hearers and illustrative anecdotes drawn from both his imagination and his experience, he held their attention and moved their emotional response.

As early as 1656 he began writing controversial tracts, but the spoken word was easier for him than the written and so he had no thought of becoming an author. With the Restoration, however, he was arrested for refusing to suspend his itinerant preaching; and from 1660 to 1672, with short intervals on parole, he was a prisoner in Bedford Jail. Here he read and reread the Bible and Foxe's *Book of Martyrs* until every sentence had sunk into his mind. Preaching to his fellow-inmates having proved an inadequate outlet for his zeal, his inner compulsion drove him to writing, and a series of didactic and controversial works ensued.

The most important of these was an autobiography, *Grace Abounding to the Chief of Sinners*, published in 1666. It showed a gift of straightforward narrative and an effortless choice of exact words within the limits of a small vocabulary. In the preface he defended his style with the doubtful claim that

> I could have stepped into a style much higher than this in which I have here discoursed, and could have adorned all things more than here I have seemed to do; but I dare not. God did not play in convincing of me; the Devil did not play in tempting of me . . . wherefore I may not play in my relating of them, but be plain and simple, and lay down the thing as it was.

As a matter of fact, it seems certain that he seldom did "lay down the thing as it was," but exaggerated his youthful follies and his spectacular conversion; but the exaggeration was due to his spiritual intensity rather than to any calculated artistic effect.

After his release in 1672 he was licensed to preach, but he was briefly imprisoned again four or five years later. During one or other of his terms in jail he accidentally discovered his real genius. His tracts were beginning to show touches of humor and imagination, with use of brief character sketches and snatches of dialogue; but he was not aware that these techniques might be used as anything more than incidental devices. Then one day while composing a tract he happened to compare the Christian life to a pilgrimage. The trite analogy seized upon his imagination, as he tells in a doggerel report of the event:

> And thus it was: I writing of the way
> And race of saints, in this our gospel-day,
> Fell suddenly into an allegory
> About their journey, and the way to glory,
> In more than twenty things, which I set down;
> This done, I twenty more had in my crown,
> And they again began to multiply
> Like sparks that from the coals of fire do fly.
> Nay then, though I, if that you breed so fast

> I'll put you by yourselves, lest you at last
> Should prove *ad infinitum*, and eat out
> This book that I already am about. . . .
> Thus I set pen to paper with delight
> And quickly had my thoughts in black and white.
> For having now my method by the end,
> Still as I pulled, it came; and so I penned
> It down, until it came at last to be
> For length and breadth the bigness that you see.

The book wrote itself so easily that he was suspicious of its merit. Apparently he suspended it midway for a fairly long interval, and when it was finished he insisted that he had worked on his "scribble" only in "vacant seasons," and with no intention of publishing: "I did it mine own self to gratify." When he experimentally showed the manuscript to his friends, some of them were horrified by his use of worldly episodes to symbolize spiritual truths. Others, however, approved of the story because of its moral teaching, and in 1678 it was published with the title, *The Pilgrim's Progress from this World to that which is to Come.*

The versified preface admitted that Bunyan expected many of his godly fellow-Baptists to disapprove of the book because it was "feigned" and lacked "solidness"; and he tried to justify it by pointing out that many religious authors had used both similitudes and dialogue, and that "Holy Writ in many places hath semblance with this method." He argued further that his concrete episodes would be easy to remember: "Then read my fancies, they will stick like burrs." Finally he adduced his simple style:

> This book is writ in such a dialect
> As may the minds of listless men affect:
> It seems a novelty, and yet contains
> Nothing but sound and honest gospel strains.

The author must have been agreeably surprised by its unprecedented popularity. Under the Puritan regime literacy had been widely extended, with the intention that even the humblest person should be able to read the Bible and thus find his own salvation; and within the comprehension and the purse of this new reading public no material was available beyond the Bible except chapbooks and the dreary tracts of Puritan evangelists. Bunyan's book, crudely printed on cheap paper, could be bought even by the poor; its short words and simple sentences offered no obstacle to the slowest reader; and in view of its religious orthodoxy it could offend none but the most austere of Puritans by its admixture of fiction.

Though most of its readers accepted *The Pilgrim's Progress* ostensibly for its moral allegory, their real enjoyment of it was for other reasons. The hazards and enemies encountered by the trustful hero supplied enough excitement and suspense to rivet attention. Bunyan's own spiritual conflict made the book ring with emotional sincerity. The fascination of the marvelous was provided by the monster Apollyon and Giant Pope and Giant Despair with his grim dungeon, figures out of the folk tales that Bunyan had heard in childhood and the chapbook romances he read in his unregenerate youth. But the essential appeal of the story was in its portrayal of familiar scenes and people. The setting was the English countryside, with its muddy lanes and flowery meadows, its lonely hillsides and busy market towns. Most of the characters, in spite of their allegorical names, were ordinary human beings such as Bunyan had seen during his military service, or on his preaching missions among the hamlets, or later when he had his own chapel in town and had to contend with troublesome parishioners. Arrogant squires, greedy merchants, hypocritical clergy, slow-witted bumpkins, brawny thieves, they parade through the pages and talk in recognizable tones — for one of the strongest merits of the book is its constant use of dialogue.

This realism of characterization, which makes the persons of the story something more than pale materializations of virtues and vices, extends to the hero also. Christian is no priggish figure of perfection, but an anxious, blundering man who suffers and weakens, boasts and despairs. In contrast, certain minor characters — Faithful and Hopeful — are simple, unimaginative souls without problems, who meet no major hazards as they journey toward the Heavenly City. These, and evil figures also, such as Mr. Worldly Wiseman, are really separate aspects of the total personality. Seen thus, the book is an analysis of the complex human individual, and the conflicts are an objectivized record of what goes on inside him.

Although *The Pilgrim's Progress* thus embodied many

qualities that later came to be characteristic of the novel, it cannot be admitted into the canon. An illusion of unity arises from the fact that a final climax — Christian's triumphant arrival at the Celestial City — is innate in the story from the outset. But otherwise the structure is essentially episodic, and Christian is the only character who is carried through from start to finish. Furthermore, the didactic purpose obtrudes persistently through the realistic surface, not only in the descriptive names of the characters but also in the rhythmical recurrence of the reminder, "I saw also in my dream," and in long, dull passages of doctrinal debate. Bunyan no doubt sustained these features throughout in order to demonstrate that the book was to be used for religious instruction, not realizing that its incredible circulation was due less to the public's desire for spiritual guidance than to their hunger for literary entertainment.

He was quite ready, however, to take advantage of his success. The book went through four large editions in its first two years, and in each edition he made revisions and expansions, adding several episodes and smoothing out some of the colloquialisms and lapses of grammar. At the same time he was writing his second book of didactic fiction, *The Life and Death of Mr. Badman,* which came out in 1680. Its theme, as he explained in the preface, occurred to him as the logical converse of the preceding book:

> As I was considering with myself what I had written concerning the Progress of the Pilgrim from this world to glory, and how it had been acceptable to many in this nation, it came again into my mind to write, as then of him that was going to Heaven, so now of the life and death of the ungodly, and of their travel from this world to Hell.

Bunyan's increased self-confidence resulting from the fame of *The Pilgrim's Progress* sounds clearly in this preface, though veiled by a decent show of Christian humility:

> The butt therefore, that at this time I shoot at, is wide; and 'twill be impossible for this book to go into several families and not to arrest some, as for the King's Messenger to rush into an house full of traitors and find none but honest men there. I cannot but think that this shot will light upon many, since our fields are so full of this game; but how many it will kill to Mr. Badman's course, and

make alive to the Pilgrim's Progress, that is not in me to determine; this secret is with the Lord our God only, and he alone knows to whom he will bless it to so good and blessed an end. However, I have put fire to the pan and doubt not but the report will quickly be heard.

Whereas *The Pilgrim's Progress* had emerged from the author's imagination unbidden, *Mr. Badman* was carefully preconceived with full awareness of literary technique.

The story was more realistic than its predecessor. Instead of spiritual symbolism through incarnations of forces of good and evil, it offered the biography of an average worldly citizen. "To the best of my rememberance," Bunyan declared, "all the things that here I discourse of, I mean as to matter of fact, have been acted upon the stage of this world, even many times before mine eyes." It was confined to the sordid details of the small-town, middle-class environment that Bunyan knew well. Probably most of his congregation recognized one another somewhere in the book.

Yet, paradoxically, *Mr. Badman* makes a less concrete impression on the reader's mind than does *The Pilgrim's Progress*, in which even the most fantastic occurrences seem real and vivid. The difference is partly due to a technical experiment in the new book, foreshadowing the present-day concern with problems of time sequence and point of view. "I have put it," Bunyan explained, "into the form of a dialogue, that I might with more ease to myself and pleasure to the reader perform the work." The entire book consists of a conversation between two of Mr. Badman's neighbors, the day after his death; the story is gradually built up out of their reminiscences of his behavior and their analysis of his character. Ingenious though the device was for supplying unity and plausibility, it deprived the story of immediacy and suspense. The end is known from the outset, and the two narrators are so relentless in condemning all the dead man's deeds that the reader never acquires that sense of identification with the action which is the first requisite for enjoying fiction. In a picaresque novel such as *The Unfortunate Traveller* the author's gusto in his hero's misdeeds soon infects the reader; but Bunyan allows no hint of such unhallowed sympathy. His severity tends to defeat its purpose: a nonpuritan reader begins secretly to champion Badman against his intolerant neighbors and to feel gratified that — no matter what the eternal destiny of his soul might be — at least in this life he lived to a ripe age and died snugly in his bed.

The Pilgrim's Progress had been equally ruthless toward sinners, but it was sustained by a spiritual fervor that is scarcely perceptible in *Mr. Badman*. In spite of tirades about the deadly sins and the will of God, the story's theme is social rather than religious. It preaches the prudential ethics of a commercial society and thus reveals the practical common sense that was so strangely mingled with the Puritan otherworldliness.

Bunyan's next book was a more ambitious undertaking; he turned back to religious allegory, but this time on an epic scale rather than through the adventures of individuals. *The Holy War Made by Shaddai upon Diabolus* (1682) is much more elaborately planned than *The Pilgrim's Progress*, with a wider range of literary background that may have included *Paradise Lost*. Its several levels of interpretation brought in contemporary political and sectarian issues as well as its cosmic theme of the struggle between the armies of God and the devil. The military scenes were based on recollections of Bunyan's years in uniform. There are some impressive imaginative passages, but the attempt to present a crisis in the destiny of the whole human race left little scope for the development of individual characters. The book's affinity is therefore with the fictionized utopias rather than with the precursors of the novel.

Bunyan probably became aware that neither his second nor his third work of fiction appealed to the public as strongly as his first one. He knew too that other writers had tried to trade on its fame by issuing spurious continuations. Accordingly he made a final effort to repeat his original triumph by writing a sequel of his own. At the beginning of *The Pilgrim's Progress* Christian had somewhat callously left his wife and family when he set out on his journey. The second part, published in 1684, narrates the parallel adventures of Christiana and her children when they in their turn go in search of the Heavenly City. They pass through the same scenes and encounter some of the same characters, so that the reader has a comfortable sense of familiarity. Several effective new personages are introduced — the Giants Grim and Maul, Mr. Brisk and Old Honest, and especially Christiana's protector, Greatheart, a probably unintentional self-portrait.

The writing shows how much ease and flexibility Bunyan had

gained in six years: there are touches of grace and humor, and the grim urgency of Christian's pilgrimage has given place to a leisurely and almost sentimental atmosphere of feminine sociability. As a famous author and efficient church administrator, Bunyan looked at the world in a different mood from that of the obstinate prisoner who had written the first part. His complacency shows in the preface, which scolds certain rigid doctrinaires for attacking his books. This relaxing of tension contributes to the sense of anticlimax that haunts the second part; but mainly the reason is that the completeness of the original story had left no suspense to carry over into the sequel, which merely repeats the well-known pattern.

When Bunyan died in 1688, the generation of militant Puritans was ending, and so there was no writer to carry on his line of work. Sophisticated literary men knew nothing about these vulgar books that were selling by thousands and were being read to shreds by the respectable middle class and the literate segment of the poor. And yet *The Pilgrim's Progress* gradually infiltrated into the very texture of English literature. In a time when few books were written expressly for children, the simple language and marvelous adventures of *The Pilgrim's Progress* suited it ideally for young readers, while its well-known moral purpose recommended it as wholesome for them. Thus it came into the hands of generations of children, even in the upper class, who absorbed it avidly with little or no awareness of the allegory. When a few of these children, a century or two after Bunyan's time, grew up to write fiction themselves, scenes and characters and phrases from *The Pilgrim's Progress* were as much a part of them as the real experiences of their youth.

At the time of Bunyan's death, however, the tone of most prose fiction was the antithesis of his. In France, as in England, the vogue of the high-minded heroic romance was declining. Satirists had plastered it with ridicule. A French novelist, Paul Scarron, revitalized the picaresque genre in *Le Roman comique*, a realistic story about a troupe of strolling actors; and Antoine Furetière followed with *Le Roman bourgeois*, in which a middle-class girl makes herself absurd by affecting the grandiloquent airs and ideals of Mlle. de Scudèry's heroines. Then the Comtesse de Lafayette published several novels, notably *La Princesse de Clèves*, which were unpretentious and reasonably brief studies of natural human behavior. Also current in France were short prose books of a less respectable description, known as *chroniques scandaleuses*, giving lurid reports of illicit love affairs and other misconduct in the highest social circle; the most notorious of them was *L'Histoire amoureuse des Gaulles*, by Bussy-Rabutin (1660). For additional plausibility they often took the form of letters supposedly exchanged between the lovers, as in the *Five Love-letters from a Nun to a Cavalier*, which was translated by Sir Roger L'Estrange (1687). While these books were perhaps closer to modern sensational journalism than to fiction, the writers had little scruple in making a good story better, and so the border line between fact and invention was not clear.

As the French influence continued to be strong in England, such books became well known there. In an attempt to revive the picaresque novel, a ne'er-do-well Irishman named Richard Head published in 1665 *The English Rogue, Described in the Life of Meriton Latroon,* which was based partly on his own exploits. It was a racy story and so indecent in places that the censor banned it and copies had to be peddled surreptitiously. Its success encouraged Francis Kirkman, a London bookseller and hack writer, to compose several additional parts for it, a tedious jumble of tales from earlier sources, crudely colored with obscene details from the London underworld.

This work had something in common with numerous cheap books that purported to give the true life-stories of notorious criminals. Writers seized upon any court trial that attracted general interest, and embroidered the evidence with sensational details of their own devising, while maintaining a pretense of strict truth. In 1663, for instance, when Mary Carleton, a hussy who masqueraded as a German princess, was tried for bigamy, a batch of little books exploited the case; and ten years later, when she was executed as a thief, the writers vied with each other in creating biographies of her. Kirkman, in particular, produced one that was largely his own invention. The significance of such books is not in any literary merit, but in the fact that their claim to be factual reports forced the writers to strive for the illusion of reality as their primary aim.

This kind of publication resulted from the emergence of authorship as a distinct profession. Previously the only writers who had been able to make a living solely by their pens had been dramatists; and this vocation had terminated with the closing of the theaters in 1642. During the Civil War both sides made wide use of printed propaganda, and various periodical bulletins of events were established. By the time of the Restoration the public had become accustomed to reading topical reports. As the trades of printing and bookselling expanded, another trade became needed for supplying them with wares. Hence developed "Grub Street," where underpaid hacks ground out the necessary product. Unconcerned with artistic values, they sought only to write in a manner that could be understood with a minimum of effort and on subjects that would have the most direct appeal. The outcome was a new corps of writers, a new class of readers, and a new sort of relationship between them.

A conspicuous sign of the change was an abrupt shortening of prose fiction. The colossal, sluggish romances were not immediately abandoned, but they met strong competition from stories that moved quickly and ended promptly. By 1670 these short prose fictions, dealing with less exalted themes, were being described by the booksellers as "novels" to distinguish them from the "romances." The word was, of course, a revival of the old term "novella," and some of the novels that flooded the market were translations or adaptations of those earlier works. A selection from the *Exemplary Novels* of Cervantes had been translated by James Mabbe in 1640, and a volume containing five from Cervantes and five from Solórzano was brought out by Sir Roger L'Estrange in 1687. With examples of this sort before them, professional writers had little trouble in following the formula.

Averaging from 10,000 to 20,000 words (but sometimes shorter) and selling for one shilling, the stories had little complexity of plot or vividness of detail. The plots usually centered upon love intrigues, and the settings were in foreign countries. Their readers were probably predominantly feminine, and women soon began to write them as well as read them.

A new freedom for women to participate in literature and the theater was a result of the Restoration. Distinguished ladies like the Duchess of Newcastle and Katherine Philips were writing copiously, though in an elegantly amateur manner, and women of lower rank found that they could enter the field professionally, just as others were appearing for the first time on the stage.

The Duchess of Newcastle's contributions to fiction were short and didactic, but in her contempt for the heroic romances she did make some effort to depict actual life, as indicated by the title of one of her books, *Nature's Pictures by Fancy's Pencil;* and in another one, the *CCXI Sociable Letters,* she achieved some plausibility by using the epistolary form for imaginary characters and actions.

On a lower social level, the first professional authoress was Mrs. Aphra Behn, whose life seems to have been as eventful as any of her writings, though her talent for fiction was so often applied to her statements about herself that the plain facts have been hard to disentangle from her embellishments. Her early life is unknown, even her maiden name is disputable, and if she ever had a husband named Behn, said to have been a Dutch merchant in London, the marriage must have been a brief interlude early in her career. At about the age of twenty she went to Surinam, in the West Indies, and lived there for several years, perhaps as the mistress of an antiroyalist plotter who fled from England at the Restoration. Later she spent some time in Antwerp, engaged in mysterious negotiations between this same refugee and the British government. After returning to London, she failed to collect a reimbursement that she expected from the authorities, and fell into such straits that she was committed to the debtors' prison. In 1670, however, she wrote a successful play, and for the next fifteen years she was known equally well for her bawdy comedies and for her promiscuous love affairs. Handsome, generous, and good-natured, she was liked by her fellow-writers, who followed the current fad of borrowing names from heroic romances by calling her "the incomparable Astrea"; but she believed nevertheless that there was prejudice against her plays because of her sex, and several of them got her into trouble for their indecency, even by the lax standards of the time. Eventually, debt-ridden and crippled, she abandoned playwriting in favor of fiction.

Her first narrative was in the epistolary form, *Love-letters between a Nobleman and his Sister* (1684), supposedly translated from the French but believed to be based on a scandal concerning Lord Grey and Lady Henrietta Berkeley. About this time she also started writing short novels, and a batch of them were published in 1687 and 1688. Upon her death in 1689 she was honored with burial in Westminster Abbey. Several additional short novels appeared posthumously.

Mrs. Behn was apt in the invention of alluring titles, and most of them indicate the melodramatic, woman-centered nature of her fiction — *The Adventure of the Black Lady, The Wandering Beauty, The Unhappy Mistake, The Unfortunate Happy Lady.* She tried to make the stories seem authentic by claiming that she had witnessed the occurrences or that they had been reported to her by a participant; but most of them used standard plot situations which she manipulated with so many coincidences and impostures that credulity soon breaks down. Nor could she wholly escape from the despotism of the heroic romance, which demanded that the characters express intolerably noble sentiments in speeches of flowery rhetoric. Only a few of the briefer stories had English settings; and these, in spite of their stock devices, contain agreeable touches of humor and naturalness.

The stories in this group end happily; for her tragedies Mrs. Behn preferred foreign settings, in Spain, Portugal, Italy, or France. *The Dumb Virgin* is a painful story in which the son of a Venetian nobleman is lost at sea in infancy, is rescued by an English ship, visits Venice when he grows up, and unwittingly commits incest with his sister, a beautiful mute. *The Nun, or The Perjured Beauty* depicts a coquette whose simultaneous love affairs with three men bring death to all three, as well as to herself and to another girl. A longer and better-handled story is *The History of the Nun, or The Fair Vow-breaker.* In it a lovely votaress elopes from the convent to marry the brother of a fellow-nun; later, believing him killed in battle, she marries his best friend; and when the first husband returns, she murders both men and is executed for the crime. In *Agnes de Castro*, based on a famous fourteenth-century event in Portugal, a virtuous prince, with an equally virtuous wife, falls in love with her lady-in-waiting, who is quite as noble as either of them; a jealous woman forges a letter to convince the wife that her husband is unfaithful to her, and she dies of grief; Agnes is finally murdered by a rejected suitor. *The Fair Jilt,* being less sentimental, comes nearer to the amoral vigor of

Mrs. Behn's own life and era. A beautiful nymphomaniac plans the murder of her sister and gets three men condemned to death for crimes of which she falsely accuses them or to which she has instigated them; yet through it all she expresses the loftiest sentiments, and she retains her reputation unspotted for a serene old age.

None of these distressful stories possessed enough vividness or naturalness to survive; but Mrs. Behn wrote one novel that became a minor classic. This was *Oroonoko, or The Royal Slave*. Here again she represented herself as an onlooker upon actual events, and this time she was successful in maintaining the illusion. The scene was Surinam, and her early sojourn in that colony not only provided touches of local color (though apparently she refreshed her memory by reading travel literature) but also inspired a personally biased picture of the administration, using the real names of residents. This adds emotional impact to a tale that would otherwise be as conventional as her others. The hero is a young African chieftain brought to the West Indies by a slave trader. Through one of Mrs. Behn's typical coincidences he meets his boyhood sweetheart; later he leads an unsuccessful revolt of the slaves and is recaptured by the governor's false promise of amnesty. To save his wife from rape he cuts her head off, and then stoically endures a slow death by torture.

In his magnificent physique, his princely rank, his honorable nature, and his eloquent speeches, Oroonoko resembled dozens of the heroes of romances, who had already represented every race and nationality that the authors could think of. Mrs. Behn was lucky enough to find a new one. The sufferings of Oroonoko and Imoinda gave plentiful opportunity for harrowing the reader's feelings; and their simple virtues were an excuse for diatribes against the vices of civilization. After Mrs. Behn's death the story won new fame when dramatized by Thomas Sotherne. In the eighteenth century the romantic cult of "the noble savage" adopted *Oroonoko* as one of its favorite works, and later the humanitarian crusade used it for antislavery propaganda.

No new writer replaced Mrs. Behn as a purveyor of fiction, though one candidate appeared briefly. In 1692, under the romantic pen name of "Cleophil," a short novel was published by

William Congreve, a twenty-two-year-old law student. Like such diverse predecessors as Sidney and Bunyan, Congreve insisted that his "trifle" was not the result of serious effort but had been "began and finished in the idle hours of a fortnight's time." The book's title was *Incognita, or Love and Duty Reconciled,* and in spite of a conventional Italian setting the characterization and the use of informal conversation lent some naturalness, while its playful irony of manner was a welcome change from Mrs. Behn's emotionalism. The preface stated how the new type of fiction differed from the heroic romance:

> Romances are generally composed of the constant loves and invincible courages of heroes, heroines, kings and queens, mortals of the first rank, and so forth; where lofty language, miraculous contingencies and impossible performances elevate and surprise the reader into a giddy delight, which leaves him flat upon the ground whenever he gives off, and vexes him to think how he had suffered himself to be pleased and transported, concerned and afflicted by the several passages which he has read, . . . when he is forced to be very well convinced that 'tis all a lie. Novels are of a more familiar nature; come near us and represent to us intrigues in practice, delight us with accidents and odd events, but not such as are wholly unusual or unprecedented, such which not being so distant from our belief bring also the pleasure nearer to us. Romances give more of wonder, novels more delight.

After pointing out that no mere narrative can rival the illusion of realism in an acted play, Congreve stated his technical innovations:

> I resolved . . . to imitate dramatic writing . . . in the design, contexture, and result of the plot. I have not observed it before in a novel. . . . I leave the reader at his leisure to consider . . . whether every obstacle does not in the progress of the story act as subservient to that purpose which at first it seems to oppose. In a comedy this would be called the unity of action; here it may pretend to no more than an unity of contrivance. The scene is continued in Florence from the commencement of the amour, and the time from first to last is but three days.

In its exact symmetry the structure perhaps goes too far in the direction of controlled form. If Congreve had continued, however, to apply his keen sense of technique to prose fiction, he might have brought the novel to artistic maturity; but his praise of drama showed the direction in which his preference lay, and he soon became the leading figure in the brilliant group that raised the comedy of manners to its apogee.

Congreve's choice was symptomatic. As long as the sophisticated theater flourished, the novel remained in the hands of hacks, with only an occasional example rising above the mediocre average. Probably the best of these was *The Adventures of Lindamira, a Lady of Quality*, published in 1702. It was described as "revised and corrected" by Thomas Brown, the prolific journalist. If Brown wrote it himself, he was successful in disguising his facetious style under what he termed in the preface "the natural softness of the female pen." It consists of a series of letters, with greater realism and suspense than in the other novels of the time. While the theme and situations were derived from the heroic romances, with an admixture of Restoration stage comedy, the author stayed within the bounds of plausibility. Equally unusual are the use of an English setting and the moral probity of attitude; it was a novel of domestic life intended for respectable middle-class readers.

Elements of realism are to be seen also in *The Generous Rivals*, an anonymous short novel of 1711, in spite of the retention of classical names for the characters — Phylastratus, Panaretus, and so forth. The setting is contemporary London, the characters are drawn with some individuality and even subtlety, and there are touches of earthy humor in a few of the minor figures.

Incognita, Lindamira, and *The Generous Rivals* suffice to prove that by the beginning of the eighteenth century prose fiction was on the threshold of becoming a valid literary genre. All that it lacked was authors of first-rate talent to put the new principles into effect.

I I I

The Discovery of Realism

(1700 – 1740)

UPPER-CLASS ENGLISH LIFE in the last quarter of the seventeenth century had been characterized by artificiality in dress, manners, and conversation — an elaborate surface of formality and grace covering a certain amount of vice and a great deal of plain silliness. The same description can apply to most of the prose fiction of the period, which was neither sincere in its assumed dignity nor frank in its underlying crudity.

By 1700 a more sensible era was setting in. The decent commercial class was increasing in prosperity and influence. The Restoration fashion of elegant depravity wore itself out and was replaced by the roistering and ribaldry that were chronicled in ruder but more honest fashion by Grub Street humorists. In the theater the brilliant outburst of sophisticated comedy had passed its peak by 1700, and gave way to the respectable, sentimental plays of Colley Cibber and Richard Steele. John Locke's empirical philosophy appealed to thoughtful readers. The best writers of the time were geniuses in the art of satire, which attacks pretension with the weapons of common sense. Journalism contributed to the change in literary modes by proving that the reading public enjoyed plain facts straightforwardly expressed. The separate ingredients for realistic novels were developing in miscellaneous forms.

Three of these semi-fictional modes are important. One was a revival of the Theophrastian character writing. A new edition of Theophrastus in English was followed by a translation of La Bruyère's *Caractères*, and in 1702 came *The English Theophrastus, or The Manners of the Age*. Tom Brown's characters of women in *A Looking Glass for Married People* were typical of the trend. Another device of fiction, the imaginary conversation, in a tradition dating back to Plato, had been used by Dryden in prefaces, and was reinforced by translations of the dialogues of Lucian, the colloquies of Erasmus, and other such works. Thirdly, the pseudo-letter was used in dozens of pamphlets and periodical articles to provide a focus for expressions of opinion. Sometimes these were combined with fantasy for satiric effect, as in Brown's *Letters from the Dead to the Living*.

The periodicals furthered the use of these devices of fiction to lend variety or to heighten interest. Sir Roger L'Estrange's *Observator* in 1681 employed dialogue to break up its expository text. John Dunton's *Athenian Gazette* in 1691 was attributed to a fictionized editorial committee. Peter Motteux cast each number of the *Gentleman's Journal* (1692–94) in the form of a letter to a friend in the country, and the contents usually included complete "novels" (i.e., short stories). Ned Ward in his monthly *London Spy* (1698–1700) not only gave a lively description of everyday life in the city but achieved definite point of view by presenting it as the experiences of a Londoner showing the sights to a visitor from the country. The prolific Tom Brown used the structure of a walk through London with an American Indian for his book, *Amusements Serious and Comical* (1700), which, like much other writing of the era, was borrowed from a French original but was skillfully adapted to the English scene.

Ward and Brown were using the same sort of material as *The English Rogue*, but they dispensed with the lurid narrative, realizing that their readers were sufficiently interested in the description of actual places and atmosphere. Fiction had temporarily retreated in favor of fact, and its retreat proved that readers did not have to be lured with violence and abnormality, if the familiar facts were reported in such a way as to arouse imaginative identification. The pages of Ward and Brown read like the settings for novels, waiting to be populated with individual characters and to be linked together by means of a plot.

The portrayal of individual characters soon ensued. Several serials by Ned Ward, such as *The Weekly Comedy*, are cast in the form of conversations among persons representing various social vocations and psychological types. These are in the Theophrastian tradition, and are also reminiscent of Jonson's comedy of "humours," as indicated by their names: Madam Manlove, "a buxom widow who lately buried her husband"; Cant, a dissenting tailor; Allcraft, a turncoat; Scribble, a newswriter; and so forth. Ward boasted that "I'll wager a man cannot go twenty yards in any street in London but he will meet some original or other, whose likeness he will find so well preserved that he may know them by their pictures."

Out of such antecedents as these, two better written periodicals emerged. The *Tatler* was begun in 1709 by Richard Steele, an improvident Irishman who had made a literary success with three comedies and had learned journalism as editor of the official *Gazette*. As fictitious editor of his new paper he invented the personality of Isaac Bickerstaff. His purpose was to amend the morals and manners of the day — "to expose the false arts of life, to pull off the disguises of cunning, vanity, and affectation, and to recommend a general simplicity in our dress, our discourse, and our behavior." He hoped to appeal to women as well as to men, and so he avoided the violence and coarseness of previous journalists, and wrote with gentle satire about current upper-class life, in drawing rooms, in coffee-houses, at the theater. Character sketches, letters from imaginary correspondents, and sentimental short stories were scattered among the essays.

By the time the *Tatler* was well established, Steele was joined by his friend from school and college days, Joseph Addison, whose more polished and ironical style lent variety; he produced several neat vignettes of social types — Ned Softley, the poetaster, and Tom Folio, the book collector, and the "political upholsterer" and his cronies. Steele's character studies were more sympathetic glimpses of everyday people, such as Mr. Bickerstaff's sister Jenny Distaff and her husband, his three nephews, and an old friend and his family whom he visits. Of such pieces

Steele remarked, "it has been a most exquisite pleasure to me to frame characters of domestic life."

The *Tatler* was suspended at the end of 1710; but two months later the pair of friends started a new journal, the *Spectator*. Expanding the fictional element from the *Tatler*, "Mr. Spectator" started off with a group of characters supposedly associated with him in the enterprise — Sir Roger de Coverley, Sir Andrew Freeport, Will Honeycomb, and others, including their lady friend Leonora. Whenever there was a dearth of news, the editors could fill a whole issue with another scene from the lives of these people. Some modern reprints give a false impression of unity by making a separate book of the "De Coverley Papers." It must be remembered that Sir Roger and his friends appeared at irregular intervals, without any comprehensive scheme. But Sir Roger, in particular, was soon invested with so much individuality and humor that both Steele and Addison enjoyed every opportunity to bring them into their pages. If happy-go-lucky Dick Steele had been gifted with enough foresight and persistence, or if dignified Mr. Addison had been less occupied with affairs of state, one or other of them might have invented a plot for these static characters, and might thus have become the first English novelist.

Although long romances had not been written in either France or England for nearly half a century, the durable volumes survived in every gentleman's library, and many had been reprinted in successive editions. Much of the comedy in Steele's play, *The Tender Husband* (1705), centered upon Biddy Tipkins, who was so steeped in them that, as another character remarked, "the young lady, by being kept from the world, has made a world of her own. She has spent all her time in reading romances, her head is full of shepherds, knights, flowery meads, groves and streams, so that if you talk like a man of this world to her, you do nothing." In 1710 Addison's list of a typical lady's library included *Cassandra*, *Astraea*, *The Grand Cyrus* (with a pin stuck in one of the middle pages), and *Clelia* (which opened of itself in the place that describes two lovers in a bower). In 1714 Pope described the hero of *The Rape of the Lock* as possessing "twelve vast French romances, nicely gilt"; and in real life Pope presented a five-volume set of *The Grand Cyrus* to his friend Martha Blount (who liked to call herself "Parthenissa"), with a playful letter saying that "it is usual with unfortunate young women to betake themselves to romances, and thereby feed and indulge that melancholy which is occasioned by the want of a lover." Clearly the romances were far from defunct; everyone knew something of them and regarded them with mild but affectionate amusement as old-fashioned and visionary. In the course of two generations they had established a permanent effect by conditioning women to the habit of reading for amusement.

Steele's decision that his paper should "have something which may be of entertainment to the Fair Sex" was justified by the increasing prominence of women both as readers and as writers. The success of the *Tatler* impelled a rival journalist to start the *Female Tatler*. Most of it was cast in the form of conversations among the guests at the salon of the fictitious editor, Mrs. Phoebe Crackenthorpe, ranging "from his Grace, my Lord Duke, to Mr. Sagathie, the spruce merchant, . . . from the Duchess to Mrs. Topsail, the sea captain's wife at Wapping." The purpose of giving a survey of social types is evident.

The real woman hidden behind the disguise of Mrs. Crackenthorpe was Mrs. Delarivière Manley, who had inherited the reputation of Aphra Behn both as an authoress and as an adventuress. Of higher social origin than Mrs. Behn, she was the daughter of a cavalier who had been knighted for his loyal services and who had some talent as a writer. After his death his daughter's reputation was tainted at an early age when she was drawn into a bigamous marriage with a cousin, and was left with a child to support. For a while she was attached to the household of the Duchess of Cleveland, former mistress of Charles II, but was dismissed when the Duchess suspected her of designs upon her son. Her first book, entitled simply *Letters Written by Mrs. Manley* (1696), was a lively report of a stagecoach journey to Exeter, with descriptions of the passengers and with short stories introduced as being told by the fellow-travelers. About the same time she produced a comedy and a tragedy. For several years she was mistress of an unscrupulous married lawyer and helped in some of his financial maneuvers. Always a Tory partisan, she wrote her first long piece of fiction during the 1705 elections, *The Secret History of Queen Zarah and the Zarazians*, an attempt to discredit the Duchess of Marlborough and the Whig politicians by depicting them, under transparent disguises, as indulging in disreputable love affairs. In the preface she explained that she merely "sweetened" the real circumstances to procure the greater credit. Acknowledging that "the romances in France have for a long time been the diversion and amusement of the whole world," she expressed satisfaction that the "vice" of reading romances was diminishing — "that fury is very much abated." In offering some of "the little histories" that "have taken the place of romances" she claimed that they were "much more agreeable to the brisk and impetuous humour of the English, who have naturally no taste for long-winded performances, for they have no sooner begun a book but they desire to see the end of it." Whatever of truth may have been in her scandalous narrative, the series of bedroom scenes had the vividness and psychological intimacy of fiction.

After four years of playwriting and journalism, hounded by bill collectors and hopefully launching new schemes for enriching herself, Mrs. Manley returned to the technique of *Queen Zarah* and published *Secret Memoirs and Manners of Several Persons of Quality of Both Sexes, from the New Atalantis, an Island in the Mediterranean.* She acknowledged her allegiance to Mrs. Behn by introducing Astrea as the investigator who visits the Mediterranean island. The book was a confused jumble of comment on all aspects of contemporary English life, cast in the form of fiction and containing torrid episodes based on notorious recent scandals. In case any reader might miss the identification of the celebrities, the author issued a key. The first volume aroused so much excitement that when the second one came out five months later it was suppressed by the authorities, and the author and the publishers were arrested for libel. After protracted hearings, at which Mrs. Manley blandly asserted that she had used no secret sources of information and had been unaware of any resemblance to actual persons, the charge was dismissed. She celebrated her victory by adding two more volumes, these being entitled *Memoirs of Europe Towards the Close of the Eighth Century.*

Mrs. Manley assumed a righteous pose as a moral reformer. Quoting Dryden's phrase, she claimed that her purpose was "scourging of vice and exhortation to virtue." She defended herself against the censure of the *Tatler* by announcing:

Whoever is withheld by consideration of fear, danger, spiteful abuses, recriminations, or the mean hopes of missing pity, has views too dastardly and mercenary for lofty, steadfast souls, who can be only agitated by true greatness, by the love of virtue and the love of glory.

The New Atalantis was widely read and enjoyed. Lady Mary Wortley Montagu, being as sensual and opinionated as Mrs. Manley herself, liked it infinitely better than Steele's gentility. Deploring Mrs. Manley's arrest, she lamented:

> Now she will serve as a scarecrow to frighten people from attempting anything but heavy panegyric; and we shall be teazed with nothing but . . . false characters, so daubed with flattery that they . . . both scandalize the writer and the subject, like that vile paper the Tatler.

Addison included *The New Atalantis* in his catalogue of Leonora's library, and Pope praised it ironically in *The Rape of the Lock,* when the Baron exults:

> While fish in streams, or birds delight in air,
> Or in a coach and six the British fair,
> As long as Atalantis shall be read, . . .
> So long my honour, name, and praise shall live!

In the flush of this fame, Mrs. Manley published her autobiography (again in the guise of fiction) in 1714, as *The Adventures of Rivella.* The fictitious narrator of her life story, Sir Charles Lovemore (believed to be a recognizable portrait of one of her real admirers), repeated her claim to merit as a conscientious truth-teller:

> She was proud of having more courage than had any of our sex, and of throwing the first stone, which might give a hint for other persons of more capacity to examine the defects and vices of some men who took a delight to impose upon the world, by the pretense of public good, whilst their true design was only to gratify and advance themselves.

Her final work of fiction was *The Power of Love, in seven novels* (1720), adapted from Painter's *Palace of Pleasure* and other Renaissance *novelle.* Though by 1712 Swift could describe her as "about forty, very homely and very fat," she was securely established as the mistress of a rich printer and London alderman, and thus she lived till 1724, cherishing the ideal of herself that she had presented in *The Adventures of Rivella:*

> . . . the only person of her sex that knows how to live, and of whom we may say, in relation to love, that she has so peculiar a genius for, and has made such notable discoveries in that passion, that it would have been a *fault in her, not to have been faulty*.

Though Mrs. Manley was blatant in her publicity-hunting and monotonous in her series of salacious stories, she has a place in the development of the novel. She made a real effort to differentiate the personalities of her characters. Breaking with the high-flown elegance of the heroic romance, she depicted the kind of contemporary life she knew best, which happened (as she boasted in her autobiography) to be sex:

> She has carried the passion farther than could be readily conceived. [Many of her erotic scenes] are such representations of nature that must warm the coldest reader; it raises high ideas of the dignity of human kind, and informs us that we have in our composition wherewith to taste sublime and transporting joys. After persuing her enchanting descriptions, which of us have not gone in search of raptures which she everywhere tells us, as happy mortals, we are capable of tasting.

Thus she flaunted her belief that fiction, if vivid enough, can directly influence the behavior of readers.

In basing fiction squarely upon contemporary events Mrs. Manley was the female counterpart of another writer who emerged from the same cut-throat turmoil of Grub Street journalism and political propaganda. Daniel Defoe, as he came to call himself, was a dozen years older than Steele and Addison and Mrs. Manley, but he had come slowly to authorship after failure in other vocations. Until he was thirty he had been satisfied with the name of "Foe", which had been that of his father, a London tallow chandler; then some obscure claim to ancient Norman blood impelled the future author to adopt the aristocratic prefix "de." The family were strict dissenters and respectable citizens; during Daniel's boyhood the father branched into the business of butcher and prospered in it. In the hope that the boy might enter the Presbyterian ministry he was sent to a good academy, where he received a grounding in science, mathematics, and terse English, as well as a smattering of the classics.

Upon leaving school he went into business in London, and for some years made an ample income by trading in tobacco, wines, and liquors as well as haberdashery, which was his chief staple. He traveled over England and Scotland on business trips, which seem to have taken him sometimes as far as France and Spain. By the time he was twenty-four he had married a girl with an ample dowry, and during the next five years he could afford a country house as well as his London residence alongside his warehouse.

He lost money, however, in ambitious speculations, and was involved in a series of lawsuits which indicate that his financial methods were not too scrupulous. The cases involved not only normal business transactions but such bizarre ventures as a civet-cat farm and a stock company to exploit a newly invented diving apparatus. In 1692 the unlucky speculator went bankrupt for a staggering sum.

Making a fresh start as a manufacturer of brick and tiles, he was successful enough during the next twelve years to pay off much of his debt. But in the same years he was giving more and more of his time to political activity. He held minor government appointments, and in some mysterious way he was advising the Whig officials in financial policy. Apparently he was acting also as a secret investigator in various parts of the country.

Before his bankruptcy he had written a few commonplace poems, and afterwards his restless interest in new inventions and social reform expressed itself in a book proposing such radical ideas as an income tax, pension and insurance systems, good roads, hospitals for the feeble-minded, a military academy, and higher education for women. Some of the schemes were not put into effect until two hundred years later; but Defoe presented them not as utopian visions but as clearly reasoned plans, complete with methods of financing and administration. This *Essay upon Projects,* published in 1697, revealed Defoe's unique genius, which may be termed "practical imagination" — the ability to develop existing facts in original directions without sacrificing plausibility. The book is notable also for its prose style, which is clear, positive, and sensible, free alike from the embellishments of the romance-writers and from the witticisms of the journalists. It was the prose of a businessman, concerned only with making himself understood.

As a political partisan with a flair for writing, Defoe was soon drawn into producing propaganda pamphlets. Through these he gained skill in emphasis and in the use of vivid examples and analogies. Being a devout dissenter, be could not bring himself to write the obscenities that were usual with Brown and Ward and most of the other professionals; but apart from this he tried every current literary mode, only to prove that for the two that were most prevalent — poetry and satire — he had little talent. His verse was pedestrian, and his most notorious piece of satire was so inept that his political enemies were able to accuse him of seditious libel and to have him imprisoned, fined, and exposed in the pillory. During his months in jail his brick business collapsed; and when he was pardoned, at the age of forty-three, deep in debt, penniless, with seven children to support, he finally committed himself wholly to the profession of letters.

His output was incredible. From 1704 to 1713 he conducted a newspaper, the *Review*, which for most of the time came out three times a week, and which he wrote almost wholly himself. His pamphlets, being anonymous, are not all identified with certainty, but may have reached a total of four hundred. As he was subsidized by politicians, he wrote almost exclusively about national affairs, but an occasional gleam of interest in individual human behavior broke through. The most notable was a pamphlet called *A True Relation of the Apparition of one Mrs. Veal* (1706). Public interest had been excited when a woman in Canterbury reported a visit from a friend who had died twenty-four hours before. Defoe's narrative was so matter-of-fact in manner and so photographic in detail that it made the supernatural episode uncannily convincing.

During most of these years he was traveling over England and Scotland, under a false name, as a government spy; and thus he sharpened his naturally keen faculty for observing details of psychology and conduct, and enriched his fertility of invention whenever he had to offer plausible evidence to conceal his identity. Not until he was almost sixty, however, did he stumble on the kind of writing that produced his masterpieces. By that time, in spite of having shifted his allegiance to serve whatever party was in power, sometimes to the extent of writing for papers of both parties at once, his political prestige was waning, and twice more he had been convicted for libels. His rugged heaith was beginning to crack, and his enemies were exulting over his downfall.

Without being aware of it, he was uniquely qualified to write in a new way. He had studied human nature from many angles: in politics, as adviser to ministers of state, and also as a devious agitator and spy; in business, as a prosperous trader and also as a ruined bankrupt. Twenty years of journalism gave him mastery of a supremely readable style. Nevertheless he seems to have arrived at the change of material by a process of elimination, rather than by choice. And he found the first of his new subjects almost accidentally.

Travels to remote and primitive regions were among the best-selling books of the early eighteenth century. Sea captains published meticulous records of their voyages; men who had been captured by Barbary pirates or Asiatic natives were sure of eager readers when they escaped to civilization; the buccaneers of the Spanish Main were popular heroes. Defoe had always shared this interest in geography and exploration, but not until 1719 did he think of making a book on the subject.

Six years earlier, the public had been fascinated with the adventures of Alexander Selkirk, who had lived alone for four years on a remote island. In 1718 the interest was revived by a new edition of the book that recounted his rescue. It is possible that Defoe had interviewed Selkirk in person. At any rate, he probably thought first of doing a short, factual report like the one on Mrs. Bargrave, who had seen the ghost of Mrs. Veal. The Veal pamphlet had been reprinted again and again. But as Defoe's "practical imagination" dwelt upon Selkirk's experiences, he began to visualize ways of giving them a stronger hold upon readers. He could lengthen the period on the island; he could add details suggested by the narratives of other castaways. Obviously, since Selkirk's real tale was well known, Defoe could not make these improvements without changing the protagonist's identity. Once this was done, the account grew far beyond the dimensions of a literal report.

The Life and Strange Surprising Adventures of Robinson Crusoe, of York, Mariner, published in 1719, contained all the elements of popular appeal. It was a story of wild adventure and yet it was told with the coolness of everyday routine. No other theme, perhaps, has as strong a psychological impact as the struggle of an individual to survive in hostile surroundings. By the simple device of telling it in the first person, Defoe gave an incomparable sense of actuality. The narrator was such an average unimaginative specimen of humanity that most readers identified themselves with him completely and automatically before they finished the first chapter. Matter-of-fact tradesmen and artisans, approving all Crusoe's efficient contrivances, reveled vicariously in his triumph over primitive hardships, and perhaps secretly envied him his remoteness from the counter and the workbench.

On the artistic side, the story's inherent requirements guaranteed unity and climax. Undeniably the opening narrative of Crusoe's early years of perils by sea and land is episodic; but this part is kept brief and can be justified as establishing his self-reliant character. Once he sets foot on his island, the tempo slows to that of his daily life; the scene contracts to the few square miles of his domain; the action moves without digression toward its only possible climax — his rescue. Though thoughtful readers had in the back of their minds the comforting certainty of this happy outcome, since Crusoe lived to tell his tale, there was terrific tension at each stage along the way, as he faced the crises of starvation, of sickness, of insanity, and then the unforgettable moment of the footprint in the sand.

Defoe's readers had no idea that they were being offered a work of fiction. The title page said that Crusoe's narrative was "written by himself," and the unsigned preface assured them that "the editor believes the thing to be a just history of fact; neither is there any appearance of fiction in it." This guarantee was intended to allay the doubts of religious-minded readers, who had been brought up in the belief that fiction was identical with lying, and thus was a device of Satan to tempt men's minds from virtue. Such readers were further reassured that "The story is told with modesty, with seriousness, and with a religious application of events to the uses to which wise men always apply them, viz., to the instruction of others by this example, and to justify and honor the wisdom of Providence in all the variety of circumstances, let them happen how they will."

Luckily Defoe did not let this latter purpose dominate the story to the extent of making it tiresomely didactic. Crusoe's occasional religious moralizing rendered him all the more plausible as a typical lower-middle-class Englishman. It was the author's other concession to his readers' austerity — the necessity of convincing them that this was "a just history of fact" — that made it a milestone in the history of the novel. Under the compulsion of his market, he produced the first long piece of prose fiction that had the primary purpose of giving the illusion of reality. After years of hiring his pen to politicians in order to impose their views upon the public, he must have been amazed to find that far more readers could be secured by simply enabling them to merge their identity in that of a fictitious character.

Though the book was ignored or despised by intellectual authors and cultivated readers, it gained unprecedented success. A satirist of the time describes Defoe as telling his friend Crusoe,

> I have made you, out of nothing, famed from Tutle Street to Limehouse Hole; there is not an old woman that can go to the price of it but buys the *Life and Adventures*, and leaves it as a legacy with the *Pilgrim's Progress*, the *Practice of Piety*, and *God's Revenge Against Murder*, to her posterity.

The businesslike author did not delay in exploiting this unforeseen triumph. Apparently, however, he failed to realize that the book's effectiveness had resided partly in its artistic unity. As with *The Pilgrim's Progress*, this quality had been inherent in the theme, rather than conceived by the author. When Defoe rushed into print with *The Farther Adventures of Robinson Crusoe*, four months after the first part, he took Crusoe back on a casual visit to his island and then on an interminable business sojourn in the East Indies, followed by a rambling journey homeward across China and Siberia. Worse still, the next year came *The Serious Reflections of Robinson Crusoe*, a volume of moralizing with no action at all.

The progressive anticlimax of the three parts not only illustrates the usual ineffectiveness of sequels, but specifically proves how little the author recognized what had given the original book its novelty. Seemingly he considered his readers to be attracted by geographical information rather than by the thrills of danger. Besides, he was worried by attacks upon the first part. Adversaries had pointed out a few inconsistencies of detail, such as that Crusoe filled his pockets with biscuit after swimming naked to the wrecked ship, an episode cited by Benjamin Hoadley to support his blunt charge that the book was "a most palpable lie from beginning to end." Even more disturbing was Charles Gildon's charge that the story did not teach a lesson: "To render any fable worthy of being received into the number of those which are truly valuable, it must naturally produce in its event some useful moral, either expressed or understood." In the preface to Part II Defoe emphasized the moral value of the first part, even at the expense of admitting that some portions were not literally true: "The just application of every incident, the religious and useful inferences to be drawn from every part, are so many testimonies to the good design of making it public, and must legitimate all the part that may be called invention or parable in the story." By the time he wrote the *Serious Reflections* he followed this idea to the absurd extreme of asserting that the first two parts were to be read as "parable or allegoric history," of which "the just and only good end" is "moral and religious improvement." On this basis he defended his use of exotic settings: "Facts that are formed to touch the mind must be done a great way off, and by somebody never heard of."

As soon as he finished *The Farther Adventures*, Defoe looked for other stories of strange experiences. His next three dealt with characters so picturesque that no veneer of invention was needed: a dumb man who suddenly gained powers of speech and prophecy at the age of fifty-eight, another deaf mute who was currently astonishing London as a fortune-teller, a pirate captain who established a temporary kingdom in Madagascar. In the same year with these three literal biographies, Defoe brought out two books which were entirely fictitious, but which derived enough precise detail from authentic sources to sound utterly convincing. One of them, *The Memoirs of a Cavalier*, was used by historians as a reliable first-hand record of the Civil War period until modern research attributed it to Defoe; the "editor" had explained plausibly that the manuscript came to light among the papers of a deceased cabinet minister. The other book, *The Life, Adventures, and Piracies of the Famous Captain Singleton*, fell into two loosely related halves. The first half was largely occupied with the hardships of a party of mutineers, abandoned on the east coast of Africa, who made their way across the heart of the continent to the west coast as their only chance of being rescued. Little was known about the interior of Africa at that time; but so thoroughly did Defoe absorb such information as he could find, and so fully did he visualize every detail, that his descriptions were not seriously invalidated by later explorations. After this epic trek, the second half of the book falls somewhat flat, though it deals with Singleton's exciting exploits of piracy, and includes a voyage around Australia, which was then as totally unknown as the central Africa of the earlier chapters. The book was an outgrowth of Defoe's research when he was writing the biography of the real pirate, Captain Avery; and he discovered a new device for plausibility when he made Captain Singleton fall in with Avery's gang. Anyone who had recently read *The King of the Pirates* would feel an immediate conviction of truth, as well as a pleasant sense of familiarity, when he met the same pirate leader figuring in another book — especially as no one suspected that both books were by the same author.

A year later Defoe displayed another burst of energy. In 1722, in addition to a long book of sanctimonious dialogues on marriage, he published two of his best fictitious biographies and also an amazing work of fiction that was not a narrative at all. England was terrified that year by a serious recurrence of plague in France. Defoe, as usual, exploited the public interest with a pamphlet, *Due Preparations for the Plague*, which told about the last great outbreak in London in 1665; and he followed this with a more remarkable book on the same subject. As he had been scarcely five years old at the time, he could have retained only the dimmest recollection of it; but in *A Journal of the Plague Year* he constructed what purported to be a first-hand account of the calamity, so successfully that the book was accepted for more than a century as the authentic diary of a saddler who was in London throughout the weeks of the crisis. Not even the chronicler, however, can be described as a character, since he is not accorded so much as the bare identification of a name; and unlike Robinson Crusoe he makes no effort to contend with circumstances, but merely records stoically from day to day the conditions that he observes around him. And yet his anonymity increases the effect, by making him a typical specimen of the thousands constituting the helpless population of London. His acceptance of the facts becomes an emotional atmosphere in its very lack of emotion: one feels that it reproduces the numb fatalism that would be the only possible way of enduring the horrors of the pestilence. Even statistics acquire artistic validity in this context.

Among the books that Defoe brought out in 1722, the one now regarded most highly is *The Fortunes and Misfortunes of the Famous Moll Flanders*. It can never rival the fame of *Robinson Crusoe* (Part I), which has been read for over two centuries by millions in virtually every language of the world because of its unsurpassed appeal to children. Even the least bookish of boys can absorb *Crusoe* and be impelled to act out the castaway's exploits in the nearest patch of woods. *Moll Flanders* is emphatically not a story for children, but its essential theme is much the same as that of *Crusoe:* the resourceful heroine, cast on the world in childhood without family or money, manages to conquer every mischance through a long lifetime, by her stubborn refusal to yield. Defoe's knowledge of the criminal class, and his realization of the ruthlessness of the struggle for survival, provide unity of impression in spite of the episodic structure.

He was aware that the autobiographic method was dangerous here. Readers might doubt whether Moll could tell her story with the clarity and restraint that were inherent in his style. His preface therefore explained that the original manuscript ("written in the year 1683") had been modified by the editor:

> The world is so taken up of late with novels and romances, that it will be hard for a private history to be taken for genuine, where the names and other circumstances of the person are concealed, and on this account we must be content to leave the reader to pass his own opinion upon the ensuing sheets. . . . It is true that the original of this story is put into new words, and the style of the famous lady we here speak of is a little altered; particularly she is made to tell her own tale in modester words than she told it at first, the copy which came first to hand having been written in language more like one still in Newgate than one grown penitent and humble, as she afterwards pretends to be.

The problem was not confined to plausibility of style, but extended also to morals. Moll's clearest trait was the complacency with which she chronicled her lawless career, and Defoe knew how repugnant this must be to the decent citizens who were his best customers. He fell back on the obvious excuse that the sordid tale would render crime disgusting and that Moll's belated repentance justified the ugly details:

> As the best use is made even of the worst story, the moral 'tis hoped will keep the reader serious, even where the story might incline him to be otherwise. To give the history of a wicked life repented of, necessarily requires that the wicked part should be made as wicked as the real history of it will bear, to illustrate and give a beauty to the penitent part.

The title page gave generous promise of viciousness by announcing that Moll "was born in Newgate, and during a life of continued variety for threescore years, besides her childhood, was twelve year a whore, five times a wife (whereof once to her own brother), twelve year a thief, eight year a transported felon in Virginia, at last grew rich, lived honest, and died a penitent." The preface dropped further tantalizing allusions to gaudy moments in the story, but the "editor" smugly explained:

> There is not a wicked action in any part of it but is first and last rendered unhappy and unfortunate; there is not a superlative villain brought upon the stage, but either he is brought to an unhappy end, or brought to be penitent; there is not an ill thing mentioned but it is condemned, even in the relation, nor a virtuous, just thing, but it carries its praise along with it.

The deft mixture of lewd particulars and moral strictures was exactly suited to the taste of Defoe's readers. Being of their own class and temperament, Defoe may have been sincere in his attitude; but if the book had been no more than this it would have small claim to survival. Its basic importance rests neither upon Moll's sins nor upon her repentance, but upon the tolerance and insight which belie the author's conventional censure and which link him with Chaucer and Shakespeare and other great humane writers. Moll is revealed as a normal human type whose behavior and standards were shaped by circumstances. Driven by an uncontrollable urge to become a "lady," she has no alternative but to drift into a life of sin; and as soon as she and her fifth husband, after their transportation to Virginia, succeed in acquiring a profitable plantation, her economic status enables her to fulfil her lifelong ambition and turn respectable.

Moll Flanders is the best of Defoe's novels because it is dominated and unified by the personality of the heroine. Whether by a feat of imaginative identification or by his innate possession of the same traits, Defoe creates a consistent and convincing portrait of a human creature whose reactions are totally materialistic, never either imaginative or spiritual. Though sensual, she has not an iota of sensibility. She never challenges the respectable middle-class standards in which she was brought up; but they are in ironic contrast with her life of crime. Financial prosperity and physical possessions are her only goal.

The narrative pattern is as loose as in Defoe's previous books, sometimes with long periods of the heroine's career summarized in a single sentence. In fact, if the reader can ever detach himself from the immediate vividness of the separate episodes, he must realize the exaggeration of the total record. The same love of excess is observable in *Robinson Crusoe,* where Selkirk's four years on the island were magnified to twenty-eight. Thus Moll enjoys some twenty lovers and gives birth to about the same number of children, along with all her other activities. But the circumstantial details, reinforced by "documents" such as bills and inventories, carry such conviction that one is seldom able to gain the perspective necessary for skepticism. In spite of this advantage of the single-line structure, however, a comment in the preface shows Defoe's glimmering of recognition that more complex effects might have been achieved if he had departed from it:

There are two of the most beautiful parts still behind, which this story gives some idea of, and lets us into the parts of them, but they are either of them too long to be brought into the same volume, and indeed are, if I may call them, whole volumes of themselves, viz.: 1, the life of her governess, as she calls her. . . . The second is the life of her transported husband.

This half promise of sequels was not fulfilled; instead of continuing with a Moll Flanders cycle, Defoe invented a sort of masculine counterpart for her in *The History and Remarkable Life of the Truly Honourable Colonel Jacque,* which came out in the same year. An illegitimate son of aristocratic parents, Jacque was brought up by a baby-farmer and became a child pickpocket. The first section of the book is a sympathetic account of a youngster living by his wits in the London under-world; but after Jacque grows up the interest wanes. After a long series of disjointed adventures as a highwayman, a deserter, a slave and an overseer on Virginia plantations, he reforms, about the middle of the book, wins promotion by bravery in the French army, and assists the Old Pretender in the rebellion of 1715. All this is interlarded with his business ventures and his marriages to five women of ill fame. The historical events in this later part are based on research, and real celebrities of the time are introduced, in the same manner as in the *Memoirs of a Cavalier*.

The last of Defoe's books with any claim to be classified as a novel was *The Fortunate Mistress*, more often known as *Roxana* (1724). In it he created a heroine as unprincipled as Moll Flanders, but placed her in the higher social plane of Colonel Jacque's later life. He may have taken hints from the notorious Mary Carleton, and the book has some affinity also with Mrs. Behn's *Fair Jilt* and Mrs. Manley's *Adventures of Rivella*. Defoe's heroine, deserted by a bankrupt husband, grows rich in several European countries as mistress to a succession of business magnates and aristocrats, sets up her establishment in London and moves in court society as a French lady of title. Toward the end of the book, when Roxana is in danger of being identified by one of the daughters of her early marriage, Defoe achieves unwonted suspense and the reader hopes that for once there will be a strong climax. But the author tires of the situation, eliminates the daughter without explaining what became of her, and ends the book with a few perfunctory sentences. One can only surmise that when he had written enough pages to make a volume he saw no reason to do another hour's work.

In the remaining six years of his life he wrote no more fiction. This was not due to any lack of success with his books in this genre. The satirists continued to point them out as the favorite reading matter of the servant class. As one lampoon said in 1729:

> Down in the kitchen honest Dick and Doll
> Are studying Colonel Jack and Flanders Moll.

Defoe's pen remained as active as ever, but apparently he had no inkling that his half-dozen books of fiction were to be his lasting monument. After 1724 he withdrew from political journalism and settled down in the country to devote himself to gardening and book collecting, along with a new partnership in a brick and tile business, which was no more successful than his earlier venture. The main result was that he wrote a textbook on how to make money in business.

The other writings of his final years included biographies of real people who were currently notorious, chiefly criminals (Jack Sheppard and Jonathan Wild) and seamen (Captain George Roberts and Captain Robert Drury). Only one of them, *The Military Memoirs of Captain George Carleton*, seems to have been a fictitious compilation from historical sources, like the *Memoirs of a Cavalier*. He also wrote several treatises on the supernatural, a subject that had always fascinated him.

The illusion of actual experience in Defoe's six novels is directly associated with the absence of customary artistic responsibility. In real life we are usually so close to our experiences that they lack proportion and logical correlation; but in fiction we expect the irrelevant to be excluded, the significant to be intensified, and an underlying pattern of causation to be revealed. In Defoe's stories, however, the events are unselected: an inventory of furniture or the menu of a meal is recorded as fully as a life-and-death crisis; elaborate preparations are often left without fulfillment, whereas a major event may occur with neither cause nor consequences. Defoe's own career with its extremes of fortune had left him no opportunity to gain the perspective that sees a logic in events.

A similar comment applies to his characterization. Because of the episodic structure, it is seldom that any character except the narrator appears at sufficient length to be fully portrayed; the large and ever-changing cast of subsidiary persons remain little more than type figures. By contrast, the narrator in each book seems to have a thoroughly developed personality; but this is simply because through all vicissitudes of fortune and all perils and strange adventures each hero or heroine persistently remains an ordinary individual, and therefore the reader automatically projects his own personality into the character and enriches it with complexities not actually stated in the narrative. This utter normality results in its turn from the fact that Defoe embodied himself in each of the central characters. Colonel Jacque's determination to rise to the social level of his forebears is a reflection of the author's adding of "de" to his surname and applying for a coat of arms and buying country houses. Moll Flanders is impelled by a psychopathic dread of Newgate Prison such as Defoe had acquired from his own months in jail. Roxana keeps a meticulous ledger of her earnings and investments as Defoe must have done in his business dealings.

All this points to the final reason why Defoe's six works of fiction are not in the category of major novels. They are based upon no analysis of life. Defoe is a chronicler of phenomena, not an interpreter of them. Hence there could be neither true comedy nor true tragedy in his stories. Their only ideological element is the revelation of the mentality of the author's time and class. His work epitomizes the newly influential bourgeoisie with their social aspirations, their financial acquisitiveness, their materialistic code of values, their utilitarian ethics, their puritan righteousness superimposed upon a primitive taste for violence and eroticism. His epitome is authentic because it is unintentional. He was not seeking either to condemn or to justify. He wrote about things as he understood them, and his readers were satisfied because it was thus that they understood things too.

Neither Defoe's materials nor his methods were entirely new in English. Four centuries earlier, the author of Mandeville's *Travels* had similarly fitted together details from other writers to construct a plausible first-personal narrative of adventures in distant lands he had never seen. Defoe's work was even more reminiscent of the "cony-catching" pamphlets of Greene. Several of Greene's best revelations of villainy had been made plausible by the device of autobiography, and Nashe had refined upon the same technique in *Jack Wilton*. In simple vocabulary and common-sense attitude Defoe's forerunner was Deloney. The difference resided in Defoe's imaginative identification. When readers were thus provided with the wherewithal for actually sharing the experiences of the imaginary performers, the one essential attribute of the novel had at last been discovered.

Since Defoe himself so readily relinquished his new literary genre after only five years, it is not surprising that no other writer went on with it. In the opinion of more cultivated authors, only the semi-literate could be satisfied with the simple interest of objective realism. The sole major work of prose fiction of the decade, although it borrowed technical hints from *Robinson Crusoe*, remained loyal to the axiom that realism must be the handmaid of an ulterior purpose. Jonathan Swift had been a competitor of Defoe in political journalism for twenty years, and had despised him as "so grave, sententious, dogmatical a rogue, that there is no enduring him." Swift had used imaginary characters and action in his early satires, *The Battle of the Books* and *A Tale of a Tub*, and when he decided, in his embittered later life, to compose an all-inclusive condemnation of human nature, prose fiction offered itself as the most suitable vehicle.

The main problem of a universal satirist is that he must entice readers to accept a piece of writing that ruthlessly attacks themselves and their most cherished assumptions. Swift sought to lull suspicions by presenting what seemed to be a harmless specimen of a currently popular type of book and to stimulate interest so promptly that by the time his true purpose emerged the reader would be too firmly captivated to desist. Accordingly he invented a Defoe-like hero, a commonplace ship's officer, and wrote in an appropriately homespun style. He even studied a treatise on navigation to ensure technical accuracy in the account of the voyage. When these plausible elements were conjoined with the first-personal point of view, readers were bound to fall into the author's trap by identifying themselves imaginatively with the narrator.

Travels into Several Remote Nations of the World, by Lemuel Gulliver, was published in 1726 in exactly the format of genuine narratives of exploration, and with no hint that the real author was the brilliant Dean Swift. An unsuspecting reader, upon reaching the second chapter and finding Gulliver a captive of the six-inch Lilliputians, would realize that the work was a fantasy, but would read further in expectation of an amusing burlesque upon exaggerated tales of adventure. And even the satire throughout the first voyage would gratify readers rather than infuriate them. By being identified with Gulliver, we share his calm self-confidence, his superhuman forbearance, his benign amusement at the Lilliputians' petty politics and petty wars. Intellectually we are aware that when we laugh at the vainglorious midgets we are laughing at our own pretensions; but emotionally we enjoy the delight of rising above human limitations with Gulliver's secure sense of wisdom and power.

In the second voyage all this abruptly changes. Inescapably identified now with the narrator, the reader has to become helpless and terrified, struggling to maintain his self-respect by pitiful bragging. At the same time, seeing the Brobdingnagians as magnified human beings, we realize that physical strength and beauty can be loathsomely coarse. The third voyage similarly destroys our faith in man's highest endowment, his brain. The way has now been prepared for the final voyage, when, still sharing Gulliver's emotions, we regard mankind as lower than animals. By no other technique than that of imaginative identification could Swift have succeeded in subverting all our inmost criteria of human superiority.

If Defoe never achieved a full-scale novel because his books lacked interpretation of life, *Gulliver's Travels* falls outside of the canon for the opposite reason. Its greatness resides in its meaning, not in its story. In external pattern it consists of four separate episodes, each complete in itself. The final powerful climax is in the mind of the reader, and not in Gulliver's career. The significance of *Gulliver's Travels* in the development of the novel is simply the fact that Swift, to accomplish his special purpose, was obliged to borrow the new realistic method as the best means of capturing the greatest number of readers. And the ultimate irony of his career is that his subordinate device came to obscure his ulterior purpose. The book was too clever to be ignored, yet too painful to be accepted. By an instinct of self-defense, posterity solved the dilemma by shutting their eyes to the intolerable satire, labeling the book a pleasant fantasy, and then eliminating the second half of it in order to make it suitable reading matter for children. Robbed of its intellectual meaning, it took its place alongside three earlier masterpieces, the *Morte Darthur*, *The Pilgrim's Progress*, and *Robinson Crusoe*, as a juvenile classic.

Apart from Defoe and Swift, the writers of prose fiction between 1720 and 1740 were undistinguished hacks, predominantly female. The most industrious was Eliza Haywood, who began to write a few months before the death of Mrs. Manley and sought to become her successor. The daughter of a London shopkeeper, she was married early to a clergyman who was many years older. After an unsuccessful debut as an actress, between 1719 and 1725 she published half-a-dozen short and melodramatic "exemplary novels," after the model set by Mrs. Behn. These were repeatedly reprinted and reached the eminence of a collected edition in 1725; perhaps it was the success of her first books that encouraged her to run away from her husband in 1721. In 1725 she turned to the scandal-mongering type of *roman à clef*, and imitated Mrs. Manley in two books that gained some notoriety, *Memoirs of a Certain Island Adjacent to the Kingdom of Utopia* and *The Secret History of the Present Intrigues of the Court of Caramania*. For many years she continued with a flood of books and pamphlets, but her chief reward was an exceptionally brutal allusion in Pope's *Dunciad*.

Like Mrs. Manley, Mrs. Haywood kept up a smug pretense of morality as justification for her erotic scenes. In her preface to *Lasselia* she rejected "that aspersion which some of my own sex have been unkind enough to throw upon me, that 'I seem to endeavor to divert more than to improve the minds of my readers.' Now, as I take it, the aim of every person who pretends to write (though in the most insignificant and ludicrous way) ought to tend at least to a good moral use." Most of the other women writers of the time went further and actually wrote tediously proper fiction. These well-meaning ladies included Jane Barker, Elizabeth Rowe, Penelope Aubin, and Arabella Plantin. The best of them, Mrs. Mary Davys, displayed some realism and humor, and sought to follow Congreve's example in adapting the unified structure of comedy. A little later Elizabeth Boyd, with *The Female Page* (1737), reverted toward Mrs. Behn's raffish lewdness.

Knowing what the novel was soon to become, we are apt to wonder at the obtuseness of the writers from 1700 to 1740 in failing to achieve the final synthesis of their material. Characters existed without plots, as in the *De Coverley Papers*; settings existed without characters, as in the *Journal of the Plague Year*; plots existed without either definite settings or believable characters; potentially effective situations were allowed to fade out in muddled anticlimaxes. Fact and fiction were inextricably confused in the "secret histories" that claimed to reveal actual intrigues under false names, and in the fictitious biographies wherein Defoe used all his skill to deceive his readers into believing that Singleton and Moll Flanders had really existed, as well as in the biographies of real people that heightened their interest by exaggerating the adventures. The best prose writer of the time, Jonathan Swift, practiced fiction only as a vehicle for philosophical satire, while the man with the potential talent of a great novelist, Alexander Pope, never wrote prose at all.

Nevertheless, the half-century marked a vital stage in the process by which the novel came to birth. The old fantastic trappings of the romances were discarded. Prose style became simple and flexible enough to be appropriate for reproducing everyday experience. Natural dialogue was used for many purposes of exposition and ridicule. A huge new reading public was being purged of the old suspicion that fiction was either a waste of time or an incitement to sin, and was becoming conditioned to enjoy the pleasure of identifying themselves with the characters and events that an author invented. Equally essential was the expansion of the book trade to a point where substantial books could be distributed in large numbers at a reasonable price. Not until all these conditions had developed was it possible for writers to conceive that long fiction might be practiced as a form of art.

I V

The First Masterpieces

(1740 – 1755)

IN ALL BRANCHES of history, important developments occur when by accident the right person is in the right circumstances at the right moment. When the novel was ready to emerge from its long prenatal development, no single individual had enough foresight to envision the opportunity clearly; but by a set of curious chances two separate men, antithetical in every trait of personality, blundered into the new genre from opposite directions and were intelligent enough to recognize what they had found.

The man who first served as catalyst for the suspended elements of the novel was not unlike the two who had come nearest to distinction in the preparatory era. Both Bunyan and Defoe originated in the tradesman class and reached middle age before external pressures impelled them to start writing fiction. Samuel Richardson differed from them only insofar as the lower middle class had become stabilized during the two generations since Bunyan's time. He was more prosperous than Defoe in the same ratio as Defoe had been more prosperous than Bunyan; and he was less devout than Defoe in the same ratio as Defoe had been less devout than Bunyan. Bunyan had been a preacher for an evangelical Puritan sect; Defoe's parents had dreamed of making him a Presbyterian minister; but Richardson's parents dreamed of making him an Anglican clergyman. The moral earnestness remained, but economic improvement brought a steady trend toward orthodoxy.

Richardson's father was a London cabinet-maker who was living somewhere in Derbyshire when his son was born. The boy's schooling did not go beyond the average training for a tradesman's son. At school, where he was nicknamed "Gravity" and "Serious," he was popular for his facility in telling stories, some derived from his reading and others from his own invention. By the time he was thirteen, various young women were confiding their secret love affairs to him and asking him for help in revising their letters to their sweethearts. At seventeen he chose to be apprenticed to a printer in London, in the hope that this vocation would allow opportunity to indulge his fondness for reading. After his seven years of apprenticeship he spent further years as typesetter, proofreader, and foreman, until when he was thirty he was able to set up his own business, and two years later he married his former employer's daughter. Cautious in his business dealings and tactful in his personal relations, he prospered steadily until he could afford the luxury of a second house in the suburbs as a week-end retreat from the printing shop.

Short, fat, and rosy-faced, fond of good food and drink until he began to worry about his health and submit to rigid diets, he was apparently a typical businessman who dabbled in authorship only because it was part of the routine of his particular trade. He compiled indexes, wrote dedications and prefaces, edited and revised manuscripts. His first independent book was a brief manual of advice to young workmen, *The Apprentice's Vade Mecum.*

A commission for a similar book came to him from two leading booksellers in 1739. This, as he reports, was to be "a little volume of letters, in a common style, on such subjects as might be of use to those country readers who were unable to indite for themselves." He set about composing the usual form-letters that could be adapted for use in typical situations, such as paying a bill, hiring a worker, and expressing congratulations or sympathy.

In accepting the assignment, Richardson proposed that the letters could be used not only as specimens of form but as moral precepts: "Will it be any harm, said I, in a piece you want to be written so low, if we should instruct them how they should think and act in common cases, as well as indite?" He soon found that this obliged him to invent specific circumstances, and his boyhood talent for story-telling proved useful. More than once he linked several letters together into a longer episode; and he relieved the prevailing tone of practicality and earnestness with an occasional humorous piece. When he came to compose a solemn letter of parental advice, "A Father to a Daughter in Service on Hearing of her Master's Attempting her Virtue," he was reminded of "the knowledge of the female heart," as he called it, that he had obtained in his youthful role as confidant to sentimental girls.

By this time, at the age of fifty, he was able to spend more than week-ends at his comfortable house in Fulham, and so he had enough leisure to suspend work upon the handbook and to start a new series of letters that would deal fully with the problem of the imperiled servant girl. His point of departure being the father's letter of counsel, the next step obviously was to have the girl write her own account of the crisis.

Once he had undertaken the story, he found that he could not restrain its growth. He was dealing with a social environment such as he had known since childhood — that of the servants in a country mansion — and with a central character who epitomized the naïve girls whom he had learned to impersonate when composing their letters for them. Having started with the epistolary form, he was committed to the first-personal point of view, with its vividness and plausibility. In fact, it gave even more immediacy to the reader's participation than Defoe's method, for the events are being reported as they occur, and not in long retrospect. And since the narrator was a girl with only a rudimentary education, the simplicity of his prose style was as appropriate as Defoe's had been. In one major respect, however, Richardson's initial scheme resulted in an effect that Defoe had never perceived. Richardson's story dealt with a single emotional relationship affecting only four or five people and existing only for the working out of its central problem of conduct. Therefore, though the book grew to a greater length than any of Defoe's, it never became episodic and disjointed, as his always did. Defoe's stories, crowded with factual detail, rushed on breathlessly from one adventure to the next; Richardson's novel, concentrating upon complexities of feeling, moved with exasperating deliberation but with unbroken suspense. Defoe gave the illusion of reality by the variety and precision of the external facts; Richardson gave it by the credibility of the internal motives and indecisions.

So far as plot goes, the whole story can be condensed into the dimensions of a sentimental stage comedy. Pamela Andrews, brought up by God-fearing parents, is a favorite maid of the wealthy Lady B——. Upon the employer's death the son and heir makes advances to her, which she indignantly repels. The bulk of the story is taken up with the cajolery, bribes, and threats by which Squire B—— tries to seduce her, until at last he is so genuinely in love with her that they are properly married.

Richardson later claimed that the story was based on an occurrence that had been reported to him by a friend fifteen years before. The statement may have been made to forestall suggestions that he had borrowed from Pierre de Marivaux's *Vie de Marianne*, which had been appearing in installments since 1731, and which also used the letter device. As Richardson could not read French, and as there is no evidence that he knew the English translation which was still in course of publication, the resemblance between the two books is probably due to the fact that both authors were adhering to the Cinderella theme, and were writing for a sentimental and mainly feminine audience. Stories with the same plot were current in broadside ballads, in periodical essays, and in *chroniques scandaleuses*. Richardson's innovation was in the psychological subtlety with which Pamela's character was revealed. For the first time in English literature a person of low social status was portrayed seriously as a complex and admirable human being.

The question remains, whether this illusion of reality can be described as the author's primary purpose. The didactic moralizing, which had given the incentive, remained persistent throughout. The heroine missed no opportunity to reaffirm her virtue and to condemn the evil conduct of her master even while she was falling in love with him. In a letter to a friend, a dozen years later, Richardson explained that "little did I think, at first, of making one — much less two — volumes of it. But when I began to recollect what had, so many years before, been told me by my friend, I thought the story, if written in an easy and natural manner, suitably to the simplicity of it, might possibly introduce a new species of writing, that might possibly turn young people into a course of reading different from the pomp and parade of romance-writing, and dismissing the improbable and marvellous, with which novels generally abound, might tend to promote the cause of religion and virtue. I therefore gave way to enlargement." Beyond a doubt, however, the "enlargement" was not due primarily to so rational a scheme. Richardson was carried away by his emotional involvement in Pamela's experiences and by the delight of probing her feelings. He wrote rapidly, completing the long manuscript in two months; and when he read it to his wife and three lady friends their enthusiasm convinced him that the story would appeal to the public by its naturalness rather than by its moral lesson.

His business connections enabled him to launch the book with unusual fanfare. A month before publication date, a long letter in a newspaper praised the forthcoming work as "an English novel with a truly English spirit of unaffected good sense, and yet with a great deal of invention and ingenuity." When it came out in November, 1740, it was prefaced not only with two fulsome letters from friends of the author but also with a foreword in which Richardson, posing like Defoe as merely the editor of genuine documents, pointed out its merits. The title page, too, offered a variety of attractions, moral, realistic, and emotional: *Pamela: or, Virtue Rewarded. In a Series of Familiar Letters from a beautiful Young Damsel, to her Parents. Now first published in order to cultivate the Principles of Virtue and Religion in the Minds of the Youth of Both Sexes. A Narrative which has its Foundation in Truth and Nature; and at the same time that it agreeably entertains, by a variety of* curious *and* affecting *Incidents, is entirely divested of all those Images, which, in too many Pieces calculated for Amusement only, tend to* inflame *the Minds they should* Instruct.

Whether or not the devices of publicity contributed to the result, *Pamela* won immediate fame. Alexander Pope sat up all night to finish it and declared that "it will do more good than a great many of the new sermons." A prominent clergyman (perhaps for a fee) lauded it in the pulpit. The *Gentleman's Magazine*, the most influential periodical of the time, reported that it was "judged in Town as great a sign of want of curiosity not to have read *Pamela* as not to have seen the French and Italian dancers." The current epigram was that Pamela "like the snow that lay last week, covers every other image with her own unbounded whiteness." Versified tributes were printed in the newspapers. Fashionable ladies flaunted copies of the book when they appeared in public, and scenes from it were reproduced upon a fan on sale in the smart shops. Letters from enthusiastic readers poured into the publishers' office. David Garrick acted in a dramatic adaptation. Within a year five large editions had come off the press, and it was being translated into French, German, and Dutch. Soon it gained the distinction of appearing on the Papal index of banned books.

The favor of the fashionable world was not by itself enough to bring such large circulation. The book was equally appreciated by people of the lowest class, who gathered in parties to hear it read aloud. One such group, in Slough, were so overjoyed upon finding that Pamela's wedding took place in their own village that they trooped off to the church and celebrated by ringing the bells. Ten years later the sardonic Lady Mary Montagu remarked that *Pamela* "is still the joy of the chambermaids of all nations."

Delighted with his triumph, Richardson made little effort to sustain the disguise of anonymous editor. He was soon basking in the flattery of genteel ladies — even a few with titles. But he found that success also brought problems. The first was that hack writers tried to share his profits. One began to issue a paraphrase in heroic couplets, while others went to work to compose continuations. Within six months of its debut, a rival firm published the first volume of *Pamela's Conduct in High Life*, and Richardson advertised that this impudent imitation had forced him unwillingly to begin writing a sequel himself. Before the end of 1741 he brought this out in two volumes, doubling the length of the whole novel. A dull series of letters between Pamela and her sister-in-law, the continuation is mainly taken up with comments on such topics as current operas and Locke's educational theories and the advisability of employing a wet-nurse for the baby, though some action is dragged in when

Pamela has to recapture her husband from the wiles of a flirtatious countess. A few scenes show that Richardson had some talent for writing comedy of manners.

As troublesome as the imitators were the attackers. Among prominent writers of the day Pope was almost alone in praising the book. The others treated it with ridicule or disgust. To men of classical education and intellectual subtlety it was incredible that a fat, middle-aged, ignorant tradesman should receive serious recognition as an author. This was the first time that such a phenomenon had bothered them. Their predecessors had ignored Bunyan's existence and dismissed Defoe with a sneer; but Richardson was not so easily obliterated. Unconsciously they may have been actuated by some envy of Richardson's earnings and some fear of his competition. But on the conscious level they were sincere in their condemnation of his obvious faults; and his naïve vanity, as shown in his publicity, enabled them to regard him as a presumptuous fool.

As they saw it, Pamela was not virtuous and innocent, but was a mealy-mouthed hypocrite and a designing minx. The upper-class characters were drawn without knowledge of how gentlefolk behaved. The language of Pamela's letters was low, and her earnest analysis of every mood and dilemma was intolerably tedious. Worst of all, the author's own standards must be as crude as those of his heroine, for the moral lesson of the whole story could be stated as "be good because it pays better."

The great age of English satire was not yet over, and so the handiest weapon against *Pamela* was ridicule. *An Apology for the Life of Mrs. Shamela Andrews* came out five months after the first edition of *Pamela*. According to this impudent parody, the heroine is really the bastard of a theater orange-woman; after various love affairs, including one with a canting evangelical clergyman, she changes her name from Shamela to Pamela and feigns piety while entrapping the stupid young squire, whose full name is now revealed to be "Booby." Though published under a pseudonym, the book was undoubtedly written by a clever lawyer and journalist whose character and background qualified him admirably to be Richardson's antagonist.

Eighteen years younger than Richardson, Henry Fielding was the great-grandson of an earl and was educated at Eton, where he became a competent classical scholar and acquired a circle of friends as witty and aristocratic as himself. At eighteen he tried unsuccessfully to elope with a young heiress, and before he was twenty-one his first comedy was produced at Drury Lane Theater. He then spent a year or two as a student at Leyden University, but by 1730 he was back in London for the opening of his second play. These first dramatic works were sophisticated comedies of manners, after the Congreve pattern of thirty years before; but Fielding soon turned to the style of drama that was currently popular and wrote a number of burlesques, as well as translating two comedies of Molière. High-spirited and hastily written, his burlesques were ingenious and original, but revealed no serious artistic purpose.

It was perhaps the financial success of these plays that encouraged him to marry and enjoy an interval of leisure at the country house of his family, until his savings and his wife's dowry were spent. Several further burlesques of his contained such open ridicule of contemporary politics that in 1737 a new Licencing Act established a censorship that could prohibit his libelous skits; and so at the age of thirty he was deprived of the income that he expected to earn by playwriting. He spent the next three years as a law student, occupying his spare time with contributing to periodicals, and he was called to the bar about four months before the date of *Pamela's* publication.

Handsome, witty, and charming, Fielding was the perfect type of the young man-about-town, with all the assurance that is conferred by good birth and education. He indulged his impulses without prudence and uttered his opinions without discretion. Richardson was not the only person who aroused his scorn in 1741. Equally disgusted with the blatant autobiography of Colley Cibber, a conceited actor and playwright, he echoed the title of *An Apology for the Life of Colley Cibber, Comedian* in that of his burlesque of *Pamela*, and the pen-name that he attached to it was "Conny Keyber."

Shamela was certainly better than the other attacks on *Pamela* that came out in the next few months, such as *Anti-Pamela, or Feigned Innocence Detected, in a Series of Syrena's Adventures*, by the egregious Mrs. Haywood, who was still busy with her pen. But Fielding must have realized that the elements of genuine satire in *Shamela* were weakened by the brutal travesty of Richardson's pathetic scenes and the lewd caricature of his erotic ones. Parody enforced a limitation precluding effective exposure of Richardson's weaknesses, and so Fielding soon started all over again. *Shamela* fulfils the same function in relation to his next book that Richardson's *Letters to and for Particular Friends* fulfils in relation to *Pamela*.

For his second onslaught Fielding conceived a more ingenious scheme. To his robust masculine mind it seemed that the sentimentality and improbability of Pamela's behavior could be rendered ludicrous by simply reversing the sexes of the two main figures. He therefore invented a brother for Pamela, as innocent and pious as herself, and depicted him as repelling the wanton advances of his rich employer, Lady Booby, an aunt of Pamela's persecutor. This brother he named Joseph, in allusion to the Old Testament youth who rebuffed Potiphar's wife.

The first ten chapters of *Joseph Andrews* took full advantage of this comic situation, with fresh jibes at Colley Cibber into the bargain. By that point the satirical effect had been achieved, and the story had no reason to continue further. But Fielding was beginning to feel the strange joy of fictional creation. In order to link his book to Richardson's he had used plausible details; and Joseph, in spite of a priggish lack of sexual impulses, was capturing his sympathy by his manly self-respect.

The satire abruptly ceased to be aimed at Richardson's bourgeois morality and widened its scope to include the injustice of class distinctions, the hypocrisy of social codes, and the selfishness of human nature. A complete change came over the book. Joseph's personality was transformed by the simple statement that he was already engaged to a girl in his home village — though previously he had explicitly denied having ever been attracted by any woman. Dismissed by his frustrated employer, he set out to make his way home across England; and thus the lascivious Lady Booby conveniently faded out of the story and a whole new cast of characters entered.

The change seems to have been accompanied, in Fielding's mind, by a perception of kinship between his undertaking and *Don Quixote*. Cervantes, too, had set out merely to ridicule a silly literary mania and had gone on to create a masterpiece of humor, realism, and wise philosophy. In the generation preceding Fielding, the Cervantes manner had been revived in the picaresque novel by Alain René Le Sage, *Gil Blas* (1715–35). In contrast with the exaggerated episodes in *Don Quixote,* Le Sage's book had been grimly realistic, and gained its strongest effect by the impartiality of the author's attitude. Good and bad persons alike were presented with humorous detachment, and though the adventures were violent enough, they never took precedence over characterization. Fielding also apparently borrowed some hints from another recent French novel, *Le Paysan parvenu,* by Marivaux (1735), in which the humor was gentler than in *Gil Blas.*

Though the larger part of *Joseph Andrews* is in simple episodic sequence, as Joseph moves through a series of mishaps and meets a variety of odd characters, the story does have a certain structure. He sets off alone, and progressively the three other major characters (by a chain of improbable coincidences) become his companions. He is motivated by the single determination to get home and marry Fanny, but the theme of his attempted seduction by Lady Booby is farcically sustained by means of the similar intention on the part of her hideous attendant, Mrs. Slipslop. These unifying elements, however, do not promise a sufficient climax. One feels that the adventures of Joseph and his traveling companions could go on indefinitely. Near the end, therefore, a second shift occurs in the handling of the story, as arbitrary as that which changed it from burlesque to realism. Fielding's theatrical experience takes control, and he introduces a series of melodramatic surprises, which heighten suspense and result in a strong denouement, but which almost vitiate the relaxed realism of the main part of the book. At the end, too, he reverts to his original theme by bringing Pamela and her husband in as participants in the climax; but he was so affected by the benevolent spirit of the happy ending that there is only the faintest touch of satire in his portrayal of them.

Among the characters the most significant is Parson Adams. Joseph and Fanny are little more than the conventional young lovers, and Mrs. Slipslop is a stock-type caricature. Mr. Adams, on the contrary, is a living human being. Almost for the first time in English fiction, a character is simultaneously comic and sympathetic. The parson is heroic in strength and nobility, and lovable in his unselfish kindness; but his unsophistication makes him the focus of the basic satiric theme — the divorce of modern life from its proclaimed Christian ideals.

One outcome of Fielding's unplanned approach to the novel was the point of view that he employed. Unlike Defoe and Richardson, he was not subservient to the middle-class suspicion of fiction, and therefore he did not need to strive for an illusion of authenticity. Instead of the first-personal method he adopted that of a superior onlooker, commenting on the characters, digressing to express his prejudices, even pausing to analyze his technical problems as inventor and manipulator of the story. It is perhaps artistically indefensible for an author thus to project himself into the very texture of what is supposed to be an objective record of actuality. Yet instead of destroying the illusion, this somehow gives it a new dimension of significance. The reader cannot fully identify himself with the story while the author insists on reminding him of its fictitiousness; but as a recompense for the loss of identification, one acquires a gratifying sense of superior insight into the meaning of experience.

A further enrichment that Fielding provided was an intellectual complexity approximating that of real life. Material that should logically belong to an essay or a lyric poem finds its way into the book. More than once, following the practice of the heroic romances, the author coolly inserts a complete short story by the simple expedient of having one character narrate it to others during a coach journey or in an inn parlor. The whole heterogeneous mass could not possibly exist in any other artistic genre, and Fielding's accidental production of it revealed the value of the novel as the only medium adequate for depicting the confused interrelationships of modern society.

By the time Fielding reached the middle of his story he was aware of the novelty and importance of what he was doing. He therefore began his second volume with a discussion that may be termed the manifesto of the modern novel. With witty paradox he declared that history should really be classified as "romance," since no two historians agree in their interpretation of events, whereas the "biographers" of fictitious characters tell essential truth: "the facts we deliver may be relied on, though we often mistake the age and country wherein they happened." As examples he cited Cervantes, Scarron, Le Sage, and Marivaux. This list of predecessors shows not only that he was trying to define a specific literary category but also that he preferred foreign models to any previous English authors. After paying

sarcastic tribute to "those persons of surprising genius, the
authors of immense romances, or the modern novel and Atalantis
writers, who, without any assistance from nature or history,
record persons who never were, or will be, and facts which
never did, nor possibly can, happen," he asserted that the authors
"who are contented to copy nature, instead of forming originals
from the confused heap of matter in their own brains" can
produce such a work as *Don Quixote*, "a history of the world
in general, at least that part which is polished by laws, arts,
and sciences; and of that from the time it was first polished to
this day; nay, and forwards as long as it shall so remain." He
went on to insist that any resemblance between his characters and
specific individuals was due only to this universal psychological
truth, and not to portrayal of actual persons; his aim was "not
to expose one pitiful wretch to the small and contemptible circle
of his acquaintance, but to hold the glass to thousands in their
closets, that they may contemplate their deformity." And lastly,
he declared that no social generalizations were intended; though
the "high people" he depicted happened to be uniformly dis-
honorable and heartless, this was not meant as an indictment of
the upper class as a whole.

Fielding discussed other aspects of his new technique in the
preface that he wrote for the first edition. In this he stated
flatly that *Joseph Andrews* represented "a species of writing
. . . hitherto unattempted in our language," and he called
it "a comic epic poem in prose." He differentiated it from
the serious epic in that it dealt with the ridiculous rather than
the sublime, and from stage comedy "in that it has more
extended action, more incidents, and greater variety of character."

In the light of subsequent developments in the novel, his
phrase was an amazingly apt definition of it. Two of the words,
however, need fuller explanation, for their implications inhere
in classical literary theory and practice. By "comic" Fielding
did not mean merely that the story should provoke laughter,
or even (as the opposite of "tragic") that it should have a
happy ending. In Greek drama, comedy was distinctive also by
dealing with contemporary actuality instead of ancient legend,
by employing characters of lower rank rather than heroic rulers,
and by presenting an intellectual analysis of social phenomena.

Because Fielding, like Aristophanes, was a satirist, he devoted much of his preface to discussing satire; but his careful discrimination of comedy from burlesque showed that he was conscious of its serious function of social observation: in comedy "we should ever confine ourselves strictly to nature, from the just imitation of which will flow all the pleasure we can this way convey to a sensible reader."

By "epic poem," also, he meant more than a long narrative of varied events. Ever since Aristotle, discussion of the epic had dwelt on its well-organized structure. As Fielding remarked, it consisted of "fable [i.e., plot], action, characters, sentiments, and diction." And, of course, his phrase "poem in prose" was not a capricious paradox, but an acceptance of the basic meaning of poem as any work of creative imagination, as Sidney had regarded it. Thus interpreted in relation to classical precedent, Fielding's words can stand with little modification as defining what the novel remained for the next two hundred years.

It was Fielding's range of knowledge, both of recent European literature and of the classics, that enabled him to give the novel for the first time a secure place in the main line of English literature. Luckily this did not occur earlier in its development, or it would have been stultified by inflexible aesthetic theories. Having grown up to this point without attracting the notice of academic critics, the novel possessed enough vitality and independence to absorb the classical tradition instead of being enslaved by it.

When published anonymously in 1742, *Joseph Andrews* did not gain the immediate popularity of *Pamela*; six months elapsed before a second edition was necessary. But men of taste and intellect found it well worth reading, as is proved by the recommendation it received from Thomas Gray, who was already addicted to the French fiction of Marivaux and Crébillon *fils*. "The incidents are ill laid and without invention," the poet said in a letter to a friend; "but the characters have a great deal of nature, which always pleases even in her lowest shapes. . . . Throughout he shows himself well read in Stage-Coaches, Country Squires, Inns, and Inns of Court. . . . However the exaltedness of some minds (or rather as I shrewdly suspect their insipidity and want of feeling or observation) may make

them insensible to these light things (I mean such as charac-
terize and paint nature), yet surely they are as weighty and
much more useful than your grave discourses upon the mind,
the passions, and what not."

Richardson and Fielding jointly achieved an immense enlargement of the readership of fiction. The moral middle class was
finally convinced by *Pamela* that fiction was not a waste of
time and a temptation to sin; the intelligentsia was convinced
by *Joseph Andrews* that it was not a tissue of silly make-believe.
Many people, of course, were able to enjoy reading both books
and thereby to realize how wide a range of effects could be
included in the genre.

Other writers did not delay in exploiting the new market. A
typical professional, Mrs. Haywood, whose first impulse had
been to attack Richardson in her *Anti-Pamela*, quickly realized
her mistake, and wrote *The Fortunate Foundlings*, which was
largely in Richardson's vein, though with some parts reminiscent
of Defoe. Like *Pamela*, it was supposed to be "a Genuine
History" based on authentic documents, unlike "the many fictions which have been lately imposed upon the world under
the specious titles of Secret Histories, Memoirs, &c"; and the
title page emphasized that it was "calculated for the entertainment and improvement of the youth of both sexes." Mrs. Haywood achieved some variety and contrast by following the
careers of both a brother and a sister.

Ironically, the best of Richardson's early disciples was none
other than Henry Fielding's sister, Sarah. Her *Adventures of
David Simple* came out in 1744. Using the traditional situation of an evil brother scheming against a good one, it depicts
the guileless hero moving through various social environments
in London, seeking vainly for true friendship, which he finally
finds in a girl as virtuous as himself. The initial stages of
David's disillusionment have satirical touches that show the
influence of the author's brother; but most of the book is as
moral and sentimental as Richardson. The new literary ideals
of realism and sentiment are defined in David's assertion that

the only way of writing well was to draw all the characters from
nature, and to affect the passions in such a manner, as that the
distresses of the good should move compassion, and the amiableness
of their actions incite men to imitate them; while the vices of the

bad stirred up indignation and rage, and made men fly their footsteps; that this was the only kind of writing useful to mankind, though there might be embellishments, and flights of imagination, to amuse and divert the reader.

Though *David Simple* is loosely episodic in structure, with irrelevant short stories inserted indiscriminately, its sincerity of feeling gives it charm, and some readers even attributed it to Henry Fielding himself. He therefore wrote a preface for the second edition, disclaiming any share in it, and lauding it handsomely:

> As the merit of this work consists in a vast penetration into human nature, a deep and profound discernment of all the mazes, windings, and labyrinths, which perplex the heart of man to such a degree, that he is himself often incapable of seeing through them; and as this is the greatest, noblest, and rarest of all the talents which constitute a genius, so a much larger share of this talent is necessary even to recognize these discoveries, when they are laid before us, than falls to the share of a common reader.

The rest of this important preface reverted to Fielding's definition of the "comic epic poem," particularly insisting upon unity of action:

> Three different ingredients . . . will be found on consideration to be always necessary to works of this kind, viz., that the main end or scope be at once amiable, ridiculous, and natural. . . . As the incidents arising from this fable, though often surprising, are everywhere natural (credibility not being once shocked through the whole) so there is one beauty very apparent . . . ; that every episode bears a manifest impression of the principal design, and chiefly turns on the perfection or imperfection of friendship.

Fielding himself was not in any hurry to produce another sustained work of fiction. He was busy with conducting newspapers and with establishing himself in his belated legal profession. His *Miscellanies*, however, published a year after *Joseph Andrews*, contained one fictional *tour de force*, which he may have partly written at an earlier date and left unfinished when he became absorbed in his novel. *The History of the Life of the Late Mr. Jonathan Wild the Great* narrated the life of an infamous highwayman who had been written about also by Defoe; but Fielding's purpose was very different. A masterpiece of satire almost worthy of Swift. the book gravely depicts the ruthless scoundrel as a hero, whose hanging is the noble climax to an illustrious career. Like all major satires, it had several levels of meaning, being aimed not only at the glorification of criminals in the pseudo-biographies issued by the gutter press, but also at the current Whig government, which Fielding regarded as unscrupulous, and at the whole human tendency to admire success without applying moral judgment. Fielding's humane generosity, his hatred of cruelty and selfishness, dictated his thesis that no ambitious conqueror or politician can be more praiseworthy than this atrocious criminal. The cold fury of his irony is the complement of his sister's sentimental exalting of unsophisticated kindliness.

Meanwhile Mr. Richardson was working steadily on his next novel, which was a far more pretentious undertaking than the first. He had been pained by the ridicule of *Pamela,* and especially by the suggestion that his heroine's speech and behavior were sometimes vulgar. The sequel had been written chiefly to remedy this defect, and for a while he thought of revising the first part of the novel to make it more refined; but then he decided to concentrate on another book which would have a higher social environment throughout. And since the story of Pamela was of a girl rewarded because she was strong-minded enough to resist evil, the obvious converse was to tell about a girl ruined because she succumbed to temptation.

Having realized the potentialities of the novel, Richardson experimented with a larger canvas. *Clarissa, or The History of a Young Lady* was nearly four times as long as the original *Pamela.* Though it had numerous characters and a carefully constructed plot, most of its vast length was occupied by analysis of personality and motive. Again the whole story was told in letters, totaling 547, but variety in point of view was achieved by having them written by many of the characters, whereas all but four of those in *Pamela* were from the pen of the heroine.

Richardson was now aware of the special effectiveness residing in the epistolary technique that he had first adopted by sheer good luck. "All the letters," he pointed out in the preface, "are written while the hearts of the writers must be supposed to be wholly engaged in their subjects (the events at the time dubious), so that they abound not only with critical situations, but with what may be called *instantaneous* descriptions and reflections." He went on to declare that this is "much more lively and affecting . . . than the dry, narrative, unanimated style of a person relating difficulties and dangers surmounted can be; the relater perfectly at ease; and if himself unmoved by his own story, not likely greatly to affect the reader."

His use of multiple correspondents, moreover, gives a fuller complexity to the epistolary technique. In *Pamela* it merely increased the suspense by keeping the reader's knowledge of the situation within the framework of the events as they developed; in *Clarissa* it maintains an excruciating anxiety by revealing the full meaning of each situation through the cumulative evidence of several points of view. The majority of the letters being from the heroine to her friend Miss Howe and from the hero-villain to his friend Belford, the reader watches with anguished foreknowledge while Clarissa walks unsuspectingly into the trap. Richardson had mastered the device of dramatic irony.

The plot may have been based on incidents in the life of a generous but dissolute gentleman who had befriended the author in his youth. Richardson's literary renown had by now gained him admission to social circles above any he had previously frequented, and so he felt better qualified to portray people of cultivated minds and manners. While working on the book he often consulted his admiring friends, though his self-esteem usually prevented him from accepting their specific suggestions. The higher social milieu was not, however, the greatest difference between his new novel and his earlier one. It was more important that *Clarissa* is a tragedy.

Clarissa Harlowe, a high-spirited beauty, is destined by her prosperous and socially ambitious family to marry an elderly and repulsive but wealthy neighbor. Meanwhile Robert Lovelace, a libertine, is courting her for her fortune; and though at first she is prejudiced against him, her family's opposition arouses her interest in him, and at last she elopes with him as the only method of escape from marriage to Solmes. Lovelace is genuinely in love with her, but he is determined to seduce her in order to have revenge on her family. By deception and drugs he accomplishes his purpose, and in an agony of shame she dies of a broken heart, after which Lovelace is killed in a duel with her cousin, and his accomplices meet with appropriately bad ends.

In this stark outline, the plot is that of a conventional melodrama. Indeed, Richardson termed the book a "Dramatic Narrative," and acknowledged its kinship with the domestic tragedies of Otway and Rowe, while in the Postscript he suggested that he had handled his theme according to the principles prescribed by Aristotle and practiced by the Greek tragedians and by Shakespeare. What extended the book far beyond the scope of the stage was the minute study of the two central characters. Superficially, Lovelace was cut to the pattern of the cynical rakes of Restoration comedy, and of Lothario in Rowe's *Fair Penitent*. It is scarcely believable that a cultivated, intelligent gentleman would discuss his own viciousness as candidly as Lovelace did, even with so loyal a friend as Belford. But Richardson devoted himself to a doubly difficult task — to supply adequate reasons for Lovelace's villainy and at the same time to suggest that he was not totally villainous, after all. "The gentlemen are not," he explained in the preface, "either infidels or scoffers; nor yet such as think themselves free from the observance of those other moral duties which bind man to man." Lovelace considers himself socially superior to the Harlowes, and therefore resents their disapproval of him; an early disappointment in love has given him a grudge against women; a vague sense of Clarissa's spiritual integrity makes him try to drag her down to his moral level, while at the same time he enjoys the "talents for stratagem and invention" by which he outwits her. By the standards accepted in his frivolous world, he has no doubt that Clarissa will marry him as soon as he has gratified his hatred for her family by violating her. He is astounded to discover that, once ravished, she regards herself as unfit for marriage, even though she has loved him deeply. To account for his hold over her, Richardson had to equip him with so much charm that the reader is apt to succumb to it too, and even to feel something like pity for him in his bewildered efforts to comprehend and overcome her scruples.

Daringly, in view of his readers' rigid moral code, Richardson set out to show that by losing her innocence a girl might be ennobled and not degraded. Indeed, the theme of the whole book was subversive to the social laws of the time — not only to the maxim that by marriage a seducer "protects the honor" of the woman he has wronged, but also to the principle of parental authority. The lack of understanding on the part of Clarissa's parents was primarily responsible for her downfall. As the title page stated, the particular theme of the novel was "the Distresses that may attend the misconduct of both Parents and Children in relation to Marriage." In the preface Richardson explained that Clarissa

> is not in all respects a perfect character. It was not only natural, but it was necessary that she should have some faults, were it only to show the reader how laudably she could mistrust and blame herself. . . . As far as is consistent with human frailty, and as far as she could be perfect, considering the people she had to deal with, and those with whom she was inseparably connected, she *is* perfect.

The same pride and independence that impelled Clarissa to loathe the prospect of a conventionally suitable marriage with Solmes also motivated her behavior in the later part of the story. So far as the plot was concerned, the final one-third of the novel could have been condensed into a few chapters; but to the author the climax was not Clarissa's seduction but the spiritual martyrdom that followed and the saintly abnegation with which she forgave all the offenses against her. It was a spectacular contrast to the worldly morality that had provoked the most damaging criticisms of *Pamela*.

The book's power does not depend upon its pathos or its puritan morals or its picture of contemporary manners. It takes on a more than life-sized magnitude not so much for its length as for the symbolic aura that accumulated around the protagonists. If Moll Flanders is to be called the quintessence of worldliness, Clarissa is the quintessence of emotional idealism. Her rebellion against a wealthy marriage and her death from shame would have seemed sheer insanity by Moll's standards. Clarissa is the archetype of inviolable spiritual purity, and Lovelace is a very incarnation of the devil, the arch-tempter whose power is challenged by the existence of an utterly virtuous woman. He wins the contest in terms of the flesh, but she triumphs in the spirit. In this view, *Clarissa* becomes as much an allegory of eternal principles as was *The Pilgrim's Progress*.

As the main theme was so painfully pathetic, the author took care to promise in the preface that there were also "such strokes of gaiety, fancy, and humor, as will entertain and divert, and at the same time both warn and instruct." In addition to these touches of comedy, the book contained a few scenes of sordid realism, such as one in a London brothel, more like some in Fielding's novels and Hogarth's paintings than in Richardson's usually genteel settings.

Clarissa was published over a period of twelve months of 1747-48. After reading the earlier volumes, many readers foresaw that the heroine was doomed to die, and some pleaded with the author to change his plans and make Lovelace reform as Mr. B— had done, so that Clarissa could conscientiously marry him. Even Fielding, who published an enthusiastic review of the first two volumes of *Clarissa*, wrote to Richardson, entreating him to spare Clarissa's life. And Laetitia Pilkington, a lively Irishwoman of scandalous reputation, reported to Richardson the hysterical raving of Colley Cibber when she broke the news to him of how the novel was to end:

> When he heard what a dreadful lot hers was to be, he lost all patience, threw down the book, and vowed he would not read another line. . . . He shuddered; nay, the tears stood in his eyes: "What! (said he) shall I, who have loved and revered the virtuous, the beautiful Clarissa, from the same motives I loved Mr. Richardson, bear to stand a patient spectator of her ruin, her final destruction? No! . . ."
>
> When I told him she must die, he said, "G-d D—n him, if she should; and that he should no longer believe Providence, or eternal Wisdom, or Goodness governed the world, if merit, innocence, and beauty were to be destroyed: nay (added he) my mind is so hurt with the thought of her being violated, that were I to see her in Heaven, sitting on the knees of the blessed Virgin, and crowned with glory, her sufferings would still make me feel horror, horror distilled."

Richardson himself had been shocked by the way Lovelace's character had developed. In the midst of writing the novel he confessed to a friend that "my libertine in the next volume proves to be so vile, that I regretted the necessity, as I may call it, which urged me to put the two former to press." But he rejected all appeals for a contrived happy ending, and remained true to his conception of the characters. He had learned the principle of letting them lead their own lives, instead of manipulating them for ulterior purposes, whether of plot or moral theme. As a result of his epistolary technique, he could not avoid discovering that everyone is justified in his own mind. As Clarissa expressed it, "There would hardly be a guilty person in the world, were each suspected or accused person to tell his or her own story, and be allowed any degree of credit."

A serious objection to the story was its inordinate length. William Shenstone, the poet, while plodding through the million words of the completed novel, muttered that it "threatens to grow extremely tedious: not but that the author is a man of genius and nice observation; but he might be less prolix." Here again the author forestalled his critics. At an early stage he complained that "I have run into such a length! — And am such a sorry pruner, tho' greatly luxuriant, that I am apt to add three pages for one I take away!" Actually, he did force himself to omit a good many passages from the first edition, but he reinserted them in the third.

It is one of the paradoxes of Richardson that his moral earnestness carried implications of prurience, as was recognized even in the first days of his fame, when Dr. Isaac Watts, the devout hymn-writer, protested to him that "the ladies complain they cannot read [*Pamela*] without blushing." More than half a century later, Coleridge burst out with exasperation, "I confess that it has cost, and still costs, my philosophy some exertion not to be vexed that I must admire, aye, greatly admire, Richardson. His mind is so very vile a mind, so oozy, so hypocritical, praise-mad, canting, envious, concupiscent!" It was this side of the worthy Mr. Richardson that degenerated into the sewage of John Cleland, whose *Fanny Hill, or The Memoirs of a Woman of Pleasure* (1748) combined Richardson's epistolary technique with such lavish obscenity that it brought the publisher £10,000 for an investment of £21, and survived for two centuries in surreptitious editions for addicts of pornography.

The same year brought proof that the methods of Fielding also could easily be vulgarized; but probably because there was an element of healthy animalism in his work that served as a safeguard against infection, there is nothing repulsive in the candid crudity of his vulgarizer, Tobias Smollett. The grandson of a Scottish laird, Smollett was educated at Glasgow University and qualified for the profession of surgery. At eighteen he wrote a tragedy and set out for London with confident hopes of literary success, but when it was rejected by the theaters he joined the navy as a surgeon's mate on a man o' war, and saw action at the disastrous siege of Carthagena in the Caribbean. The naval service at that time was particularly brutal and disorganized. Officers were incompetent, food and sanitation loathsome, sailors insubordinate, and constant floggings the only method of controlling crews largely made up of ex-criminals. When these conditions were combined with the discomforts of tropical climates and the horrors of primitive surgery in a ship's cockpit, it is no wonder that Smollett developed a tough hide to shield his originally poetic disposition. After the failure of the siege, he spent some time in Jamaica, where he fell in love with the pretty daughter of a planter, and their marriage brought him enough resources to enable him to quit the service and set up as a surgeon in the West End of London.

Unsuccessful again in his efforts to have his tragedy produced, Smollett acquired a bitter outlook that intensified his natural traits of pride, belligerence, and sarcasm; and he published verse satires on contemporary literature and politics. Then, during eight months of 1747, at the age of twenty-six, he wrote a long novel, *The Adventures of Roderick Random*, which came out anonymously in January, 1748.

The story closely follows Smollett's own experiences. The young hero, a surgeon's apprentice, makes his way from Scotland to London, with numerous adventures, some dangerous and some ludicrous. The press gang sends him to sea for the Carthagena expedition; he enjoys a romantic interlude with a beautiful girl while employed as a footman by her fantastic aunt, before going on to rascally exploits of soldiering on the Continent, gambling in London, and a commercial voyage to South America, till at last he meets his long-lost father, now a rich Spanish subject, and marries the lovely Narcissa. Even Smollett's struggle with the theatrical managers is introduced as the interpolated narrative of a minor character.

The book has obvious resemblances to those of Defoe, in its autobiographic technique, its expeditions to foreign shores, and its disjointed series of adventures among seafarers, soldiers, and metropolitan scoundrels. But Smollett differs from Defoe in two important respects. The scenes of action derive validity from personal experience, and they are interspersed with comic episodes.

The antecedents for the comedy are to be found in *Don Quixote* and *Gil Blas*, as Smollett admitted in his preface. Starting with the inevitable diatribe against "romance," which "owes its origin to ignorance, vanity, and superstition," he lauded Cervantes who "by an inimitable piece of ridicule reformed the taste of mankind, . . . converting romance to purposes far more useful and entertaining, by making it . . . point out the follies of ordinary life." Le Sage too, he said, "has described the knavery and foibles of life with infinite humor and sagacity. The following sheets I have modeled on his plan, taking the liberty, however, to differ from him in the execution, where I thought his particular situations were uncommon, extravagant, or peculiar to the country in which the scene is laid." The preface repeatedly claimed a high moral purpose: to show "the contrast between dejected virtue and insulting vice," to inspire "that generous indignation which ought to animate the reader, against the sordid and vicious disposition of this world"; and a justification was put forth also for the unvarnished depiction of squalor:

Though I foresee that some people will be offended at the mean scenes in which [Roderick] is involved, I persuade myself the judicious will not only perceive the necessity of describing those situations to which he must of course be confined, in his low estate, but also find entertainment in viewing those parts of life, where the humours and passions are undisguised by affectation, ceremony, or education; and the whimsical peculiarities of disposition appear as nature has implanted them.

The same double defense — realism and moral correction — was offered for the profanity in the dialogue: "Nothing could more effectually expose the absurdity of such miserable expletives, than a natural and verbal representation of the discourse in which they occur."

In claiming to be "representing familiar scenes in an uncommon and amusing point of view," Smollett felt obliged to protect himself against charges of libel: "I have not deviated from nature, in the facts, which are all true in the main, although the circumstances are altered and disguised to avoid personal satire." His method of characterization indeed varied between two ex-

tremes. Many of the persons in the story were caricatures of
living originals, ranging from David Garrick to obscure innkeepers and booksellers; but others were exaggerated embodiments of
peculiar traits, in a tradition that reached back through Jonson's
comedy of humours to the personified vices of the morality
plays.

Smollett's experiences in surgery and warfare had made him
callous toward pain and outspoken about the physical functions of
the human body. His treatment of these matters usually seems
gross if not positively sadistic, especially in the comic scenes.
His humor is sometimes sheer buffoonery and at other times
savage satire, but it usually tends to be brutal or obscene, and thus
obscures his genuine regard for simple human integrity, his hatred
of oppression and conceit.

Roderick Random met with immediate success, and several
large printings were called for. Some readers attributed it to
Fielding, on the basis of resemblances to *Joseph Andrews*. The
comic characterizations were not much more exaggerated than
Parson Adams, Parson Trulliber, or Mrs. Slipslop; the broad farce
was not much coarser than the fight at Tow-wowse's inn; the
episodic structure and contrived ending were not much less coherent than those of Fielding's book. The author's angry humanitarianism, too, had something in common with Fielding's.
A year later, however, Fielding brought out his own second novel,
which proved that his genius had matured far beyond the range of
Smollett's lively but heavy-handed story-telling.

In the seven years since *Joseph Andrews*, Fielding had been
occupied with his professional duties at the bar and with political
journalism. His reluctance to write another novel was due in
part to fear that his status in the law would be impaired if he were
known to be a writer of fiction. His personal life during this time
was painful: his extravagant habits burdened him with debts; he
suffered acute gout and other illnesses; one or more of his children
died young, and the death of his much-loved wife caused him
violent grief. In 1747 he married his wife's former maid, a plain
woman who looked after him faithfully.

With the fading of his hopes for legal eminence, he began to
think of writing another "comic epic in prose," under the urging
of his friend George Lyttelton, a prominent politician and author.
Fielding said that he "employed some thousands of hours in the

composing," which probably extended over two and a half years. In December, 1748, he became a police magistrate in London, and his new book appeared soon afterwards, with the title, *The History of Tom Jones, a Foundling.*

Like Richardson, Fielding had profited by his experience with his first novel. The new one was three times as long as *Joseph Andrews;* but in contrast with that loose-jointed story it was carefully integrated throughout. Coleridge rated it for structure besides Sophocles' *Oedipus Tyrannus* and Jonson's *Alchemist,* calling them "the three most perfect plots ever planned." Thackeray termed the book "the most astounding production of human ingenuity. . . . There is not an incident ever so trifling but advances the story, grows out of former incidents, and is connected with the whole. Such a literary *providence,* if we may use such a word, is not to be seen in any other work of fiction. . . . It is marvellous to think how the author could have built and carried all the structure in his brain, as he must have done, before he began to put it to paper."

Superficially *Tom Jones* resembled Fielding's earlier novel in many ways. There is a mystery about Tom's parentage, as about Joseph's; both heroes make long journeys across England, encountering odd characters and dangerous mishaps; Benjamin Partridge accompanies Tom as faithfully as Parson Adams accompanied Joseph. Basically, however, the two books are totally unlike. One feels that the author chose to rework the same material in order to prove how much better he could do it. Instead of having the one-line structure inherited from picaresque fiction, *Tom Jones* offers a complex pattern of interaction among persons who are kept in conflict with steady tension. Even the minor characters contribute directly to the unfolding of the plot. Therefore, when the carefully preserved secret of Tom's parentage is finally revealed, it has none of the implausibility of an afterthought concocted by the author to bring the story to a spectacular end. Instead, it seems as inevitable as the "discovery" at the climax of a classical Greek tragedy, which Aristotle prescribed as an essential element of plot. Aristophanes, Shakespeare, and Molière are among the authors whom Fielding extols in his frequent critical digressions; and his handling of the story has the tight construction of a well-made play.

Although Tom's life is narrated from infancy to the age of

twenty-one, the first twenty years occupy only about one-eighth of the whole, the events of the next year are told somewhat more fully, and the remaining two-thirds of the book cover but five weeks, with every day and almost every hour accurately accounted for. The proportions are classically symmetrical: the first six books take place at the Allworthy manor in Somerset, the next six along the road, the last six in London. To enhance realism, Fielding provided recognizable details of both time and place. The main action occurs during the Jacobite rebellion, little more than three years before the book was published; from time to time readers are deftly reminded of the atmosphere of national danger and public excitement. Similarly, the geographical locations are always precise — the towns and inns along Tom's route from Glastonbury to London, the streets and taverns and theaters of the metropolis. While Fielding does not indulge in much description of landscape for its own sake he always makes the setting recognizable.

The main power of the book, of course, is in characterization. The central character is not the conventionally perfect hero of romance. A weakness of *Joseph Andrews* had been the author's inability to depart from his initial concept of Joseph as an absurd paragon of moral purity. Tom Jones, on the contrary, is a normal young man, good-natured, generous, and brave, but impulsive and sensual. Though he sincerely loves Sophia Western, he indulges in casual affairs with three other women. If Fielding had been writing a tragedy in the vein of Euripides or Shakespeare, this would be termed Tom's "tragic flaw." He is cured of his incontinence only after the shocking experience of believing for a while that one of the women with whom he has had sexual relations may prove to be his mother.

The heroine, Sophia, is in the same predicament as Clarissa Harlowe: she is threatened with a repulsive marriage, and yet she cannot decide to defy her father and marry the man she loves. Though she has more practical sense than Clarissa, her inner motives and conflicts are not revealed with the subtlety that made Richardson's heroine convincing. Having modeled Sophia upon the idolized girl who had been his first wife, Fielding was so handicapped by his devotion to her memory that he could not portray Sophia quite impartially.

The other characters were not inherently very different from the old stock types representing "humours." Blifil is the self-seeking hypocrite, Squire Western the irascible autocrat, Squire Allworthy the honorable benefactor, Partridge the loyal and comical servant, and so on. Fielding was able to give them individuality, however, by several methods. For one thing, he borrowed traits from living people. He announced in the dedication that Allworthy was based partly on his own two generous friends, Lyttelton and Ralph Allen. Squire Western may have been suggested by a bluff sportsman and landowner in the neighborhood where Fielding grew up. The tutors, Square and Thwackum, derived traits from two Salisbury worthies. Lady Bellaston is said to have some resemblance to a notorious society woman, Lady Townshend.

Secondly, the author gained plausibility by showing some admixture in every character. Squire Allworthy's magnanimous nature has its logical defects in his gullibility and his humorless tediousness. Squire Western's obstinacy is offset by occasional rough kindliness and by real affection for his daughter. Even the two tutors are not merely mouthpieces for opposing prejudices in religious dogma, but show glimmerings of intelligence and integrity.

Finally, Fielding's success in characterization is enhanced by his method of portrayal. He used dialogue more fully and naturally than previous novelists had done, and thus the people are gradually revealed through their own words and actions rather than by explicit commentary. Hence Fielding became the first novelist to give the impression of frankly and fully recording normal behavior. Byron called him "the prose Homer of Human Nature," and Hazlitt said that "he has brought together a greater variety of characters in common life, marked with more distinct peculiarities, and without an atom of caricature, than any other novel writer whatever."

Fielding was well aware of his momentous achievement. As in his previous book, he frequently discussed his own methods; and here again he had grown more systematic. Instead of being occasional and digressive, the critical passages are complete essays, inserted as the opening chapters of all the eighteen books; and he composed them with care, confessing, "I can with less pains write one of the books of this history, than the prefatory chapter to each of them." He realized that readers might be bored by the disquisitions, but justified them as "so many scenes of Serious artfully interwoven, in order to contrast and set off the rest. . . . And after this warning, if [the reader] shall be of opinion that he can find enough of Serious in other parts of this history, he may pass over these, in which we profess to be laboriously dull."

The personality of the author thus becomes as familiar to the reader as are those of his characters. He hovers in the background, ready to step forward at intervals with his urbane, ironical comments on literary art. If they were extracted and printed separately, they would form a treatise on his theory of novel-writing. Again and again he reiterated that "our business is only to record truth," and "it is our province to relate facts, and we shall leave causes to persons of much higher genius." Therefore he scorned the unrestricted freedom of imagination indulged in by romance-writers: "Truth distinguishes our writings from those idle romances which are filled with monsters, the productions, not of nature, but of distempered brains." To compensate for this absence of imaginative material, he felt that his style had to be saved from dullness by "interspersing through the whole sundry similes, descriptions, and other kind of poetical embellishments. . . . Without interruptions of this kind the best narrative of plain matter of fact must overpower every reader [with sleepiness]; for nothing but the everlasting watchfulness, which Homer has ascribed only to Jove himself, can be proof against a newspaper of many volumes." These poetical embellishments are usually mock-heroic passages, rich in classical echoes and allusions.

Repeatedly declaring himself a disciple of Lucian, Rabelais, Cervantes, and Swift, he poured contempt upon his fiction-writing contemporaries for their lack of scholarship and of critical theory:

The favorable reception which two or three authors have lately procured for their works of this nature from the public, will probably serve as an encouragement to many others to undertake the like. Thus a swarm of foolish novels and monstrous romances will be produced. . . . To the composition of novels and romances, nothing is necessary but paper, pens, and ink, with the manual capacity of using them. This, I conceive, their productions show to be the opinion of the authors themselves: and this must be the opinion of their readers, if indeed there be any such. . . . And it is the apprehension of this contempt that hath made us so cautiously avoid the term romance, a name with which we might otherwise have been well enough contented.

In spite of his emphasis on literary background, Fielding did not doubt that his special advantage was his familiarity with people of all classes: "A true knowledge of the world is gained only by conversation, and the manners of every rank must be seen in order to be known." A mock-epic invocation of his muses lists his inspirations as love of fame and need of money, and his necessary endowments as genius, humanity, learning, and, as the climax,

> Lastly, come Experience, long conversant with the wise, the good, the learned, and the polite. Nor with them only, but with every kind of character, from the minister at his levee, to the bailiff in his sponging-house; from the duchess at her drum, to the landlady behind her bar. From thee only can the manners of mankind be known; to which the recluse pedant, however great his parts or extensive his learning may be, hath ever been a stranger.

Fielding's glorification of "Truth" and "Human Nature" was always accompanied by assertion of serious moral purpose. It was announced unequivocally in the dedicatory epistle:

> The reader . . . will find in the whole course of it nothing prejudicial to the cause of religion and virtue, nothing inconsistent with the strictest rules of decency, nor which can offend even the chastest eye in the perusal. On the contrary, I declare, that to recommend goodness and innocence hath been my sincere endeavor in this history. . . . For these purposes I have employed all the wit and humor of which I am master in the following history; wherein I have endeavored to laugh mankind out of their favorite follies and vices.

Derived mainly from the Bible, Cicero, and Shaftesbury, his ethical creed maintained that "the natural goodness of the heart" is more important than rigid righteousness; that the reward of virtuous conduct is inward peace of mind; and that, so long as a person's innate instincts are right, forgiveness ought to be extended to the moral lapses to which fallible human nature is all too prone. His doctrine thus differs from Richardson's, which centered in a standardized code of right and wrong, enforced by the sanctions of respectability and prosperity. Richardson's ethics were external, Fielding's were subjective. It is not too paradoxical to say that Fielding, for all his rowdy realism, was ideologically more sentimental than Richardson. The latter insisted on worldly matters of conduct and on inflexible formulas, whereas Fielding's sole criterion was "feeling." In the year that *Tom Jones* was published, Jean-Jacques Rousseau won a prize in France with an essay in which he promulgated a similar theory.

Fielding's scholarship and vigorous intellect gave his novel prestige with the social sophisticates, who had little respect for the piety of Richardson or the violence of Smollett. The great William Pitt was one who read some of the manuscript and spread praise of the book among his friends before publication. The author was paid the substantial sum of £600, and the sale of the first edition was so lively that the binders could not keep up with the demand. As usual, hack writers produced spurious continuations (*Tom Jones in his Married State*) and imitations (*The History of Charlotte Summers, the Fortunate Parish Girl*). Within a year a "Tom Jones" was the current slang for a "boy friend," and young gentlemen were using "Sophia" as the pet name for a sweetheart or a favorite puppy.

In spite of its popularity, however, the book was reviled by two groups of antagonists — by the Tory journalists who hated Fielding for supporting the House of Hanover, and by Richardson and his coterie who regarded Fielding (in Richardson's words) as "a very indelicate, a very impetuous, an unyielding-spirited man." The principal basis of the attack was "lewdness," and the adverse critics spared no ugly words in abusing him as a filthy and immoral writer. This was extended to include personal slander of him as a slovenly, drunken, bribe-taking magistrate who had married his cook.

Following the success of *Clarissa* and *Tom Jones*, the middle year of the eighteenth century may be regarded as the point where the novel won recognition as a distinct genre. In February, 1750, the preface to *Charlotte Summers* spoke of Richardson and Fielding as "the two inimitable moderns." A month later Samuel Johnson, then just coming into his power as a critic, devoted the fourth *Rambler* to a study of the new fiction, which he defined with his usual clarity:

> The works of fiction with which the present generation seems more
> particularly delighted are such as exhibit life in its true state,

diversified only by the accidents that daily happen in the world, and influenced by those passions and qualities which are really to be found in conversing with mankind. This kind of writing may be termed not improperly *the comedy of romance,* and is to be conducted nearly by the rules of comic poetry. Its province is to bring about natural events by easy means, and to keep up curiosity without the help of wonder; it is therefore precluded from the machines and expedients of the heroic romance.

To Johnson, ever the moralist, the popular appeal of the new novels entailed a solemn responsibility:

These books are written chiefly for the young, the ignorant, and the idle, to whom they serve as lectures of conduct and introductions into life. . . . When an adventurer is leveled with the rest of the world and acts in such scenes of the universal drama as may be the lot of any other man, young spectators fix their eyes upon him with closer attention, and hope, by observing his behavior and success, to regulate their own practice when they shall be engaged in the like part.

Obviously referring to Fielding and Smollett, he went on:

It is therefore not a sufficient vindication of a character, that it is drawn as it appears, for many characters ought never to be drawn; nor of a narrative, that the train of events is agreeable to observation and experience, for that observation which is called knowledge of the world will be found much more frequently to make men cunning than good.

Johnson's essay is significant, not only as a recognition of the importance and influence of the new novels, but as a plain statement of the moralistic criterion that continued to dominate much criticism of fiction down to the present time. Till the end of his life, he retained a preference for Richardson over Fielding. He admitted, to be sure, that "if you were to read Richardson for the story, your impatience would be so much fretted that you would hang yourself. But you must read him for the sentiment." On the latter ground, he declared that "there is more knowledge of the heart in one letter of Richardson's than in all *Tom Jones.*" And again, "Richardson has picked the kernel of life, while Fielding was contented with the husk."

Further evidence that the novel had now established itself can be seen in the increased output. Publishers took prompt advantage of the vogue, and the neat duodecimo volumes of fiction

became a staple in their business. Another commercial development was the circulating library, which sprang into existence all
over England to provide a constant flow of novels to the insatiable reading public. A motley brigade of writers hastened
to supply material to satisfy the demand.

One was Charlotte Ramsay Lennox, daughter of a British officer
stationed in New York; she came to England at the age of fifteen,
tried unsuccessfully to become an actress, and then turned to the
profession of authorship. Her marriage to a ne'er-do-well
merely intensified her need of earning money with her pen.
The Life of Harriot Stuart was a highly dramatized version of
her early career. After a childhood on the New York frontier,
the heroine (like Clarissa Harlowe and Sophia Western) flees
from a domineering father and a hateful suitor, escapes kidnapping
by Indians and pirates, and survives varied perils in England
and France. Sam Johnson celebrated the novel's publication in
1750 with an all-night party for the Lennoxes at the Devil Tavern,
and during twelve hours of tea, coffee, and lemonade he crowned
the guest of honor with a laurel wreath. Lady Mary Montagu,
however, found Harriot to be "a jilt and a fool in every page."

Sarah Robinson (later Mrs. Scott), sister of the bluestocking
Elizabeth Montagu, came out with a serious story in the vein of
Marivaux, *The History of Cornelia*. An elderly London attorney,
Robert Paltock, contributed a more original book, *The Adventures of Peter Wilkins*, which combined an imaginary voyage in
the *Gulliver* tradition with a good deal of Richardsonian sentiment to produce an eccentric but rather charming effect. The
Rev. Francis Coventry, an admirer of Fielding, also offered an
attractive novelty in *The History of Pompey the Little*, a short
novel in which the central character is a lap-dog.

The veteran Mrs. Haywood continued her adherence to Richardson in *The History of Miss Betsy Thoughtless*, her best novel,
in which a vain, impulsive girl marries the wrong man, nurses him
through his last illness, and in the end becomes the wife of a rich
and worthy gentleman. For its placid style and attention to commonplace detail it has been termed the first "domestic novel"
in English. A more unsavory writer, John Hill, a fantastic
charlatan, brought out two slipshod, salacious works of fiction,
The Adventures of Mr. Loveill and *The Adventures of Mr. George
Edwards, a Creole*. John Cleland, too, produced another novel,

The Memoirs of a Coxcomb, which was somewhat less indecent than his *Fanny Hill.*

Above the ruck of mediocre fiction of 1750–51, Smollett's second novel stands out sharply. In the interval since *Roderick Random* he had graduated from surgery to medicine by receiving the M.D. degree at Aberdeen, and had translated *Gil Blas* and begun a translation of *Don Quixote.* The new novel, *The Adventures of Peregrine Pickle,* was much longer than its predecessor, and was further extended by a 50,000-word interpolation, "The Memoir of a Lady of Quality," the authentic confessions of the notorious Lady Vane. The rest of the book was sprinkled with Smollett's personal digressions, reflecting his numerous enmities. The more offensive of these attacks on Fielding, Lyttelton, Garrick, and others, were eliminated from the second edition seven years later; but even when thus tightened up, *Peregrine Pickle* showed no marked advance over *Roderick Random.* Obviously written in haste, it keeps the picaresque unilinear construction, and Peregrine is a more sordid rogue than Roderick. As a student at Winchester and Oxford, Peregrine develops his penchant for mischievous pranks; and later, after falling out with his parents, he is adopted by a crusty retired naval officer. His ramblings in France with the inevitable comic attendant gave Smollett a chance to introduce local color obtained during a recent trip to Paris. In the background, of course, there is a love story, with a conventionally virtuous and beautiful girl whom Peregrine tries to seduce, and eventually marries. The story is crammed with brutal practical jokes and farcical escapades, but Smollett's gift of lively narrative keeps it readable, and several of the grotesque characters are richly comic in his usual vein of caricature.

The author's objective manner gives a callous effect but makes even the most exaggerated occurrences seem plausible, and is in pleasing contrast with the moralizing that pervaded much fiction at the time. This merit Smollett mockingly pointed out on the occasion of Peregrine's first sojourn in jail:

> I might here, in imitation of some celebrated writers, furnish out a page or two with the reflections which he made upon the stability of human affairs, the treachery of the world, and the temerity of youth, and endeavor to decoy the reader into a smile by some quaint observation of my own, touching the sagacious moralizer.

But, besides that I look upon this practice as an impertinent anticipation of the peruser's thoughts, I have too much matter of importance upon my hands to give the reader the least reason to
believe that I am driven to such paltry shifts in order to eke out
the volume.

Fielding, meanwhile, had been working hard on his next book,
which was very different in tone from *Tom Jones.* His duties
as magistrate had brought him close to the squalor and depravity
of the London underworld, and he was advocating drastic reforms
in law enforcement. Though handicapped by illness, he took a
prominent and sometimes courageous part in suppressing a serious
crime wave. This intimate experience with lawlessness modified
the light-hearted attitude toward misconduct that had been perceptible in *Tom Jones.* Besides, he could not have been immune
to the ferocious attacks on the alleged immorality of that novel.
In the preface to *Amelia* he sounded his new note of earnestness
by declaring that

> as histories of this kind may properly be called models of human
> life, so by observing minutely the several incidents which tend
> to the catastrophe or completion of the whole, and the minute
> causes whence those incidents are produced, we shall best be in-
> structed in this most useful of all the arts, which I call the Art
> of Life.

When *Amelia* was published in 1751, the whole first impression
was sold in a single day; but a decline in sales soon showed that
readers were not well pleased on finding that it lacked the humor
and energy of Fielding's previous books. A month later, in his
new periodical, the *Covent Garden Journal,* he portrayed himself
as Amelia's father testifying in her defense against a charge of
dullness:

> Of all my offspring she is my favorite child. I can truly say
> that I bestowed a more than ordinary pains in her education,
> in which, I will venture to affirm, I followed the rules of all
> those who are acknowledged to have writ best on the subject;
> and if her conduct be fairly examined, she will be found to
> deviate very little from the strictest observation of all those rules;
> neither Homer nor Virgil pursued them with greater care than
> myself, and the candid and learned reader will see that the latter
> was the noble model, which I made use of on this occasion.

He ended the plea with an offer of compromise, solemnly declaring "that I will trouble the world no more with any children of mine by the same muse."

Unlike Fielding's other fiction, *Amelia* had a woman as the central character, and it offered a predominantly unhappy picture of domestic life. The passage of time had deepened his idealization of his first wife. In Sophia Western he had portrayed her generous, high-spirited girlhood, with himself providing some traits of her thoughtless lover; now there was an element of penitence in his picture of her as the self-sacrificing wife of an irresponsible husband.

It was the first English novel to deal wholly with the married life of a couple. Lieutenant Booth, invalided out of the army on a tiny pension, is deeply in debt. At the beginning of the novel he engages in an affair with another woman, in the sordid surroundings of a London jail, while his wife and children are in the country. The rest of the story is a record of ever-increasing destitution, with the feckless husband frequently in and out of prison and the wife exposed to the evil designs of two unscrupulous gentlemen. The atmosphere of gloom points to a tragic ending as inevitable; but Fielding was too fond of his heroine to doom her to disaster and so he invented an implausible happy outcome. Amelia unexpectedly inherits a fortune, and her weak-willed husband — as a result of reading a volume of sermons — is converted from skepticism and becomes a respectable citizen.

The inartistic conclusion is the novel's only flaw. The plot, while less complex than that of *Tom Jones*, is well organized, and the emotional unity is firmly sustained. The characters are drawn without the touches of caricature that Fielding formerly used. The most remarkable feature, however, is his change of outlook. The dominant purpose is an earnest social crusade, the principal mood is tender pathos, and the morality is that of orthodox Christianity.

In spite of his unwonted seriousness, he failed to mollify Richardson, who reported to one of his women friends that he had been unable to read beyond the first volume: "I found the characters and situations so wretchedly low and dirty, that I imagined I could not be interested for any one of them; and to read and not to care what became of the hero and heroine is a task that I thought I would leave to those who had more leisure than I am blessed with." He went on to prove his thesis that Fielding had "little or no invention" by listing characters and settings in his three novels that were "all drawn from what he has seen or known." In *Amelia* "he designed to be good, but knew not how, and lost his genius — low humor — in the attempt."

Amelia was Fielding's last novel. During the next year he was busy with the *Covent Garden Journal*. Then illness obliged him to resign his magistracy, and he went abroad for his health, dying in Lisbon in his forty-eighth year, in 1754.

The publication of *Amelia* marks the triumph of the new realistic fiction. This development was signalized in 1752 in the theme of Charlotte Lennox's second novel, *The Female Quixote, or The Adventures of Arabella*. Like Biddy Tipkins in Steele's play, half a century before, the heroine has grown up reading nothing but the old romances and believing that they give a literal picture of real life. Absurd misunderstandings and deceptions are needed to cure her of her fantasies and persuade her to accept a sensible suitor. Since the heroic romances still offered some rivalry to the new realism, *The Female Quixote* was welcomed by all the realists. Johnson wrote the dedication for her and is suspected of having contributed one chapter to the book. Richardson said that "the writer has genius," and Fielding reviewed it enthusiastically, terming it "a most extraordinary and most excellent performance."

Smollett, in his third novel, tried to depart from his established pattern. In his previous books he had exhausted the material from his own experience; in the later part of *Peregrine Pickle* he had obviously started to repeat himself. Though both of his earlier heroes were brazen young rascals, he apparently regarded them with indulgent affection. Now in *The Adventures of Ferdinand, Count Fathom* he tried the experiment of writing about an unmitigated scoundrel, as Fielding did in *Jonathan Wild*. His preface defended his portrayal of the "disgrace and discomfiture of vice, which is always an example of extensive use and influence, because it leaves a deep impression of terror upon the minds of those who were not confirmed in the pursuit of morality and virtue." But this argument is weakened when at the end of the story his specimen of vice repents and becomes respectable and prosperous.

The early part is a simple picaresque series of exploits in

which a self-styled "count" imposes on gullible victims all over
Europe, especially people who are kind to him. Later the focus
shifts to some of these better characters in order to achieve a
complicated climax. The most noteworthy passages are two in
which Smollett produces genuinely powerful effects of terror,
once by tricking the reader into believing that supernatural
forces are at work.

Ferdinand, Count Fathom is thus an inartistic farrago, and yet
the preface contains a definition of the novel that suggests a
clearer sense of form in the author's mind than any he achieved in
his works:

> A novel is a large diffused picture, comprehending the characters
> of life, disposed in different groups and exhibited in various
> attitudes, for the purposes of a uniform plan. This plan cannot
> be executed with propriety, probability, or success, without a
> principal personage to attract the attention, unite the incidents,
> unwind the clue of the labyrinth, and at last close the scene,
> by virtue of his own importance.

This statement proves that by 1753 the biographical structure was
firmly established; thereafter for almost a century it was accepted
as the only possible pattern for long fiction.

Richardson, with his usual deliberation, spent five years in
writing his third novel. As before, he tried to escape from the
limitations of his previous work. In the preface, with his customary air of omniscience, safely based on hindsight, he explained
that the present novel fulfilled a plan that he had had in mind
ever since he began to write *Pamela*. His two earlier novels had
used different social strata and different plots for the single purpose of inculcating virtue. Precarious health and the pressure of
business had then led him to fear that he would have to desist;
but the insistence of his friends had compelled him to "complete
his first design"; and he warned that "the present collection is
not published ultimately, nor even principally, any more than
the other two, for the sake of entertainment only. A much
nobler end is in view."

In each of the previous books the central character was a
woman, and the principal men were selfish and sensual. In social
status his characters had ranged from the servant level up to the
country squirearchy and the wealthy upper-middle class. It re-

mained for him to show that he could write understandingly and favorably about the aristocracy and about a man. His friends were pleading with him to provide an antidote both for the insidious charm of his own Lovelace and for the moral laxity of Tom Jones. His new hero, Sir Charles Grandison, was therefore conceived as a counterpart to his saintly Clarissa, but without the feminine helplessness that had led to her downfall.

Richardson was venturing not only into a higher social sphere but into a wider geographical area, for part of the action takes place abroad, a fact that the author naïvely advertised by a prefatory roster of the characters divided into "men," "women," and "Italians."

The book inevitably suffers from two handicaps. The hero is so immaculately perfect that he repels the sympathy of ordinary readers, who find him an intolerable prig; and his combination of virtue and prudence renders him so invulnerable to disaster that the book lacks the emotional tension arising from the possibility of a tragic outcome. This lack of intensity is partly due to the persistent goodness of the main characters. Only one secondary figure is a roué of the Lovelace type, and his effort to abduct the heroine is easily thwarted. Perhaps it is a merit of the story that its main conflicts are not between good and evil forces but between people who are all equally worthy and altruistic. But what it gains in sweetness it loses in contrast and power.

In spite of its limitations, the book has been regarded by some critics as Richardson's masterpiece. By this time he was a master of technical skill, and he manipulated a cast of characters much larger than before. Though not quite so long as *Clarissa*, it replaces the dramatic unity of that book with a more panoramic view of society. Nevertheless, as Richardson boasted, the structure was carefully planned: "There is not one episode in the whole, nor, after Sir Charles Grandison is introduced, one letter inserted but what tends to illustrate the principal design." In its variety of subplots, its range of secondary performers, its minute study of genteel behavior, and its use of social predicaments as the basis for the action, *Sir Charles Grandison* set a lasting model for the "novel of manners."

The dialogue is consistently lively and natural. To sustain the atmosphere of sophisticated society, the author gave freer rein to his comic talent, which had appeared only faintly in the second part of *Pamela* and in *Clarissa*; but it is still incidental, for Sir Charles himself is too austere to indulge in wit.

In the handling of the hero, the epistolary method caused some difficulties. Sir Charles is too intelligent to be unaware of his own merits, and too truthful to assume a false humility; and so the discussion of his conduct and motives is bound to seem egotistical. Tedious repetition ensues when the author tries to offset this by having his virtues further extolled through other characters, chiefly Harriet Byron, a pretty heiress who falls in love with him. Though Harriet is the nominal heroine of the story, Richardson was in danger of becoming more interested in Clementina della Porretta, an emotional Italian lady whose love for Grandison is doomed to disappointment because of their difference in religion. Her pathetic plight has some resemblance to Clarissa's. But as the balance of the book would be disturbed if Clementina were to monopolize too much sympathy, she is saved from her dramatic determination to become a nun, and meekly accepts the suitable Catholic husband selected by her parents.

The ultimate strength of the book resides in the portrait of Grandison himself. No matter how much the reader may rebel against the baronet's monotonous perfection, the blame must rest on Richardson's purpose and not on his execution of it. He succeeded completely in presenting a paragon of integrity in the Protestant Christian model, for whom even the most recalcitrant reader gradually acquires respect. If one says that Grandison is an idealized self-portrait, one is not scoffing at the fictitious character so much as extolling the author. The sententious, benevolent gentleman, modestly aware that every woman falls in love with him at sight, is an authentic projection of the personality concealed under the deceptive exterior of the fat little printer of Fulham with his circle of adoring bluestocking friends.

The History of Sir Charles Grandison in a Series of Letters Published from the Originals came out in seven volumes in 1753–54. It had been so much talked about in advance that one of the hack writers had been able to forestall it by almost a year with *The Memoirs of Sir Charles Goodville*. Before *Grandison* had ended its six months' publication, some critics were objecting to the hero's unbelievable perfection, and so Richardson added a "Concluding Note" to his final volume, restating his principle: "The Editor thinks human nature has often, of late, been shown in a light too degrading; and he hopes from this series of letters it will be seen that characters may be good without being unnatural." After defending in detail the plausibility of Grandison's conduct, and digressing to condemn the practice of dueling, he returned to the charge against his contemporaries of having "given success (and *happiness*, as it is called) to their heroes of vicious, if not of profligate, characters."

Although some readers complained of the book's wordiness, Richardson's admirers pestered him for a continuation until he was obliged to issue a public refusal:

> The conclusion of a *single story* is indeed generally some great and decisive event, as a Death or a Marriage; but in scenes of life carried down nearly to the present time, and in which a *variety of interesting characters* is introduced, all events cannot be decided . . . ; since persons presumed to be still living must be supposed liable to the various turns of human affairs.

Thus Richardson maintained until the end the pretense that he was merely serving as editor for actual letters of living people. He made no move to start another book. In the full assurance that he had outdistanced his hated rival, Fielding, he complacently enjoyed his fame until his death in 1761. As Dr. Johnson remarked, he "died merely for want of change among his flatterers."

Fielding and Richardson had been absolute antitheses when they began writing fiction; but a sort of magnetic attraction drew their work steadily closer together, until Fielding's third novel might almost have been written by Richardson, and *vice versa*. *Amelia* told a pathetic story about a noble-souled woman abused by a selfish man, while *Grandison* dealt urbanely and sometimes wittily with social *mores*. The imitators of the two authors maintained the distinct styles of their earlier books, and thus the "masculine" and the "feminine" types of fiction survived as separate species; but the final achievement of both masters showed that the essential English novel could stand somewhere between.

The novel emerged in the middle of the eighteenth century as the artistic fulfilment of the neoclassical era. For a hundred years the major authors had been occupied with precise observation of facts, with analysis of the structure of society, with attempts to understand human personality. But so long as they employed traditional literary genres they were handicapped by an incompatibility between the material and the form. The new genre of the novel had the range, the flexibility, the naturalness of style, to be a fitting medium for depicting the new social environment that was dominated by industrial and commercial expansion, by facilities of transportation, by rapid changes of social status, and by conflict of ideas that challenged the old simple axioms about religion, government, and even human nature. The "age of reason," after striving vainly to cram all this into the ancient literary molds of expository treatises, personal essays, poems, or plays, finally gave birth to a new medium that satisfied the need.

V

Establishing the Tradition

(1755 – 1775)

THE EMERGENCE OF THE NOVEL as a new literary genre occupied only fourteen years, from *Pamela* to *Sir Charles Grandison*. After that amazing era of experiment and definition a pause ensued, as though authors needed to absorb the new principles and decide what to do with them. For six years after *Grandison*, even Smollett did not write another novel, being busy with editing magazines and composing a massive work on English history. And during those same years no new novelist of any stature appeared.

Meanwhile prose fiction was gaining form and prestige in France. Alongside the success of Marivaux, even greater popularity had been won by the Abbé Prévost, whose *Memoirs et aventures d'un homme de qualité* came out between 1728 and 1731. The last volume contained a short separate narrative, *Manon Lescaut*, which came to be regarded as a masterpiece of tender pathos. Having lived in London as a political refugee, Prévost chose British settings for his next two books, *Le Philosophe Anglais, ou l'histoire de M. Cleveland* (1733–39) and *Le*

120

Doyen de Killerine (1735–40). His heroes and heroines suffer their way through an incredible series of woeful complications; and the reader's emotions are further harrowed by sensational perils and nightmare scenes of horror and gloom.

The prevailing tone of the French novels is usually called "sensibility," to distinguish it from the moral sentimentalism of Richardson and his disciples. The French authors were not trying to inculcate strict ethical principles; they made a cult of emotional self-consciousness for its own sake. Hence among respectable English readers their novels gained a reputation for immorality; and one of the most successful French writers, Crébillon fils, certainly reveled in lewdness in *Le Sopha* (1740). Marivaux and Crébillon wrote comedy, while Prévost preferred the pathetic mood; but all three give an illusion of realism by their detachment from moral preoccupations. Actually, however, their stories are less realistic than Richardson's, because their purpose of perpetually keeping the reader at a tense emotional pitch impelled them to strain credulity with melodramatic situations, especially when Prévost's type of story settled into a formula in the hands of his followers, Baculard d'Arnaud and Mme. Riccoboni.

As Richardson's verbose solemnity began to lose its hold on the English public, translations and adaptations of the shorter and livelier French novels of sensibility gained currency in England. Conversely, the English novels, particularly Richardson's, were immensely popular in France. Horace Walpole remarked that the French "had adopted the two dullest things we have, whist and Richardson's novels." *Clarissa* and *Grandison* were translated by Prévost, and an enthusiastic *Éloge de Richardson* was written by Denis Diderot, the great encyclopedist. The interplay between the French and English novel unquestionably furthered the artistic development of the form.

The vogue of prose fiction encouraged the two outstanding French thinkers of the mid-century to adopt this form as the best vehicle for their most potent opinions. Beginning with *Zadig* in 1747, Voltaire wrote a series of brief *contes philosophiques* mainly with oriental settings, and he used fiction also for a longer satire, *Candide* (1759), in which he followed the well-worn pattern of *Don Quixote* and *Gil Blas*, but made every episode of the story contribute to his hero's disillusionment and reinforce the author's onslaught upon optimism and dogma. In contrast with Voltaire's cynical wit, Jean-Jacques Rousseau followed Richardson's model in the two books in which he set forth his ideals of love and education — *Julie, ou la nouvelle Héloïse* and *Émile*. In his preface to *Julie* he admitted that he had chosen fiction as his vehicle because "spectacular shows are necessary in big cities and novels for corrupt publics." To illustrate his theory of innate virtue and the evils of sophistication, he depicted a pair of high-souled lovers whose impulses broke through conventional restraints. The cult of sensibility, already launched by Prévost and his disciples, was here expanded into a doctrine that exalted emotion at the expense of reason and formal morality. The ardor of Rousseau's passionate scenes combined with his radical doctrines to give these books immense notoriety.

The united impact of Voltaire and Rousseau added an important dimension to the novel by making it an instrument of propaganda. Earlier writers of fiction had often, indeed, been didactic. But in an era of fixed intellectual standards they had merely reaffirmed familiar dogmas. The whole basis of thought was changed in the middle of the eighteenth century by the new concept of progress; and along with it came the corollary that progress can be guided and accelerated by individual thinkers. Immutable laws, whether of God or government, were yielding to unstable concepts of human welfare and political action; and every theorist with a new panacea, no matter how extravagant, yearned to illustrate it in a novel that would appeal to the imagination and sympathy of the widest reading public.

An imitator of Smollett wrote the first topical propaganda novel in English. Dr. John Shebbeare was a surgeon who turned political agitator; when Parliament passed a law regulating various abuses of marriage, Shebbeare wrote *The Marriage Act* (1754), attacking the new law in a farrago of episodes that mingled Smollett's coarseness with Richardsonian sentiment. Its publication led to Shebbeare's arrest for disrespect of the government. His next novel, *Lydia, or Filial Piety*, was an indiscriminate assault on various doctrines that had roused his Tory ire. The remarkable feature of this book was the noble pair of Indian lovers, Canassetego and Yarico, used as a contrast with the contemptible British characters. Though stolen shamelessly from

Mrs. Behn's *Oroonoko*, the episode foreshadowed the glorification of the uncivilized man that was soon to be launched by Rousseau.

The next English example of the propagandistic purpose is one of the most eccentric novels ever written. Thomas Amory was a learned old recluse whose demented work of fiction, *The Life and Opinions of John Buncle, Esq.*, came out in two volumes ten years apart, 1756 and 1766. It is a shapeless jumble of crotchety prejudices on all sorts of subjects, written in a pedantic style and equipped with vast footnotes. The hero wanders through life with a clear objective: "to see if I could find another good country girl for a wife, and get a little more money; as these were the only two things united that could secure me from melancholy and confer real happiness." Before the book ends he has married eight times, winning each bride by the eloquence and abstruseness of his philosophical and scientific discourses. In spite of its naïve absurdity, the book has charm and power in the matter-of-fact vividness of its style and in the self-portrayal of a supreme egotist. Buncle writes as extensively and enthusiastically about a good meal or a picturesque landscape as about the lovely and virtuous girls with whom he falls in love. With utter solemnity Amory produced a comic masterpiece.

A more distinguished writer also turned to fiction as a medium for expounding his philosophy. Samuel Johnson at the age of fifty had written satirical poems, a poetic tragedy, and numerous volumes of essays, as well as compiling his dictionary; but he was still an underpaid literary drudge. When his mother died he did not have enough money for her funeral expenses and so he laid aside his journalistic work during the evenings of one week and wrote a short book that he hoped would appeal to the public taste. Not bothering to read over the manuscript, he sent it off to a publisher and received £100 for the copyright.

The History of Rasselas, Prince of Abyssinia (1759) is an oriental tale in the manner of Voltaire's *Zadig*. In theme and structure it more closely resembles *Candide*, but Johnson cannot have read the French story, as the two books appeared almost simultaneously. Less satiric and skeptical than Voltaire's, Johnson's story is just as positive a refutation of the current optimism. His royal Abyssinian hero escapes with his sister from the secluded, uneventful luxury of a "Happy Valley" in the hope of learning the true values and aims of life. His experiences teach him that imaginative literature, romantic love, philosophical theories, and scientific discoveries are equally deceptive because they stimulate false hopes and conceal the essential grimness of existence. The story advocates a rational recognition of the futility of human wishes and a Christian stoicism under the yoke of destiny. This means that although Johnson used the external trappings of romance, his philosophical outlook was more uncompromisingly realistic than that of Richardson, Fielding, and Smollett, since they subscribed to the principle of "poetic justice" with a happy ending in which virtue triumphs and evil is punished.

Johnson made little effort to provide local color or even to make the story conform with African conditions. As the writers of heroic romances had done, he chose an exotic setting as a flimsy covering for characters and conversations of his own time and country. Although the action appears episodic, it is actually well organized to bring out the central theme, working up to a climax of the idea rather than of the plot, like the structure of *Gulliver's Travels*. Johnson's style is too formal for lively story-telling, but in some passages he achieves a simplicity and strength that make *Rasselas* the most readable of his works. Composed at a time of sorrow, it was bound to be gloomy, but it had none of the sentimental melancholy that was fashionable in other writings of the period. And in the face of the new-fangled concern with human welfare and of the faith that it could be promoted by benevolence, Johnson sternly reasserted the orthodox doctrine that earthly life is inherently painful and cannot be changed — the doctrine that Pope had crystalized in his austere dictum, "Whatever is, is right."

If *Rasselas* is to be regarded as a step toward the acceptance of the novel as a medium for intellectual exposition, an equally significant but totally different example of the same tendency appeared a few months later. This was the first two volumes of *The Life and Opinions of Tristram Shandy, Gent.*, by the Rev. Laurence Sterne. Sterne was a devotee of sentiment, but he differed from the other members of the cult in possessing an irrepressible sense of humor and a keen and subtle mind.

Sterne's father, though a grandson of an Archbishop of York, was a penniless army ensign. His son Laurence was born in

barracks in Ireland and spent his childhood at military posts in
various parts of Ireland and England. From the age of ten he
was at school under the supervision of relations, and saw nothing
of his parents. As an undergraduate at Cambridge he acquired
convivial habits and showed first symptoms of tuberculosis.
Without any perceptible religious bent, he entered the clergy
and spent twenty years as a rural vicar in the vicinity of York.
He married an unattractive woman for her money, and their
home life was unhappy. His local reputation was based on his
eccentric dress and habits, his mordant wit, and his fund of in-
decorous anecdotes. He developed his conversational skill among
the guests of a college friend, an amateur author of obscene
rhymes and a devotee of Rabelais, who kept open house in his
ramshackle castle near Sterne's parish.

Not until he was forty-five did Sterne write anything beyond
a few local newspaper squibs. Then he discovered his literary
talent when an ecclesiastical squabble led him to compose a
satirical pamphlet, closely modeled on Swift. The pamphlet
was suppressed; but Sterne had learned the joy of creating comic
narrative, and launched into a more ambitious project. In the
spring of 1759 he wrote the first volume of *Tristram Shandy;*
and when York booksellers rejected it on the grounds of its
erratic form and its libelous local references, he sent the manuscript to a London publisher. A second installment was written
in the midst of a flirtation with a pretty concert-singer, and the
two volumes were published in December.

Tristram Shandy shows many signs of its capricious origin.
Caricatures of Sterne's adversaries in the diocesan politics of
York appear among the characters, and several of his friends
and relations were also used as models. So far as the "opinions"
of the retrospective narrator Tristram are concerned, the book
was intimately personal, and Sterne also introduced an objective
self-portrait as Parson Yorick. Thus he depicted himself from
the inside and the outside simultaneously.

His lifetime experiences had prepared him to be a disillusioned
onlooker at life. He only dimly remembered his father, and had
been alienated from his mother since childhood. The incompatibility with his wife had grown worse and she was lapsing into
insanity. His feeble health led him to believe that he would not
live long, and his beloved only daughter was also sickly. He had

been disappointed in expectations of patronage or legacies from influential relations. Efforts to gain preferment through the petty schemes and jealousies of church functionaries had ended in failure, and he was still stuck in a dull country parish. Well aware of the resemblance between his career and Swift's, he felt ready to express himself frankly even though friends warned him of the danger to his professional standing.

His own tastes and interests color every page. Rabelais and Cervantes and Robert Burton, his favorite authors, affected the digressive technique and the colloquial vocabulary. His other favorite, Swift, determined the main purpose, which was to satirize everything in general and current intellectual pretensions in particular. "The plan," Sterne explained in a letter to the publisher, "is a most extensive one, — taking in not only the weak part of the sciences, in which the true point of ridicule lies — but everything else which I find laugh-at-able in my way."

A master of paradox, he was capable of laughing at himself and at the main source of his ideas. Since his college days he had known John Locke's *Essay Concerning Human Understanding*, which propagated a theory of the association of ideas: "Whenever two or more impressions chance to enter the mind simultaneously, they will thereafter always keep in company, and the one no sooner at any time comes into the understanding, but its associate appears with it." In his fourth chapter Sterne points out that the "strange combination of ideas, the sagacious Locke, who certainly understood the nature of these things better than most men, affirms to have produced more wry actions than all other sources of prejudice whatsoever." Sterne set out to show how the workings of every individual brain are controlled by a different pattern of irrelevant associations and personal quirks.

While borrowing ideas from Locke, however, he ridiculed his solemn rationalism. Locke's associative theory had been merely a step in his procedure of establishing sound and clear communication, but Sterne sees it as an insurmountable barrier to any real meeting of minds whatsoever. The very basis of Locke's argument is that we can never know the reality of things outside our own perceptions of them, and that language merely increases the confusion by substituting words for things. Hence, Sterne implies, Locke is foolish in believing that any two minds can have a dependable point of contact at all.

This generalization includes the author and the reader. If no accepted logical arrangement of ideas can be justified, Sterne offers in its place an "impressionistic" technique that at first glance looks like nonsense. He warns his readers not to expect any conventional form in the book. "In writing what I have set about, I shall confine myself neither to [Horace's] rules, nor to any man's rules that ever lived." He ended his first volume thus: "If I thought you was able to form the least judgment or probable conjecture to yourself, of what was to come in the next page, — I would tear it out of my book." And later he boasted that "of all the several ways of beginning a book which are now in practice throughout the known world, I am confident my own way of doing it is the best. — I'm sure it is the most religious, — for I begin with writing the first sentence, — and trusting to Almighty God for the second."

A mere turning of the pages was enough to show that the book was freakish. Italics, capitals, and Gothic type occurred indiscriminately. Brackets, asterisks, and other visual devices abounded, and punctuation was largely by dashes, sometimes varied with rows of dots. French and Latin passages were interspersed. One chapter was barely four lines in length. Midway occurred a blank dedication that the author offered to fill in with the name of the first person who would pay fifty guineas.

Following the initial effect of typographical novelty, the next impression conveyed by the book was incoherence, with its perpetual digressions and abrupt suspensions. At the end of the first two volumes the hero was not yet born. Some readers gave up in bewilderment. "You will laugh at me, I suppose," Sir Horace Mann wrote to Horace Walpole, "when I say I don't understand it. It was probably the intention that nobody *should*. It seems to me *humbugging*." On one level of meaning, Sterne was indeed consciously employing nonsense, in order to ridicule the biographical structure of current novels, the solemn logic of scientific thinkers, and the whole assumption that a writer ought to make organized sense out of the confused jumble of experience.

Many readers, however, were encouraged to dig further when they realized that they might uncover a rich vein of indecency. Sterne wrote about sex and anatomy quite as freely as Fielding and Smollett had done, and the response of readers ranged from the horror of respectable folk on finding a clergyman guilty of such lewdness to the delight of frivolous folk on recognizing his mastery of innuendo, by which he often left one wondering whether the lewdness was actually on the page or merely in the reader's prurient inferences. Thus *Tristram Shandy* won a lasting reputation as a "naughty" book. No doubt Sterne relished ribaldry and wanted to shock prudes; but again this is only one view of the complex structure.

Other readers were impressed by the author's miscellaneous learning, and found a pastime in identifying his allusions. *Tristram Shandy* thus gained favor with scholarly men who had felt little interest in previous novels. By most of his contemporaries, however, Sterne's claim to a deeper philosophical purpose was not taken seriously. The favorable terms applied to his book were "whimsical," "fanciful," "quaint"; while Goldsmith censured it outright for "bawdy and pertness." Richardson, as might be expected, called the volumes "execrable," and remarked, "One extenuating circumstance attends his works, that they are too gross to be inflaming." Nevertheless, he had to concede that "unaccountable wildness, whimsical digressions, comical incoherencies, all with an air of novelty, has catched the reader's attention, and applause has flown from one to another, till it is almost singular to disapprove."

The novelty of the book undeniably made it the season's best seller, and two months after it came out the author traveled to London to enjoy his triumph. He signed a lucrative contract with the publishers for the future volumes of the story, which he promised to furnish "as long as he lived." With no apparent recognition of inappropriateness, a collection of his sermons was brought out as *The Sermons of Mr. Yorick*. Noblemen vied in entertaining him. Lord Chesterfield and Bishop Warburton patronized him, Garrick sponsored him, Reynolds painted his portrait, Hogarth undertook to supply illustrations, the Prime Minister (William Pitt) accepted the dedication of the second edition. Never before had a work of fiction thus brought social prestige to its author. Sterne traveled home to York in a new-bought carriage and plunged into the next volumes of his story. These continued to appear at intervals during the eight years of life that remained to him. At the time of his death he was also in the midst of writing a second book, *A Sentimental Journey through France and Italy*, which claimed to be a literal diary of travel but which contained something like the same mixture of autobiography and fiction that characterized *Tristram Shandy*.

His original intention of writing a general satire in the manner of Swift indicates that he did not start *Tristram Shandy* as a novel. The title and opening scenes were borrowed from the current fashion of prose fiction in the same way that Swift borrowed from Defoe for *Gulliver's Travels*. But Sterne soon displayed the one talent that is essential for the novelist — the power to create characters. Uncle Toby and Corporal Trim, Mr. Yorick and Widow Wadman, even the grotesque sketches of his enemies as Didius and Dr. Slop, were more than lay figures for the expression of the author's ideas. He portrayed them with a mixture of ridicule and sympathy, recording idiosyncracies and absurdities that are surprising because they are utterly plausible. He had an uncanny knack of catching the fragmentary, repetitive movement of everyday speech. He made action come to life in the reader's imagination by combining dialogue with precise notation of gesture and posture, often inserting these in the middle of a spoken sentence. As soon as the characters grew distinct and familiar to the reader the book became essentially a novel in spite of lacking the accepted sort of narrative continuity.

Yet while in this basic sense it is a significant novel, it remains also a sort of gigantic personal essay, in which the author chats with the reader about everything that interests him, in the manner of Montaigne and Burton. As in all other personal essays, the ultimate reason for its appeal is the personality that it discloses. Sterne is one of the fascinating eccentrics of literature, a tantalizing mocker who leaves us uncertain whether he is a cynic wearing a mask of sympathy or a sentimentalist wearing a mask of cynicism. He is not in the true category of satirists, because he sees both sides of every case. Rather he is a disillusioned onlooker who mocks at himself and the reader as often as at the characters of his tale. And the mockery is not an end in itself. After demonstrating that logical communication between minds is impossible, he turns to sympathy as the alternative. Even though people cannot understand each other's notions, there is no reason why they should not maintain mutual affection and tolerance. The reader is constantly drawn into the texture of the book and made to realize that he, too, is blindly devoted to his particular hobbyhorse and is as deserving of laughter and of sympathy as the characters are.

Sterne, in fact, made a more original contribution to the technique of fiction than any other single author has ever done. His theories were implied in his burlesque of his contemporaries. The interspersed tales in Fielding and Smollett are parodied by the even more irrelevant ones in *Tristram Shandy*. Tristram's meticulous recording of events preceding his birth piles ridicule on the standard autobiographical convention by which a narrator assumed the right to chronicle every word of conversations occurring years before. And basically Sterne challenged the assumption that straight chronological order is the only possible structure for narrative. He saw that the meaning of experience is revealed only by its subsequent significance in the consciousness of a retrospective analyzer, and that this can be shown best by rearranging widely dispersed details into a simultaneous array.

In spite of all the nonsense and exaggeration in *Tristram Shandy* the book is essentially realistic, not merely for its characterization but because in the absence of plot the reader's interest is maintained chiefly by the vividness of the trivial details. Sterne did more than any writer since Defoe to prove that a work of fiction could satisfy the reader through his recognition of familiar things as fully as by tragic crises or hair-raising dangers.

Of plot, in the usual sense, there could be little, if any; no climax was possible so long as the author intended to continue writing the book until his death and could not foresee when that event might occur. Yet he protested that there was an inherent unity:

> I fly off from what I am about, as far, and as often too, as any writer in Great Britain; yet I constantly take care to order affairs so that my main business does not stand still in my absence . . . By this contrivance, the machinery of my work is of a species by itself; two contrary motions are introduced into it, and reconciled, which were thought to be at variance with each other. In a word, my work is digressive, and it is progressive too — and at the same time.

Modern critics agree that the book has artistic structure of its own sort. Whereas previous novels had strung a series of incidents upon the straight thread of a central character's life, Sterne interwove an elaborate pattern of themes and persons. In view of his knowledge of music it might be compared to a symphony or a fugue. He made perpetual use of contrast: between the theorizing Walter Shandy and his matter-of-fact wife; between Walter's chilly logic and his brother Toby's sensibility; between Toby's impulsiveness and Corporal Trim's stability. These are all essential elements because they exist together in the mind of Tristram; and if the record could have continued until he reached maturity, the significance of the whole complex might have been plainer. The interplay of personalities upon each other, the importance of heredity and environment for the understanding of character, the irrational vagaries of the human mind — these form the texture of the book.

One of the ideas that Sterne adapted from Locke was that time is a subjective, relative thing, governed by the succession of our ideas, and therefore moving swiftly or slowly in response to our moods. At some points he tried to prove this to the reader by retarding or hastening the speed of narration. This in turn was connected with the assumption of the whole book that external things have no actual scale of importance in themselves, but are significant insofar as they impress themselves on the observer's mind. Sterne created his impressionistic or relativistic method to demonstrate his belief that "the circumstances with which everything in this world is begirt give everything in this world its size and shape." The truth about the thing itself must be conveyed by telling all the begirding circumstances rather than by isolating it in a factual description.

From his reading of Locke, Sterne became a precursor of modern pragmatism and the science of psychology. One of his central themes — used for comic effect but basically a serious argument — is the absurdity of the abstract deductive logic of the Shandy brothers when it encounters the intractable phenomena of real life. He struck a final blow in Rabelais' battle against dialectical scholasticism, just as his contemporaries struck a final blow in Cervantes' battle against idealized romance.

Sterne always retained a sort of youthful naïveté; his kinswoman Mrs. Montagu remarked of him that "he is full of the milk of human kindness, harmless as a child, but often a naughty boy, and a little apt to dirty his frock. . . . He has a world of good nature, he never hurt anyone with his wit." Hence, in spite of all his equivocation and coarseness, he wore the guise of a sentimentalist. The dominating figure in the book, Uncle Toby, the military expert who was too tenderhearted to kill a housefly, superficially resembles Parson Adams in his unworldly kindliness; but his mild sensibility is basically different from the pugnacious obstinacy of Fielding's parson. Throughout the book Sterne was always ready to mingle a tear with a sneer, or to insert a paean of platonic love in the midst of bawdiness. He declared that his major purpose was to use laughter for the promotion of loving-kindness:

> If 'tis wrote against anything — 'tis wrote, an' please your Worships, against the spleen; in order, by a more frequent and more convulsive elevation and depression of the diaphragm, and the succussations of the intercostal and abdominal muscles in laughter, to drive the *gall* and other *bitter juices* from the gall-bladder, liver, and sweetbread of his majesty's subjects, with all the inimicitious passions which belong to them, down into their duodenums.

Because of this emphasis upon universal benevolence, *Tristram Shandy* came to be regarded, crammed though it was with indecency and farce, as a monument of sentimentalism. Yet each passage of sensibility ends so inevitably in an anticlimax or in a sly phrase of double implication that one cannot help suspecting Sterne of intentionally burlesquing the novel of sentiment just as mischievously as he burlesqued deductive logic and the novel of virility.

Many devoted admirers have found the book inexhaustibly fascinating, but to other readers it is peculiarly offensive, a blend of tediousness, egotism, and insincerity. In the paradoxical world of Shandyism, both views can be accepted as valid. The interminable talks between author and reader sometimes become boresome, and Sterne flaunts his learning and his sophistication blatantly. His physical illness, his social ambitions, his dallyings with pretty grass-widows contributed to an abnormal tone. Yet it is hard to ignore the courage and gaiety with which he defied his disease, the cleverness with which he kept pace with his eminent friends, and the good nature that seemed to be mingled so strangely with his vanity.

During 1760, while the first two volumes of *Tristram Shandy* were the sensation of the London season, several other successful novels came out. In January Smollett began to publish his newest work as a serial in the *British Magazine* — the first novel ever to appear in this way. Entitled *The Adventures of Sir*

Launcelot Greaves, it had been written during a three months' imprisonment for libel. Probably remembering that *Don Quixote*, which he had translated not long before, had also been written in prison, Smollett modeled his story directly upon Cervantes' masterpiece. Shorter than his other novels, it was obviously fantastic in sending a knight in armor out on quests in the contemporary English scene. Smollett went Cervantes one better by suppling a second knight-errant also, a naval captain who provided the opportunity for the author's usual display of seafaring lingo. Much of the story is effectively conveyed through dialogue rather than by straight narration. The indiscriminate satire is aimed at various sorts of political and religious chicanery.

A more peculiar book, full of scurrilous satire, was *Chrysal, or The Adventures of a Guinea*, by Charles Johnstone. A coin which passes through many transactions has a supernatural insight into the despicable motives of the people involved, and readers could easily identify the characters with prominent personages in public life. As the guinea ranges across the world from Peru to London, and through many social groups — the church, the army, the law, the government — the picture of human depravity would seem intolerably cynical were there not indications that Johnstone hid a genuine reforming purpose beneath his indictment of society. Resembling some other books of the same era, such as *Pompey the Little*, *Chrysal* represents a type of fiction that was tangential to the true course of the novel. Too much of the significance was ephemeral, owing to its concern with current personalities and scandals; and the use of an inanimate object as narrator, though an ingenious variation of the picaresque form, obviated any illusion of reality.

By this time novel-reading had become such a mania that even the tolerant Goldsmith, in a letter of 1759, insisted that his young nephew should never be allowed to "touch a romance or novel; those paint beauty in colours more charming than nature, and describe happiness that man never tastes. . . . They teach the youthful mind to sigh after beauty and happiness which never existed, to despise that little good which fortune has mixed in our cup, by expecting more than she ever gave." On a similar basis, but with a lighter touch, the flood of sentimental fiction was ridiculed by George Colman in his play, *Polly Honeycomb*, which used the same situation as Mrs. Lennox's *Female Quixote*, except

134 The English Novel

that after eight years the target of ridicule was no longer the implausible romances but the new kind of novel with its seductive illusion of reality. Colman's heroine, refusing to marry a respectable businessman, compares herself to Clarissa Harlowe and Sophia Western, and terms her suitor "as deceitful as Blifil, as rude as the Harlowes, and as ugly as Dr. Slop." Colman appended a list of nearly two hundred novels representing the current staple of the circulating libraries, and in the prologue he summed up the theme of the play:

> But now, the dear delight of later years,
> The younger sister of Romance appears:
> Less solemn is her air, her drift the same,
> And NOVEL her enchanting, charming name.
> Romance might strike our grave forefathers' pomp,
> But Novel for our buck and lively romp!
> Cassandra's folios now no longer read,
> See, two neat pocket-volumes in their stead!
> And then so *sentimental* is the style,
> So chaste, yet so bewitching all the while!
> Plot, and elopement, passion, rape, and rapture,
> The total sum of every dear, dear chapter. . . .
> Miss reads — she melts — she sighs — Love steals upon her —
> And then — Alas, poor girl! — good night, poor honor!

The writer who had so gaily satirized the old romances, Mrs. Lennox, contributed to the new sentimental genre with *Henrietta* (1758) and *Sophia* (1760–61), in which virtuous heroines undergo cumulative misfortunes. A better novel in the same vein is *Memoirs of Miss Sidney Bidulph* (1761), by Frances Sheridan, whose husband, a well-known actor and educational theorist, was a friend of Dr. Johnson. An epistolary novel, written at the instigation of Richardson and dedicated to him, it showed also the influence of the French novelists of sensibility. The misery of the lovers was so prolonged that Johnson grumbled to the author, "I know not, madam, that you have a right, upon moral principles, to make your readers suffer so much." In spite of its exploitation of pathos, however, the book is an improvement on the others of its class. Mrs. Sheridan admitted that it would annoy some readers by failing to gratify their expectations of "poetic justice":

> We are disappointed in the catastrophe of a fable, if everybody concerned in it be not disposed of according to the sentence

of that judge which we have set up in our own breasts. The contrary we know happens in real life; let us not then condemn what is drawn from real life.

Like Fielding's Amelia, the heroine is a long-suffering wife and mother; and the complexity of a woman's emotional responses is shown convincingly enough to make Sidney something more than merely the traditional patient Griselda.

A rival for Mrs. Sheridan's book was *The History of Lady Julia Mandeville* (1763), by Frances Brooke, who had mastered the method by translating one of Mme. Riccoboni's novels. Her pathetic chronicle of aristocratic lovers, full of refined feelings and high-minded misunderstandings, has fewer melodramatic incidents than the others of its type. Much of it is devoted to the idyllic life of an English country house, until it ends in an outburst of tragedy.

Mrs. Sarah Scott, who had published two other works of sentimental fiction since her *History of Cornelia*, wrote *A Description of Millennium Hall* (1762), depicting a group of middle-aged ladies who have retreated from fashionable life to organize an institution for training cripples and misfits to become self-supporting. Though lapsing into the usual sentimentalism in narrating the ladies' past experiences, the book shows a new trend in its didactic humanitarianism.

The dominance of sentimentalism in the fiction of the time cannot be attributed merely to the success of Sterne or to the innate softheartedness of the women who were active practitioners. Its affiliation with Rousseau provides the clue to its being a symptom of the new romantic cult of the individual. Fielding and his contemporaries, adhering to the neoclassical dictum that literature should deal with universals, had insisted that their characters must be regarded as representatives of general types; but the new school gave precedence to the whims and emotional responses of the individual.

Novels of sensibility, however, did not have a monopoly of the market. Following in the footsteps of *Rasselas* came moralistic "oriental tales," such as *Almoran and Hamet* (1761), by John Hawkesworth, a friend of Johnson, and *Solyman and Almena* (1762), by the Rev. John Langhorne, a poet and classical scholar. An innovation was provided in 1762 with *Longsword, Earl of Salisbury, an Historical Romance*, by John Leland, an Irish clergyman, who set the action in the time of Henry II and introduced some historical personages in his romantic plot. Not since Nashe's *Unfortunate Traveller* and Deloney's *Thomas of Reading* had an English author established a work of fiction in a specific earlier era. Though Leland later wrote treatises on history, he allowed his imagination free play in *Longsword*, and warned readers in his preface not to expect either historical accuracy or moral preachment in his tale of adventure. His nearest predecessor, both in use of history for a background and in exploitation of exciting intrigue, was Prévost.

In 1764 a distinguished amateur wandered into the field of fiction. Horace Walpole was the embodiment of eighteenth-century dilettantism. Rich and well-born, the son of a famous Prime Minister, he devoted his life to his hobbies, of which the chief was the purveying of gossip in both conversation and letter-writing. He dabbled in scholarly research, compiling *A Catalogue of Royal and Noble Authors* and *Anecdotes of Painting in England*. When "Gothic" architecture became a fashionable craze, he rebuilt his country house near London in the guise of a medieval castle and surrounded it with a miniature forest containing a tiny "hermit's chapel." After he had spent ten years in this pastime, it is not surprising that one night he had a vivid dream about glimpsing a giant's armored hand on the stair-rail of an ancient castle. The next day, he tells us, "I sat down and began to write, without knowing in the least what I intended to say or relate. The work grew on my hands, and I grew fond of it. . . . I was so engrossed with my tale, which I completed in less than two months, that one evening I wrote from the time I had drunk my tea, about six o'clock, till half an hour after one in the morning, when my hands and fingers were so weary that I could not hold the pen to finish the sentence."

When the short book was finished, Walpole added a preface asserting that "the following work was found in the library of an ancient Catholic family in the north of England. It was printed at Naples, in the black letter, in the year 1529." He published it as *The Castle of Otranto*, "translated by William Marshall, Gent., from the original Italian of Onuphrio Muralto, Canon of the Church of St. Nicholas at Otranto." No doubt this disguise was partly intended to enhance the plausibility of the fantastic story; but one cannot help suspecting that Walpole wanted also to conceal his authorship of a work that was so unlike the neat reference books he had previously compiled and so remote from the world of cultivated wit in which he resided.

The pretense of a translation further enabled the author to praise his own work brazenly. After justifying the "air of the miraculous" on the ground that "belief in every kind of prodigy was so established in those dark ages," the preface went on:

> Allow the possibility of the facts, and all the actors comport themselves as persons would do in their situation. There is no bombast, no similes, digressions, or unnecessary descriptions. Every thing tends directly to the catastrophe. Never is the reader's attention relaxed. The rules of the drama are almost observed throughout the conduct of the piece. The characters are well drawn, and still better maintained. Terror, the author's principal engine, prevents the story from ever languishing; and it is so often contrasted by pity, that the mind is kept up in a constant vicissitude of interesting passions.

While admitting that the book's moral teaching was not forceful, Walpole yet insisted that "the piety that reigns throughout, the lessons of virtue that are inculcated, and the rigid purity of the sentiments, exempts this work from the censure to which romances are but too liable."

He was right in claiming that the story's effectiveness was chiefly due to its being short and free of ornamentation. As it could be read in a few hours, the emotional tension would build up without long interruptions to break the spell and arouse incredulity. It seized upon the reader's curiosity at the beginning and offered no solution to the mystery until the very end. And it gained a sort of imaginative consistency from the absence of everyday modern details. Although laid in medieval times, it lacked even the rudimentary connection with recognizable dates and personages that Leland provided for *Longsword*. The action takes place sometime during the Crusades (which lasted for two hundred years) and ostensibly in Italy, though some of the names are German and Spanish. This vague setting in a past age and a foreign scene gave it a certain resemblance to the romances that flourished in the preceding century; and a few of the episodes — abduction by pirates, and recognition of a lost son by a birthmark — were standard equipment in them; but Walpole's story differed in its brevity and in its evocation of supernatural terror.

The author showed some skill in the use of atmosphere — pale moonlight, shadowy vaults, blasts of wind. For this attempt to play on the reader's imagination and superstition the nearest antecedent is to be seen in Prévost.

To a modern reader the portents and apparitions are laughable rather than terrifying: a giant in armor, a skeleton perambulating in a hermit's cowl, a statue that drips blood, a picture that comes to life. But Walpole's contemporaries found them delightfully gruesome; "it engages our attention here," his friend the poet Gray reported from Cambridge University, "makes some of us cry a little, and all in general afraid to go to bed o' nights." The book was so well received that Walpole confessed his authorship when the second edition came out, and he wrote a new preface to assert that he was not merely harking back to the outmoded genre:

> It was an attempt to blend the two kinds of romance, the ancient and the modern. In the former, all was imagination and improbability; in the latter, nature is always intended to be, and sometimes has been, copied with success. Invention has not been wanting; but the great resources of fancy have been dammed up by a strict adherence to common life. . . . The author of the following pages thought it possible to reconcile the two kinds. Desirous of leaving the powers of fancy at liberty to expatiate through the boundless realms of invention, and thence of creating more interesting situations, he wished to conduct the moral agents in his drama according to the rules of probability; in short, to make them think, speak, and act, as it might be supposed mere men and women would do in extraordinary positions.

These claims to naturalness in characterization were scarcely borne out by the story, in which all the persons are thoroughly wooden. The real link between *The Castle of Otranto* and the other fiction of the decade was in the prolonged miseries endured by the hero and heroine before the happy ending. Its prime significance was in the very fact that it did revert to the kind of implausible romance that was believed to have been exterminated by the realism of Richardson, Fielding, and Smollett only twenty years before. Walpole proved that reason and common sense had not succeeded in eliminating the public craving for the exotic and the marvelous.

This does not mean that the book at once started a trend.

Readers enjoyed the delicious sense of horror that it aroused, but only as a momentary escape from the comfortable routine of practical life. It was regarded as an ingenious bit of make-believe, like the battlements and stained glass of Walpole's counterfeit castle at Strawberry Hill. He himself made no move to write another book in the same manner; and even the hack writers, usually prompt to exploit a new success, did not try to imitate it.

More characteristic of the time was another work of fiction, the first volume of which came out in 1766. Henry Brooke was just the sort of man to appreciate the new potency of the novel as a vehicle for personal theories. An Irish lawyer, he had written a long mystical poem on *Universal Beauty*, a tragedy that was withdrawn from the stage at the last moment because of its supposed treasonable application to the government, and pamphlets counseling tolerance in Ireland's bitter conflict of religions. Past sixty years of age, he was a quixotic character with a headful of visionary theories when he began to write *The Fool of Quality, or The History of Henry Earl of Moreland.*

If the Rev. Abraham Adams or Captain Toby Shandy had written a novel, it would have been something like *The Fool of Quality.* It is as crammed with the author's prejudices as *John Buncle* and as digressive as *Tristram Shandy;* the difference is that Brooke has nothing of Amory's arrogance or Sterne's lubricity. The theme is the education of an ideal nobleman by a rich and equally ideal man of business. Eleven other stories are interwoven with the central narrative of Harry Clinton's training, and many short tales from history are interspersed to illustrate its moral lessons. Besides, all action frequently stands still while long discussions of philosophical and social topics grow into complete essays, some cast in the form of dialogues between the author and a friend.

The basis of the book is Rousseau's belief in the innate goodness of the "natural man." The wise Mr. Fenton develops Harry's noble nature by constant appeals to his emotions. The good characters weep copiously throughout, either from sympathy with suffering or from admiration of virtue. Harry is incredibly magnanimous in his juvenile acts of courage and generosity. After the innocent characters have suffered repeated injustices at the hands of the unscrupulous ones, they emerge triumphant at the end.

In spite of its absurdities the book has genuine merits. The author was well aware that it would seem implausible to worldly readers, as he indicated in the title and in the interspersed comments. Touches of humor prevent the sensibility from becoming mawkish. Furthermore, Harry's excessive magnanimity does not hinder his coming to life as a real lovable boy. Fortunately he does not grow up until almost the end of the story; and Brooke in his sixties was still enough of a child to reproduce a boy's outlook convincingly. The spiritual earnestness of the book recommended it to religious-minded readers who seldom condescended to read fiction. An abridgment was edited by no less a person than John Wesley.

Such books as *John Buncle*, *Tristram Shandy*, and *The Fool of Quality* indicate that the newly established integrity of the novel as an art form was in peril of dissolving into the vague laxity of a medium for expounding personal fads. In the same year as Brooke's first volume and Amory's last one, however, a more skillful author brought out a masterpiece of controlled art. Oliver Goldsmith had an uncanny knack of accepting the current techniques of any literary genre and yet subtly transforming them into something peculiarly his own. He had relieved the tediousness of the periodical essay with humorous fictitious characters in *The Citizen of the World*. Later, in his poems, he was able to relax the epigrammatic rigidity of the heroic couplet into easy-flowing and mildly idealized recollections of his travels abroad and of his childhood home. When he turned to drama he produced the two most spontaneous and merry comedies of the century. This very versatility, combined with the pressure of hack-writing, prevented him from concentrating upon any one literary type as his life work. His only venture in the novel was written early in his career, and like all his other work it was full of self-portraiture and informal reminiscence.

He seems to have written *The Vicar of Wakefield* in 1761-62, when he was still a harried and little-known hack writer. Subsequently he was threatened with imprisonment for debt, and sent a desperate appeal to his friend Dr. Johnson, who came to his lodgings, looked over his jumble of manuscripts, and picked out *The Vicar of Wakefield* as being good enough to offer to a publisher. It brought the author what seemed to him a magnificent sum — sixty pounds; but the buyer was so doubtful of his bargain that he withheld it from the press until 1766, after Goldsmith had won some fame with his poem, *The Traveler*.

The reason for the publisher's hesitation is not hard to see. The book was shorter than most of the successful novels of the time, and was deficient in melodramatic action. The characters did not go through tear-compelling agonies. The humor was gentle and tolerant, devoid of either satire or obscenity. It could not be put into the category of propaganda fiction, for the author recommended nothing more remarkable than family affection and Christian goodwill. But when it got into print, these negative qualities proved to be its positive virtues. Because there was little suspense or excitement in the plot, the reader's interest was held by the characters. Instead of rhetorical scenes of grief and despair there was genuine pathos, all the more effective because it was implied rather than exploited. The absence of ideology meant that the story was not dated by contemporary notions. As a simple chronicle of a good man's fortitude in the face of worldly pressures, it had much in common with *The Pilgrim's Progress*, and its difference from Bunyan's book is a good measure of how far prose fiction had moved in ninety years.

The author's intentions were set forth honestly in a brief preface (signed by Goldsmith but sounding more like Johnson):

> The hero of this piece unites in himself the three greatest characters upon earth; he is a priest, an husbandman, and the father of a family. He is drawn as ready to teach, and ready to obey, as simple in affluence, and majestic in adversity. In this age of opulence and refinement whom can such a character please? Such as are fond of high life, will turn with disdain from the simplicity of his country fire-side. Such as mistake ribaldry for humor, will find no wit in his harmless conversation; and such as have been taught to deride religion, will laugh at one whose chief stores of comfort are drawn from futurity.

The story was not free of faults. Traces of haste and carelessness are easy to see: it has been suspected that one or two whole episodes were left out altogether. The climax is as implausible as that of *The Fool of Quality*. The defects, however, are offset by fundamental advantages — admirable prose style, vivid characterization, an idyllic atmosphere, and the implicit idealism and tolerance supplied by the author's personality.

His main technical *coup* was his adoption of the first-personal point of view for a subtle effect. The elderly vicar would be a standard comic figure of the Parson Adams model if he were seen from the outside; but when he tells the story himself his unworldly benevolence becomes convincing and lovable. Goldsmith's unaffected prose is natural as Dr. Primrose's medium of expression. Beyond this, the appeal of the characters arises from their fidelity to the author's experience. His father and brothers and sisters, in addition to himself, are represented in a whimsically idealized manner in every page. Thus *The Vicar of Wakefield* became the archetype of middle-class domestic fiction.

It is not too much to say that this is the first completely "normal" novel. The era of experimentation being at an end, a man of first-rate talent but little creative originality, such as Goldsmith, could write a book that had all the essential merits and no eccentricities. He derived in almost equal measure from the two diverse schools that had originated with Richardson and Fielding. He was akin to the former in his moral earnestness, and to the latter in his genial humor. The two most serious episodes of his plot are likewise divided: the seduction of Olivia Primrose by the dastardly Squire Thornhill points back to *Pamela* and *Clarissa;* the sufferings of Dr. Primrose in the debtors' prison point back to *Amelia*.

The reward of normality was that *The Vicar of Wakefield* remained for more than a hundred years the most widely read of the eighteenth-century novels. When Fielding and Smollett came to be too licentious for nineteenth-century prudery, Richardson and Mrs. Sheridan too emotional for nineteenth-century apathy, and Walpole too supernatural for nineteenth-century rationalism, Goldsmith's clear and simple style, his convincing characters, and his sunny humor continued to appeal to readers of all ages and backgrounds.

For several years after *The Vicar of Wakefield* the output of novels was copious but undistinguished. Feeble imitations of *Tristram Shandy* vied with tearful tales of sentiment. Among the better of the sentimental novels were Sarah Scott's *Man of*

Real Sensibility, or The History of Sir George Ellison,
Hugh Kelly's *Memoirs of a Magdalen, or The History of
Louisa Mildmay,* and Elizabeth Griffith's *Delicate Distress.*
Mrs. Sheridan, just before her untimely death in 1766, experimented with the oriental apologue in *The History of Nourjahad,* perhaps the most charming specimen of its type. A touch
of novelty appeared in Frances Brooke's second novel, *The
History of Emily Montague* (1769), because of its unusual
setting. Shortly after her *Lady Julia Mandeville* came out, her
husband was appointed chaplain of the forces in Quebec, and she
spent several years with him in Canada. She therefore provided
Emily Montague with a regional background, including both
the picturesque Canadian scenery and the unconventional habits
of the people. Most other novelists of the time felt no need for
much description of setting, since their books were laid either
in the contemporary England that the readers knew familiarly
or else in remote oriental lands that the authors knew not at all.
Emily Montague can be termed the first novel of local color.

In 1771 Smollett published his fifth and last novel. Though
no more than twenty-three years had elapsed since his first
one, and ten since his fourth, *The Expedition of Humphry
Clinker* seemed like an apparition from a defunct era. Smollett
was only fifty years old; but illness, overwork, and bitter
quarrels had deepened his misanthropy, and the new vogue of
sensibility was to him merely a broad target for ridicule. He
had been living in France and Italy for several years, in search
of health, and in 1766 had published a book about his travels.
Naturally, then, the new novel dealt with travel and health
resorts, though the travel was confined to Britain and the resorts were Bath and Harrogate. Not only the itinerary but also
some of the episodes were based on Smollett's own last visit
to England and Scotland. Several living people were introduced
under their real names. Other episodes and characters were
suggested by a successful recent poem, *The New Bath Guide,*
by Christopher Anstey; and from it Smollett derived also the
technical device of having the same events reported in the letters of several comic characters, who thus reveal their own
idiosyncracies. His transmuting of his personal experience into
fiction owed something to Sterne's *Sentimental Journey* and the
last books of *Tristram Shandy.*

The plot of *Humphry Clinker* was as disjointed as Smollett's previous ones, and he still resorted at times to heavy-handed caricature. His years as journalist and historian impelled him to include factual information about the places visited, which was out of keeping with comic fiction. This expository padding and his borrowing from Anstey's satire suggest that his originality was running dry. Yet in some ways this is Smollett's best novel. The comic episodes entail less of sadistic violence, and the characters are more complex and more appealing. Matthew Bramble, the chief letter-writer, is to some degree a self-portrait of the irascible middle-aged Smollett, as Roderick Random and Peregrine Pickle had been self-portraits of the headstrong young one. Bramble's sister, Tabitha, is an aggressive spinster; his friend, Lieutenant Lismahago, conceals good sense and self-respect under his ungainly appearance and grotesque behavior; the maid, Winifred Jenkins, pours out her muddled impressions in phonetic spelling and distorted vocabulary; even Miss Bramble's dog Chowder becomes a personality. Humphry Clinker, though filling the title role, is a secondary character, a loyal servant who finally (in a parody of Tom Jones) turns out to be Mr. Bramble's bastard son. The use of local color, in descriptions of Bath and Edinburgh, adds a dimension of reality.

In the same year that *Humphry Clinker* maintained the anti-sentimental ferocity of the Fielding school, another novel served to represent the *reductio ad absurdum* of Richardsonian sentimentality. *The Man of Feeling* was composed between the ages of twenty-one and twenty-five by Henry Mackenzie, an Edinburgh lawyer of good family and education, who published it anonymously. When its spectacular success tempted an obscure clergyman to claim the authorship, Mackenzie admitted having written the book.

More clearly than the other novels of sensibility, Mackenzie's reveals a philosophical foundation. At Edinburgh University he had encountered the teachings of Francis Hutcheson, who in turn was a disciple of the Earl of Shaftesbury in believing that a moral sense is innate in man and impels him to approve virtuous actions and despise vicious ones, with a corollary that a "public sense" makes us "pleased with the happiness of others and uneasy at their misery." The resemblances between Mackenzie's hero and St. Preux in Rousseau's *Nouvelle Héloïse* or

Yorick in *Tristram Shandy* are modified by the Shaftesbury-Hutcheson influence, which insisted that sensibility should not merely be enjoyed for its own sake but should result in humanitarian action.

Among literary antecedents for *The Man of Feeling*, the most immediate was the *Contes moraux* of Jean François Marmontel, who was a follower of Rousseau and whom Mackenzie ranked alongside of Richardson. He was not simply imitating earlier writers, however, for in his memoirs he confessed that his hero was in part a self-portrait:

> Some of the incidents I had a certain degree of share in myself. I was often the martyr of that shyness which Harley is stated as being affected by in his intercourse with mankind, and I had likewise the disgust at some parts of the legal profession to which I was destined.

The hero goes to London to pursue humanitarian schemes, and investigates criminals, prostitutes, and lunatics. Though endlessly imposed upon by the vicious characters he encounters, he never abates his generosity to the poor and the oppressed. Tears and guineas flow from him in equal profusion. He is so exquisitely modest that he never can disclose his love to the girl he adores, except by clinging to her hand when she visits him on his deathbed.

Mackenzie's luxuriating in sensibility shows kinship with Sterne, as does his capricious, digressive technique — he pretends that his manuscript has been haphazardly reassembled from fragments used as gun-wads; but the effect is totally different because of the absence of comedy. On this point he felt nothing but contempt for Sterne, who, he says, "often wants the dignity of wit. I do not speak of his licentiousness, but he often is on the very verge of buffoonery, which is the bathos of wit, and the fool's coat is half upon him." In *The Man of Feeling* there is not even the gentle humor that makes *The Fool of Quality* and *The Vicar of Wakefield*, with equally naïve heroes, endurable to the modern reader.

The spiritual earnestness and humanitarian zeal of Brooke and Mackenzie had close relationship with the spread of Methodism and of the Evangelical movement within the Church of England, which were a reaction against the irresponsible con-

duct of many clergymen of the time. A typical specimen of
the pleasure-loving vicars, the Rev. Richard Graves, was roused
to write a novel ridiculing the solemn enthusiasts. In *The Spiritual Quixote* he fell back on the hackneyed device of imitating
Cervantes, with an Oxford-educated country squire as his knight-
errant and a village cobbler as the inevitable attendant. Geoffrey
Wildgoose sets out to preach the Methodist gospel, only to encounter absurd misadventures and eventual disillusionment. The
story is more plausible than Smollett's *Sir Launcelot Greaves,*
having closer affinities with Fielding and Sterne; but Graves was
an anachronism in 1772, when the public taste was all for the
didactic.

While *The Man of Feeling* ran through edition after edition,
Mackenzie made haste with his next work of fiction. Like some
other novelists, he obviously found the theme for it by invert-
ing the previous one. *The Man of the World* (1773) centers
upon a character as selfish and unscrupulous as the other was
altruistic. This wicked baronet seduces the daughter of a country vicar, and years later almost repeats the procedure with another girl, who turns out to be his own daughter. There is better
structure and more dramatic action than in *The Man of Feeling,*
but the echoes of *Pamela* and *Clarissa* and *The Vicar of Wakefield* are obvious. The most interesting episode, though no
more plausible than the rest of the book, is a digression dealing
with a cultivated young Englishman, a misfit in his proper social
sphere, who is captured by Cherokee Indians while serving in
the army in America, and finds happiness and wisdom among
the redskins.

Mackenzie's third novel, *Julia de Roubigné*, was intended to
be more realistic than *The Man of the World* by having no
villain whatsoever, but showing a group of virtuous characters
drawn into a tragic catastrophe through excessive indulgence
in their emotions. Thus it teaches the Shaftesbury-Hutcheson
theory negatively, as *The Man of Feeling* taught it positively:
the characters in *Julia de Roubigné*, blameless though they may
be, are destroyed by their sensibility because it has no humanitarian outlet. As a melodramatic tragedy, this is the best unified
of Mackenzie's three novels; but for this very reason it is the
worst of them, because it gives least scope for his talent for
depicting shades of feeling and conduct.

Mackenzie was only thirty-two when he published *Julia de Roubigné*, and fifty-four years of life remained to him; but he wrote no more novels, devoting himself instead to essays, poetic drama, and literary friendships. The last significant disciple of Richardson, he realized that the novel was moving in directions that he was not competent to follow.

VI

Terror and Edification

(1775 – 1800)

WHEN SMOLLETT DIED in 1771, the last of the "founding fathers" of the novel vanished from the scene. No one was left to carry on the sort of virile, rowdy fiction that had originated with Fielding. And in the same year the other major type — the sentimental, moralistic manner of Richardson — reached its apogee in *The Man of Feeling*.

Having survived for thirty years, the novel was facing a crisis. New lines of development were essential if it was to avoid premature decay. The blight of standardization already afflicted it. In 1769 the *London Magazine* accused a publishing firm of "keeping in pay a set of needy authors to furnish a sufficient supply of new novels for publication," and this evoked an angry denial in the preface of the next novel the firm brought out. On the contrary, they asserted, many of their novels were "written by persons of rank, property, and fortune, above accepting any other return for their labors than a few printed copies for themselves and friends." Similarly, one of the minor characters in *Humphry Clinker*, Tom Cropdale, writes novels at £5 a volume, but complains sarcastically of the competition from ladies "who publish merely for the propagation of virtue, with so much ease and spirit, and delicacy, and knowledge of the human heart, and all of the serene tranquility of high life, that the reader is not only enchanted by their genius but reformed by their morality." Mass production, whether by needy professionals or by incompetent amateurs, could result only in mediocrity.

Meanwhile, the feeble emotional novels were under constant fire from two adversaries — from satirists for their silliness, and from moralists for their deleterious effect on adolescent girls. Lydia Languish, in Sheridan's comedy, *The Rivals* (1775), is portrayed as an avid reader of current fiction, which shapes her conduct so completely that Sir Anthony Absolute grumbles, "A circulating library in a town is as an evergreen tree of diabolical knowledge! It blossoms through the year! And depend on it, Mrs. Malaprop, that they who are so fond of handling the leaves will long for the fruit at last." And William Cowper lamented in "The Progress of Error":

> Ye writers of what none with safety reads,
> Footing it in the dance that fancy leads:
> Ye novelists, who mar what ye would mend,
> Snivelling and drivelling folly without end;
> Whose corresponding misses fill the ream
> With sentimental frippery and dream,
> Caught in a delicate soft silken net
> By some lewd earl, or rake-hell baronet:
> Ye pimps, who, under Virtue's fair pretense,
> Steal to the closet of young Innocence,
> And teach her, inexperienced yet and green,
> To scribble as you scribbled at fifteen;
> Who, kindling a combustion of desire,
> With some cold moral think to quench the fire;
> Though all your engineering proves in vain,
> The dribbling stream ne'er puts it out again.
> Oh that a verse had power, and could command
> Far, far away, those flesh-flies of the land,
> Who fasten without mercy on the fair,
> And suck, and leave a craving maggot there.
> Howe'er disguised th'inflammatory tale,
> And covered with a fine-spun specious veil,
> Such writers, and such readers, owe the gust
> And relish of their pleasure all to lust.

During the next decade four or five new lines of development emerged. Starting points for all of them can be identified in books before 1777, but only in that year did the tendencies become positive. The most potent was a delayed reaction to *The Castle of Otranto*. About the same time as Walpole's book, two literary works of another type, both intended for a limited scholarly audience, had astonished their authors by becoming best sellers: James Macpherson's pseudo-translation of primitive Gaelic folk epics and Thomas Percy's edition of an old manuscript of popular ballads. Later a similar success was won by Chatterton's imitations of medieval poetry. All of these aroused a frenzy of admiration for their atmosphere of a vaguely feudal past, which was summed up in the epithets "Gothic" and "romantic." Richard Hurd, in his *Letters on Chivalry and Romance* (1762), provided critical sanction for the new vogue by defending the imaginative validity of the medieval romances.

Past ages had appeared in prose fiction only in Walpole's story and in Leland's *Longsword;* and the concomitant mood of mystery and terror had figured to only a minor degree in Smollett's *Ferdinand Count Fathom* and in a few sentimental novels imitative of Prévost. Not until 1777 did another novelist devote a whole novel to a historical epoch and to the mood of terror.

Clara Reeve was a spinster who made her literary debut with a "romance" in the earlier sense of the word by publishing a new translation of Barclay's seventeenth-century *Argenis*. This led her to defend prose fiction against the critics who, in her view, were inconsistent in sneering at it while they exalted the epic. She asserted that the old romances "are only epics in prose."

> The business of romance is, first, to excite the attention, and secondly to divert it to some useful or at least innocent end. Happy the writer who attains both these points, like Richardson! and not unfortunate, or undeserving praise, he who gains only the latter, and furnishes out an entertainment for the reader.

Citing Walpole's statement of his objective in *The Castle of Otranto*, she remarked that, in order to combine the merits of "the ancient Romance and the modern Novel, . . . there is required a sufficient degree of the marvellous to excite attention; enough of the manners of real life to give an air of probability to the work, and enough of the pathetic to engage the heart in its behalf." Walpole's book, in her opinion, suffered from "a redundancy" in the first of these requisites: "The machinery is so violent that it destroys the effect it is intended to excite. Had the story been kept within the utmost *verge* of probability, the effect had been preserved, without losing the least circumstance that excites or detains the attention."

Miss Reeve undertook to show how it ought to have been done, by using a similar setting and the same central plot *motif*, but providing a rational explanation for each apparently supernatural event. Her book was first entitled *The Champion of Virtue: A Gothic Story;* but when its success led to a second edition in 1778, she adopted a name that suggested its historical atmosphere: *The Old English Baron.* The action was laid in the reign of Henry VI, and an effect of naturalness was produced by occasional everyday details — her knights suffer from toothache and eat bacon-and-eggs. Miss Reeve was as austere a moralist as Richardson; the eerie phenomena are used strictly for enforcing the lesson that crime never goes unpunished.

While Miss Reeve was justified in her objection to Walpole's gross horrors, she adopted the wrong way for correcting them. She might have built up a mood of terror by means of psychological suggestion; instead she conscientiously follows each gruesome moment with the matter-of-fact circumstances that produced it. The result is that the reader either is annoyed at having been imposed upon or else laughs at the anticlimax. If Miss Reeve had intended a burlesque of the tale of terror, this method of incongruity would be justified; but apparently she was striving for a perfectly serious effect. Walpole, who, as might be expected, was not gratified by her attempt to improve upon his method, pointed out its ineffectualness. "It is so probable," he grumbled, "that any trial for murder at the Old Bailey would make a more interesting story."

A second type of fiction that emerged in the late seventies was the novel of manners. Tentative glimpses of it had appeared as early as *Sir Charles Grandison;* and several of the better novels of sensibility by women writers, notably Mrs. Sheridan and Mrs. Brooke, occasionally allowed social comedy to mingle with the agonies. Mrs. Brooke's third novel, *The Excursion,* in 1777, tried to deal quietly with the everyday experiences of a girl making her first acquaintance with high society and finding it less elegant than she expected.

If Mrs. Brooke had been blessed with greater liveliness of

style and vividness of characterization, *The Excursion* might take rank as the first novel of a new type. Actually, however, the distinction goes to one that came out a year later, the work of a younger and cleverer woman. Like Mrs. Lennox, Mrs. Brooke, and Mrs. Sheridan, the author became a member of Dr. Johnson's literary circle; but she had the additional advantage, as the daughter of a learned musicologist, of having lived among literary people all her life. Thus she was indoctrinated from her girlhood with wit, common sense, and good conversation.

In her early teens Fanny Burney composed short tales and one full-length novel, which was in the current sentimental mode; the heroine married the usual dissolute baronet and died in giving birth to a daughter after he had deserted her. Fanny's practical-minded stepmother, however, discovering that she was wasting her time so frivolously, insisted on a bonfire of all the manuscripts. Thereafter Fanny devoted herself to keeping a voluminous journal, and thus gained facility in the accurate recording of everyday behavior and talk. She went often to the theater to see her friend Garrick perform; and she read many novels, finding fault with any that were "very enthusiastick" or "so romantick that every word betrays improbability." In her diary she stated what she liked in fiction: "I cannot be much pleased without an appearance of truth; or at least of possibility — I wish the story to be natural though the sentiments are refined; and the characters to be probable though their behavior is excelling."

Though she had destroyed her juvenile novel, the subject of it lingered in her memory; when she began secretly to write another, she started where it had left off, making her new heroine the daughter of her former one. The plot centers upon the girl's efforts to prove her legitimacy and upon her dilemmas in repelling a profligate baronet and encouraging a high-minded nobleman. These sentimental matters, however, are overshadowed throughout by the social comedy.

The novels of Richardson and his disciples had been concerned primarily with moral standards; those of the school of sensibility with emotional ones. Miss Burney's was the first in which the essential standards were social. Her heroine is careful of her virtue, to be sure; but she is not passionate enough to incur any real danger in that direction. Hers are the comic perils of errors in etiquette and of imprudence in associating with the wrong people. There is much comedy, therefore, throughout the book — partly mild satire at the expense of vulgarity and pretension, partly the inherent absurdity of the contrasts in outlook among diversified people in an artificial environment. For this sort of writing the author's lack of emotional experience was no handicap. She was a bright girl with a sharp eye for the way people behave and a keen ear for the way they talk. Out of this material she made a graceful and amusing picture of contemporary manners.

Being a modest young woman, Miss Burney was doubtful as to the propriety of publishing a novel, and so she took elaborate precautions to conceal her identity, going so far as to copy the manuscript in a disguised handwriting to prevent even the publisher from recognizing it. Early in 1778, when she was twenty-five, the book appeared under the title of *Evelina, or A Young Lady's Entrance into the World.* The preface announced her realistic intention:

> To draw characters from nature, though not from life, and to mark the manners of the times, is the attempted plan of the following letters. . . . The heroine of these memoirs, young, artless, and inexperienced, is "No faultless Monster, that the world ne'er saw," but the offspring of Nature, and Nature in her simplest attire.

Favorable reviews appeared, and Fanny was overjoyed to hear that the book was being talked about everywhere. When she learned that Dr. Johnson had said there were "passages in the book which might do honor to Richardson," the news "almost crazed her with agreeable surprise," so that she "danced a jig without any preparation, music, or explanation." *Evelina* was soon being attributed to various well-known writers; and when the publisher was besieged with inquiries as to the author's identity he concealed his own ignorance by hinting that it was the work of a prominent gentleman who could not let himself be known.

The book's popularity was due to its real novelty, even though it showed traces of earlier literary models. The epistolary technique derives straight from Richardson, and several of the serious characters follow types that he originated. The comic naval officer, on the other hand, with his nautical vocabulary and his crude practical jokes, is a modified borrowing from Smollett. Some of the other characterization and action probably came from the comedies that Fanny loved to see on the stage. But she combined these effectively with her own observation of people around her; she wrote the fictitious letters in the lively style of her own diary rather than the rhetoric of Richardson and Mrs. Sheridan; and her knowledge of the theater enabled her to handle the dialogue with neat timing. Another merit was the topographical accuracy; she knew London well, and readers enjoyed recognizing the familiar settings — Snow Hill, Hampstead, Ranelagh, Kensington Gardens.

The fundamental appeal, however, was in the naturalness and lack of pretension. As Fanny noted in her diary, "I have not pretended to show the world what it actually *is*, but what it appears to a girl of seventeen: — and so far as that, surely any girl who is *past* seventeen may safely do?" Evelina's agonized embarrassment over social blunders that make her conspicuous is so convincing that one sympathizes with her sense of irreparable tragedy while smiling at it; and the characters insist on lingering in the reader's memory like real people. When the authorship came to be known among the friends of the Burney family, Fanny was repeatedly, though deliciously, disconcerted to hear Johnson and Reynolds and Mrs. Thrale and others quoting phrases from the conversations in the novel or remarking how mannerisms of the characters appeared in actual people they met.

Finally, *Evelina* was successful because the time was ripe for satirical social comedy. The bourgeois class had reached a stage of prosperity and ambition that led them to imitate the behavior of gentlefolk, and people like the Burneys and their friends were becoming aware of a challenge to their exclusive prerogatives. They laughed at the Branghton family in Fanny's book, with its bungling efforts to appreciate the arts and to master the mysteries of etiquette; but they recognized that the subject was adequate as the theme of a novel. Though the word "snobbery" had not yet come into use, the phenomenon was clearly to be seen.

For this reason Miss Burney's comedy of manners has an underlying connection with another kind of fiction which became prominent about the same time — the novel of social theory. These were the years when the startling new doctrine of liberty, equality, and political democracy, originated by the French *philosophes*, was being put into practical form in the American Declaration of Independence and Constitution; and the topics were being discussed fervently in England by Paine, Wilkes, Burke, and others. Rousseau, the most influential progenitor of the doctrine, had set the example of using fiction to popularize his theories, and Brooke and Mackenzie had done likewise. Even *The Vicar of Wakefield*, setting out to be a sentimental domestic comedy, veered into serious discussion of crime and law when Dr. Primrose was committed to prison. In Germany, too, when the twenty-five-year-old Goethe wrote his first novel, *The Sorrows of Young Werther* (1774), he took Rousseau as his model in giving a highly emotionalized version of his own early experiences and using it as the vehicle for suggesting his social philosophy.

The first thoroughgoing English radical to become a novelist was a peddler's son, Thomas Holcroft, who educated himself at night while he was a stableboy at a race track, then worked for a while as a shoemaker, and later became an actor and playwright. His first novel, *Alwyn, or The Gentleman Comedian* (1780), is less occupied with ideology than his later ones, but it is distinctly proletarian in its portrayal of a company of strolling players. The story stays close to the author's own experience, and he had known enough of poverty and discrimination to give a convincing picture of the seamy side of contemporary life.

Another strongly humanitarian writer, Robert Bage, was a paper manufacturer who, like Defoe, turned to authorship after a failure in business. He was past fifty when he wrote his first novel, *Mount Henneth* (1781), a rambling mixture of dangerous foreign exploits, pathetic love stories, and doctrinaire argument. His hero begins as a young adventurer in India and ends as a rich nabob with a castle in Wales where he collects his friends together and solves their problems for them. This philanthropist stands somewhere midway between Smollett's cantankerous Matthew Bramble and Mackenzie's maudlin Harley. In the course of the book the author campaigns against such varied adversaries as sectarian intolerance, the American war, the British exploitation of India, and the ostracism of ravished women. As a former businessman, Bage argued always in favor of commerce and industry; his opposition to war was based on the practical consideration that it hampered trade.

A fourth new line of development for fiction was exotic Eastern fantasy. The oriental tale in its previous form, as represented by *Rasselas* and Mrs. Sheridan's *Nourjahad,* had used a picturesque, remote setting merely as a flimsy disguise for a moral allegory. By 1780, however, public interest in Asia had been stimulated by the British conquest of India, and the colorful life of the Middle East was imaginatively familiar through *The Arabian Nights,* one of the most popular of books for children.

Appropriately, the first fantastic oriental romance was written by a man with some resemblance to the Caliph Haroun Al-Raschid. William Beckford was the only legitimate child of a West Indian planter who became a Liberal politician, Lord Mayor of London, and the richest man in England. At the age of eleven William inherited his father's fortune and gigantic mansion in Wiltshire. Dominated by an aristocratic mother, he was educated privately, studying music under Mozart and painting under a self-claimed bastard of Peter the Great. It is not surprising that the pampered young millionaire rebelled against the formal conduct and the rational tenets that he was expected to adopt. He vowed himself to Rousseau's gospel of unbridled imaginative and emotional indulgence. Just as Walpole had dreamed a medieval ghost story to fit his pseudo-Gothic castle at Strawberry Hill, Beckford as naturally dreamed Arabian Nights fantasies to fit his gorgeous palace at Fonthill. At the age of seventeen he started to write a long prose tale of oriental mystery, but left it unfinished. He may have gone so far as to experiment with Eastern sorcery before he composed another story, when he was twenty-one. This one was written in French and was completed with the same sort of creative urgency that had produced *The Castle of Otranto.* Beckford withheld it from publication for four years while he made desultory attempts to invent additional episodes for it; but in 1786 an English translation of the manuscript was surreptitiously issued as *The History of the Caliph Vathek,* with the implication that it was a genuine Arabian legend. Beckford was then obliged to print the French text to establish his authorship.

Vathek, like *The Castle of Otranto*, is too short and too fantastic to be included in any strict definition of the novel; but both books made a distinct contribution to the art of prose fiction by their unity of emotional tone and by their strong climax. Of the two, *Vathek* impresses the modern reader more deeply; there was a thin streak of genius in Beckford, and the morbid weirdness of his tale reproduces his tortured personality with uncomfortable power.

With so many new tendencies appearing in fiction, it is not surprising to find some critical discussion of the novel as a literary type. The word "romance" was still in general use for all prose fiction, rather than the new-fangled word "novel"; and Holcroft in the introduction to his *Alwyn* tried to differentiate between the two terms. He did not contrast "romance" with "realism," as later critics were to do; his stage experience made him conscious of structure, and so he proposed applying "romance" to all loose-jointed, episodic stories, the picaresque accounts of real life as well as the artificial ones of remote times or places, while he restricted "novel" to stories with "unity of design" such as *Tom Jones*.

In the eighties the novel had become accepted to the extent that several learned historians of literature included it in their treatises, notably Lord Monboddo (*Of the Origin and Progress of Language*), Hugh Blair (*Lectures on Rhetoric and Belles Lettres*), and James Beattie (*Dissertations Moral and Critical*). It remained for Clara Reeve, however, following up the ideas she had voiced in the preface to *The Old English Baron*, to write the first book in English devoted solely to the history of prose fiction. This was *The Progress of Romance*, published in 1785.

Miss Reeve was a conscientious scholar, though not a brilliant critic; she read widely in preparation for her book, and announced that her intention was "to trace Romance to its origin, to follow its progress through the different periods to its declension, to show how the modern Novel sprung up out of its ruins, to examine and compare the merits of both, and to remark upon the effects of them." She points out that the vogue of the French heroic romances ended about half a century earlier and that "to us they appear dull, heavy, and uninteresting. . . . These books are now become the lumber of a bookseller's shop, and

are frequently seen to wrap a pound of sugar from the grocer's."
She then undertakes to set up a clear distinction between Romances and Novels, "though they have lately been confounded
together and are frequently mistaken for each other":

> The Novel is a picture of real life and manners, and of the
> time in which it is written. . . . The Novel gives a familiar
> relation of such things as pass every day before our eyes, such
> as may happen to our friend, or to ourselves; and the perfection
> of it is, to represent every scene in so easy and natural a manner,
> and to make them appear so probable, as to deceive us into a
> persuasion (at least while we are reading) that all is real, until
> we are affected by the joys or distresses of the persons in the
> story, as if they were our own.

This is a competent definition, and Miss Reeve used it intel-
ligently in her survey of realistic novels from Cervantes and
Defoe through Richardson and Fielding to her own contemporaries, her opinions being only intermittently colored by her own
prejudices, chiefly her concern over the moral influence of literature and her belligerent defense of women as fiction-writers and
fiction-readers against the supposedly superior attitude of male
critics.

To avoid evaluating current books, Miss Reeve ended her
survey with 1770; but she could see that even by that date there
were new trends in fiction that did not fit into her definition of
the novel. She grouped together Brooke's *Fool of Quality* and
several other books as primarily didactic, "to convey to the
young and flexible heart wholesome truths that it refused to
receive under the form of moral precepts and instructions." She
admitted that *Longsword* was "a Romance, in reality, and not
a Novel." And she made a special category for Eastern Tales,
which "are indeed so far out of the bounds of Nature and
probability that it is difficult to judge of them by rules drawn
from these sources."

Though the levelheaded Miss Reeve was thus baffled by the
extravagances of the new tendencies, they represented the insurgent power of romanticism, against which a losing battle
was being waged by the comedy of manners which remained
in the eighteenth-century tradition of rationality and wit. Fanny
Burney's second novel, *Cecilia, or The Memoirs of an Heiress*
(1782), was inferior to *Evelina*. In spite of her modesty, she

could not escape being influenced by the admiration heaped on her both by her literary friends and by the reading public. *Cecilia* was twice as long as *Evelina* and its theme was handled more formally and obviously. Even her style lost its easy sprightliness. The conflict of caste prejudice against human feeling was displayed in the love story of a wealthy girl and a proud but poor young gentleman. The too-numerous characters tended to be comic or melodramatic stereotypes rather than individuals, and the author ventured beyond her range of experience when she strove for intensity, as in the suicide of Cecilia's guardian or the apoplectic stroke induced in the hero's mother by his opposition to her parental control. Cecilia is such a sensible girl that her temporary insanity in the later part of the story seems an unconvincing attempt at Richardsonian pathos. There was enough comedy, suspense, and moral preachment, however, to satisfy the public, and so *Cecilia* added to its author's profits and reputation. People took sides and argued angrily about the ethical and social conflicts in the situation; and the pathetic passages proved irresistible. A friend reported to Fanny's sister that

> *Cecilia* sends us into people's houses with our eyes swelled out of our heads with weeping. We take the book into the carriage, and read and weep. . . . During Cecilia's delirium, anyone coming into the room would have been surprised. . . . The children wept and sobbed aloud; my heart was bursting with agony! and we all seemed in despair.

No novel since *Clarissa* and *La Nouvelle Héloïse* had reduced readers to such delightful misery.

All the debate over the social issues in *Cecilia* proves that the public taste was inclining toward didactic fiction. A notable example of this genre appeared a year later. Its author was Thomas Day, a wealthy philanthropist resembling Bage's Mr. Foston. After leaving Oxford, Day had forgathered with the political radicals who were agitating for parliamentary reform and abolition of slavery, with the scientific experimenters who were widening the horizon of knowledge, and with the inventors who were inaugurating the Industrial Revolution. A zealous adherent of Rousseau, he flaunted his defiance of social convention even in dress and manners; and to put the educational theories of

Émile into practice he adopted two little girls from an orphanage and set about bringing them up to despise rank and fashion and all the false idols of modern culture, with the expectation that one of them would turn out to be a suitable wife for him. This and various other Quixotic schemes collapsed ludicrously, but Day doggedly went on with his campaigns for remaking society. In 1783, in the midst of political pamphleteering, he published a small volume entitled *The History of Sandford and Merton: a Work Intended for the Use of Children.* A second volume followed in 1786, and a third in 1789.

It was based partly on *Émile* and partly on *The Fool of Quality*, which was Day's favorite novel. From Brooke's book he borrowed the contrast between two little boys — one generous and manly, the other pampered and selfish — and the figure of the wise tutor who trains them with tales of noble conduct from history and legend. The chief difference from *The Fool of Quality* is Day's intentional catering to youthful readers. Previously children had adopted books not originally meant for them, such as *The Pilgrim's Progress* and *Robinson Crusoe.* Here at last was one that used the effective techniques of fiction directly for the child. There was a naïveté in Day that gave his writing a genuine appeal to the juvenile mind, and for the next hundred years *Sandford and Merton* was perhaps the most popular of all children's books. Some readers, indeed, on reaching years of discretion, looked back on Harry Sandford as a smug little prig and ridiculed the author's solemn moralizing; but actually there was enough lively action in the story to hold a boy's interest, and possibly this book did as much as any other to shape the standards of ethics and behavior that have prevailed in Anglo-American life ever since. Day wrote one other book for children, *The Story of Little Jack* (1788), which traced the rise of a poor foundling through honesty and hard work, thus initiating all the "rags to riches" stories that culminated in Horatio Alger.

While Day was thus teaching democracy and self-reliance to the most impressionable class of readers, other liberals were continuing to write propaganda fiction for adults. Bage brought out *Barham Downs* in 1784 and *James Wallace* in 1788, in each of which a wise philosopher gives good advice to an assortment of people with extreme prejudices. A writer with a more polished and scholarly style, Dr. John Moore, won renown with *Zeluco* (1786), which had the explicit subtitle, "Various Views of Human Nature Taken from Life and Manners, Foreign and Domestic." Moore was a Scottish-born physician, a friend and admirer of Smollett; he had seen the world as an army doctor in the Flanders campaign and as resident physician at the British embassy in Paris. The great impact of his book arose from the fact that its central character was a thoroughly evil man. Dr. Moore had enough psychological insight to portray his villain-hero with touches of subtlety that prevent this vicious Sicilian from being an incredible monster of lust, cruelty, and revenge. The sadistic scenes link the book with the Gothic tales of horror, but it also offers more realistic pictures of contemporary European life, and has a few amusing minor characters. Its main ideological targets are the Roman Catholic Church and Negro slavery.

There was a more impelling propaganda theme in *Mary, a Fiction* (1788), by Mary Wollstonecraft, who was a militant proponent of both political and emotional freedom for women. Largely an idealized autobiography, the story accepted the theories of Rousseau to the fullest in showing how a girl of strong intelligence defies the tyranny of convention and gradually gains a wise and unselfish personality. A sort of feminine counterpart of Goethe's *Werther*, it would have been a better novel if the author had not indulged so copiously in passionate sensibility.

Miss Wollstonecraft was not the only woman who used fiction as a vehicle for personal vindication. The same motive, in less aggressive form, can be seen in the novels of Charlotte Smith, who was regarded in her own day as the nearest rival to Fanny Burney. Yoked with an irresponsible husband who frittered away his inheritance while fathering a dozen children, Mrs. Smith finally separated from him and turned to authorship as her only means of supporting the large family. She first unburdened her heart of its griefs in a volume of sonnets and then had recourse to the more profitable medium of fiction. In rapid succession came *Emmeline, or The Orphan of the Castle* (1788), *Ethelinde, or The Recluse of the Lake* (1789), and *Celestina* (1791). Primarily based on Richardson, these novels show also the influences of Prévost and of *Cecilia*. The incidental social satire, however, differs from Miss Burney's in being obviously the outcome of personal bitterness. Somewhere in each book occurs a reproduction of Mrs. Smith's own misfortunes: she herself serves repeatedly as model for a high-born, sensitive girl trapped into an unworthy marriage; her ne'er-do-well spouse and his vulgar commercial family are portrayed with asperity again and again.

The conventional plots and didactic morality in Mrs. Smith's stories show that the novel of sensibility was firmly standardized. Nevertheless, traces of the new romanticism can be detected, if not improving them, at least giving a touch of freshness. Though the action takes place in her own time, she occasionally uses Gothic castles and gloomy corridors as backgrounds for her distressed heroines; and when Ethelinde feels that the spirit of her dead father is present to comfort her misery, the author is venturing close to the supernatural. Being a poet, she makes extensive use of scenery to enhance the moods of her characters. The Lake District provides landscapes for her second novel, and Provence for her third. Not only for her prolific output, but also for her mingling of current tendencies, Mrs. Smith can be regarded as the best representative of her period.

The decade of the eighties was marked also by the full emergence of the Gothic romance. Horace Walpole by this time was embarrassed by the renown of his solitary experiment in fiction. In a letter to Hannah More in 1784 he apologized for *The Castle of Otranto:*

> It was fit for nothing but the age in which it was written; an age in which much was known; that required only to be amused, nor cared whether its amusements were conformable to truth and the models of good sense; that could not be spoiled; was in no danger of being too credulous; and rather wanted to be brought back to imagination, than to be led astray by it.

Walpole's protests, however, could not deflect the trend. *The Recess, or A Tale of Other Times* (1785), by Sophia Lee, followed the lead of Miss Reeve's *Old English Baron* in using a specific background of English history. The author's sister claimed that it was "the first English romance that blended interesting fiction with historical events and characters, embellishing both by picturesque description." This meant that, unlike Miss Reeve, Miss Lee showed no scruples about mingling her imaginary characters freely with real ones: her heroines

are twin daughters of Mary Queen of Scots by a secret marriage, and have love affairs with the Earls of Leicester and Essex,
respectively. Almost all the celebrities of the era parade through
the story, but the chronology is sadly mixed — the Spanish
Armada occurs before the execution of Mary Stuart. Though
the setting is Renaissance rather than medieval, the melodramatic tragedies of the plot and the gloomy terrors of dungeons
and ruins strengthened the Gothic vogue. Miss Lee's book was
widely admired and imitated during the next five years. Clara
Reeve, for example, in her next novel, *The Exiles, or Memoirs
of the Count de Cronstadt*, departed from the placidity of her
Old English Baron in favor of emotional despair and terrifying
perils.

At this point a younger writer, picking up hints from Walpole, Miss Lee, and Mrs. Smith, carried the tale of Gothic terror
to new extremes. The wife of a journalist, Ann Radcliffe was
twenty-five when she published anonymously her first book, *The
Castles of Athlin and Dunbayne* (1789). Its action takes place in
the Scottish Highlands in a vaguely feudal era, but there is little
local color or historical connection. The plot is close to that of
The Castle of Otranto and *The Old English Baron*, with a young
hero, brought up as a peasant, who is finally recognized by a
strawberry mark on his arm as the rightful heir to the estate
and titles of his wicked uncle. The machinery of trap-doors,
underground passages, and so forth, was already becoming standard equipment. There is a certain amount of exciting action in
the way of clan fights and abducted heroines; but the next
year Mrs. Radcliffe achieved stronger melodrama in *A Sicilian
Romance*, in which the heroine's father has imprisoned his
wife in the depths of his castle and installed a young mistress in
her place. There are many mysterious portents and hairbreadth
escapes before the happy ending occurs.

By the time Mrs. Radcliffe wrote *The Romance of the Forest*
(1791) she was gaining greater skill in producing her effects: her
heroine is dragged about France and Switzerland, and is involved
in several mysteries that are all neatly unraveled at the end.
There are not so many irrelevant adventures as in *A Sicilian
Romance*, but suspense is not legitimately sustained because the
author withholds too many essential facts in order to produce a
grand final surprise.

The second edition of this novel revealed the author's name

for the first time; but already, with three books in three years, the unidentified young woman had established herself as the most popular novelist of the epoch. It was not merely the demand at the circulating libraries that attested to her power. The critics of the *Monthly Review* and the *Critical Review,* usually contemptuous of novels, praised her to the skies. Influential men of letters joined the chorus: T. J. Mathias called her a "mighty magician, bred and nourished by the Florentine Muses," and Nathan Drake dubbed her "the Shakespeare of Romance Writers." Anna Seward, the leading bluestocking of the day, who adored Richardson but said, "I have an absolute horror at the idea of wasting my time upon modern novels," raved over Mrs. Radcliffe's "genius."

Mrs. Radcliffe had led a sheltered life, and the material for her fiction was derived entirely from her reading. Her books are virtually identical in plots and characters. Always there is a melancholy, swooning, poetry-quoting heroine and a generous, headstrong hero who is overshadowed by a gloomy villain of superhuman ferocity. They all converse in stilted rhetoric. In each novel the heroine or her relations are imprisoned in an ancient castle or a ruined abbey, which is on a precipice or in a dense forest. The mystery always centers upon the true parentage of a main character. Like Miss Reeve, Mrs. Radcliffe avoided actual supernatural occurrences: the characters merely misinterpret events under stress of terror, and after being deluded for a while the reader is finally given a rational explanation for every strange phenomenon.

Probably from Charlotte Smith she picked up the use of atmospheric description, but she went much further in the inclusion of elaborate detail. Having seen none of the regions she depicted, she was not hampered by demands of accuracy, but drew upon the gloomy landscapes painted by Claude Lorraine and Salvator Rosa. The principal function of the scenery is to evoke spiritual rhapsodies from the heroines and heroes.

In view of her stereotyped plots, characters, and settings, her anticlimactic exposures of the supernatural illusions, and the schoolgirlish naïveté of her outlook, one may wonder why her stories so fascinated her public. In part, the answer is that they combined in an extreme degree three of the main elements of romanticism that had been developing separately during the pre-

vious half-century — the melancholy natural scenery first popularized by the "graveyard school" of poetry, the emotional
excesses fostered by the novel of sensibility, and the savagery
of feudalism exploited in Macpherson's *Ossian* and Chatterton's
Rowley poems and Percy's folk ballads. Yet, like Walpole, Mrs.
Radcliffe was still a rationalist of the age of enlightenment, and
she did not discard the Richardsonian tradition: the theme of the
imprisoned heroine came straight from *Pamela* and *Clarissa*.
The emotional tension is always produced by a well-calculated
antithesis of two powerful feelings, love and fear.

   This explanation, however, is not fully adequate. The impact
of her novels was stronger than a mere accumulation of elements already well known. The further clue must be sought
through modern psychology. In departing from realism Mrs.
Radcliffe stumbled upon the whole realm of the unconscious.
The standard situations in her stories are those which recur in
everyone's nightmares — wandering alone in an unrecognizable,
eerie place, or trying to flee from unidentified but frightful
pursuers in an endless tunnel or staircase, or being imprisoned
in a tiny cell that seems to be closing in. No matter how crudely
Mrs. Radcliffe described these things, she had the knack of stimulating the reader's own dream-making function, which then took
over and supplied the private horrors of each individual imagination. Probably, too, her central theme — a pure, pale maiden
persecuted by a vicious but dominating sadist — became a powerful sex symbol for both male and female readers. Unuttered
risks of incest sometimes hover around the heroine through the
uncertainty of her parentage. Even the heroine's excessive refinement, preventing the slightest mention of crime or of any
strong emotion, helps to strengthen the morbid suggestiveness.

   With her fourth book, *The Mysteries of Udolpho* (1794), Mrs.
Radcliffe reached the apex of her fame. The harried heroine is
imprisoned in a castle high in the Apennines, and she travels
also through picturesque scenery of Gascony and the Pyrenees,
thus giving occasion for leisurely descriptions that provide relief
from the crises of terror and danger. The supposed date of the
action is 1584, but anachronisms abound. For suspense Mrs.
Radcliffe still depended upon the indefensible device of concealing vital information, as in the celebrated scenes when Emily
is horrified by a sentence she reads while burning her father's

papers and later when she faints after raising the black veil that masks a picture frame. Though the reader is sharing Emily's restricted point of view, what she saw in either case is not divulged until the end of the book.

By this time Mrs. Radcliffe had a flock of imitators, who exaggerated her gruesome details and omitted her touches of poetic imagination. Only one of them became a serious rival. This was Matthew Gregory Lewis, a clever young man of twenty who had all the effrontery and sophistication that Mrs. Radcliffe lacked. Resembling Beckford in some respects, he was the son of a rich West Indian proprietor, and while an undergraduate at Oxford he spent his vacations on the Continent, studying foreign languages and absorbing current German literature — the soulful agonies of Goethe's *Werther,* the gloomy perils of Schiller's *Robbers,* and the blood-curdling horrors of the *Schauersromane* ("shudder-novels"). At nineteen he became an attaché to the British embassy in Holland, where he read *The Mysteries of Udolpho* as soon as it was published, and admired it so much that he spent ten weeks in composing a book in emulation.

He went directly contrary to Mrs. Radcliffe's practice, however, in two respects. Instead of her excessive moral delicacy, he offered gross voluptuousness; and instead of her carefully rational explanations of her uncanny effects, he indulged in crude supernaturalism, rising to a grotesque climax borrowed from *Dr. Faustus,* when a demon rescues the villain-hero from execution, only to fly high in the air with him and drop him to his death on jagged rocks. In the course of the book Lewis introduced some of the most durable horrors from history and legend — the Wandering Jew, the bleeding nun, and the atrocities of the Inquisition. His Teutonic models led him to depend solely upon scenes of physical agony and unbridled lust, adorned with such properties as rotting corpses.

When *Ambrosio, or The Monk* was published in 1796, it caused such a sensation that it was banned for immorality, and Lewis brought out a revised edition in which he toned down some of the lurid details of Ambrosio's abnormalities. Though Mrs. Radcliffe must have been outraged by the libidinous and nauseating elements in Lewis's book, there can be little doubt that it influenced her choice of subject for her next one, *The Italian, or The Confessional of the Black Penitents* (1797). The criminal monk, the girl imprisoned in a convent, the terrors of the Inquisition, all reappear here; but Mrs. Radcliffe's high moral tone is maintained, and even Schedoni, the evil monk, eventually repents and helps the noble lovers to escape. Once again the power of the book comes from its evocation of a half-suppressed dread already present in her readers. Two hundred years of militant Protestantism had imbued the average Englishman with a vague but deep conviction that the Roman Church encouraged secret and frightful vices, and so there was an automatic response to the lecherous monk, the tyrannical abbess, the convent dungeons, and all the other Catholic paraphernalia of *The Italian.*

Apart from Lewis, the only competitor of Mrs. Radcliffe whose work is ever remembered is Regina Maria Roche, whose best known book, *The Children of the Abbey,* contains no fewer than four Gothic buildings, two in Ireland and one each in Scotland and Wales. Mrs. Roche was equally excessive with the tears of her heroines, the rhetoric of her love scenes, and all the other clichés of the genre.

While several of the chief components of romanticism were combined in the Gothic novels, one other principal component, perhaps the most potent of all, which could not be accommodated in tales of the feudal past, dominated a separate set of novels. This was the doctrine of democracy, progress, and perfectibility, which gained fresh impetus after 1789 as a result of the French Revolution.

In Robert Bage's fifth novel, *Man as He Is* (1792), the author's independent mind ranges widely over contemporary life and ideas. The American and French republics come in for approbation, and the whole book is based on Rousseau's theory of the evil influence of society upon the naturally noble human spirit. The hero is an impulsive young baronet, who has been badly brought up by a silly mother and who tours Europe, blundering into many dissipations before the long-suffering heroine decides to marry him in the hope of reforming him. This is perhaps Bage's best book on account of its lively comedy of manners and its panorama of English and foreign society, with characters ranging from doctrinaires to spendthrifts.

Thomas Holcroft took the social upheaval more seriously than Bage did. Since his first novel, he had written some successful plays, and in *Anna St. Ives* (1792) his stage experience is per-

ceptible in his vigorous use of dialogue and his strong melodramatic scenes, though he is hampered by adherence to the old
epistolary method. His intellectual heroine falls in love with a
man whose social theories are as radical as hers, and who is of
lowly origin. Unlike the heroes of the Gothic romances, he
remains the bailiff's son till the end, instead of proving to be an
aristocrat kidnapped in infancy. His high-born rival remarks in
contemptuous amazement:

> "He stands as erect, and speaks with as little embarrassment, and
> as loudly as the best of us; nay, boldly asserts, that neither riches,
> rank, nor birth have any claim. . . . Among the most ridiculous
> of what he calls first principles is that of the equality of man-
> kind. . . . The savage, the wild man of the woods, is his
> true liberty-boy; and the orangoutang, his first cousin. A lord is
> a merry-andrew, a duke a jack-pudding, and a king a tom-fool;
> his name is man!"

Thus Frank Henley is the first proletarian hero in an English
novel; and the man of rank is not allowed the status of an impressive villain, even when, like Lovelace, he is so frustrated by
the girl's mental and moral superiority that he kidnaps her with
intention of rape. In his capitulation to two stronger characters
the long snobbishness of English fiction had its first setback.
Whereas Lovelace and the many others drawn in imitation of
him had carried with them the glitter of their social prestige,
Holcroft represents Coke Clifton as merely pitiable for his mistaken values.

In the same year even Charlotte Smith succumbed to the
ferment of the new ideas. She was no political theorist, but her
personal disillusionment with English justice and the English
social code made her susceptible to the French vision of universal
equality. Also, she had lived for a while in France and seen the
oppression of the peasantry. In *Desmond* her hero travels
through France and reports his observations in long letters. He
discusses the political issues with French and English friends of
all shades of opinion; and thus Mrs. Smith, like Bage, may be said
to present both sides of the case, though her sympathy is obviously with the revolution, which she terms "the cause of truth,
reason, and humanity." The story also touches upon problems of
the relation between the sexes, but in this matter her attitude
is more conventional. The heroine flees from a depraved husband who wants her to become the mistress of a duke. She is

sheltered by Desmond and they fall in love. Nevertheless Geraldine returns to nurse her spouse when he is wounded by robbers, while Desmond, in spite of his adoration for her, begets a child in a transient affair with a French woman, exactly as young William Wordsworth was doing in that very year. Mrs. Smith does not question either Geraldine's wifely duty to a brutal husband or Desmond's devotion to her, but rewards them at the end with a happy marriage.

Mrs. Smith's next book, *The Old Manor House* (1793), is her best piece of work, containing good social satire and well-drawn comic characters. The main setting, a decaying country house with the usual sliding panels and suits of armor, shows traces of the Gothic vogue; but the supposed ghosts soon prove to be smugglers. The author had by this time mastered the technique of using description of scenery as an integral part of her effects, so that it unobtrusively enhanced the moods of the characters.

A further merit of *The Old Manor House* is that the political ideology is well subordinated to the story. The change in English society is shown in the contrast between the hero's aristocratic old cousin, brooding on her family traditions, and his parents, who are of the prosperous business class. When he goes to fight against the American colonists, the author gives a favorable view of the revolutionary cause. And Rousseau's theory of the noble savage is illustrated when her hero falls into the hands of the Iroquois and makes friends with a young brave.

The events of 1793–94 shocked all but the most zealous disciples of the French Revolution. After the bloody purges of the Reign of Terror, and the subsequent military aggression against neighboring states, a moderate observer like Mrs. Smith had no hesitation in changing her opinion. No doubt she was influenced also by the marriage of one of her daughters to a French refugee, who probably served as model for the hero of her novel, *The Banished Man* (1794). Mrs. Smith had not given up her faith in the ideals that motivated the French Revolution; her book is devoted to proving that the leaders of the new France betrayed those ideals by indulging in cruelty, tyranny, and war. Though she holds England up as the only country where real freedom exists, she does not unduly idealize the English, but attacks the smugness that makes them intolerant toward other nationalities.

Thomas Holcroft was too deeply dedicated a radical to modify his creed. His activity in a propaganda group led to his arrest in 1794 for high treason. After two months' imprisonment his release without a trial left him more bitter than ever, for he felt that he ought to have been vindicated of the charge. The first half of his novel *Hugh Trevor* appeared in that year, and the remainder in 1797. A statement in the preface shows that Holcroft had formed a concept of the novel not unlike that which Goethe was to exemplify in Germany a year later with *Wilhelm Meisters Lehrjahre*. Holcroft remarked that his story was intended to reveal "the growth of intellect" through "the lessons received by the principal character, the changes they produced in him, and the progress of his understanding. . . . In my opinion, all well-written books that discuss the actions of men are in reality so many histories of the progress of mind."

After a boyhood of poverty and overwork, Trevor is sent to Oxford by a wealthy grandfather and is soon disillusioned by the depravity of students and tutors alike. When he enters public life in London he is shocked by the dishonesty of politicians and the corruption of church dignitaries. Upon falling out with these powerful people he is persecuted until he is unable to earn a living. Yet, in spite of the wholesale indictment of Parliament and aristocracy, church and university, the book's message is Fabian rather than revolutionary. A wise friend persuades Trevor to renounce all thought of violence and to work for moral betterment and the education of the masses.

The best-written novel of radical doctrine was by an associate of Holcroft who had thought more profoundly about the principles of reform. William Godwin's father had been a Calvinistic preacher; and the son, while being trained for the ministry, adopted the tenets of an even more rigid sect. After preaching for a few years, however, he came across the ideas of the French philosophers, gave up his pulpit, and moved to London to become a writer, convinced that by a reasoned exposition of the tyranny of all existing institutions — social, political, and religious — he could reform society and promote universal welfare. Among his earlier writings were three mediocre works of fiction; but he devoted most of his time to composing a monumental book on social theory, *An Enquiry Concerning Political Justice*, which condemned every form of organized control over individual liberty, such as taxation, private property, marriage, and any sort of legal punishment for crime. In reaction from the determinism of his Calvinist upbringing, which taught that the majority of human souls are doomed to sin in this life and eternal torment thereafter, he became just as dogmatic in the new creed that believed in the exact opposite — the innate goodness of human nature and the capacity of mankind to live virtuously by the light of pure reason.

Realizing that his exhaustive and expensive book could reach only the minority whose minds were trained to follow abstract reasoning, Godwin turned to fiction as a medium that could reach a wider public. *Caleb Williams, or Things as They Are* (1794) was identified plainly in the preface as a political tract:

> What is now presented to the public is no refined and abstract speculation; it is a study and delineation of things passing in the moral world. It is but of late that the inestimable importance of political principles has been adequately apprehended. It is now known to philosophers that the spirit and character of the Government intrudes itself into every rank of society. But this is a truth highly worthy to be communicated to persons whom books of philosophy and science are never likely to reach.

The publishers were so terrified by this statement, at the moment when Holcroft and his friends had been arrested for treason, that they refused to print the preface, which did not appear until a year later, when the excitement had cooled.

The author's unworldliness prevented him from giving a fully convincing picture of human conduct, and yet his sheer intellectual power makes the book more than just another propaganda treatise in fictional guise. Godwin thought seriously about problems of technique and left a detailed statement of his intentions. For one thing, he realized that characterization is a matter of inner processes rather than of visible peculiarities: "The thing in which my imagination reveled most freely was the analysis of the private and internal operations of the mind." This led him to consider the question of point of view. The narrative begins in the third person, but changes to the autobiographical method as "infinitely the best adapted" to his purpose.

Secondly, in a day when novels were loose and rambling in structure, Godwin was unique in planning the whole thing carefully; he first conceived the final climax and then worked backward so that the earlier stages should lead up to it. The plot centers upon a murder and its detection, but the main purpose is not to mystify the reader as to who committed the crime but is to analyze the psychology of the murderer and the detective, and through this to imply a criticism of the inequities of justice and social prestige — or, as the preface announced, "to comprehend, as far as the progressive nature of a single story would allow, a general review of the modes of domestic and unrecorded despotism by which man becomes the destroyer of man."

The story starts with a charming aristocrat, Falkland, who is so imbued with the ideals presented in the heroic romances that he feels compelled to kill a man who has insulted him. Though Godwin intended to show here that pride and honor are social conventions leading to evil results, Falkland's motives are so clearly drawn, and his victim is so thoroughly hateful, that the reader's sympathy identifies itself with the murderer.

Still humanly believable is Falkland's passively allowing others to be executed for the crime. Even here Godwin was pursuing one of his crusades; disapproving of capital punishment, he attributed Falkland's behavior to his terror of the gallows. Falkland thinks he has escaped all suspicion, but his secretary, Caleb Williams, ferrets out the secret. The irony of the situation is that, instead of being an instrument of justice, Caleb at once becomes the victim of Falkland's persecution. The story thus arrives at the part which had been Godwin's starting point, "a series of adventures of flight and pursuit; the fugitive in perpetual apprehension of being overwhelmed with the worst calamities, and the pursuer, by his ingenuity and resources, keeping his victim in a state of the most fearful alarm." Caleb's hopeless efforts to evade his enemy establish a mood of painful suspense. Prolonged fear destroys his confidence to the point that when he is brought into court, charged with theft, he lacks the courage to accuse Falkland of the murder. While thus illustrating Godwin's thesis that rank and wealth tyrannize over humble honesty, the book also excels the Gothic tales in their own purpose of creating terror by psychological tension.

While Holcroft and Godwin were publishing their strongest novels of radical doctrine, the satirical Bage wrote a brilliant survey of the whole clash of ideas. The hero of *Hermsprong, or Man as He Is Not* (1796) is the embodiment of Rousseau's primitivism, having been brought up among the Indians of

Michillimakinac. When Hermsprong comes to England his naïve and rational mind rejects all the absurdities of social convention, and he startles the public with his indiscreet truthfulness as well as with his personal habits of early rising, water-drinking, athletic feats, and frequent baths. In spite of the exposure of pride and pretension, however, the book is not aggressively proletarian like Holcroft's and Godwin's. Hermsprong is wealthy, and at the end — when he is on the point of leading several like-minded admirers across the Atlantic to found "a society of friends" on the banks of the Potomac — he proves to be the lost heir to a title and estates. He is as outspoken in warning the mob against revolution as in unmasking the supposed superiority of the upper class.

Charlotte Smith also moved toward primitivism as the only alternative to political injustice. In *Marchmont* (1796) she was still preoccupied with the excesses of French republicanism: when her hero goes to France to escape his creditors he witnesses terrible scenes of wartime frenzy and economic collapse. But this does not imply satisfaction with the state of her own country; she is more virulent than ever in her attacks on lawyers, and her hero says many angry things about the English Constitution. Her last significant novel, *The Young Philosopher* (1798), is her most visionary in its proposal of a utopian substitute for contemporary culture. Her hero begins as a precocious child who is trained to believe in individual liberty and the inherent dignity of man. At Eton and Oxford he gains influence among his fellows by his independence and benevolence. By the time he graduates, he is such a devout adherent of Rousseau that he cannot adapt himself to any career in England, and repulses the bold advances of an heiress who wants to marry him. He finds his only acceptable friends in an American family, and finally marries the unsophisticated American girl and sets off to find a new simple life on the frontier.

The mediocrity of the English novel in the decade 1790–1800 was due mainly to ineffectual characterization. In the Gothic novels the characters were puppets adopting attitudes of terror or nobility; in the novels of doctrine they were specimens of social tendencies or mouthpieces for the author's opinions. Mrs. Smith stands out as the most respectable novelist of the period, in spite of her badly constructed plots and the distortions

resulting from her personal animosities, because she had some
ability to give lifelike touches to her characters.

Something of the same talent lent distinction to a less prolific
novelist of the decade, Elizabeth Inchbald. Like Mrs. Smith, she
had known hardship and was writing to earn a living. Both
were opposed to existing social evils less from ideological conviction than from personal experience and sympathy for the unfortunate. A beautiful, red-headed daughter of a farmer, she
ran away from home to go on the stage, and married an actor.
Though continuing to perform for nearly twenty years, she was
handicapped by a lisp and eventually turned to playwriting and
then to fiction. She had little idea of how to put a novel together,
but thanks to her practice in drama she could write effective
dialogue and develop gripping scenes.

Her first novel, *A Simple Story* (1791), tries to teach a lesson
in prudence through the contrasted behavior of a mother and
her daughter — the one vain and flighty, the other unselfish and
discreet. To bring out her thesis, the author had to split the
story into two halves, with a lapse of seventeen years while
the daughter grows up. Another defect is sectarian bias. As a
devout Roman Catholic, Mrs. Inchbald insists that the weak girl's
character had been ruined by attending a Protestant school; and
she stretches the reader's credulity by having her hero begin as
a priest and then become free to marry because he is released
from his vows upon inheriting an earldom. Nevertheless, the
story is genuinely pathetic, without the worst excesses of the
novel of sensibility. There is some sound psychology: the
frivolous girl falls in love with the ex-priest, who is her guardian,
but after their marriage she cannot live up to his austere moral
standards and becomes unfaithful to him, so that after agonies
of conscience he has to repudiate her. There is naturalness also
in the account of how the daughter gradually weans him from
the bitterness that her mother's conduct induced.

The method of contrast and the problem of proper education
recur in Mrs. Inchbald's other novel, *Nature and Art* (1796).
Here she deals with two cousins, representing opposite types,
in the manner of *The Fool of Quality* and *Sandford and Merton*.
Her hero has been brought up among savages in Africa, and
comes to England, like Hermsprong, to apply a simple but devastating frankness to all the social conventions in the household of

his uncle, a worldly clergyman. Mrs. Inchbald rationalizes her own troubled life in her insistence that the poor are happier than the rich and in her portrayal of the hero's kindly parents as social outcasts because they are professional musicians. The later part of the book goes off on another of the author's crusades — the ostracism of the "fallen woman." The selfish cousin seduces a village girl and leaves her to poverty and crime; and eventually, when he has become a judge, there is a dramatic scene when she is arraigned for forgery in his court and he coldly condemns her to death.

The most depressing feature of the fiction of the 1790's is the decline of the one surviving author who had previously shown real ability. Shortly after the publication of *Cecilia*, Fanny Burney had been rewarded for her literary eminence by appointment as a lady companion to the queen. Six years of life in the royal court ought to have widened her social insights; but instead her duties proved so intolerably boresome that she resigned and married a penniless French *émigré*, Alexandre d'Arblay. High public anticipation attended her third novel, *Camilla, or A Picture of Youth* (1796), and by publishing it by subscription she earned the unprecedented sum of £2000. In comparison with her two previous books, however, it was a sad disappointment. Not a trace of her youthful gaiety survived. The action and characters repeated those that she had used before, and the mass of everyday detail, instead of being agreeably recognizable, was unutterably tedious. Worst of all, her admiration for Dr. Johnson had led her to imitate his worst traits of pomposity and wordiness. No glimmer of natural behavior could penetrate the murky style.

The most interesting novels of the decade are those of radical doctrine, but not because of superiority in literary art. They are valuable as documents of social history, revealing the confused ferment of ideas that were soon to dominate the nineteenth century. Probably the novels contributed to the spread of the ideas to a point where public pressure began to eventuate in action. Latent in these tensions was the material for great fiction, but the writers were not capable of fusing it into the convincing experience of individuals.

All discussions of the novel at the time, by reviewers and authors alike, assumed that the only readers of fiction were those on the lowest intellectual level — impressionable adolescents and scatterbrained women. Novels were attacked for their pernicious influence on these innocents, and were defended as offering models of virtue for imitation and cautionary examples of vice to be avoided. It is a basic paradox of fiction — all the more obvious here from being on such a low artistic plane — that both the attacks and the defenses were valid. The popular novels were full of smug and pompous moral preachments, but the plots centered upon cruelty and lust and other evil passions. The moral issue was the only ground on which fiction was judged. Neither the authors nor the critics indicated that any literary standards of originality or technical skill applied to novel writing. It was a mass-production business, in which the purveyor merely satisfied the requirements of an undiscriminating market.

Thus a vicious circle had come into operation. Writers of ability were ashamed to venture into such a contemptible vocation; and the more they shunned it, the more the remaining output deserved the disdain of intelligent people. After a bare sixty years the novel seemed to be on the brink of extinction.

VII

Recovery of Prestige

(1800 – 1820)

AT THE DAWN of the nineteenth century the literary status of
the novel could not have been lower. Feeble Gothic romances
glutted the circulating libraries to such an extent that one publishing house, the Minerva Press, grew wealthy through producing
virtually nothing else. But the better authors even in this vein had
ceased to write. Mrs. Radcliffe, perhaps because her husband was
prospering in his profession, published nothing after 1797. William Beckford, with a more fantastic imagination than all the
Gothic novelists put together, did not follow *Vathek* with anything else in the same style, and in fact burlesqued the current
craze for the emotional and the supernatural in two skits, *Modern
Novel Writing, or The Elegant Enthusiast* (1796) and *Azemia*
(1797). Matthew Lewis, now universally called "Monk" Lewis
because of his notorious book, wrote no more fiction, but became,
like Beckford, a Member of Parliament, and confined his literary
ambition to playwriting.

Godwin, who could not afford the luxury of a dignified withdrawal from fiction, was obliged to give in to the demand for

sensationalism. His second novel, *St. Leon* (1799), dealt with a sixteenth-century alchemist, and in the preface he grumbled that "the hearts and the curiosity of readers have been assailed in so many ways that we writers who bring up the rear of our illustrious predecessors must be content to arrive at novelty in whatever mode we are able." It is a powerful but uneven story, with a hero who has conquered death and gained the philosopher's stone but who — like Midas or Faustus — meets only disaster and frustration.

To comprehend the reasons for the collapse of the novel, one must remember that it occurred simultaneously with an abrupt advance in other literary genres, especially poetry. The romantic impulses of emotionalism, fantasy, and self-expression, which had intruded awkwardly into the novel and had hastened its decline, became the essential merits of the poetic revival. The manifesto of the new poetry, written by Wordsworth as the preface to the second edition of *Lyrical Ballads* in 1800, is full of implications about prose fiction, though the only direct allusion is a sneer that "the invaluable works of our elder writers are driven into neglect by frantic novels." His statement of his purpose in his poetry would serve just as well as the creed of a serious novelist:

> The principal object . . . was to choose incidents and situations from common life, and to relate or describe them throughout, as far as was possible, in a selection of language really used by men, and, at the same time, to throw over them a certain coloring of imagination, whereby ordinary things should be presented to the mind in an unusual aspect; and further, and above all, to make these incidents and situations interesting by tracing in them, truly though not ostentatiously, the primary laws of our nature.

It may be assuming too much to suggest that Wordsworth might not have thought of these objectives had not the prose fiction of half a century already practiced them; but whether intentionally or not the poets certainly invaded the field of the novel and temporarily annexed it. Crabbe's *Parish Register* and *The Borough* were grimly matter-of-fact; Wordsworth dealt realistically with everyday experiences in his shorter poems and probed into psychological complexities in *The Prelude;* Coleridge borrowed the material of the tale of terror and gave it imaginative validity in

"The Ancient Mariner" and "Christabel"; Southey's *Thalaba the Destroyer* was a more vivid oriental tale than any since *Vathek*. When Walter Scott published *The Lay of the Last Minstrel* in 1805, he proved that a story of adventure could move in verse with more speed and energy than any prose narrative had yet achieved. Later, Byron took over the heroic villains of Gothic romance and brought them to life with the breath of his own fiery nature.

Whenever a romantic author thought of producing a work more complex and objective than a poem, he turned not to fiction but to drama. Every one of the major poets of the era composed at least one play; and the consistent failure of all their efforts suggests that they might have been equally inept if they had attempted novels. But drama, like poetry, retained its traditional prestige, while the novel was so contemptible that the thought of writing one never entered their heads.

As fiction-writing was mainly in the hands of women, it is not surprising that the only new novelists of any merit who emerged immediately after 1800 were feminine. The first two were both protégées of the established doctrinaire writers. Mrs. Amelia Opie was the daughter of a physician who had retained his radical views through all the reactionary pressure that followed the Reign of Terror. She herself attended the treason trials of Holcroft's associates. When she settled in London as the wife of a popular painter, she was already an intimate friend of Godwin and his wife, Mary Wollstonecraft. Her novel, *The Father and Daughter* (1801), which dealt with a girl's seduction and death from shame, in the well-tried tradition of *Clarissa*, was much admired for its extreme pathos. It was followed in 1804 by *Adelina Mowbray, or The Mother and Daughter*, a livelier book with touches of satire. Like Mrs. Inchbald, she suggested basic problems of education by contrasting a parent and her child; Mary Wollstonecraft probably served as the model. Mrs. Mowbray is an egotistical woman who wins a reputation for genius by reading radical books and expounding progressive theories while she neglects her daughter and extends no charitable aid to the unfortunate. The daughter grows up to be equally intellectual but more practical, and gets into tragic difficulties when she tries to apply the revolutionary doctrines to everday life, especially as regards marriage.

The other new writer was Maria Edgeworth, whose father, a wealthy Irish landowner, had been a friend of Thomas Day, the author of *Sandford and Merton*, and had participated in Day's social experiments. A witty, kindly woman, Maria collaborated with her father in writing *Practical Education*, a treatise seeking to uphold the theories of Rousseau and Day by means of a record of the behavior of Mr. Edgeworth's numerous children by four wives. She also wrote a book in favor of education for women, and *The Parent's Assistant*, a collection of stories for children, which grew out of the experiences in the family nursery. When she was thirty-three she published her first work of adult fiction, a short book entitled *Castle Rackrent* (1800).

When she first went to live on the Irish estate, at the age of sixteen, she had already imbibed social consciousness from her father and Mr. Day, and so she observed the local conditions with an analytical eye; and later, while helping to manage the property, she became familiar with the whole way of life that she depicted in her book. *Castle Rackrent* scarcely falls within the strict definition of a novel, as it covers the events of many years in a summarized form, with little complexity of action. It should rather be considered an expanded character sketch, because the story is colored throughout by the personality of the narrator, an illiterate old servant who reveals all the follies and selfishness of his successive employers while naïvely expressing loyal admiration for them. The author had an underlying social purpose, for the Edgeworths were conscientious landlords and disapproved of the heartless exploitation practiced by many of their neighbors; but Maria's picture of incompetence and extravagance was invested with so much whimsical humor and good nature that the propaganda was not conspicuous.

Her skillful handling of point of view was an innovation in fiction, and the book was admired also for giving a truthful picture of Irish life instead of the stereotyped "Paddy" characters that had infested English drama in the eighteenth century. *Castle Rackrent* therefore has perhaps a better claim than Mrs. Brooke's *Emily Montague* to be the first real local-color story, imbued with the distinctive customs and outlook of a particular region.

Miss Edgeworth did not, however, continue to use her new technique in her next book. *Belinda* is a London drawing-room comedy in the manner of Fanny Burney. The theme is not unlike that of *Evelina* — a girl's first adjustment to sophisticated society. There are incidental moral themes in the reformation of the unhappy woman of fashion who introduces the heroine to society, and in the troubles of a friend of Belinda's whose reputation is endangered by scandal. A reminiscence of Thomas Day can be seen in the hero, who has tried to bring up a girl as a "child of nature" after the precepts of Rousseau. Structurally the story follows a mechanical pattern of antitheses, in which pairs of characters represent opposite types to illustrate good and bad attitudes, mainly in marital relations, through which the hero and heroine learn true social values.

After the publication of this book the Edgeworths spent some time in France; and Maria's next significant novel, *Leonora*, which reverted to the old-fashioned epistolary technique, shows the influence of Mme. de Staël's popular *Delphine*. Intended to serve as a warning against the still-surviving vogue of sensibility, the story tells how a selfish coquette almost succeeds in stealing a trustful gentleman from his ultra-proper wife. Not until 1809, in *Ennui*, did Miss Edgeworth return to the Irish setting, and even here it was subordinated to episodes of fashionable life. More openly than in *Castle Rackrent*, she emphasizes the neglect of duty by Irish aristocrats who wasted their time and money in London while dishonest agents looted their estates. The virtuosity in point of view also recalls *Castle Rackrent*, as her bored, rich hero tells his own story and unintentionally reveals his weaknesses.

It remained for a less disciplined woman writer to exploit the theme of Irish national consciousness to the full. The topic had become acute as a result of the administrative union of Ireland with England in 1801. Humiliated by the loss of their local parliament, the Irish people turned for consolation to the glories of their traditions. The Edgeworths, after all, were of the unpopular Anglo-Irish landowning class; and although Maria loved the native Celts and satirized the absentee landlords who dominated them, she was nevertheless identified with the alien "ascendancy party."

A very different sort of person was Sydney Owenson, the daughter of an improvident Dublin actor who was loved by the public for his singing of old ballads. She had to find employment as a governess when barely out of her teens, and she later made influential friends through her impudent wit and her performances of folk dances and folk music. Intensely ambitious, she published a book of poetry and then an epistolary novel, *St. Clair* (1803). It was full of effusive sensibility, after the manner of *La Nouvelle Héloïse, Werther,* and *Paul et Virginie,* but it used picturesque Irish scenery and expatiated on Irish history, and the heroine was a refreshingly independent, outspoken girl, obviously a glorified self-portrait. Miss Owenson's next novel was a French historical romance, and then in 1806 she won a spectacular success with *The Wild Irish Girl.* The central characters were of the old native nobility, utterly different from the peasants and servants who were the main Celtic representatives in Miss Edgeworth's stories. The novel told how a sophisticated English aristocrat, unwillingly fascinated by the "Princess of Inishmore," is converted from his anti-Irish prejudice and becomes an enthusiast for Irish culture and a crusader for cooperation between the opposing religious and social forces in the country.

Miss Owenson never took the trouble to overcome the defects of her sketchy education. Her style remained pretentious and slipshod, and her conceited self-portrayals in her heroines were as monotonous as Mrs. Manley's had been, a century before. The influential critics, infuriated by her anti-English bias, ridiculed these qualities unmercifully; but there was a sheer energy and conviction in her writing that made her the outstanding doctrinaire novelist of the decade.

Her lead was followed by another Dublin author, the Rev. Charles Robert Maturin, an eccentric young clergyman, whose first novel, *The Fatal Revenge, or The Family of Montorio* (1807), was a Gothic romance of the purest Radcliffe-Lewis vintage. Believing that terror is a more universal emotion than love, he announced that "I have presumed to found the interest of a romance on the passion of supernatural fear, and on that almost alone." Corpses, counterfeit apparitions, and rites of black magic abound throughout the book. In his next novel, however, Maturin deserted Lewis in order to attempt the impossible feat of imitating Miss Owenson and Miss Edgeworth at the same time. The grotesquely exaggerated attack upon fashionable society and its degrading influence upon an impressionable youth is a sort of masculine counterpart of *Belinda,* while the title — *The Wild Irish Boy* —

and the character of an old Irish nobleman are taken straight from Miss Owenson.

Of the other purveyors of sensational fiction, the only one occasionally remembered is Charlotte Dacre, whose pen name was "Rosa Matilda," and whose best novel, *Zafloya, or The Moor* (1806), is a sadistic story modeled upon Lewis's *Monk,* dealing with a murderous Italian beauty and her dusky accomplice who is actually Satan in disguise. The fascinating horrors of Miss Dacre made a deep impression on the youthful mind of Percy Bysshe Shelley, and before he was twenty he published two Gothic tales, *Zastrossi* and *St. Irvine, or The Rosicrucian.* In a fantastic mixture they combined the agonized lovers and ferocious villains of the tales of terror with Godwin's doctrines about free love and the tyranny of wealth.

The best romantic novels of the decade were those by two sisters, Anna Maria and Jane Porter. They tried to give genuine historical accuracy and local background to their fiction, and avoided excessive use of terror. Jane Porter's *Thaddeus of Warsaw* (1803) won lasting fame for its heroic adventures. Her sister's best books were *The Hungarian Brother* (1807) and *Don Sebastian* (1809). As they had spent their girlhood in Edinburgh, Miss Owenson's Irish nationalistic stories gave them the idea of doing something similar for Scotland. In 1810 Jane Porter published *The Scottish Chiefs,* a historical novel about Wallace and Bruce. Full of patriotic fervor, it was a favorite book of young readers throughout the nineteenth century and did much to establish the popular conception of Scotland's heroic past.

A few of the older writers continued to publish novels occasionally during these years. Godwin brought out *Fleetwood* and Holcroft *The Memoirs of Bryan Perdue* in 1805; and Fanny Burney, after nearly twenty years of silence, produced *The Wanderer, or Female Difficulties,* as late as 1814. None of these books added anything to the fame of their authors.

By 1810 the novelists of the new generation were in the full tide of success. Miss Owenson temporarily deserted her Irish scenes to imagine herself an intellectual Greek girl in *Woman, or Ida of Athens* (1809) and a Brahmin priestess in *The Missionary* (1811). Inspired by Mme. de Staël's immensely successful *Corinne,* Miss Owenson was for a while even more excited about moral equality for her sex than about political equality for Ireland: the heroine of *Woman* is a freethinker and deep in men's intrigues for the liberation of Greece. The other novel turned its attention to religious intolerance. Borrowing ideas from Mme. Cottin's *Mathilde* and Chateaubriand's *Atala*, Miss Owenson tells of the love between the Indian priestess and a Roman Catholic monk which brings them both to disaster. The story entranced Shelley and may have helped to provide the Kashmiri background for Thomas Moore's poem *Lalla Rookh*.

Maturin, meanwhile, aligned himself fully with the Irish national theme in *The Milesian Chief* (1812); but even here the episodes of armed insurrection are overshadowed by the emotional torments of the central characters, one of whom is a girl who has been brought up as a boy and discovers her sex only after she has fallen in love with a young man. The story ends with the hero executed for treason, his sweetheart committing suicide, and the other heroine losing her mind and dying of a broken heart.

In contrast with Maturin and Miss Owenson, who both reveled in melodramatic extravagance, the two writers of domestic fiction, Mrs. Opie and Miss Edgeworth, became more placid with each successive volume, inculcating moral conduct by displaying the absurdity of affectation and the dissoluteness of the aristocracy. Mrs. Opie brought out *Temper* in 1812 and *Tales of Real Life* in 1813. Miss Edgeworth's short novels appeared under the general title of *Tales of Fashionable Life* (first series, 1809; second series, 1812). The best of them is *The Absentee*, in which she achieves her most effective contrast between the spendthrift life of the Irish landlords in London and the mismanagement of their estates without their supervision. In this book the antithetical type-characters are more skilfully blended with the action than in her earlier works. They have greater individuality and more influence upon each other, and their various attitudes are revealed through dialogue rather than by exposition.

Being an unpretentious little woman, Maria never ceased to be amazed at finding herself a celebrity, and always allowed her father to claim the main credit on the ground that he was her literary mentor. His influence may have been responsible for some of the heavy-handed moralizing that mingled with her humorous and sympathetic understanding of human nature. Her next long novel, *Patronage* (1814), had first been written twenty years earlier and was revised so often that it lacked much of her usual buoyancy.

Another novelist in the moralistic vein, Mary Brunton, who was temporarily regarded as a rival of Miss Edgeworth, harked back to the sentimentalism and melodrama of Henry Mackenzie. Born in the north of Scotland and married to a Presbyterian minister, Mrs. Brunton published *Self-Control* in 1811. Her hero and heroine are incredibly perfect and her villain monstrously base; in the climax of the plot the virtuous girl is abducted to Canada and escapes from Indian captors by going over the Montmorenci Falls in a canoe. Mrs. Brunton's other novel, *Discipline* (1814), is not quite so violent in action, but is just as rigid in its religious dogmas.

As we look back with the perspective of a hundred and fifty years to the irreparably faded novels of the nineteenth century's first decade, we see the irony of the fact that during all that time a quiet spinster had manuscripts in her desk that were eventually to obliterate the fame of her contemporaries. Jane Austen was the seventh child of a country rector and spent her girlhood in the rural parsonage. After writing short burlesques for the amusement of the family, she composed her first full-length novel about 1795, when she was twenty, in the epistolary form, with the title of *Elinor and Marianne*. Its main purpose was to show the absurdity of the sentimental fiction then current. She followed it with another, which she called *First Impressions*; and in 1797 she wrote a third, originally entitled *Susan*, which was intended to ridicule the vogue of the Gothic romances. About the same time she rewrote *Elinor and Marianne* as a straight narrative instead of a series of letters. Her father offered the manuscript of *First Impressions* to a publisher, but it was so totally unlike the prevalent tales of sensibility or terror that it was summarily rejected. In 1803 another publisher accepted *Susan*, and even announced it as forthcoming, but then lost confidence and put the manuscript away in his files.

In 1801 the family moved to Bath, and after the father's death in 1805 the widow and her two unmarried daughters settled in Southampton in genteel poverty. These two old-fashioned communities were the only towns they ever lived in, and in 1809 the household retired to the country, not far from where Jane had spent her youth. For ten years or more she seems to have written nothing except the beginning of a novel called *The Watsons,* which was soon abandoned; but in the withdrawal from Southampton she apparently came across the manuscripts of her first two stories, and her pleasure in getting back to rural life stimulated her to rework them. *Elinor and Marianne,* under the new title of *Sense and Sensibility,* "by a Lady," was brought out by a London publisher in 1811, at the author's expense, and proved sufficiently profitable to warrant the appearance of *Pride and Prejudice* — the new name for *First Impressions* — in 1813.

It must be borne in mind that three of Jane Austen's novels — half of her total output — were first written before the end of the eighteenth century. There is no evidence as to how extensive her later revisions were; but they must have been concerned with technical details rather than with basic themes and characters. Not only did she begin writing in the eighteenth century, but also her environment until the end of her life retained the atmosphere of that century intact. She belonged to the social class that was most obstinately opposed both to new ideas and to unseemly display of emotion, the minor country gentry, who were untouched by the social or economic ambitions of the commercial class and were immune to aristocratic habits of self-indulgence. The men of her family were either priests of the Church of England or officers in the navy, two professions that are innately conservative. Apart from some brief schooling in Oxford and Reading before she was nine, her whole life was spent in tiny villages or drowsy country towns of Southwest England, far from the stirrings of the Industrial Revolution. In this environment her few intimate acquaintances were either young women as untraveled as herself or else elderly people of settled habits and convictions. Her novels therefore expressed the very essence of the eighteenth century — its sense of permanent social and moral standards, its suspicion of uncontrolled emotion or imagination, its precise observation of immediate fact.

These were the qualities that set her apart from the other women novelists whose subject matter superficially resembled hers, Miss Burney and Miss Edgeworth, Mrs. Inchbald and Mrs. Opie. Like them, Miss Austen wrote about young women and their problems of social adjustment in the setting of upper-middle-class family life. The very titles of her first two novels suggest Mrs. Brunton's *Self-Control* and *Discipline* or Mrs. Opie's *Temper.*

The husband-hunting theme of *Pride and Prejudice* has a parallel in *Manoeuvring*, one of Miss Edgeworth's *Tales of Fashionable Life*. But these other writers were all touched in some degree with the cult of sensibility, with the evangelical urge to reform behavior, and with the radicals' hatred of the aristocracy, while Jane Austen was perfectly content to accept life as she saw it and to analyze it with cool wit and invincible common sense. Besides, they all repeatedly moved outside of what they knew, to invent exaggerated pictures of dissolute noblemen and unconvincing tragedies arising out of needless misunderstandings, whereas she stayed strictly within the narrow limits of her experience. Her characters were so much a part of her accepted pattern of life that she seldom felt any need of describing their appearance. They reveal their individuality wholly by conversation and behavior, and yet they are so fully individualized that each one stands out as a complete portrait.

She had been so much encouraged by the publication of *Sense and Sensibility* that she went to work on a new novel, *Mansfield Park*, which came out in 1814. A symptom of the limited but increasing fame of her books was the acceptance of the next one by John Murray, the most influential publisher of the time, who issued it in 1816. Entitled *Emma*, it is a more subtle psychological study, centering upon a self-willed girl who gradually learns consideration for other people. Miss Austen was now at the height of her technical skill, and this is the most perfectly constructed of her books.

Though her name was still kept off the title pages, the knowledge of her identity was spreading, and the librarian of the Prince Regent transmitted to her a royal message that she was "at liberty to dedicate any future book to H.R.H." The librarian also took it upon himself to offer suggestions of what she might write about next — "an historical romance illustrative of the august House of Cobourg." She knew her own talent well enough to reject the idea with ridicule. "I could no more write a romance than an epic poem. I could not sit down seriously to write a serious romance under any other motive than to save my life; and if it were indispensable for me to keep it up and never relax into laughing at myself or at any other, I am sure I should be hung before I had finished the first chapter. I must keep to my own style and go on in my own way."

Staying within her established range, she started a new novel,

Persuasion; and also she thought about the unpublished work that she had sold in 1803. Her brother regained the manuscript by paying back the ten pounds that had been originally given for it. Naturally he did not reveal that it had been written by the now successful author of *Pride and Prejudice.* She made some revisions in the story and renamed it *Northanger Abbey,* but she postponed publishing it. In 1817 her health began to give way. The family moved to Winchester, where she died a few weeks later. *Northanger Abbey* and *Persuasion* were published together the next year.

She had never adopted any airs of a professional writer. All her books were composed in the family sitting-room, with the household activities going on around her. She wrote on slips of paper that could be dropped into a drawer or slid under a sheet of notepaper if visitors came in. She was always ready to interrupt her work to pay a visit, or play cards, or take her share in the tasks of dressmaking and cooking, or tell "long circumstantial fairy tales" to nephews and nieces. The natural style of her writing was maintained by its never being divorced from the daily life around her. Her characters were so real in her imagination that they mingled comfortably with her actual surroundings: in her letters and conversations she mentioned people in her novels in the same tone as her neighbors, and included additional details not in the books.

Her novels are so much alike in theme and setting, and were written (or rewritten) during such a comparatively brief period, that they can be discussed as a group. It is sometimes objected that the central plot of all six is essentially the same: an eligible young man comes into a village and eventually secures the most suitable wife, while other and less desirable gentlemen are temporarily admired before being disclosed at their true value. But this does not mean any monotonous resemblance among the six books. In Miss Austen's real surroundings, marriage and inheritance of property and maintenance of social prestige were the only important issues in life, for her own experience had taught her the grimness of inadequate means and of mother-dominated spinsterhood. She could make these things all the more authentically crucial in her stories when they occurred in rural isolation. "Such a spot is the delight of my life," she remarked; "three or four families in a country village is the very thing to work on."

Another school of criticism admits the validity of her picture of the life she knew, but finds it distasteful — selfish, materialistic, and class-conscious, without a gleam of spirituality or an impulse of social responsibility. Again her justification is her incorruptible realism: she portrayed people as she saw them, and the burden of proof is on the objectors if they believe average human beings to be basically different, then or now.

Miss Austen had read fairly widely, and by intuitive good taste she was able to absorb the best elements in eighteenth-century fiction, from Richardson and Fielding to Miss Burney, without acquiring the excesses that their imitators indulged in. Her comments on current novels consistently expressed disapproval of extravagant language, affected sentiment, improbable characters, incoherent plot, and violent incidents. Nor did she accept literary tradition as a substitute for personal observation. Aware of her limitations, she confined herself to comedy. "Let other pens dwell on guilt and misery," she said in *Mansfield Park;* "I quit such odious subjects as soon as I can." And in a letter she described her fiction as "the little bit (two inches wide) of ivory on which I work with so fine a brush as produces little effect after much labor." For example, her knowledge of masculine behavior was so limited that she avoided presenting any scene of men together without women present. But this serves actually to enhance her particular effect, for each story is kept strictly in focus upon the feminine characters, and they naturally would have no insight into male conversations.

The absence of passion is a graver limitation, since the dominant theme of all her novels is love. She is so suspicious of emotion that when a scene of strong feeling is imperative she tries to avoid narrating it. At the climax of *Sense and Sensibility* — Edward Ferrars' long-delayed proposal to Elinor Dashwood — she coolly remarks:

> How soon he had walked himself into a proper resolution, however, how soon an opportunity of exercising it occurred, in what manner he expressed himself, and how he was received, need not be particularly told. This only need be said: — that when they all sat down to table at four o'clock, about three hours after his arrival, he had secured his lady, engaged her mother's consent, and was not only in the rapturous profession of the lover, but in the reality of reason and truth, one of the happiest of men.

Of the sixteen kisses mentioned in the novels, not one is exchanged by a pair of lovers. Her heroines are so sensible and self-controlled that even in their secret thoughts they do not allow sex to intrude. Prudish this may be, but in such an honest woman as Jane Austen it cannot be termed hypocritical. The suppression of passion had been implanted in her from infancy, and was strengthened by her contempt for the meretricious emotionalism of popular fiction. She simply did not comprehend the primitivism of her century, proclaimed by the disciples of Rousseau, and she would have had as little grasp of the naturalism proclaimed a hundred years later by the disciples of Darwin. The truth of human nature, as she understood it, had nothing to do with blind animal instincts, but was the elaborate code of custom and manners, built up through the ages by complex social intercourse.

Within her narrow bounds, however, she achieved something not far from perfection. Her modest description of herself as a miniature-painter is true so far as her range and precision are concerned, but says nothing about the depth of her penetration. There was just as much suspense and crisis arising out of her situations — the misjudgment of character and the conflicts of family opinion — as in the gruesome mysteries and tragic climaxes of her contemporaries. A girl neglected at a dance, or jealous of a rival, suffered perfectly genuine agonies under her prim mask. Jane Austen recorded these unuttered tensions with absolute fidelity because she had gone through them herself.

This raises the question of the personal element in her stories. In contrast with the other novelists from Richardson and Fielding down to her own day, she appears uniquely objective. She does not talk to the reader about her technical methods, as did Fielding, or moralize upon ethical problems, as did Richardson and his offspring, or idealize herself in a beautiful or brilliant or martyred heroine, as did many of the women novelists. And yet closer familiarity reveals her as more individual than any of them, for most of the didactic discourses were trite generalizations, and most of the glorified self-portraits were standardized paragons, whereas Jane Austen remained incorrigibly herself. Her brief comments on the action are so mildly phrased that one needs to take a second look before recognizing their gentle sarcasm or their incisive truth. Her preoccupation with human follies provides a touch of satire, but she has nothing of the impatience and arrogance that impelled the great satirists like Swift and Voltaire. She was too well adjusted to life to be guilty of intolerance. Sometimes she has been likened to Chaucer and Shakespeare for her affectionate amusement at even her least attractive characters, Mr. Collins or Mr. Woodhouse or Mrs. Norris. She shows how much they annoy the people they encounter, but she herself does not lose her temper with them. Just as she is too sensible to portray ultra-noble heroes and heroines, so also is she incapable of creating hateful villains. Willoughby and Wickham and Henry Crawford are stupid in their selfishness, but not inherently evil, and she inflicts no worse punishment on them than obscurity and boredom. Egoism is in her view the dominant vice of human beings, because an intelligent person ought to realize that he is no more important than anyone else.

It follows that although she portrayed herself in her heroines quite as much as any other woman author ever did, she produced a different effect because she did not take herself seriously. Her heroines, like herself, have a sense of humor and can smile at their own foibles; and their power of reasoning is strong enough to make them learn by experience. Elizabeth Bennet comes to realize the folly of her intolerant atitude; and Emma Woodhouse — a more complex study — begins by believing herself wise enough to arrange the lives of other people, and eventually finds out how mistaken she can be, even about her own affairs. Fanny Price in *Mansfield Park* and Anne Elliot in *Persuasion* are gentler souls, but with qualities of fortitude and independence underlying their meekness. Some part of the author's personality entered into each of her main characters. She could be considerate and patient, like Fanny and Anne; she could be witty and critical, like Elizabeth and Emma; she could be severely rational, like Elinor Dashwood, and impulsively imaginative, like Marianne Dashwood and Catherine Morland. But, though all these girls are close to her heart, and though she keeps them at the center of the reader's attention, she remains detached from them, observing them with serene amusement.

The texture of the novels is so uniform that no firm basis exists for discriminating among them. Most readers, however, incline to feel that *Sense and Sensibility* and *Northanger Abbey* are not as satisfactory as the other four. Both of them originated in an impulse to satirize the extravagances of current fiction in the 1790's; and even though, like all good novels, they outgrew their initial limited objective, they retained some trace of it. *Sense and Sensibility* is a trifle rigid in sustaining the antithesis expressed in its title: Elinor Dashwood is so austere in her prudence that one's sympathy is likely to veer toward her more extroverted sister, although Marianne's tears of sympathy for sorrow and her raptures over scenery become tedious. Of all Miss Austen's novels, this one is nearest in method to Fanny Burney's, with its caricatures of vulgar or stupid people and its episode of the two heroines' going to London to "see the world." The brief *Northanger Abbey*, for all the skill in its telling, cannot quite overcome the element of burlesque inherent in a rather obvious idea which had already been used less subtly in *The Female Quixote* and in Colman's play, *Polly Honeycomb*. In the interval between the first writing and the belated printing of *Northanger Abbey*, several other books had used the same device to ridicule the vogue of sensational fiction, notably *Romance Readers and Romance Writers*, by Sarah Green (1810), and *The Heroine, or Adventures of Cherubina*, a slashing burlesque by Eaton Stannard Barrett (1813).

Among Jane Austen's remaining four books each has its contingent of enthusiasts. *Pride and Prejudice* is the most widely read, for its consistent humor and its balanced portrayal of the whole Bennet family — father, mother, and four daughters. It was the first English novel to take a family unit as its central theme. *Mansfield Park* ventures into a wider range of social observation, with its clear-sighted picture of the Price household in its poverty. *Emma* shows an increased confidence in psychological analysis. "I am going to take a heroine whom no one but myself will much like," Miss Austen remarked; and she succeeds in winning the reader's grudging sympathy for the headstrong girl. The sustained irony of the story, as Emma plunges on from one misapprehension to another, is as masterly on its comic level as the tragic irony in a play by Sophocles. In these two novels the author's youthful gaiety and hardness were perceptibly fading, and by the time she reached *Persuasion* she was acquiring a mellow tenderness that some readers find particularly appealing. If Elizabeth Bennet is the best portrait of the youthful Jane Austen, with her wit and common sense, Anne Elliot is the companion picture showing the author in her maturity, resigned to the obscure existence of a spinster aunt.

In her lifetime, and for many years after, her fame was limited to the few who appreciate subtlety. In 1814 *Mansfield Park* was overshadowed by Miss Edgeworth's *Patronage* and by *O'Donnel*, the current success of the former Miss Owenson, who was now Lady Morgan, having married a reticent physician after refusing to do so until she had cajoled the Lord Lieutenant of Ireland into granting him a knighthood. Perhaps under her husband's tutelage, or through her new experiences in cultivated society, this novel was more restrained than her previous ones, and contained some lively comic scenes. It marked a vigorous return to her theme of Irish nationalism.

Another book of that year, however, threw all its competitors into the shade. This was *Waverley*, which came out anonymously and aroused intense curiosity as to who wrote it. There were various reasons why its author went to extraordinary lengths to conceal himself.

As the son of a prosperous Edinburgh attorney, Walter Scott was destined by environment and temperament to a pleasant, undistinguished life in the paternal profession, or perhaps in the army, which would have been his preference. Physically energetic and socially gregarious, he would have been an athlete at school and college and a popular guest at parties when he grew up. But the whole course of his life was deflected by an illness (probably polio) when he was eighteen months old. It left him with a crippled right leg. His childhood was therefore spent not in the streets and schoolrooms of the city, but mainly at his grandfather's farm in the Border country. Here he lived on friendly terms with the peasantry and absorbed the local legends and folk songs. Here too he realized that his ancestors had once been leaders in the fierce feuds among the landowning families and in the recurrent wars with England. His innate energy, being denied physical outlet, became concentrated in imagination. He learned to read by spelling out a book of local history. Later, at school in Edinburgh, he was popular with the boys for his gift of story-telling. After attending Edinburgh University he studied law and was called to the bar.

Edinburgh at that time had a pleasant literary coterie, presided over by the genial Henry Mackenzie. While in his teens Scott came to know a number of authors, including Burns; and at the age of twenty-five he translated several fantastic ballads by the German romantic poets, then greatly in fashion. This led him to compose ballads of his own, and to collect a volume of the folk poetry that he had known since boyhood. *The Minstrelsy of the Scottish Border,* published in 1802, won him a measure of literary reputation. Soon afterwards he started to write a ballad on a Scottish folk tale about a mischievous hobgoblin, and it grew in his imagination into a book-length historical poem, *The Lay of the Last Minstrel,* which was immensely successful when it came out in 1805.

Scott was by this time thirty-four, a man of established social standing, with a sinecure appointment as sheriff-depute of a county near Edinburgh. After an unlucky love affair he had married happily and set up a household. The popularity of the *Lay* made him realize that he had drifted into a career of authorship that he liked better than his nominal profession.

He made a start on a prose story at this time, but a friend who read the opening chapters found it uninteresting and persuaded him to return to verse. The success of *Marmion* (1808) and *The Lady of the Lake* (1810) was unprecedented. These two poems are an approach to the achievement of that hybrid genre, the novel in verse. In each there are a well-knit plot, clearly marked characters, precise detail in the description of settings, and even touches of humor. The rapid octosyllabic verse is well suited to the action.

On the strength of his huge profits Scott committed himself to two ambitious undertakings. He invested heavily in a new publishing business founded by a former schoolmate, and he gratified his most cherished dream by buying a large acreage in the Border region and starting to build a baronial mansion. These responsibilities forced him to assume a heavy burden of literary work. He applied himself to vast scholarly tasks of editing historical documents and the works of famous authors. He helped to found the *Edinburgh Review* and later the *Quarterly* and wrote many articles for them. And all the time he kept up the strenuous social program that he considered essential to his position as a wealthy "laird."

It was partly this overwork that led to deterioration in his poetry. But also there was a fatal limitation in his poetic range.

He had never been obliged to master technical finesse, and by the time his fourth long poem appeared the public was getting tired of the sameness in his manner. Besides, Lord Byron had emerged as an even more popular poet, who borrowed some of Scott's methods and enriched them by the romantic passion of his plots and the exotic luxury of his scenes. Hence came a disastrous decline in Scott's income, at a time when he had to pour more money into the publishing firm to stave off bankruptcy.

Obviously, if he was to maintain his extravagant way of life by literary earning, he must find a new medium. One of his hack jobs in 1808 had been the completion of an unfinished romance, *Queenhoo Hall,* by Joseph Strutt, a learned antiquary who had weighed the book down with exhaustive research. This had made Scott aware of the potentialities of historical fiction. In 1810, when looking for some fishing tackle, he chanced upon the seven chapters that he had written five years before, and showed them to his publisher; but at that time the colossal sales of *The Lady of the Lake* convinced the man of business that no new experiment should be attempted.

By 1813, however, the situation was so different that Scott took out the old manuscript again and decided to go on with it. But he was uncertain as to its value. After being hailed as the best poet of the age he felt that it would be a sad humiliation to become a mere novelist, even if a successful one; and there was much likelihood that he might be a failure. His novel fell outside all the categories that were then in vogue. Its setting was historical, but not far enough back in the past to have acquired the glamour of remoteness; it dealt with the Jacobite uprising of 1745, and in Scott's boyhood he had known survivors of that episode. His historian's conscience forced him to keep strictly to the facts, and his travels in the Highlands rendered his backgrounds authentic. Still less had the book any of the emotional hysteria of the Gothic romances; Scott's robust humor and common sense precluded him from indulging in gruesome horrors or superstitious figments. Finally, being perfectly well satisfied with life as he found it, he had no impulse toward reforming manners or morals. In view of these negative qualities, the book belonged in the realm of realism.

Nevertheless, in another light Scott was incurably romantic.

In boyhood he had devoured the romances of chivalry and even "the ponderous folios of *Cyrus* and *Cassandra*," and the tales he spun for his classmates were all about enchantments and knight-errantry. This was normal boyish love of adventure and heroism; but in Scott it had an added psychological motive because he could thus live vicariously the life of action that his lameness denied him in actuality. Further, he was convinced that his own ancestors had been the same sort of doughty fighters and hospitable hosts that populated the romances. Therefore his youthful acceptance of the romantic outlook was too deeply rooted to be outgrown. The whole tragicomedy of his career stems from his belief in the chivalric ideals and his insistence upon putting them into practice.

It was not a mere passing fancy that had led him in his first long poem to identify himself with the last of the feudal minstrels. Since their time few authors had devoted themselves exclusively to the function of telling a fascinating story. In English fiction Defoe was probably the only one — if we disregard his claim that he was writing to promote morality — and it is significant that Scott was the first critic to accord Defoe much recognition as a novelist.

This does not mean that Scott had no purpose whatsoever beyond spinning a good yarn. For one thing, he was motivated by patriotism. He admired what Miss Edgeworth had done in using distinctively Irish material and he enjoyed even the cruder national propaganda of Miss Owenson. He responded to the patriotic fervor in Jane Porter's *Scottish Chiefs* in spite of its hackneyed rhetoric. His friends were disturbed by the decline of Scottish tradition under the political and economic dominance of England. Obviously there was an opening for him to do something for his country's cause by reviving a knowledge of its former glories.

In choosing the last Jacobite rebellion as his topic, he went straight to the heart of this problem. "The Forty-five" was more than an attempt by the Stuart dynasty to regain the British crown. It was also the final attempt of Scotland to assert her equality in the United Kingdom. And within Scotland itself it was the last struggle of feudalism, as represented by the Highland clans, against the modern urban and commercial civilization of the Lowland region.

Scott's attitude toward this conflict is the key to his nature. When the popularity of *Waverley* led to a sentimental cult of the Stuart regime and a flood of tourists into the picturesque Highlands, Scott came to be thought of as a champion of lost causes and a Rousseauistic devotee of primitive people and of scenic solitude. On the contrary, there was nowhere a more loyal subject of the House of Hanover, and as an orthodox Protestant he looked suspiciously on the Catholic Jacobites. Nor was he ever in revolt against the modern economic solidity represented by his thrifty farmer-grandfather and his practical lawyer-father. He had no wish to set the clock back to a simpler age. But his intuition taught him the inherent effectiveness of the struggle between two ways of life and the dramatic pathos in the inevitable defeat inflicted upon the archaic one. Actually, he recorded the historic significance of the new era of progress with more profound interpretation than did the radical novelists, such as Holcroft and Godwin, who were preaching specific doctrines. Scott perceived an epic theme in the central fact that social change had become inevitable and that change entails conflict and tragedy. Scottish history provided a microcosm of this universal process.

Also, his dominant traits of kindliness and humor obliged him to see the situation in terms of human beings. Neither cause was right or wrong; people were sincere on both sides. Scott depicted the whole range of types and outlooks, from the noblemen all the way to the peasantry. He brought fiction back to its fundamental function of telling an interesting story in a convincing fashion, through characters who took on the reality of living people. Any wider meaning was implicit in the picture of a plausible situation, instead of obviously dictating the behavior of characters and the sequence of events.

To bring out his theme he followed a method used by Miss Owenson by choosing as his hero a conventional young Englishman whose attitude would be like that of his average reader. At the beginning Edward Waverley is as much deluded by romantic sensibility as was Jane Austen's Marianne Dashwood. As he becomes more and more deeply involved in the war and learns to understand Scottish ways and the Scottish point of view, the reader undergoes a conversion along with him. The theme is exemplified even in the love element, which concerns Waverley's hesitation between two charming girls — the imperious daughter of a Highland chief and the domesticated daughter of a Lowland laird.

The diffidence with which Scott put out his first novel was perfectly sincere. He was over forty years old, an easygoing soul who was writing for profit rather than in hope of fame or in conviction of superior talent. Even the offer of appointment as Poet Laureate had not deluded him into thinking himself a genius and the decline in his popularity had been disillusioning. He was making headway in his secondary vocation of the law: he had been appointed Clerk of Session, which might be a step toward a judgeship. The novel was a desperate venture into new territory. Why endanger his status by being identified as a writer in a genre that serious readers and critics labeled "trash"? Therefore when *Waverley, or 'Tis Sixty Years Since* came out in 1814, scarcely anybody but the publisher knew who had written it. Even after it began to attract attention, Scott was still so dubious that he made the irrevocable mistake of flatly denying his authorship.

In comparison with his subsequent books, the story was slow-moving and the manner formal. But it was so superior to the average fiction of the time that it captivated all types of readers. Whereas the other realistic novelists dealt with the artificial life in drawing rooms and the conflicts of caste in sophisticated society, Scott offered an equally convincing picture of adventure and danger in the heather-scented open air of the mountains. Readers realized that the historical and topographical details were authentic, and so they had the satisfaction of feeling that they were learning useful facts under the pleasant guise of entertainment. Humor added its appeal throughout, and it was a kindly, sympathetic humor, without any sour flavor of satire. For these reasons *Waverley* appealed to every sort of person. Cultivated folk appreciated the author's sound scholarship and his naturally easy style. Men of affairs responded to the vigor of the action and the absence of preachment, and yet serious-minded people found nothing that offended their sense of propriety. For his enduring influence, probably the greatest fact was that young people could enjoy the excitement of the plot and identify themselves with the uncomplicated central characters.

The unexpected triumph of *Waverley* convinced Scott that he had found his *métier*. His memory was crammed with the varied reading of a lifetime, and besides he could recall scores of quaint characters that he had known and liked. His next novel, *Guy Mannering*, was composed in six weeks. Though again the action takes place in the eighteenth century, there are no public events involved, and so the attention is centered upon characterization and local customs. This time it is the economic decay of an aristocratic family that provides the antithesis between archaic traditions and the practical modern world. The stereotyped plot concerning a missing heir serves merely as framework for a gallery of lovingly elaborated portraits — a schoolmaster, a lawyer, a farmer, a smuggler, and a wild gypsy woman. Some traces of the old comedy of humours can be detected in his method; but his wide acquaintance with eccentrics gave individuality to each figure.

In the third novel, *The Antiquary*, he came down to within twenty years of the date of writing. For his strong effects he depended upon weirdness and gloom — a violent storm, a midnight burial, a candle-lit scene in a fisherman's hut. These elements have some kinship with the tales of terror, but Scott kept away from the gruesome and the supernatural. In fact, *The Antiquary* is the most consistently comic of his novels. The plot, again concerning a missing heir and a particularly colorless pair of young lovers, is melodramatic throughout, building up to a sort of general transformation scene in the happy ending. But many of the characters, especially the heroic old beggar, Edie Ochiltree, and the half-crazy peasant crone, Elspeth, are unforgettable; and the elderly antiquary, Jonathan Oldbuck, has touches of humorous self-portraiture.

In the same year with *The Antiquary* came two other stories, published together under the title *Tales of My Landlord*. One of them, *The Black Dwarf*, was an experiment in Gothic grotesquerie that proved so unsatisfactory that the author cut it off short. But the other is probably his greatest work of historical fiction. *Old Mortality* dealt with the uprising of the Presbyterian Covenanters in 1679, and he went to unusual trouble to verify his historical data and merge them with the fictitious narrative. The portrait of Graham of Claverhouse is especially impressive. The invented characters are carefully developed to illustrate the various points of view in the conflict. Though

Scott is unsparing toward the fanaticism of the extreme Covenanters and the brutality of their conquerors, he shows that there
were more moderate men in both camps. His hero, like Waverley,
is a conscientious young man who is drawn into the struggle
and tries vainly to conciliate the bitter adversaries. Only near
the end does Scott allow the demands of melodrama to overshadow the historical validity of the action.

In combining two novels under one inclusive title, and in
continuing the practice for the next four years, Scott created a
cumbersome mechanism. He invented a fictitious editor, Jedediah
Cleishbotham, a pompous schoolmaster, who is supposed to be
presenting stories originally told by the local innkeeper and then
transcribed by the schoolmaster's assistant, Peter Pattieson. In
Old Mortality there is even a fourth transmitter, the old tomb-
stone-restorer whose enthusiasm for the Covenanters led him to
collect traditional tales about them. By all this framework Scott
was seeking to add an illusion of historical authenticity by
bridging the gap between his own day and the past. But modern
readers, accustomed to historical fiction, find the preliminary
gambits merely tedious. Unless the reader starts at the beginning
of the series, with the inferior *Black Dwarf*, he never gets any
clear idea of who these irrelevant characters are, or why they
intrude in the later books with introductory remarks, concluding apologies, and explanatory footnotes. In part the device was
intended to increase the mystification as to the authorship, for
the title page did not carry the phrase "By the Author of *Waverley*" as had the two intervening books. Few readers, however,
believed for a moment that any other writer could display the
same sort of power; and by this time it was widely known or
suspected that "the Great Unknown" was Walter Scott. Occasionally, it is true, some other claimant was suggested, and the
resulting argument added extra publicity for the books. Scott
watched the confusion with a mixture of embarrassment and
amusement, and at this point he increased it by contributing a
favorable critique of *Tales of My Landlord* to the *Quarterly
Review*.

To keep up the pretense that he was a gentleman of private
wealth, he was forced into an arduous double life. His great
house at Abbotsford was now finished, and he crammed it with
ancient weapons, armor, and antique folios. Here he held open

house for a constant parade of guests, with whom he spent his days in fishing, shooting, and riding. He maintained the routine of his official legal duties, and continued to compose the sort of respectable literature that could appear under his name — poetry, antiquarian treatises, a play. Therefore he had to sit up most nights to write the novels, pushing his pen at top speed to keep up with his flow of ideas. Little wonder that in 1817 he began to suffer intestinal agonies, probably from stomach ulcers. But in spite of attacks of pain he continued with his stories, dictating to a secretary when he felt too ill to hold a pen. Thus there was no perceptible lag before the next novel, *Rob Roy*, came out at the end of 1817.

Using as its title the name of a real Highland outlaw, *Rob Roy* forms a natural parallel with *Waverley*, as it deals with the other great Jacobite rebellion, thirty years earlier than that of "Bonnie Prince Charlie," and it even uses the same device, an English visitor stumbling into the midst of the uprising. It therefore serves as evidence of how far Scott had advanced in narrative skill. The faults of hasty writing and catering to popular demands are obvious: the plot is improbable and sometimes confused, and the happy ending is both logically and artistically inept. On the other hand, Scott enhanced the vividness of effect by using, for the first time, the autobiographic form. With real psychological skill he reveals the transformation of Frank Osbaldistone from conventional-minded brashness to mature judgment. The Highlanders are portrayed in all their ruthlessness and superstition, with Helen Macgregor as an unforgettable embodiment of feminine ferocity. Furthermore, Diana Vernon, who is probably a reminiscence of the girl Scott loved and lost in his youth, is an intelligent and courageous heroine, a refreshing change from the sweet, modest girls he usually portrayed. She and a group of splendid comic characters make *Rob Roy* one of Scott's best-loved books.

Immediately reverting to his *alter ego*, he brought out the second series of *Tales of My Landlord*, consisting of only one novel, *The Heart of Midlothian*, which has been placed by modern critics in the highest rank of his work. The historical starting point is a local event in Edinburgh, the Porteous riots of 1736; but this is subordinated to the personal story of Jeanie Deans and her heroic walk to London to win a royal amnesty for her sister, convicted of child murder. This was based upon an actual case, and Scott combined it expertly with the events of the rioting. The few comic characters are kept in the background, and the book is more somber in tone than any he had previously written. If he had ended with the granting of the pardon, it would be a realistic masterpiece of pathos and nobility in humble life; but Scott felt the need to include some of his customary romantic picturesqueness and so he shifted the subsequent scenes to the Highlands and introduced a farrago of melodramatic adventure.

A third series of *Tales of My Landlord* followed in 1819. In one of them, *The Bride of Lammermoor*, he went further in the direction implied in *The Heart of Midlothian* and ventured upon unrelieved tragedy. Its new atmosphere of gloom and cruelty may be due to the fact that it was dictated during a crisis of his illness, when he was sometimes semi-delirious with pain. When he read the printed book he "did not recollect one single incident, character, or conversation," and felt that on any page he might be "startled by meeting something altogether glaring and fantastic." It was so unlike his normal manner that he did not care for it: "I felt it monstrous gross and grotesque." The hopelessness of the situation and the morbid passivity of the main characters make it his only depressing novel; but many nineteenth-century men of letters considered it his best. The use of superstitions and omens to heighten the sense of doom, and the solid reality of the grim castles that are the principal setting, render it a fulfillment of the purpose toward which the Gothic novelists had groped.

The other story that was published along with it, *A Legend of Montrose*, was brighter in tone. Dealing with the fighting in the Highlands incidental to the English civil war of the 1640's, it is adventurous and colorful, without much depth. It is chiefly notable for the character of Dugald Dalgetty, who dominates most of the story; but one feels the lack of that special mixture of sympathy and laughter that brings Scott's best comic characters to life. The boastful captain is a caricature in the manner of Smollett.

This thinness of texture betrays the fact that Scott's original reservoir of material was almost exhausted. He had covered a century and a half of Scottish history, had ranged through the best scenic spots in all corners of the country, had portrayed the best specimens of eccentric characters that he had ever met or heard of, and had exploited his supply of local legends and family traditions. He therefore put an end to *Tales of My Landlord* and launched out into a different sort of historical fiction, in which invention and research replaced memory and observation.

The creation of nine novels in five years was a marvel of sheer productivity and hard work, expecially when one considers the author's multifarious other activities. The defects in the novels are inevitable results of this speed, for they were improvised without planning and printed without revision. But their merits outweigh their blemishes. A born story-teller, Scott was gifted with the instinct of how to hold the reader engrossed. And he possessed in equal measure the other requisite of a good novelist, the power to create three-dimensional characters and to endow them with life. In regard to style, his very speed of composition was an advantage, for he wrote with the fluency of speech, whereas more laborious novelists felt obliged to be rhetorical and decorative. The author's personality never obtrudes itself, for he was a modest man; but one grows aware of the pervasive spirit of the stories, which must be the author's own — a spirit of generosity, honesty, and loyalty that even the most cynical reader finds hard to resist.

It was the attitude and manner of the writer, as much as the novelty of his settings and historical data, that made the reading of "the Waverley novels" seem like entrance into a new world. To be sure, one comes away from them with a clear impression of Scottish scenes and customs, dialects and beliefs, and one has acquired unforgettable portraits of important personages and set-pieces of battles and controversies. But one has been reading not for ethnological and historical information but for the delight of sharing in adventures and laughing affectionately at odd characters. These qualities won for Scott a tribute of personal gratitude and devotion from millions of people in all countries for at least a century. His popular designation, "the Wizard of the North," was an epitome of the enchantment he cast upon readers of every mentality and every age.

In the practical view, too, his achievement was a landmark. No previous author in any genre had earned anything like the thousands of pounds that flowed in upon him. The entire relationship of author and publisher was revolutionized, as various firms bid against each other for the privilege of issuing his books. The natural result was that able and ambitious young writers, who are bound to be influenced by hope of wealth as well as of fame, realized that prose fiction might be the medium best suited to their talents.

The reversal of taste and opinion was summed up in the fact that Walter Scott was the first professional author ever to receive a title in recognition of literary eminence. In March, 1820, the new king, George IV, raised him to the rank of baronet. Since the real reason for the distinction could not be mentioned, because of Scott's absurd refusal to acknowledge the authorship of the novels, it had to be conferred on him nominally for his long-faded reputation as a poet and his insignificant service as a county official. For Scott personally it was the one triumph that could gratify his inmost dreams, for it raised him to the status of the minor nobility and provided a hereditary title to be handed on to his son. And he had won it by writing novels, the class of literature that only five years before had been universally despised.

VIII

Expansion of Scope

(1820 – 1830)

SCOTT'S SUPERIOR HANDLING of the traits that he borrowed from the Gothic romances — historical background, dangerous adventures, taut suspense — did not obliterate the cruder type of fiction. In fact, two of the best tales of terror came out at the very height of his triumph. One was *Frankenstein*, by Mary Shelley, published in 1818. As the daughter of William Godwin and Mary Wollstonecraft and the wife of Percy Bysshe Shelley, she could hardly avoid being drawn into authorship. Her writing of the book resulted from a playful contest when she was nineteen. She was in Switzerland with her husband and Byron, and for a pastime several members of the group decided to write supernatural tales. Byron left his effort unfinished; but his physician, Dr. Polidori, wrote a fairly good one entitled *The Vampire*, and Mrs. Shelley's proved to be a minor masterpiece. Her choice of subject was influenced by the "Rosicrucian romances" — her father's *St. Leon* and her husband's *St. Irvyne*. In her story a scientist constructs a human figure and discovers the secret of bringing it to life, only to find that he has created a murderous monster. Perhaps more by luck than by judgment, she had taken a theme with deep symbolic suggestion, linking back to the ancient Greek legend of Pygmalion and forward to the twentieth century's anxiety about man's subjugation to the machine. She made the story more effective than the Gothic romances by setting it near her own day, by using the first-personal point of view, and by enclosing it in a "frame", in which a matter-of-fact sea captain reports how he obtained the unhappy scientist's confession. There is real pathos in the predicament of the artificial man, who turns against society because it despises him. This echoes her father's humanitarian themes and the Rousseauistic idea of the noble savage. Just at the same time her father's *Mandeville* (1817) used much the same theme, without the supernatural device: it too deals with a victim of social injustice who develops psychopathic vengefulness against more fortunate people.

Mrs. Shelley wrote several other imaginative stories, the best being *Valperga* (1823), a historical romance, and *The Last Man* (1826), which is a startling forecast of the extinction of the human race by pestilence in 2073, and which has additional interest because her husband is portrayed in one of the characters.

The other notable belated Gothic romance was the work of Maturin. For five years after *The Milesian Chief* he devoted himself to playwriting; and his next novel, *Women, or Pour et Contre* (1818), showed an improvement over his previous work, in which, as he admitted in the preface, "the characters, situations, and language are drawn merely from imagination; my limited acquaintance with life denied me any other resource." In *Women* there is some realism, especially in the depiction of an intolerant Calvinist family, and there are even a few scenes of amusing social satire. The main plot, however, is sufficiently melodramatic: the rather spineless hero deserts his saintly fiancée in favor of a world-famous actress, who is eventually discovered to be the girl's long-lost mother.

Instead of continuing to depict contemporary society, however, Maturin reverted to the supernatural terrors that he had started with, as though he felt a compulsion to show how far he could now excel his first work. *Melmoth the Wanderer* has a good claim to be the best of the English horror novels. Though concocted from some of the most overworked ingredients, it is invested with a sort of eerie vividness and distorted plausibility, like an El Greco painting. For one thing, like *Frankenstein* it has a modern setting and an oblique approach that reveals the ghastly story piecemeal as it comes to the knowledge of the narrator. In common with many of the romantic authors, Maturin was fascinated by the Faust theme. Combining this with the legend of the Wandering Jew, he invented a man who has sold his soul to the devil in the seventeenth century and thereafter travels endlessly in search of someone who can be tempted to become his substitute. One of his descendants, a college student in Dublin, stumbles across a hint of the awful truth. Thereafter the book's effectiveness resides in the contrast between the realistic modern framework and the series of episodes, sometimes transmitted through several intermediaries, which reveal Melmoth's fearsome progress across the continents and the centuries. These inserted stories use a number of standard themes, some pathetic, others frightful, ranging from the idyllic life of a nature-girl on a tropical island to the tortures of the Inquisition.

Another remarkable tale in the romantic vein, which came out in 1819, was *Anastasius, or The Memoirs of a Modern Greek.* It was the only work of fiction by its author, Thomas Hope, a wealthy art connoisseur. Son of a Scottish merchant in Amsterdam, Hope had traveled through Europe and parts of Africa and Asia before he was twenty, collecting objects of art; and when he set up a mansion in London his style of furnishing, and a book that he wrote about it, exerted a lasting influence on theories of interior decorating. His character and career resemble those of Horace Walpole, Beckford, and Lewis; and like them he found escape from his life of wealth and ease by writing a fantastic story. The change in fashion is illustrated by his choice of subject: instead of the horrors of feudal cruelty he preferred the sensuous colors and luxurious indulgences of the Near East, as popularized by Byron. From Byron, too, he inherited the figure of his brooding, introspective villain-hero. Indeed, when the book appeared anonymously it was widely attributed to Byron, who confessed that when he read it he shed tears of annoyance because he had not written it. Though embroidered with the fashionable Levantine patterns, the story was basically a throwback to the old picaresque tales of clever rascality.

At the time when these culminating specimens of romantic

fantasy were being published, another man was writing in an utterly contrary mood. Thomas Love Peacock may be set beside Jane Austen as a belated survival of eighteenth-century rationalism, appealing to a limited audience with a taste for good sense and wit. Like her, he kept to a narrow range of subject because it was the only one he knew. An omnivorous reader, he found books more interesting than ordinary people, and his friendships were confined to a few writers and scholars. There is some doubt whether his books may be properly termed novels at all; like *Tristram Shandy*, they might be classified as personal essays disguised as fiction. The plots are negligible, the characters are dummies set up to voice opposing points of view, the subject matter is satiric dissection of current ideology. Peacock is not propagating any theory, but is simply ridiculing the unreasonableness of the doctrine-mongers. Yet by reviving the element of critical intelligence and urbane scholarship in fiction, he won a restricted but honorable place in the history of the novel.

For deciding that he disliked the new-fangled ideas of progress, science, and democracy, Peacock was equipped with ample evidence through being a friend of Shelley. Privately educated and financially independent, he adopted authorship as an entertaining hobby. Between the ages of nineteen and twenty-seven he published four books of mediocre verse in neoclassical style. Then in his first prose work, *Headlong Hall*, which came out anonymously in 1816, he established the model that he was to follow in much of his later work. An assorted group of characters, assembled in a comfortable country house, spend their time in arguing over their pet hypotheses. In this they are reminiscent of Walter and Toby Shandy, and of Smollett's "humours" characters. Scarcely anything happens in the course of the brief story, and the abrupt outbreak of engagements in the last chapter is so little prepared for that it reads like a burlesque on conventional fiction.

As his literary antecedents Peacock claimed the classical and neoclassical satirists — Petronius, Rabelais, Swift, and Voltaire. His immediate models were the apologues of the French *philosophes*, such as Marmontel's *Contes moraux*. Firmly based on his love of the classics, his attitude may be described as humanistic: to put the intellectual and artistic fads of the moment into proper perspective, he measured them against the accumulated thought of past centuries. Believing in the free play of the intelligence, he was contemptuous of hypocrisy, dogma, and prejudice. The chief characters in *Headlong Hall* are three philosophers — a "perfectibilian," a "deteriorationist," and a "statu-quo-ite." The other disputants include a phrenologist, several poets and critics, and a worldly clergyman who thinks only of food and wine. All of them hold forth endlessly, with a liberal sprinkling of Greek phrases and other scholarly allusions.

Peacock's second novel, *Melincourt*, is longer and has a livelier comic plot, though with no gain in plausibility, since it deals with an amateur anthropologist's success in educating an orang-outang, who becomes an English baronet and a candidate for Parliament. The satire on the "noble savage" doctrine is obvious, and the book thus forms an interesting contrast with *Frankenstein*, which was written about the same time. In this novel Peacock gives greater individuality to his characters by making them recognizable caricatures of celebrities of the day. Mr. Mystic is an impudent sketch of Coleridge, Mr. Paperstamp of Wordsworth, and Mr. Feathernest of Southey. In Mr. Anyside Antijack the author lampooned George Canning, a distinguished Tory cabinet minister.

His next novel, *Nightmare Abbey*, came closer to a conventional romantic plot in the midst of its farce. Here again he depicted several leading contemporaries. Mr. Flosky is another caricature of Coleridge, Mr. Cypress is Byron, and Scythrop Glowry is a tolerant sketch of Peacock's friend Shelley. As some of the sarcasm is directed toward the Gothic cult of gloom and haunted ruins, there is another coincidence in the fact that this book came out in 1818, the same year that saw the long-delayed publication of *Northanger Abbey*.

Peacock's representation of real people under thin disguises was typical of a tendency that was newly cropping out in English fiction. It first attracted attention in *Glenarvon* (1816), which was written by Lady Caroline Lamb, a clever and unstable woman who had been one of Byron's mistresses. The book is negligible as literature, but it was avidly read because everybody knew that it told the intimate story of Lady Caroline's notorious love affair.

This kind of fictionized scandal-mongering had an ancestor in the "secret histories" of Mrs. Manley. Its revival in the nineteenth century must be attributed to the cult of personality practiced by the romantic writers. The novelists of the mid-eighteenth century had been explicitly opposed to such a practice. Fielding and the others insisted that they were depicting types and not drawing portraits of individuals. But the neoclassical doctrine of generalities was replaced by the assumption that the individual was all-important. With Wordsworth, Byron, Lamb, Hazlitt, and De Quincey talking about themselves in everything they wrote, it was not long until novels also began to be written about and by conspicuous people.

Such stories appealed to the public's insatiable curiosity about celebrities, especially those of high rank. The moralistic novels of the preceding generation had succeeded in implanting a belief that aristocrats led a life of sumptuous sin. Instead of being revolted by the idea, however, the mass of average readers were captivated by the glittering contrast with their own drab existence, and they welcomed first-hand revelations of passion in high life. On their side, such writers realized that this demand offered them a golden opportunity to vindicate themselves and vilify their enemies. The new note is conspicuous in *Florence Macarthy* (1818), the next novel by Lady Morgan, who had now become a friend of Lady Caroline Lamb and of other fashionable figures. The heroine is an even closer self-portrait than usual, and much of the book is devoted to her feud with an unscrupulous critic, Conway Crawley, an unmistakable likeness of John Wilson Croker, who had disparaged Lady Morgan's books and character in the *Quarterly Review*.

The trend of fiction was being strongly influenced by changes in the book-production trade. With expansion of the reading public, publishing had become a prosperous and competitive business. The unwieldy eighteenth-century combines of booksellers had given place to powerful London firms that struggled ruthlessly for the market. Longmans, Murray, and Constable with the higher quality of literary commodities, Richard Phillips and John Stockdale on the popular level, had emerged soon after the century opened. They were followed by Henry Colburn, the most enterprising of them all. Concerned only with what would sell, Colburn used high-pressure methods of publicity and offered lavish payment to any writer with a famous name. As a medium for publishers' advertising, the *Literary Gazette* was started in 1817, the first weekly paper confined to reviews of current books.

The price of books, however, remained high. A novel was usually stretched to three or more volumes by the use of large type, wide margins, and heavy paper. Therefore the distribution of fiction remained largely in the hands of the circulating libraries. A different form of publication was essential if novels were to become widely available to people who could not afford even a library subscription.

The potential profits in this larger public were demonstrated by the success of a vigorous but undignified writer named Pierce Egan, who was a sports reporter for a weekly paper. His first book, *The Mistress of Royalty* (1814), was an *exposé* of the Prince Regent's notorious love life. He followed this with *Boxiana*, a series of biographies of popular pugilists, which was issued in monthly installments at a shilling each; and it proved so popular that in 1821–24 he produced a work of fiction, brought out in the same format. This was *Tom and Jerry: Life in London, or the Day and Night Scenes of Jerry Hawthorn, Esq. and his Elegant Friend, Corinthian Tom, Accompanied by Bob Logic, the Oxonian, in their Rambles and Sprees through the Metropolis.*

This was much like the books that Ned Ward and Tom Brown had written more than a century earlier. An authority on underworld slang, Egan gave a raffish, picaresque series of violent and farcical incidents. His heroes were the irresponsible young "bucks" who flourished in the reign of the "First Gentleman of Europe." In fact, the book was dedicated to George IV, with an assertion that "an accurate knowledge of the manners, habits, and feelings of a brave and free people is not acquired in the closet." There is certainly nothing of either the study or the drawing room in Egan's world, which is devoted to gambling, horse-racing, coach-driving, boxing, and other strenuous pastimes, interspersed with drinking bouts and rioting in the streets. The author's rapid, journalistic style and outrageous puns produced the necessary effect of crude energy, as did the comic illustrations by George Cruikshank, who had inherited the mantle of Hogarth and Rowlandson.

Egan's phenomenal success on its vulgar level paralleled that of Scott in the polite sphere. Within a year of its first appearance *Tom and Jerry* was dramatized in no less than ten London theaters, and imitations proliferated. Egan published another work of fiction, *The Life of an Actor*, in 1824–25, and then returned to his former theme and produced the further adventures of Tom and Jerry in 1828, unwisely attempting to introduce a more serious note.

High above these other enterprises in fiction Scott remained secure upon his throne. In 1820, with his average quota of three novels, he broke away from his previous type of material. With *Ivanhoe* he deserted Scotland for England, and went all the way back to the Middle Ages. Consequently he had to abandon the elements of local color and humorous characterization, and produce an elaborate historical reconstruction. It was this book that extended his fame for the first time to the Continent. The scenes of feudal chivalry, centering on the heroic figure of Richard Coeur de Lion, fixed the public conception of the chivalric age in a permanent mold. Unfortunately Scott's desire for a richly varied panorama led him to shift Robin Hood and his outlaws two centuries backward, on the worthless authority of an Elizabethan play.

His other two novels of 1820, *The Monastery* and *The Abbot*, revert to a Scottish setting, but as they deal with the middle of the sixteenth century they also are historical constructs rather than pictures of anything the author knew. *The Monastery* is marred by tedious analysis of the causes for the Reformation, and by an inept attempt at the supernatural. Its sequel, *The Abbot*, which uses some of the same settings and characters, is a better book, thanks to its success in portraying the tragic figure of Mary Stuart. This novel led inevitably to *Kenilworth* (1821), written in response to a demand from his publishers that he deal with Queen Elizabeth as he had just dealt with her Scottish rival. The pathetic story of Amy Robsart is told with dramatic force, and the complex personality of Elizabeth is well drawn. The year 1822 again brought three books. *The Pirate* is chiefly notable for its magnificent scenery of the islands north of Scotland. *The Fortunes of Nigel* combines a thrilling adventure story with realistic scenes of London life in the early seventeenth century and a first-rate study of the paradoxical character of James I. *Peveril of the Peak* (the longest of his novels) continues the royal portrait gallery by presenting Charles II, in a story with many melodramatic trappings.

In the next year came what is perhaps the most brilliant of Scott's strictly historical novels, *Quentin Durward*. By this time he had his new technique under perfect control, and the adventures of a young Scottish gentleman at the French court combine the archetypal themes of a fairy tale with the precision of detail and depth of characterization that enforce credulity. The miserly, cowardly King Louis XI, in the midst of the sword-play and bravado, provides not only humor but an ironic antidote to the romantic view of life.

The next book, *St. Ronan's Well*, is unique among Scott's works in having a contemporary subject. There are some amusing scenes of social satire, but they are awkwardly combined with a tragic plot, and the latter is further weakened by the fact that the author had to make last-moment changes. When the publishers discovered that the principal woman character gave birth to an illegitimate child, they refused to accept the episode; and as Scott lacked the leisure for rewriting the whole book, he merely revised a few pages, leaving his readers sadly mystified. He was the first novelist to learn the penalty of being popular: the author becomes a slave to the taboos of the majority.

In the same year he wrote the last of his novels on eighteenth-century Scotland, *Redgauntlet*, returning to the historical theme of *Waverley* by telling about a belated and pathetically hopeless effort to organize a third Jacobite uprising. A good mystery plot is combined with richness of local color and quaint characters; in this novel, more than in any other, Scott allowed personal memories and emotions to cast a mellow glow over the scene, and he portrayed himself to some extent both in Darsie Latimer and in Alan Fairford, a young lawyer. Meanwhile the whole elaborate structure is carefully correlated with the collapse of Prince Charlie's cause. A comparison with *Waverley* will show how far Scott had developed in ten years. His increased interest in the mechanics of narrative can be seen in his experiment with a mixed method: some of the book is a diary, some a collection of letters, some a straight narrative. The best-known pages are not part of the main structure at all, being a short story, Wandering Willie's Tale, inserted by the old device of having one character tell it to others.

In 1825 Scott published two stories under a joint title, *Tales of the Crusaders*, consisting of *The Betrothed*, an attempt at psychological tragedy that was not altogether successful, and *The Talisman*, a rather mechanical specimen of historical romance. At this point his incredible career broke down in disaster. The Ballantine publishing firm failed, and Scott, as a partner, was responsible for debts to a gigantic total of £130,000. His pride prevented him from going through the bankruptcy court, or even receiving financial help from friends and admirers. He vowed he would pay off the whole sum by his own earnings. The previous happiness of his domestic life was destroyed about the same time by the death of his wife and the discovery that his beloved little grandson was incurably ill.

Doggedly he undertook an even more back-breaking load than before. He compiled a huge *Life of Napoleon* that entailed onerous research, and wrote a *History of Scotland* and other miscellaneous works, while keeping up his superhuman output of fiction. His next novel, *Woodstock*, filled a gap in his coverage of English history by dealing with Charles I and the conflict of Royalists against Parliamentarians. Most of his subsequent stories appeared under joint titles, two series of *Chronicles of the Canongate* and a final fourth series of *Tales of My Landlord*. Though none of these equaled his best work, they included several effective short stories and one strong novel, *The Fair Maid of Perth*, which revealed the brutality of medieval life more frankly than he had ever done before. No man's strength could stand such unremitting overwork, and his last stories were dictated after he was partially disabled in 1830 by a paralytic stroke. He died in 1832, having paid off more than half of the debt. In seventeen years he had written twenty-nine novels of varying length, and had changed the whole course of English fiction.

Scott was a more complex writer than appears on the surface. His novels are not to be dismissed as an incongruous mixture of high-flown heroism with homely practicality, of conventional noble sentiments with earthy common sense. The combination of these two opposite views of life was indeed the principal reason for his extraordinary popularity, since it made his novels attractive to disparate types of readers. But it served also a more serious artistic purpose. The fact that each attitude can exist in the minds of numerous people proves that both have widespread significance. Previous novelists had associated themselves exclusively with one outlook or the other. By the accidents of temperament and early experience, Scott happened to share the two outlooks in approximately equal proportions, and he juxtaposed them in such a way that they shed revealing light on each other. The balance gradually shifted: before 1820 the realistic element predominated, and after that date the romantic; but both are present in every novel and provide the conflict that is the underlying theme, deep below the uproar of clashing swords and the display of opposing banners. The final implication of each story is that heroic enterprises — strongly though they appeal to our sympathy and our love of excitement — are not only less useful but also less admirable than the achievements of sensible people who are able to withstand the pressures of everyday life.

The extent and uniqueness of Scott's achievement can be judged by the fact that his literary disciples divided into two categories that have survived to the present. From his earlier novels sprang a school of local-color humor and pathos, first in Scotland, then in Ireland and elsewhere; and from his later novels sprang the innumerable horde of historical romances.

The first Scottish writer to show traces of his influence was more directly akin to Maria Edgeworth, if not to Jane Austen. This was Susan Edmonstone Ferrier, who was a personal friend of Scott's, her father having been one of his fellow-officials of the Court of Session. Her three novels are *Marriage* (1818), *The Inheritance* (1824), and *Destiny* (1831). Published anonymously, the first two aroused curiosity as to the authorship, as the *Waverley* novels did. In fact, the general uncertainty led some people to suggest that they were the work of the same writer. Scott, who admired Miss Ferrier's novels almost as highly as Miss Austen's, was amused by the notion, and referred to her in a preface to *Tales of My Landlord* as "my sister shadow."

Her first novel cannot have been much affected by either Scott or Jane Austen, for it was almost finished in 1810, though not published till eight years later. Like Scott in *Waverley*, she derived from Miss Edgeworth and Miss Owenson the device of bringing an English character into the alien environment — in this case, a fashionable girl whose marriage to a Highland laird places her in the midst of manners that seem uncouth to her sophisticated London taste. Miss Ferrier's second novel, *The In-*

heritance, has greater certainty of characterization, but is marred by lapsing into an outworn melodramatic plot device, when the heroine discovers that she was adopted in childhood and therefore has no claim to the fortune and title she has inherited.

Miss Ferrier had a more boisterous sense of humor than Miss Austen, and none of her delicate irony. To the snobbery and greed of upper-class Scottish society she applied the harsh hand of caricature, and some of her readers in Edinburgh claimed that they could recognize individual models for several of her characters. Her comedy was too high-spirited, however, to be malicious, and her representation of defective conduct lacked Miss Edgeworth's moralizing.

A more varied picture of Scottish life was given in the fiction of John Galt. He had gone through unusual experiences before becoming a novelist. During the Napoleonic period he traveled in Europe in an effort to maintain trade relations in evasion of wartime restrictions. Thus he made friends with Byron when the poet was on his Childe Harold pilgrimage about the Mediterranean. At intervals he tried to become an author, making little success with poetry, plays, biography, and journalism. Nor did he do any better with two works of fiction — incoherent, sensational romances in the Gothic vein, with Continental settings. There could not be better proof of how completely a writer's natural talent can be smothered by his trying to follow a prevailing mode that does not suit him. At last, when he was forty, Galt found his vocation with *The Ayrshire Legatees,* which came out in *Blackwood's Magazine* in 1820. Modeled on Smollett's *Humphry Clinker,* this brief book was in the form of a series of letters written by the members of a Scottish family visiting London. Galt's journalistic experience prompted him to use the current events most interesting to the public — the accession of George IV and his litigation with his wife; and the humor and irony of the story arise out of the visitors' naïve reports of these great doings. A new device in epistolary fiction was added by narrative links between the letters, telling how they affected the recipients in the Scottish village. Having originated as a series of sketches for a magazine, the story has a minimum of plot, and gains its effect solely by the naturalness and sympathy of characterization.

Galt hurried on to a longer book, *The Annals of the Parish*

(1822). He had pondered this for many years, and had even shown a draft to a publisher as early as 1813, only to be told that the public would not accept such an uneventful narrative. It was derived as directly from *The Vicar of Wakefield* as his preceding book was derived from *Humphry Clinker*. Like Goldsmith, Galt chooses as his narrator an unworldly country minister, and thus adds plausibility to the record of life in a quiet neighborhood over a period of fifty years. One is reminded also of Miss Edgeworth's Thady in *Castle Rackrent*, for the Rev. Mr. Balwhidder does not grasp much of the true import of what he chronicles; but his kindly interest in his parishioners supplies the necessary unity for the book, and his seriousness enhances the humor of the comic episodes. There is no central plot, but an illusion of real life emerges from the jumble of unconnected events. This is the first English novel that takes a whole community as its subject, rather than an individual or a single family. In fact, Galt remarked later that "to myself it has ever been a kind of treatise on the history of society in the West of Scotland during the reign of King George the Third; and when it was written, I had no idea it would ever have been received as a novel."

Having found that his readers regarded him as a novelist, Galt went on to write books which retained the realistic and humorous Scottish atmosphere but added a firmer structure of action. His next significant book, *The Provost* (1822), set out "to be a companion to *The Annals of the Parish*" by showing "the progress of improvement" not in a rural district but in a flourishing town. It is presented as the autobiography of a self-made politician whose career supplies the backbone of the plot as he rises to the top of the civic administration. Galt's next two books display his fullest mastery of the art of fiction, and both set up themes that have been used repeatedly by subsequent novelists. In *Sir Andrew Wylie* (1822) an enterprising Scottish lad rises to fame and fortune in London. *The Entail* (1823), Galt's most ambitious attempt to handle a complex plot, covers three generations of a Scottish family which is dominated by determination to enlarge their property. As *The Annals of the Parish* is the first novel centering upon a community, *The Entail* is the first one (except the sketchy *Castle Rackrent*) centering upon the history of a family.

The success of his five works of fiction ought to have convinced Galt that he should continue; but his old ambition for business enterprise reasserted itself. He organized a company for developing the resources of Upper Canada, and spent much of his time in the colony during the years 1825–29. He founded two towns and did other valuable pioneer work, but he lacked administrative ability and failed to obtain financial backing. When he resigned as secretary of the Canada Company in 1829, he was a disillusioned and impoverished man. His last two novels of any importance, *Laurie Todd* (1830) and *Bogle Corbet* (1831), deal with his Canadian experiences.

Next to Galt, the Scottish novelist who made the best use of local color was Sir Walter Scott's son-in-law, John Gibson Lockhart, a brilliant, sardonic journalist. His two short novels are as grimly tragic as Galt's are sunnily happy. *Some Passages in the Life of Adam Blair* (1822) tells of a Calvinist minister convicted of adultery, and *The History of Matthew Wald* (1824) is the autobiography of a weakling, written long after he has brought disaster on his friends and temporary insanity on himself. As psychopathic studies they were preceded only by Godwin's novels. In the same year as *Matthew Wald* came a still more horrific novel on a similar theme, written by James Hogg, a friend of Lockhart and Scott, *The Private Memoirs and Confessions of a Justified Sinner*, an amazing *tour de force*, in which a fanatical Calvinist reveals the internal conflicts that accompanied his life of hatred and murder.

Soon after Galt and Lockhart and Miss Ferrier developed their subtypes of the local-color novel in Scotland, other writers attempted the same thing in Ireland. Departing both from Miss Edgeworth's upper-class comedy and from Miss Owenson's strident nationalism, the brothers Michael and John Banim decided to collaborate in a series of stories that would depict Irish life as truthfully as the Waverley novels depicted Scotland. Borrowing from Scott's *Tales of My Landlord* the device of a unifying frame and title, they issued the *Tales of the O'Hara Family* in three series, 1825–29. They also wrote a number of longer stories. Of peasant origin, the brothers were determined to show the life and sufferings of the Catholic country-people; but they laid on the Irish scenery and customs too lavishly, and tried to command attention with violent melodrama. Besides, the bitterness of their propaganda distorted the emphasis. Similar subjects were used by Gerald Griffin in his three series of *Tales of the Munster Festivals* (1827–32) and in one powerful tragic novel, *The Collegians* (1828). Slightly later came a more gifted writer, William Carleton, who had struggled upward from rural poverty with greater difficulty than the Banims, and who depicted what he knew best in *Traits and Stories of the Irish Peasantry* (1830–33). All these authors were at their best in shorter tales; their full-length novels show defects in structure and plausibility. The main significance of the Irish group is that for the first time fiction was being centered in the life of the peasantry as known at first hand.

Life in England seemed so ordinary in contrast with the odd habits of the Scottish and the Irish that no English author at that time consciously devoted himself to local color. Something not unlike Galt's *Annals of the Parish*, however, can be seen in *Our Village*, by Mary Russell Mitford, who thought that her claim to literary fame would rest in her verse dramas. The series of sketches that she contributed to the *Lady's Magazine* and collected in five volumes (1824–32) consisted of unpretentious observations of country life, with only occasional moments when anything happens. *Our Village* reads like the background of a Jane Austen novel, without sustained characterization or plot; but the unhurried naturalness produces a pleasant illusion of reality, and the book helped to prove that a work of fiction could be enjoyable for that reason alone.

The trend toward local color had emerged from the novels written by Scott before 1820. When he went on, after that date, to yet greater popularity with his historical romances, it was inevitable that other authors should soon imitate him. Some of those already mentioned tried their hands at the new method. Lockhart's first novel was *Valerius* (1821), an unsuccessful attempt to recreate the period of the Roman occupation of Britain. Galt paused in the midst of his series of humorous books to publish four historical romances between 1823 and 1830. The Banims and Carleton chose historical themes for several of their longer novels. Maturin brought out an immensely long example, *The Albigenses* (1824). Fifty-year-old Horace Smith, a wealthy stockbroker who had made his literary reputation with verse parodies in 1812, wrote a competent historical novel, *Brambletye*

House (1826), and followed it with some twenty others. But the most remarkable symptom of the new tendency was that Peacock deserted his satirical dialogues in favor of two historical stories. They were short, of course, and predominantly comic; but the author was not ridiculing the vogue of historical romance so much as showing that human behavior was laughable in the past as much as in the present. His first, *Maid Marian* (1822), has a specific link with *Ivanhoe* by dealing with Robin Hood and his outlaw band. The other was *The Misfortunes of Elphin* (1829), based on medieval Welsh legends and displaying greater depth of irony and brilliance of style than Peacock had previously shown. The two books have a genuinely romantic flavor, and moreover they seem in some ways truer to life than the laboriously documented works of the serious authors.

Though the school of Scott commanded such widespread attention throughout the twenties, there was an equally active movement in fiction that took its leadership from the other eminently popular author, Lord Byron. Indeed, Byron's own last and greatest poem, *Don Juan*, was essentially in the central tradition of the English novel, with its satirical realism, its picaresque series of adventures, and its complex panorama of contemporary society. Even the digressive comments are in the manner of Fielding. One cannot help thinking that if Byron had lived longer he might have followed Scott in shifting from verse to prose, and could have become the great realistic novelist of the early Victorian era. At any rate, it is further evidence of the resurgence of the novel that Byron had no important poetic imitators; his chief disciples expressed themselves in prose fiction.

In the use of picturesque Near Eastern material, the only noteworthy successor to Byron is James Justinian Morier, whose first novel, *The Adventures of Hajji Baba of Ispahan*, appeared in 1824. Born in Smyrna, the son of a British consul, Morier served in the diplomatic corps in Egypt and Persia and wrote two books about his travels before turning to fiction. His book mingled memories of *The Arabian Nights* with broadly comic realism derived from his own experience. The Persian ambassador in London officially protested that it gave an unfavorable impression of his country. In the picaresque manner of *Gil Blas* it records the exploits of a shrewd barber who gets involved in many kinds of roguery. A less successful sequel was *The Adventures of Hajji Baba in England* (1828).

Closer to the main current of fiction were the novelists who identified themselves with another side of Byron's self-portrayal — the cynical aristocrat who mingles in fashionable society while defying conventional standards of behavior. Lady Caroline Lamb's *Glenarvon* had pointed the way, but ten years elapsed before the "fashionable novel" suddenly came into vogue. The man who launched it was Theodore Hook, who had been a schoolmate of Byron at Harrow and later was a leader of the "Regency wits," famous for his epigrams, his hoaxes, his ability to improvise comic songs while accompanying himself on the piano. He had thus become a celebrity before he began to write books. As editor of *John Bull*, a political weekly, he sprayed scurrilous propaganda against the Whigs. Then in 1824 he published a collection of four novelettes, *Sayings and Doings, a Series of Sketches from Life*, which was followed by a second series the next year, and a third in 1828. The general title was derived from an artificial device of making each story illustrate a familiar proverb; but the didactic implication was less obvious than the author's intimate acquaintance with the sparkling life of London drawing rooms. Hook wrote hastily and carelessly, using trite melodramatic plots and stereotyped central characters. But his worldly manner and lively comedy (sometimes slipping into farce) produced an effect of masculine aplomb unlike the propriety of Miss Edgeworth and other ladies who had depicted aristocratic life.

Immediately after Hook came two gentlemen who gave the fashionable novel its intellectual pretensions. In 1825 Colburn the publisher used all his devices of publicity to launch an anonymous novel, *Tremaine, or The Man of Refinement*, suggesting that it was the work of some prominent public figure. Actually the author was Robert Plumer Ward, a successful lawyer and former Member of Parliament, who had written treatises on jurisprudence and international policy before turning to fiction at the age of sixty. Shocked by the frivolity of recent novels, he tried to set a good example by going back to the serious style of the eighteenth century. Not only the subtitle but the whole outlook of the book recalls Mackenzie's *Man of Feeling*. The hero is morally so scrupulous that he has found all modern girls too indelicate to be worth marrying. Disillusioned with travel, politics, and society, he withdraws to his country estate to devote himself to study; but a saintly clergyman and his equally earnest daughter convert him to orthodox religion and matrimony. It is paradoxical that this novel, so reactionary both in opinions and in style, should have set a new literary fashion among sophisticated people. A modern reader finds the interminable debates on abstract ethical problems unbearably tedious. It is a prolonged and humorless counterpart of Peacock's concise and witty *Headlong Hall*. But Ward was obviously sincere, and as obviously a scholar and a gentleman. The upper class felt that it had acquired a dignified literary spokesman.

Ward's success was duplicated the next year by a younger man of similar social background, Thomas Henry Lister. His book, *Granby*, was more frivolous than Ward's, being chiefly a disjointed chronicle of balls, operas, ballets, gambling parties, and other fashionable pastimes, with recognizable portraits of social celebrities such as Lady Caroline Lamb. The sprightly wit of the dialogue is consistent with the prevailing tone of contempt for bourgeois stuffiness and provincial naïveté.

Both Ward and Lister promptly produced second novels. Ward's *De Vere, or The Man of Independence*, has a political theme, telling how a rich young idealist adjusts himself to a career in Parliament. Traits of the best-known party leaders were recognizable in some of the characters. Both of Ward's books, in spite of his ponderous manner, did something unusual in fiction by undertaking a reasoned analysis of social ideas. Lister's second novel, *Herbert Lacy* (1828), and his third, *Arlington* (1832), elaborated his first picture of smart society. Though neither author had much creative talent, each contributed an ingredient to the new formula for the fashionable novel, Ward's contribution being good taste, Lister's the witty sneer.

Within two years after *Tremaine* appeared, the genre had taken such definite form that William Hazlitt ridiculed "the dandy school" in the *Examiner*. The first nobleman to participate was the Earl of Mulgrave (later Marquess of Normanby), with *Matilda* (1825), followed by *Yes and No* (1827) and several others. Equally well born was Lady Charlotte Bury, daughter of a duke; she had seen court life as a Lady-in-Waiting to the Princess of Wales, and had published several sentimental stories before finding success at fifty-three with her first fashionable novels, *Flirtation* and *A Marriage in High Life*, both in 1828. Another lady of good family, Marianne Spencer-Stanhope, published *Almack's* (1826), naming it for the exclusive assembly rooms where fashionable balls were held; and this book was so popular that another writer, Charles White, traded upon its title in *Almack's Revisited* (1828).

These "silver-fork novels," as they were nicknamed, were not of high literary merit, but they did something toward the restoration of realism by treating a peculiar segment of contemporary life with superficial verisimilitude. Heinrich Heine, visiting England in 1828, observed sourly that

> The London presses are abundantly employed with fashionable writings, with novels that move in the glittering sphere of "high life" or reflect it, as, for instance, *Almack's, Vivian Grey, Tremaine, The Guards, Flirtation*, which latter novel would be the best example for the whole species, for its flirtation with foreign manners and phrases, its coarse refinement, ponderous lightness, sour sweetness, elegant rudeness, in short for the whole disagreeable conduct of those wooden butterflies that flutter in the salons of the West End of London.

The books are monotonous in theme because the conditions that they depicted were rigidly standardized, and they had little depth of characterization because the dominant trait of their characters was an artificial pose that concealed natural behavior. They are of value chiefly as social history, for their meticulous record of dress, food, etiquette, and conversation in fashionable circles under George IV. And they have a further significance as providing the literary debut of two men who later rose to eminence both in fiction-writing and in public life.

One of these, Benjamin Disraeli, was a brilliant, ambitious youth whose Spanish-Jewish family had moved from Italy to England eighty years earlier. His father, Isaac, was an amateur literary historian who had written several mediocre novels and had become acquainted with Byron and other authors. Fiercely determined to obtain money and fame as quickly as possible, young Benjamin tried speculation in newspaper publishing and the stock market, and adopted the role of a dandy; and when dandyism found its voice in the fashionable novels he saw his opportunity to turn his literary flair to account. He modeled his first book on *Tremaine* but gave it a youthful swagger that changed its whole tone. *Vivian Grey* was written before the author reached his twenty-first birthday and was published anonymously by Colburn in 1826, with the usual fanfare about the eminence of its mysterious author and the identity of its characters with current notables. At first these ruses brought wide attention, but there was an angry reaction when the truth leaked out that the author was not an ex-cabinet minister but a Jewish boy of twenty-two. Nevertheless, he completed the story with a second part in 1827.

The precocious, epigrammatic hero is unquestionably an idealized self-portrait. The first part deals with Vivian Grey's meteoric career in politics and his organizing of a new faction to compete with the old parties. The second part is less effective, ranging from serious philosophizing to melodrama. A jealous woman wrecks Grey's political movement, and after killing a former supporter in a duel he goes on a long tour through Germany (as Disraeli had recently done), with disjointed adventures in the "Childe Harold" tradition. Grey's accidental death in an avalanche has no justification except the need of bringing the book to an end. In fact, we are left in some doubt as to whether he was actually killed or not.

As an artistic work of fiction *Vivian Grey* is a failure because it tries to do too many different things. When a beautiful girl dies from the shock of the hero's proposal of marriage, we are carried back to the excessive sensibility of Mackenzie's *Man of Feeling;* in Vivian's debates about the theory of government with the prime minister of a German state, we are reminded of Ward's *Tremaine;* as a record of a young man's education through experience, the story is modeled on Goethe's *Wilhelm Meister.* The book's validity for modern readers is in its portrayal of the hero's impudent self-assurance and his lust for power through political manipulation. The rest is derivative, but this is Disraeli himself.

Close on Disraeli's heels came Edward Lytton Bulwer, one year older and equally ambitious. Proud of his descent from ancient families, he imitated Byron in early sentimental poems and love affairs. As soon as he left Cambridge and made the grand tour he established himself among the London dandies and gained a reputation for immorality with a brief epistolary novel, *Falkland* (1827), which was in the old vein of sensibility.

In his first full-length book, *Pelham, or The Adventures of a Gentleman* (1828), he aligned himself with the fashionable novel. It included a murder mystery borrowed from *Caleb Williams* and some macabre touches reminiscent of Mrs. Radcliffe; but it won its popularity by modifying the Satanic type of Byron's heroes into that of a worldly young man who combines serious social ideas with his cynicism, and intellect with his foppery. The witty and polished Henry Pelham is contrasted with Richard Glanville, whose defiance of moral principles has led him into crime. Bulwer later boasted that the book helped "to put an end to the Satanic mania, — to turn the thoughts and ambitions of young gentlemen without neckcloths, and young clerks who were sallow, from playing the Corsair, and boasting that they were villains." Its direct effect is proved by one ridiculous example. Pelham's mother happened to remark to him, "You look best in black, which is a great compliment, for people must be very distinguished in appearance to do so." Immediately the wearing of colored coats went out of style, and black remained the only acceptable color in men's formal attire for more than a century.

In spite of affectations and incoherencies, *Pelham*, like *Vivian Grey*, was a phenomenon of permanent significance. Both books are *Bildungsromane* — studies of a young man's coming to grips with reality — but with the English spirit of compromise and humorous common sense replacing Goethe's romantic intensity. The vogue of these two books gave general currency to a special type of fiction that may be termed the intellectual novel. It is primarily interested in ideas, and differs from the propaganda novel in having no particular crusade. The author of an intellectual novel is not trying to win the reader's adherence to a cause by playing upon his sympathy. Instead he is trying to arouse the reader to think independently upon matters of lasting importance. To achieve such a difficult result, shock treatments are requisite. Satire, scandal, and flouting of convention are justified as means to this end. Sterne was a forerunner of the intellectual novel in the eighteenth century, and Peacock its first practitioner in the nineteenth. But the brash impudence of Disraeli and Bulwer was needed to make it palatable to casual readers.

Apart from some of Scott's, none of the novels written between 1820 and 1830 are first-rate. Nevertheless the decade was crucial in the development of the novel. Financial profit and social acceptability now combined to make fiction-writing so attractive that a wide variety of people were drawn into the practice of it. Elderly professional and business men like Plumer Ward and Horace Smith, noblemen like Lord Mulgrave, ambitious young gentlemen like Disraeli and Bulwer, journalists like Egan and Hook, ladies of rank and fashion, all tried their hand. The apparent ease of composing novels and the lack of critical standards encouraged careless, unorganized work; but these same conditions had a certain value in allowing free scope for experimentation.

Even the preferable length for a novel was undecided. Some of the most original work of the period was in the middle length, thirty thousand to fifty thousand words. In this class are the tales by the Banims and Griffin, the *Saying and Doings* of Hook, the satires of Peacock, and Bulwer's *Falkland*. By 1830, however, a larger size became obligatory. Hook in that year published *Maxwell*, a full-length novel, and never went back to the novelette. Similarly the Irish folk-authors gave up their series of tales in favor of three-volume works. Thereafter, fiction of intermediate length, deprived of opportunity for publication, had little chance of survival.

Techniques of fiction were affected also by the increase in serial publication. A new type of popular magazine was coming into existence by 1820, and editors found that the inclusion of a serial story helped to attract subscribers. Hence novelists were stimulated to write fiction with strongly marked characters and lively episodes, so that readers' interest could easily be revived at monthly intervals. As the first installment usually appeared before the rest of the story was written, the author concerned himself more with the effectiveness of the separate units than with any over-all structural plan.

Fundamentally, however, the revitalization of the novel was due to the ebbing of the tide of romanticism. A quarter-century of great poetry and personal essays had absorbed the pressure of emotional turmoil, imaginative visions, and introspective egotism which could not adjust itself to the pedestrian tempo of the novel. After the Congress of Vienna in 1816, the era of political upheaval came to a halt, and the average person welcomed a reversion to normal settled conditions. Relieved from many years of wartime emergency, the British public enjoyed indulging in frivolous pastimes and admired its social leaders for doing likewise. A half-century of industrialism had shifted the balance of power into the hands of the practical, unexcitable bourgeoisie. These circumstances promoted the precise observation of external detail, the dispassionate examination of behavior and ideas, and the enjoyment of humor and satire, which all find their best medium in prose fiction.

In fact, fictional methods gained such pre-eminence that some writers applied them to material that was not naturally amenable to such handling. The dividing line between the novel and other types of prose was for a while obscured. Some of the books already mentioned in this chapter are close to the boundary. Galt thought that his *Annals of the Parish* ought to be classified as social history. Ward and Peacock were discussing political and ethical problems. The fashionable novels were not far removed from gossip-column journalism. It is not surprising that at the same period there is a body of what may be called "semi-fiction," lying outside any workable definition of the novel and yet borrowing many of its methods. A notable example is the series of "Noctes Ambrosianae" which appeared in *Blackwood's Magazine* between 1819 and 1835. The editor, John Wilson, and several of his regular contributors collaborated in this, creating fictitious names and personalities for themselves and using dialogue and narrative as a framework for comments on current literature, political events, and social customs. Readers of the magazine acquired a feeling of personal friendship with Christopher North, Ensign O'Doherty, Timothy Tickler, and the other convivial souls who held forth so humorously in the private room of Ambrose's tavern. In the same category fall Walter Savage Landor's *Imaginary Conversations*, published at intervals from 1824 to 1829; in these Landor used the dialogue form and fictitious episodes to convey his interpretation of historical celebrities and forces. Robert Southey employed fictitious dialogue for the same purpose in his *Colloquies* (1829) and wrote a sort of plotless fiction in *The Doctor* (1834–47), a vast accumulation of opinions and anecdotes, containing, as Southey said, "a little of Rabelais, but not much; more of Tristram Shandy, somewhat of Burton, and perhaps more of Montaigne." The most remarkable example of semi-fiction was Carlyle's *Sartor Resartus*, started in 1830 and published serially in 1833. Though primarily a crypto-autobiography and an exposition of metaphysical philosophy, it was given the form of a plotless novel, with fictitious characters and German local color. This and some of the other semi-fiction had higher literary merit than the novels published during the same years, and probably helped to bring distinction of style and complexity of thought into the major novels that were soon to follow.

 **I X**

Humor and Melodrama

(1830 – 1845)

A DECADE OF EXPANSION and experiment ended in 1830. By that
date the less effective varieties of fiction were fading out, leaving certain recognizable types of method and subject matter to
serve as models. A competent writer could choose whichever
kind of novel suited him best and could feel reasonably sure of
an income if he continued to produce new works at regular intervals. This does not mean, however, that the men and women
with the best talent for fiction were intuitively certain of their
vocation. On the contrary, almost all the good novelists began
with other kinds of writing, or in callings unconnected with
authorship, and wandered into fiction by devious routes.

In spite of the experimentation during the twenties, there
remained several important fields for novelists to invade. We
can now see that the two most tremendous historical occurrences
of the preceding half-century were the Napoleonic Wars and the
Industrial Revolution, but neither of these had been touched in
fiction. They were so vast and so complex that the contemporary
writers lacked perspective for observing them. Jane Austen vir-

tually ignored the great war that was going on all the time she was writing, even though her brothers were on active service; and all the other authors of fiction were equally oblivious. Though Scott wrote a biography of Napoleon, he did not think of composing a romance on those most crucial years of European history. The novelists at home in Britain did not know enough about the war to deal with it; the fighting men had neither the leisure nor the training to do so.

Not until ten years after the war ended did a veteran put his experiences into fiction. Then George Robert Gleig wrote *The Subaltern* (1825), which closely followed his own military career. As a young officer he had been wounded three times in the Peninsular campaign and three more times in America in 1814. After leaving the service he had completed his university education and become a clergyman. A similar novel is *The Youth and Manhood of Cyril Thornton* (1827), by Thomas Hamilton, who also had been wounded in Spain. This was Captain Hamilton's only work of fiction, but Gleig went on with a number of others during the next twenty years.

These first narrators of army life in fiction were soon overshadowed by a more gifted writer who dealt with the navy. Frederick Marryat had started as a midshipman at the age of fourteen, taken part in fifty engagements, been wounded three times, risen to the rank of captain, and been decorated for his services. His blunt criticism of naval policy retarded his further promotion, and so he began to look for an alternative career. In 1829 he published *Frank Mildmay, or The Naval Officer*, and he followed it the next year with *The King's Own*. These were successful enough to encourage him to retire on a pension, at the age of thirty-eight, and devote himself to authorship. During the next seven years he wrote all his best works, notably *Peter Simple* (1834), *Jacob Faithful* (1834), *Japhet in Search of a Father* (1836), *Mr. Midshipman Easy* (1836), and *Snarley-Yow, or The Dog Fiend* (1837).

Captain Marryat enjoyed the advantage of being able to express himself in his novels without restraint. Twenty-five years of naval service in war and peace had given him a huge fund of anecdotes, character types, and recollections of foreign ports. He wrote a vigorous, unpretentious prose and diversified the dangerous adventures with broad comedy, often of the slapstick variety. His literary ancestor was Smollett, whom he followed both in his callous narrating of cruelty and degradation and violent death and in his characterization by humours. His young heroes are naïve, plucky, and incorrigibly mischievous, with a heartless addiction to practical jokes. As a concession to sentimental readers he usually includes a conventional love story, but it is kept in the background, and his heroines do not come to life. His innate conservatism dictates the satire on egalitarian doctrines which sometimes emerges in *Mr. Midshipman Easy*, as Jack learns by hard experience the advantages of inequality and the absurdity of his father's democratic notions; yet occasionally one can glimpse a trace of sympathy toward the common seamen for the primitive conditions of the forecastle and the tyranny of the officers. Marryat's patriotic enthusiasm helped to build up the tradition that the English navy was the world's best fighting service, in which the toughness of all ranks necessarily entailed brutality.

Though devoid of technical dexterity, Marryat was endowed with the essential gift of always being able to tell an exciting story. Men of action enjoyed his books because they recognized the truth of his material, and landlubbers were equally fascinated because they felt that they were sharing a new kind of experience. It was typical of the interest in his stories that when *Japhet* was coming out serially an American ship stopped a British merchantman in mid-ocean and ran up a flag-signal to ask, "Has Japhet found his father yet?" By 1836, however, Marryat's supply of naval reminiscences was running low. *Japhet* is a picaresque story that takes place ashore, and *Snarley-Yow* (which some critics consider his best novel) uses a historical background and mingles Gothic grotesquerie with the farce. Already his success had brought a school of imitators who grasped the opportunity of making a profit from their seafaring experiences. These included Michael Scott (*Tom Cringle's Log, The Cruise of "The Midge"*), Frederick Chamier (*The Life of a Sailor, Ben Brace, Tom Bowling*), the Hon. Edward Howard (*Rattlin the Reefer, The Old Commodore*), and William J. Neale (*Cavendish, The Port Admiral, The Naval Surgeon*). Throughout the thirties these novels vied in popularity with the historical romances.

Perhaps the most remarkable historical novel of the time was the Rev. George Croly's *Salathiel* (1829), which dealt with the destruction of Jerusalem by the Romans under Titus. Influenced by Maturin, Croly used the theme of the Wandering Jew, and the book has a kind of gloomy power through the sheer magnitude of devastation and dread. This, however, was a belated specimen of the Gothic mode. A more typical historical novelist was George Payne Rainsford James, who reduced Scott's technique to a simple formula. His grandfather, a physician who made a fortune through a patent medicine, was a friend of Dr. Johnson and Goldsmith, and G.P.R. James in his boyhood met and admired Byron. As a young man-about-town and dilettante writer he began a historical novel; and later, when the unfinished manuscript was shown to Scott, the master advised James to continue. This book, *Richelieu*, came out in 1829, and thereafter James was a prolific professional, bringing out two or three stereotyped novels every year. He estimated his normal output as five pages an hour, four hours a day. A few of his titles will suffice to indicate how thoroughly he covered European history: *Darnley, or The Field of the Cloth of Gold; Philip Augustus, or The Brothers in Arms; Henry Masterton, or The Adventures of a Young Cavalier; Mary of Burgundy, or The Revolt of Ghent.*

Slightly younger than James was William Harrison Ainsworth, later to become his greatest rival in historical fiction. At the age of sixteen, when he was beginning law studies in Manchester, Ainsworth started writing copiously for magazines; and three years later he moved to London, supposedly to complete his law course but mainly to fling himself into literary and fashionable life. Handsome and self-assured, he dressed in the extreme style of the dandies, and in 1826, when he was twenty-one, he published a historical romance, *Sir John Chiverton*, written in collaboration with a friend. It led Scott to remark that he was becoming "hard pressed by these imitators, who must put the thing out of fashion at last." In spite of this successful debut, Ainworth went into the business of publishing and did not find time to write another novel for eight years. By then, new forces were affecting historical fiction.

For one thing, the popularity of Scott on the Continent had incited several able authors to write in this genre. The most important were Honoré de Balzac, with *Les Chouans* (1829) and

La Peau de chagrin (1831), and Victor Hugo, with *Notre Dame de Paris* (1831). These showed greater dramatic power and intellectual breadth than the English imitators of Scott possessed. And among English authors, Disraeli and Bulwer were breaking away from the fashionable novel and turning their restless imaginations in directions that affected historical fiction.

The heyday of the fashionable novel was brief. Its vogue was of the sudden, intense sort that collapses as quickly as it flares up, and the subject matter was so narrow that later books seemed monotonous echoes of previous ones. Besides, the material was highly topical, and the social milieu underwent a change after the death of George IV in 1830 and the passage of the First Reform Bill in 1832. The upper class lost the irresponsible gaiety that gave a kind of flippant charm to the silver-fork novels. Politics became a serious business, and intelligent people could no longer ignore the social and economic problems raised by the new industrialism. Carlyle preached the funeral sermon of the fashionable novel in his chapter on "The Dandiacal Body" in *Sartor Resartus*.

The writing of fashionable novels did not cease, but it fell into the hands of third-rate women authors who endlessly repeated the old effects. Lady Charlotte Bury continued all through the thirties, and was joined by the Countess of Blessington, who ground out novels in an effort to earn the money necessary for keeping up her London salon. A woman who wrote with more wit and technical skill, to compensate for her lack of a title, was Mrs. Caroline Frances Gore, who, after three mediocre historical novels, turned to fashionable fiction with *Women as They Are, or Manners of the Day* (1830), and poured forth a stream of similar books for the next thirty years, the best of them being *Cecil, or The Adventures of a Coxcomb* and its sequel, *Cecil, a Peer* (both 1841).

Bulwer and Disraeli were too clever to remain identified with this sort of tinsel. But in departing from it they could not decide where to go. Their impulse to write satirical fiction was deflected by other forces — the assumption that the plot of a novel needed mystery and violent action, the romantic compulsion toward self-revelation, and the desire to propagate social doctrines. Untouched by such irrelevancies, Peacock remained as the sole purveyor of the novel of pure intellect. In 1831 he published *Crotchet Castle,* which used the theme and technique of his three earliest books with a mellower maturity of spirit and a slight shifting of his aim away from literary targets and toward the new economic and educational theories. But after this sally against slogan-mongers, Peacock — now a high official in the East India Company — withdrew from the unequal conflict and did not write another novel until thirty years later.

Bulwer's novels after *Pelham* reveal desperate experimentation with every type of fiction he could think of. With an extravagant wife and an expensive London house to maintain, he was driving his pen to the limit. *The Disowned* (1828) was written too hastily and suffered from inflated style and confused melodramatic action. The fashionable aristocrats, with their lofty Norman names and artificial manners, are still there; but instead of satirizing them, as in *Pelham,* Bulwer takes them seriously and mingles them with a romantic sojourn among the gypsies (based an an episode of his own boyhood). The setting was the days of Dr. Johnson; and in his next novel, *Devereux,* he moved back to the first half of the eighteenth century and introduced all the literary and social celebrities of that previous era of wit and polish. His purpose, he said, was "to portray a man flourishing in the last century, with the train of mind and sentiment peculiar to the present."

In both books Bulwer was trying to combine the fashionable novel with the historical, and in the second he was trying also to work out his political philosophy. For his next novel he undertook something entirely different. The aged Godwin, whom he admired, suggested that he borrow from *The Beggar's Opera* the device of satirizing political leaders under the guise of criminals. Bulwer was also anxious to attack the harshness of English justice, and he combined these two purposes in *Paul Clifford* (1830), the story of a young highwayman and his gang. The publisher's advertising made much of the satiric identification of the underworld characters with the king and his chief ministers; but the public enjoyed the book as a thrilling story of crime, which sounded convincing because the author had studied actual criminal records, and inserted gobbets of thieves' jargon.

Shortly afterwards Bulwer was elected to Parliament, and also undertook to edit a popular magazine; but there was no interruption in his output of fiction. *Eugene Aram* (1832) dealt with a famous murder case of the mid-eighteenth century. It is reminiscent of *Caleb Williams* in depicting the mental strain of an undetected murderer.

Though Bulwer's two crime stories delighted the public as a novelty, they actually had a long ancestry, starting with the rogue tales of the Renaissance and coming down through Defoe and even Scott, who was always inclined to be sympathetic toward lawbreakers, whether the noble outlaw Robin Hood or the smugglers and gypsies of recent Scotland. In the eighteenth century the favorite reading matter of the semi-literate class was the *Newgate Calendar*, sensational reports of the careers and executions of criminals, and this was revived in the *New Newgate Calendar* (1824–26). The adventures of Egan's Tom and Jerry helped to cast a literary glamour over lawlessness, and on a higher level there were the Byronic heroes with their contempt for social conformity. Bulwer merely gave these elements a fresh literary pretension with his rhetorical style, his historical research, and an admixture of Gothic gloom.

It is surprising, therefore, that his two novels incurred violent attack. In part, the reason was personal dislike for Bulwer among the professional writers, who were annoyed because this elegant young gentleman, with his dandified clothes and condescending manner, had won quick success in their calling; and his earlier books were easy to ridicule for their egotistical digressions and florid style. But the gravity of the accusations against *Paul Clifford* and *Eugene Aram* showed more than mere spite. The books were charged with portraying criminals sympathetically and thus encouraging crime. The indication is not merely that a new note of social consciousness was coming into book reviewing but also that the critics recognized the increasing influence of fiction upon public attitudes.

The attacks may account for Bulwer's attempt to conceal his authorship of his next novel, *Godolphin* (1833), which he did not acknowledge until seven years later. It was a return to the subject matter of *Pelham*, but showed greater maturity in its analysis of society and politics, and a strong interest in the occult. His next book, which proved to be his most lastingly famous, was *The Last Days of Pompeii*, a subject that occurred to him during a tour of Italy. It was regarded as a powerful tragedy and an impressive reconstruction of ancient history. This was followed by another historical novel that grew out of his Italian travels, *Rienzi* (1835), dealing with fourteenth-century Rome.

Disraeli, meanwhile, suffering from ill health and not being under such financial pressure as Bulwer, was more deliberate in following *Vivian Grey* with other novels. *The Young Duke* (1831) was a *reductio ad absurdum* of the fashionable novel, with a lavish display of luxurious furnishings and dissipated noblemen, spiced with cynical asides in the manner of *Don Juan*. "The Young Duke!" snorted the author's father. "What does Ben know of dukes?" Indeed the atmosphere sometimes seems that of *The Arabian Nights* rather than of modern England; and yet in spite of all its exaggeration, the book contains perceptive comments on political theories and issues. The happy ending comes when the hero, reformed by the love of an intelligent girl, assumes his duties in the House of Lords and makes an eloquent speech in favor of a progressive measure. Like Bulwer in *Devereux*, Disraeli was trying to shape a program of action for his own career by putting it in the form of fiction so that he could see it clearly.

His profits from *The Young Duke* enabled him to make a tour of the Near East, in the approved Childe Harold manner, and while there he wrote *Contarini Fleming, a Psychological Romance* (1832), in which the influence of Byron was pre-eminent. In tracing "the development and formation of the poetic character" Disraeli followed the model of *Wilhelm Meister*, and again the autobiographical element was strong. Written in the first person, it is an intimate transcript of Disraeli's inmost emotions and aspirations, but passionate where *Vivian Grey* had been cynical. The hero's father is a Scandinavian statesman of German parentage and his mother is Italian. This rootlessness renders Contarini moody and defiant. He gets into trouble through publishing a novel satirizing the court; he runs away from college to become leader of a band of brigands; he loves and loses an Italian cousin with whom he shares telepathic communication; and he wanders gloomily about the East before finally deciding to enter politics.

Disraeli used the Levantine setting also for *The Wondrous Tale of Alroy*, a historical romance of the twelfth century. In his previous books he had idealized several facets of his personality — the cynical dandy, the political innovator, the ambitious author; here he undertook to glorify his racial origin by dealing with a heroic Jewish prince leading a revolt against the Moslems.

Disraeli's prose had been becoming more ornate in each novel, and parts of *Alroy* lapsed into irregular meter and rhyme. In *Henrietta Temple* (1836), however, he wrote a more conventional book, confining himself to an ardent love story based on his own affair with Lady Sykes. This was followed by *Venetia* (1837), chiefly interesting as a fictional interpretation of the personalities of Byron and Shelley. In that year he achieved the first major step in his public career by being elected to Parliament, and withdrew from authorship for seven years.

The early novels of Bulwer and Disraeli are readable as the work of dynamic, versatile young men trying to use fiction for objectivizing their inner urges and their intellectual probings. In contrast, the work of less aspiring authors often has less vitality, but it is apt to be better controlled and to stay closer to the novelist's business of telling an effective story. Ainsworth in 1834 resumed fiction-writing with *Rookwood*, which was influenced by Bulwer's two novels of crime. Like *Paul Clifford*, Ainsworth's leading character is an eighteenth-century highwayman, and his achievements overshadow the other elements of the plot. Ainsworth frankly borrowed the atmosphere of terror from the leading practitioner of Gothic romance:

> I resolved to attempt a story in the bygone style of Mrs. Radcliffe (which had always inexpressible charms for me), substituting an old English squire, an old English manorial residence, and an old English highwayman for the Italian marchese, the castle, and the brigand of the great mistress of Romance.

By interspersing underworld slang culled from handbooks on the subject, Ainsworth invested this antiquated material with an illusion of realism, so that the episode of Dick Turpin's ride to York was widely accepted as a genuine occurrence.

Ainsworth's next novel, *Crichton* (1837), was centered upon a famous Scottish adventurer of the sixteenth century, and was full of cloak-and-sword exploits at the French court. Then came *Jack Sheppard* (1839), dealing with another highwayman, who had first been written about by Defoe. On the strength of these three books Ainsworth established himself as Bulwer's chief rival in melodramatic romance. Indeed, during the later 1830's Bulwer partly relinquished fiction in favor of playwriting, in which he was highly successful. In consequence, his only novels in the five years after *Rienzi* showed neater manipulation of plot and less grandiloquence of style. These were *Ernest Maltravers* (1837) and its sequel, *Alice, or The Mysteries* (1838), wherein sensational action served as a skeleton for studying the modern questing philosopher in Maltravers and the naïve child of nature in Alice Darvil. Bulwer put much of his own experience into the two books, and there is extensive discussion of such current issues as the condition of the poor and the need for the secret ballot, in which Bulwer was playing an active role in his parliamentary career. The cynical epigrams of *Pelham*, written in the gay Georgian reign, give place to wise (if sometimes obvious) apothegms, ushering in the earnest era of Victoria. In the year of the publication of *Alice*, Bulwer was created a baronet.

In the varied fiction of the early thirties the only common trait is not mastery of technique but exploitation of personal interests and experiences. Perhaps the best illustration of this fortuitous quality is Robert Smith Surtees, who became a novelist through his enthusiasm for a subject that no one else was writing about. The son of a country squire in the north of England, he was educated to be a solicitor; but his consuming interest, like that of his forefathers before him, was fox-hunting. In 1831, when he was twenty-eight, he published a compendium of the legal knowledge needed by horse-dealers, and about the same time he became part owner of the *New Sporting Magazine*. In it he published between 1831 and 1834 a series of anecdotes about a London grocer who wanted to be a fox-hunter. These proved so popular that they were eventually reprinted in book form in 1838, with the title, *The Jaunts and Jollities of that Renowned Sporting Citizen, Mr. John Jorrocks*.

As the title indicates, it consists of separate episodes without unified plot; but the characters of Jorrocks and his friends hold it together. The unselfconscious colloquial style and the boisterous humor, in perfect accord with the subject, make it the antithesis of the turgid rhetoric and worldly wit of the fashionable novels. Not only the technical details of fox-hunting, but all the traditional life of the English countryside, are recorded with easy familiarity. In his way, Surtees was akin to Peacock in his contempt for the vulgar new world of commerce and social experiment. For his direct antecedents, however, we have to go back *via* Pierce Egan to the eighteenth-century fiction of the Smollett school, with its farcical satire and its utter absence of sentiment.

While so many novels were dealing with special departments of life — the navy, fashionable society, politics, fox-hunting — only one author of the early thirties concerned himself with average middle-class conditions. This was Theodore Hook, who, in the midst of journalism and debt and alcoholism and an endless round of noblemen's parties, ground out *The Parson's Daughter* (1833), *Gilbert Gurney* (1836), and *Jack Brag* (1837). There is something irredeemably vulgar in his buffoonery, his sarcastic sneers at human follies and stupidities, his exaggerated type-characters; but there is also something uncomfortably realistic in his detailed picture of the narrow mediocrity of ordinary experiences that other novelists ignored. Heavy eating and drinking, sordid greed for money, petty dishonesty of many sorts, hypocritical catering to rank and power — these are pictured against an accurate topographical background of London. Repetitive and nonselective though he was, Hook helped to bring fiction to terms with real life.

With a score of authors producing competent though aesthetically inadequate books, it might seem that any young man with a talent for fiction would have no difficulty in recognizing his vocation. Yet the master novelist who emerged at this juncture blundered into his first book as accidentally as Richardson and Fielding had done a century before.

The early years of Charles Dickens not only provided material for much of his writing but also shaped his personality. His grandmother, the housekeeper in a nobleman's country mansion, was able to provide her son with enough education for a minor government clerkship. But John Dickens was too impractical and dilatory to rise in the service. When Charles was two years old the family moved from his birthplace, Portsea, a shabby naval station, to London, and three years later they moved again, to Chatham, a shabby dockyard town. As his parents made little effort to provide him with schooling, he got most of his elementary education by precocious reading of old novels, chiefly *Don Quixote, Gil Blas, Tom Jones,* and the works of Smollett. When he was ten, he and his five brothers and sisters were taken to London, where they lived in anxious poverty. The repeated removals must have already given the little boy a sense of insecurity, and before long John Dickens was sent to prison for debt. As was customary, his wife and younger children lived with him in the Marshalsea, but the twelve-year-old Charles was considered old enough to occupy lodgings alone and to earn money by working in a warehouse, where he glued labels on bottles of shoe polish. After a few months John Dickens inherited some money at his mother's death, and was released from prison; but Charles was left at his labor for another month or more before being sent to a cheap school, where he remained until his fifteenth birthday.

With only this sketchy education he became an office boy in a legal firm, supposedly the first step toward eventual qualification as an attorney. His years in the gloomy precincts of the London law courts taught him the stark facts about crime and increased the contempt for the machinery of justice that had already been implanted in him by the illogical law that kept a debtor in prison until he somehow obtained enough money to satisfy his creditors.

John Dickens, meanwhile, had retired from government service and found employment as a newspaper reporter. In the hope of qualifying for this more interesting career, his son taught himself shorthand and supported himself for three years as a court stenographer. During this time he fell in love with a pretty coquette, but she and her family rejected him as socially unacceptable. For a while he was eager to go on the stage, and took lessons in acting; but no manager hired him, and at the age of twenty he became political reporter for a newspaper.

Circumstances had admirably prepared him to be a novelist. He had learned about poverty and hard work through participation, in the early years when his sensitive and imaginative temperament registered every impression indelibly. He had acquired a law clerk's disrespectful familiarity with official processes and a reporter's keen eye and ear for significant details. His practice in acting gave him a sense of dialogue and a realization that every scene needs to be clearly visualized.

Negatively, too, his preparation had been helpful, for his intermittent education had not encumbered him with traditional literary formalities. Instead, at an early age he had steeped himself in some of the best fiction ever written, so that the great novelists were his direct models.

Even with this background, however, to say nothing of his determination to earn money with his pen, he did not think of undertaking to write a novel. His contact with fiction came as a by-product of his reporting, when he began to write brief narrative and descriptive sketches for his newspaper and for popular magazines, using the pen name "Boz." Some of these were short stories, but most were studies of the odd characters he observed in his ramblings through London byways, and word-pictures of taverns, shops, playhouses, police courts, and other city scenes. Their nearest literary antecedents were not in fiction but in the essays of Lamb and Leigh Hunt. In 1836 they were reissued in book form as *Sketches by Boz*. Lamb having recently died, Boz seemed to be Elia's natural successor as the whimsical essayist of the metropolis.

At this juncture a popular humorous artist, Robert Seymour, conceived the idea of an illustrated serial in monthly parts, in the style of *Tom and Jerry*. His plan was to portray a "Nimrod Club" in which town-dwellers would meet with ludicrous misadventures when they attempted shooting, fishing, and other sports. He sold his idea to an enterprising new publishing firm, Chapman & Hall. Merely secondary in the scheme was to be the letterpress narrating the events; and after several professional authors, including Hook, had rejected the contract, it was offered to the unknown Boz, who accepted with alacrity. Barely twenty-four, and on the verge of getting married, he found that the moderate payment would mean a fifty per cent increase in his income. With youthful bumptiousness, however, he insisted on modifying Seymour's plan and allowing himself freedom to avoid monotony by ranging over everything he considered comic in contemporary life. Seymour grudgingly consented, and the first number of *The Posthumous Papers of the Pickwick Club* came out on March 31, 1836.

The uneasy division of creative responsibility lasted only through the second number, at which point the moody Seymour committed suicide. Unwilling to give up the project, the publishers searched for a substitute illustrator, but no established artist would assume the task, and so they had to be content with a twenty-year-old youth, recently out of art school, Hablôt Knight Browne. From that moment Dickens was in full control.

Begun so casually, the opening chapters were awkward and uncertain. The word "Papers" in the title indicated no plan for a continuous plot. The satire on amateur scientists and on parliamentary oratory was feeble enough, and Mr. Pickwick and his friends were no more than type-caricatures of a kind that Hook and other authors could produce at will. Success was so doubtful that Dicken's rate of pay was reduced by almost one-third. But in the fourth number Sam Weller, the impudent cockney handyman, caught the public fancy, and the circulation took a gigantic leap.

The miraculous discovery had occurred, as so often before: the author found himself developing characters that breathed the breath of life and weaving them into a pattern that had depth and meaning. His material was not particularly original. The basic scheme is like that of Surtees' serial, though Mr. Pickwick is more genteel and kindly than the assertive Jorrocks. The background of stagecoaches, inns, and country farmhouses also resembled that of Surtees. The motley crew of rascally lawyers, venal editors, stupid magistrates, irascible militia officers, *et al.* had appeared in comic fiction from Smollett to Hook. But Dickens's treatment is warmer and more tolerant. Even the most minor characters, sketched in a few sentences, take on individuality. The author describes them with such irrepressible gusto that the reader feels affection for them even while laughing at them. The shallow facetiousness of the opening chapters mellowed into a flexible comic style that moves with tireless vitality.

Since each monthly part went to press as soon as it was written, the author could not go back and revise the early chapters to conform with later developments. But perhaps this is just as well, for the reader undergoes a process of deepening comprehension; characters who were first observed merely through their physical features and their external mannerisms are imperceptibly transformed into people with a lifelike mixture of pathos and absurdity, of generous impulses and foolish mistakes. Mr. Pickwick and Sam Weller assume the archetypal roles of Don Quixote and Sancho, the eternal trustful idealist and the eternal disillusioned realist, journeying unscathed through pitfalls of knavery and vice. Pickwick's three comrades (mystic number) cease to be merely an incompetent braggart, a posturing poet, and a flirtatious old bachelor, and become gentlemen of fidelity and dignity. The story is no longer a reporter's panorama of contemporary life in its infinite variety, but an apologue of the discovery of evil by a man who has innocently believed that human beings are innately good and that virtue prevails. Mr. Pickwick is a belated specimen of the eighteenth-century "man of feeling."

Having endowed his characters with life, Dickens became aware that he was in the midst of writing a novel, and therefore that he needed some sort of unifying plot. The earlier episodes had to remain as isolated units, but from the time of Mr. Pickwick's entanglement with Mrs. Bardell there is preparation for a major climax; and alongside it the author introduced secondary threads with conventional love affairs for Winkle and Snodgrass and even for Sam Weller.

One other element that filtered gradually in was social criticism. In the Rev. Mr. Stiggins and in the Eatanswill election, under the surface of genial ridicule, one can perceive Dickens's contempt for evangelical intolerance and for political chicanery. And as soon as Mr. Pickwick becomes involved in the lawsuit that leads him to the Fleet prison, the author is drawn into a crusade against injustice. Mr. Pickwick becomes a veritable (though temporary) martyr in the cause of conscience, and the picture of the imprisoned debtors is disturbingly grim in the midst of so merry a book.

Long before *The Pickwick Papers* had completed their eighteen installments, the circulation reached 40,000, and it seemed as though everyone in England, from street urchins to judges and bishops, were quoting phrases from the story. Groups of people too poor to pay even the monthly shilling would rent a copy and read it aloud. Before he was twenty-five Dickens was being hailed as the greatest novelist since Scott. His payment had been repeatedly increased, and he was besieged with offers from other publishers. While the last numbers were still being written he resigned from the newspaper and committed himself to half-a-dozen literary ventures. He wrote an operetta and a farce and became editor of a new popular magazine, *Bentley's Miscellany*, in which his second novel began to appear serially in February, 1837.

With this story, *Oliver Twist*, Dickens tried to demonstrate that he was not a man of a single style. *Pickwick* had been praised exclusively for its humor; most of *Oliver Twist* is harshly serious. *Pickwick* had ranged widely over English towns and countryside; *Oliver Twist* has its principal setting in the slums of London. *Pickwick* was episodic; *Oliver Twist* has a carefully planned mystery to hold it together. And the social consciousness which had been an intrusion in *Pickwick* is the dominating theme of the new book.

The workhouse scenes in the early chapters, and the later exploitation of Oliver by a gang of pickpockets, were bound up with current controversies over the Poor Laws and the care of abandoned children. Dickens's recollections of his months as a child laborer gave authenticity to what might otherwise have been sentimental propaganda. Similarly, in dealing with the London underworld *Oliver Twist* had affinities with the crime stories of Bulwer and Ainsworth; but Dickens's first-hand observation as court stenographer and reporter resulted in something quite different. There is no glorifying of criminals in the sinister Fagin or the brutal Sikes, though even they acquire a degree of human appeal when Dickens finally enters their minds to reveal how hallucinations and external impressions are mingled under stress of guilty terror.

For his plot Dickens relied on the overworked theme of the missing heir; but he handled it with effective suspense and foreshadowing that disguised the implausible coincidences. He conferred literary validity upon grisly episodes of violence such as he had absorbed from *The Terrific Register*, a penny paper that he had devoured every week as a schoolboy. The conversations are unnatural because of a pretentious style of speech borrowed from the cheap theater, and Oliver's inviolable saintliness is hard to credit; nevertheless, in spite of inflated rhetoric, the later scenes, culminating in the deaths of Nancy, Sikes, and Fagin, generate compelling power. Dickens had discovered that the effect of terror did not have to depend on remote times and places, as in the Gothic tales; it was made all the more gruesome when revealed as existing in the reader's own environment. *Oliver Twist* survives its handicaps of sentimentality and melodrama because it objectivizes a profound emotional state — the solitude felt by an individual who has no place within the framework of society. The dark cellars and garrets, the tottering tenements and hungry river currents, the moments of mob violence, all lend weird vividness to the theme of the social outcast.

Magazine serialization caused this novel to be shorter than *Pickwick,* but for his next story Dickens resumed the larger canvas and more relaxed tempo of monthly parts. Its opening portion developed from the theme of *Oliver Twist.* Having dealt with the plight of unwanted children in workhouses, Dickens turned his attention to the cheap boarding schools where bastards and sons of broken homes could be left to suffer disease and cruelty. As a good reporter, he made a trip to Yorkshire to investigate the conditions for himself.

Nicholas Nickleby differs from both the previous novels in several respects. It is his first to have a conventional young hero and heroine. Indeed, with his usual prodigality he provides two of each, for the separate experiences of Nicholas and his sister, with their respective love stories, are carried along side by side. Both *Pickwick* and *Oliver Twist* had departed from this stereotype of the novel by keeping the young lovers in the background while the central personage was, in one, a fat old retired businessman, and, in the other, a homeless little boy. Nicholas and his sister are inevitably colorless, being normal, well-intentioned young people; and because they have as little knowledge of the world as either Samuel Pickwick or Oliver Twist, they provide the same contrast between the pure in heart and the menacing evil around them, while of course the reader has the comfortable certainty that innocence will triumph.

The mood of the book strikes an average between the extremes represented by the earlier ones. The geographical settings are almost as diversified as in *The Pickwick Papers.* The humor is rich and hearty, but not so persistently farcical as in *Pickwick;* the pathos is sometimes genuinely moving, but never so gloomy and terrifying as in *Oliver Twist.* After Nicholas breaks away from his teaching at Dotheboys Hall he joins a traveling theatrical company, and here Dickens laughs indulgently at his own thwarted ambition to be an actor. Meanwhile, Kate's misadventures as a lady's companion and as a milliner's assistant form a pioneer study of the problems of a girl trying to earn her living honestly.

The chief weakness of *Nicholas Nickleby* is the attempt to

portray the upper class. Dickens had not yet seen much of good society, and Sir Mulberry Hawk and Lord Frederick Verisopht are not much more than standard stage puppets of the wicked baronet and the degenerate aristocrat. Fortunately they play smaller roles than the inexhaustible array of middle- and lower-class characters — the Mantalinis, Miss La Creevy, the Kenwigs family, and dozens of others, including the scatterbrained Mrs. Nickleby, a kindly if unfilial portrait of the author's mother. Dickens enjoys the talk and the antics of these irrelevant individuals so much more than the dastardly intrigues of his villains that he often lets the complicated and implausible plot fade almost out of sight.

By this time he had perfected his individual style, which no other novelist ever rivaled. Often condemned as rhetorical or grotesque, it maintains a lurid vividness, chiefly through perpetual embroidery of simile and metaphor, including a trick of describing inanimate objects in terms of living creatures. In addition to this power of imaginative projection into every scene, his sheer exuberance of creative power, his undisciplined mixture of farce, melodrama, picaresque adventure, and trite moralizing, his mingling of stock types with sharply drawn individuals, are seen in *Nicholas Nickleby* in fullest efflorescence; and while these traits leave it open to critical cavil they make it irresistibly readable. But Dickens was determined not to settle down to a formula, no matter how successful. He was eager to try the experiment of a weekly periodical selling at threepence instead of a serial in monthly parts at a shilling. He named it *Master Humphrey's Clock* and intended it to be a *mélange* of short stories, essays, and so forth, after the model of *The Spectator*. For the introductory framework he injudiciously revived Mr. Pickwick and Sam Weller, in conversation with an old London eccentric who collects miscellaneous manuscripts in his clock-case. The first one was to be a short story entitled *The Old Curiosity Shop;* but as soon as it started it began to take hold of Dickens's imagination. Besides, he found that sales dropped off as soon as the public discovered that this was not another novel.

He therefore abandoned his original scheme and let *The Old Curiosity Shop* develop as it would. Hence, when reprinted in volume form, without the prefatory sketch, it begins with Master Humphrey as an unidentified narrator who soon drops out of the story. The complete novel never acquired much plot structure, and the brevity of weekly installments made the episodes even more scrappy than usual. Nor did it contain any specific attack on social abuses. Like *Oliver Twist* it has a child as the central figure — in this case Little Nell, a young girl so virtuous and so responsible that modern readers find her incredible. The emotional aura surrounding her was transferred from the excessive love that Dickens had felt for his girlish sister-in-law, who had recently died in his arms at the age of seventeen. This lack of objectivity was responsible also for the mawkish sentimentality that affects the language whenever Nell appears, especially in her death scene, where the sentences lapse into meter.

For these reasons *The Old Curiosity Shop* is sometimes termed Dickens's worst novel. And yet it has its own sort of imaginative power. Its realism is not that of literal fact but of poetic insight. The wanderings of Nell and her senile grandfather across England give the picaresque technique a new quality, so that the story becomes a sort of allegory, a *Pilgrim's Progress*, the fullest expression of Dickens's recurrent theme of innocence surviving amid the hideousness of greed and lust. If Nell is represented as a saint, she has her antithesis in the dwarf Quilp, who is positively a devil, grotesque but all the more horrifying because of being half comic, with Sampson and Sally Brass as his auxiliary demons. The charm of the book resides in a sort of idyllic quality, arising not so much from the preponderance of rural scenes as from its presentation of the patient heroism and kindliness of the poor, as represented in the Nubbins family, in the irrepressible Dick Swiveller, and in the illiterate little drudge he befriends.

Though the general title of *Master Humphrey's Clock* had lost its significance, Dickens retained it for his next novel, *Barnaby Rudge*, which was his first venture into historical fiction. He went back to the Gordon Riots of 1780, an anti-Catholic outbreak in London, and produced a story that came closer than before to the Gothic weirdness of Ainsworth's books. The plot, as usual, is the melodramatic one of unidentified parentage, and once more the central character is not a handsome young hero: Dickens went to a dangerous extreme in focusing the story upon a lad who is mentally deranged. Barnaby is a fantastic, pathetic creature, not unlike Madge Wildfire in Scott's *Heart of Midlothian*, which also dealt with urban riots and an attack on a jail. The whole mingling of comic realism and romantic mystery, in fact, is reminiscent of Scott. One of the book's most popular features was Dolly Varden, who can scarcely be called the heroine, as she is so selfish a coquette, but who is a welcome change from the meek heroines of Dickens's previous novels.

England at that time was undergoing an acute political crisis, the collapse of the Chartist movement having been followed by unemployment and strikes. This gave a topical application to the portrayal of unrest and mob violence and parliamentary bungling. The book shows a transition in Dickens from impulsive assaults on individual abuses to anxious assessment of his political philosophy.

Serial publication of *Barnaby Rudge* ended in November, 1841. For five and a half years Dickens's five long novels had been coming out without interruption, sometimes even overlapping. The weekly issues of the last two had kept him under excessive tension. He therefore took a half year's holiday for a tour of the United States, where he was welcomed with enthusiasm and sometimes embarrassing curiosity. On his return to England he wrote an account of his travels, *American Notes,* and then started his sixth novel, *Martin Chuzzlewit.*

Not only by being published in monthly parts, but also in its structure and atmosphere, it resembled *Nicholas Nickleby* so closely that Dickens seemed at last to be running out of new ideas and starting to repeat himself. The humorous characters were as memorable as ever; but the conventional hero, trying to find a career for himself and struggling blindly against mysterious plotting by his own relations, while carrying on an obstacle-strewn wooing of a mild young lady, was Nicholas over again.

The realization of this tendency prompted Dickens midway in the book to enliven it and use his own recent observations by sending his hero to America. His impressions of that country had not been wholly favorable: as an English radical, he had expected the young republic to be an ideal region of liberty and equality, and he was disillusioned by finding that these slogans meant liberty to be unscrupulous in business and equality of bad manners and obtrusiveness. Personally, too, he was embittered by his failure in advocating an international copyright law that would have ensured him some profit from the American printing of his books. Therefore, although he had made warm friends among American authors, he felt impelled to depict in extravagant satire the crudities of American society and the dishonesty of real-estate projects on the frontier. He was fully as ruthless toward the unsavory features of life in his own country; but the American press was outraged, and condemned him for ingratitude and malice.

Artistically the American interlude is questionable in that it breaks in upon the continuity of the action and introduces a group of characters with no relevance to the rest of the book. Being emotionally involved in the situation himself, Dickens was unable to see it in proper perspective, and episodes out of his experience as a visiting celebrity become absurdly improbable when transferred without alteration to an unknown young steerage passenger. These chapters can be justified, however, as contributing to the thematic pattern. The story had been planned as an elaborate study of selfishness, and this finds its epitome in the picture of a whole society that makes a virtue of the aggressive motives of boastfulness, acquisitiveness, and cut-throat competition. Throughout the book the moral theme merges into a more abstract question than Dickens perhaps realized. Selfishness cannot be defined without consideration of what constitutes the self. Therefore the mystery of identity is pervasive. Pecksniff's sleek duplicity, Mrs. Gamp's imaginary alternative ego, Jonas Chuzzlewit's secret murderous sorties, old Martin's pretense of senility, Montague Tigg's transformation into the fraudulent company promoter, Tigg Montague — all exemplify the baffling ambiguity of personality.

The tone of the book is less buoyant than Dickens's previous work. The selfish characters predominate throughout, even Martin being headstrong and opinionated until chastened by hard experience; and the few examples of cheerful unselfishness — Tom and Ruth Pinch and Mark Tapley — are too good to be convincing. There is a hint of a jeer in the comedy, so that even two of Dickens's greatest comic figures, Pecksniff and Mrs. Gamp, are drawn with some asperity as embodiments of smug and heartless egoism.

With this book Dickens emerged from his youthful resilience. He had been able to produce six novels at top speed, in the midst of other activities, because he relied wholly on his fecundity in creating characters, his immense knowledge of English life and scenery, his hilarious comic sense, and his innate narrative skill. These were great gifts, but they could not result in first-rate works of art if he were to remain almost oblivious to technical considerations. He was so far superior to the other novelists writing during these eight years that no competition spurred him to self-criticism. After he passed the age of thirty, however, his exuberance began to flag, and a few rivals appeared in the offing. The result was a three years' interruption, during which he was occupied mainly with journalism; apart from a book of travels in Italy he produced only his short annual Christmas tales, which enhanced his income and popularity but which do not belong to a study of the novel.

Among the new authors who were now enjoying a share of the public favor, the most astonishing was a woman old enough to be Dickens's mother. Mrs. Frances Trollope was only five years younger than Jane Austen, and until she was over fifty she devoted herself wholly to an unsuccessful lawyer-husband and a family of six children. In a fantastic effort to restore their fortunes, the Trollopes in 1827 emigrated to the United States to open a department store in the frontier town of Cincinnati. After four years of futile effort they returned to England, penniless and disillusioned; and Mrs. Trollope set out to earn a living by her pen. Her first book, *The Domestic Manners of the Americans*, was widely read for its outspoken condemnation of the uncouth *mores* of the new world. Three mediocre novels followed, one being the inevitable historical romance. In her fourth novel, *Jonathan Jefferson Whitlaw*, she began to find her aptitude for social controversy by launching an attack on Negro slavery in America. She was a woman of unbridled prejudices, and a long-standing feud with the clergyman of her parish inspired her next book, *The Vicar of Wrexhill* (1837), a ferocious satire upon the Evangelical party in the Church of England. In the vicar she portrays a licentious hypocrite even more contemptible than Stiggins in *Pickwick*, which was appearing at the same time. Encouraged by the angry arguments that the book provoked, she continued her ridiculing of middle-class vulgarity in *The Widow Barnaby* (1839) and its sequel, *The Widow Married* (1840). In the latter year she also brought out a powerful study of child labor in *Michael Armstrong, the Factory Boy*, one of the first books to face the ugly facts about industrialism. Lord Ashley was introducing legislation for shortening the working hours of children, and Mrs. Trollope visited Manchester to observe the factory conditions for herself. In *Jessie Phillips* (1843) she was equally outspoken about the evils of the Poor Laws. Mrs. Trollope never learned how to manage a plot effectively, or even how to control her syntax; but she had a fund of sarcastic humor and a sharp eye for human foibles. The sheer force of her personality galvanized her novels into life, and she produced a total of thirty-four before she died aged eighty-three.

While she was paralleling Dickens with sensational stories uncovering social abuses, other writers were following the example of his comic technique. When the reprinting of *Jorrocks's Jaunts and Jollities* convinced Surtees that he had delighted the public, he kept Jorrocks alive in two full-scale novels. *Handley Cross* appeared in his magazine in 1838–39, and was brought out in three volumes in 1843. Like Mr. Pickwick, Jorrocks underwent a transformation, ceasing to be an object of ridicule and becoming shrewd and independent, though still gloriously vulgar. There is a good deal of satire on the incompetence and fraud of legal practice, also reminiscent of *Pickwick*. The beginning seemed to promise a study of the social changes in a town as the result of industrialization; and Jorrocks might have been analyzed as a specimen of the current phenomenon, the rise of the middle class in the social scale. But Surtees was not burdened with much social consciousness: the joys of hunting soon dominated the action, and in later editions the author inserted additional episodes with little relevance to the main plot.

Hillingdon Hall (1845) completes the metamorphosis of Jorrocks, who buys a country estate, becomes a Justice of the Peace, and is elected to Parliament. These events were based on recent experiences of the author's, and he even succumbed to the pressure of current controversies to the extent of including attacks on the Anti-Corn-Law League. It was not these inklings of political thought, however, but the breakneck adventures and blunt satire in Surtees' first three works of fiction that installed him as the favorite novelist of the country squires.

In much the same way Charles Lever started with a magazine serial that was little more than a stringing together of farcical anecdotes, and soon discovered that it was developing into a novel. Lever was an Irishman of English descent, who as a student at Trinity College, Dublin, indulged in merry pranks and conviviality. A period of wandering in the American backwoods, and medical study at Göttingen and Heidelberg, enlarged his stock of good stories, and by the time he received his medical degree in Dublin he was a popular raconteur. He settled down as a country doctor in Northern Ireland and in 1837 began an irregular serial in the *Dublin University Magazine* with the title, *The Confessions of Harry Lorrequer*. The first-personal method added to the liveliness of the devil-may-care comedy, and by 1839 a Dublin publisher decided that the story was worth reissuing in monthly parts, in a format imitating that of the *Pickwick Papers*.

Lever's subject matter was the improvident, sport-loving Anglo-Irish landowning gentry, the same that had been depicted by Maria Edgeworth; but in place of her prim irony and moral disapproval he was motivated by unalloyed delight in their dueling and horse-racing, their practical jokes and wrong-headed prejudices, their loquacity and their reckless flouting of common sense.

There is a slight military flavor in the story, as the hero is an officer, and some of the events occur in garrison life; but during most of the book Lorrequer is roaming about Ireland on leave. In the course of its serial publication, however, Lever had gone to practice medicine in Brussels, where he was surrounded by survivors of the Napoleonic campaigns; and when he was offered the inevitable contract for another novel he decided to deal mainly with army life. *Charles O'Malley, the Irish Dragoon* begins with country sports in Galway and high jinks at Trinity College, but soon shifts to the Peninsular campaign and proceeds to Waterloo, including some vigorous battle scenes that won approval from the aged Duke of Wellington himself; but even the perils of war could not depress the spirit of reckless courage and exuberant fun, so that the book has to be classified less as a historical novel than as another Irish comic chronicle. It was so immensely popular that Edgar Allan Poe, in an unfavorable review, had to admit that "in this respect it has surpassed even the inimitable compositions of Mr. Dickens."

Lever's next two novels appeared in their serial form under the joint title of *Our Mess*. The first one, *Jack Hinton, the Guardsman* (1842), is another farrago of harum-scarum exploits in Ireland, while the second, *Tom Burke of Ours* (1843–44) forms a companion piece to *Charles O'Malley* by showing the French side of the great war, in the adventures of an Irish soldier of fortune who serves under Napoleon. The latter story came out concurrently with another, *The Wanderings and Ponderings of Arthur O'Leary*, a mere string of separate episodes mainly based on the author's experiences on the Continent and in America.

By this time Lever had given up his medical career in favor of authorship and had become editor of the *Dublin University Magazine*. Closer contact with the animosities of Irish politics at the height of Daniel O'Connell's agitation convinced him that his former carefree accounts of his native country had shown only one side of the picture. Furthermore his fund of funny anecdotes was running low. During a tour of the west of Ireland he became more familiar with the life of the Celtic poor and the role of the Catholic parish priests. Accordingly his next novel, *The O'Donohue* (1845), was a new departure, not only in its coherence of plot but in its somber tone. Like Lady Morgan's novels, it dealt with an old native aristocrat in his crumbling castle, and there was insight in the analysis of the antipathies leading up to the Irish uprising of 1798.

Lever here moved closer to the type of fiction that was being written by William Carleton, then at the height of his career. His first full-length novel, *Fardarougha the Miser*, serialized in the *Dublin University Magazine* simultaneously with *Harry Lorrequer*, is a morbid psychopathic study against a background of peasant poverty. In spite of the implausibility of Carleton's melodramatic plots, he succeeded in conveying powerful impressions of hardship and oppression. *Valentine McClutchy, the Irish Land Agent* (1845) goes far beyond Miss Edgeworth in censuring the absentee landlords and the avarice of their local representatives, as exemplified in a highly emotional scene of the eviction of tenants. In *The Black Prophet, a Tale of the Irish Famine* (1846) he deals gruesomely with the typhus epidemic and starvation of 1817, with the ulterior purpose of rousing the English government to undertake relief measures for the similar crisis prevailing when the book was written. *The Emigrants of Ahadarra* (1847) gives a poignant picture of the exodus that resulted from extortionate rents.

Carleton was not a religious or patriotic fanatic, but was searching urgently for a solution to the woes of his country. This led him to changes of allegiance; he early left the Roman Catholic faith and wrote for Protestant papers, but later counseled tolerance for the Catholics. Nor was he blind to the defects of his own people. During those angry years of turmoil his stories overstepped the restraints of fictional art in their savage condemnation of the national curses of dirtiness, laziness, and drink, and in their enmity toward the terroristic secret societies of both factions. Thus he incurred disfavor from all sides.

Similarly, in 1845 Lever came to the decision that a moderate, tolerant man could achieve nothing among the embittered extremists in Dublin. He resigned from his editorship and took his family to the Continent, where he became a well-known figure in the expatriate society of Florence and later received an appointment in the consular service. His next novel, *The Knight of Gwynne* (1846–47), was more deeply pondered than any of his previous books. In it he studied the political conflict over the union of England and Ireland in 1801, intending to convey implications about the current difficulties between the two countries. For the first time he planned the plot in advance so that it developed logically. He drew the characters with greater subtlety and kept the humor under restraint. This refusal to continue repeating the kind of fiction that had made him famous indicates that Lever had the makings of a major novelist in him; but his spendthrift nature, his convivial habits, and his expensive family kept him writing desperately against time, never allowing him opportunity to organize or polish his material.

Captain Marryat, by contrast, did not succeed in making the change to a more mature outlook. There had been an adolescent quality even in his best books, and after 1840 his only significant stories — *Masterman Ready*, *The Settlers in Canada*, and *The Children of the New Forest* — were frankly intended for juvenile readers.

Ainsworth also settled into a routine, though it was not so naïve as Marryat's. Borrowing from Hugo's *Notre Dame de Paris* the use of a historic building as the unifying device, he wrote *The Tower of London* in 1840, and followed it in rapid succession with *Guy Fawkes*, *Old St. Paul's*, *Windsor Castle*, *St. James's*, and *The Lancashire Witches*. His use of English local color gave his novels a certain solidity in contrast with those of his rival, G.P.R. James, who remained faithful to foreign settings; but Ainsworth's Gothic melodrama seemed more and more outmoded when other novelists were coming closer to the actualities of life.

Bulwer, on the other hand, maintained an illusion of originality by rotating three or four types. *Night and Morning* (1841) is a melodrama of the most sensational description, full of unbelievable coincidences and missing documents, well seasoned with violence and crime. Immediately after this he turned to the Rosicrucian romance and the theme of the Wandering Jew, even though earlier writers from Godwin to Croly had exploited these materials so relentlessly that no vitality might be expected to survive. Bulwer was fascinated by the occult, and had experimented with astrology, clairvoyance, necromancy, and other esoteric arts. He had already revealed traces of this interest in *Godolphin* and *Ernest Maltravers;* and now *Zanoni*, which he considered to be his masterpiece, gave a peculiar sense of conviction to the story of a man who conquers death on the condition of relinquishing all human sympathy, and who after five thousand years breaks the compact by saving a beautiful girl during the Reign of Terror, which was beginning to replace the Spanish Inquisition as the most dependable historical stimulus for curdling the reader's blood. In contrast with this excursion into the supernatural, Bulwer's next book, *The Last of the Barons* (1843), was a sound and scholarly historical novel. In this year, upon inheriting his mother's ancestral estate, he added "Lytton" to the end of his name.

At this juncture Benjamin Disraeli reappeared as a novelist. During his seven years of concentration upon politics he had more than fulfilled the program set forth in *Vivian Grey*, for the fictitious young politician had failed in his scheme for starting a new faction to seize control of one of the old parties, whereas in his actual career Disraeli was now the acknowledged leader of the "Young England" bloc which was challenging Sir Robert Peel's leadership of the Tories. Peel had been catering to the new capitalistic class that emerged from the Industrial Revolution and gained influence through the first Reform Bill. Disraeli's platform emphasized that the Crown, the Established Church, and the hereditary landowners ought to protect the national welfare by preventing the factory owners from exploiting the urban workers. As the most effective way to put his policies before the public Disraeli decided to embody them in a series of three novels.

The first one, *Coningsby, or The New Generation*, came out in 1844. As in his earlier books, many of the characters were drawn from living originals, but the purpose was no longer satire or gossip, but was analysis of political forces. The real plot of the story is the course of English administration in the twelve years since the Reform Bill, with prolonged conversations devoted to the theories and issues involved. The basic social philosophy is akin to Carlyle's, in its contempt for utilitarian economics, its insistence upon leadership by great men, and its faith in the priority of emotion over reason as expressed in the slogan that "man was made to adore and to obey." The author's spokesman is Sidonia, a Jewish multi-millionaire of mysterious antecedents, who combines high-minded idealism with cynical intellectual isolation from human sympathies.

The second book of the trilogy, *Sybil, or The Two Nations,* comes to grips with the evils of the new industrialism. Disraeli gives first-hand accounts of the impoverished hand-loom weavers and the enslaved miners; he asserts the potential danger in strikes and radical trades unions and the futility of the legislative remedies currently being proposed by the Chartists. To symbolize the need for cooperation between the highest and lowest classes he tells the love story of a young nobleman and the doctrinaire daughter of a workingman who is a Chartist agitator. Unfortunately the author shirks the full impact of his situation by relapsing into the old cliché of the missing documents that prove Sybil and her father to be aristocrats too. The social theme of the book is that the rich and the poor in England constitute "two nations between whom there is no intercourse and no sympathy; who are as ignorant of each other's habits, thoughts, and feelings, as if they were dwellers in different zones, or inhabitants of different planets."

Since legislation and economic theory seemed powerless to find a solution, Disraeli in the third book offered religion as the alternative. His original plan intended this to deal with the role of the Church of England, but actually it took a wider theme. The hero of *Tancred* is another young aristocrat, who is encouraged by Sidonia to make a tour of the Holy Land in search of the origins of his Christian faith. Disraeli's pride in his Jewish forebears and his belief that Christianity was the fulfillment of Hebraism provide the central theme; but it is overlaid with fantastic adventures and opulent descriptions in which his oriental imagination had free rein. The lovely Palestinian heroine is an even more articulate theorist than Sybil was, but the mystical message of the need for a spiritual revival is not very convincingly conveyed. By 1847, the year when *Tancred* was published, Disraeli had succeeded in dislodging Peel and becoming an influential leader of the Tories, with opportunities to put his visions into effect.

Disraeli's trilogy impressively illustrates the change that had occurred in the English novel during the decade after Victoria came to the throne. Crucial political and social issues could not be ignored in any serious study of contemporary life. The Chartist movement, the repeal of the Corn Laws, the nationalist agitation

in Ireland, the campaign of Lord Ashley against child labor —
these and kindred problems filled the newspapers and daily conversation, and found their literary utterance through Mrs. Trollope
with her impulsive crusading, Carleton with his lifelong experience
of poverty and oppression, Disraeli with his ambitious schemes for
political leadership, Dickens with his bitter memories of an under-
privileged childhood. The pressure was so irresistible that even
such jesters as Surtees and Lever began to succumb.

X

Social Consciousness

(1845 – 1850)

DURING THE WHOLE TEN YEARS while Dickens and Lever held the public captive with a series of diffuse but entertaining novels, another writer was fumbling his way toward mastery of the art of fiction. William Makepeace Thackeray was seven months older than Dickens, and his background was utterly different. His ancestors for several generations had been civil and military officials in India; when he was four years old his father died, leaving him well provided for, and a year later he was sent from Calcutta, his birthplace, to be educated in England. Awkward and shortsighted, he was unhappy in his preparatory schools and felt miserably isolated. His nose was broken when he was ten, rendering his face irresistibly comic. By the time he entered Charterhouse School he had learned to mask his sensitiveness with a sarcastic manner, and he became popular through his ability to tell amusing stories and to draw absurd sketches; but the brutality of school life left him prejudiced against stupidity and unkindness. At Cambridge University he was an indolent student, more interested in wine parties and card-playing than in scholarship, and he left without taking a degree. Visits to Paris and a winter in Germany made him at home in cosmopolitan society, and a dilatory interval as a law student was relinquished as soon as he became twenty-one and gained control of his finances.

Though he had incurred heavy gambling debts at college, he felt no doubt as to the adequacy of his income; his devoted mother and stepfather, now settled in England, encouraged the assumption that he was a young gentleman of leisure who could indulge his whims at will. He sank some of his inheritance in a weekly paper, which soon collapsed. Meanwhile his facility in caricaturing led him to become an art student in Paris, where at twenty-five he married a pretty, penniless girl with a mild disposition. Within a year the ineptness of his stepfather's investments resulted in loss of the family resources, and Thackeray faced the necessity of earning a living.

He made a few efforts to find employment as an illustrator of books, including an application to provide the drawings for *The Pickwick Papers* after the suicide of Seymour; but his amateurish sketches could not compete with the work of professionals. As he had dabbled in journalism ever since his school days, he turned to authorship as a last resort. For him, as for Dickens, the expansion of newspapers and magazines provided a varied market for his writings.

The events of his life all combined to equip him with the disillusioned outlook of a social satirist. Early separation from his home and even from his native country left a sense of rootlessness. In spite of his mother's lavish affection he never regained the confidence in her that was lost through her remarriage and her absence during his childhood, though his attitude toward her and his stepfather was never so exasperated as was that of Dickens toward his parents. His financial mishaps proved his incompatibility with the methods and standards of the dominant world of business. Aware that he was likely to be laughed at for his grotesque appearance, since exceptional height made him conspicuous, he had formed the defensive habit of ridiculing himself and everyone else. When he had to adjust himself to the stresses of economic insecurity he was further hurt by discovering that most of his prosperous and fashionable acquaintances ignored him as soon as he became poor. Being innately warm-hearted, he came to cherish inordinately the few friends who remained sympathetic and loyal, and to despise the selfishness and hypocrisy that he saw in most other people. Thus he combined an inside knowledge of the *mores* of the upper middle class and the aristocracy with an emotional alienation from them.

Elements of fiction first entered Thackeray's writing as devices for lending savor to the ordinarily dull routine of journalism. In order to ridicule a stupid book by a social climber, he reviewed it in the disguise of a semi-literate footman, James Yellowplush, whose phonetic spelling reproduced the oddities of cockney speech. This comic figure reappeared in subsequent contributions to *Fraser's Magazine*, acquiring fuller traits of character and environment; and two or three of the sketches, such as "Dimond Cut Dimond," emerge as full-fledged short stories. It is enlightening to compare this conceited, cynical footman with Sam Weller, another cockney-speaking manservant, who was flourishing in *The Pickwick Papers* during the same months.

Having discovered that a fictitious spokesman helped him to invent lively material from month to month, Thackeray created others. For the *New Monthly* he wrote as Major Goliah Gahagan, a braggart narrating his heroic exploits in the Indian army; in *Fraser's* his art criticisms were attributed to Michael Angelo Titmarsh, a cocksure little connoisseur. These various impersonations, while reminiscent of the Isaac Bickerstaff and Mr. Spectator of Steele and Addison, were consistent with the current vogue of pseudonymous editors and fictitious contributors, and so the reading public had no suspicion that Yellowplush, Gahagan, and Titmarsh were false faces of one man.

Unlike Dickens, who quickly discarded the pen name of "Boz," Thackeray had no wish for personal recognition. His sense of caste made him dimly ashamed of earning his living as a professional writer, especially in the rough-and-tumble arena of journalism. Yet at the same time an inversion of this feeling endowed him with a realistic pride in his new vocation, so that he despised the pretensions of authors like Bulwer and Disraeli, who put on airs of superiority. As a book reviewer, Thackeray had to plow through the current output of novels, many of which nauseated him with their turgid style and their falsification of experience. Even Dickens seemed to him vulgarly ostentatious and melodramatic. Thackeray was obsessed with the journalist's duty of reporting unvarnished facts.

This revulsion against what he considered shoddy in fiction drove him to try to demolish it by parody. His immediate incitement came from the vogue of "Newgate Calendar" novels as represented by *Eugene Aram, Oliver Twist*, and *Jack Sheppard*. His burlesque, entitled *Catherine* and attributed to "Ikey Solomons, Jr.," came out serially in *Fraser's* during 1839. In order to strip off the glamour that Bulwer and Ainsworth had conferred upon robbers and murderers, Thackeray set out to depict crime with disgusting frankness, and so he chose the career of a brutal murderess who had been contemporary with Ainsworth's Jack Sheppard. Like Fielding with *Joseph Andrews*, however, the author found that the characters began to win his sympathy as he developed them, so that he could not sustain his intention of making them totally vile. Caught in this dilemma, he ended the undertaking after six installments, and never reprinted it.

Burdened with miscellaneous writing — travel sketches, book reviews, occasional short stories — he started another serial in *Fraser's* in 1840, *A Shabby Genteel Story*, dealing with the sordid affairs of the lower middle class with almost the coarseness of Theodore Hook. There was some good farcical characterization, but the structure was defective, probably because the author's personal troubles were mounting to a crisis. A second daughter had died in infancy, and after the birth of a third child Mrs. Thackeray lost her mind. The serial story was abruptly terminated at the ninth chapter, the household was broken up, and after months of agonizing confusion Thackeray adjusted himself to a solitary life in London clubs and taverns.

The psychological effect of the disaster can be seen in his next effort at an extended piece of fiction, *The History of Samuel Titmarsh and the Great Hoggarty Diamond*, which included characters and episodes based on his own experiences and in which his sardonic swagger and scorn were tempered with a more mature sympathy for human weakness. Again serialized in *Fraser's*, this melancholy story had little appeal to readers, and the author did not develop it to the dimensions of a novel; but its increased clarity of characterization and firmness of construction indicated that he was learning how to write fiction.

He found what seemed to be a more suitable medium for his talent when he was appointed to the staff of *Punch*, the comic weekly that had recently been established. For it he could easily toss off short satirical essays, singly and in series. He also undertook to write two books of travel, one on Ireland and the other on the Near East. In 1844, however, he made another attempt at a sustained narrative. As in his three previous ones, the central character of *Barry Lyndon* is a scoundrel; but this time Thackeray undertook a technical *tour de force* by making the scoundrel tell his own story. Undoubtedly it was modeled upon Fielding's *Jonathan Wild*, and it survives the test of comparison with that minor masterpiece. Sustained irony results from the complacency with which the narrator, an eighteenth-century Irish adventurer, boasts about his shameful actions, and from the contempt that he heaps on other characters whom the reader soon admires. By this device the book is transformed from a picaresque adventure story into a subtle study of character, with an underlying moral purpose of displaying worldly standards of success and honor as inherently vicious. Thackeray did some serious historical research for it, and found the labor highly distasteful. Yet once again the readers of *Fraser's Magazine* did not enjoy the serial; once again the author cut it short; and once again he found no publisher to bring it out as a volume.

He had used a more absurd pseudonym than usual, "George Savage Fitzboodle," and his identity was still unknown to the public. During the next three years two of his contributions to *Punch* were significant in the final shaping of him to be a novelist. One was *The Snobs of England*, a long series of satirical portraits of types, in the tradition of the Theophrastian characters. Though this tended to become monotonous because of the rigid formula, it established Thackeray for the first time as a general satirist of contemporary society. Glimpses of personality and fragmentary episodes were couched in an urbane, conversational style that suited the theme. The word "snob" had been undergraduate slang for townspeople when Thackeray was at Cambridge, and his series put it into general circulation. The phenomenon of bourgeois social pretension had become so predominant in early-Victorian England that an epithet for it was needed, and Thackeray both analyzed and named it for his generation.

His other series was *Mr. Punch's Prize Novelists*, a group of parodies of popular authors — G. P. R. James, Lever, Disraeli, Mrs. Gore. The mischievous aptness of his exaggerations was a genuine form of criticism, conveying not only the deficiencies of the novel as then practiced but also by implication what Thackeray thought it ought to be. When he was writing these parodies in the early months of 1847 he had already begun to publish in monthly parts his own first ambitious work of fiction.

His ten years of trial-and-error had taught him much about the writing of novels. Unlike any other novelist of the time, he had formulated critical theories on the subject. His book reviews, his apparently irresponsible parodies, his handling of narrative and dialogue in essays and travel sketches were as much a part of his preparation as were his unsuccessful works of fiction. Equally important was his sense of identification with the eighteenth century, and with Fielding in particular. He felt pride in the achievements of his ancestors; he had attended a school and a college where celebrities of the previous century had preceded him; his favorite authors included Addison and Steele and Goldsmith. He resembled Fielding in being an impoverished gentleman and convivial London clubman who had been trained in the law before becoming a journalist. Fielding's suave, intimate style, humane sympathies, and disillusioned irony were congenial to him. And as a modern Fielding upholding the elegance and dignity of authorship, he saw the modern equivalent of Richardson in Dickens, the popular exponent of bourgeois sentiment.

He began his first real novel, therefore, with a clear sense of what he wanted to avoid, though he was not confident as to what he could achieve. After several false starts he convinced the firm of Bradbury & Evans that the book might be profitable in monthly parts, though as yet only the first few chapters were written; and the first number appeared on January 1, 1847. The title, *Vanity Fair*, borrowed from *The Pilgrim's Progress*, suggested that the story was to be an indictment of worldliness; and the subtitle, "Pen and Pencil Sketches of Modern Society," announced not only that the author was supplying his own illustrations but also that the whole thing might turn out to be a mere series of episodes, an expanded version of his *Book of Snobs*. After a few installments, however, discriminating readers realized that a new major talent had emerged, and Thackeray knew that he was committed to a novel on the grand scale.

The implications of the title were maintained by its panoramic scope. Departing from the biographical pattern that had prevailed ever since the works of Defoe, Thackeray interwove the careers of several contrasted characters, rather after the model of the seventeenth-century romances. His own interest, and that of most readers, was primarily engaged with Becky Sharp, an anti-heroine whose courage and cleverness compel admiration in spite of her unscrupulousness. But her sequence of admirers and her involvement with the Sedley, Osborne, and Crawley families enable Thackeray to range over a wide area of upper-class life, both in England and abroad. He set the time thirty years back, amid the tawdry glitter and feeble depravity of the Regency, but except for a characteristically oblique glimpse of the Battle of Waterloo he paid no attention to historical events. Instead, he was concerned with the indefinable conflicts of social change: the aristocracy striving blindly to preserve its prerogatives and the new business class torn between its desire for material advancement and its devotion to puritan morality. Becky Sharp, an adventuress without social anchorage, is able to clamber almost to the top in this unstable structure.

To most readers Thackeray appeared to be a cynic and an iconoclast. Rebellious souls hailed him rapturously as an intrepid assailant of entrenched traditions. On the other hand, conventional-minded people upbraided him for subverting the necessary principles of social intercourse. They complained that most of his clever characters were vicious, most of his virtuous characters were stupid, and the chief exceptions were people like Rawdon Crawley and Jos Sedley who were stupid and vicious in an equal degree. This effect was heightened by his pose of aloofness, as expressed in his favorite metaphor of himself as a puppet-master manipulating his manikins. He seemed to take heartless joy in human misfortunes. In a perpetual running commentary the author made fun of his readers' prejudices almost as freely as he ridiculed the characters in the story.

A subsequent revulsion of feeling condemned him for diametrically opposite reasons. He came to be scorned as a shallow sentimentalist, naïvely lavishing compassion on commonplace beings. He was accused of prudishly evading scenes of sex and passion. His interpretative remarks were regarded as an intolerable intrusion, destroying any possible illusion of reality.

A more equitable assessment can allow him credit for solid achievements. He created a gallery of lifelike characters, in a milieu that seems to be a complete reconstruction of actuality.

From the first chapter the reader enters this world with confidence because it offers the complexity and the leisurely movement of daily experience. On this basis a defense can be found for Thackeray's commentary, in that it reinforces the intimacy between reader and subject. The commentator is not quite Mr. Thackeray, a disparate author; rather he figures as an unnamed and unidentified member of the group among whom the action occurs, and records the responses of time and class, like a superlative gossip. Thackeray had previously invented objective narrators with a distinct though minor connection with the occurrences — Yellowplush, Titmarsh, Fitzboodle; now he merged the onlooker with his own identity to produce a *persona* with whom the reader enjoys identifying himself — a sophisticated man of the world who is capable of pity and yet not blinded by illusions. Like most normal people, he is wary of displaying emotion and masks his embarrassment by lapsing into a jest. Reader and narrator alike are *l'homme moyen sensuel*, seeking to comprehend the baffling flow of experience all about them.

The grace of Thackeray's manner, spontaneous as it appeared, implied a cultivated background and a discriminating taste. These qualities recommended his novel to people of similar disposition, for whom no writer of fiction since Fielding and Sterne, except Peacock, had catered. But it had its roots in other antecedent types of fiction as well. Its satiric picture of fashionable life, with identifiable portraits, affiliated it with the "silver-fork novels" that Thackeray had ridiculed as meretricious. In some degree it can be related to an earlier genre, the picaresque tale, insofar as the reader is induced to feel a guilty satisfaction in Becky's triumphs. But Thackeray endowed these comparatively naïve types with maturity. In spite of occasional inconsistencies of tone, he advanced the novel toward both distinction of style and realism of material.

The realism was largely due to the author's familiarity with the world he depicted. Many of the characters were drawn directly from real people, either public figures like Lord Hertford (Lord Steyne) or members of his own circle like his grandmother (Miss Sedley) and a cousin (Jos Sedley). Among the principal characters, Amelia Sedley was largely derived from his wife, and Captain Dobbin had some resemblance to Thackeray himself. Indeed the uncomfortable emotional effect of the story, which gives readers a sense of involvement and yet leaves them undecided where their sympathy ought to reside, arose from Thackeray's complicated personal connection with his material. Toward Amelia he displays a protective affection as toward a child, and yet this is intermittently mixed with futile exasperation at her weakness and stupidity, ending with a downright scolding of her for complacent selfishness. Critics have disagreed sharply on this point, some insisting that he suffers from inexcusable uncertainty in his presentation of an important element in his theme, others arguing that he despises Amelia throughout and that his praise of her is wholly sarcastic. Without settling the question of its artistic effectiveness, one can suggest that at least his attitude is true to human nature, since it is an accurate representation of his own contradictory feelings toward his ineffectual wife and also toward another woman. When he was writing *Vanity Fair* his emotional conflict had come to a crisis because he realized that he was falling in love with Jane Brookfield, the wife of one of his closest friends. The predicament was unresolvable, for Mrs. Brookfield was loyal to her clergyman-husband and Thackeray had no prospect of release from his insane wife. Traces of his bafflement crept into the novel, with Amelia in this regard serving as surrogate for Mrs. Brookfield, devoted to an insensitive husband and silently adored by the husband's comrade. The author's immoderate contempt for George Osborne and his mounting impatience with Amelia can be understood as an unintentional releasing of his personal misery. This feeling was probably complicated by a literary reminiscence, for Amelia's name suggests a resemblance to the heroine of Fielding's third novel, who was also meek under the affliction of an unhappy marriage.

The ambivalence of Thackeray's attitude, however, was not confined to his handling of individual characters; it was inherent also in his interpretation of the whole social scene. His political sympathies were liberal and humanitarian, and like most of the Victorian authors he was antagonistic to the smug materialism of the bourgeois mentality. Nevertheless, he appreciated the comforts of civilized living and the company of cultivated people. The lower social strata were almost totally ignored in the book. Hence he was widely accused of snobbery, the vice that he most often condemned. He attacked no social abuses with the zeal of Dickens, because he lacked faith in a campaign of reform: to him the abuses were inherent in human nature, and so he satirized the failings of individuals in all classes. His family pride and his love of the eighteenth century rendered him nostalgic for the old days of assured distinctions in rank, when gracious manners had a chance to flourish; yet, like Scott, he was aware that basic changes in the social structure were occurring and could not be withstood. Since he proclaimed no program and championed no cause, idealistic readers have found him deficient in earnestness. He was not egotistic enough to think that he knew any solutions to the crucial problems of his time.

His assumptions about his function as a disillusioned onlooker rather than as a molder of opinion had their effect also upon his technique. When the book was complete he gave it a new subtitle, "A Novel Without a Hero," which can be interpreted in two senses — either that it has only a heroine, Becky Sharp, or that it contains no conventionally heroic character. This ambiguity is ironic in either sense: if Becky is the "heroine," she is the antithesis of all traditional heroic virtue; if the whole panorama of society contains no heroic figure, this is proof that the idealistic world of the epic poets has given place to drab mediocrity. He could have called it with equal truth "a novel without a villain." Consequently the story is not constructed about a central monumental figure or a simple conflict of good against evil, but is fitted together in a series of contrasts and parallels that imply the author's concepts. Impersonal social trends and caste attitudes are the hero and the villain alike.

When *Vanity Fair* began to appear, Dickens had resumed the writing of fiction after an interval of more than two years. The first installment of his *Dombey and Son* came out three months before the first issue of Thackeray's story, and the two ran their monthly course side by side. In some respects it was plain that Dickens had moved a long way in the direction of what Thackeray was so soon to write. The main characters in *Dombey and Son* are principally of the prosperous class. Although there are several comic characters who rank with Dickens's best, the comedy is usually less farcical than before, and verges upon social satire in such figures as Major Bagstock and Mrs. Skewton. There is less melodramatic bombast, too, in spite of the impossible theatrical dialogue in the climactic scene between Edith Dombey and Carker. The last hours of little Paul seem mawkish to modern taste, but less so than the death of Little Nell, and the chapter was hailed as a masterpiece of pathos by such unimpressionable readers as Lord Jeffrey and Thackeray himself. Most significant of all is the fact that the book has a firm central theme, which includes both social and psychological analysis. On the social side, Mr. Dombey is a serious study of the wealthy businessman, who had never before figured so convincingly in fiction. His power over other people's lives and his pride in the integrity of his firm can be paralleled at the present day. This connects with the psychological validity of the portrait: his commercial success has rendered him positive that his opinions are always right, so that his determination to transmit the business to a son leads to the ruin of the little boy's health, to an incompatible second marriage, and to alienation from his daughter. There are elements of tragic dignity in Mr. Dombey's pride and its humiliation.

A wider significance of the theme is its discrediting of the current utilitarian philosophy. Dombey is the natural product of a system based on logic and on material gain. His rigorous plans for his son's training and his exaltation of economic principles above human feelings are consistent with the detailed setting of the new industrial prosperity, in which railways are being built in every direction and stock-exchange speculation is a principal basis of wealth. Dombey's self-centered concern with money-making and the somber respectability of his associates are contrasted with the outgoing warmth of the working-class characters. Dickens was beginning to look at the society around him with analytical intelligence instead of with emotional impulses.

The structure of the story, too, shows an abrupt access of thoughtfulness, with all the episodes integrated into the central theme and neatly balanced to intensify the required effects. For the first time, Dickens had prepared an outline of the whole story before beginning to write, instead of improvising each installment at the last moment. Elaborate patterns of recurrent symbols and phrasal echoes can be traced throughout. Dickens was becoming conscious of artistic technique as well as gaining awareness of basic social issues.

While these serial novels of the two veteran journalists, Dickens and Thackeray, were competing for public preference, an utterly different kind of fiction emerged from a most improbable source. In October, 1847, *Jane Eyre*, by Currer Bell, was published in three volumes; and three months later another firm brought out two shorter novels jointly — *Wuthering Heights*, by Ellis Bell, and *Agnes Grey*, by Acton Bell. Even the publishers did not know that these apparently masculine names concealed the identity of three young women in a remote Yorkshire parsonage.

Charlotte Brontë was thirty-one, and her sisters Emily and Anne were twenty-nine and twenty-seven. Their experience was limited to the bleak northern moors and to a few years as pupils and teachers in shabby boarding schools; but they observed their restricted environment with poetic intensity and interpreted it with concentrated emotion.

Their father, Patrick Brunty, the son of a poor farming family in Northern Ireland, had succeeded in graduating from Cambridge and being ordained in the Church of England. To conceal his humble Irish origin, he changed his name to Brontë, taken from the Italian dukedom conferred upon Lord Nelson. Shortly after he became curate of Haworth his wife died of cancer, leaving him with six children. He sent four of the little girls to a cheap boarding school where they were ill-used, and the two eldest soon died of tuberculosis. The other two were brought back to the rectory, where Anne and their brother Branwell had remained; but even there they saw little of their egotistical, moody father. Whenever he emerged from his study he regaled them with tales of murders and other atrocities, both from Ireland and from their own Yorkshire vicinity. Their mother's sister, who kept house for them, tried to inculcate the gloomy and emotional theology of Methodist revivalism.

The children spent most of their time in exploring the moorland, reading without supervision, and inventing interminable stories, which they transcribed in tiny handwriting in miniature books. Driven in upon their own imaginations for entertainment, they prolonged these fantasies beyond the normal age of childish make-believe, and identified themselves passionately with the fictitious characters. A complete geography and history were invented for Angria, a nation supposedly in West Africa; the genealogy and biography of its rulers and generals were elaborately worked out, and actual personages such as the Duke of Wellington were reshaped into Byronic heroes and villains. When Charlotte, who had been the leader of the project, went away to school again at fifteen, Emily refused to collaborate with Branwell, and so she and Anne started a new cycle, located in a Pacific island named Gondal. A Gothic atmosphere of violence, terror, and sexual misconduct prevailed in both cycles.

At her second boarding school Charlotte spent a reasonably happy year, before returning to Haworth to instruct the other two girls. When she was nineteen she went back to the same school as a teacher for a few months, taking Emily with her as a pupil, but the latter was so unhappy that she went home, and Anne came in her place. Soon afterwards, in spite of their sketchy schooling, Charlotte and Anne took positions as governesses; but Emily was unwilling to venture away from Haworth. Branwell, though gifted with cleverness and charm, had been hopelessly distorted by isolation and lack of discipline; his sisters' earnings were wasted upon his futile studies to become a painter, and he drifted into drunkenness and low company. Charlotte, though small and drab in appearance, shortsighted and painfully shy, had rejected proposals of marriage from two curates by the time she was twenty-five; she preferred even the dull work of a governess to the companionship of an insipid young clergyman. Emily was more striking looking, being tall, thin, and dark, but she was too silent to make friends and found her only pleasure in lonely walks on the moors. Anne was the mildest and most melancholy of the three. Charlotte's inconspicuous physique masked an inflexible will and a capacity for hard work, and she was ambitious to raise the family out of its indigent obscurity. Hoping to qualify themselves to open a school of their own, she and Emily went to study in Brussels in 1842, but after some months Emily again found a pretext for fleeing homeward. Charlotte, having formed a strong affection for the headmistress's husband, who gave her lessons in French, stayed on at the Belgian institution for another year as a student-teacher. The sisters never succeeded in enrolling any pupils for their projected school, but in 1845 a new possibility was opened to them when Charlotte discovered that Emily and Anne had been writing poetry, as she also was doing. They paid for the publication of a volume of their verse, but only two copies were sold.

Branwell had already started to write a novel, and in the hope of producing something more profitable than the poems, each of the girls proceeded to do likewise.

The books were composed under the most disheartening conditions. Their father was going blind; both Emily and Anne were showing consumptive symptoms; and Branwell, after being dismissed from more than one employment, was drinking himself to death at the village tavern. These circumstances, however, merely intensified the morbid influences that had dominated their whole lives. The deaths of their mother and sisters, the struggle with poverty, the eccentric habits of their father, and the lack of normal association with people of their own age and interests had all combined to give their imaginations a gloomy cast. Hence their novels were a unique mixture of realistic vividness with the weird and tortured fantasy of their Angrian and Gondalian tales, which they had continued to compose until the time they started their serious works. The writing of several million words in fifteen years had given them an assured narrative style, and their imaginative identification with the heroes and heroines of their youthful tales enabled them to feel an equally subjective intimacy with the central characters in their novels.

Charlotte undertook a bold experiment by writing hers from a man's first-personal point of view. Entitled *The Professor*, it was based upon her experiences in Brussels. Since leaving the Pensionnat Héger she had idealized her former tutor more and more, and in candid letters to him she poured out her loneliness and frustration until, afraid that his wife might become jealous, he asked Charlotte not to address the letters to his residence. Reversing the nationalities of the two main characters, she wrote the novel as an Englishman who teaches in a Brussels school and wins the love of a Swiss pupil-teacher. Apart from this change, the two are reasonably accurate portraits of M. Héger and Charlotte Brontë, and in Mlle. Reuter she had her revenge on Héger's suspicious wife. To solace her yearning, she ended the fictional love story with a happy marriage. The plot lacks complication, perhaps the best part of the book being some astringent but irrelevant portraits of teachers and pupils; there is a refreshing lack of sentimentality in the depiction of feminine character, and a good deal of common sense in the discussion of educational methods. The early chapters give a harsh glimpse of a Yorkshire manufacturing town; and the character of Yorke Hunsden, though inadequately developed, is an interesting sketch of a radical theorizer. The melodramatic scenes at the beginning are unlike the intimate realism of the rest of the book, and for a sufficient reason: they were transferred with little change from Angrian stories that Charlotte and Branwell had written years before. Once the artificial opening chapters are left behind, the book is distinctive for its uncompromising emphasis upon the emotional tensions of apparently commonplace people, the unspoken interplay between one personality and another.

The Professor was rejected by several publishers, and at last one of them explained that it was deficient in incident, and too brief for three-volume publication, but that he would like to see another manuscript from the same author. Charlotte hastened to finish *Jane Eyre*, and it won immediate fame. Within a few months it went through several editions, arousing controversy over its moral implications and widespread curiosity as to the author.

This second novel contained as much personal experience as the first, but it was combined now with a plot that possessed conflict and suspense, sometimes to the degree of melodrama. Elements from the Angrian tales mingled inextricably with the impressions of real life. Again the vividness of the story was intensified by use of the first-personal point of view; but this time the narrator was a young woman and so plausibility was better sustained. The penniless governess, plain-looking but proud and outspoken, was largely a self-portrait; and even the austere moralizing, which intruded strangely amid love scenes, contributed to the characterization of an independent and intolerant young woman. The early episodes, when she is a friendless child in a harsh school, are vitalized by Charlotte's hatred of the institution that she blamed for the deaths of her elder sisters. A child's outlook is convincingly conveyed in these scenes.

Once Jane becomes governess at Thornfield, the figure of Rochester steps straight out of Angria, where he had been the Byronic Duke of Zamorna. The lonely house, the ferocious gentleman, and the mysterious glimpses that are later explained as resulting from the incarceration of his insane wife on the top floor, all sound like a belated revival of the Gothic tale of terror. The horrible death of the maniac in the burning mansion was borrowed from a scene in *Ivanhoe*. Later, the telepathic communication that calls Jane back to Rochester introduces a touch of the supernatural — or, at any rate, of the extrasensory — and Charlotte had first used this occurrence in an Angrian story when she was fourteen. But somehow in *Jane Eyre* she makes the phantasmagoria believable by her abundant use of familiar detail, and especially by Jane's matter-of-fact attitude through all her perils. An odd feature of *The Professor* had been the bluntness of speech practiced by most of the characters: not only did Crimsworth and Hunsden indicate their friendship by exchanging insults, but even the lovers usually conversed in brusque terms. This trait, which may be attributable to Yorkshire reticence, reappears in the interviews between Jane and Rochester, and serves as an antidote to sentimentalism or bombast.

What chiefly gives the book its power is Charlotte's faculty for creating atmosphere. Her practice in poetry had trained her to choose the connotative words and similes that evoke sense impressions as one reads. Rhythmic structure of sentences also contributes to the emotional impact. Many of the original readers were so strongly affected that they accepted the story as a literal record of experience rather than as a projection of the writer's wishes. Hence arose the bewildered protests on moral grounds. After Rochester's cynical project of committing bigamy, his invitation to Jane to become his mistress, and his confession of previous sexual adventures, it was shocking that he finally be rewarded with a happy marriage. Though Jane tediously reiterated strict religious principles, she also uttered her passionate love to Rochester without restraint. Even more disturbing was the assumption throughout the book that women have a claim to absolute independence, both in earning their own living and in displaying their emotions. As Jane is an orphan, the problem of a girl's dependence on her parents is not introduced: she is portrayed as fighting a single-handed war for recognition and for spiritual equality with men. In the same year Tennyson published *The Princess* and F. D. Maurice announced the establishing of Queen's College to provide (for the first time) higher education for women. These symptoms of a new concept of women's rights were profoundly distressing to conventional-minded people. To them Jane Eyre was an intolerable renegade from all the standards of behavior expected of respectable girls.

While Charlotte was thus concerned with one of the major social issues of the century, her two sisters wrote their novels with
single-minded concentration upon personal emotions. Both their
books had been finished before Charlotte started to write *Jane
Eyre*, but their publisher was so dilatory that its appearance preceded theirs. When *Wuthering Heights* and *Agnes Grey* came
out, the similarity of the three stories in setting and in the authors'
pen names indicated some sort of connection and added to the
general puzzlement. Neither book won anything like the success
of *Jane Eyre*. *Wuthering Heights*, in particular, was condemned
both for brutality of feeling and for incompetence of structure.
In both respects it was so individual that the better part of a
century elapsed before it was adequately assessed.

Emily had already demonstrated her superiority over her sisters
as a poet. The poems, however, intense though they are, seem
seldom if ever to have been direct expressions of her own feelings, but to have been created out of the dramatic situations in
her Gondal stories. All attempts to provide her with a love affair
have failed. Apparently she found emotional satisfaction, to the
extent of a sort of mystical rapture, in her solitary walks on the
moorland, in her affection for animals, and even in her silent competence as a housekeeper. She was so taciturn and self-sufficient
that even Charlotte did not feel sure she understood Emily's temperament. Emily's *Wuthering Heights* also is a strangely impersonal novel, in contrast with the excessive subjectivity of
Charlotte's *Jane Eyre*. Though it centers upon an overmastering
love, it is devoid of sexual passion; the love between Heathcliff
and Cathy is sometimes almost indistinguishable from hate. Not
handicapped by any admixture of her own experiences, Emily
was able to imagine a story that is terrible and beautiful, seeming to be a symbolic embodiment of elemental forces rather
than a record of normal human behavior. In contrast, too, with
Charlotte's didacticism, Emily offers no moral judgments, but
displays the tragic action with fatalistic impassiveness.

The materials for the story were undoubtedly derived from
the local tales of hatred and revenge and pathological personalities that both her father and her brother enjoyed collecting
and recounting. These took on an accretion of passion from the
unbridled love scenes and ruthless feuds in the Gondal cycle.
Heathcliff is a more inhuman specimen of Gothic violence than

Rochester; but within the framework of the novel he is more believable because the setting and the other characters all sustain the tone. Emily had conversed so little with the country people that she had but slight knowledge of their everyday lives. The little group of inbred sadists and victims seems to exist in utter isolation from the world of ordinary social values.

It is here that Emily's extraordinary technical experiment proves its worth. If the story had been narrated from the customary omniscient point of view it might have been another implausible tale of terror. Instead it is filtered through the minds and words of two onlookers, who are the only approximately normal people in the situation. This device enables the author also to avoid a pitfall in the handling of time, for the action extends over thirty years and there is a change of heroine in the middle. What would otherwise be a disjointed sequence of events is unified and placed in perspective by starting the account almost at the end, when the mild Mr. Lockwood arrives as a stranger in the lonely district and grows inquisitive about his eccentric neighbor, Heathcliff. In a series of interviews with Nelly Dean, the housekeeper of Wuthering Heights, who is the only person who has witnessed the whole action, he ekes out his fragmentary impressions, and thus the reader is held by an ever-mounting suspense and by an inescapable illusion of actuality. The emotional agonies of the chief characters seem all the more intense in the consistent understatement of the commonplace reporters.

Logical minds may complain that Nelly's style is too eloquent for a simple countrywoman, but she has a quiet shrewdness that is sufficiently in character. Indeed, it is typical of Emily's impartial attitude that Nelly's personality and her share of responsibility in the events remain equivocal. Most readers accept her on her own terms as a well-meaning but helpless bystander, but a recent critic stigmatizes her as the real villain, whose mischief-making brings on the catastrophe. If this be the case, Emily achieves with great subtlety the effect that Thackeray attempted in *Barry Lyndon*, in which a vicious character smugly betrays his own evil nature. Whatever Nelly's role may be, the reader ends with a strange feeling that he comprehends the tragic situation with deeper insight than either of the transmitters possesses.

As in *Jane Eyre*, but to a greater degree, the book's effect is intensified by its poetic style. The natural setting constantly colors the mood, the moors through the changing seasons being described with a poet's observation and a poet's sense of the inevitable word. The tempestuous passions of the characters are thus tranquilized by being shown against the eternal background of nature's impersonal processes. Hence the final effect of the story, though both the principal characters die, is not one of melancholy, but of exaltation. Emily achieved something of the rare power of the highest tragedy by showing people of potential nobility ruined by some flaw in their nature and yet spiritually triumphant over death.

The author's uncanny skill is conspicuous in her ability to arouse a sense of the unseen. Nothing in the story can positively be labeled as supernatural, but the recurrent dreams and hallucinations take on an effect of actuality. The young Brontës were positive that on occasions in the Haworth rectory they had seen the ghost of their dead sister, and their genuine superstition lends conviction to the psychic phenomena in both *Jane Eyre* and *Wuthering Heights*. When Heathcliff's dead body lies drenched with the rain that blew in through the open window, the effect is more authentically eerie than all the palpable atrocities in the tales of terror. The only other writer of fiction who achieved anything like this convincing use of Gothic material was also a poet, Edgar Allan Poe, who was writing in almost the same years; and even he confined himself to short stories instead of attempting the more difficult task of maintaining the imaginative pitch through a whole novel. *Wuthering Heights*, in short, is a belated masterpiece of romanticism. Just as Jane Austen had been an anachronistic eighteenth-century rationalist in the romantic heyday, so Emily Brontë was an anachronistic romantic visionary amid Victorian practicality.

Alongside of her ferocious story, the one by her gentle sister Anne, which shared the three-volume set, seems pallid and conventional. *Agnes Grey* consists of the same sort of material as *Jane Eyre*, and in its quiet way is as sincere and outspoken; but it lacks both the melodramatic plot and the passionate assertiveness of Charlotte's novel. This heroine, too, is a governess, and falls too deeply in love to indulge in conventional sentimentalism; but she is inarticulate with shyness, and the hero is a good-hearted curate, an idealization of a young clergyman who briefly brought gaiety into the Haworth household and then prematurely died. The happy ending was a sort of compensation for that sorrow in real life, and Anne did not wholly succeed in transmuting her actual experience into a work of art. In place of her sisters' vehemence, her prevailing mood is patience, relieved with touches of amiable humor.

Her second novel, *The Tenant of Wildfell Hall*, was a more ambitious attempt, and holds the same relationship to *Wuthering Heights* as her preceding one held to *Jane Eyre*. She even tried something like Emily's experiment with time, by starting the story in the middle and using flash-backs. The portrait of a man ruining his life with dissipation was derived from her brother, who was killing himself with alcohol and drugs. Agonized by this close view of moral disintegration, Anne intended her novel to be a terrible warning against sin and self-indulgence. She chose a more violent plot than that of her other story, introduced episodes of cruelty, and confronted some of the unhappy aspects of the relations between the sexes. Unprecedented in English fiction was a scene in which the heroine locks her bedroom door against her brutal husband, or a later episode when after a dinner party the drunken men invade the privacy of their wives. The author's intention was to shock her readers and she succeeded in shocking her sister Charlotte also. The obvious moral purpose and the author's self-torture in writing the book produce an effect that is painful rather than tragic.

The Tenant of Wildfell Hall was published in June, 1848. Three months later Branwell died miserably, and by that time — though they were not aware of it — both Emily and Anne were in advanced stages of consumption. Emily died just before Christmas, and Anne's death followed within six months.

During this year of family tragedy Charlotte had forced herself to go on with writing her next book. Emboldened by the incredible success of *Jane Eyre*, she had undertaken the new work with a more pretentious conception of the novelist's function. She had been so fascinated by *Vanity Fair* that she dedicated the second edition of *Jane Eyre* to Thackeray as "the first social regenerator of the day." In *Shirley* she followed his example by building the story around two contrasted heroines, by using them as the focus for a panoramic view of society, and even by adopting at times a satiric tone. She had imbibed from her father a prejudice against both High Churchmen and Dissenters, which prompted sarcastic digressions about effete curates and revival meetings. The claims of women's rights are debated lengthily instead of being implicit as in *Jane Eyre*. Already in *The Professor* she had revealed some awareness of the class conflicts that were brewing in the new industrial towns, only a few miles away from her moorland hamlet, and now she brought this theme into the center of her story. Again following the example of *Vanity Fair*, she went back thirty-five years for her time-setting, and studied old newspapers for details of the machine-wrecking Luddite riots.

This burden of social consciousness threatened to throw the book out of balance, especially as the second and by far the more interesting heroine did not appear until almost half way through. The original plan called for a tragic ending; but after the series of bereavements in her family Charlotte could not bring herself to inflict misery on her imagined characters and so she contrived a perfunctory happy conclusion. The intolerant moral judgments and the general distrust of beauty and pleasure give the book an almost repellent austerity; yet, in spite of these handicaps, it has power and its own kind of beauty, arising particularly from the second heroine, the outspoken and untamably independent Shirley Keeldar, who is a fairly faithful portrait of Emily Brontë, though she retains traces of an Angrian original. Unity of theme is provided by the contrast between the emotional, self-centered characters of the Brontë type — the two heroines and their lovers — and the impassive, worldly people around them. Even Robert Moore, though a successful businessman, is simply a new embodiment of the Byronic rebel. The exaltation of love in defiance of convention, the ecstatic communing with nature, the acceptance of pain as a concomitant of love, all set the story's dominant mood. But in spite of the romantic preference for those who obey the dictates of their feelings, Charlotte pays lip service to the new fetish of realism, warning her readers:

> Do you anticipate sentiment, and poetry, and reverie? Do you expect passion, and stimulus, and melodrama? Calm your expectations; reduce them to a lowly standard. Something real, cool, and solid lies before you; something unromantic as Monday morning. . . . The first dish set upon the table . . . shall be cold lentils and vinegar without oil; it shall be unleavened bread and bitter herbs, and no roast lamb.

Though the Brontës were the most gifted of the new novelists who emerged in 1847–48, they were not the only ones. The increased prestige of the novel made it a potent medium for influencing public opinion, and this attracted a band of writers with theories and with missions.

One of these earnest souls was Elizabeth Cleghorn Gaskell, the wife of a Unitarian minister in Manchester. After a happy, sheltered childhood in a Cheshire village she was horrified by the poverty and vice that she found in her husband's slum parish. She had no thought of writing fiction, however, until she was thirty-five, and then it was suggested by her husband as a possible antidote for her grief over the death of a baby son. Her first novel, *Mary Barton*, had a strong appeal through its warm sympathy and touches of humor, and thus made many people conscious of the underlying causes for unrest among the poor. This was 1848, when the country was terrified by an epidemic of revolutions on the Continent and the abortive Chartist uprising in England. Mrs. Gaskell's intention being "to give some utterance to the agony which, from time to time, convulses this dumb people; the agony of suffering without the sympathy of the happy," she slanted the story in favor of the laboring class. Like Dickens, however, she did not believe in organizations as a remedy for their troubles. The real villain of the story is the labor union, which in the denouement is disclosed as having compelled John Barton to murder the employer's son who had been making love to his daughter. The handling of the story is amateurish, falling back on melodramatic action to sustain interest, and sometimes condensing a crucial scene into flat exposition. As a social treatise it is invalidated by the author's naïve optimism: her thesis is simply that if everyone would ignore class distinctions and economic rivalries, the modern world could be perfectly happy, accepting the text that "we are all members one of another." This is symbolized at the close of the novel when the rich father of the murdered youth comes to the murderer's deathbed to forgive him.

Yet *Mary Barton* survives because Mrs. Gaskell had the essential power of creating characters who enlist the reader's emotional participation. They are not caricatures, and the author's kindness and intuitive understanding endow them with life. Harriet Martineau had been using fiction to reinforce her radical opinions ever since her nine volumes of *Illustrations of Political Economy* in 1832–34, followed by *Poor Laws and Paupers Illustrated* and *Illustrations of Taxation*. With characteristic candor, Miss Martineau used titles that could not be accused of disguising her propaganda purpose under a pretense of entertainment. Later Mrs. Trollope, in *Michael Armstrong*, had depicted the Manchester slums and factories with greater vigor than Mrs. Gaskell's; and Disraeli, in *Sybil*, had warned of the peril inherent in industrial strife, with clearer understanding of the basic issues. But Mrs. Gaskell was the first to regard these topics in the simple light of common humanity. Dickens expressed the opinion of many readers when he called it "a book that most profoundly affected and impressed me."

In the same year another author produced a first novel that emerged out of somewhat similar antecedents. Charles Kingsley, too, had enjoyed a tranquil childhood in the country, and discovered the plight of the poor through undertaking parochial duties, though in his case it was rural rather than industrial conditions that shocked him. The shy, stammering, and emotionally intense son of a clergyman, he had been so repelled by his parents' conventional piety that in boyhood he lost his respect for the Bible and devoted himself to geology and athletic sports. While an undergraduate at Cambridge, however, he fell in love with a devoutly High-Church young woman, who restored his Christian faith. Upon taking holy orders he became curate and afterwards rector at Eversley, an impoverished parish in Hampshire. The vice and ignorance that he found rampant there impelled him to organize schooling for the children and elementary measures for cleanliness and health.

Kingsley's reason was completely subordinated to his emotions. Impractical and impulsive, he formed passionate opinions on the basis of personal feeling, without regard for consistency. His reading of Carlyle shaped his belief in the nobility of work and in the spiritual essence immanent in the universe. His reading of Frederic Denison Maurice convinced him that Christianity has a pragmatic sanction by promoting happiness and physical welfare. Because he had to dissuade his sweetheart from entering an Anglican sisterhood before she would consent to marry him, he became prejudiced against asceticism and celibacy, regarding these as a major evil of the Roman Catholic faith. Because

the patron of his living refused to repair the rectory, he grew
fanatical about the selfishness of landlords and the imperative
need for good sanitation.

His first literary work was a poetic drama, *The Saint's Tragedy*,
an attack upon the ascetic ideal of Catholicism. Immediately after
it was published he plunged into the political crisis of the day and
wrote a series of "Letters to the Chartists" for a propaganda
paper, signing them "Parson Lot." While deploring violence,
he proclaimed his adherence to the cause, indeed insisting that
"my only quarrel with the Charter is that it does not go
far enough in reform." At the same time he was sitting up at
nights after his parochial duties to write a novel. *Yeast, or The
Thoughts, Sayings, and Doings of Lancelot Smith, Gentleman*
came out as an anonymous serial in *Fraser's Magazine* during the
second half of 1848.

It is an incoherent, vehement story. The title, *Yeast*, was
meant to suggest the social and intellectual ferment of the time,
and this was some justification for the lack of order in the book.
But mainly its strength and its weakness come from its being
a record of the author's personality and opinions. The ugly
hero and the theologically minded heroine are portraits of Mr.
and Mrs. Kingsley; the episode of her converting him from youthful skepticism is reproduced in full. The wealthy Lancelot
Smith shares Kingsley's enthusiasm for scientific inquiry and
for field sports, especially fox-hunting. Three varieties of landlords are used as the vehicle for an analysis of the causes for
agricultural misery, while the peasantry are idealized in a manly,
verse-writing gamekeeper. Alongside of the assault upon the
vested interests of the landowners, Kingsley vented his contempt
for the Tractarian movement in the character of the hero's
cousin Luke, a convert to Romanism.

The radicalism of the serial aroused disfavor to such an extent
that country squires began canceling their subscriptions to the
magazine, and the publisher begged Kingsley to hasten the conclusion. Three years elapsed before it was brought out in volume form. On the other hand, to many people it was stimulating
and inspiring. Worried young men found in it a sympathetic
record of their doubts, while sportsmen appreciated the strenuous action of the hunting scenes.

Yeast was not the only work of fiction that tried to come to grips with the controversies of the moment. James Anthony Froude, a friend of Kingsley's and soon afterwards his brother-in-law, wrote two fictional accounts of his split with the Tractarians and his becoming a freethinker. The first, *Shadows of the Clouds* (1847), was brief but belligerent; the second, *The Nemesis of Faith* (1849), was considered so blasphemous that one of Froude's Oxford colleagues burned a copy in front of the students in his lecture room, with the natural result that the book was more talked about than ever. In the intervening year John Henry Newman made his first attempt to defend himself from the attacks on his joining the Roman Church, in the form of a novel, *Loss and Gain,* which was intended to be a "suitable answer" to Froude's "wantonly and preposterously fanciful" book. Newman gave a picture of how the High Church movement had affected Oxford, and included many autobiographical details in the portrayal of the hero, Charles Reding.

Of Froude's and Newman's books it is enough to say that they serve to induce a more favorable opinion of *Yeast.* In some passages Kingsley did show his potentialities as a writer of fiction by vivid descriptions of setting and vigorous movement of narrative. The whole group of books, however, incompetent though they were in technique, contributed to the development of the novel by dealing seriously with major topics of immediate concern. The conflicts inherent in social change are valid subjects for fiction, and England was going through a social change more fundamental and rapid than any had ever been. People interested in ideas began to regard novels with more respect. Disraeli and Mrs. Gaskell and Kingsley and the others brought fiction into closer relationship with the dominant forces of their time.

X I

The Domestic Scene

(1850 – 1855)

THE PRINCIPAL NOVELISTS now were pushed forward by the pressure of active competition as well as by their own accumulated experience. The market for fiction had expanded to unprecedented dimensions, not only as people in the upper intellectual strata were attracted by the sophistication of Thackeray or by the political zeal of Disraeli and Kingsley, but also as a vast semi-literate public was being catered to with crude but highly readable narratives. The best-selling novelist of the forties and fifties was not Dickens but George W. M. Reynolds, a Chartist agitator and editor of a Radical newspaper, whose lurid tales came out in penny parts. He wrote dozens of cheap novels with such titles as *Wagner, the Wehr-Wolf* and *The Slaves of England* (*No. 1, The Seamstress*). Never quite crossing the line into pornography, his *Mysteries of London* (1845–46), imitated from Eugène Sue's *Mystères de Paris,* combined salaciousness and brutality with diatribes against the aristocracy and the clergy.

About the same time, broad farce brought immense popularity to the novels of Henry Cockton, *Valentine Vox, the Ventriloquist* (1840) and *Sylvester Sound, the Somnambulist* (1844). Imitators of Dickens formed a sort of "Cockney School" of fiction, the first of them being Samuel Warren, whose *Ten Thousand a Year* (1841) tells the adventures of a draper's assistant who temporarily inherits a fortune and ends as a lunatic. In the same vein of crude comedy and sensationalism are the works of Albert Smith, *The Adventures of Mr. Ledbury* (1844), *The Fortunes of the Scattergood Family* (1845), and *The Struggles and Adventures of Christopher Tadpole* (1848). One of the incentives driving Dickens to undertake new experiments was the need of keeping far in advance of these plodding disciples.

The expansion of the market was accompanied by growth in all the commercial machinery of fiction-distribution. When the publishing firm of Chapman & Hall waxed rich on the profits of serials by Dickens, Lever, and others, new firms such as Bradbury & Evans and Smith, Elder & Co. challenged their priority. Low-priced magazines like the *Family Herald* serialized stories that were irreproachably moral and fulsomely sentimental. The bookselling trade profited, Mudie's and other circulating libraries flourished, novels were widely advertised and reviewed in a growing assortment of literary periodicals.

The better English novelists, aware that they were not merely inventing stories to entertain casual readers but were also shaping a significant new genre of literary art, paid more attention to the parallel development across the Channel. Most English readers knew something of the crudely realistic novels of Parisian bourgeois life that were written by Paul de Kock in the twenties and later; but few had heard of Stendhal, though *Le Rouge et le noir* dated from 1830. Another name, however, eventually set up impressive reverberations. In 1833 Honoré de Balzac had turned from romanticism to realism with *Eugénie Grandet,* and in 1842 he formed the grandiose scheme of linking a huge series of novels into *La Comédie humaine,* a panorama of contemporary French life. By the time he died in 1850 he had proved the feasibility of using novels as documents for social observation and analysis. And while he was formulating a new concept of realism, George Sand was attracting quite as much attention by her uninhibited novels of passion. Beginning with *Indiana* in 1832, she fascinated and shocked the world with *Lélia, Consuelo, La Comtesse de Rudolstadt,* and other amorphous but fiery stories that proclaimed her creed of emotional independence for women.

The majority of English people were probably content with second-hand opinions that Balzac and George Sand were "immoral" and "disgusting"; but the cultivated minority, accustomed to keeping abreast of French literature, read their books as a matter of course. Thackeray's disillusioned survey of society certainly owed' something to Balzac; specific resemblances have been observed between *Vanity Fair* and *La Cousine Bette,* which appeared in France the previous year. And though the Brontës would have felt outraged by any comparison with the sensual George Sand, their novels had an affinity with hers in their preoccupation with love and their ardor for feminine emancipation.

The new themes and methods, both English and foreign, the cheapening of his early manner by obtuse imitators, the improved criticism of fiction, and his own compulsive need to achieve deeper understanding of man and society, all brought Dickens to the fullness of his achievement with *David Copperfield,* which began serial publication in May, 1849. It did not contain as much crusading against specific abuses as most of his previous books; but his preoccupation with the problems of opportunity and social prejudice was under the surface throughout. The examination of the English class structure that he had begun in *Dombey and Son* was developed through the handicaps faced by David in getting an education, the ugly yet somehow pathetic schemes of Uriah Heep to rise above his base origin, the helplessness of Micawber with his nimble mind and his lack of practical sense, the gentlemanly arrogance of Steerforth, the snobbery of the Spenlows, and the honest fidelity of the illiterate Peggotty family.

Dickens had thought at one time of writing his autobiography and had drafted some pages dealing with his childhood. When he gave up the project, he transferred the material into the life of David Copperfield. By employing the first-personal point of view he conveyed a stronger impression of unity and probability than in his preceding novels. Though children had figured prominently as characters in *Oliver Twist, The Old Curiosity*

Shop, and *Dombey and Son,* this was his first attempt to enter
a child's mind and trace the growth of his understanding. Under
the guise of his fictitious narrator he was able to reveal the
bitterest experiences of his own early days, which he could
never bring himself to confide fully even to his closest friends.
His humiliation at his father's sojourn in the debtors' prison,
his heartsick disappointment in being denied regular schooling,
his loathing of his months of drudgery in the blacking warehouse, his grudge against the adults responsible for inflicting
these miseries upon him, all appeared in the life of the child
David and grasped the reader's sympathy with a peculiar intensity that came from the personal emotions that were being
vented. Another suppressed passage in his life provided the
tragicomic chapters about David's love for Dora Spenlow, which
reproduced Charles Dickens's adolescent bondage to the flirtatious Maria Beadnell. His struggles as a law clerk and a shorthand
reporter also figured in the novel. All these first-hand experiences, however, were assimilated into a completely invented
plot. His practice in his seven preceding novels saved him
from the pitfall of reproducing actual persons and episodes too
literally. Micawber had many traits in common with the author's
father; but he was both less and more than a portrait of John
Dickens. By being simplified and magnified he took on an im-
mortal identity of his own. In short, Dickens's technique of
characterization by humours was still rife in *David Copperfield,*
and had reached its highest pitch of creativeness. Micawber immediately became the standard specimen of the incorrigible
optimist, and Uriah Heep of the fawning hypocrite.

In making David tell the story in person, Dickens incurred a
more difficult psychological task than he had ever faced before.
David is not a particularly complex or percipient young man;
but there is real subtlety in the tracing of his emergence from
childhood through youth into maturity. His early idealization
of Steerforth reluctantly yields to the admission that this model
of the Byronic hero is actually a selfish cad, and that the true
paragon of friendship is the ridiculous, loyal Tommy Traddles;
and in the same way his idealization of Dora gives place by
degrees to recognition that she is shallow and silly, and that
the truly lovable woman is the quietly competent Agnes Wickfield.

The autobiographical method also obliged Dickens to restrain the more florid flights of rhetoric in his style; and the authorial comments that annoy some readers in his other books are no longer censurable when they form part of the hero's retrospect of his own career. Whether or not the more conversational tone was due wholly to the requirement of simulated reminiscences, it appeared to Thackeray like a deliberate adoption of his manner, and he predicted somewhat complacently that *"David Copperfield* will be improved by taking a lesson from *Vanity Fair."*

Thackeray's own second novel, *The History of Pendennis*, ran its serial course side by side with *David Copperfield*, and the coincidental resemblances between them were amazingly close. Each was a *Bildungsroman* based squarely upon the author's own life, and recording a young man's education, his successive love affairs, and his adoption of authorship as a profession. The functions of various characters in the two novels can be easily equated: Steerforth and Warrington, Micawber and Major Pendennis, Agnes Wickfield and Laura Bell. These obvious parallels, however, serve to emphasize the differences between the two authors. Dickens devotes one-third of the story to David's childhood, whereas Thackeray starts when Arthur Pendennis is leaving school and preparing to enter university. Thackeray devotes many chapters to a detailed satiric picture of London publishers and hack writers, containing recognizable portraits of people he had known when beginning his own career. As the hero's mentor, the worldly Major Pendennis is an antithesis of the feckless Mr. Micawber. The love affairs are also wide apart. Fanny Bolton, in *Pendennis*, resembles Dickens's Little Em'ly in social rank, but plays a less prominent part in the story, and Pendennis's relations with her stand somewhere midway between Copperfield's and Steerforth's with Em'ly. Pendennis's abortive engagement to Blanche Amory occupies the same place in his maturing process as David's marriage with Dora, and both girls are selfish and affected; but otherwise the clever coquette is totally unlike the immature "child-wife." Indeed, by ironical chance, Dora is more like Thackeray's ineffectual young wife than is anyone in Pendennis's series of involvements with the opposite sex. Pen's first affair of the heart, with Emily Costigan, affords some of the most amusing scenes in the book; and for a Dickensian comparison it is necessary to go back to *Nicholas Nickleby* to find an equally comic picture of an itinerant dramatic company.

The two novels use elements of intrigue and mystery to keep the action moving; but the scandal in the Clavering family is more worldly and less implausible than either the abduction of Em'ly or Uriah Heep's plot to gain control over the Wickfields. It is only in the typical Victorian heroines, Agnes and Laura, waiting patiently in the background to reward the heroes at the end with domestic tranquility, that the two novels intermittently inhabit the same world.

Thackeray started writing *Pendennis* with the intention of exposing the real nature of a young man with complete frankness. He drew an allegorical cover design in which his hero stands irresolute: on one side is a luscious mermaid attended by baby fauns, on the other a respectable wife and children. There was as much personal confession in the record of Pen's conflicting impulses as there had been in Dickens's account of David's early sufferings; the difference is that Dickens's attitude was unequivocal — he abominated the selfish people who impeded David's rise — whereas Thackeray, himself poised between the worldly and the domestic, portrayed attractive features of both. Though he had no doubt which side would eventually win, he meant to reveal Pen's dissipations without reserve.

The first half of the book, however, necessarily showed him as a boyish idealist, as Thackeray looked back with indulgent irony on his own early self; and by the time the story should move into a lewd phase the author modified his plan. Disheartened by the accusations of misanthropy that were hurled at *Vanity Fair*, he wanted to prove that he did not divide all human beings into two classes — knaves and fools. Besides, he suffered a dangerous illness at the mid-point of writing the novel, and the brush with death had a sobering effect. The tone of the story therefore changed perceptibly, so that Pen's involvements with Blanche and Fanny, and his participation in the shady dealings of Clavering and Altamont, were far from vicious.

Nevertheless, Thackeray felt frustrated by his failure to produce a realistic work that could rank with Fielding's. In a preface that he added when the serial issues reached their end, he grumbled:

Since the author of "Tom Jones" was buried, no writer of fiction among us has been permitted to depict to his utmost power a MAN. We must drape him, and give him a certain conventional simper. Society will not tolerate the Natural in our Art. Many ladies have remonstrated and subscribers left me, because, in the course of the story, I described a young man resisting and affected by temptation. My object was to say that he had the passions to feel, and the manliness and generosity to overcome them. . . . A little more frankness than is customary has been attempted in this story; with no bad desire on the writer's part, it is hoped, and with no ill consequence to any reader. If truth is not always pleasant, at any rate truth is best.

These almost despondent words initiated a debate over realism in fiction that was to rage for half a century.

The new vogue for social and domestic analysis was proved by the adherence of Bulwer-Lytton, always prompt to follow the trends of public preference. Three years previously his *Lucretia, or The Children of the Night*, based upon the career of the forger and poisoner Thomas Wainewright, had reverted to the type of crime story that he had written a dozen years before; and it provoked the same attacks for exerting a bad moral influence through arousing sympathy for a criminal. Though Lytton defended himself in a vigorous pamphlet, he turned for his next novel to the safer ground of a historical romance, *Harold, or The Last of the Saxon Kings*. But already, several years before these two, he had begun working desultorily on *The Caxtons, a Family Picture*, which was a departure from all his previous styles, and which came out as a serial in *Blackwood's Magazine* in 1848–49. As he did not attach his name to it, there were various wild guesses as to the authorship. Just as Thackeray had affiliated himself with Fielding, Lytton unexpectedly affiliated himself with Sterne, and produced the only book that ever succeeded in capturing something of the flavor of *Tristram Shandy*. Pisistratus Caxton tells the story of his life, and the early part contains many recollections of Lytton's boyhood. As soon as he grows up, Pisistratus rebels against the petty affairs of his family and seeks adventure in Australia. The life there was described so pleasantly that the book was credited with doing much to give the English public a favorable impression of the new colony. Nevertheless, after recouping the family fortunes Pisistratus returns to England, having learned the lesson "that, whatever our wanderings, our happiness will always be found in a narrow compass, and amidst the objects more immediately within our reach."

The announced purpose of the story was "to imply the influences of Home upon the conduct and career of Youth"; but it treated this serious topic with whimsical humor, which had not been foreshadowed by either the supercilious wit of *Pelham* or the solemn gloom of *Zanoni*. Lytton admitted to a friend that "the art employed in *The Caxtons* is a very simple one, and within the reach of all. It is just that of creating agreeable emotions. Now to do this, we have only to abandon attempts at many subtle and deep emotions, which produce uneasiness and pain, and see that the smile is without sarcasm and the tears without bitterness. That is one branch of art and rarely fails to be popular."

Further evidence of the prevailing taste was the success of *Frank Fairlegh*, by Frank E. Smedley, which began as a magazine serial in 1846–47, with the title "Scenes from the Life of a Private Pupil," then was reissued in monthly parts, and finally came out in volume form in 1850. Smedley was a malformed cripple from infancy; and the life of action, sport, and comic pranks, from which he was debarred in the real world, was idealized in this story and the two that followed it, *Lewis Arundel* and *Harry Coverdale's Courtship*. He retained the conventional types of haughty heroes and fragile heroines, just when Dickens was abandoning them; but otherwise his three novels give a sufficiently plausible picture of the healthy, complacent upper classes in mid-Victorian days — clergy, university students, landed gentry, all comfortably ensconced in a permanent pattern of fishing and fox-hunting on country estates, dining in town houses and going to the theater and riding in the Park, or varying the routine with leisurely tours on the Continent.

The geniality of Smedley's outlook is conspicuous by contrast with the current novel of the veteran Surtees, which dealt with a similar environment in an utterly different mood. *Mr. Sponge's Sporting Tour* ran in the *New Monthly Magazine* in 1849–50 and then in monthly parts before achieving book form. It was more widely acclaimed than any of his previous books. His new hero, "Soapey" Sponge, is as vivid a comic creation as Jorrocks; but Surtees acknowledged the ascendancy of social morality by announcing that "the author will be glad if it serves to put the rising generation on their guard against specious, promiscuous acquaintance, and trains them on to the noble sport of hunting, to the exclusion of its mercenary, illegitimate offshoots." Surtees' method of carrying out this cautionary function was to create a complete gallery of blackguards. The rascally hero, however, is so amusing and buoyant that he wins the reader's affection and apparently the author's too. A sort of male equivalent to Becky Sharp, Soapey flourishes by imposing on the stupidity and egoism of respectable people. The episodic construction gives little indication that Surtees had gained any of the new awareness of technique, and his mingling of farce and violence is still insensitive, as evidenced by the ending of the story with a leading character killed in a steeplechase.

The irresponsible picture of English life drawn by Surtees and Smedley is worlds away from the depressing grimness and zealous reforming spirit of Kingsley's second work of fiction. Entitled *Alton Locke, Tailor and Poet,* and published anonymously in 1850, it was ostensibly the autobiography of a self-educated radical propagandist. It closely followed the career of a living contemporary, Thomas Cooper, who taught himself Greek, Latin, and Hebrew while a shoemaker's apprentice, and later became a schoolmaster and then a journalist, taking part in Chartist agitations. While spending two years in jail for organizing a strike, Cooper wrote a political epic; but later his revolutionary fanaticism waned and he turned to lecturing on history and educational theory, whereby he became known to Kingsley, who undertook to wean him from his religious skepticism.

The poverty and sectarian bigotry of Alton Locke's childhood in the London slums, the squalor of the sweatshop where he works, are conveyed with a mingling of blunt simplicity and rhapsodical emotion that sounds plausibly like the style in which a proletarian poet might write. The ideas and mannerisms of Carlyle are conspicuous throughout, and Carlyle personally served as the model for Sandy Mackaye, a Scottish bookseller who gives Alton his first lessons in social consciousness. Kingsley's attempts to convert Cooper are reproduced in the scenes between Alton and Dean Winnstay, a broad-minded clergyman.

The heroine is a beautiful and saintly countess who delivers orations upon human brotherhood.

The story has power because it sprang from Kingsley's blazing excitement about major problems of the time. We may not believe in the coincidence by which the hero's rich, heartless cousin catches fatal typhus from an overcoat infected in the pest-holes where his own employees work; and we may not be deeply moved by the tritely pathetic ending, when the heroine dies of consumption and the hero — emigrating to Texas to start a new life — dies also before he can disembark at Galveston; but we are compelled to respond to the despair of the Chartists after the collapse of their final uprising, and we are nauseated by the description of the foul purlieus of Bermondsey, which Kingsley derived directly from current newspaper reports.

It is interesting to compare *Alton Locke* with another pseudo-autobiography of a self-taught genius, which was published a year later, and which offered a different view of the life of the poor. This was *Lavengro*, by George Borrow, a fantastic vagabond and self-trained philologist. The son of an army sergeant, he spent his childhood in encampments throughout the British Isles, and became fascinated with the gypsies. In addition to learning their language he picked up some thirty others, and published translations of Danish ballads, Russian poems, and Turkish humor. As a pretext for rambling in out-of-the way regions he became a salesman for the Bible Society in Russia, Spain, Portugal, and North Africa; and he gained some literary renown with *The Bible in Spain* (1843). Then at the age of forty-eight he brought out *Lavengro*, after working on it intermittently for ten years.

It is an easy paradox to say that *The Bible in Spain* claims to be a travel book but contains some invented material that should be termed fiction, whereas *Lavengro* claims to be a novel but consists mainly of real experience. The problem of the dividing line between factual narrative and fiction is well illustrated by Borrow's works. A man whose emotional reactions were violent and who dramatized himself throughout his life, he naturally adorned the account of his travels with breathless adventures and glowing descriptions which probably improved upon the truth. It is obvious, too, that *Lavengro* and its sequel, *The Romany Rye* (1857), adhere closely to the facts of Borrow's career and seem to lack artistic selectivity. Having an old-fashioned contempt for novels, which he considered shallow and frivolous, he did not claim this category for his pair of books. Instead, he asserted in the preface to *Lavengro* that "I have endeavored to describe a dream, partly of study, partly of adventure." He announced also that "amongst the many things attempted in this book is the encouragement of charity, and free and genial manners, and the exposure of humbug."

Yet if *Lavengro* and *The Romany Rye* are considered together as a unit they do prove to fall within the tradition of the English novel. They are perhaps the last genuine example of the picaresque. Borrow even reverted to such a primitive practice as inserting the life stories of six characters whom Lavengro encounters in his wanderings. He originally planned the work, undoubtedly, as straight autobiography; but he was an admirer of Defoe, and as early as 1844 he was mentioning it as being "in the Robinson Crusoe style." The major difference from Defoe is that Borrow was a bundle of ferocious prejudices, and he perpetually digressed into diatribes against Roman Catholics, radicals, and other bugbears, or into paeans of praise for tinkers and prize-fighters, instead of remaining an impartial recorder. His factual material included portraits (sometimes libelous) of people he had known, ranging from Sir Richard Phillips the publisher to Thurtell the murderer.

What transforms the hodge-podge of crotchets and anecdotes into a novel is the steady unfolding of the hero's personality. It is as veritable a *Bildungsroman* as *David Copperfield* or *Pendennis*. Indeed, some of Lavengro's experiences as a young hack writer in London are comparable with those of Dickens's and Thackeray's heroes. Lavengro, however, learns his best lessons not from urban intellectuals but from gypsy vagabonds and from "the wind on the heath." The characters and episodes fall into a symbolic design, with the gypsies representing the hedonistic life of sensation, the evangelist and the Jesuit representing types of religious dogma, and the narrator finding his particular key to the riddle of existence in philology. Thus the pair of books have a unifying structure: under the apparently casual surface there is an integration of recurrent themes and interlocking situations.

A long ramble across England had served as an adequate

skeleton for notable earlier novels, from *The Pilgrim's Progress* through *Joseph Andrews* to *The Old Curiosity Shop*; but it seemed archaic in 1851, the era of railways and industrial cities. The basic reason, however, why *Lavengro* found little favor with the critics was its unmitigated romanticism. The super-human physical and mental powers of the hero, the independence and passion of the "child of nature" who is the heroine, the uninhibited indulgence in emotion, the lyrical rhapsodies over nature — all these qualities put it in the category of the other underestimated masterpiece of that epoch, *Wuthering Heights*.

More congenial to the current taste was Mrs. Gaskell's second work of fiction, though it also was so rudimentary in plot and so closely based on reminiscence that it can be admitted only marginally to the genre of the novel. Dickens, having launched an ambitious weekly paper, *Household Words*, had been so favorably impressed by *Mary Barton* that he invited Mrs. Gaskell to be a regular contributor. Not conceived as a serial story, her group of sketches of life in a drowsy village appeared intermittently between December, 1851, and May, 1853. When issued in book form as *Cranford*, there proved to be a frail thread of continuity; but the story's chief claim to artistic unity was in its atmosphere. Mrs. Gaskell recreated with loving detail the society of Knutsford as she had known it in her childhood. It is the most placid book in English fiction: Jane Austen's novels, with a similar social milieu, are energetic by comparison. Instead of Miss Austen's acerbity, Mrs. Gaskell manifests only gentle humor in portraying the impoverished spinsters and the dictators of rural society, whose stratagems provide the mild trickle of action. The book lives because its sympathetic insight into everyday predicaments never degenerates into sentimentality and because its events, trivial though they are, capture something of the pathos inherent in ordinary people. Its special significance in 1853 is as a symptom of the triumph of domestic tranquility as a fictional mood.

Even Charles Lever departed at this time from his Irish eccentrics and swashbuckling adventurers, and devoted his next serials to what he called "the quiet homely narrative style of German romance writers." *The Daltons, or Three Roads in Life* (1851–52) was written with unwonted care as to consistency of details, and many of the characters were modeled upon people whom the author knew. This was followed by *The Dodd Family Abroad*, in which Lever fell back on the antiquated epistolary method to give an amusing account of a typical British family on the grand tour, with a minimum of plot and a maximum of sensible comment on the customs of the various foreign countries. Lever had now settled down in Florence, and had acquired something like Thackeray's cosmopolitan perspective toward the snobbery and parochialism of his compatriots.

Thackeray himself, on the other hand, was unwilling to be identified solely as an observer of contemporary *mores,* and he broke away by turning to historical romance. He had reached a point of financial security that enabled him to complete a whole novel before it went to press, instead of writing installments with the printer's devil waiting at the door; and consequently he was able to plan this one more coherently.

As he had recently been delivering a series of lectures on "The English Humorists of the Eighteenth Century," his affection for that era was intensified by the research entailed in preparing them. He became so saturated with the Augustan age, not only with its events and personalities but even with its language and literary techniques, that he felt as though he had been "living in the last century for weeks past — all day that is — going at night as usual into the present age." In *The History of Henry Esmond* he undertook the experiment of writing a pseudo-autobiography, which meant that he had to imitate the eighteenth-century style throughout. He had already done this on a smaller scale ten years before in *Barry Lyndon;* but that had been merely an ingenious *pastiche* in the manner of Fielding. With *Esmond* he had the harder task of revealing the whole character of a complex, moody, intelligent man, while at the same time sustaining the historical accuracy of every detail and phrase.

In spite of the remoteness of the time-setting and the outer circumstances, the book was in one sense more intimately personal than anything he had yet written. *Pendennis* had followed the outlines of his earlier life, but *Esmond* revealed an emotional crisis that he was enduring even while he wrote. His devotion to Mrs. Brookfield, which had already colored some of his attitudes in *Vanity Fair*, had now moved into a more painful phase. William Brookfield had finally protested against Jane's intimacy with Thackeray, and as a faithful wife she had accepted the ban upon their friendship. Thackeray found relief for his anguish by depicting in Lady Castlewood another woman who was so loyal to her marriage vows that she would not admit even to herself that she might love someone else. And as in *Vanity Fair*, Thackeray was able to remove the obnoxious husband and eventually reward the true lovers with marriage, an outcome that was impossible in the real-life situation. To avoid too close a parallel with his own plight, he did not depict Esmond as also fettered by the existence of a wife. Instead he established other barriers, in that Esmond was eight years younger than Lady Castlewood and believed himself to be hopelessly in love with her fascinating daughter, Beatrix. Like *Vanity Fair*, therefore, the story is built upon the contrast between two women of opposite types, one gentle and compliant, the other selfish and brilliantly clever. In Beatrix, Thackeray created one of the most captivating young women in all fiction. And he did not succumb to the temptation to sentimentalize the conclusion by letting her finally respond to Esmond's love.

Many readers have been disturbed by this central theme, either because they find something psychologically unhealthy in the mixture of maternal and sexual love that Lady Castlewood feels for Henry, or else simply because a love affair with a widow eight years older than the man appears to be unromantic. In rebuttal it may be pointed out that the dividing line between sexual and parental love can seldom be absolutely drawn, and further that Thackeray was intentionally demonstrating what he considered to be the plain fact that domestic affection based upon compatibility is superior to the kind of ultra-romantic idealization exemplified in Esmond's infatuation with Beatrix. Since historical fiction was ordinarily the particular domain of the romantic concept of love, Thackeray's defiance of this convention was part of his campaign for realism.

This story of emotional cross-purposes is deployed against a richly elaborated background of English history for twenty years covering the reigns of William III and Queen Anne. The battles in the war with France, the political intrigues in England, and the literary coterie of London are all included in Esmond's experiences. Several of the incidents are based on real occurrences, notably Viscount Castlewood's duel with Lord Mohun; but the climax of the political action, when James Stuart comes secretly to England in hope of seizing the throne when Queen Anne dies, has no historical foundation.

Most of the leading public figures of the time are introduced, and Thackeray has sometimes been censured for bias in certain of his portrayals. The belittlement of Swift is connected with Thackeray's dislike for the dean's black misanthropy, and the unflattering view of Marlborough can be explained because one of the author's collateral ancestors was General Webb, whose quarrel with the duke is incorporated into the story. Though such judgments may be unfair as strict historical verdicts, they add to the authentic effect, for it was an age of strong partisanship, and Esmond could not represent his time without having prejudices.

Primarily the distinction of the book depends upon its central character. Esmond is modest, reticent, melancholy almost to morbidity; and yet Thackeray succeeds in having him reveal his own virtues of loyalty, unselfishness, and self-respect without making him seem either a prig or a hypocrite. With his sensitive honor and his abhorrence of pretension, Esmond demonstrates Thackeray's obsessive concern over the attributes of the true gentleman. It may be conceded that here he has come at least as near to depicting a perfect gentleman as Richardson did in Grandison.

Insofar as technical skill is concerned, *Esmond* is certainly Thackeray's masterpiece. And criticism is now tending toward a similar opinion regarding *Bleak House,* the novel of Dickens that was written at the same time. Apart from the peculiar choice of title, which has little relevance to the main scenes and themes of the book, it is an amazing display of stylistic virtuosity and architectural design. Though published in the customary monthly parts, it was planned with such consummate care that every detail in the vast picture falls into exact relationship with all the others.

On the basis of plausibility, this feature of *Bleak House* is open to objection. The loose ends and superfluous characters in Dickens's earlier novels are closer to real experience than this controlled mosaic of interlocking pieces. But the inherent improbability is cunningly concealed, chiefly by the fact that the *dramatis personae* are so numerous and so diversified that through much of the book they seem to have no possible relationship with each other, and by the time their mutual dependencies are revealed the reader's imagination has submitted to the author's spell and cannot rebel against it. At the end, when we look back and realize the ingenuity of the whole structure, we are too deeply gratified by the sense of unity and pattern to be capable of protesting that real life is never so tidy. We enjoy the illusion of god-like superiority that discovers a tight web of cause and effect beneath the apparent chaos of daily affairs.

It is for this reason, as well as because it deals with the actual solving of mysterious crimes and contains a character who is a police investigator, that *Bleak House* has been termed the first detective novel. Indeed, it is two detective novels merged into one. The main plot line concerns the unveiling of Lady Dedlock's hidden past and the identity of her vanished husband. In this investigation the lawyer, Mr. Tulkinghorn, plays the main detective role, though he is abetted by half-a-dozen other characters who for their own reasons are digging into corners of the same complicated mystery. Then, when Tulkinghorn is murdered, the plain-clothes officer, Inspector Bucket, takes over, and practices the patient analysis of clues which makes this the archetypal detective story. The reader becomes pleasurably aware that every detail conceals some hint of the facts, and he begins to match his wits against the author's in foreseeing the outcome. No previous novelist had realized how readers can be held in ever-mounting suspense through a confusing multiplicity of evidence, while the author manipulates his array of clues so elusively as to deceive the eye.

The social diversity of the multifarious characters contributes more to the book than a mysterious plot. They also constitute an unsurpassed panorama of the English social scene. Dickens in his personal life had by this time become sufficiently intimate with people of rank to venture to include them in his story. Sir Leicester Dedlock has infinitely more verisimilitude than Sir Mulberry Hawk in *Nicholas Nickleby*. The Dedlocks and their country estate and their fashionable friends belong to the social level which Thackeray customarily depicted. Sir Leicester is less a caricature and more an authentic specimen of a gentleman than Sir Pitt Crawley. And in its range downward to the very dregs of society *Bleak House* displays abysses of degradation and ignorance that Thackeray knew nothing of.

Like *Vanity Fair*, too, this novel of Dickens has neither a hero nor a single heroine, but is constructed around two major feminine figures, Lady Dedlock and Esther, the hardened woman of the world and the gentle denizen of the home. Certainly none of the masculine characters can lay claim to be the hero. Esther's lover is a shadowy figure who appears in only a few chapters. Richard Carstone seems cast for the hero's role in the early part, but his degeneration into psychopathic frustration is one of the book's best tragic components. John Jarndyce, with his kindliness and insight, remains, like Thackeray's Major Dobbin, a background figure who is too good to be quite human. Many of the secondary characters exemplify the author's pet phobias. Mrs. Jellyby and her henchmen are a satire upon impractical welfare projects; the Smallweed family are a horribly comic instance of the utilitarian ideal in education; Mr. Chadband is another specimen of the hypocritical evangelists first represented by Stiggins in *Pickwick*.

The wide range of Dickens's survey enabled him to imply much about the transformation that was occurring in the class system. This comes to a focus in the interview between Sir Leicester, the ultra-conservative exponent of the landowning aristocracy, with its feudal sense of privilege and its rigid ideal of family honor, and the newly rich industrialist, Rouncewell. Proof of Dickens's maturity is that he represents both of them sympathetically while yet showing that their principles are irreconcilable. The significance is emphasized by the fact that Rouncewell's mother is Sir Leicester's housekeeper, a family retainer of the type that was becoming obsolete. A further dimension of irony has developed since it has been discovered that Mrs. Rouncewell is a portrait of Dickens's own grandmother.

This situation is but one of several that probe into the transition from a romantic to a materialistic ideology. In offering two of his case histories Dickens incurred some censure by portraying eminent contemporaries. Hitherto the real people who had served him as models had been his own relations and other obscure individuals whom he happened to know; but now Lawrence Boythorn was drawn openly from Walter Savage Landor, and Harold Skimpole was an equally accurate picture of Leigh Hunt. These two men were the last survivors of the great generation of romantic poets, and their counterparts in *Bleak House* both in their different ways illustrate the defeat of romantic individualism by the conformist pressures of the Victorian age. Boythorn wages stubborn but futile battle against convention, whether by his boisterous manners or by his defiance of magistrates; Skimpole evades responsibility by neglecting to earn a living. The use of Landor as a model was not obnoxious, since Boythorn is made lovable as well as absurd; but the reflection upon Hunt was undeniably cruel, particularly because Skimpole finally behaves not merely foolishly but unscrupulously. In defense of Dickens it can be insisted that a fictitious character may derive traits of manner from a real person without becoming factually identical with him; but an ethical problem still remains in the fact that Hunt had been an enthusiastic friend to Dickens when the support of an influential critic was of great help in the young writer's early success; and Hunt was grieved by what he considered a betrayal. Two basic dilemmas of every novelist are here illustrated: must realism be confined to observation of individual cases? and, if so, does the compulsion of artistic creation take precedence over gratitude and other gentlemanly standards?

This novel marked a major change in Dickens's social consciousness. A concern with the underlying reasons for inequity and poverty instead of with surface phenomena had begun to appear in *Dombey and Son;* but in *Bleak House* for the first time Dickens based his book's whole fabric overtly upon what he considered a cankerous evil in the social system. In doing so, he selected one that would shock many of his contemporaries profoundly. Englishmen were willing to admit that their political parties and their charitable institutions and even their business economy were vulnerable to criticism; but the traditional superiority of English justice was sacrosanct. Yet Dickens aimed his full barrage at the Court of Chancery, a cornerstone of English law. His smattering of legal training enabled him to cite specific examples of the court's incompetence and to sketch the whole inhuman mechanism of litigation with deadly precision.

This theme provides a second structural framework for the story. Not only are all the characters somehow involved in the unraveling of Lady Dedlock's past; also they are all held fast in the tentacles of the Chancery Court. The confident young heirs whose lives are blighted with disappointment, the old litigants driven to madness and suicide, the myriad of lawyers and officials who batten upon the interminable cases, the fetid slums that are administered under court authority, all add up to a horrifying indictment of the Chancery organization.

In addition to its unity of both plot and theme, *Bleak House* is extraordinary in its style. Each of the principal settings is invested with a distinctive atmosphere. The opening chapter is a descriptive *tour de force*, with its general picture of London wrapped in fog and then the focus on the law courts at the heart of the obscurity. This symbolic use of the fog is paralleled by the rain that serves as the keynote of the scenes at Chesney Wold, by the allegorical ceiling of Tulkinghorn's chambers, by the cluttered darkness of Krook's rag-and-bone shop, and by the polluted decay of "Tom-All-Alone's," which rivals the Bermondsey slum in *Alton Locke*. Throughout the book recurrent phrases and metaphors mark the interwoven texture of motifs and clues.

The most astonishing feature, however, is that parts of the story are presented as the personal narrative of Esther Summerson. The reader is not warned of the mingling of individual with universal point of view, either when it first occurs or at the points where the viewpoint shifts back and forth; there are no transitional phrases, and even the chapter titles seldom give a hint. And the undertaking is rendered all the more hazardous by the author's obligation to assume the manner and outlook of an unsophisticated girl. Complete success in the attempt was impossible; Esther's innocent revelations of her own unselfishness and modesty are bound to sound insincere. Neverthless, the mild serenity of her reports and the massive power of the scenes that are presented impersonally heighten each other. Dickens almost achieves his ambitious purpose of deriving the best advantage from both techniques — the immediacy of personal observation and the insight of the omniscient interpreter. The use of the present tense throughout the omniscient scenes makes them seem to be happening while we read, in contrast with the tranquil backward gaze of Esther's reminiscences. Only a master novelist at the height of his power could carry off such a venture with so much bravura.

During the same months that *Bleak House* was coming out

serially, Bulwer-Lytton's latest work was running in *Blackwood's;*
and it too had as an underlying theme the transfer of privilege
from the hereditary landowners to the new business class. Its
peculiar title, *My Novel,* is explained by its being supposedly
written by Pisistratus Caxton, the hero of Lytton's preceding
book; and members of the Caxton family are introduced in an
initial chapter to each division of the story, in Shandean discussions of the characters and action as Pisistratus creates them.
Though it is an ingenious device, its aristic validity is questionable. Like a *trompe l'oeil* painting, which uses tricks of perspective to make the picture appear to project beyond the
limits of the canvas, it gives an illusion that the Caxtons are
actual people, existing outside the novel in which they had been
major figures; but on the other hand it calls attention to the
author's inventive function in the story in hand. Perhaps it is
chiefly significant as revealing a psychological quirk that tends
to develop in a novelist as he comes closer to real life and trans-
mutes more of his past experience into fiction: he becomes
fond of his invented characters and these beings take on an
independent identity and refuse to vanish from his mind at
the end of a book. Balzac used this as a method for making
his series of novels seem like an actual transcript of current
events, and Thackeray was constantly transferring characters
from one story to another, even to the extent of introducing
people in *Esmond* as ancestors of others who figured in *Vanity
Fair* and *Pendennis.*

The plot of *My Novel* is somewhat less tenuous than that of
The Caxtons, but still the main purpose is to depict what is
stated in the subtitle as "Varieties in English Life," and especially
to vindicate the upper class against the strictures of radical
authors. Mr. Caxton remarks:

> "I really think that while, as I am told, many popular writers
> are doing their best, especially in France, and perhaps a little
> in England, to set class against class, and pick up every stone
> in the kennel to shy at a gentleman with a good coat on his
> back, something useful might be done by a few good-humored
> sketches of those innocent criminals a little better off than their
> neighbors."

Thus *My Novel* contributes to the atmosphere of complacent
domesticity that dominated so much of the fiction of the fifties.

The year 1853, in which both *Bleak House* and *My Novel* appeared in volume form, was remarkable for its crop of noteworthy novels. Charlotte Brontë's *Villette* was in some ways her masterpiece. She centered it upon her two years at the Pensionnat Héger in Brussels, and so it uses again the experiences that had underlain her first book, *The Professor*, which was still unprinted. But her art had matured in six years. This is the first-personal narrative of Lucy Snowe, who, like Charlotte Brontë, goes to teach in a Belgian school, has trouble in disciplining her pupils, dislikes the other teachers, and is intolerant toward such foreign immoralities as shameless lying and nude paintings in the art galleries. Gradually she falls in love with Paul Emanuel, a ferocious-tempered but unselfish fellow-teacher, but she believes that he is devoted to a pretty girl who is his ward.

The handling of the action still lacks assurance. Some of the characters who seem important in the early chapters are allowed to fade out of the story and then are implausibly dragged in again. No details are given as to the disaster that deprives Lucy of her family and sends her out to earn a living. At the end, when Paul has arranged for Lucy to conduct a school of her own and finally reveals his love for her, he leaves the country for an unexplained reason; three years later, when he is expected back, a terrible storm occurs, and the reader is left without a positive statement as to whether Paul survives it.

All this awkwardness is counterbalanced by the story's emotional power. As before, it was generated by a strange mingling of personal experience with the imaginative fantasies that survived from the youthful tales of Angria. Paul Emanuel seems to be a blending of two characters in the cycle. The handsome, self-assured Dr. John Bretton, who contrasts so strongly with the nervous little Belgian, and whom Lucy adores while she thinks she hates Paul, is derived from Zamorna, the principal Angrian hero; and the lovely Paulina Home can be regarded as a composite of Zamorna's two wives. Even the otherwise unaccountable hurricane at the end is reminiscent of various tempests in the Angrian tales.

But at the same time, most of these characters are portraits of people in Charlotte's own life. Paul Emanuel is M. Héger; Mme. Beck is Héger's wife; and Dr. Bretton is George Smith, a publisher who won Charlotte's affection by his thoughtful management of her affairs. The chapter describing a performance by a great tragic actress has resemblances to a fictitious account of Mrs. Siddons acting in the national theater of Angria; but it is also a report on the French tragedienne Rachel as Charlotte actually saw her in London. The episode in which the fiercely Protestant Lucy, at a moment of intolerable stress, goes into a Catholic church and makes confession to the priest, is a literal transcript of an act performed by Charlotte herself during her tribulations in Brussels.

Villette thus becomes a primary exhibit in any inquiry into the nature of the "autobiographical novel." Because the youthful manuscripts survive to prove how much of reverie and romantic invention underlies the story, we are able to see that the observation of real people and the adapting of personal experience served mainly as a basis for selection and a source of verisimilitude. One is tempted to say that in such cases life imitates art — that Charlotte Brontë felt as she did toward M. Héger and George Smith because she identified them with already existing figments of her daydreams. This evidence is relevant to the discussion of *David Copperfield* or *Pendennis* or *Lavengro* or any of the other books that are taken to be disguised autobiographies.

Villette was Charlotte Brontë's last piece of writing. She had produced it slowly and painfully, tormented by anxiety lest it should not be as good as her previous books. Soon after it was published she married one of her father's curates, and within a year she died in childbirth. *The Professor,* her first-written novel, came out posthumously in 1857.

Mrs. Gaskell, meanwhile, had returned to social reforming in her next novel, *Ruth,* which seemed startlingly unconventional to readers in 1853, as it made a heroine of the mother of an illegitimate child. There had been many seductions in the novels of Dickens and other contemporaries, but in them the betrayed woman suffered either death or bitter remorse as her punishment. When Ruth, a working girl, is about to have her child in a strange town, a liberal-minded minister persuades his sister to take her into their home; and with their help she brings up her son and is accepted as a respectable member of the community. Her lover, a man of higher social rank, reappears and offers to marry her, but she refuses on the ground that he would be an unsuitable father for the boy. Upon her secret becoming known, the minister's intolerant parishioners turn against her and her benefactors, but she vindicates herself by nursing her seducer and some of the persecuting neighbors in a typhoid epidemic and by dying as soon as they all recover.

As in *Mary Barton*, the social and moral questions are over-simplified; and Mrs. Gaskell did not know enough about human passions to make the beginning of the story effective. She tells about the seduction without conveying any understanding of the impulses that caused it. *Mary Barton* and *Ruth* are so inferior to *Cranford* that they seem like the work of a different author, simply because in them Mrs. Gaskell was writing about characters and events which she did not know at first hand. She was profoundly aware that the poor suffered injustice and misery, but she had observed it only from her sheltered seclusion, even though she fulfilled the duties of a minister's wife by dispensing charity. She sympathized sincerely with a girl like Ruth who was a victim of social prejudice; but as a well-loved wife and the mother of half-a-dozen children she could not truly conceive the agonies of desertion and disgrace. Nevertheless, her innocence contributes something to the story's appeal: it is a sort of fairy tale made up by a sensitive child who has heard about a world in which painful things happen.

Ruth is another indication of the unrest over women's place in society, which had lent stimulus to Charlotte Brontë's books. Mrs. Gaskell's warm-hearted plea for tolerance and her condemnation of the double standard of morality were courageous for her day. Indeed, this novel helped to persuade a contemporary young woman, Josephine Butler, to take the lead in reforming the English laws regarding prostitution and in seeking to control the "white slave traffic."

Kingsley's third novel marked a departure from his previous ones in being a historical romance. But under its pageantry of an ancient era *Hypatia* was tense with concern about the issues of his own day, as he emphasized in the subtitle, "New Foes with an Old Face." The setting is Alexandria of the early fifth century, and the heroine is a beautiful, intellectual girl who tries to maintain a philosophical academy on the old Greek model amid the turmoil of expanding Christianity. In a remarkable feat of reconstruction, Kingsley draws an obvious parallel between

Alexandria and Victorian London — a vast commercial city, the financial capital of the world, with luxurious theaters and brilliant lecture halls, but with swarming slums jostling the fashionable mansions. Every major cult of antiquity is represented: the ascetic monks of the desert; the sensual Roman administrators with a veneer of official Christianity; the Greek minority, cultivating a sterile neo-Platonic pedantry; the prosperous Jews, proud of their traditional wisdom and law, and sneering at the upstart Christians; the humble African converts, cherishing little tribal idols for secret rites. A sense of urgency is contributed by the realization that Rome has recently fallen to the Goths, whose forerunners arrive in Alexandria in the innocuous form of a sightseeing party who voyage up the Nile to discover whether the Valley of the Kings is the Asgard of their Norse mythology.

One of the problems implied in the story is the educational and moral emancipation of women, as represented by Hypatia, who tries vainly to maintain her aloof wisdom against the demands of sexual passion. She and her disciples also represent something else that Kingsley disliked in his own age — the abstract transcendentalism that he had already caricatured in an Emersonian lecturer in *Alton Locke*. He establishes a parallel between this and the equally ascetic ideal of the Christian hermits, implying that both, being a denial of human ardor, are impractical and even sinful.

Another contemporary application of the story was that of sectarian rivalry. England was in a frenzy over the re-establishment of the Roman Catholic hierarchy, which had begun with the appointment of Nicholas Wiseman as archbishop in 1850. As a fanatical Protestant, Kingsley wanted to adduce historical evidence against the "papal aggression"; and so he implied a resemblance between Wiseman and Cyril, the Bishop of Alexandria in his story, who was an ambitious administrator and a wily ecclesiastical politician. To embody the opposite view he used another historical personage, Synesius, Bishop of Cyrene, who shared Kingsley's humanitarian sympathy, blunt common sense, love of outdoor sports, and belief that a priest ought to have a wife and children.

In achieving his massive effect of social ferment and ideological conflicts Kingsley painted some thrilling mob scenes; but the direct story line is often submerged as the reader tries to follow the adventures of too many separate characters or becomes entangled in theological arguments. The young renegade monk, Philammon, serves as a link to hold the diverse action together, but he is too passively involved in it to be properly nominated as the hero. The most interesting character, Raphael Aben-Ezra, was modeled upon a Jewish friend of Kingsley's who had recently joined the Church of England. A spiritual kinsman of Carlyle's Teufelsdröckh, he passes from elegant cynicism through a black night of negation before finding for himself an "everlasting yea."

Kingsley's purpose in writing the novel had been to vindicate Christianity as "the only really democratic creed," in opposition to transcendentalist philosophy, which he condemned as "the most exclusively aristocratic creed." But he was honest enough to refrain from presenting an impossible antithesis of good and evil. To prove that neo-Platonic hedonism was a dangerous fallacy, he had to display its attractive features; and while insisting that Christianity endures because it has at its heart the welfare of all the people, he had to admit that it is handicapped by the errors and rivalries of its leaders and by the blind enthusiasms of their followers. Kingsley's reputation as a subversive radical, already established by his previous novels and by his preaching of "Christian Socialism," was thus enhanced. "*Hypatia* was written with my heart's blood," he lamented, "and was received with curses from many of the very churchmen whom I was trying to warn and save." Nor was this the book's only offense. Partly from his fidelity to history, but also because of his belief in the wholesomeness of normal impulses, Kingsley described the sexual indulgences of Alexandria warmly enough to incur a charge of immorality, which was still so strong ten years later that it was a pretext for denying him an honorary degree at Oxford.

It was probably the impact of *Hypatia* that incited Newman to desist from his theological studies long enough to write a second novel; his *Callista* (1856) is as neatly counterbalanced against *Hypatia* as his *Loss and Gain* had been opposed to *Shadows of the Clouds* and *Yeast*. The scene is also in North Africa, two generations before Hypatia's time, and the heroine is also a beautiful pagan Greek girl. Callista, however, is converted to Christianity and dies while undergoing torture, where-

upon her body works miraculous cures. There are a few effective scenes, but nothing of the vigorous story-telling that sustains
Hypatia. Newman's propaganda purpose is too obvious in long
dialogues and expository passages. Though the psychology of
the main characters is developed with some insight, the author
evades the love scenes that ought to play a pivotal role in the
plot.

In the same year with *Ruth* and *Villette* and *Hypatia,* two
new novelists joined the ranks of best-sellers, and between them
typified the norm of fiction-reading taste for the period. One
of these was Charlotte Mary Yonge, a devout and modest young
woman who had already published six works of fiction, and who
now at the age of thirty produced one of the best-loved novels
of the century in *The Heir of Redclyffe.* Its immense popularity
was due to a perfect balance between romantic sentiment, religious earnestness, and the atmosphere of placid domesticity
that had come into vogue.

Like Jane Austen, Miss Yonge lived out her life in a Hampshire village; but she had none of Jane's acid detachment. Instead,
she was a parishioner and friend of John Keble, the saintly
leader of the High-Church Anglicans, and his spirit was reflected in all her works. One of her earliest books had been
intended for young girls, and in 1851 she became editor of a
magazine for juvenile readers, *The Monthly Packet,* which she
conducted for forty years. The strongest recommendation of her
novels was their suitability for family reading. The admirers
of *The Heir of Redclyffe,* however, were not confined to adolescents and their parents; such unregenerate men as Dante
Rossetti and William Morris wept over its pathos, and it was a
favorite book among the soldiers in the Crimean trenches. Miss
Yonge had the mysterious gift of creating living characters,
so that even the most pious actions of her hero, Sir Guy Mor-
ville, who would not take his horse with him to Oxford for
fear his groom might be polluted by the worldliness of the
college town, are not those of a sententious prig. He has all
the romantic charm of the Byronic hero, though it is chastened
with religious zeal and moral probity. Family life is idealized
in *The Heir of Redclyffe* and all her other books; filial obedience
is the foundation stone of her ethics and the spiritual exercises
of the Church of England are the basic law of life.

Within the next two or three years Miss Yonge consolidated her fame with *Heartsease* and *The Daisy Chain,* and in the half-century of life that remained to her she wrote some 150 books, many of them being linked together by Thackeray's device of recurrent characters and family ramifications. Several of her best works were historical romances, such as *The Dove in the Eagle's Nest* (1866). But her permanent contribution to English fiction is her genuine chronicle of the upper-class homes in the halcyon years of the mid-century, and what a recent biographer calls "her particular gift to make ordinary everyday goodness appear the most exciting thing in the world."

The other popular success of 1853 was *Captain Digby Grand,* which was first serialized in *Fraser's Magazine.* The author was George John Whyte-Melville, the grandson of a duke. He had been educated at Eton and was a captain in the Coldstream Guards when he retired from the army in 1849. Before turning to fiction he published some agreeable verse and a translation of Horace. The fox-hunting and steeple-chasing episodes in his novel suggest a link with Surtees; but a comparison of *Digby Grand* with *Mr. Sponge's Sporting Tour* emphasizes how archaic Surtees had become. Melville's novel was not particularly well constructed or original, since it used the hackneyed form of a young roué's memoirs of his army service and his fashionable pastimes, echoing the silver-fork novels and Lever's military tales; but it had a sophisticated ease of manner that aligned it with *Pendennis* and *The Caxtons.* Nonliterary gentlemen liked it because it was obviously produced by a member of their own caste, in contrast with the persistent vulgarity of Surtees' characters and methods.

In spite of a brief return to military service in the Crimea, Melville lost no time in taking advantage of his success with a series of similar stories. *Tilbury Nogo, General Bounce,* and *Kate Coventry,* published between 1854 and 1856, standardized his mixture of humor and romance, adventure and moralizing. He lived the sort of life he described, consorted with no other authors, and donated his earnings to charities connected with fox-hunting.

In seeing Miss Yonge and Captain Whyte-Melville as the representative novelists of the fifties, we recognize the two basic types of fiction that had endured for three centuries — the "feminine" novels of Sidney and Richardson, the "masculine" novels of Nashe and Fielding. It is a measure of the greatness of Dickens and Thackeray that they both rise above these facile categories.

Thackeray's new serial, *The Newcomes*, which began in October, 1853, was indeed a family chronicle, but it was not in the current mood of domestic serenity. Like his previous novels, it gives an uncomfortable impression because it contains so much of his personal frustration. In its autobiographical elements it is a companion piece to *Pendennis*, filling in the parts of Thackeray's early life that had been omitted from that book. Clive Newcome is sent home to England from India as a small boy and is educated at Charterhouse School (here called Grey Friars) as Thackeray had been. He becomes an art student, and his experiences in the studios are close to Thackeray's own, just as was Pendennis's London journalism. His marriage to meek little Rosie Mackenzie, and the character of her domineering mother, are parallel to Thackeray's calamitous married life. And the heroine, Ethel Newcome, was also drawn from life. She is usually considered to be the most attractive of the young women in his novels, possessing the vivacity and intelligence of Becky Sharp and Beatrix Esmond without their selfish hardness. After conquering his attachment to Jane Brookfield, Thackeray had gone on a lecture tour to the United States, where he was captivated by a pretty girl in New York, Sally Baxter. Though his feeling for her was playful rather than passionate, he found her American frankness such a delightful contrast to the affectation of young women in English society that his imagination warmed to the dream of being her suitor if only he were fifteen years younger and a bachelor. As usual, he provided fulfillment in his novel for the wish that had to be suppressed in real life; Clive Newcome's immature wife conveniently dies, Ethel decides at the last moment not to marry the nobleman to whom she has become engaged from motives of worldly ambition, and so Thackeray's surrogate has a chance to win the fictional equivalent of Sally Baxter as his wife.

Another of the personal elements is the character of Colonel Newcome, a full-length portrait of Thackeray's stepfather. In this courageous and unworldly soldier Thackeray came nearest to fulfilling his ambition of depicting an ideal gentleman, as he had previously attempted in Dobbin and Esmond. There are traces of Don Quixote and Parson Adams and Dr. Primrose in the colonel, but he is less caricatured than any of them in his boyish trustfulness and innate dignity. Though readers may be no longer deeply moved by his old age and death, he is still one of the few convincing figures of unalloyed goodness in fiction. And for this very reason he emphasizes the bitter tone of the book, through his unlikeness to most of his scheming and hypocritical kindred. The central irony of the situation is that this paragon of honesty and candor cannot survive in the competitive struggle of modern business.

As his technical method of handling the point of view, Thackeray borrowed the device that Lytton had recently used in *My Novel*. The narrator is Arthur Pendennis, who is a friend of Clive Newcome's and plays a minor role in the action. A specific identity is thus given to the onlooker who tells the story, instead of his being merely a nameless *alter ego* of the author, as in *Vanity Fair* and *Pendennis*. The action moves sluggishly and the plot is not neatly integrated; but Thackeray's sense of the reality of his characters transmits itself to the reader. The Newcome family itself is the unifying element, and their rise in wealth and rank through four generations makes this one of the great studies of English bourgeois society at its apogee. Thackeray's contempt for selfishness, snobbery, and narrow-minded respectability is illustrated from every angle before the story reaches its powerful final scenes.

In contrast with the diffuse opulence of *The Newcomes*, Dickens's novel of the same year was his briefest and most concentrated. This was partly due to its being published in short weekly installments in *Household Words*, but another reason was that *Hard Times* is more strictly centered upon a single social theme than his other novels, and that he had not absorbed this theme through his pores from childhood onward. He began with the conscious purpose of examining the relationship between industrialists and workers in the new manufacturing cities, and of discrediting the utilitarian philosophy which was the ideological basis of current capitalism. This had been foreshadowed in *Dombey and Son* and *Bleak House*. But in those novels he had started with characters and evolved the social implications; in *Hard Times* the characters are obviously invented to demonstrate the theory. It contains none of the richly elaborated comic figures that live so heartily in his other books. With unwonted caution, Dickens began by studying the reports of the newly organized national system of education, and by visiting a strike-bound midland town to observe industrial conflict at first hand. The characters in the novel are neatly arranged in symmetrical groups, either to represent labor *vs.* capital or to contrast the re-pressed children of a practical school with the fun-loving deni-zens of a circus.

The angry scorn for utilitarian economics was derived straight from Carlyle, to whom the novel was dedicated. Mr. Gradgrind, with his gospel of facts and statistics, is a perfect embodiment of Carlyle's chief bogy, the ruthless "logic-grinder." And Dickens is caught in the same dilemma that afflicts much of Carlyle's thinking: being as strong a believer in individual responsibility and freedom of choice as were the proponents of *laissez-faire*, he had no faith in any organized system for promoting human welfare. In the past he had assailed charitable institutions and the Poor Laws; now he turned his guns on the new phenomenon of the labor unions, which he saw as an unwarrantable denial of the worker's right to choose his job. Perhaps the least convincing character in the story is the demagogic union organizer. But almost equally lacking in verisimilitude is the nominal hero, Stephen Blackpool, the honest workman who is sacrificed between the conflicting interests of the union and the employers.

Being the only novel of Dickens that is openly revolutionary in its implications, *Hard Times* was admired by such radical social thinkers as Ruskin and Bernard Shaw; and for its tightly organized structure it has been praised by some modern critics who exalt form as the main criterion of fiction. But most readers have always ranked it lower than Dickens's other works, not for its subversive economic views or even for its depressing picture of human greed, but simply because its characters fail to come alive.

Basically the same theme was treated in Mrs. Gaskell's *North and South*, which appeared about the same time; but her invin-cible sympathy and hopefulness produce an effect very different from Dickens's grim despondency. This novel marks an advance over her previous treatment of similar material in *Mary Barton*. In the intervening years she had made friends among wealthy employers, through whom she learned that the problems were more complex than she had imagined. The theme is better in-tegrated with the action, and the plot depends less on coincidence and melodrama. There is wider variety and naturalness in characterization, and the distress of the poor is presented through the experiences of the characters rather than by the author's disquisitions. She shows equal sympathy for the self-made employer's certainty that he is justified in managing his industry in his own way and for the workers' belief in the righteousness of unionized mass action as the only way to gain better conditions. Her proposed solution for social conflict, however, is still a simple insistence upon Christian generosity and the innate goodness of mankind. "The most depraved," she declares, "have also their Seed of the Holiness that shall one day overcome their evil." Her attempt to be tolerant to all parties deprives the story of any strong appeal to the reader's moral judgment. She implies that her ideal of mutual understanding is adequately fulfilled at the end when John Thornton, the manufacturer, modifies his intransigent stand after he marries Margaret, who is familiar with the misery of his employees.

Kingsley, meanwhile, who had begun writing fiction at the same time as Mrs. Gaskell and with similar motives, remained aloof in his new role of historical romancer. *Westward Ho!* is his most popular book, though it is regarded as more suitable for young people than for adults. His vivid historical imagination, his happy memories of the North Devon coast where he spent some of his childhood, his love of physical action, and his idealization of such simple virtues as courage and loyalty combine to make this one of the great adventure stories. The author's religious prejudices lurk below the surface, for in this tale of the war with Spain in Elizabeth's time he glorifies the English Protestants in contrast with the dastardly schemes of the Roman Catholics; but as the bias is consistent with the patriotic fervor of the characters it is not obtrusive. Free from overt didactic preoccupations, Kingsley showed his talent for telling a thrilling story.

The patriotic feeling in *Westward Ho!* was particularly intense because the novel was written during the Crimean War. England's first major war in forty years, it was unpopular with a segment of the public, especially with the politicians of the Manchester school, for both humanitarian and economic reasons. Kingsley's ardent and simple enthusiasm for his country and for heroic actions aroused him to fury against such pusillanimity, as he considered it, and the crisis changed him from an incendiary radical to a conservative imperialist. For the moment he contented himself

with the contrast implicit in his story of the noble national
spirit in the days of Drake and Raleigh; but he was impelled also
to write a novel on the contemporary situation.

It was published in 1857, with the inept title *Two Years Ago,*
which was intended to emphasize its topical application to the
recent war. The book is a farrago of all the things that Kingsley
was most excited about — not only the Crimean War, but American abolitionism, public health, the value of scientific research,
and, of course, the heresies of Tractarians and Dissenters, particularly what Kingsley regarded as the pernicious doctrine of
torments in hell. Incidentally, as a defense for his habit of writing
didactic fiction, he inflicts terrific retribution on one of the characters, a minor poet, who has changed his name from John Briggs
to Elsley Vavasour, and who, as a believer in art for art's sake,
admires a shipwreck for its aesthetic values.

The hero, a headstrong young doctor, after years of adventure
in wild regions, settles down in a Devonshire village and falls
in love with an incredibly saintly schoolmistress. To check an
epidemic of cholera, he forces sanitation upon the unwilling vil-
lagers. He then goes to serve at the Crimean front, where the
beautiful Grace Harvey also appears as a nurse. His arrogance is
chastened by the rigors of a Tartar prison, and Grace is converted from her fanatical terror of hell-fire. Meanwhile a beautiful mulatto, who escaped from slavery with the doctor's help, becomes a world-famous actress and marries a rich, sophisticated
American as soon as he dedicates himself to abolitionism at her
urging. The whole extravagant mixture is rendered readable by
the author's impassioned faith in its essential truth. It has much in
common with Henry Brooke's *Fool of Quality,* which was Kingsley's favorite novel.

Almost as wide a range of social causes figures in Dickens's
novel, *Little Dorrit,* which came out between December, 1855,
and June, 1857. With the return to monthly parts Dickens resumed his customary vast, crowded survey. Structurally *Little
Dorrit* resembles *Bleak House* in consisting of several apparently
unrelated threads of action which are eventually woven together.
The scenes are even more widely diversified, for one of the
narrative threads begins in Marseilles, and the Dorrits later go to
Italy. Having paid several long visits to the Continent, Dickens
was now able to describe foreign scenes with the sharpness of
observation that had previously been confined to English settings.

The atmosphere of the story, too, has points of contact with that of *Bleak House*, with Bleeding Heart Yard as the equivalent of Tom-All-Alone's, and the feeling of Gothic terror culminating in the collapse of Mrs. Clennam's old house, somewhat like the spontaneous combustion of Krook in the other story. And this book again was a full-scale assault on an entrenched part of the administrative system — this time the civil service, with its incompetent staff appointed through family influence. Dickens's disgust was dictated partly by the blundering of the authorities during the Crimean War, as well as by personal annoyances. The Circumlocution Office took its place in popular terminology as the symbol for all governmental dilatoriness and meaningless routine.

There is an equally elaborate exposure of financial corruption, whether represented by Mr. Casby, the moralizing humanitarian who derives his income from slum rentals, or by Mr. Merdle, the millionaire speculator who is lauded by bishops and noblemen, but whose fraudulent dealings lead him to bankruptcy and suicide. This part of the story was taken from the case of John Sadleir, a company promoter who killed himself in 1856 (Lever also used the Sadleir affair for his novel, *Davenport Dunn*, in 1857–59).

As an unmasking of the dishonesty rampant in the supposedly respectable world of finance, *Little Dorrit* is akin to *The Newcomes*. Mr. Dorrit, indeed, is a sort of inverted image of Colonel Newcome, beginning in the debtors' prison and suddenly inheriting wealth, instead of losing wealth and ending in a charitable institution. But whereas the Colonel's dignity and unworldliness are magnificent, Mr. Dorrit's are merely absurd.

Perhaps the most interesting feature of *Little Dorrit* is the author's return to his own early life as a source. Much of this had already been worked in preceding novels, and his second adaptation of the same data offers an opportunity for judging the changes that had occurred in his feelings. The scenes in the Marshalsea prison are a fuller record of the humiliating misfortune of his parents that he had pictured in *David Copperfield;* and Mr. Dorrit plays the role that Dickens's father occupied in real life. Dorrit, in other words, is a second version of Micawber; but everything that was lovably comic in Micawber's financial incompetence and pompous rhetoric and affection for his children becomes contemptible and faintly sinister in the more subtle and realistic portrait of Dorrit.

A more ironical sequel to *David Copperfield* is to be seen in the character of Flora Finching. The boyhood sweetheart who had been the model for Dora Spenlow had unexpectedly written to Dickens with sentimental memories of old times; and in some dim hope of reviving past happiness he had arranged to see her. The shock was distressing: the once fascinating Maria was now fat, talkative, and silly. Faced with the truth about his advancing years and his former gullibility, Dickens took an unfair revenge on the unoffending woman by giving a wryly comic picture of her in his next book.

This, however, is only a minor facet of the emotional crisis that underlies the story. Dickens had been married for nearly twenty years, and his wife had borne ten children, but she had failed to keep pace with his intellectual interests or his social advancement; and as a man of intense vitality he was in a state of revulsion against his domestic life and the condition of middle-aged inertia that it implied. Hence in the novel he explores the possibility of a love affair between a young girl and a man in his forties (Dickens's own age). Admittedly, the moody and self-distrustful Arthur Clennam is unlike the extroverted Charles Dickens; nevertheless the psychological identification gives the book something of the disturbing aura that a similar personal involvement gave to *Henry Esmond*.

Because of Dickens's mood of mutiny, as well as his disillusionment with Parliament and the ruling class, themes of imprisonment and impotence run through the story until the whole of society seems to be symbolized as a universal jail. As an indictment of the economic and political system and as a collection of case histories illustrating frustration and irrational fears, *Little Dorrit* — in spite of a few gleams of comedy — is the most despondent of Dickens's novels.

The most noteworthy proof of the prestige that the novel had acquired in the fifties was its influence upon the poets. A shift in the balance of power was recognized in 1853 by Arthur Hugh Clough, who remarked that the romantic themes and techniques of poetry were losing their appeal:

> It is plain and patent enough that people much prefer Vanity Fair and Bleak House. . . . Is it that to be widely popular, to gain the ear of multitudes, poetry should deal more with general wants, ordinary feelings, the obvious rather than the rare

facts of human nature? . . . The modern novel is preferred to the modern poem, because we do here feel an attempt to include these indispensable latest addenda, these phenomena which, if we forget on Sunday, we must remember on Monday — these positive matters of fact, which people who are not verse-writers are obliged to have to do with.

In an effort to protect the ancient supremacy of poetry from this upstart rival, many poets tried to adapt the novelists' material to their own uses. Tennyson employed realistic detail, character analysis, and contemporary social problems in such poems as "Locksley Hall" and "Aylmer's Field," and especially in his study of abnormal psychology, "Maud." Browning evolved the dramatic monologue as a medium for concentrating the complexities of a novel into the dimensions of a poem, and subsequently expanded this again into his epic in monologues, *The Ring and the Book*, which is a realistic murder-melodrama studied in terms of motive. Clough tried to deal whimsically with everyday life in the hexameters of "The Bothie of Tober-na-Vuolich" and "Amours de Voyage." Two self-proclaimed "novels in verse," *Aurora Leigh* (1856), by Elizabeth Barrett Browning, and *Lucile* (1860), by Bulwer-Lytton's son Robert, who used the pen name "Owen Meredith," sold as widely as the most popular prose novels. These hybrid productions, however, serve mainly to prove that the novel could not abandon the medium of prose. Familiar details seem comically incongruous when adorned with poetic metaphor, and conversation cannot sound natural in the confines of meter and rhyme.

This incompatibility was the more obvious because *Aurora Leigh* and *Lucile* partook of the prosaic quality that dominated the fiction of the fifties. The novels of this decade reached the apex of one particular development — the synoptic picture of the contemporary social scene. Dickens, Thackeray, Kingsley, Mrs. Gaskell, even Surtees, surveyed its fraudulence and its conflicts. Lytton, Miss Yonge, and Smedley represented the happier aspects of benevolence, family solidarity, and moral assurance. Though most of these authors continued to write novels in subsequent years, their pre-eminence was soon modified by the increasing significance of others who were introducing different techniques and attitudes.

XII

Intellectual Maturity

(1855 – 1860)

THE AUTHORS WHO SOUNDED new notes at this juncture had been writing inconspicuously for several years before each established his individual manner. The most notable of them, Anthony Trollope, conquered a series of obstacles and failures, and was forty years old before he produced his first distinguished novel.

His initial handicap was the fame of his mother, who was still publishing fiction as copiously as ever. Anthony, the fourth of her sons, was regarded as the family dunce. He did not participate in the exciting though disastrous expedition to America, but was left forlornly at school in England. Intermittently enrolled in two good schools — Harrow and Winchester — he was unhappy because he realized the family's financial instability and because he was slovenly and awkward and always at the foot of the class. With no prospect of entering a university, he was appointed as a junior clerk in the postal service when he was nineteen, a position that offered nothing but monotonous work and low salary.

For seven years he was employed in the London General Post

Office, living in cheap lodgings and making few friends, one of the faceless crowd both in the office and in the streets. He ran into debt, neglected his duties, and annoyed his superiors with crude pranks. But there was a substratum of fortitude in the surly young man, and he was unconsciously acquiring self-dependence and a tolerant understanding of human beings. In 1840 he suffered a dangerous illness and the next year he was transferred to a remote region of Ireland. Here an amazing transformation occurred. As a deputy inspector he covered a wide district and dealt with people on his own responsibility. He became a good rider and discovered the joys of fox-hunting. The salary seemed munificent after his London poverty. He got along famously with the Irish as soon as their warmth broke through his shyness. For the first time in his life he was self-confident and happy, and within a year of his arrival he was engaged to be married.

By this time his elder brother Tom had taken up the parental profession of authorship, and Anthony too felt a revival of a long-suppressed ambition to write. He began a novel in 1843, but it was not finished until 1845 and then waited two more years for publication. Naturally he turned to his immediate surroundings for his subject, and gave a faithful picture of Irish conditions as he saw them. Although he had read the novels of Lady Morgan and Miss Edgeworth and Lever, he could not accept either the humorous or the romantically patriotic view of the country. The "hungry forties" were a period of misery among the Irish poor, and so Trollope's report was closer to the unrelieved gloom of William Carleton. *The Macdermots of Ballycloran* is a tragic story of a landowning family's decay; a second novel, *The Kellys and the O'Kellys* (1848), includes more comedy but is handicapped by artificiality of plot. Both books contain some effective character drawing, but they are burdened with their obvious effort to expound the causes of Ireland's wretchedness. As this problem held no appeal for English readers, neither novel won any success.

The Continental upheavals of 1848 then attracted Trollope's thoughts to the French Revolution, and he wrote a historical novel, *La Vendée*, which was essentially a political treatise on the evils of tyranny, with none of the glamour that readers expected in stories of the past. It was as flat a failure as the Irish books had been. At this point Trollope seemed to be a mediocre didactic novelist, deficient in the infectious zeal and the creative imagination that sustained the polemics of Dickens and Kingsley and Mrs. Gaskell.

Discouraged by his three failures, he wrote no more fiction for several years. By the time he resumed it he had gained promotion in the postal service; and during two years of organizing delivery service in the southwest of England he became familiar with the everyday manner of English life. Chancing to take a walk in the cathedral town of Salisbury one evening, he was reminded of his school days in Winchester and of a controversy over the administration of an almshouse there. The result was a short and unpretentious novel, *The Warden*, written at intervals over more than two years. It centered upon a muddle-headed but generous old clergyman who becomes the victim of a newspaper outcry about the financial affairs of the old men's home of which he is superintendent. The Rev. Septimus Harding is a minor version of the type of unworldly gentleman that Thackeray had exalted to heroic stature in Colonel Newcome. Around him seethe the petty rivalries and maneuvers of the hierarchy in a Church of England diocese. This microcosm, isolated from the wider world by geography, by vocation, and by leisurely and tradition-bound procedures, was a perfect specimen for the analysis of human behavior in relation to social patterns. It is like a slow-motion film which reveals unsuspected complexity in familiar activities.

Trollope wrote in the muted tone of everyday discourse, with the amused impartiality of a sensible onlooker who has learned to be neither exasperated by human absurdity nor enticed into advocating reform of the social fabric, no matter how defective it may be. He had moved closer to his mother's type of fiction, with its matter-of-fact recording of contemporary life; indeed, *The Warden* shows specific resemblances to one of her recent novels, *Petticoat Government*. But he avoided her tendency to indulge in assertive social criticism. Having ejected the didactic virus from his blood in his first three novels, he was now interested in individual behavior without concern over theories. He made a point of dissociating himself from propagandistic writing by including gratuitous and heavy-handed caricatures of Dickens and Carlyle, ridiculing their self-elected function as arbiters of public morals.

When *The Warden* was published in one volume in 1855, Trollope had no thought of doing anything more with the subject. But the characters that he had invented, and the cathedral town that he had visualized in such detail, refused to fade from his mind, and so he wrote a longer novel, *Barchester Towers*, with the same setting. In order to introduce new characters he had to deal summarily with some of the former ones. At the end of *The Warden* Mr. Harding's younger daughter had married a local surgeon; between the two books this man conveniently dies, leaving his widow free to engage in more complicated love affairs. The old bishop is also killed off, because the main theme of the new novel is the impact of a less diplomatic prelate upon the community. The husband of Mr. Harding's other daughter, Archdeacon Grantly, develops into a more complex and more admirable character to become a principal protagonist. The exotic Stanhope family is introduced to emphasize the seclusion of Barchester by the contrast with sophisticated cosmopolitans.

It might be expected that in a book dealing with ecclesiastical matters some of the great contemporary controversies would loom large, when the Church of England was being torn by the battles of the High, Low, and Broad factions. Trollope indeed betrays his sympathies by his ridicule of the Low-Church Bishop and Mrs. Proudie and especially of the Bishop's hypocritical chaplain, Mr. Slope. But there is nothing like Kingsley's passionate concern over the spiritual values involved. Trollope ignores historical and doctrinal issues. He merely dislikes Mrs. Proudie because she is aggressive and Mr. Slope because he is crass. The other clergy are preferable because they have gracious manners and are not in an unseemly state of fervor.

This novel shows the full development of Trollope's skill in characterization and his ability to make commonplace details interesting. Also he had found that he could produce novels at a rapid pace without encroaching on his official duties. When *Barchester Towers* was published in 1857 he was already in the midst of another full-length book, which came out later in the year. This was *The Three Clerks*, which contains some revealing glimpses of his unhappy years in London, but which is overloaded with complications of plot, marred by bad taste in style, and disfigured with spiteful caricatures of the author's official superiors. Trollope wrote at his best only as long as he could sustain a disengaged attitude toward his material; in this book he was hampered by too much personal involvement.

As quickly as possible he returned to the region that he knew as an onlooker, and which was already growing in his mind beyond the central town into a whole county with a topography so complete that he drew a precise map of it. He moved out into the rural villages with this third Barsetshire novel, *Doctor Thorne,* and also widened the social picture by centering the story upon a physician in place of the clergy. The whole 200,000 words were written in about five months, even though for part of the time Trollope was traveling on an official mission in Egypt and Palestine. Nevertheless it is well unified in structure and atmosphere. There is a noteworthy heroine, Mary Thorne, an unsurpassed portrait of a natural, gentle English girl. The whole social and political system of the county is sketched in as background. Even the theme of the new capitalism is introduced through Roger Scatcherd, an ex-convict, who began life as a stonemason and ends as a millionaire railway contractor and a baronet. The plot contains elements of conventional melodrama — the secret of the heroine's parentage, the rich boy in love with the poor girl and the final reversal of their positions — but this is subordinate to the series of perfectly natural dilemmas that beset all the characters.

In his next two novels Trollope deserted the Barsetshire scene; and both of them were of inferior quality. *The Bertrams* deals with an unhappy marriage, suffers from a contrived happy ending, and includes too many irrelevancies. In *Castle Richmond* he reverted to the Irish setting and to the dreary and didactic strain of his first book. Meanwhile in 1859 he was requested to provide the first serial for the *Cornhill Magazine,* which was being launched with Thackeray as the editor. Trollope was enraptured by this recognition from the man whom he considered the foremost novelist of the age, and he contributed a fourth Barsetshire novel, *Framley Parsonage,* which proved to be a major cause for the magazine's unprecedented success.

Within six years Trollope had published seven novels and established himself among the leading novelists. Yet he remained obstinately an "ordinary man." His appearance and demeanor gave no hint of the artist: he was burly and bald-headed, with a loud voice and bluntly cordial manners. He much preferred his days in the hunting field and his evenings of whist to the company of authors. His chief pride was in the businesslike efficiency with which he held to his schedule of writing — three hours a day, 1000 words an hour, with the finished book always of the stipulated length and in the printer's hands on the promised date. He was equally practical in his attention to his contracts and profits.

It is this quality of normality that gives his novels their particular effect. His style is so devoid of subtlety and grace that the reader is seldom aware of any distinctive voice of the author. Instead, one has the gratified feeling that this is the way things actually happened, without manipulation by an ingenious intermediary. This does not mean that Trollope adopted an impersonal attitude. He frequently discusses the characters and their behavior, but his comments are so sensible that they seem to be the reader's own reaction and not an intrusion that weakens the objectivity.

The events of the story are seldom sensational, and whenever the plot does arrive at an emotional crisis, the author seems embarrassed, and resorts to a sort of gruff understatement that leaves the reader to infer the tragic undertones for himself. Trollope also had a horror of rhetorical elaboration such as Dickens practiced; and he avoided also Dickens's methods of suspense. He laid down a positive policy in *Barchester Towers:*

> Our doctrine is, that the author and the reader should move along together in full confidence with each other. Let the personages of the drama undergo ever so completely a comedy of errors among themselves, but let the spectator never mistake the Syracusan for the Ephesian; otherwise he is one of the dupes, and the part of a dupe is never dignified.

Therefore, with a kind of stubborn frankness, Trollope insisted upon forewarning his reader of the outcome whenever a situation could conceivably arouse anxiety or doubt.

Trollope was a devout admirer of Thackeray, though he had little of his master's emotional involvement with the story and less of his mordant irony and urbane style. Labeling him a disciple of Thackeray only discloses his lack of genius. It is fairer to place him in the category of the domestic novelists, with Frank Smedley and Charlotte Yonge. He used their type of material and produced their atmosphere, but with immeasurably superior verisimilitude. If realism be regarded as the interesting presentation of familiar material, Trollope is the third great realist in English fiction, in succession to Defoe and Jane Austen. The only advantage in terming him a follower of Thackeray is a convenient antithesis with two other novelists who achieved prominence at the same time, Wilkie Collins and Charles Reade, both of whom are closely affiliated with Dickens.

Wilkie Collins was the son of a successful portrait painter. At the age of seventeen he was apprenticed to a London tea-broker; and before he was twenty he sought to vary the monotony of his work by writing an erotic novel about native life in Tahiti. Though the manuscript never found a publisher, Collins went on to compose a historical romance about the fall of the Roman Empire. On the strength of the opening section of it, his father allowed him to give up the uncongenial tea business and enroll as a law student. At this juncture the senior Collins died, and the son carried out his wishes by writing a biography of him, which was published in 1848 at the family's expense. Although he continued with his legal studies long enough to be called to the bar, he had now no intention of following any other career than authorship. He analyzed the literary profession and decided that the most profitable branch was fiction.

For the moment, unlike most of the other novelists, he was not under the troublesome necessity of earning a living. By staying at home with his mother he found his inheritance ample for his modest needs. In physique he was small and underdeveloped, with an abnormally large head, and his eyesight was painfully defective. Apart from a love of amateur acting, he had no impulse to attract public notice.

His first novel, *Antonina, or The Fall of Rome,* came out in 1850, when he was twenty-six. It was a conventional romance after the model of *The Last Days of Pompeii,* with the material derived largely from Gibbon. Its most notable feature was a series of panoramic tableaux and landscapes, showing the influence of his life among pictorial artists. His next novel, *Basil,* also had a historical source — Lord Chesterfield's relations with his son and with Dr. Dodd, the forger; but Collins transformed this into a story of his own day, with a detailed realistic setting which he obtained conscientiously by ranging over London in omnibuses and eavesdropping on conversations. Large parts of the novel also had an autobiographical basis. The first-personal technique of narrative lent plausibility to what was otherwise a melodrama of violence, crime, a dark secret, and passionate love and hatred. Collins had worked out a theory that "the Novel and the Play are twin-sisters in the family of Fiction: that the one is a drama narrated, as the other is a drama acted." Admiring the sensational plays of the French stage, he insisted that "those extraordinary accidents and events which happen to few men seemed to me to be as legitimate materials for fiction to work with . . . as the ordinary accidents and events which may, and do, happen to us all." The preface to *Basil*, in which he enunciated this theory, is the manifesto of a new type of fiction that came to be termed "the sensation novel."

By this time he had become a friend of Dickens through playing roles in the amateur theatricals that Dickens loved to organize. The mutual influence of the two writers on each other is hard to determine. Collins was still at work on *Basil* when Dickens began publishing *Bleak House*, his first novel to make integral use of suspense and mystification. Thereafter the two authors moved side by side in perfecting a technique for retaining the effect of Gothic gloom and terror while rendering it plausible with familiar settings.

For his third novel, *Hide and Seek*, Collins borrowed from *Bleak House* the mystery of an illegitimate girl's parentage as his plot motif. As a result of an accident as a child performer in a circus she becomes a deaf-mute, and after she grows up she falls in love with a young man who turns out to be her half-brother. Collins tried to invade the domain of domestic fiction in the first half of the book, reserving the detection of the mystery for the later part. Recollections of his own youth provided scenes of a narrowly religious household and a dreary tea-warehouse, and a great deal about artists and their work. This mixture of the tranquil and the sensational was not successful, and Collins devoted himself for a while to writing short stories, in which he aimed solely at suspense and morbid horror. Not until 1857 did he start to write another full-length novel, *The Dead Secret*, which came out serially in *Household Words*. Though the plot was rather thin, the writing was better than his previous work in tension and in directness of approach, and several of the characters showed an effort to follow the methods of Dickens. For the first time Collins made a marked success with the public.

By this time he had overcome an obsession with his own early days, which had appeared in his four previous novels in the form of a domineering father who does not appreciate a sensitive son (or daughter). A new theme was now available in his personal life. One night in 1855, when he was walking in a London suburb with his brother and Millais, the painter, a young woman rushed out of a house, screaming. Upon going to her aid, Collins found that she was escaping from a brutal husband. Subsequently Collins provided quarters for her and her baby daughter, and came to regard her as his unofficial wife. Traces of this affair appeared in more than one of his short stories, and when he began to write another novel in 1859, he built it around the startling scene of his first encounter with the distraught woman. In a collection of French trials he found various cases of mistaken identity. A chance letter from a stranger suggested the terrifying possibility of wrongful detention in a lunatic asylum. At the same time he conceived the technical device of imitating a court trial by presenting the story through the testimony of various witnesses. As each tells his version of the events on the basis of his limited knowledge, the truth is gradually revealed with an acute sense of reality and a concomitant revelation of the separate characters. Collins plays on the reader's imagination with ominous details that are all the more disturbing because they are so trivial. The main characters feel unexplainable premonitions; people moan and shriek in their sleep; a spaniel is mysteriously shot the first day Marian Halcombe is at the Glydes' estate; another dog cringes in terror when Sir Percival pets it; even landscape and houses are described in foreboding phrases. In addition to these novelties Collins provided a new type of villain in Count Fosco, who was not only suave and witty but also fat. The combination of a nerve-racking plot, natural characters, and a fresh mode of narration gave *The Woman in White* unprecedented impact. It appeared as a magazine serial in New York and Paris simultaneously with its London publication in Dickens's new weekly, *All the Year Round*. By the time the story reached its end Collins was an international celebrity.

Collins was almost the first significant novelist to enter the profession by conscious choice, instead of blundering into it by way of other vocations. After making his decision, he mastered the craft through ten years of trial-and-error, during which he published five commonplace novels. Like Trollope he had little feeling for style. His first four novels were wordy and bombastic, until experiments with drama and the short story taught him economy and natural dialogue. Like Trollope, too, he regarded novel-writing strictly as a business; he collected his material with cool efficiency, and devoted attention as seriously to the financial transactions and the publicity for his books as to the creative process. He wrote laboriously and pointed out his technical innovations in complacent prefaces. His function, as he understood it, was to entertain; he announced defiantly that "I have always held the old-fashioned opinion that the primary object of a work of fiction should be to tell a story."

The other important innovator of the sensation novel was ten years older than Collins, but he was slow in discovering his *métier*. The son of an Oxfordshire squire, Charles Reade studied at Magdalen College, Oxford, and remained a Fellow of the college all his life, not because he had any affection for the academic world, but because the fellowship assured him an income. Two disagreeable conditions, however, were attached: he was not permitted to marry, and he was obliged to enter one of the three "learned" professions — the church, law, or medicine. The dull duties of a clergyman had no appeal for him, and an interlude as a medical student in Edinburgh ended when he found he could not endure the sight of blood. As a last resort he settled down in London to read law.

At the time of his graduation from college he started making notes for possible use in writing fiction, but he modestly doubted his ability to be an author. Instead he completed his law studies, was called to the bar, and took the degree of D.C.L. Concurrently he served terms as junior dean, then bursar, and eventually vice-president of his college. He invested in a herring fishery in Scotland and carried on a business in London as an importer of antique violins. His deepest interest, however, was in the theater, in both London and Paris, and at last he decided to be a playwright. Starting at the age of thirty-six, he wrote or translated a dozen plays, alone or in collaboration, between 1851 and 1855. One of these, entitled *Masks and Faces*, he expanded into a short novel, *Peg Woffington*, which dealt romantically with the real career of an eighteenth-century actress. Another of his early plays, *Christie Johnstone*, which was similarly transformed into fiction, depicted the Scottish fisher-folk whom he knew through his herring business; indeed, there is some evidence that it is based on a love affair between Reade and a pretty fisher lass.

English drama in the mid-century was highly artificial, and in these two stories Reade stayed close to the stage practice by presenting a series of spectacular scenes, with little regard for coherent development. Sometimes a whole page of conversation was printed in the same form as the dialogue of a play. The books were moderately successful, and he went on to develop another of his plays into fiction, on a larger scale.

Reade's tardiness in becoming a novelist suggests that he felt no strong inner compulsion. When he adopted the vocation as a way of earning a living he was equipped with habits acquired through his previous training. As a university scholar he had learned the methods of research; as a lawyer he knew the value of a well-prepared brief. Accordingly, he kept a vast system of notebooks and files of newspaper clippings, and to verify a single fact he would plow through half-a-dozen long books. Half of each page of his manuscript would be left empty for inserting corrections of detail.

His play *Gold* dealt with the topical subject of the Australian diggings. In turning it into a full-length novel he interviewed everyone he could find who had been to the new country. As he was also introducing another theme, the English penal system, he visited prisons in search of accurate information, and was shocked by what he observed. When the novel was published in 1856, with the title *It Is Never Too Late to Mend* (subtitled "A Matter-of-fact Romance"), its depiction of the mistreatment of prisoners aroused a newspaper controversy, in which Reade took active part. This public uproar, combined with the melodramatic plot, made the book hugely successful. The structure of the story is mechanical enough, with the parallel narration of two men's careers and a contrived climax; but the prison scenes are powerful, and the hypothesis that a criminal might be redeemed by considerate treatment was a startling new idea a century ago. Reade's experience as a playwright gives an almost inhuman externality to his manner: the characters are shown through outward behavior rather than by revelation of their inner processes.

Reade's next two novels were inferior potboilers, as were two volumes of short stories reprinted from magazines. He devoted his energy chiefly to a series of lawsuits in which he tried more courageously than discreetly to obtain better terms for authors from publishers and better protection from plagiarists. He was equally ready to wage war on reviewers by pointing out their misrepresentations. Obstinate and short-tempered, he made powerful enemies, and he lost money by most of his suits, even when he won the verdict. But his fanatical devotion to justice, which inspired these campaigns as much as it inspired his novels, would accept no compromise; and the ultimate result can be seen in the modern safeguards of copyright.

It is ironical that his next novel — which turned out to be his masterpiece — grew out of a characteristic quarrel. When Dickens arbitrarily discontinued *Household Words* in 1859 and issued his new weekly through another firm, his former publishers started *Once a Week* in competition; and since the success of Dickens's paper was due largely to its including his own new novel as a serial, the editor of *Once a Week* wished to start off with a serial by the most popular novelist he could find. Collins was a henchman of Dickens, and Trollope was engaged by the *Cornhill Magazine;* therefore the offer was made to the author of *It Is Never Too Late to Mend.*

Being interested at the moment in fifteenth-century history, Reade began to write a short serial entitled *A Good Fight*, based on an episode in the early life of the father of Erasmus. Soon he was embroiled in disputes with the editor, whom he accused of tampering with his text, and when it had run for three months he brought the story to an abrupt end. With his usual stubbornness he then decided to vindicate himself by rewriting it on a larger scale. He secluded himself at Oxford for two years of diligent research, and produced *The Cloister and the Hearth,* five times the length of the serial.

The structure of this novel was fairly primitive, harking back to the picaresque form as it followed Gerard Eliason's route across Europe from Rotterdam to Rome. But Reade's experience with the sensation novel enabled him to exploit each adventure to its maximum effect. Humor and pathos abound, and the excitement is sometimes almost intolerably acute. One idiosyncracy, which had already appeared in his previous books, was the use of typographical tricks: important passages were printed all in capital letters, secret whispers were in minuscule type, illustrative diagrams were inserted in the text. Such devices reflect the dramatist's desire to achieve something like the auditory and visual effects that inhere in stage production. His narrative techniques, too, are still mainly theatrical: the vividness of each episode, whether for excitement or for farce, depends upon its pictorial composition, its sequence of physical action, and its abrupt "curtain" at a climactic moment.

The book's greatest value is its embodiment of the spirit that was about to produce the Renaissance and the Reformation. Its geographical range enabled the author to survey the whole Western culture of the era, and he captured its zest and intellectual curiosity to the full. The burden of scholarly precision is never wearisome, for Reade worked all his details of food and dress, customs and pastimes, medicine and law and painting, into the lively action of the story.

He was proud of its authenticity, and contemptuous of his contemporaries for writing so-called historical fiction about modern people in fancy dress. Yet *The Cloister and the Hearth* is more essentially of the nineteenth century than any of the cloak-and-sword romances that he scorned. The ferment of curiosity and experiment, the excitement over new inventions, was the typical mood of his own time. And the particular theme of the novel — the evils of celibacy, which separated the young friar Gerard from his sweetheart and brought a tragic outcome for them both — was even more intimately personal with Reade than with Kingsley. In condemning the unnatural asceticism of the Romanist discipline, Reade was taking his revenge upon its anachronistic survival in the university regulation that had brought emotional frustration into his own life.

The three new men of English fiction in the later fifties had much in common. All of them developed the mechanical routines of their craft as a substitute for creative invention — Trollope with his three thousand words a day, Collins with his omnibus expeditions, Reade with his notebooks and clippings. All were committed to the cause of realism, though with Trollope it was an end in itself, whereas Collins and Reade used it as a means for strengthening the impact of the abnormal events that they narrated. And all were aware of the value of firm plot structure, though Collins was the only one who made this his chief claim to fame.

One reason for these changes was the decline of publication in monthly parts. For twenty years this practice had brought huge profits to the most popular novelists; but by 1860 serial publication was being taken over by the new mass-circulation monthly and weekly magazines. Thackeray's last novel in parts was *The Virginians* (1857–59), Lever's was *Luttrell of Arran* (1863–65). Dickens and Trollope occasionally used the method until the seventies.

This form of publication had required a degree of completeness and an individual climax for each part. Magazine serialization was less demanding; installments were briefer, and when the serial was only one among many contributions the sales of each issue did not fluctuate so identifiably on the basis of readers' reactions. Hence the author could build a better integrated plot and maintain a more consistent atmosphere.

Several other popular authors also emerged in the mid-fifties. One was Dinah Maria Mulock, who won immense success in 1856 with her fifth novel, *John Halifax, Gentleman*. Her father had been an eccentric religious fanatic, and she had grown up in an environment of evangelical piety. Her novel presented the ideals of the nonconformists with the same sincerity as Miss Yonge's depiction of High-Church Anglicanism. At the same time, by telling the story of a poor farm lad who becomes rich and socially accepted through hard work and self-respect, Miss Mulock embodied the cherished ambition of the lower middle class. Her book vindicated the solid virtues of a way of life that was being ridiculed by other authors as narrow-minded or materialistic, and it did much to make fiction respectable in the eyes of the devout Evangelical party. Her next book, *A Life for a Life*, which was an attack on capital punishment, followed in the wake of Reade's exposure of barbarous discipline in prisons.

Another work of fiction that was tremendously successful, though it cannot be counted as a novel for adults, was *Tom Brown's School Days* (1857), by Thomas Hughes, a barrister who had been educated at Rugby under the famous Dr. Arnold and who later was associated with Kingsley and Maurice in

their campaign for Christian Socialism and workmen's education. The book was an idealized version of his own boyhood, and
its simple standards of loyalty, generosity, and friendship expressed the spirit of the domestic fiction of the decade with an
admixture of bullying, fisticuffs, athletics, and pranks that made
it palatable to young readers. A sequel, *Tom Brown at Oxford*,
has never been so popular but provides a good picture of the
intellectual ferment among the undergraduates of the forties, as
a complement to Kingsley's *Yeast* and Newman's *Loss and Gain*.
Meanwhile Hughes's picture of life at a boys' school had been
developed into a sentimental stereotype by Frederick William
Farrar, a schoolmaster who later became a famous preacher.
His *Eric, or Little by Little* (1858), *Julian Home* (1859), and
St. Winifred's, or the World of School (1862) were inflicted on
boys as models of conduct and virtue, and consequently they
came to be universally ridiculed by later generations.

Offsetting this mawkish trend, a former schoolmate of Hughes
at Rugby, George Alfred Lawrence, took to writing novels that
exaggerated the cult of physical strength and reckless courage.
His first book, *Guy Livingstone, or Thorough*, published anonymously in 1857, was widely read, as was *Sword and Gown* (1859),
in which the hero is killed in the charge of the Light Brigade.
The masculine ideal of hardness and the total absence of intellectual subtlety made Lawrence's stories the prototype of the
novel of action.

Meanwhile, the two senior novelists, Dickens and Thackeray,
both resorted to historical fiction. Thackeray was becoming anxious about the deterioration of his creative power; he felt that
he was in danger of reworking his own experience monoto-
nously. Accordingly he decided upon writing a sequel to *Esmond*, dealing with the American grandsons of his former hero
and their participation in the War of Independence. During a
second lecture tour in the United States he consulted two American novelists, John Esten Cooke and John Pendleton Kennedy,
for help in keeping his details accurate. His original plan would
have produced a neatly constructed story, with the brothers taking opposite sides in the Revolution and both falling in love with
the same girl. But when he started to write he allowed his
interest in characters and historical atmosphere to override the
requirements of structure. He got one of the young men out

of the way by having him captured by the Indians, and then he brought the other to England to visit his noble kinsfolk. This provided an opportunity for Thackeray's usual contrast between a naïve, impulsive character and a group of selfish worldlings. The chief connection with the earlier book was the reappearance of Beatrix Esmond, now an embittered old woman whose ambitions have brought her no happiness. In this portrait and in that of the kindly Lambert family — a sketch of Thackeray's home life with his daughters — the moralizing tendency becomes unduly obvious. So many chapters are occupied with static depiction of the social and literary world in London, including glimpses of General Wolfe, Dr. Johnson, and other celebrities, that the American Revolution has to be crowded into a few pages near the end. An attempt to achieve vividness by having some chapters cast in the form of the elder brother's journal merely produces confusion in the point of view. Yet, in spite of weaknesses, *The Virginians* has its own special charm in its mood of middle-aged disenchantment and whimsical melancholy.

As his serial to launch his new periodical, Dickens wrote a novel of the French Revolution, *A Tale of Two Cities*. In unity and structure it was superior to *Barnaby Rudge*, his previous venture into historical fiction, which had centered upon a somewhat similar occurrence in England about the same time — a proletarian uprising and the burning of a prison by the mob. The situation of a physical likeness between two men which enables one to be substituted for the other resembles those that were being used by Collins; but the book was raised above the level of the sensation novels by its effectively tragic ending and by the amplitude of the historical scene. Dickens had studied Carlyle's *French Revolution* assiduously, and he caught something of the panoramic vision of that epic book. His opening chapter is a remarkable condensation of a historical era in imaginative phrases. Throughout, the brevity of the chapters and the conciseness of the descriptive passages make the story move with unusual rapidity. As the title indicates, the structural pattern depends upon parallelism and antithesis. "It was the best of times, it was the worst of times"; Dr. Manette is recalled to life at the beginning, and Charles Darnay at the end; trial scenes are counterbalanced in the two cities; Jarvis Lorry and Sidney Carton are opposite in character but function similarly in the action. Balanced contrasts also pervade the theme and the figures of speech.

Sydney Carton, the hero, was a departure from the conventional pattern. A drunkard and a cynic, he was almost an open affront to the moral standards of the day, and as such he represented a step in the direction of realism, though his nobly unselfish action in giving his life for another man who is to marry the girl they both love is strictly in the romantic tradition.

By this time the English novel was ready for the final development in its advance toward equality with the other major genres of literature. Technical expertness had been acquired, but still lacking was a conscious perception of the novel as a form of art. Likewise, though opinions and theories on all sorts of specific subjects were if anything too plentiful in novels, no author had yet shown much evidence of capacity for serious and consistent thought.

In France the situation was similar. Balzac had established the prestige of massive realism, and Alexandre Dumas had exploited the potentialities of suspense and excitement. But not until 1857, when Gustave Flaubert published *Madame Bovary*, did a novelist combine meticulous realism with perfection of literary form and with a concern for general ideas that gave his novel permanent significance as an interpretation of the human predicament. Flaubert's influence on the subsequent development of fiction was tremendous. On one hand, his minute attention to phrase, imagery, and structure proved that a novel could be a work of art every bit as dextrous as any poem or drama. On the other, he gave a new and distasteful connotation to the word "realism," because of his conviction that human behavior is incurably vicious. Claiming that he was merely facing the unpalatable truth, he implied in his novels that all hope of happiness or even of comprehension is a stupid illusion. *Madame Bovary* and *L'Education sentimentale* showed that satisfaction cannot be found in love; *La Tentation de Saint-Antoine* and *Bouvard et Pécuchet* disqualified religion and philosophy; and to abolish the romantic escape from the hideousness of the present day, he wrote *Salammbô* to show that antiquity was just as brainlessly brutal.

While Flaubert's first novel was winning startled attention — and being banned in France as immoral — two English writers were on the threshold of work that was to bring equivalent maturity to the novel in their country. One was a woman approaching middle age, an associate of some of the most independent thinkers of the time; the other was a strenuous young man with grandiose hopes of being a poet.

Mary Ann Evans (eventually famous as George Eliot) is the most incredible figure in the gallery of English novelists. No other overcame so many social and personal handicaps to attain eminence in this vocation. Her origin was unlikely to produce an author, more unlikely to produce a woman author, and fantastically unlikely to produce a woman author of independent intellectual doctrines. Her father, as the manager of a rich squire's estates in Warwickshire, belonged to the rural lower middle class, which unquestioningly accepted the traditions of the caste system, of the pre-industrial agricultural economy, and of the Church of England. In the *mores* of this class, no axiom was more basic than that woman's place was in the home. The Evans family were deeply devoted to each other, and in her childhood Mary Ann often accompanied her father as he drove about the countryside to inspect the properties under his charge. She was equally fond of her brother, three years her senior.

A sensitive, awkward, conscientious child, she attended boarding schools in neighboring towns until the age of sixteen, receiving a conventional education in a strictly religious atmosphere. Upon the death of her mother she went home to be her father's housekeeper, and worked faithfully at her duties of cooking, sewing, and supervising the dairy. Also, however, she read widely, studied history, acquired fluency in Italian and German, became a skilled pianist, and wrote some mild poetry. For a while she was so pious that she doubted whether she ought to continue reading novels, though she had loved Scott's since childhood. When she was twenty-two her father retired and they moved into the town of Coventry. Here she made friends with a family of wide literary and intellectual interests, under whose tutelage she studied Greek, Latin, and Hebrew, and discovered the existence of liberal theories about human personality and the Christian religion. Straightway she gave up the evangelical orthodoxy in which she had been brought up.

Almost grotesquely ugly, with her large features and sallow complexion, she was quiet in manner and yet so earnestly enthusiastic in her response to new ideas that she won esteem from men of literary and scholarly distinction, including Emerson, who frequented her friends' home. By the time she was twenty-five she was translating *Leben Jesu*, by David Friedrich Strauss, the most notorious of the German scholars who were applying rational analysis to Christianity. Her translation was published, without her name, in 1846. Though her father was distressed by her freethinking, she nursed him through his lingering final illness. Her own health was never robust, and after his death she was saved from emotional and physical breakdown when her friends took her to the Continent. Eight months alone in Geneva endowed her with so much self-reliance that on her return she decided to make her living in London as a professional writer. She took lodgings in the home of John Chapman, a radical publisher, as sub-editor of his periodical, the *Westminster Review*, and applied herself to book reviewing and translating.

Women who supported themselves and lived away from home were still regarded with some prejudice in 1851; and the literary profession was particularly suspect. It took courage for this spinster of thirty-two to break away from a sheltered family life and undertake an independent career. Even more remarkable was the fact that the plain, sickly, self-educated provincial woman was accepted on equal footing by some of the most eminent thinkers of the day, such as Carlyle and Herbert Spencer. One of her strongest traits, in spite of her mental power, was her dependence on more forceful personalities to provide her with confidence and incentive. When John Chapman proved inadequate in this role, she turned to Spencer, who was of the same age and background as herself and was at this time beginning his life work of synthesizing all the sciences and laying philosophical foundations for the theory of evolution. He had published *Social Statistics* in 1850, and his *Principles of Psychology* was to follow in 1855. Miss Evans was profoundly impressed by his application of scientific methods to the study of human behavior and by his reasoned exposition that the principle of progress was the basic law of the universe.

Through Spencer she met George Henry Lewes, a less exhaustive and more versatile writer. He had published several novels and was probably the best dramatic critic of the time;

but his interest was now turning toward biological and psychological research. Also he was a disciple of Auguste Comte, and in his *History of Philosophy* he had persuasively presented the doctrines of positivism. Marian (as she now spelled her name) was immediately converted to this "religion of humanity" which filled the void that had been left by her loss of orthodox Christianity.

Lewes was undergoing a domestic crisis: his wife had deserted him for another man, leaving him with three young sons; and because he had refrained from expelling her upon first discovering her unfaithfulness, he was regarded by the law as having condoned her conduct and therefore there were no grounds for divorce. Miss Evans became, in everything but a legal sense, a wife to Lewes and a mother to his boys. After her second translation of a rationalistic book, Feuerbach's *Wesen des Christentums*, was published in 1854, she went to Germany with Lewes, and on their return they established a home together in London.

This was the last in a series of major ethical decisions that Mary Ann Evans had faced. First was her break with the religious faith in which she grew up and which she still respected; next came her submission to duty in the years of her father's illness, when she had to postpone her scholarly ambitions; this final dilemma was more painful because it entailed estrangement from her beloved brother.

The situation was richly ironic. Her deepest concern had always been with morality. The moral discipline of her religious youth had merely been replaced by equally rigorous standards of ethical philosophy (at this period she was translating Spinoza's *Ethics*). A sense of duty was at least as strong as sexual attraction in leading her to her technically immoral union with Lewes, who needed her to take care of his household. Similarly, his inability to obtain a divorce resulted from the virtue of forgiveness toward his wife's misconduct. A further irony was that Miss Evans displayed no particular zeal for the abstract ideal of women's rights, which was espoused by so proper a woman as Charlotte Brontë; and yet she put it into practical effect to a degree that the others merely advocated in their writings. Yet more ironical was the fact that many of the leading masculine writers and other prominent personages were

equally irregular in their sexual affairs, but remained socially
acceptable because they kept their infidelities decently concealed, whereas Miss Evans and Lewes were penalized because
they adhered to the virtue of honesty. As a model of the mutual
trust and understanding and the parental love that were idealized
in the domestic fiction of the decade, their home was more
adequate than were many that enjoyed the sanction of respectability. Their radical friends, of course, remained loyal to
them, and in the course of time most of the authors and intellectuals frequented their famous weekly receptions; but ladies
who were subservient to propriety did not endanger their repu-
tations by recognizing these moral outcasts.

Lewes was so charmed with the humor and sympathy with
which Marian narrated recollections of her girlhood that he encouraged her to recast them in fictional form, and she diffidently
produced three stories of intermediate length; the first was of
30,000 words, the second 45,000, the third 60,000. They appeared as short serials in *Blackwood's Magazine* during 1857, and
were then published in two volumes as *Scenes of Clerical Life*.
The author's identity was not disclosed, and when the publisher
demanded a name it was given as "George Eliot."

In setting and characters the three stories were derived from
Marian's childhood surroundings in Warwickshire. With quiet humor and pathos she depicted crises in the lives of ordinary people
with normal weaknesses. Although superficially resembling the
domestic fiction of the decade, the stories had deeper qualities
of naturalness and insight. They were praised by several leading
authors, and Dickens alone suspected that the writer was a woman.
The increasing length of the stories showed her development
toward the larger scope of the novel, and she soon felt hampered
by the monotony imposed by her plan of centering each story
upon a clergyman's family. By the time *Scenes of Clerical Life*
was published she was at work upon a full-scale novel.

The strength and validity of even the early stories came from
the author's unique qualifications. Nearing the age of forty, she
had gained an uncommon degree of mature wisdom. During her
first twenty years she had known English rural life more intimately than any author since Bunyan; but her later cosmopolitan
experience enabled her to look back on it with wide perspective.
Her emotional dilemmas had given her comprehension of the

conflicts that can occur in apparently placid lives. Her philosophical studies and her friendship with analytical thinkers had taught her to regard human behavior in a social and psychological context. Finally, as a literary critic she had formulated positive opinions about the art of fiction; one of her last contributions to the *Westminster Review* before writing *Scenes of Clerical Life* was a trenchant attack on "Silly Novels by Lady Novelists," condemning their trite language, their snobbish attitudes, their slipshod methods and pretentious ignorance.

In writing her first novel, *Adam Bede*, she remained as faithful to her childhood environment as she had been in *Scenes of Clerical Life*. By dating the action in 1799–1800, she emphasized her representation of English country life as it had been for centuries, before its serenity was invaded by nineteenth-century innovations. Her central character was a portrait of her father as she imagined him to have been in his youth, while still a village carpenter in Staffordshire. As the model for her heroine, Dinah Morris, she used an aunt who had been in her early days a Methodist preacher, and who must now have acquired new significance to her as a woman who had incurred censure both by breaking from the established church and by adopting a vocation ordinarily reserved for men. This aunt once told the young Mary Ann about how she had prayed in the prison cell of a girl accused of poisoning her illegitimate infant and even had accompanied her on the way to execution. George Eliot used this tale as the plot of her novel, though she made the ending less grim by having the girl reprieved from the gallows.

This climax, when the remorseful seducer arrives with the reprieve at the last moment, is the only touch of melodrama in the novel. Otherwise the emotions are under the traditional English restraint, and the action moves with the deliberate pace of the farmer's routine and the cycle of the seasons. The author's abiding love for the countryside and her photographic memory make the local color authentic. Unlike any previous novelist, she was able to draw rustic characters humorously without a trace of condescension: the sententious Mrs. Poyser, in particular, partly based on the author's mother, is a noteworthy comic characterization.

The central situation has some resemblance to that of *The Scarlet Letter*, by Nathaniel Hawthorne, the only novelist who had hitherto conveyed anything like George Eliot's impression of ethical earnestness. It is more closely reminiscent of *The Heart of Midlothian*, but its firm structure is unlike Scott's rambling story. Indeed, it moves with such steadily increasing momentum toward the climax that the sense of inevitability becomes oppressive. Though all relevant facts seem to be presented with scrupulous fairness, the author actually conveys several important occurrences by skillful indirection. The seduction of Hetty Sorrel is indicated by Arthur's action in searching for her pink neckerchief and hiding it; the birth and death of the baby are suggested in advance through a long account of her state of mind, and are later reconstructed through legal evidence; in the final chapters, after Hetty's conviction, suspense is strengthened by the reader's ignorance of Arthur's efforts to obtain her reprieve. In these portions George Eliot borrowed technical devices from the sensation novels.

The book's style is not quite so admirable as its construction. Though the general effect is straightforward and unpretentious, some phrases and similes betray the author's scholarly and scientific interests; and here and there a self-consciously elaborate reference to literature or mythology obtrudes incongruously in the homespun context. There is also a monotonous mannerism of admonishing the reader: "you remember," "you perceive," "possibly you think," "yes, the house must be inhabited, and we will see by whom; for imagination is a licenced trespasser: it has no fear of dogs, but may climb over walls and peep in at windows with impunity. Put your face to one of the glass panes in the right-hand window: what do you see?" These minor infelicities are the only indications that the author was still a novice in writing fiction.

The novel's strength resides in its impression of being true to life not only in external details but also in the intricacies of character. This arises partly from the author's attitude of tolerant understanding. Arthur Donnithorne is neither a Byronic hero nor a lecherous villain, but a confused, well-meaning young man who lets a casual flirtation go too far. Hetty is not treated with either conventional censure or the sentimental sympathy that had replaced it in such a novel as Mrs. Gaskell's *Ruth;* she appears as shallow and conceited, but not inherently vicious. The Rev. Mr. Irwine, fitting no stereotype of the clergyman in fiction, is considerate but inadequate when a crisis occurs among his parishioners. Admittedly, the author's affection for the real people who were the originals of Adam and Dinah made her idealize these two in some degree; but they are not incredibly perfect, for George Eliot no longer shared Dinah's religious inflexibility or Adam's subservience to "the gentry."

The impression of objectivity results mainly from the attention given to inward processes of thought and feeling. Hetty's glittering visions of rank and wealth, and then her blind desperation during her solitary journey across the country; Arthur's helpless dismay when he realizes the consequences of his behavior; the absurd mixture of rage and affection in the relationship of Arthur and Adam when they fight — the reader shares these emotional states instead of merely being told that they exist.

It is surprising that this unspectacular novel was at once acclaimed as a masterpiece. A slow-moving story of stolid country folk, it nevertheless was so suffused with the author's nostalgia for the secure way of life that she had lost for ever, and with the sober love of simple people that she shared with her favorite poet, Wordsworth, that even the most sophisticated readers were captivated. The placid scenery, the weather, the rustic festivals and superstitions, were woven into the texture of the story. Aware that she had relinquished the picturesqueness and excitement that were customary in novels, George Eliot inserted a manifesto of her artistic purpose:

> My strongest effort is . . . to give a faithful account of men and things as they have mirrored themselves in my mind. . . . I feel as much bound to tell you as precisely as I can what that reflection is, as if I were in the witness-box narrating my experience on oath. . . . So I am content to tell my simple story, without trying to make things seem better than they were; dreading nothing, indeed, but falsity. . . . It is for this rare, precious quality of truthfulness that I delight in many Dutch paintings, which lofty-minded people despise. I find a source of delicious sympathy in these faithful pictures of a monotonous homely existence, which has been the fate of so many more among my fellow-mortals than a life of pomp or of absolute indigence, of tragic suffering or of world-stirring actions.

To be sure, many novelists since Defoe and Fielding had affirmed their devotion to truth; but George Eliot succeeded in giving truth a third dimension by revealing it in depth as well as on the surface.

The fame of her book was so phenomenal, and the curiosity about George Eliot's identity was so acute, that one Joseph Liggins, a resident of Coventry, coyly admitted the authorship; and when his adherents wrote to the *Times* on his behalf, the real author felt obliged to make herself known. In view of her equivocal position, however, which rendered either "Miss Evans" or "Mrs. Lewes" equally unsuitable, the pen name remained in general use.

The other epoch-making novel of 1859 was *The Ordeal of Richard Feverel*, by George Meredith; but it met with a totally different reception. Eight years younger than George Eliot, Meredith originated in a comparable social stratum, though in a provincial town instead of the countryside. His grandfather had prospered as a tailor in Portsmouth by supplying naval uniforms during the Napoleonic Wars. Being handsome, witty, and urbane, the tailor had become popular among the local gentry, and was in the habit of claiming descent from Welsh princes. His son inherited his good looks and aristocratic manners, but lacked business acumen, and by the time George was born the tailor shop was running into debt. George's mother died when he was five years old. Five years later his father was declared bankrupt and went to find employment in London, soon afterwards marrying a servant girl who had been his housekeeper. A small inheritance from his mother enabled George to attend obscure private schools, and later he spent a year and a half at an inexpensive school at Neuwied on the Rhine. At the age of eighteen he was articled to a London solicitor.

Handsome and virile, proud of his Celtic and possibly royal ancestry and ashamed of his father's failure and degradation, he was eager to distinguish himself in some calling that would be remote from social prejudices. The best opportunity for such a career seemed to be offered in authorship. Soon he and several other young men were exchanging and discussing their essays and poems. One of these new friends was a son of Thomas Love Peacock, who was exactly the sort of author that Meredith admired most, a subtle and learned satirist of bourgeois stupidities. Young Peacock had a sister, a widow who possessed something of her father's wit. Though she was seven years older than

Meredith, he married her as soon as he reached the age of twenty-one. Giving up his desultory legal studies, he set out to earn their living by writing.

The next few years were a period of miserable tension. Meredith issued a book of poems that won a few good reviews but brought in no money. The young couple were perpetually in debt, in spite of financial aid from Peacock; but Meredith stubbornly refused to acknowledge defeat by taking a salaried position. Only when he had to give up all hope that his poetry might prove salable did he turn reluctantly to prose.

His first two works of fiction do not fall within the definition of the novel; but they are important for an understanding of his later writings. *The Shaving of Shagpat*, published in 1855, was an elaborate imitation of *The Arabian Nights*. Not since Beckford's *Vathek* had an English writer so successfully reproduced the ornate fantasy of the oriental tale. Meredith's book contains enough horror to be classified as a belated Gothic tale and enough comedy to classified as a burlesque. Essentially it is an allegory, embodying a group of serious ideas. The dominant theme is that the greatest evil in human nature is egoism: only by overcoming his selfishness and conceit does the hero achieve true manhood and the power to defeat the tyrannical Shagpat, who symbolizes the illusions of worldly pretension. His main help comes from a wise and intuitive woman who loves him, and the turning point occurs when he learns to laugh at himself.

In a second short book, *Farina* (1857), Meredith created a similar apologue, modeled this time upon the medieval folklore of the Rhineland. On the surface it is a whimsical retelling of the legendary origin of *eau de Cologne*, but also it is another version of the eternal struggle against the powers of darkness and materialism.

By the time this book appeared, Meredith's domestic troubles were at a crisis. His wife had fallen in love with one of their friends, a young painter, and she eventually went away with him to Italy, deserting her husband and their small son. This disaster had a double influence upon Meredith's literary work; it not only obliged him to attempt to produce a more profitable kind of book, but also incited him to analyze the psychological bases of personal conflicts. The outcome was a full-length novel of contemporary life.

To a man of his pathologically sensitive pride, this second humiliation was even more bitter than his early loss of respect for his father. He felt that he was partly to blame for the failure of his marriage, in that he had been wrapped up in his self-importance, ignoring the symptoms of his wife's unrest. They had both clung blindly to the romantic concept of love, which prevented them from making a sensible adjustment to the stresses of married life. He decided that egoism expressed itself in a particularly vicious form under the guise of sentimentality.

The Ordeal of Richard Feverel was an effort to see his personal problem objectively. At the beginning of the story Sir Austin Feverel has been left with a little son after his wife's elopement with a dilettante poet. The theme of the novel emerges from this situation. As a salve for his wounded pride, Sir Austin asserts that all women are fickle, and he determines to train his son according to a planned program that will guard him against the temptations of sex. The pampered young heir becomes arrogant and headstrong, vaguely rebellious against his father's authority: the two love one another but cannot communicate their feelings. When Richard meets the pretty niece of a farmer on the estate, they fall desperately in love and are secretly married, just when Sir Austin, in pursuit of his project, is searching for a eugenically suitable wife for his son. In the hope of reconciliation with his father, Richard lives apart from his bride and they are both exposed to the wiles of seducers. Lucy eventually wins Sir Austin's approval and Richard belatedly returns, only to undertake a duel with the nobleman who tried to make love to his wife, and she meanwhile dies.

Thus outlined, the plot sounds conventional and melodramatic; but Meredith invested it with new features. His emphasis throughout is psychological; he is concerned with the ambiguous motives, the suppressions and self-deceptions that occur in a complex social relationship. His psychological analysis differs from George Eliot's because he is dealing with more sophisticated people. There may be some truth in the charge that Meredith chose to write about aristocrats because he was eager to obliterate his plebeian origin; but it is more important that he found the subtleties of conduct in a highly cultivated society more interesting than the simple rustic behavior that George Eliot believed to reveal what Wordsworth called "the primary laws of our nature."

Nor can Meredith be accused of worshiping rank and fashion. He was a true successor to Rousseau in believing that civilization faces catastrophe because it inhibits natural impulses by an artificial code of manners. The principal doctrine of the book is that Richard's marriage with the wholesome country girl is the best thing that can happen to the overbred Feverels, and that Sir Austin is responsible for the whole tragedy by his abnormal repression of his son's emotions.

The other basic theory in the book had already appeared in *The Shaving of Shagpat*. Again Meredith asserts that maturity can be reached only through a harsh test by suffering (the "ordeal" of the title), which proves whether a man can develop wisdom and unselfishness or must remain a sentimentalist and an egoist. Again a direct, generous young woman shows greater strength of character than the hero and enables him to endure his trial.

The Ordeal of Richard Feverel, then, is a psychological study based upon vital opinions about human nature. It is also experimental in method. For one thing, it presents its serious theories and its tragic story in terms of high comedy. Meredith believed that a sense of humor is a prime antidote to egoism, and also that comedy is the intellectual attitude best suited for giving a dispassionate revelation of truth. Besides, the formalities of etiquette among the English upper class, and their oblique habits of speech, lent themselves better to comic than to solemn treatment. Meredith's use of comic irony, however, was more disturbing to readers than Thackeray's had been, because Thackeray's was allied with warmth of sympathy whereas Meredith usually maintained an aloof detachment that seemed inhumanly hard.

His particular brand of high comedy, moreover, was conveyed in a style that was ornate and bafflingly allusive, ranging from witty epigrams to extravagant poetic imagery. Mannerisms that seemed acceptable in the literary *pastiche* of his two previous prose works became obtrusive in a novel dealing with contemporary life. Meredith was a brilliant conversationalist, and many of the apparent obscurities in his style are of the sort that in spoken discourse are illuminated by intonation, by pauses, or by gesture and facial expression. He omits transitional phrases, he passes casually over details that later prove to be vital to the story. But these conversational techniques are intermingled with poetical devices, particularly the use of metaphor. Figurative language in prose is usually couched in the more readily comprehensible form of the simile; Meredith maintains such a glittering flow of metaphors that readers are apt to become confused between the literal narrative and the images through which it is being conveyed. Some of the metaphors recur through the book to form a symbolic pattern; these include various attributes of time and frequent allusions to the Garden of Eden and the forbidden fruit.

Part of Meredith's intention was to diversify the style in conformity with the changing moods of the story. The dialogue is usually closer to real talk than that of any previous novelist had been; he tried to give the appropriate tone to each of his characters, from ignorant farm hands to elegant aphorists. But his own narrative and descriptive passages vary almost as widely. The most conspicuous chapters are two that are crucial for demonstrating his belief in the importance of allowing primitive natural forces to guide human conduct. The first recounts the passionate love-making between Richard and Lucy in a summer wood; the second tells how Richard gains his self-mastery while walking all night through a storm in the Rhineland hills. These two counterbalanced scenes are written in lyrical rhythms and emotive phrases that contrast sharply with the cerebral allusiveness of their context.

These idiosyncrasies of style were no doubt due partly to Meredith's determination to show his superiority to the journeyman writers of his time. Since he was obliged to produce fiction, he would elevate it to aesthetic equality with poetry. But he was not merely displaying his virtuosity as an artist in words. He felt sure that a novel of serious analysis ought to be read thoughtfully and that therefore it must keep the reader's mind constantly alert. An obvious, explicit style, he believed, would quickly bore an intelligent reader or at best would lull him into inattentive skimming.

In adopting this theory Meredith broke with the tradition of English fiction since the time of Defoe. The writers of courtly romance, such as Lyly and Sidney, had composed their works consciously for a small, cultivated audience that could enjoy learned allusions and baroque ornament. Thereafter it was assumed that the purpose of a novel was to entertain by telling a good story in a manner that made minimum demands on the reader's attention. The writers who used fiction with a serious purpose of promulgating social theories were as eager as any others to reach the widest possible public through the attractions of readability. Only Sterne, and to some extent Meredith's father-in-law, Peacock, had ignored this axiom in favor of employing subtle innuendo and abstruse allusions. Meredith was prepared to sacrifice popularity in order to address his novels to an intellectual elite. Readers expecting facile amusement would be so bewildered by his opening chapter that they would penetrate no further.

As a matter of fact, the unfavorable reception of *The Ordeal of Richard Feverel* was based not so much upon its obscurity as upon its immorality. Though its treatment of sex seems to modern readers wholly innocuous, it was so shockingly frank by Victorian standards that it was banned by Mudie's chain of circulating libraries, which had the power to establish or to destroy the reputation of a new novelist. Meredith had taken an incautious step toward that truthful picture of "the gentlemen of our age, . . . with the notorious foibles and selfishness of their lives and their education," which Thackeray, as he admitted in his preface to *Pendennis*, a decade earlier, had found himself forbidden to achieve.

XIII

Realism Dominant

(1860 – 1870)

IT IS SIGNIFICANT that 1859, when English fiction arrived at artistic and intellectual maturity with the first novels of George Eliot and George Meredith, was also the year when the whole climate of ideas was changed by the publication of Darwin's *Origin of Species*. As soon as the implications of that book emerged, the material of fiction was transformed. It was not only that the religious code of morality was weakened by skepticism regarding the literal credibility of the Bible. Much more it was the realization that mankind must be regarded on the same basis as all other physical phenomena and that therefore human behavior is susceptible of scientific analysis. Herbert Spencer, working parallel with Darwin and reinforcing his evolutionary hypothesis, established the social sciences, and in so doing he invaded the territory of fiction, which falls into two broad categories — the motives and actions of individuals, and the relationships of these individuals with one another. Both categories became accepted as sciences, under the names of psychology and sociology.

Though the novel had reached a stage of development that

qualified it to perceive and absorb this revolutionary change of attitude toward its subject matter, the adjustment was too fundamental to be quick or easy. George Eliot and Meredith were the only novelists with an active interest in what was happening in philosophy and science, and even to them the full significance of the new evangel became apparent only gradually. Perhaps this is why English fiction during the decade of the 1860's was on a sort of plateau. More well-written novels were published than ever before; the chief figures of the older generation were prolific, side by side with their juniors; but no new novelist of major importance appeared till after 1870, and neither George Eliot nor Meredith reached full stature before that date.

It is hard to realize how brief was the span in which the novel had moved forward to its pre-eminence. The clearest proof of it came in 1860 when Peacock, after a thirty-year silence, brought out his final novel, *Gryll Grange*. There was a timeless quality in his ironic detachment that preserved this book from seeming archaic, though it showed no deviation from his previous manner; but the amazing fact was that he had published his first work of fiction in the same year as *The Antiquary* and *Emma*.

The high productivity of novelists during this decade owed something to the competition among the popular magazines, which bid for public favor by providing serial stories for which they paid liberally. Even *Gryll Grange* came out serially in *Fraser's*. The veteran Harrison Ainsworth had serials running without intermission in *Bentley's Miscellany* or the *New Monthly Magazine* or *Bow Bells* until 1878. Charles Lever, too, abandoned monthly parts in favor of serialization in *Blackwood's* and the *Cornhill* for his later novels, *Tony Butler*, *The Bramleighs of Bishop's Folly*, and others. Surtees remained faithful to the obsolescent monthly parts for his last three novels, *Ask Mamma*, *Plain or Ringlets?*, and *Mr. Romford's Hounds;* but even he modified his primordial violence somewhat, in deference to the vogue of domestic fiction. Women characters are more prominent than in his previous books, and the construction is sturdier. All three stories offer variations of a single plot — a wealthy and rather foolish young man seeking to gain social success and to court pretty girls.

By this time Thackeray was nearing the end of his career.

His editorial responsibilities on the *Cornhill* weighed heavily upon him until he resigned in 1862. He felt obligated to write serials for the magazine, though he was happier in contributing personal essays in the eighteenth-century manner, under the title of *The Roundabout Papers*. A short novel that ran for six months in 1860, *Lovel the Widower,* was interesting chiefly for the handling of the narrator, an amateur of psychology who studies the idiosyncracies of the main characters. The story begins in a serious vein, and on the scale of a full-length novel, only to decline precipitately into farce. In his next serial, *The Adventures of Philip on his Way through the World,* he resumed his former type of novel, with Arthur Pendennis once more as narrator and with some of Thackeray's own experience introduced under a thin veneer of fiction. He revived some of the characters who had been left half-drawn when his wife's breakdown forced him to discontinue *A Shabby-Genteel Story* twenty years earlier. Perhaps it was this that led him to shape the middle part of the story closely upon his own marriage, when his poverty and his overbearing mother-in-law made life miserable for the young couple. His style and characterization are as skillful as ever; but as a whole the book adds nothing to what he had done as well — if not better — in *Pendennis* and *The Newcomes,* and a pervasive sense of effort and discouragement gives it a depressing tone.

In 1863 he started a novel of a different type, *Denis Duval,* which reverted to his favorite eighteenth-century setting and to the autobiographical technique that had been so brilliantly handled in *Esmond.* A livelier tale of adventure than any of his other novels, it promised to rank among his best; but when less than four installments had been written he died in December, 1863, white-haired and broken in health at the age of fifty-two.

Dickens was working far harder than Thackeray, but his superhuman vitality was unexhausted. As autocratic editor of his weekly he selected contributors, assigned subjects, even rewrote articles; and he also gave much time after 1858 to dramatic readings from his books. In tours all over Britain his solo performances held huge audiences enthralled with selections including both comic and melodramatic scenes, and proved that the success of his novels had been due to their closeness to the techniques of the theater.

His next novel, *Great Expectations*, which ran in *All the Year Round* during the first half of 1861, was his masterpiece of form and structure. For the first time since *David Copperfield* he used the autobiographical method, and therefore it illustrates how far he had developed in subtlety of characterization and unity of construction in ten years. It is symmetrically built around two examples of a single situation — an embittered person adopting a child and molding its personality to be a compensation for the foster-parent's frustrations. Magwitch, the exiled convict, devotes all his savings and endangers his life to make a fine gentleman of the crude village boy who is the only person ever to have treated him kindly. Miss Havisham, the jilted bride, brings up Estella to be a heartless coquette so that she may be an instrument of revenge on the male sex. These two counterpoised stories are ironically linked together: for the first half of the book, Pip believes that Miss Havisham is his benefactor; and even at the end Estella is unaware that she is the daughter of the convict.

For sheer efficiency of engineering, with every girder bolted securely into place, no novel was ever better built. If analyzed rationally, both the symmetry and the interlocking are too neat to be credible; but the implausibility is well masked on two levels. One is the expert handling of mystery and suspense, in which Dickens now brought the sensation novel to its apex. Thanks to the first-personal point of view, the reader learns the facts only as Pip discovers them, and yet clues are sufficiently well distributed to prevent the surprises from seeming factitious.

The other source of verisimilitude is in the characterization. Pip reveals himself as being gradually seduced by snobbery and selfishness to the point where he is contemptuous of the kindly, illiterate blacksmith who served as a father to him in his childhood. When faced with the shocking discovery that his second surrogate father is an even more illiterate social outcast — the convict — he is faced with alternative temptations: either to accept the man's wealth in shameful silence or to turn him over to the law. An innate strain of honor enables him to choose a less ignoble course and to sacrifice everything in an effort to save the man from capture.

Estella also represents a fresh character type in Dickens's work. In contrast with his sweet, gentle heroines, who culminated in Esther Summerson and Little Dorrit, she is an intelligent but callous beauty, more like Beatrix Esmond. Recent biographers suggest that this new feminine personality was modeled upon Ellen Ternan, a young actress with whom Dickens became infatuated after his separation from his wife. The logic of the story, and the psychological consistency of Estella, both pointed to an ending that would complete the ironic pattern by having Pip recover from his devotion to the frigid heartbreaker, as Henry Esmond did in Thackeray's novel; but Dickens's friends (and perhaps his own affection for Estella's original) impelled him to change the final paragraphs and imply a conventional happy ending in marriage without actually stating it.

Perhaps the most difficult achievement in the book is the portrayal of the two monomaniacs, Magwitch and Miss Havisham, who are rendered believable and even pathetic as specimens of personalities hopelessly warped by circumstances. This may be due partly to the absence of Dickens's usual crusading. The depiction of Magwitch's life as a convict is not an indictment of the prisons like Reade's in *It Is Never Too Late to Mend*. But in another sense this novel strikes at the heart of the English social system by challenging the sanctity of caste. Being elevated in the social scale brings nothing but misery to Pip and Estella alike. The brutal Bentley Drummle and the ineffectual Mrs. Pocket, both proud of being gentlefolk, are contrasted with hard-working Joe Gargery in his forge and serene Wemmick cultivating his suburban garden. This was not a new theme in English fiction, but it had become acute by 1860, when the old assured structure of society was under new stresses; and possibly Dickens was also making a personal confession of guilt for having so eagerly courted social and financial success and for having felt ashamed of his humble origin.

If the sequence of events in the attempt to smuggle Magwitch out of England ranks as one of the highest achievements of the sensation novel, it had keen rivalry in other books written about the same time. Wilkie Collins's *No Name* (1862) combined ingenuity of plot with several eccentric characters that almost reach the comic level of Dickens. Centering upon the troubles of a girl who is driven to the brink of suicide after being left penniless upon the death of her parents because they were not married at the time of her birth, it includes a diatribe against the laws penalizing illegitimacy.

Collins's next novel, *Armadale*, which ran in the *Cornhill* in 1864, shows a marked increase in morbidity. By this time he was indulging in laudanum as a relief for painful illness, and something of the weird vividness of a drug-addict's dreams makes the novel gruesomely powerful. Collins's use of atmospheric setting was an outcome of his early association with landscape painting. It was a device that had been practiced by Mrs. Radcliffe, but he brought it to its highest pitch of effectiveness. When he decided upon a suitable geographical background for any portion of a story he would spend weeks in exploring the region thoroughly. Several scenes in *Armadale* — on a derelict ship, in a library during a storm, on the bleak Norfolk Broads — supply eerie intensity. A supernatural touch is added by having the action foretold at the beginning in dreams. The author leaves us to wonder whether a real doom is being fulfilled or the psychology of autosuggestion is forcing the characters to carry out the premonition.

A principal character is a pretty blonde drug-addict who engages in theft and forgery and plans to kill a man with poison gas. Ranging from an abortion clinic to a disreputable mental institution, both in supposedly respectable districts of London, the sustained exploration of the shady half-world below the prosperous surface of modern life was far more realistic and shocking than had been the Newgate novels of Ainsworth and Bulwer thirty years before.

Charles Reade did not try to continue with historical fiction after *The Cloister and the Hearth*, but returned belligerently to contemporary abuses. Having been personally involved in gaining freedom for a young man whose relations had committed him to a lunatic asylum, Reade used this as the central theme for *Hard Cash*, which was serialized in *All the Year Round* in 1863. The victim's sufferings in a private asylum are described with the same horrifying distinctness as had been the prison tortures in *It Is Never Too Late to Mend;* and again this is counterbalanced with another character's exciting adventures in a different part of the world. This structure gave Reade a chance for one of his favorite devices of suspense — the abrupt switch from one story line to another. Thus, when Captain Dodd has apparently died at sea and his corpse is about to be dropped overboard, the story reverts to the English episodes, and many chapters elapse before we are told that the Captain came to life just before his body went over the rail. Reade's stated axiom was that "I never knew an interesting story allowed to proceed without a whole system of interruption."

His method had another advantage, in enabling him to maintain a constantly fast tempo of action. In contrast with Collins's leisurely building up of portentous landscapes and everyday details, Reade rushes onward at a breakneck pace that would become intolerable if it were not moderated by the distribution among more than one concurrent series of events.

Another contrast with Collins is illustrated by the handling of the madhouse theme. Anne Catherick in *The Woman in White* had been shut up in an institution by scheming relations, just as Alfred Hardie was in *Hard Cash;* and some scenes in *Armadale* (two years after Reade's book) also occur in an asylum. But Collins is mainly concerned with the emotional potency of the situation, whereas Reade is emphatic about the social and legal implications, indicting the dangerous power that was vested in the Commissioners in Lunacy.

His next novel, *Griffith Gaunt* (1866), showed an effort toward more subtle characterization, and the first part of the book resembles the domestic novel in its account of a courtship; but after the couple are married, the theme of bigamy brings in the usual melodramatic complications. The story was serialized in a new magazine, the *Argosy*, and in the *Atlantic Monthly;* Dickens considered some episodes too indelicate for the family circle to which his paper appealed. When Reade was preparing to sue an American reviewer for libel because he had called the story "an indecent publication" dealing with "adultery, bigamy, and nameless social crimes," so that "the modesty and purity of women cannot survive the perusal" of it, Dickens was unwilling to testify in the author's favor, explaining that "I should say that what was pure to an artist might be impurely suggestive to inferior minds." He cited "those passages about Gaunt's going up to his wife's bed drunk and that last child's being conceived," and "the passage where Kate and Mercy have the illegitimate child upon their laps and look over its little points together." In Dickens's opinion the ending, when Gaunt chooses one wife and lets his rival take the other, was "extremely coarse and disagreeable."

The spectacular success of Reade and Collins produced a shoal of imitators, such as James Payn, who made his reputation with *Lost Sir Massingberd* (1864). An industrious magazine editor and fiction-monger, Payn wrote about a hundred novels in all. The most successful of the new sensation novelists, however, were women, especially Mrs. Henry Wood. The daughter of a businessman in a country town, she grew up a fragile hunchback, and after her marriage she lived in France for twenty years until her husband's failure in business forced her to earn a living. Her first novel, *Danesbury House*, was written in a month to be submitted for a prize of a hundred pounds offered by the Scottish Temperance League for a novel illustrating the evils of drink. She won the prize, and the publishers enjoyed the profits of a sale that eventually reached a hundred thousand copies.

Her next novel, *East Lynne*, which ran as a magazine serial in 1861, became one of the best sellers of all time, and when made into a play was equally successful on the stage. This improbable story of a rejected wife who returns in disguise to bring up her children as their governess contained exactly the balance of melodrama and tears that appealed to the average mind. By maintaining the rigidly moral dogmas in which she had been brought up, Mrs. Wood was able to make sensational material — even adultery and bigamy — acceptable to a large segment of the public that was repelled by the more flagrant situations in Collins and Reade.

Her closest rival, Mary Elizabeth Braddon, was twenty-three years younger and much less goody-goody. She started writing fiction of the "penny-dreadful" variety when she was eighteen; and seven years later, in 1862, her *Lady Audley's Secret* became second only to *East Lynne* as a best seller. Its central character is a beautiful woman who has murdered the father of her illegitimate child by pushing him into a well. In this and subsequent novels, such as *Aurora Floyd*, Miss Braddon used situations that implied sexual irregularity, but by implausible manipulation of the plot she always avoided openly improper occurrences. While virtue always triumphed and the transgressors were punished, she did not indulge in such smugly pious homilies as Mrs. Wood, but instead maintained a faintly ironic tone that suggested she did not take her readers' moral prejudices altogether seriously. As a result, she was accused of being "a corrupter of youth" and "a purveyor of poisonous sensuality."

Mrs. Wood and Miss Braddon immediately engaged in a headlong race. In seven years after *East Lynne* Mrs. Wood published fifteen novels, some of which ran simultaneously in different magazines. The best of them were *The Channings, Mrs. Halliburton's Troubles, Verner's Pride,* and *The Shadow of Ashlydyat.* Miss Braddon was equally prolific, and by the time she died in 1915 she had written over eighty novels. Each lady acquired a magazine in which to publish her own stories and others of the same sort. Mrs. Wood took over the *Argosy* when the original proprietor relinquished it after the scandal over Reade's *Griffith Gaunt,* and about the same time Miss Braddon assumed control of *Belgravia.*

Next to the sensation novels in popularity came the stories of manly adventure. Whyte-Melville was at the height of his vogue, and his *Market Harborough* (1861), though loosely put together, is probably the best of his novels about fox-hunting. He produced historical fiction with equal success in *Holmby House* (1860), *The Queen's Maries* (1862), and *The Gladiators* (1863). Along with him may be mentioned Charles Kingsley's younger brother, Henry, who became the chief representative of the wholesome school of muscular Christianity. A more unstable character than his brother and without the compulsive urge toward social polemics, he had left his Oxford studies unfinished to go seeking his fortune in the Australian gold fields. After five unsuccessful years he returned to England and used his experiences as the basis for his first novel, *The Adventures of Geoffrey Hamlyn* (1859). This was followed by *Ravenshoe,* which included episodes of the Crimean War, and *The Hillyars and the Burtons,* another Australian story. His idealistic devotion to noble conduct conflicts with the realism of his settings, and his novels are weak in structure, but they are readable for their vigorous action and their attractive characters.

In the adventure novel, as in the sensation novel, a formidable competitor soon appeared in the person of a woman. A story entitled *Gaston de Vigne,* by "Ouida," ran in the *New Monthly* along with *East Lynne,* and was retitled *Held in Bondage* when it came out in three-volume form in 1863. The author was Louise Ramé, daughter of a French expatriate of somewhat mysterious proclivities. Devoid of beauty and social status, but endowed with enormous egoism and ambition, she grew up in a dull provincial town, escaping from the unpropitious realities into a dream world of wealth and sophistication, in which she could be a heroine. She changed her name to "de la Ramée" and hinted that her irresponsible father had been an exiled aristocrat.

When she began to write fiction she poured her fantasies of grandeur into torrid love stories in which uninhibited beauties were wooed by magnificent officers of the Guards amid surroundings of exotic luxury. Nor is there any lack of excitement and danger: in the midst of *Held in Bondage* the hero and his comrades are transported to the Crimean War and take part — inevitably — in the charge of the Light Brigade. Her first novel was followed in rapid succession by *Strathmore, Chandos,* and *Under Two Flags,* each more lavish than the last in recounting the debauches and the daring exploits of her opulent and high-born heroes. Unhampered by any knowledge of actual life among the nobility, she wrote vividly enough to give equally uninformed readers an illusion of experience. Her florid style was no handicap to her immense story-telling ability, and her frank allusions to sex won her a reputation for immorality that soon overshadowed Miss Braddon's.

It is paradoxical that the sensation novels, remote though they were from normal events, exerted a powerful influence in preparing the way for greater realism in fiction. Collins, Reade, and Ouida all felt that they were dedicated battlers for truth and for the demolition of taboos that prevented honest talking about sex and about violence or brutality. During the same years Swinburne was incurring even more ferocious censure for the indecency of his poetry; and it is worth noting that he was an admirer of the sensation novelists. The narrative energy of these books allured countless readers in spite of the flouting of conventional reticence.

While the sensationalists were promoting the extension of realism by touching on forbidden topics, the chroniclers of the commonplace were also gaining ground. Here again the novel was moving side by side with other literary forces. Matthew Arnold had begun to decry the vogue of romantic poetry and to insist upon the primary necessity of "seeing the object as in itself it really is." Browning carried his interest in psychological subtleties and in the relativity of truth to its apex in his vast investigation of motives and prejudices in *The Ring and the Book.* These influences aligned themselves with the ever-in-

creasing pressure of scientific rationalism and the experimental
approach to social phenomena.

The growth of realism in the domestic novel is illustrated by
the last works of Mrs. Gaskell, who had relinquished social propaganda and settled down to the tranquil mood of *Cranford*. In
Sylvia's Lovers she deals with the Yorkshire town of Whitby at
the end of the eighteenth century, but it is not much more of a
historical novel than *Adam Bede*, which was set in the same
years. The smuggling and whaling and the activities of the
press gang were as much a permanent part of life in a seaport
town as the harvesting and revival meetings belonged to the in-
land setting of George Eliot's book. As Mrs. Gaskell was dealing
with a way of life that she did not know at first hand, it required unwonted effort on her part. She is not at her best in
the adventurous passages, but otherwise the book is delightful for
its local color and for the character of Sylvia Robson, a strong-
willed, unforgiving woman, whose ordeal of unhappiness and
eventual growth into mature integrity are as true to reality as
anything in George Eliot.

There is less complication of plot in *Cousin Phillis*, a novelette
of idyllic sweetness; and Mrs. Gaskell's final novel, *Wives and
Daughters*, though her longest book, is almost devoid of action.
It is a subtly developed study of two contrasted women, the
daughters of a country doctor and his two successive wives.
In the characterization of this family and in the picture of their
community Mrs. Gaskell comes closest to the quiet irony and
tolerant insight of Trollope at his best. *Wives and Daughters* is
certainly her masterpiece, even though the last chapter remained
unfinished when she died in 1865.

The most notable new figure in domestic fiction was Margaret
Wilson Oliphant. She had been publishing novels since 1849,
mainly dealing with the Scottish life that she had known in her
girlhood; but not until 1861, when she had been left a widow with
several sickly children to support, did she win wide recognition.
Then her stories in *Blackwood's Magazine*, "The Rector" and
"The Doctor's Family," showed a sympathetic and humorous eye
for ordinary human beings and their affairs. Her next serial,
Salem Chapel, was highly praised, and many readers became convinced that the anonymous stories were the work of George Eliot.
Along with *The Perpetual Curate* (1864) and *Miss Marjoribanks*

(1866), these came to be known as "The Chronicles of Carling-
ford," in which Mrs. Oliphant created a picture of a typical
English community akin to Mrs. Gaskell's Cranford and Trollope's Barchester. Like Trollope and George Eliot, she paid particular attention to the clergy, both Anglican and Nonconformist;
but she enlivened her drowsy setting with incongruous elements
of mystery borrowed from the sensation novels. If she had not
been perpetually overworked in the job of earning a living by
writing some hundred and twenty books of all sorts, she might
rank among the major novelists.

Another author of much the same caliber was George Mac-
Donald. The son of a Highland farmer, he was brought up in
strict Calvinism, but became a Congregational minister and developed a vein of mysticism that manifested itself in his earliest
books, two volumes of poems and a remarkable "faerie romance
for men and women," *Phantastes* (1858). His first novel, *David
Elginbrod* (1863), was based upon the character of his father and
contained picturesque contrasts between the life of Highland cot-
tagers and that of the English middle class. The author's interest in the occult appeared in episodes dealing with telepathy and
suggestion. By this time he was associated with F. D. Maurice
in Christian Socialism and adult education; he joined the Church
of England and became a popular lecturer. In subsequent novels,
Alec Forbes of Howglen (1865), *Annals of a Quiet Neighborhood* (1866), and *Robert Falconer* (1867), he established himself as a faithful recorder of Scottish rural life and an exponent of
deep spiritual values. His novels revived the tradition of Scottish
local color that had been initiated by John Galt a generation
earlier.

Meanwhile Trollope was at the height of his triumph. With
promotion to a position of authority in the postal service, he had
settled his family in a pleasant country house near London; but
he went abroad from time to time on official business — to the
West Indies in 1858, to the United States in 1861. With customary efficiency he exploited his overseas impressions by writing
travel books; but nothing interfered with his steady output of
fiction. After *Framley Parsonage* he temporarily abandoned Barsetshire in *Orley Farm,* a long novel which came out in monthly
parts (1861–62) and which consequently betrays some of the defects of that method — episodic structure and sudden shifts

from serious to comic scenes. The central theme, however, is a persuasive and touching study of a woman placed in an intolerable moral dilemma. With *The Small House at Allington* (1862–64) he returned to Barsetshire, and created a natural and charming heroine in Lily Dale, while her tongue-tied admirer, Johnny Eames, is a wry portrait of Trollope himself in his clumsy youth. The story of these two was completed in *The Last Chronicle of Barset* (1867), wherein Trollope violated a sacred canon of sentimental fiction by leaving their love unfulfilled and letting the delightful Lily remain unmarried. He was more conventional in an intervening novel, *Can You Forgive Her?*, in which the heroine jilts a virtuous but colorless fiancé in favor of her attractive scamp of a cousin, only to repent of her mutiny and end by marrying the faultless John Gray. In two other novels of these years, *The Claverings* and *The Belton Estate*, Trollope's particular method is at its maximum proficiency: with apparently ingenuous and almost aimless simplicity he subtly reveals the complicated embarrassments and hesitations that beset commonplace people, maintaining the reader's sympathy even for the least praiseworthy characters, such as the disillusioned coquette, Julia Ongar, in *The Claverings*. As in Jane Austen's novels, the plot always centers in two interlocking problems — a girl's choice between contrasted suitors and the contrary temptations of personal compatibility and financial advantage; but though Trollope explores every facet of the dilemmas with leisurely thoroughness, the suspense and the verisimilitude never relax.

Altogether, Trollope published ten novels between 1861 and 1867 in addition to three volumes of short stories and four works of nonfiction. His versatility is shown by several of the shorter novels in this total — *Rachel Ray* and *Miss Mackenzie*, which are social satires in a light vein, and *Nina Balatka, The Story of a Maiden of Prague*, which is picturesque and unblushingly romantic. The major novel that marks the end of this stage of his career shows symptoms of impending change. By calling it *The Last Chronicle of Barset* he gave public notice that he was abandoning the placid atmosphere that had become identified with his name; and the main plot deals at vast length with a drab and somewhat grim situation in which a middle-aged, underpaid curate is suspected of stealing a check. The Rev. Josiah Crawley, tactless and absent-minded as he is, takes on some dimensions of a true tragic hero.

Dickens, for three years after *Great Expectations* was finished, wrote no fiction except Christmas supplements for *All the Year Round*, and occupied himself chiefly with his reading tours. Then in 1864 he started another of his mammoth novels in monthly parts, *Our Mutual Friend*. It contained all his familiar ingredients — grotesque comic characters, elaborate atmospheric settings, melodramatic mystery, an interlinked pattern of concurrent lines of action. The social satire is still mordant, and the book's total effect is as depressing as that of the two with which it is most readily comparable — *Bleak House* and *Little Dorrit*.

The two story lines that provide suspense are far from plausible, as they both depend upon disguise: John Harmon is hiding his true identity and Noddy Boffin is pretending to be a miser. But, as usual, Dickens conceals any weakness in his plot by the infinitely varied panorama of character and scene. His knowledge of upper-class life had continued to mature, and in Eugene Wrayburn he gives a good portrait of a young gentleman, whose dilettante indolence is contrasted with the morbid violence of Bradley Headstone, the frustrated intellectual of humble origin. Headstone's complex suppressions and antagonisms, and his symbolic involvement with the atrocious Riderhood, render him more convincing than the standard villains of previous fiction. The heroine, Bella Wilfer, is a shallower version of the selfish coquette he had previously drawn in *Great Expectations*. Mr. Podsnap is another relentless dissection of a smug businessman, reminiscent of Dombey, Merdle, and Gradgrind.

Dickens's inexhaustible familiarity with the shabby quarters of London provides the principal settings — the fetid mud-flats and sluggish waters of the Thames, where Hexam trawls for drowned corpses, and the monstrous garbage dumps from which Boffin derives his wealth. But these nauseous settings are not used solely to create an atmosphere of horror such as graveyards and dungeons had provided for the Gothic romances. Instead they are basic to the symbolism that dominates the book. Hexam and Boffin draw their livelihood from death and decay, but the wealthy and powerful are fully as dependent upon the rotting substructure of society. Even the disguises cease to be merely a melodramatic device and link themselves with more subtle deceptions: the Veneerings pretend to be gentlefolk; the ancient Lady Tippins pretends to be young and beautiful; Sophronia Akershem and Alfred Lammle pretend to be rich, and marry each other under this misapprehension. Everything is greed and sham, and the illiterate old dustman is the only genuinely noble personage in the story. An essentially poetic and mythopoeic tendency had been expanding in Dickens's work ever since *Oliver Twist*. In *Our Mutual Friend* it engulfs the whole novel and turns it into a terrifying epic of a doomed society. With its gigantic bulk and sumptuous embellishment, this book moves like a galleon among the sleek pinnaces of the other novelists.

While Dickens was thus retaining the leadership that he had held for almost thirty years, George Eliot had risen spectacularly to be the chief claimant for second place. After *Adam Bede* she wrote another novel which was even more intimately identified with her childhood. The previous book had drawn upon the reminiscences of her father and aunt about their early life, but *The Mill on the Floss* depicts herself and her brother and parents with almost painful fidelity. Maggie Tulliver, with her rebellious emotions and her insatiable intellectual curiosity, reveals all that we can hope to know about young Mary Ann Evans's inner life. The author's insight into a child's feelings is keener than any previous novelist had displayed. Psychologists can approve the implication that Maggie's early subjection to her brother affected her behavior toward the two men she falls in love with after she grows up. Maggie comes to see all the faults in the smug, self-righteous Tom, and in a burst of anger she can call him an uncomprehending, unimaginative Pharisee; but he always holds first place in her affection.

It has been suggested that Philip Wakem, the brilliant hunchback who liberates her mind with his range of scholarly knowledge, is partly derived from a crippled Swiss painter who was Miss Evans's chief friend during her lonely months in Geneva, just as Paul Emanuel in *Villette* emerged from a similar episode in the life of Charlotte Brontë. Philip probably also contains traces of John Chapman and Herbert Spencer, each of whom for a while held sway in Miss Evans's susceptible heart. Maggie then develops a still deeper love for the handsome Stephen Guest, who is engaged to her cousin, and who can be regarded as the fictional counterpart of Lewes. These situations are significant not merely for flouting the sentimental doctrine of female constancy and showing that a girl can change the object of her love; they also parallel Mary Ann Evans's own ethical dilemmas. Maggie knows that if she were to marry Philip she would bring agony to her father, who has a feud with the Wakem family; and when she turns toward Stephen, she is not only betraying Philip but is also on the verge of treachery to her cousin.

The conclusion of the novel, when Maggie and Tom are drowned together in a flood, has sometimes been condemned as a melodramatic trick, dragged in to provide a solution to the impasse. Actually, however, it is a fulfillment of the story's whole theme, for when Maggie gives her life in an effort to save her brother she displays the unselfish devotion to him that has been her compelling motive ever since infancy. Besides, the climax has been·prepared for by the use of the river as a recurrent symbol throughout the book. George Eliot was no longer willing to offer a meretricious happy ending as she had done in *Adam Bede.*

The Mill on the Floss, then, is not merely a fervent investigation of love from a woman's point of view, but is also a truthful unveiling of the author's inmost feelings. Perhaps it is this extreme degree of personal involvement that prevents it from being one of her best novels. Unable to restrain her sympathy for Maggie, even when making exasperated comments on her faults, she did not maintain the impartial attitude that gives her other stories their particular power. This defect may have been brought home to her by several unfavorable reviews, which were probably influenced by the knowledge that George Eliot was the scandalous woman who was living with a married man. At any rate, her next novel scrupulously avoided personal elements.

Silas Marner is briefer than its two predecessors, and is tidily constructed around a simple situation that takes on some qualities of an allegory. The tale of a poor weaver who becomes a miser in compensation for being rejected by his community, and who is redeemed through adopting a lost child that miraculously wanders into his cottage after his gold has been stolen, it is a rustic idyl in the Wordsworthian tradition, with roots deep in folk legends. The psychology, however, is as sound as in her other books, and there is mellow earthy humor in her sketches of unsophisticated types.

Three novels in three years had displayed George Eliot's unmatched familiarity with the English country life that she had absorbed in her early years. In this sense, as well as in her per-

ception of psychological complexities, she deserves the appel-
lation of realist, though her realism is in the English tradition
that believes in the inherent goodness of human nature and
presents the moral consciousness of individuals rather than their
animal instincts. She protested that she was not a didactic novelist because she did not advocate specific doctrines but merely
portrayed situations in such a way that the reader's emotional
response led him to think earnestly about them. She was certain, she said in *The Mill on the Floss*, that "the mysterious complexity of our life is not to be embraced by maxims," because
"moral judgments must remain false and hollow, unless they are
checked and enlightened by a perpetual reference to the special
circumstances that mark the individual lot." Therefore she depicts no character as innately evil, but shows how harmful effects
result from inadequate foresight. As Adam Bede remarks, "you
never can do what's wrong without breeding sin and trouble
more than you can ever see"; or as Mr. Irwine phrases it,
"men's lives are as thoroughly blended with each other as the
air they breathe: evil spreads as necessarily as disease." In each
novel a principal character — Adam Bede, Maggie Tulliver, Silas
Marner — is redeemed from self-righteous intolerance. It was perhaps her study of Spinoza that convinced George Eliot that selfishness is the root of all evil and renunciation the highest good.

There was another side of George Eliot's mind, however,
which was unrevealed in her nostalgic reminiscences of the countryside or in her simple ethical creed that "no man is an ilande."
She was also a well-trained scholar and a more than amateur
philosopher. For her fourth novel she sought a subject that
would give full scope for her intellectual gifts; and she turned,
somewhat unexpectedly, to history.

She and Lewes made a trip to Italy for local color and to
take notes in the Magliabecchian Library in Florence. After a half
year of exhaustive research in Italian sources she began *Romola*,
a story of Florentine life in the fifteenth century. She received
the unprecedented sum of £7000 from the proprietor of the *Cornhill*, in which the story ran in 1862–63. Because it dealt with the
same era of European history, it was inevitably compared with
The Cloister and the Hearth, which had come out a year earlier;
though both are based on immense research, they are diametrically unlike, Reade's book being essentially romantic in its strenu-

ous adventures and pathetic love story, whilst George Eliot's is essentially realistic in its concentration upon mental processes.

Like Browning in some of his best dramatic monologues, she was probing for a clue to the paradoxes of the Italian Renaissance. The central character, Tito Melema, begins as a pleasure-loving young man who uses his charm and cleverness to make life more comfortable for himself, and who degenerates into an unscrupulous and ruthless schemer. In contrast, his wife Romola is a nobly unselfish woman who eventually leaves him and becomes a worker in Savonarola's religious revival. The historical background is provided by the conflicts between Savonarola and the Medici and by the glittering society of artists and scholars of the 1490's.

While admitting George Eliot's erudition as displayed in the setting, and her moral earnestness in the analysis of the characters, some critics have caviled at important elements in the story. One is the handling of plot. When Romola's spiritual strength is exhausted by prolonged anguish she restores it by ministering to victims of the plague. Swinburne condemned the "puerile insufficiency" of "the casually empty boat, which drifts her away to a casually plague-stricken village, there to play the part of a casual angel of mercy dropped down from the sky by providential caprice, at the very nick of time when the novelist was helplessly at a loss for a more plausible contrivance, among a set of people equally strange to the reader and herself." The characterization also has been challenged. Lord David Cecil holds that in this novel "she comes a dreadful crash" because "the human beings . . . are inevitably the sort of human beings who inhabited the Victorian Midlands, narrow, prudish, steady, and prosaic; about as much like the contemporaries of Leonardo da Vinci and Lucrezia Borgia as they are like the man in the moon." Other readers lose sympathy with the heroine because of her oppressive magnanimity.

On the other hand, Romola is not a static model of perfection. At first a pagan humanist, she is converted by Savonarola to a creed of self-sacrifice, which is actually more like Comte's religion of humanity than like the great Friar's Catholic mysticism. But she retains her freedom of conscience, and in spite of her dependence on his spiritual strength she repudiates him when he tries to become a political dictator. And beyond question Tito Melema is one of the most effective studies of a vicious character in all fiction, in that he is not a monster of gratuitous evil but is a victim of his own moral inadequacy. George Eliot had already sketched self-indulgent weaklings in Arthur Donnithorne in *Adam Bede* and Godfrey Cass in *Silas Marner;* now she showed how — given opportune circumstances — this type of personality could lapse into total depravity.

Her three years of work on *Romola* undermined George Eliot's never robust health; the labor, she said, had made an old woman of her, and she did not start her next novel for two years. In it she returned to English provincial life, though not to idyllic rural scenes. The vitality of *Felix Holt, the Radical* is lower than that of any of her other books. It is concerned with English political affairs at the time of the first Reform Bill; but George Eliot, looking at human conduct always in the light of permanent principles, lacked the excitement over public issues that can engender a good political novel. Because her plot was more complicated than usual, suggesting the sensation novels in its use of a double mystery of parentage and a disputed inheritance, she studied Blackstone for legal details and verified them with Frederic Harrison. The chief charm of *Felix Holt* is in the love story, wherein a frivolous girl is weaned away from her selfish pastimes by her affection for the idealistic radical.

While George Eliot was occupying the summit of fame and rewards, George Meredith remained in obscurity. When his second novel was accepted as a serial for *Once a Week* he made a distinct effort toward gratifying popular taste by including Dickensian comic characters and a fairly conventional love story. Nevertheless, the importance of *Evan Harrington* resides in elements that are characteristically Meredith's own. Like George Eliot in *The Mill on the Floss* in the same year, he gives a frank description of his own family, all the more astonishing in view of his extreme reticence about this matter in real life. In the early part of the story the hero is a faithful picture of Meredith's father — the handsome, self-conscious youth with pretensions to gentility, son of a genial tailor and his businesslike wife, brother of three women who are socially ambitious. The account was so literally accurate that Meredith's aunts and their families took offense at what they considered to be unflattering portraits.

As the story progresses and Evan is accepted as a guest in a country mansion, the material comes closer to Meredith's own current experiences. Living with his little boy in a rural cottage, he had become friendly with Sir Alexander and Lady Duff Gordon, who were the center of a lively intellectual group; and he fell half in love with their forthright seventeen-year-old daughter, though the existence of his renegade wife, as well as fifteen years' difference in age, made any serious affair unthinkable. He portrayed the Duff Gordons as the Jocelyns, and his feelings toward Janet lent poignance to the scene in which Evan renounces Rose Jocelyn's love because of his inferior rank.

Meredith tried to keep the story in the mood of high comedy throughout; and the Countess de Saldar, Evan's unscrupulous sister, is a triumph of witty characterization. But he is obviously preoccupied with the serious theme of class distinctions. Evan's ordeal by ridicule is totally different from Richard Feverel's emotional torture, but it is as significant in bringing him to maturity; and the lesson he learns is the same that Pip learned in *Great Expectations* — the falsity of social ambition.

Though the style of *Evan Harrington* is less ornate than that of Meredith's previous novel, he was still addicted to the abstruse and the oblique; and this quality, combined with lack of vigorous movement in the story, prevented it from being widely admired. Shortly after finishing it, Meredith became reader for the firm of Chapman & Hall, a position that earned him a meager income and required him to read stacks of inferior fiction. He acquired a pathological contempt for the sentimental excesses of Mrs. Henry Wood and Ouida; and his next three novels show him in search of a form of fiction suitable to his idiosyncracies. In *Emilia in England* (later renamed *Sandra Belloni*), on which he worked painfully for four years, he undertook the difficult task of portraying the artistic temperament. His heroine, the daughter of an Italian street-musician in London, is gifted with a magnificent singing voice that attracts the attention of the three Pole sisters, the socially ambitious daughters of a rich but unpolished businessman. This gives Meredith an opportunity to expound his theory that the primary vice of contemporary society is sentimentalism — a conscious cultivation of artificial attitudes that results from lack of assurance in the newly influential middle class. The Pole girls with their anxious pose of aesthetic sensibility, and their brother with his stiff diffidence, are contrasted with Emilia's vitality and impulsiveness. Though Meredith, like Dickens, believed that social pretension based on wealth spells the doom of civilization, his kindly, vulgar Mr. Pole is a more likable person than Merdle or Podsnap because of Meredith's theory that the only good people are those who live according to the dictates of nature.

When he went on to his next novel Meredith made an unwonted invasion of George Eliot's territory. The main setting of *Rhoda Fleming* is a farming community, and the central situation is close to that of *Adam Bede*. The difference between the two authors is thus brought out. Dahlia Fleming, the farmer's daughter seduced by a young gentleman, is depicted more sympathetically than Hetty Sorrel; her sister Rhoda's integrity and determination seem ruthless to the verge of sadism, whereas in Dinah Morris the same traits were entirely noble; and certainly the principal male character, Robert Armstrong, is unlike Adam Bede, for he has been a drunkard and is afflicted with a vile temper. In these respects *Rhoda Fleming* must be called more realistic than the Eliot novel had been. It stands apart from the rest of Meredith's work not only in its rustic milieu but also in its relatively straightforward narration and unadorned style.

After this interlude Meredith wrote a sequel to *Sandra Belloni*, though it is a totally different sort of book. The previous one was high comedy, but *Vittoria* is his nearest approach to a full-dress historical romance. Emilia has now become a great prima donna and her girlish impetuousness has ripened into spiritual intensity. She dedicates herself to the Italian uprising against Austria in 1848. While writing this novel Meredith witnessed the more successful revolt of 1866 in the capacity of a war correspondent, and therefore felt qualified to give a large panorama of the conspiracies and battles of the earlier affair. The resulting complexity is sometimes difficult to follow; but the essential atmosphere of suspicion and frustration is brilliantly evoked, and several big scenes, such as that in which Emilia gives the signal for the revolt while singing in La Scala, are magnificent.

This novel provides a good example of Meredith's ambiguous position between realism and romanticism. Revolution against tyranny is among the most cherished of romantic themes; and Meredith idealizes his heroine to such a degree that she becomes a symbolic figure rather than a credible human being. Nevertheless he abstains from committing himself or his readers to wholehearted sympathy with the cause. Instead he remains aloof, emphasizing the ironical contrasts between the professed magnanimity of the revolutionaries and their actual traits of jealousy, cruelty, and incompetence; and he insists on the uncomfortable fact that many people kept up their personal relationships with both sides. It is this sort of ambivalence that makes Meredith's novels distasteful to some readers, who object to being suspended between the romantic and realistic modes.

In his next book he departed from this attitude of ironic remoteness, mainly because for once he adopted the first-personal narrative method. The result was a sharp increase in the romantic element. *The Adventures of Harry Richmond* appeared anonymously in the *Cornhill Magazine* in 1870–71, and was so unlike Meredith's usual manner that his authorship was not suspected. In order to sustain the illusion that the story was actually being told by a rather ordinary young man, Meredith was obliged to moderate his indulgence in epigram and recondite allusion. The most remarkable effect of the autobiographic technique is a magnification of the principal character, Harry Richmond's father. Richmond Roy, as he calls himself, is a fascinating adventurer, who insists that he is the true heir to the British throne and by his flamboyant effrontery convinces many people that his claim is genuine. Seeing him always through the admiring but embarrassed eyes of his son, who is dragged helplessly in his wake, we are never sure whether Roy is an impudent pretender or a self-deluded megalomaniac — or whether perhaps his claim is valid after all. Unscrupulous though he is, he assumes truly heroic proportions in his indomitable campaigns to marry his son to a German princess or to find him a seat in Parliament.

The lovely and intellectual Princess Ottilia is another of Meredith's attempts to prove that women can be wiser and more unselfish than men if they have a chance to display their true individuality, and as such she is somewhat too perfect to be believable; but she is effectively contrasted with Janet Ilchester, an outspoken English girl. Harry Richmond's irresolute love for these two charmers is thoroughly natural.

Much of the charm of this novel derives from the settings. Meredith's memories of his schooldays on the Rhine provided the

idyllic scenes in a German principality, where Harry becomes
involved in court intrigues; but even more appealing to most
readers' imaginations are the episodes among the gypsies in the
English countryside. By the use of these beguiling backgrounds,
along with the avoidance of deep psychological probing, Meredith hoped that he might at last win a measure of popular esteem.

   Harry Richmond was not the only novel that indicated a resurgence of the romantic mood at the end of the sixties. A more
thoroughgoing romance had been published in the previous year;
and though it was so unlike the current fashions that it was not
immediately acclaimed, it grew steadily in favor. The author was
Richard Doddridge Blackmore, an Oxford graduate and London barrister who found that he liked gardening better than
law, and retired to a quiet village. When almost forty he wrote
his first novel, *Clara Vaughan*, a sensational story of murder
and apparitions of the Wilkie Collins stamp. This vein, however,
proved uncongenial to him, and his next book, *Cradock Nowell,
a Tale of the New Forest*, was a gentle story with an overload
of classical scholarship in the style. Then in 1869 he brought out
Lorna Doone, a Romance of Exmoor. He had known and loved
the West Country in his schooldays, and he captured its picturesqueness in descriptions of the Doone Valley. A ferocious
clan of outlaws, with their lovely, high-spirited daughter, are
suitable inhabitants for the wild region, and the Monmouth rebellion of 1685 provides an exciting historical framework. The
peculiar attractiveness of the story lies in its being narrated by
the hero, John Ridd, whose sturdy honesty and rustic
humor are conveyed in his rhythmic, colloquial speech. Before
long *Lorna Doone* took its place as one of the century's best-
loved novels.

   Lorna Doone and *Harry Richmond* are isolated outcroppings of
romance in a decade when realism was entrenching itself in the
English novel. It must also be observed, however, that the
same decade witnessed a remarkable output of fantasy. Indeed,
not until then is fantasy (when not used merely as a device for
satire) identifiable as a distinct mode in English prose fiction.
Two important novelists, Meredith and MacDonald, had begun
in the later fifties by writing fantasies of originality and beauty.
Charles Kingsley, who published no novel after 1857 except
Hereward the Wake (1866), a conventional historical romance,

brought out *The Water Babies* in 1863; and two years later Lewis Carroll produced *Alice's Adventures in Wonderland*, which was followed in 1872 by *Through the Looking Glass*. While the books by Kingsley and Carroll were nominally addressed to children, they contained depths of satire, imaginative suggestion, and philosophical symbolism which only adults could fully appreciate. George MacDonald entered this field of symbolic fairy tales in 1871 with *At the Back of the North Wind*, and followed it with *The Princess and the Goblin*.

Another type of fantasy — this one positively not for children — was the weird tale. Its fresh impetus came partly from Bulwer-Lytton, who abandoned the domestic novel after another one attributed to Pisistratus Caxton, *What Will He Do with It?*, which came out in *Blackwood's* in 1858–59. He had already turned to the supernatural in 1857 in a powerful novelette of horror, *The Haunters and the Haunted;* and this vein was resumed in *A Strange Story* (1862). In place of the Gothic grotesquerie of *Zanoni* he now employed the realistic details of the sensation novel skillfully enough to make Collins grumble that "he beats one on one's own ground." Busy with his parliamentary career, which in 1858 had raised him to the Secretaryship for the Colonies and in 1866 earned him a peerage as Baron Lytton of Knebworth, he wrote no more fiction until 1871, when he brought out *The Coming Race,* an eerie picture of the remote future, when people live underground and have mastered all the present human problems of caste and sex.

The chief master of supernatural fiction in this epoch was Joseph Sheridan Le Fanu, a scholarly Irish journalist and poet, who began with historical novels and then produced a series of uncanny stories for the *Dublin University Magazine*, of which he was editor. The best of these are *The House by the Churchyard* (1861–62), *Wylder's Hand* (1863–64), and *Uncle Silas* (1864). Le Fanu's expert knowledge of occult lore, his sense of atmosphere, and his mastery of suspense make these perhaps the best book-length ghost stories in the language. He lived so intimately with his spooks that in later life he became a recluse and surrendered to his nightmares and demons to the exclusion of normal human relationships.

Similar psychopathic symptoms were beginning to afflict Wilkie Collins, who was succumbing more and more to laudanum and

was experimenting also with opium-smoking. This artificial influence lent a sort of unearthly clarity to *The Moonstone* (1868),
which rivals *The Woman in White* for the rank of his masterpiece. Again he used the device of telling the story through the
composite narratives of several participants, so that the reader
feels like a spectator at a trial. This time Collins gives an even
more convincing touch by allowing the police investigators to
play a major part in solving the mystery. It was fifteen years
since Dickens had invented the first English fictional detective,
Inspector Bucket in *Bleak House*, but it was *The Moonstone* that
set the permanent pattern of the detective story.

The immense success of *The Moonstone* depended also upon
another factor: into his usual atmosphere of everyday English
life Collins inserted a band of East Indian priests, searching for
the great diamond that has been stolen from the idol in their
temple. Thus he invoked all sorts of superstitious fears about
the cruel and mysterious Orient, guaranteed to make any reader's
blood run cold. *The Moonstone* combines so many effective elements that its triumph was inevitable: the murder of a man who
lived a double life; a girl's suicide for unrequited love; a crime
committed under the influence of drugs; a love affair developing
in the midst of danger; the superstitious terror of the curse upon
the stolen jewel; the cool, logical inductions of Sergeant Cuff;
the psychological reactions of the diversified people who become involved in the mystery; and generous touches of farcical
humor.

Dickens was undoubtedly influenced by the fame of *The Moonstone* when he planned his next novel. The very title emphasized
the adoption of Collins's method, for he called it *The Mystery
of Edwin Drood*. Ominous Asiatic strangers and gruesome opium
dreams are introduced at the beginning, and Dickens follows
Collins also when he heightens his effect by contrasting these
exotic horrors with a familiar English environment — this time
a quiet cathedral town much like Trollope's Barchester. The most
notable feature, however, is the attention to abnormal psychology. The villain, John Jasper, with his schizophrenic and homosexual symptoms, is a more subtle study of a murderer than had
been Dickens's earlier portrayals of the same type, Jonas Chuzzlewit and Bradley Headstone; and Dickens seems to have intended to present the climax in the form of a psychopathic confession.

He remained loyal to his old system of publication in parts, and the first six numbers came out during the middle months of 1870. His power showed no sign of diminution in these chapters, but without warning he suffered the penalty for years of overdriving his physical and mental energy: on June 9 he died of a paralytic stroke.

His characteristic methods of work brought an ironic sequel. As usual, he had written each installment shortly before it went to press; and he was so determined to keep the outcome a secret that he did not confide it even to his closest friends. *The Mystery of Edwin Drood* therefore remains for ever a tantalizing mystery in a sense that Dickens did not foresee. Countless continuations and analyses have tried to solve the puzzle. Mediumistic communication has been invoked to wrest the answers from the author himself. The literary detectives are hopelessly divided as to whether a murder occurred at all; there is just as much controversy as to the method of the crime (if it occurred) and the identity of the detective (if one has appeared in the story as far as it goes). Since a perfect crime is one in which the perpetrator is never suspected, perhaps on similar grounds we are justified in calling *Edwin Drood* a perfect mystery story.

XIV

Recognition of Technique

(1870 – 1880)

THE DEATH OF DICKENS marked the end of an epoch. For thirty-five years he had held unchallenged supremacy in the novel; and even though his methods had grown vastly more subtle, keeping pace with the experiments of his competitors, he retained his fundamental traits of sensational action, unrestrained outbursts of sentiment, interludes of farce, and comic characterization by "humours." With his death, this type of fiction became archaic, and even his principal disciples showed an abrupt decline in creative energy. Reade continued to write until 1884 and Collins until 1889, but neither came anywhere close to repeating his earlier successes.

Reade kept to his formula of melodramatic violence plus factual verisimilitude plus social polemics. *Foul Play* (1868) was an attack on the practice of overloading unseaworthy cargo ships. He made an exhaustive study of seamanship to be certain that his indictment could not be impugned as untrue to facts. A charming love story and an idyllic interlude on a desert island contributed to the book's popular appeal; but its main impact was made

374

by the grim depiction of wealthy shipowners who welcome the loss of a ship because it is overinsured, oblivious to the sufferings of the crew. The book had a direct result in the parliamentary campaign of Samuel Plimsoll that led to reform of the maritime laws.

Reade's next novel was equally topical. This was *Put Yourself in His Place,* in which he came to grips with what he considered to be the tyrannical power exerted by labor unions, and their ruthless tactics of sabotage. His view resembled that of Dickens in *Hard Times,* but Reade as usual embodied it in a quick-moving sequence of spectacular "big scenes," ending with a terrific flood rendered with the breathless immediacy of a newspaper report.

The bane of the sensation novelist is the need for perpetually increasing the voltage of his shocks. Inevitably this leads to overstepping whatever may be the currently accepted bounds of propriety. Reade had already been accused of salaciousness in *Griffith Gaunt,* and fiercer condemnation was incurred by *A Terrible Temptation,* which came out in 1871. The specific target of this book was again the iniquity of private lunatic asylums, which Reade had already assailed in *Hard Cash;* but what attracted most attention was the revelation of scandalous conduct in high life. Reade coolly tells how a baronet discards his mistress when he is about to make a suitable marriage, and how the bride's family accepts his conduct quite serenely. The intimate description of the seductive mistress stirred up a storm of moral indignation among reviewers, who stigmatized Reade with such epithets as "a slimy, snaky, poisonous literary reptile."

To modern readers the most interesting feature of the book is the complacent self-portrait of the author as Mr. Rolfe, who writes novels by Reade's elaborate system of selecting the necessary ingredients from a vast accumulation of "facts, incidents, living dialogue, pictures, reflections, situations," all classified on filing cards. Reade defiantly justifies his method through Rolfe's declaration that "I feign probabilities, I record improbabilities." When the hero is committed to an asylum by his cousin, Rolfe is recommended to the distressed wife as the only person who can help:

"What we want is a man of genius, of invention; a man who will see every chance, take every chance, lawful or unlawful, and fight

with all manner of weapons. . . . He is a writer; and opinions vary
as to his merit. Some say he has talent; others say it is all eccen-
tricity and affectation. One thing is certain — his books bring
about the changes he demands. And then he is in earnest."

Few writers would have the effrontery to proclaim their merits
so blatantly; but this invincible self-confidence is a main source
of Reade's strength.

Among Reade's subsequent novels, the only one of some interest is *A Woman Hater* (1877), not so much for its exposure
of unsanitary conditions in cottages as for the characterization
of a woman physician who exemplifies the new independence
of her sex in professional and public life.

Whereas Reade's novels after 1870 are of diminishing importance because he was merely repeating the pattern of his earlier
work, Wilkie Collins suffered a disastrous decline because he
shifted into a different mode. With *Man and Wife*, in 1870, he
flung himself into propaganda fiction: he attacked what he considered to be inequities in English marriage law, and for good
measure he included a brisk foray against the cult of athletic
sports. At first sight, his humanitarian novels resemble Reade's;
but in inner spirit they are quite unlike. Reade gives the impression of a kind-hearted, short-tempered man who flails im-
petuously at every abuse that catches his attention. Collins is
frigidly rational, like a visitor from another planet who has become aware of the contemptible follies of mankind and exposes
them with a sort of exasperated pity.

In large measure this attitude was due to Collins's remoteness from normal human habits. His bad eyesight, his physical
frailty, and his complicated array of maladies excluded him
from many activities, and his drug-taking made him all the more
detached. His personal relations, too, were unconventional: when
the original "woman in white" terminated their companionship
after fourteen years and married a plumber, Collins installed in
her stead a younger woman who bore him three children. Thus
many reasons combined to put him totally out of sympathy
with current conventions and prejudices.

His later propaganda novels include *The New Magdalen* (1872),
the story of a streetwalker who rescues herself by stealing the
identity of a respectable girl; *The Fallen Leaves,* also on the

problem of prostitution, combined with advocacy of socialism; *The Black Robe*, a diatribe against the machinations of the Jesuits; and *Heart and Science*, a condemnation of vivisection. All of these retained enough of his sensational plots and his vivid settings to hold the public interest. What could be more startling than the central situation of *Poor Miss Finch*, the marriage of a blind girl to a man who has turned blue from silver-nitrate treatment for his epilepsy? Or what more bizarre than a prominent character in *The Law and the Lady*, a legless but lecherous maniac who trundles about in a wheel chair? Nevertheless, the intrusion of social conscience was a disappointment to his old admirers, as expressed by Swinburne in a plaintive couplet:

> What brought good Wilkie's genius nigh perdition?
> Some demon whispered, "Wilkie! Have a mission!"

While the sensation novel was lapsing into decrepitude, Trollope tranquilly continued with his chronicles of everyday life. In 1867–69 he serialized a novel which broke new ground by dealing with politics. This was *Phineas Finn, the Irish Member*, which is not one of his greatest achievements, but which occupies a key position in his second major series of linked stories. One of the subsidiary plots in an earlier novel, *Can You Forgive Her?*, had concerned a certain Lady Glencora Palliser, who is married to a dull, conscientious Member of Parliament, and who comes close to eloping with a handsome philanderer. In this story the political element was negligible; but some of the same characters reappear in *Phineas Finn*, now interwoven with full details of election campaigns and parliamentary sessions. The author himself, having resigned from the postal service in 1867, stood as a candidate in the election of the next year, and though defeated he learned the unvarnished facts of political life.

During the next thirteen years the "parliamentary series" accumulated to six novels (the same total as the Barsetshire chronicles), but, as before, Trollope had no preconceived plan for a sequence, and no less than thirteen other novels were interspersed among them. In the third book in the series, *The Eustace Diamonds*, the political element again is subordinate, for the story centers in an unscrupulous woman and the detection of an ingenious theft; it is Trollope's nearest approach to the Collins technique of mystification. Some of the parliamentary characters, however, reappear in it, and the next book of the series brought them back to the foreground. At the end of *Phineas Finn* the hero's career was blighted because he stood trial for murder; but in *Phineas Redux* he returns to Parliament and wins himself a clever wife.

The characters who figure consistently in these four novels are Plantagenet Palliser and his wife, and in *The Prime Minister* (1875–76) they move to the center of the stage. In *Can You Forgive Her?* Lady Glencora was a sophisticated young woman with more charm than self-discipline, and Palliser a colorless though conscientious public servant, who arouses in the reader a mixture of respect and annoyance when he quietly ignores his wife's escapade and accepts her without reproach when she gives up her lover. Gradually in the subsequent novels the couple's characters become more complex and mature, until Palliser rises to heroic stature by his integrity and his sense of duty, though never in fiction had a hero been so drab. When he becomes Prime Minister he soon loses his office because he will not stoop to political compromises; and in the last novel of the group, *The Duke's Children* (1880), as a lonely widower, he struggles with the emotional problems of his son and daughter and acquiesces in their marriages to a brisk American girl and a young man with neither rank nor wealth. Shy and hypersensitive to the end, he represents the everyday tragedy of the introvert.

The parliamentary novels are not entirely dissociated from Barsetshire, since the Duke of Omnium, the great landowner of that county, plays some part in the new series; and Plantagenet Palliser, his nephew, had first appeared in *The Small House at Allington*. Thus the whole set of twelve novels forms a compendious view of English social life in the principal professions — the church, politics, law, medicine — and in typical environments — London, a provincial town, and the countryside. Certain important aspects are omitted, especially the working class and the new manufacturing cities with the industrial system that they represented. The picture is therefore distorted insofar as it gives a misleading impression of permanence and security, without recognition of the forces of change that were soon to render Trollope's England as archaic as that of Surtees.

The gap is only partly filled by *The Way We Live Now* (1874–75), which deals with corruption in business. Trollope had become sickened with what he considered the monstrous greed and self-seeking of current life, with its flouting of ethical standards, and he wove as many as five separate narrative strands into this long novel in order to give an inclusive array of profligates and cheats. Not since *Vanity Fair* had an English novelist offered so savage an indictment of human nature, and the reviewers were as annoyed as they had been by Thackeray's so-called misanthropy. Though an undertone of similar contempt can be detected in several of Trollope's other late novels, he evaded the risk of alienating his public by another overt offensive against their entrenched bias.

It is impractical to speak individually of all Trollope's forty-seven novels; and his general average of competence is so high that critics are hopelessly at odds in nominating his best ones. Among the others that appeared after 1868, high rating can be assigned to *He Knew He Was Right* (a grim psychopathic study), *The American Senator* (a perceptive contrast of Old World and New World attitudes), and *Dr. Wortle's School* (a sympathetic treatment of bigamy). Even his last completed novel, *Mr. Scarborough's Family* (1883), which is a return to his cynical mood, can be ranked among his successes.

Shortly after Trollope finished the Barsetshire series, and while he was beginning to embark on the parliamentary novels, George Eliot wrote her largest and most ambitious book, *Middlemarch*, which was first published in eight monthly volumes in 1871–72. Closely modeled upon Coventry and its environment as George Eliot had known the region in her early life, *Middlemarch* can almost be regarded as an attempt to rival the whole Barsetshire panorama within the limits of a single work; indeed it was originally conceived as two separate novels. In spite of being now regarded as the greatest living novelist in England, she still felt uncertain of her ability and endured miserable discouragement whilst she was at work on a book. Though historical events play no direct part in the action, she studied newspapers of the years 1830–33 and compiled elaborate notebooks in order that the incidental allusions to current events should be accurate. The same careful planning is perceptible also in the structure of the novel, which intertwines the two major stories and several secondary ones so as to give a survey of the principal social classes and the typical vocations of the region.

The individual story lines have just the right degree of separateness and intermittent contact to reproduce the caste system. The Brooke family is of the country gentry, not rich but secure in the possession of a landed estate and ancestral prestige, and living much the sort of life depicted by Jane Austen. The Vincys are of the newly prosperous bourgeois class, with the practical vigor of the parents beginning to degenerate into the snobbish ambitions of the daughter and the irresolute self-indulgence of the son. The Garths represent the stolid but dependable yeoman farmers.

George Eliot tries valiantly to maintain an attitude of judicial impartiality, but her personal bias keeps breaking through. She is fond of the Garth household because it resembles her childhood home. She sympathizes with Lydgate because he symbolizes the new spirit of scientific research and its application to human welfare. Above all, she tends to idealize Dorothea Brooke, who is as much a portrait of the mature George Eliot as Maggie Tulliver had been a portrait of adolescent Mary Ann Evans. In the same way she is antagonistic toward Casaubon because he is a desiccated pedant who lacks humanitarian sympathy; and the handling of Rosamond Vincy recalls that of Hetty Sorrel in its contempt for a pretty girl's shallow selfishness.

Nevertheless the author's sense of justice restrains her prepossessions. She allows Rosamond to behave with temporary generosity under the impact of Dorothea's appeal to her better nature; and while Casaubon is never endowed with the touches of nobility that Trollope eventually granted to Palliser, the reader does begin to feel some pity for his introverted isolation. Similarly, George Eliot develops real psychological complexity in Lydgate by showing how his dedication to science and public health is frustrated by the pressures of political expediency and worldly ambition. She even admits that Dorothea is impractical and actually egotistical in her stubborn idealism.

The action of the novel moves slowly and without much drama. There is a trace of sensation fiction only in one of the secondary plots, involving a banker with a disgraceful secret and an unscrupulous rascal who threatens to expose him; but in such a wide survey of a community a single example of criminal intrigue seems like a necessary touch of realism rather than a concession to melodrama.

The novel as a whole acquires its unity not so much from the occasional linking of the separate plot lines or from the geographically restricted setting as from the paralleling of certain major themes. The most significant of these is that of compatibility in marriage. This topic had been of primary concern to Jane Austen also; the difference is that in her novels the main characters discover their danger in time to avoid matrimony, whereas in *Middlemarch* the two principal couples get married early in the story, while totally deluded as to one another's real personality. Dorothea admires Casaubon as a great scholar; he thinks that she will be a compliant and industrious servitor. Lydgate is attracted to Rosamond because she is pretty and vivacious, while she expects him to achieve social and professional eminence. The main body of the novel traces how all four of them slowly and painfully discover the truth.

Sentimental fiction would have developed a feeling of affinity between Dorothea and Lydgate, and might have ended by pairing them off after some opportune loss of their spouses. Avoiding this obvious gambit, George Eliot surprises her readers by introducing Will Ladislaw, an apparently unstable young man who turns out to be a suitable second husband for Dorothea, while Lydgate is abandoned to a miserable life of material success and spiritual stultification under his wife's relentless compulsion. Though critics are inclined to grumble that Dorothea's marriage to Ladislaw is an unconvincing effort toward a conventional happy ending, the author could have justified it in terms of her own experience: Ladislaw in many ways resembles the lively, versatile G. H. Lewes, while Casaubon was perhaps a somewhat resentful portrait of Herbert Spencer, who had been so unresponsive to Miss Evans's hero worship. Since the unconventionality of the Eliot-Lewes union could not well be used in the novel, she found an equivalent by giving Ladislaw other handicaps than a renegade wife — foreign blood, low social origin, and poverty.

This leads into the second unifying theme of the novel — the impact of the outsider on a tightly closed society. Ladislaw outrages Middlemarch by having a Polish father, an actress mother, and a cosmopolitan wit. Having no predetermined place in the social structure of the town, he serves the technical function of tying several main lines of the action together. The theme of the intruder is repeated in Lydgate, who is as earnest as Ladislaw is frivolous, but who also falls foul of the local vested interests when he tries to impose alien standards upon the routines of the community. And the sensational mystery element of Bulstrode and Raffles depends upon their being invaders from the unpredictable world outside, like Satan in a complacent Eden. In this view *Middlemarch* is indeed a microcosm of the Victorian age, showing the disturbing encroachment of unorthodox new ideas upon doctrines and ways of life that seemed impregnable.

Middlemarch was the masterpiece of George Eliot's realistic method. She lived for eight years longer but she wrote only one more novel, *Daniel Deronda*, and it cannot be counted among her best books. She concocted it intellectually, without recourse to memories of her early days, and consequently it fails to come to life. The central topic has interest at the present day, being the project for a Jewish state in Palestine, a cause for which she felt deep sympathy; but she embodied it in too much sensational mystery and sentimental romance. Deronda is an incredibly perfect character who discovers his Jewish ancestry only after he rescues a lovely young Jewess when she is on the verge of suicide as an escape from starvation. They fall in love and dedicate themselves ardently to Zionism.

There is more psychological subtlety in the characterization of Gwendolyn Harleth, at the outset a selfish girl who marries a wealthy man for reasons of ambition, against the warnings of a woman who is the mother of his children. Gwendolyn becomes addicted to gambling and hates her husband so bitterly for his cruelty that she refrains from going to his aid when he is drowning; and in a revulsion of feeling she accuses herself of being guilty of his death. Being in love with the impeccable Deronda, she is now susceptible to his urging that she should discard her selfish attitude, and her repentance turns her into an admirable person.

In her final years, afflicted with frail health, George Eliot wrote some poetry as well as a volume of mildly satirical essays, *The Impressions of Theophrastus Such*. Lewes died in 1878, and after seventeen months of grief George Eliot married John W. Cross, a bank official from New York. She was sixty and he was thirty-nine. She enjoyed only seven months of her belated status as a legal wife before she caught a chill and died.

The year 1871, when *Middlemarch* began to appear, witnessed also the first book by a new author who was destined to be George Eliot's successor in chronicling the problems and tragedies of English rural life. Thomas Hardy sprang from the same sort of yeoman stock as she did. The tiny village in which he was born gives a misleading impression of rural isolation and poverty. Actually the Hardys lived comfortably by the standards of the time and were proud of having flourished for centuries in the same region of Dorsetshire. A kinsman was the captain of Lord Nelson's flagship, and rose to the rank of admiral and baronet.

In childhood Thomas Hardy absorbed a sense of the ageless past that invested every acre of the countryside with reminders of the Roman conquerors and the Anglo-Saxon invaders. In his early days the ancient patterns of living were almost untouched by modern changes; but the region had been disturbed by the threat of Napoleonic invasion in the opening years of the century and Hardy was fascinated by the reminiscences of that crisis that he heard all around him. Another formative influence was music, as his father and grandfather played in the old-fashioned church orchestra. The father being a building contractor, young Hardy was apprenticed to an architect in Dorchester at the age of sixteen. The firm specialized in ecclesiastical work, and Hardy made many drawings of village churches that were being restored. By the time he was twenty-two his work was good enough to gain him an appointment as assistant to one of the most eminent architects in London, and the next year he won two important prizes. In spite of this auspicious beginning for a career, however, he disliked life in the metropolis and felt more drawn to the profession of letters. He had been writing poems and essays since his teens, and at the age of twenty-seven he went home to his native territory and set to work upon a novel.

When he submitted the manuscript to Chapman & Hall it was

read by George Meredith, who told the young author that it contained too much radical propaganda and indiscriminate satire, and advised him to strive for a stronger element of plot. Hardy conformed by imitating the Collins type of intricate structure in *Desperate Remedies*, which came out in 1871. The story is redeemed from its sensationalism by some evidences of poetic sensibility and philosophic meditation; but the chief recognition that it received was a devastating review in the *Spectator*, accusing it of immorality, because it included a wealthy unmarried lady with an illegitimate son.

For his next book Hardy went so far in the opposite direction that it contained only a slender trickle of narrative, scarcely justifying its being classified as a novel at all. The title was *Under the Greenwood Tree*, and it was accurately described in the subtitle as "a rural painting of the Dutch school," for, like George Eliot in *Adam Bede*, he had lavished his greatest care on the simple details of country life. The charm and humor in his pictures of the parish choir and the love affairs of a village coquette showed that he had found his *métier*.

He tried a more dramatic situation in *A Pair of Blue Eyes* — a sentimental title for a story of painful irony, in which a young woman vacillates between two lovers and ends by alienating both. The denouement comes as a hideous shock, when both men, upon returning to England from abroad, decide to seek reconciliation with her and find themselves traveling in the same train, only to discover that her dead body, en route to her funeral, is in the luggage car. A final ironical twist is the revelation that she has married a nobleman during their absence.

Hardy at this time was wooing a young lady in Cornwall, sister-in-law of a rector whose church he had helped to restore; and traces of this experience appear both in the Cornish scenery of the novel and in the cast of characters — a clergyman and his daughter, a literary man, and a young architect of humble birth. Both the suitors contain some traits of Hardy himself, and Elfride's exasperating indecision in the novel reflects the fluctuations of Hardy's love affair, for Miss Gifford had a strong sense of her social status and doubted the wisdom of encouraging a penniless young man who could not decide whether to be an architect or an author.

The gravest defect in *A Pair of Blue Eyes* is the style, which is intolerably pretentious and awkward, full of long words and scholarly allusions. The conversation, particularly, is too formal and ponderous to be credible.

The modest success of *Under the Greenwood Tree* had brought Hardy an invitation to contribute a serial to the *Cornhill Magazine*, and *Far from the Madding Crowd* came out in it during 1874. Like the three previous stories, it was anonymous, and some readers were positive that it was by George Eliot. When published in volume form it carried the author's name, and Hardy's fame was established.

The book was written at his father's home in the country, and when Hardy ran out of paper he would use large dead leaves, chips left by woodcutters, and fragments of slate or stone. An intimate feeling for nature and primitive life seemed to pass through these media into the very texture of the novel. It combined the idyllic rural setting of *Under the Greenwood Tree* with an adequately dramatic plot, and the ending was not too tragic to gratify the average reader. The greatest advance, however, was in characterization. The heroine, Bathsheba Everdene, is a woman of passionate temperament, in revolt against the restrictions of stolid country life; the masterful Sergeant Troy is a fitting foil for her; and the farm workers provide a comic chorus for the drama. After Bathsheba marries Troy and is ill-used by him, the dashing sergeant is murdered by Farmer Boldwood, who has been driven half insane by frustrated desire for the capricious Bathsheba. With Boldwood safely in a madhouse, she is free to marry Gabriel Oak, a loyal shepherd who has always worshiped her in silence.

When the popularity of this book led to a request for another serial in the same magazine, Hardy tried comedy in *The Hand of Ethelberta*. Again the central character is a woman of strong determination, but this is the only novel of Hardy's in which the central woman character is guided by common sense instead of by emotion, and therefore achieves her purpose instead of being the victim of circumstance. A less unscrupulous version of Becky Sharp, Ethelberta is an ex-governess who married her employers' son and was soon left a widow with limited means. She struggles to hold a place in society and to conceal the fact that her father was a butler. We admire her humor and tenacity and enjoy her triumph when she marries a dissolute old peer; but the author's attempts at social satire suffer from his inadequate familiarity with fashionable society.

In each of his five novels Hardy had undertaken a different genre — tragedy and comedy, melodrama and idyl. With his sixth one he combined the best features of them all into a homogeneous work of art. The increased stature of *The Return of the Native* is partly due to the maturing of his philosophical outlook. Brought up in the Church of England, he always retained an affection for its ritual, its music, and its Gothic architecture. As soon as he grew up, however, his interest in science made it impossible for him to accept the Bible literally, while his human sympathies led him to reject the Old Testament concept of a God of Wrath. He was nineteen when *The Origin of Species* came out, and from the evolutionary theory he drew the inference that the universe is ruled by blind chance rather than by any conscious power, either benevolent or malign. He was perpetually aware of the ruthless struggle for survival, as exemplified among plants and animals, so that nature for him was not the kindly foster-mother that Wordsworth loved, but a horrifying spectacle of incessant destruction. To him the most tragic outcome of the whole accidental process was the development of the human mind, since it makes man conscious of his helpless predicament and endows him with wishes and hopes that stand no chance of fulfillment.

The scientific theories made Hardy cognizant of the incalculable size and age of the universe, with its geological strata and its astronomical light-years. Long discussions of fossils and prehistoric monsters intrude digressively in *A Pair of Blue Eyes*. Against this background of time and space the ambitions and agonies of any individual become ludicrously trivial. And yet Hardy was abnormally responsive to human suffering, so that his own relatively comfortable and untroubled life rendered him all the more keenly aware of other people's unhappiness. Every instance of frustration or unmerited misery seemed to him to be further proof of the callous injustice of circumstances. In defending himself from the charge of being too gloomy in his novels, he explained: "Differing natures find their tongue in the presence of differing spectacles. Some natures become vocal at tragedy, some are made vocal by comedy, and it seems to me that to whichever of these aspects of life a

writer's instinct for expression the more readily responds, to
that he should allow it to respond."

Therefore he saw the persons in his fiction as embodiments of
the elemental life force, struggling futilely against the influences of heredity and environment. Wider reading ultimately
made him aware of the pessimistic doctrines of Schopenhauer and
von Hartmann; and these reinforced his own vision of mankind
as the helpless victim of cosmic forces.

This concept of man's relationship with nature contributes
to another distinctive merit of *The Return of the Native* —
its imaginative and symbolic use of landscape. It is often said
that Egdon Heath is the most important character in the story.
By this time Hardy had applied to his native region its historic
name of Wessex, the Anglo-Saxon kingdom that covered four
or five modern counties of southwest England. He retained all
its geographical features in his novels, merely giving fictitious
names to actual places. This is different from Trollope's Barsetshire, which was a composite of various counties, with an imaginary though precise topography. Nevertheless the recurrence of
familiar places throughout Hardy's later novels adds to the illusion of reality as in Trollope's series, because the reader is
reminded of the previous stories which took place in the same
area.

But Hardy's Wessex provides more than realistic details or
even a picturesque background to enhance the emotional effect
in crucial scenes, in the tradition that goes back through Collins
all the way to Mrs. Radcliffe. As well as serving these purposes,
the setting always symbolizes the timeless, unchanging power
of nature itself. The opening chapter of *The Return of the
Native* describes the Heath, without a human character in sight;
and the description not only uses images that suggest a colossal
living creature but also emphasizes that this is "a face on which
time makes but little impression." The Rainbarrow, on which
the first action occurs, is not only a large conspicuous hill that
dwarfs the human beings who stand on it; it is also a Celtic
burial mound of prehistoric date. The structure of the story, too,
is adjusted to the rhythms of the Heath, for it covers exactly a
year and a day, and the episodes fit into the cycle of the seasons
and the variations of weather.

A similar function is served by the superstitions that figure repeatedly in the story. Hardy inserts them not merely for local color or as curiosities of folklore. The Guy Fawkes Day bonfires and the Christmas mummers' play go back to immemorial pagan rituals, and Susan Nunsuch's melting of a wax model of Eustacia is a form of black magic that is world-wide. These age-old observances are linked with crucial moments in the life of Eustacia, the rebellious woman who dares to oppose the dominance of the Heath; and the reader cannot help feeling a twinge of credulity when her death follows so promptly upon Susan's witchcraft, though Hardy sees only a touch of grim comedy in Susan's prospective pride in accomplishing something which actually results from sheer coincidence.

This word "coincidence" points to another manifestation of his philosophy in his novels. A casual critic could accuse him of crudely overworking a typical melodramatic device, for coincidences occur again and again as the controlling influence in the action. But analysis shows that they are not used as in sensation fiction, to provide surprise or to keep the action moving neatly and vigorously forward, nor are they usually employed to help some character out of a predicament or to produce a happy ending. Instead, pure chance invariably steps in at the one moment when it can defeat the intentions of the characters and doom them to disaster. In Hardy the *deus ex machina* has become a *diabolus ex machina*. As first exemplified in the pitiless ending of *A Pair of Blue Eyes*, these climactic coincidences evoke an overpowering sense of irony — not the sly detachment of an intelligent onlooker, such as we term "irony" in Jane Austen, but the "irony of fate," the inherent perverseness of life that thwarts human reason and human desires.

The ironic implication is all the more distressing because the chance occurrence is in itself trivial, in grotesque contrast with the magnitude of its consequences. When Mrs. Yeobright goes to her son's cottage for a reconciliation with him and his wife (an action that could have resolved all the conflicts of the story), the timing of Wildeve's visit, her arrival, Clym's return home and his falling asleep, Eustacia's mistaken belief that he has heard his mother knock at the door, and Mrs. Yeobright's sitting down beside an adder, all combine to cause her death; while the further coincidence that a boy was picking flowers in the lonely spot provides the final misunderstanding, when his report leads

Clym to believe that his wife intentionally kept his mother out of the house.

It is this ascendancy of blind chance that gives Hardy's major novels the fatalistic dignity of Greek tragedy. Just as every Greek tragedy centers upon someone who offends the gods by overweening pride and self-confidence, so in each of his novels the main character tries to exert his will against the forces of environment, and incurs defeat. Eustacia not only destroys herself but brings suffering to everyone within her orbit, whereas the compliant Tomasin and the unselfish Diggory Venn win through to a measure of happiness, and Clym Yeobright achieves stoic endurance by identifying himself wholly with the Heath.

Hardy must have been aware of the parallel between Clym and himself. Both of them went counter to worldly standards by renouncing what promised to be a prosperous career in a great city and returned to the obscure surroundings of their origin. Clym's eventual vocation as an evangelist is thus equivalent to Hardy's developing his creed of resignation.

His style in *The Return of the Native* is still stiffly formal and learnedly archaic; but instead of being clumsy as in *A Pair of Blue Eyes* it has become appropriate to his total effect. Poetic use of metaphor combines with the sonorous vocabulary to produce a prose form with something of the stateliness of blank verse; and the unlikeness to contemporary speech reinforces the impression of timelessness.

The doctrines that Hardy deduced from the Darwinian hypothesis are basically similar to those of Meredith; but the antithetical personalities of the two authors led them to different conclusions. They both saw that man's dethronement from preeminence in the cosmos as the favorite protégé of a benevolent creator meant that his ideals and desires have no guarantee of fulfillment. But Hardy emphasized the tragic irony of inevitable frustration, whereas Meredith sought to use comic irony to show his readers how to sublimate their selfish aggressiveness.

In presenting this idea Meredith was faced with a paradox. On one hand, he believed in the virtue of natural human impulses and the viciousness of convention, hypocrisy, sentimentality — all the artificial pretenses of modern civilization. On the other hand, self-assertion is undeniably a natural human impulse, and yet he regarded it as the chief cause of evil in social relations.

He resolves the paradox by insisting that self-assertion is a stupid survival of pre-human brutality, susceptible to control in anyone who uses his reason to recognize his own unimportance and the rights of others. Thus even when Meredith tells stories of defeat and disillusionment he is asking the reader not to pity characters caught in a hopeless trap but to recognize how they have blundered into it by losing their sense of proportion. Each of his novels is the chronicle of an "ordeal" by which the main character is taught the lesson of rational self-restraint.

Beauchamp's Career (1874–75) ends with an episode that seems to resemble Hardy's capitulation to blind chance, when the noble-spirited hero is drowned in saving the life of a cottager's child. But the implication of the story is essentially different. Nevil Beauchamp, like Richard Feverel, is a headstrong young aristocrat whose humanitarian visions become inextricably entangled with his emotional life. He was modeled upon Meredith's dearest friend, Captain Frederick Maxse, who gave up a naval career in favor of Quixotic campaigns for political reform. Meredith helped him in an unsuccessful candidacy for Parliament, thus obtaining material for a detailed account of an election in the novel. This theme gives it some contact with Trollope's political series, which belongs to the same years. Meredith, however, is not concerned mainly with the exposure of corruption or stupidity in public affairs. His topic is the tragic absurdity of Beauchamp's inadequate powers of judgment.

The early chapters include an idyllic love story with scenic backgrounds in Italy and France. But the lovely French girl's family has arranged her marriage with an elderly nobleman, and so Beauchamp returns to England to fling himself into radical politics. When later Renée comes to him in flight from her unhappy marriage, he callously sends her home, partly through high moral rectitude but also because a scandal would be disastrous to his party. By this time he has quarreled with his reactionary family, who abominate his theories; and a rich English girl who loves him is important to him only because her money could be useful in his campaign. Thus he is tormented by conflicts between his personal feelings and his ideal of duty toward humanity; and his final heroic deed is his one successful service to his fellow-beings. But even though he has proved the impracticality of a single-handed assault on the established social system, he has gone through his ordeal and conquered himself.

In contrast with the romantic fervor of *Harry Richmond*, the disillusioned astringency of *Beauchamp's Career* seems coldblooded. Meredith insisted that he was neither a romanticist nor a realist; an important digression in *Beauchamp's Career* defines his stand:

> Those happy tales of mystery are as much my envy as the popular narratives of the deeds of bread and cheese people, for they both create a tide-way in the attentive mind; the mysterious pricking our credulous flesh to creep, the familiar urging our obese imagination to constitutional exercise. And, oh, the refreshment there is in dealing with characters either contemptibly beneath us or supernaturally above! My way is like a Rhone island in the summer drought, stony, unattractive, and difficult between the two forceful streams of the unreal and the over-real, which delight mankind — honor to the conjurors. My people conquer nothing, win none; they are actual, yet uncommon. It is the clock-work of the brain that they are directed to set in motion, and — poor troop of actors to vacant benches! — the conscience residing in thoughtfulness which they would appeal to; and if you are impervious to them, we are lost.

The sarcastic tone in this and similar comments indicates that by now Meredith had relinquished all hope of winning a popular following. A lecture that he delivered in 1877 on "The Idea of Comedy and the Uses of the Comic Spirit" served to crystallize his ideas on the value of laughter as a form of intellectual clarification and emotional therapy. He held that perfect comedy is neither satire nor burlesque, but a dispassionate and clear-sighted perception of folly, sentimentality, and conceit. This attitude in his novels is partly responsible for the disfavor they evoke in some readers. He holds himself aloof from his characters and observes them with Olympian mockery at moments when the reader would prefer an illusion of sympathetic identification.

As an outcome of this critical theory, Meredith's next novel, *The Egoist*, is his most consistently intellectual work. As though to serve as a barricade against ill-qualified readers, the first chapter is a condensation of his lecture on comedy, couched in his most elusive phrases and embellished with parodies of the styles of other authors. The book's subtitle is "A Comedy in Narrative," and it is constructed with strict adherence to the unities of time, place, and action. The main setting is Sir Willoughby Patterne's estate, and everything happens in about six weeks. As in a play, the story is presented largely in dialogue, even the chapter titles being often merely a list of the characters who appear in the particular scene. The tone of high comedy is maintained throughout, and yet the theme is the one that Meredith took most seriously — the masculine aggressiveness that forces women to suppress their natural impulses and intelligence with a pretense of helplessness. Sir Willoughby seems to have all the best gifts — rank, wealth, brains, good looks, athletic prowess; and from infancy he has been encouraged to believe in his own perfection. Three young women, however, successively discover that his unadulterated egoism renders him intolerable as a prospective husband. The most important of them is Clara Middleton, a clever, charming girl who accepts his proposal of marriage under the usual romantic illusions. By the conventions of their caste in Victorian days, a broken engagement was almost as shameful as a broken marriage, and so Clara can find no one to understand her desperate determination to retract her promise.

Very little happens. The nearest approach to overt action is when Clara walks two miles in the rain to a railway station, intending to go away to London, but is then persuaded to come back again. But in the prolonged sequence of conversations and subtle maneuvers, every facet of half-a-dozen principal characters is revealed in their relationships with one another.

Sir Willoughby, in particular, is anatomized as no previous character in fiction had been. The author apparently despises him to the verge of loathing, and yet makes us realize that his contemptible behavior springs from traits that are present in every man. Sir Willoughby is not a villain. In the eyes of most people — including himself — he is a paragon. His final humiliation, like that of Malvolio in *Twelfth Night*, awakens our pity more than our satisfaction. In his case Meredith's "ordeal" situation is reversed: because Sir Willoughby lacks any latent quality of nobility, his painful crisis merely reduces him to woeful absurdity instead of releasing him to spiritual freedom. Clara, on the other hand, survives the test triumphantly; and Vernon Whitford, the man she finally marries, has already endured his purgation before the story begins.

As usual, the novel includes much of the author's own experience. Like Sir Austin Feverel, Sir Willoughby is in a predicament resembling Meredith's relationship with his first wife; the situation is kept within the limits of comedy merely because the conflict occurs before marriage instead of after. Clara and her father have many traits drawn from the first Mrs. Meredith and Thomas Love Peacock. Whitford is an exact portrait of Leslie Stephen, the critic, who was one of Meredith's favorite friends.

The technical methods in *The Egoist* show the full development of Meredith's individual manner. His love of apothegms is fulfilled by citations from an imaginary "Book of Egoism." Every paragraph of the novel is adorned with figurative language, including recurrent symbols and metaphors that supply a unifying pattern. The most persistent of these is the tribe of sardonic imps that are mentioned as persecuting any human being whose conduct becomes irrational. Other details that acquire symbolic value are fragile porcelain, the Alps, and a double-blossomed cherry tree. In contrast with the ornateness of the descriptive passages, the dialogue seeks to reproduce the inconsequential abruptness of real conversation, with its fragmentary phrases and vague digressions and delayed reactions.

To Meredith's astonishment, *The Egoist* was better received than any of his previous books. The reason was not solely that it was under better artistic control. Influence was now passing into the hands of a new generation of critics who had grown up during the twenty years since Meredith and George Eliot had published their first novels, and who thus had absorbed the concept of fiction as a subtle intellectual medium. Dissatisfied with the standardized product of the popular novelists, they acclaimed Meredith as their ideal.

The contrast between his work and that of the current best sellers was obvious enough. Not only Reade and Collins but even Harrison Ainsworth was still prolific. A more astonishing apparition from the past was Disraeli, whose flair for fiction had merely been suspended during his years of political leadership. Twenty-three years elapsed between *Tancred* and his next novel, *Lothair*, which came out in 1870 during an interval when his party was out of power. Then there was another ten-year lapse while he served a further term as Prime Minister, but his final retirement in 1880 enabled him to finish a last work, *Endymion*. Both these late novels deal with social, religious, and political questions in his old vein of sophisticated wit. Indeed, they have more resemblance to Meredith's novels than to the average output of the prolific professional novelists of the seventies.

These were fixed in a pattern of competent entertainment, ranging between the sensational and the domestic types. Ouida and Miss Braddon and James Payn were at the peak of their success. Blackmore brought out a series of tales distinguished chiefly by the local color of different parts of England — the South Downs, Yorkshire, Dartmoor. The most popular newcomer in the field was William Black, a journalist from Scotland whose formula was a mixture of picturesque scenery, open-air adventure, and wholesome heroines, as in *A Daughter of Heth* and *A Princess of Thule*. Melodrama and Dickensian humor played a larger part in the collaborative novels of Walter Besant and James Rice, especially *Ready-Money Mortiboy* and *The Golden Butterfly* (a story about an American oil millionaire in Europe).

A few young novelists, however, were venturing into the Meredithian type of intellectual comedy. William Hurrell Mallock aroused some controversy with *The New Republic* (1877), which harked back to Peacock's use of country-house conversation in order to satirize current theories, and followed Peacock also in introducing recognizable caricatures of contemporary writers, such as Arnold, Pater, Mark Pattison, and W. K. Clifford. In *The New Paul and Virginia* he employed the same method to attack the opinions of the Positivists. A more gifted young satirist who was beginning his literary career at that date was George Bernard Shaw. Between 1879 and 1883 he wrote five clever, unorthodox novels in which he made fun of contemporary prejudices and proclaimed his cocksure opinions. The first, *Immaturity*, was rejected by Meredith in his capacity of publisher's reader; and no firm could be persuaded to accept it or the subsequent stories. Four of them, however, got into print in 1884–88 as serials in obscure journals.

The dominant new figure in the late seventies is one who does not fit neatly into the scope of the present book. Henry James is usually classified as an American novelist, because he was born in New York, studied at Harvard, and retained American citizenship until the last year of his life. Nevertheless, he was not domiciled in the United States after he grew up, and from

1868 onward he lived mainly in England, with intervals in France and Italy. His friendship with English authors, and his advocacy of certain positive theories of fiction, not only by his practice in his novels but also in critical essays, made him the most influential personage in English fiction through the next half-century.

James's familiarity with English and Continental life, originating in visits during his boyhood, gave him a unique opportunity to contrast the manners and outlook of the Old and New Worlds, and this topic dominated the novels that he published between 1876 and 1881 — *Roderick Hudson, The American, The Europeans, The Portrait of a Lady*. He dealt with the same social group as Thackeray and Meredith — the wealthy, cultivated people who talk well, read books, and travel abroad. His innovation was in centering each story upon a candid, idealistic American who comes to Europe and painfully discovers the intangible differences between his or her background and that of the sophisticated denizens of an old, established society.

The importance of James was not so much in the novelty of his subject matter as in his method of handling it. The James family was endowed with an almost clinical curiosity about human behavior, which led the novelist's brother William to become the founder of the science of psychology in the United States. Henry James was the first novelist to recognize clearly that the materials of fiction and of scientific psychology are identical. He insisted that a novelist's primary duty is to reveal exactly what goes on in the inner workings of a character's personality. Furthermore, he condemned almost all preceding novelists for injecting their own interpretations into their books, whether by explicit comments to the reader or merely by idiosyncrasies of style. The novelist's function, James believed, was to keep himself invisible and to let the story seem to tell itself, giving the reader the illusion of analyzing the situation unaided. Like George Eliot, James was primarily interested in ethical dilemmas; but he did not seek, as she did, to discuss them in a philosophical context.

One of James's contributions to fiction in English was his connecting it with the main current of European literature. Although most English authors since the beginning of the novel had read foreign fiction, they had remained essentially provincial in their own work. From boyhood onward, James had been as familiar with French literature as with English. By his standards the greatest of novelists were the French realists, Balzac and Flaubert; and he was interested too in the recent work of the brothers Edmond and Jules de Goncourt, who in *Renée Mauperin* and *Germinie Lacerteux* had written what is termed "impressionistic" fiction, trying to reproduce the way in which experience is actually perceived by the individual through his senses.

By this time the French authors were becoming acquainted with the novels of the Russians, especially Turgeniev, who frequented the Parisian literary salons. Turgeniev's simplicity and naturalness of style, Tolstoi's massive realism, and Dostoievski's psychological insight all helped to prove that fiction could represent real life with truth and subtlety. The Russians were not employing realistic vividness merely as an end in itself, but seemed to believe that the novel was a valid medium for setting forth a profound interpretation of existence.

From the French and the Russians, James acquired the conviction that the writing of fiction is a serious form of art. English novelists, with the exception of Meredith, still regarded their work primarily as a form of entertainment, governed by the practical consideration of giving the public what it liked. When they thought more seriously about their function, the Puritan tradition led them to teach moral lessons or promote humanitarian reforms. At this time, however, a few critics and poets, with Walter Pater as their spokesman, were preaching the doctrine of "art for art's sake," which meant that the artist should concern himself solely with conveying sensations of pleasure and beauty, unaffected by social or moral values. James's temperament made him a detached onlooker on life, and so he dedicated himself to this aesthetic creed insofar as it could be applied to fiction.

Neither the material nor the manner of his writing can be called beautiful in any popular sense. There is nothing picturesque about his characters or their behavior; and when compared with other novels of his era, his stories seem sluggish in movement and deficient in energy. His precise vocabulary and formal sentence structures produce an effect of woodenness. But in his insistence upon the author's impartiality and upon the importance of technical skill, James brought the English novel into the camp of the aesthetes.

X V

Ethical Problems and Exotic Adventures

(1880 – 1895)

WITH THE DECLINE of the sensational and domestic types of fiction, a new genre that came into prominence was the problem novel. Deriving mainly from George Eliot, and paralleling the development of the problem play in the wake of Ibsen, it reflected the ever-expanding controversies over religious belief, the bases of morality, the status of women, and other fundamental matters, wherein accepted axioms were being challenged and overturned. Earnest authors depicted equally earnest characters making momentous decisions over their creeds.

A remarkable example was *John Inglesant*, by Joseph Henry Shorthouse, a middle-aged chemical manufacturer in Birmingham, who had gone through a difficult transition at the age of twenty-seven when he gave up the Quaker faith of his parents and entered the Church of England. This conversion supplied the inner validity for his story of an aristocratic young Englishman of the time of Charles I, trained by the Jesuits, who remains loyal to the royalist cause and slowly learns the Christian law of forgiveness until in the end he spares the murderer of his brother, on whom he had vowed vengeance. After working over it for ten years, Shorthouse made a privately printed edition of 100 copies of the novel in 1880. It was promptly bought by Macmillan & Company, and enthusiastic praise from Gladstone helped to give it immense circulation. Though it rivals *Henry Esmond* as a convincing reconstruction of a past epoch, with Hobbes, Crashaw, and other celebrities playing minor roles, the book's real value is its sincere study of spiritual dedication. Shorthouse said that his purpose was "to exalt culture above fanaticism of every kind."

A similar *pastiche* of historical material can be seen in *Marius the Epicurean*, by Walter Pater, which came out in 1885 after five years of gestation. Giving a scholarly picture of Roman life in the second century, it is so remote from the melodramatic violence of *The Last Days of Pompeii* or *Hypatia* that it seems almost devoid of plot. The hero is a self-portrait of Pater, and the interest is centered in his intellectual and emotional dilemmas, under the conflicting attractions of Christianity and rationalism, the love of beauty and the craving for spiritual insight.

Another serious novel about religious faith, and also based on the author's own experience, came out in the same year as *John Inglesant* — 1881. This was *The Autobiography of Mark Rutherford*, "edited by Reuben Shapcott." The real author, whose identity was long kept secret, was William Hale White. Born in Bedford, where his parents were zealous adherents of the Bunyan meeting-house, White gave up his studies for the Congregational ministry when he found himself questioning the orthodox tenets, and settled down to a dull career in the Civil Service. In this book and its sequel, *Mark Rutherford's Deliverance* (1885), he fictionized his struggle to escape from a gloomy Calvinism. The sensitive hero gains no spectacular victory, and has to school himself in stoic agnosticism, suppressing all impulse to challenge the inscrutable ways of God. Though this is based on premises quite different from the mystical quietism of John Inglesant, it reflects a similar rejection of sectarian dogmatism. White's next novel, *The Revolution in Tanner's Lane*, is an effort at historical fiction, depicting the poverty and unrest in England after the close of the Napoleonic Wars. The author's manifest sincerity gives his novels a somber power, in spite of colorless style and lack of technical dexterity.

Though White was primarily occupied with religious doctrines, he also described the cultural bleakness of lower-middle-class life in English cities. This latter theme was developed with greater intensity by George Gissing, who discovered the cruelty of modern urban existence through long and bitter hardship. A sensitive, artistic dreamer, like Mark Rutherford, he too originated in the Midlands, and after attending a Quaker school he won a scholarship at Owens College, Manchester, where he learned to love the classics. At this time, however, he became involved with a prostitute, and in a Quixotic effort to rescue her from degradation he began to pilfer money from fellow-students to buy her a sewing machine. Too impractical to be a skillful thief, he was soon arrested and convicted.

In the hope of living down this disgrace he took refuge in the United States, where neither teaching in a high school nor contributing short stories to the *Chicago Tribune* proved adequate as sources of income, and he came close to starvation and suicide. He went back to England, still believing in the possible redemption of the miserable streetwalker; he married her and they spent several years of squalid poverty in London garrets and cellars. After she left him he went on supplying her with funds until she died of alcoholism.

The miseries of this marriage can be recognized in his first novel, *Workers in the Dawn*, in which an idealistic young man patiently and vainly tries to give his ignorant, resentful wife an elementary education and to cure her of drinking. This is only one strand, however, in the long, incoherent novel, which Gissing brought out at his own expense in 1880 when no publisher would accept it. A second story of the same type, *The Unclassed*, came out in 1884, and in it he divided the story of his marital disaster into two separate episodes: in one a young prostitute is redeemed by her pure love for a socially insurgent schoolmaster; in the other, a depraved girl ruins the life of her visionary cousin by making him marry her through appealing to his generosity.

Since Gissing was writing primarily to earn a living, he accepted such current techniques of the popular novel as improbable coincidences, elaborate interweaving of several plot lines, and explicit commentary on the action. An admirer of Dickens, he followed his master's method of exaggeration in portrayal of characters, whether they were virtuous, criminal, or comic. His material, too, was superficially comparable with that of Dickens, since both depicted life in the slums. But the total effect of a Gissing novel is entirely different. Instead of Dickens's irrepressible energy and abundant kindliness, Gissing seldom departs from a drably hopeless mood. Though not openly expressed, his self-pity provides a querulous undertone and prevents him from fully understanding or sympathizing with the poor and illiterate people he describes; his attitude toward them partakes too much of disgust. He was actuated by no reforming zeal, because he did not believe that the lower class was capable of improvement. Repeatedly he portrayed an angry young man who sets out to remodel society, but he did not share any such faith in socialism or even in democracy; instead, he dreaded the result of putting political power in the hands of the proletariat.

On this basis of passive endurance he conceived the writing of novels to be a task of representing accurately "the collection of phenomena" that he observed around him. One of the characters of *Workers in the Dawn* advises another: "Paint a faithful picture of the crowd we have watched, be a successor of Hogarth, and give us the true image of our social dress, as he did of those of his own day"; and to this idea he added, in *The Unclassed,* that "art now-a-days must be the mouthpiece of misery, for misery is the keynote of modern life." Osmond Waymark, in this book, a poverty-stricken young teacher and would-be novelist, who is obviously a self-portrait, announces:

> "The novel of everyday life is getting worn out. We must dig deeper, get into untouched social strata. Dickens felt this, but he had not the courage to face his subjects. . . . Not *virginibus puerisque* will be my book, I assure you, but for men and women who like to look beneath the surface, and who understand that only as artistic material has human life any significance."

Indeed, two years before *The Unclassed* Gissing had written another novel, *Mrs. Grundy's Enemies,* which was never published because its treatment of sex was regarded as too daring. These tenets would seem to link Gissing with James as an uncompromising realist. But he differed from James in one essential respect: he was unwilling to probe into the psychology of his characters. In the preface to his third published novel, *Isabel Clarendon*, which was about people of a higher social caste, he explicitly denied any interpretative purpose, saying that a novelist

> must not pretend to do more than exhibit facts and draw at times justifiable inference. He is not a creator of human beings, with eyes to behold the very heart of the machine he has himself pieced together; merely one who takes trouble to trace certain lines of human experience, and, working here on grounds of knowledge, there by and of analogy, here again in the way of colder speculation, spins his tale with what skill he may till the threads are used up.

This mingling of modesty and contempt toward his vocation is a clue to the inherent coldness that afflicts all Gissing's novels, no matter how sincerely he tried to record what he saw as the reality of life.

Closer to Henry James in temperament and material was another new novelist who began to write about the same time as Gissing. George Moore's family owned large debt-ridden estates in the far west of Ireland, and he was educated at a Jesuit school; but he rebelled against his parents' social and religious standards, and when he was twenty he went to Paris as an art student. Seven years in France made him an ardent disciple of the erotic poets and naturalistic novelists who were then in vogue; he made friends with prominent painters and writers, and returned to England with a determination to imitate the work of the French authors. Thus, like James, he was an alien in the traditional English literary milieu; and he resembled James also in being a detached literary observer, controlled by artistic theories rather than by creative fervor.

The latest conspicuous figure in French fiction was Émile Zola, who had transformed the realism of Balzac into a grimmer and more brutal frankness by rigorous application of scientific theory. Zola declared that the novelist's procedures ought to be identical with those of the surgeon. Since the evolutionary hypothesis classified mankind as one of the genera of animals, Zola accepted the axiom that human behavior is motivated by the primitive compulsions of survival and propagation. Necessarily, then, his novels dealt with the crudest manifestations of cruelty and lust. After attracting attention in 1867 by the gruesome vividness of *Thérèse Raquin*, Zola set out to rival Balzac's *Comédie humaine* by writing a vast series of novels all dealing with a single family, which would not only be a panorama of recent French society but would also illustrate the workings of the law of heredity. Beginning in 1871, the Rougon-Macquart chronicles in the next twenty-two years totaled twenty volumes. The critics named this new phenomenon *un roman fleuve*, "a flowing novel." The author's great notoriety came with *L'Assommoir* (1878), dealing with drink, and *Nana* (1880), the story of a greedy, promiscuous burlesque-star whose only talent is the strip-tease.

For two or three centuries, in the minds of respectable Englishmen, French fiction had been synonymous with indecency. When George Moore brazenly proclaimed himself a disciple of Zola and Gautier, the public was prepared to be shocked. His first novel, *A Modern Lover*, used frank terms in telling the story of an egotistical painter and three women of different social classes who sacrifice themselves on his behalf. The most noticeable quality of the book, however, is not so much its impropriety as its atrocious literary style, even worse than Hardy's early awkwardness. At school Moore had been such an unwilling pupil that he had learned little even of grammar and spelling; and after his years abroad his idiom was a mixture of Irish, English, and French.

His second novel, *A Mummer's Wife*, was somewhat better written; but it gained more notoriety because Moore went to nauseating extremes in his physiological details. He had decided to portray a drab industrial town, a subject of which he knew nothing. When reporters told him that Hanley, in the pottery district of Staffordshire, was the ugliest town in England, he followed Zola's procedure by going there with a notebook and compiling exhaustive data. As his story was to deal also with shabby theatrical life, he spent some weeks in traveling with a light-opera troupe. On the basis of this research he constructed his story of a woman rebelling against narrow piety and a nagging husband; she elopes with an actor and after brief success on the stage she drinks herself to death.

Because *A Modern Lover* had been banned by the circulating libraries, Moore's publishers challenged their monopoly by departing from the expensive three-volume format and issuing *A Mummer's Wife* in a cheap single volume; and when this incurred the same treatment they inserted an advertising slip announcing that "this book has been placed on the Index Expurgatorius of the 'Select' Circulating Libraries of Messrs. Mudie and W. H. Smith & Son." Moore wrote a scathing pamphlet, "Literature at Nurse," defying all censorship of fiction:

> To analyse, you must have a subject; a religious or sensual passion is as necessary to a realistic novelist as a disease is to a physician. The dissection of a healthy subject would not, as a rule, prove interesting, and if the right to probe and comment on humanity's failings be granted, what becomes of the pretty schoolroom with its piano tinkling away at "The Maiden's Prayer"?

In his next novel, *A Drama in Muslin*, which he called "a study of the life of a group of girl-friends," he dealt just as openly with the sexual frustrations of young women in the struggle to find mates.

The whole development of the "problem novel," in fact, can be identified with changes in the relationship between the sexes. Apart from a few novels dealing with religious doubts, the central theme always concerned women. The principal reasons for this obsessive interest were both the breakdown of rigid moral standards based on religious dogmas and the new legal, economic, and educational status that women were acquiring. The Marriage Act of 1858 had given average people their first suggestion of the possibility of divorce. Important financial rights were granted by the Married Women's Property Act of 1882. Female suffrage was almost included in the Reform Bill of 1884, and was extended on the level of county politics in 1888. Elementary education for girls became compulsory in 1870 and women's colleges were established at Cambridge during the next decade. New careers were opening: women were admitted to medical practice in 1876.

The cumulative effect of these and other forces destroyed the conventional literary picture of innocent maidens needing the protection of generous men and achieving it by matrimony in the last chapter. George Eliot foreshadowed the change by her portraits of independent-spirited women — Dinah Morris, Maggie Tulliver, Dorothea Brooke; but these still sought refuge in marriage. Meredith was more positive in insisting that a marriage can be successful only when the wife enjoys intellectual and emotional freedom. Hardy emphasized the negative side of the case by showing the thwarted struggles of passionate women like Bathsheba Everdene and Eustacia Vye to break the shackles of their environment. Gissing and Moore marked the final abandonment of traditional reticence in their clinical reports of the emotional urges of both men and women.

Perhaps the most remarkable example of the new outspokenness was *The Story of an African Farm*, by Olive Schreiner, a South African girl who came to England when she was twenty-six, bringing the manuscript of her novel, which she had written while working as a governess in remote regions of the veldt. Instead of the sentimentality expected of a young woman or the picturesqueness expected of a story about the colonial frontier, it was a somber, resentful summary of all the chief themes of the problem novel — religious doubt, sexual antagonism, and women's rights. Not since Charlotte Brontë had a young governess vented her frustrations and her grudges with such intensity. When it was published in 1883 Miss Schreiner was acclaimed as a heroine of the radical intelligentsia, but she never wrote another novel of any consequence.

Neither Meredith nor Hardy produced a masterpiece during the early eighties. Meredith undertook another study of egoism in *The Tragic Comedians* (1881), but he hampered his creative freedom by basing the action upon the love affair of Ferdinand Lassalle, a German Socialist leader, and Helena von Dönniges, which had occurred only fifteen years previously. Using dramatic unity and condensation as rigorously as in *The Egoist*, Meredith displays the doomed course of an affair between two sentimentalists who are of antithetical social and racial backgrounds and who both are innately conceited and selfish.

Hardy at this time wrote two novels of the class that he labeled "Romances and Fantasies" (*The Trumpet-Major* and *Two on a Tower*) and one "Novel of Ingenuity" (*A Laodicean*). The action of *The Trumpet-Major* takes place during the Napoleonic Wars, and the story is more romantic than anything else he wrote, with a charming heroine of the conventional model and a good deal of genial farce. *A Laodicean*, which followed, was written during an illness to fulfill a contract for a magazine serial. Much of Hardy's early career went into this story of a young architect who makes drawings of village churches, sub-

mits plans in a competition, and marries the woman who com-
missioned the new building. There is prolonged discussion of
architectural topics, and the plot is unconvincingly sensational.
Two on a Tower is notable as the most extreme example of
Hardy's symbolic use of vast and ageless settings to minimize
the importance of human miseries. The hero is a young astron-
omer, and the stellar universe forms the "stupendous background" for "two infinitesimal lives" as he pursues a painful love
affair with a woman many years older than he is, who secretly
marries him and later learns that her missing husband was still
alive at the time. This novel came in for some of the current
condemnation of immoral fiction, and it was attacked also as a
subversive satire on the Church of England because the heroine
marries a bishop to provide a father for her unborn child.

Meredith's *Diana of the Crossways,* in 1884, became more popular than any of his previous books. It reverted toward the silver-
fork school in being a polished *roman à clef* of life in high society, with Lord Melbourne, Sidney Herbert, John Delane, and
other eminent early Victorians as originals for the characters.
As in *The Tragic Comedians,* the defects arise from using the
intractable material of an actual occurrence — this time, a notorious political scandal of forty years earlier, in which the Hon.
Mrs. Norton was blamed for having learned a crucial Cabinet
secret from her lover and betrayed it to the editor of the
Times. Meredith followed the legend faithfully; but when
Mrs. Norton's aristocratic relations protested that he had resuscitated a baseless slander he felt obliged to insert a note in later
editions insisting that the story "is to be read as fiction." The
ironical consequence is that some critics find inconsistency in
actions of the heroine which occur in the story because the
author believed that they had occurred in actuality. The charge
of inconsistency, however, can be refuted in terms of Meredith's
purpose. He chose the subject as an illustration of how a beautiful and clever woman can commit egregious blunders because her
emotional impulses have never been regulated by systematic education and social responsibility. He was so successful in depicting Diana Warwick's generosity and charm that readers were
misled into the belief that he intended her as a paragon of perfection. Newly emancipated young women, in particular, adopted
the book as their manifesto because Diana had the spunk to leave
an intolerable husband and support herself in a man's world as a

writer. These self-elected champions then complained because she is depicted as selling a state secret. But Meredith's thesis was that even so brilliant a woman as Diana was incapable of acting discreetly because the false position of women in society rendered her unstable. Like most of his other heroes and heroines, she goes through an agonizing ordeal before she learns self-discipline.

Hardy's next novel, *The Mayor of Casterbridge*, is also a study of a strong but unstable character; but Michael Henchard's problem is neither religious faith nor sexual relations, but self-control. Physical strength, mental ability, personal magnetism, and ambition enable the itinerant laborer to become a rich businessman and impressive civic dignitary. His will power is strong enough to control his craving for liquor after he sells his wife and baby to another man in a drunken rage; but it is not strong enough to conquer his pride and his savage temper when he meets with business reverses and well-organized rivalry.

This is the only one of the Wessex novels in which the action occurs mainly in a town, and therefore there is greater complexity in the situations. But Casterbridge (Dorchester) is an ancient market town with Roman remains in its outskirts and farmlands all around, and from these Hardy derives his usual effects of nature's indifference and the folk-memories of the remote past. Several of the sensational episodes, such as involuntary bigamy, had already been used by Hardy in other novels, and the involved series of coincidences that cause Henchard's downfall become almost absurd in their pertinacity. This cannot be attributed solely to Hardy's fatalistic philosophy: he admitted that it resulted partly from writing the story as a serial for the weekly *Graphic* and "aiming to get an incident into almost every week's part, causing him in his own judgment to add events to the narrative somewhat too freely." Yet in spite of defects, the picture of a potentially noble character ruined by tragic flaws and standing in solitary defiance against all his adversaries has something of the magnificence of Greek or Shakespearian tragedy.

This novel was followed immediately by another that ranks among Hardy's best, *The Woodlanders*. By choosing a wooded section of his territory he was able to make the natural background particularly expressive of the relentless struggle for survival that he saw as the primary law of nature. In no other novel is he more explicit in commenting on the "Unfulfilled Intention" — the mechanistic control over the "great web of human doings." Inclusion of humor and folk customs, however, prevents the tone from being altogether somber. The illiterate peasant girl, Marty South, is a genuinely true-hearted character, contrasted with the genteel Grace Melbury, who gives up her laborer-sweetheart in order to marry the dissolute Dr. Fitzpiers because of his higher social rank. In this novel Hardy came closer to the problems of woman's freedom that were exercising Meredith and Moore, by explicitly condemning the rigor of the marriage laws that yoke Grace with her unfaithful husband. And yet he is scrupulously fair in showing that no character is individually to blame for what happens; all have good qualities, and even the seducer Fitzpiers cannot be held responsible for his fascination for women.

An evidence of the new artistic self-consciousness of novelists is an epidemic of essays in which they expounded their theories, whereas those of earlier generations had been satisfied with brief prefaces or with digressive comments within the stories. Meredith had led off with his Essay on Comedy. Other examples were Moore's "Literature at Nurse," Hardy's "Candour in English Fiction" (1890), and Gissing's "Realism in Fiction" (1895). The most significant were two that came out in 1884, and which set the lines for an open battle between the realistic and romantic factions. One was Henry James's article entitled "The Art of Fiction," which asserted that

> the only reason for the existence of a novel is that it does attempt to represent life. . . . The air of reality (solidity of specification) seems to me to be the supreme virtue of a novel. . . . Catching the very note and trick, the strange irregular rhythm of life, that is the attempt whose strenuous force keeps Fiction upon her feet. In proportion as in what she offers us we see life *without* rearrangement do we feel that we are touching the truth; in proportion as we see it *with* rearrangement do we feel that we are being put off with a substitute, a compromise and convention.

This postulate was challenged in "A Humble Remonstrance," by Robert Louis Stevenson, who declared that no art does "compete with life." Man's one method, whether he reasons or creates, is to half-shut his eyes against the dazzle and confusion of reality. . . . The novel, which is a work of art, exists, not by its resemblances to life, which are forced and material, as a shoe must still consist of leather, but by its immeasurable difference from life, which is designed and significant, and is both the method and the meaning of the work.

In this essay and others that followed, especially "A Gossip on Romance" and "The Lantern Bearers," Stevenson proved himself a doughty spokesman for the antagonists of realism. With a background like Walter Scott's — birth and education in Edinburgh and pride in Scotland's heroic past — he combined a mercurial temperament and a poetic flair. Like George Moore, he had studied in a French artists' colony, but his was in the idyllic Forest of Fontainebleau and not the grubby attics of Montmartre. Intensely aware of the color of words and the rhythm of sentences, he perfected his prose style by assiduous practice, chiefly through imitating the manner of various authors that he admired. After publishing two easy-going, humorous books of travel he brought out *The New Arabian Nights* in 1882, containing a group of stories contributed to magazines during the preceding four years. The situations in these partook of the sensationalism of Collins, but the graceful style and sophisticated wit banished the cruder elements of horror or sadism. In 1881 also, under the pen name of "Captain George North," Stevenson wrote two serials for a weekly paper for children. These were *Treasure Island* and *The Black Arrow*, which were soon recognized by adults as displaying more technical skill than average juvenile fiction. In 1885 came *Prince Otto*, which he openly labeled "A Romance" and which depicted a mythical mid-European country in a manner reminiscent of Meredith's *Harry Richmond*.

These books inaugurated a spate of stories that exploited the standard romantic ingredients — exciting adventure, reckless heroes, lovely heroines, exotic settings. Many of the books were historical romances, but they abandoned the ponderous gait of Scott, Ainsworth, and Bulwer-Lytton in favor of the gay vitality of Alexandre Dumas. The dominant note in all of them was a sheer zest for active life which appealed to readers who were depressed by the drabness of realism and the solemnity of problem novels.

The first of these young romancers was Henry Rider Haggard, who had spent several years in the British administration in South Africa. He began with *Dawn*, a conventional melodrama, and *The Witch's Head*, which is redeemed by some vivid scenes of the bloodthirsty Zulu war of 1879. His immense popularity came with *King Solomon's Mines* (1885), which he wrote in imitation of *Treasure Island*, employing the same irresistible theme of lost treasure and combining it with the weird ruined city of Zimbabwe that had recently been discovered in East Africa. This was followed by *She*, with the equally enthralling theme of a white sorceress ruling over a savage empire. *Allan Quatermain* and many other books maintained Haggard's popularity among lovers of vicarious adventure, and he was less successful whenever he tried to write more adult stories about English society.

Another devotee of Stevenson was Stanley J. Weyman, a barrister whose first historical romance, *The House of the Wolf*, came out serially in 1883, and was followed by *A Gentleman of France*, *Under the Red Robe*, and many others. A more charming style distinguished the novels of Arthur Quiller-Couch, who, after a brilliant career at Oxford, became a book reviewer and published his first novel, *Dead Man's Rock*, in 1887, when he was twenty-four. He continued with *Troy Town*, which is full of the local color of his native Cornwall, and *The Splendid Spur*, a story of the English Civil War.

The most successful of all the Stevensonians was Arthur Conan Doyle. He was practicing as a physician when he wrote *A Study in Scarlet* (1887), which combined Collins's technique of the mystery story with the sprightly style of *The New Arabian Nights*. In France Émile Gaboriau had written vastly popular detective novels between 1866 and 1873. Doyle's detective, Sherlock Holmes, was modeled upon one of his medical professors at Edinburgh University, who had fascinated the students with his powers of induction. A second story of Holmes's ingenious solving of mysteries was *The Sign of Four* (1889). Doyle's real ambition was to write historical romances, and he produced two masterpieces in this genre, *Micah Clarke* and *The White Company*. But the public was so avid for more stories about the sardonic detective that he had to continue supplying the demand.

The vogue of these popular novelists was enhanced by changes in methods of publication. George Moore's rebellion against the three-volume format spread quickly among the publishers. *Treasure Island, King Solomon's Mines,* and most of the other books of this description came out in one volume selling at five or six shillings, and consequently their total sales soared to unprecedented heights. By 1892 the "three-decker" was extinct. An equally profitable expansion of the market came with a new type of mass-circulation magazine, with smooth paper and lavish illustrations, notably *Macmillan's, Longman's,* and the *Strand.* They paid generously for serial fiction, but their chief influence was their demand for short stories.

Until the eighties the short story in England had been mediocre. Poe and Hawthorne in America, Mérimée and Maupassant in France, had proved its artistic potentialities; but even such masters of fiction as Dickens, Thackeray, Trollope, and Meredith, when they attempted to work in such a limited area, produced pathetic abortions. The new magazine market, however, encouraged the best authors to undertake short-story writing; and the opportunity for vivid word-painting and single emotional effect made it the ideal medium for Stevenson, whose greatest achievements are in this form.

Conan Doyle, too, found it perfectly suited for providing variety, suspense, and surprise while retaining the central characters of Holmes and Dr. Watson, and the now-familiar quarters at 221A Baker Street. The short stories were collected at intervals into volumes, which eventually totaled five, while *The Hound of the Baskervilles* was a third book-length story. In the last tale of *Memoirs of Sherlock Holmes* (1892), the detective met with a spectacular death (to the author's manifest relief); but the public protested so vehemently that he was soon resuscitated, and the final volume of the series did not come out until 1927. Few fictitious characters have ever assumed such a living identity in the minds of countless readers.

The most accomplished of the romantic story-tellers confined himself almost wholly to the short story. Rudyard Kipling was uniquely equipped with exotic settings through his familiarity with India, where he spent his first five years and whither he returned after his schooling in England, when his bad eyesight excluded him from the army. As a reporter on an Allahabad newspaper he observed the English army officers and civilian administrators with a cynical eye, and became aware of the infinite contrasts between the European and native ways of life. The incisive short stories that he wrote for Indian papers were collected in seven cheap volumes in 1888, when he was twenty-two; within a few months they became known in London and New York, and his fame was instantaneous.

Kipling's versatility and curiosity, his journalistic impudence and cynicism, his genius for making an unfamiliar scene vivid through expertly selected words and details, rendered him a master of the short story. His popularity, however, encouraged him to undertake a novel, *The Light that Failed*, which, though it is a skillful performance for a young man of twenty-four, lacks the emotional depth and psychological insight that the topic demanded. The scenes of London journalistic life and of desert warfare in Africa have reportorial effectiveness; but the idealizing of the army and of men of action — a compensation for the author's frustration in being debarred from a military career — betrays a tone of immaturity that is less perceptible in his short stories, even when they convey the same values. The portrayal of a hero who goes blind but still manages to live the strenuous life has some poignancy insofar as it reveals Kipling's inner anxiety. He was mercenary enough to provide a conventional happy ending for the American serial issue, while retaining in the volume form the tragic conclusion that the situation demanded.

Two years later Kipling attempted another novel, *The Naulakha*, in collaboration with his American brother-in-law, but this was not successful. His major significance in fiction, like Conan Doyle's, is in the new genre, volumes of short stories in which the same characters become familiar as they reappear in separate episodes. Mulvaney, Ortheris, and Learoyd in *Soldiers Three*, eternal types of the hard-drinking, loose-talking men in the ranks; Corkran, M'Turk, and Beetle in *Stalky & Co.*, shattering the pious tradition of *Tom Brown's School Days* by revealing the obstreperous and brutal side of English school life; Mowgli, Baloo, and Bagheera in *The Jungle Books*, lovable characters even though two are quadrupeds — it is through these that Kipling survives. He wrote only two other full-length narratives, *Captains Courageous*, an adventure yarn for boys, and *Kim*, perhaps his masterpiece as a panorama of native life in

India, which reverts to the episodic story line of the picaresque romance.

Stevenson was more persistent in trying to produce a major novel; but his writing of fiction was interspersed with essays, travel books, poetry, and plays; and the ten years of life that remained to him after *Treasure Island* were broken into by long journeys in search of health — to California, the Adirondacks, and finally the South Seas. In *Kidnapped* and its sequel *Catriona* (American title *David Balfour*) he was still producing books of adventure for boys, but with increasing attention to psychological truth and historical detail, and with the warmth of emotional identification that Scottish writers ever since Scott have felt when dealing with the Jacobite uprising. In 1888 came *The Master of Ballantrae*, his first fully adult novel and in some respects his best work. It too deals with the collapse of Prince Charlie's doomed enterprise, but now with a sinister gloom reminiscent of *The Bride of Lammermoor*.

As a technician, Stevenson was always experimenting with point of view. The gripping reality of *Treasure Island*, like that of *Robinson Crusoe*, arises from its being told by a participant, and it has a dimension of irony in that young Jim Hawkins is often unaware of the full significance of what he observes. The device, however, is defective at one point, when the plot requires the inclusion of occurrences at which Jim is not present. Readers who have by this time identified themselves with him are forced to shift abruptly to another narrator, with only a chapter heading to warn them. *Kidnapped* and its sequel are cast as memoirs, and almost equal *Henry Esmond* in imitating the style of an earlier century. In *The Master of Ballantrae* Stevenson borrows rather from *Castle Rackrent* and *Wuthering Heights* to achieve both vividness and irony by presenting the story in the words of the old steward, Mackellar, who is fanatically loyal to his scoundrel of a master. Again, however, Stevenson was baffled by the problem of how to include episodes that the narrator could not have observed, and he had to insert long excerpts from the recollections of the Chevalier de Burke.

Discussion of Stevenson's novels must entail references to previous authors, since his art was so consciously cultivated. In explaining the genesis of *The Master of Ballantrae* he did not mention Scott or Maria Edgeworth or Emily Brontë, and paid

merely incidental tribute to Thackeray's *Barry Lyndon;* his starting point was a less gifted novelist, Captain Marryat. "I had just
finished my third or fourth perusal of *The Phantom Ship.*
'Come,' said I to my engine, 'let us make a tale, a story of many
years and countries, of the sea and the land, savagery and
civilization; a story that shall have the same large features and
may be treated in the same summary elliptic method as the book
you have been reading and admiring.' " The whole of this prefatory note is a valuable record of how a novelist's mind works,
revealed with all Stevenson's disarming candor; but his catalogue
of diverse sources and influences is a clue to the book's structural
weakness. It breaks abruptly in the middle, where there is a
seven-year lapse of time; and the Indian fakir, necessary for providing the superphysical episodes, is a synthetic figure. Nevertheless the story illustrates Stevenson's characteristic ability to use
settings for heightening emotional tension. Ranging from Scotland to India and the American wilderness, it demonstrates his
theory that the atmosphere of a particular place can be the de-
termining element in fiction: "Certain dank gardens cry aloud
for a murder; certain old houses demand to be haunted; certain
coasts are set apart for shipwreck."

In the next few years Stevenson wrote three melodramatic
novels in collaboration with his stepson, Lloyd Osbourne —
The Wrong Box, The Wrecker, and *The Ebb-Tide.* But it was
becoming apparent that his forte was the short story, wherein
his verbal and atmospheric skill had full effect, without the
novelist's responsibility for greater depth and firmer structure.
He excelled equally in psychological studies like "Markheim,"
gay comedy like "The Treasure of Franchard," romantic incidents like "The Merry Men," and — above all — subtly terrifying
stories of superstition like "Thrawn Janet." It is noteworthy that
his most famous piece of fiction, *Doctor Jekyll and Mr. Hyde,*
is one of the few admirable works ever to emerge from the
limbo of middle length between short story and novel. A mystery
story in its suspense, a supernatural tale in its horror, a moral
allegory in its implications, it has been admitted into the select
precincts of modern folklore.

Whether the reason was his failing health or inherent dilettantism, Stevenson never achieved the major novel that he hoped to
write. When he died he left half-a-dozen manuscripts in various

stages of development, two of them being far enough along to be printed. *St. Ives*, a vivacious romance of a Napoleonic prisoner in Scotland, was completed for publication by Quiller-Couch; and *Weir of Hermiston*, so far as it went, promised to be his greatest work, again set in eighteenth-century Scotland, but with more solidity of characterization than he had previously attained.

The romanticism of Stevenson, Kipling, and their school cannot be described in the old terms of implausibly perfect characters and unrealistic remoteness of scene. Stevenson did not hesitate to show his heroes suffering from vanity or fright, and Kipling allowed his to get drunk or feel vengeful. Both authors make their settings immediate by graphic and precise details. A clue to their fascination was supplied by Stevenson in "A Gossip on Romance":

> In anything fit to be called by the name of reading, the process itself should be absorbing and voluptuous; we should gloat over a book, be rapt clean out of ourselves, and rise from the perusal, our mind filled with the busiest, kaleidoscopic dance of images, incapable of sleep or of continuous thought. . . . The great creative writer shows us the realization and the apotheosis of the day-dreams of common men. His stories may be nourished with the realities of life, but their true mark is to satisfy the nameless longings of the reader, and to obey the ideal laws of the day-dream.

Perhaps it was because physical disabilities debarred both Stevenson and Kipling from careers in the world of action that their particular daydreams acquired the necessary vividness to enrapture countless readers "clean out of themselves."

While the romance-writers were riding the wave of popular adulation, the realists kept doggedly on with their analysis of the commonplace. Gissing's attempt to depict a higher social environment in *Isabel Clarendon* and *A Life's Morning* evoked a friendly suggestion from Meredith that he might hope for "a foremost place in fiction" only if he would pursue "the low-life themes." Thus encouraged, he wrote *Demos*, a bitter portrayal of Socialist agitation, which came out opportunely in 1886, when the newspapers were reporting proletarian riots and looting in London's West End. This timeliness brought the book a wider sale than any of Gissing's previous work, and rescued him from his deepest poverty and vindictiveness.

The hero of *Demos* is an ambitious and intelligent workman, who inherits a prosperous business (by the outworn melodramatic device of a capricious will) and sets out to share his profits with his employees. Gissing does not idealize the brash Mutimer, however, but emphasizes the conceit that drives him to abandon his working-class sweetheart in favor of a genteel girl who marries him for his money. Indeed, Gissing's own pretension to gentility enlists his sympathy with the mercenary wife and the elegant dilettante who is her lover. But in spite of the author's apparent hostility to Mutimer's confident visions of leadership, the story eventually gains something like the tragic dignity of *The Mayor of Casterbridge* as Mutimer's business collapses and he is attacked by a mob of the workers he tried to help.

This book was followed by *Thyrza*, a more sympathetic novel, dealing with a working girl of superior sensitivity and some musical talent who is undecided between two suitors, a thoughtful workman trying to acquire culture and an idealistic businessman ineptly hoping to improve slum conditions by extension lectures on literature. In contrast with this gentle story, Gissing's next, *The Nether World*, is the most sordid and pessimistic of his works, almost rivaling Zola in its delineation of sensual behavior and the bestial violence of crowds. Every character is impelled by the crassest sort of self-interest except perhaps one man who feebly tries to escape from the general squalor, only to be dragged back by dim loyalty to a spiritless wife. Throughout the book the weak characters are helpless and the strong ones have merely an animal energy.

Having explored the lowest social depths in three novels, Gissing turned to the white-collar class, and at the same time he undertook a greater degree of psychological analysis. About this time he read some treatises on clinical psychology, as well as the fiction of the Goncourts, Maupassant, and Dostoievski. These new influences are perceptible in *The Emancipated* (1890), which is one of his less effective books, partly because it was another attempt to deal with people of some wealth and refinement, but also because he adopted a Jamesian situation without James's talent for revealing the slow growth of self-understanding. Immediately afterwards, however, came what is perhaps Gissing's best novel, *New Grub Street*, based on his own experiences as a struggling writer. Eugene Reardon, the author's counterpart, is contrasted with Jasper Milvain, a cocksure professional, who describes Reardon scornfully:

"He is the old type of unpractical artist. . . . He won't make concessions, or rather, he can't make them; he can't supply the market. . . . Literature nowadays is a trade. Putting aside men of genius, who may succeed by mere cosmic force, your successful man of letters is your skillful tradesman. He thinks first and foremost of the realities; when one kind of goods begins to go off slackly, he is ready with something new and appetizing."

Reardon, who prefers to discuss Greek poetry with a scholarly friend, and whose novels are "almost purely psychological," fails not only as a writer, because his work seems dull to the public, but also in social relations, because poverty makes him self-conscious and awkward, and as a husband, because he cannot earn enough to keep his wife happy.

Probably the greatest weakness in Gissing's novels is the unconvincing treatment of sex, in spite of his pose of frankness. Partly this may have been due to his fear of antagonizing the critics and libraries, but also it must be attributed to the ineptness of his own relations with women. Three years after his miserable wife died he married a quiet young woman whom he met in a coffee shop, and soon found that she was incompetent and shrewish. The women in his novels are apt to be either drunken wantons like his first wife, or querulous naggers like his second, unless they are incredibly intellectual and altruistic, reflecting his dazzled admiration for two or three ladies of refinement who were courteous to him.

While Gissing was painfully documenting the frustrations of poverty, a new writer sprang into prominence with an equally somber report of spiritual frustration among the cultivated and the prosperous. Mrs. Humphry Ward was a perfect embodiment of the upper-class assurance that Gissing envied from afar. Born Mary Augusta Arnold, she was a niece of Matthew Arnold and was brought up in the rarefied intellectual atmosphere of Oxford, where she married a scholarly tutor. She was a personal friend of both George Eliot and Henry James. Her first books were a children's story, an insignificant novel about an actress, and a translation of Amiel's *Journal Intime*. Then in 1888 she won notoriety with *Robert Elsmere*, a novel which had something of George Eliot's moral earnestness in its account of the torments of conscience endured by a sensitive clergyman who finds his religious faith being destroyed by scientific rationalism and the higher criticism of the Bible. This problem, which had distressed the author's uncle and other brilliant men, such as Arthur Clough and Leslie Stephen, for thirty years past, was now seeping into the minds of the general public, and her novel had just the right balance of serious discussion and dramatic emotion to impress the average reader. In the conclusion Elsmere leaves the church and undertakes social work in a London slum, where he dies in the high Victorian tradition of renunciation and humanitarian service.

Robert Elsmere gained extraneous interest through the rumor that the characters accurately portrayed the Oxford circle of thinkers, including Mark Pattison, Thomas Hill Green, and Walter Pater, who had been treated satirically by Mallock in *The New Republic*. The book's fame was assured when Gladstone, who had become a literary oracle in his old age, wrote an extensive article deploring its religious skepticism, and Huxley (whose son was married to Mrs. Ward's sister) defended it. Seldom before had any novel become the topic of so much ideological discussion.

The scenes of London poverty at the end of *Robert Elsmere* link Mrs. Ward's novel with Gissing; and in her next, *The History of David Grieve*, she uses his type of situation — a poor youth whose intellectual ambitions are endangered by sensual temptation. The difference is that Mrs. Ward's hero survives his perils and achieves a serene "natural religion." By this time Mrs. Ward had herself founded a rescue mission in London's grimy East End, and realized that her influence with the public might be used on behalf of her objectives. Therefore *Marcella* (1894) and *Sir George Tressady* (1896) are political novels advocating legislation to improve the conditions of the poor. In *Helbeck of Bannisdale* she deals with the problem of mixed marriage between a Roman Catholic and a Protestant.

Mrs. Ward was deficient not only in humor but in a novelist's essential gift of being able to create living characters. Her people are seldom more than dummy figures to express conflicting opinions. Nevertheless she captured the mood of her decade so completely and her books were so solidly constructed and so tolerantly reasonable that Tolstoi was not alone in declaring her to be the greatest living English novelist. Henry James, on the other hand, was aware of her shortcomings and patiently lectured her on the art of fiction, though he confessed that he doubted whether the good lady comprehended one word of what he told her. He must have been wryly aware, too, that each of her novels, wooden though it might be, automatically became a best seller, whereas his subtle psychological studies were appreciated by an ever-narrowing audience.

James's earlier and relatively straightforward manner ended in 1886 with *The Bostonians,* one of his few stories dealing wholly with the American scene; and he moved into a more complex style in *The Tragic Muse* (1890), his first that was restricted to England in both setting and characters. The difficulty in reading this and his subsequent novels arose partly from his theory that the action must be presented through the consciousness of one character only, and partly from his effort to achieve the exact shade of meaning in each sentence by labyrinthine qualifications and parentheses.

Meanwhile Gissing seemed to be providing a disillusioned antidote to Mrs. Ward's idealistic view of moral dilemmas. *Born in Exile* inverts the problem of *Robert Elsmere* by showing a young clergyman of humble origin who is determined to use his profession as a means for social advancement. Totally lacking in religious conviction, Godwin Peak is equally ready to satirize or to extol the reconciling of theology with science, as circumstances warrant. His opportunism is unsuccessful: discredited by the church, he loses his influential friends and the girl who seemed ready to marry him, and ends in the social limbo he started from. Gissing has enough fellow-feeling for Peak to give a tolerant record of the interior monologues in which he rationalizes his casuistry and his defeat.

From the church Gissing turned to politics, as Mrs. Ward did, and in *Denzil Quarrier,* a hastily written novel, he uses an election campaign as the setting for a study of envy in which a would-be candidate ruins his rival by revealing that he is bigamously married to the wife of a convict. *The Odd Women* (1893) is also marred by melodramatic complications of plot, but it has a significant social theme — the excess of women in the English population and the inadequacy of opportunities for them to support themselves. Three daughters of a doctor, left penniless and untrained at his death, suffer a variety of degradations.

The most effective element in the novel, bringing it into contact with Meredith's recent work, is the character of Rhoda Nunn, a strong-minded girl who believes in complete freedom for women, not only politically and economically but also in sexual relations. Gissing's incompetent manipulation of plot is equally conspicuous in his next book, *In the Year of Jubilee*, a vigorous but diffuse attack on bourgeois vulgarity and pretension.

While Gissing was wrestling indecisively with the difficulties of construction, George Moore was slowly mastering the mechanics of English prose style. Oscar Wilde remarked that "Moore conducts his education in public." Falling under the spell of the melodious language and hedonistic doctrine in Pater's philosophical semi-novel, *Marius the Epicurean*, Moore abjured the ponderous manner and calculated brutality of Zola; but his new aesthetic sensibility produced several inferior novels. His best work at this stage of his career is an egotistical autobiography, *Confessions of a Young Man* (1888), in which, with the realistic precision of fiction, he narrates (and perhaps exaggerates) his Parisian exploits. In contrast with it, his *Spring Days* is a shoddy portrayal of suburban vulgarity and the sex problems of silly girls; and *Mike Fletcher*, tracing the degradation of an insatiable sensualist, reads like a burlesque. Adverse criticism of these two novels inspired an unwonted mood of self-distrust, and in *Vain Fortune* he gives a revealing study of a writer whose talent is inadequate for his grandiose pretensions.

Of the older novelists, only Meredith and Hardy survived, and both were nearing the end of their careers in fiction. The success of *Diana of the Crossways*, especially in the United States, had drawn belated attention to Meredith's previous work, and he was acclaimed as the greatest living English novelist. Finding himself with an income sufficient for his modest needs, he was able to end his thirty years of servitude as publishers' reader; and though handicapped by increasing deafness and paralysis, he gained legendary renown as a brilliant talker. The verbal agility and oracular allusiveness of his conversation are evident in his last major novel, *One of Our Conquerors* (1891), which is the extremest specimen of his cryptic style. Even the title is sarcastic, for the central character is a business magnate representing the opportunism that seemed to Meredith to be obliterating all ethical standards. Victor Radnor is no vulgar money-grubber; he has great personal charm and a real appreciation of the arts. But he is another Meredithian sentimental egoist, who is living biga- mously with a lovely and unselfish woman under constant peril of exposure by his legal wife, many years his senior, whom he married for her money in order to start his career. The novel's main implication is the inhumanity of rigid marriage laws, as demonstrated by Radnor's degeneration of character as a result of his incompatible early marriage, and also by the perpetual nervous tension that eventually kills his Nataly with a heart attack, by the illegitimacy that overshadows their delightful daughter, and by the ironic parallel when she too falls in love with an unhappily married man. Rather than being a propa- ganda treatise for easier divorce, however, the book is a subtle psychological study of Radnor, using whole chapters of interior monologue to reveal how his genial prodigality masks the in- tolerable double strain of financial speculations and illegal marital status, leading to final insanity.

After this brilliant and difficult novel Meredith brought out two more that are something of an anticlimax. *Lord Ormont and His Aminta* treats again of incompatibility in marriage: a roman- tic girl marries an aged general through admiration of his mili- tary heroism and later elopes with a childhood sweetheart who is establishing a progressive school in Switzerland. *The Amazing Marriage*, which Meredith had partially written a dozen years ear- lier, was completed and published in 1895. It too begins with the marriage of a beautiful young girl and a picturesque old adven- turer, but unlike the preceding story, their romance is bliss- fully happy. The theme of loveless wedlock comes later, when their high-spirited daughter is treated ignominiously by her ar- rogant nobleman-husband.

Though the two final novels are below Meredith's highest achievements of psychological analysis, they mark a recurrence of the romantic charm and the gusto for life that characterized *Richard Feverel* and *Harry Richmond*. In his sixties, and a widower for the second time, Meredith retained a strong attrac- tiveness for women, and there is more than a trace of personal identification in these two stories of mating between an old man and a young girl. No longer able to indulge in athletic exercise, he poured all his love of muscular energy into his youthful characters, and gave radiant descriptions of the mountain and ocean scenery that he could never again enjoy.

Hardy's final novels were synchronous with Meredith's in date, but antithetical in spirit. *Tess of the d'Urbervilles* (1891) became the most widely read of all his books. The old comparison of his work with George Eliot's was revived, not merely by the setting of lush farmland (unlike the bleak heath and the choked woods of his preceding rural stories) but also by a situation reminiscent of *Adam Bede*, the seduction of a naïve dairymaid by a selfish young gentleman, and her eventual trial for murder. The obvious difference is that Hardy's sympathy is entirely with the girl, as indicated by his defiant subtitle, "A Pure Woman Faithfully Presented." Equally significant is the deterministic principle that dominates the course of the action. The most notorious of all Hardy's crucial coincidences is that in which Tess's letter to Angel Clare, which would have enlightened him about her past, is slipped under his door and vanishes beneath the rug. And unlike George Eliot's melodramatic ending, when Hetty is saved from the gallows at the last minute, Tess goes hopelessly to her doom. Hardy's habit of using ancient relics to symbolize human insignificance is almost over-obvious when Tess spends her last night of freedom on a sacrificial altar in Stonehenge. With a somberly triumphant flourish of rhetoric, he composed the final sentence, which has been quoted ever since as the quintessence of his fatalism: "The President of the Immortals had finished his sport with Tess."

This callous sport proceeds inexorably from the first chapter, when the lazy laborer, Jack Durbeyfield, discovers that he is descended from the ancient landowning family of the district, and his daughter Tess thus comes to the notice of Alec d'Urberville, the heir of the usurpers now possessing the name and estates. The agent of disaster, however, is neither Alec nor Tess, who are driven by normal impulses in their sexual relations, but Angel Clare, the ineffectual idealist, whose humanitarian doctrine is not strong enough to withstand the shock of learning that Tess has been "defiled," and who merely confuses her mind with his rationalism.

There are improbabilities in the story. Tess is implausibly noble; Alec's later behavior is psychologically inconsistent, first in his religious zeal and then in his backsliding when he listens to Tess's muddled version of Angel's tenets; and when she stabs him the scene is taken too directly from newspaper crime stories. But Hardy succeeds in his purpose of demonstrating that Tess is a spiritually healthy character, even though she forfeits her chastity and later commits murder; and it was this theme, rather than any outspokenness about sex, that made the book seem outrageously immoral.

By this time Moore's battle against prudish suppression of truth in fiction was being won. His publisher served a term in prison in 1889 for bringing out allegedly obscene translations of Zola; but public sentiment was veering against the censors. Nevertheless, *Tess of the d'Urbervilles* was rejected as immoral by two magazine editors who had been competing for the serial rights until they read the manuscript; and a third accepted it only on the stipulation that Hardy eliminate the most offensive passages.

Under this compulsion of satisfying the profitable magazine market, Hardy next wrote one of his "fantasies," *The Well-Beloved,* which came out serially in 1892, though not in book form until five years later. This story does not overtly flout conventional morals; but if it is considered as a literal rather than a symbolic narrative it certainly deals with psychological abnormality, for the hero falls in love successively with a beautiful woman, her daughter, and her granddaughter. Hardy made it plain that he intended the situation to represent a Platonic search for the ideal and not a series of fleshly amours.

In his next novel, however, *Jude the Obscure,* he incensed conventional readers on no less than three grounds. In addition to sexual irregularities and an utterly hopeless determinism he included a note of social protest that had not been perceptible in his previous work, in which poverty was taken for granted as an unavoidable fact of life. Jude Fawley is more like a Gissing character in being a young workman with intellectual and artistic gifts, who dreams of being able to study at the great university of Christminster. He is thwarted not only by poverty and caste barriers, but also by his involvements with women. He is seduced at an early age by a lascivious country wench and marries her. When she deserts him he falls in love with Sue Bridehead, a neurotic young woman of advanced ideas, who leaves her husband and comes to live with Jude. The climax of their misery occurs when Jude's precocious little son hangs his half-sister and half-brother and himself, leaving a note that reads, "Done because we are too menny." The sheer grotesqueness of this calamity robs it of tragic power, leaving it merely repulsive; and its improbability is heightened by the author's emphasis on its allegorical significance: the child is nicknamed "Little Father Time" and Hardy remarks that he typifies "the beginning of the coming universal wish not to live."

The perversely black pessimism in this novel alienated many even of Hardy's former admirers; and the coarseness of the sex episodes outraged the general public, who stigmatized them as Zola at his worst. Refusing to truckle to popular pressure, Hardy made up his mind that he would write no more fiction.

While Hardy was moving closer to French naturalism, Moore took a decisive step in the opposite direction. Scornful of all English novelists, past and present, he particularly despised Hardy, asserting that the scenes of passion in *Tess* were feeble and evasive. In order to show how the subject ought to have been handled, he decided to write a novel with the same plot. For some years he had been planning a story about an illiterate servant girl, totally crude and stupid, after the manner of the Goncourts' *Germinie Lacerteux,* and he made elaborate clinical observations of the drudge in his lodgings; but his renunciation of naturalism now impelled him to assume a sympathetic attitude. *Esther Waters* (1894) shows how thoroughly he could adapt himself to a new manner. The settings are still drawn with meticulous accuracy — the scullery maid's work in a country mansion, the routines of managing a tavern, the anxious calculations of race-track touts — but now the atmosphere is genial and the characters are almost lovable.

Avoiding Hardy's sensationalism, Moore confines the action to normal, matter-of-fact behavior. Unlike *Adam Bede,* in which Hetty murdered her illegitimate baby, and *Tess,* in which it conveniently died, *Esther Waters* shows the mother's love and care for the child as the motive controlling her later actions. When she happens to meet her seducer, she returns to him simply because she likes him better than the respectable young man who wants to marry her. She helps him faithfully in his efforts to earn a living as innkeeper and horserace bookmaker, she nurses him in his lingering illness, and when he dies she goes placidly back to her original job in the scullery.

Moore was sardonically amused at the revulsion of feeling that was evoked by his "good" book. Gladstone praised it in print, and the circulating libraries grudgingly put it on their shelves. Moore believed that its exposure of brutal "baby farms" led to prosecution of this sordid business and to endowment of refuges for unwed mothers.

Moore is probably more important as a phenomenon than as a major novelist. It is unlikely that his fiction will ever again be widely read. But he was uniquely qualified to be the storm center in the destruction of the bourgeois monopoly in the novel. He was a natural antagonist to the smug English middle class on three counts. His origin in the Irish country gentry made him contemptuous of their social and financial circumspectness; his Roman Catholic training immunized him from their Protestant puritanism; and his French bohemianism gave him a supreme scorn for their lack of aesthetic taste. With these attributes he combined an exhibitionistic, aggressive temperament that he shared with his fellow-Irishmen, Wilde and Shaw. Meredith and James had widened the scope of fiction by probing the inner complexities of sophisticated characters in novels that demanded alert intelligence, and Hardy and Gissing had defied the taboos of refinement by telling distasteful truths about cruelty and poverty, both rural and urban; but it was Moore who gleefully touched off the dynamite by his blunt talk about sex. The measure of his achievement was the critical approval accorded to *Esther Waters* even though it treated sex relations with a nonchalance that would have evoked howls of protest a decade earlier. From this time onward, English fiction remained split into the two irreconcilable segments that Gissing had described through the words of Milvain: popular novels that gratify the Philistine hankering for entertainment, and cerebral novels that possess artistic integrity and serious concern for truth.

XVI

The Anatomy of Society

(1895 – 1915)

THE YEAR 1895 marks a decisive break in the continuity of English fiction. After publishing their final novels in that year, Meredith and Hardy devoted their remaining years to poetry, which had been their preferred medium from the outset, and in which they could embody their philosophical ideas about life without the trammels of story-telling. The established novelists who continued to write during the next decade underwent pronounced changes in method or material.

Henry James's "late manner" reached its full efflorescence in his final group of novels, *The Awkward Age, The Wings of the Dove, The Ambassadors,* and *The Golden Bowl,* between 1899 and 1904. The cult of stylistic refinement and psychological complexity, which restricted the cerebral novel to a select audience of disciplined admirers, attained its apogee in these books.

Moore went through a somewhat similar development. Embarrassed by the cordial reception of *Esther Waters,* he retreated into subtler analysis of cultivated characters in *Evelyn Innes*

425

(1898), dealing with a girl of musical talent. As Moore knew little about music, he gathered data from experts; and his desire to give an inclusive picture of the artistic world led him to include two of the current fads — mystical occultism, represented by a visionary Celtic poet modeled upon W. B. Yeats, and aesthetic hedonism, represented by an art-fancying baronet modeled upon Sir William Eden. The novel is written in the tone of elegant sophistication that had been brought into vogue by the newly launched quarterly, *The Yellow Book.* A synthetic quality in Moore's display of technical jargon and witty epigrams detracts from the real insight into character that underlies it.

The story of Evelyn Innes's career as a concert singer had been so much obscured by the other elements in the novel that Moore continued it in a sequel, *Sister Teresa* (1901), a more restrained study of personality. He comes closer to James's method as he reveals his heroine's dilemmas, her self-deceptions, and her reluctant acceptance of failure. When she enters a convent, Moore displays unexpected delicacy and humor in his picture of the naïve nuns.

This pair of novels is significant not only for the understanding of Evelyn's emotional conflicts, but also as marking Moore's final mastery of prose style. After conquering his early clumsiness he had employed a functional simplicity of manner in *Esther Waters;* but he spent three years in writing each of the books about Evelyn Innes in order to polish every phrase and enrich every cadence. His concern with style and form became obsessive as he grew older, and in later years he rewrote all his novels, radically changing not only the language but even important plot elements. In the final version of *Sister Teresa,* for instance, Evelyn ends by leaving the convent instead of finding spiritual peace there. The only new fiction that Moore wrote after 1901 moved so far in the direction of symbolism that it passes out of the strict category of the novel altogether. *The Lake* (1905) is still partly realistic in its story of an Irish priest who abandons his vocation upon realizing his sexual attraction toward a young schoolmistress of doubtful morals: but Moore insisted that the book should be regarded as "a sun myth." His late fiction, especially *The Brook Kerith,* is in the realm of allegory and poetic prose.

Gissing's transformation after 1895 was as decisive as Moore's. One reason was the elimination of the three-volume novel. Freed from the tyranny of prolix description and intricate plots, he was able to write with compact vigor. He celebrated his emancipation by publishing three short novels in 1895, and — even more astonishing — one of them was sheer comedy. Entitled *The Paying Guest*, it is a farcical account of how an irrepressible young woman boarder disrupts a decorous family. *Sleeping Fires* and *Eve's Ransom* are serious studies of motive, but the terse style redeems them from Gissing's former turgidity. *The Whirlpool* (1897) is a more ambitious novel, and one of his best, with firm structure, sustained irony, and a wide range of social observation. His heroine, like Moore's Evelyn Innes, strives for a career in music, but finds her talent inadequate and her love life devastated. Instead of entering a nunnery, she commits suicide.

At this juncture Gissing ended his domestic misery by separating from his intolerable wife, and soon afterwards he formed a liaison with an intelligent French girl who admired his books. For his remaining five years he lived with her and her mother, chiefly in France, and enjoyed good food and tranquility for the first time in his adult life. Though he wrote several more novels, the only book of any consequence produced in this serene atmosphere was not fiction but a mellow volume of scholarly reflections, *The Private Papers of Henry Ryecroft*. When he died of consumption at forty-six he was in the midst of the book he had always wanted to write, *Veranilda*, a historical novel about the fall of Rome.

While naturalism was evaporating from the work of Moore and Gissing, the problem novel also was losing momentum. After 1900 Mrs. Humphry Ward shifted from earnest ethical debates to the depiction of high society, and converted well-known historical scandals into fiction with a modern setting. Thus Chateaubriand's affair with Mme. de Beaumont became *Eleanor* (1900), Mme. du Deffand's rivalry with Julie de Lespinasse became *Lady Rose's Daughter* (1903), Byron's involvement with William and Caroline Lamb became *The Marriage of William Ashe* (1905), and Lady Hamilton's enchantment of the painter Romney became *Fenwick's Career* (1906). Only in 1911, with *The Case of Richard Meynell*, did Mrs. Ward revert to her original theme; in this book she depicts Robert Elsmere's son-in-law remaining in the church as a modernist. The leading place in popular favor was still firmly held by Stevensonian romance. Stevenson died in Samoa in the last month of 1894, but his disciples continued to produce their profitable commodity with machine-like precision. The chief new recruit to their ranks was Anthony Hope, who exploited the theme of *Harry Richmond* and *Prince Otto* to its utmost popular appeal in *The Prisoner of Zenda* (1894).

Another offshoot of Stevenson was a revival of the tale of horror, which was enjoying a new prestige in France in the poetry and fiction of the Symbolist school. *Dr. Jekyll and Mr. Hyde* had proved that modern readers can still enjoy being terrified so long as some illusion of reality is sustained. The current vogue of Theosophy, spiritualism, and kindred cults was exploited by Marie Corelli (real name, Minnie Mackay), a pathologically conceited woman who wrote in a flamboyant style that outdistanced the wildest excesses of Ouida. In *A Romance of Two Worlds* (1887) she offered a theory of "The Electric Origin of the Universe" through an occultist hero claiming descent from the Magi. Her subsequent books were accepted as philosophical revelations by a vast semi-literate public, and are said to have held the interest of Queen Victoria, Gladstone, Tennyson, and Oscar Wilde. An immense popular triumph was achieved by Bram Stoker's *Dracula* (1897), a vampire story rendered plausible by documentary devices imitated from Collins.

On a superior level of literary art was Oscar Wilde's novel, *The Picture of Dorian Gray* (1890), which used the *Jekyll and Hyde* formula for an allegory of moral degeneration. The most remarkable writer of plausible fantasy, however, was George du Maurier. Half French by parentage, he spent his early years in Paris, and became a leading black-and-white artist, both as an illustrator of novels and as a mellow satirist of English society in *Punch*. In 1892, when he was near sixty, he published *Peter Ibbetson*, which combined a charming picture of a boyhood in France with a fantasy about a pair of lovers who share the same dreams. He won international fame two years later with *Trilby*, using the same formula of establishing verisimilitude by autobiographical material (in this case, his art-student days in Montmartre) and then introducing a para-psychological theme, when the beautiful, tone-deaf model is transformed into a prima donna by the hypnotic power of Svengali. Du Maurier's third and last novel, *The Martian*, was more improbable in its attempt to depict telepathic communication with a denizen of another planet, but it too has much originality and charm. An admirer of Thackeray, du Maurier adopted his conversational, discursive style.

An utterly different manifestation of Stevenson's influence was a group of Scottish local-color writers that came to be called "The Kailyard School." This term was derived from one of the successful books in the genre, *Beside the Bonnie Brier Bush* (1894), a collection of fictional sketches by a Presbyterian minister, Dr. John Watson, who used the pseudonym "Ian Maclaren." The title of his book came from one of Burns's songs:

> There grows a bonnie brier bush in oor kailyard.

A kailyard is a cabbage patch, and the phrase "Kailyard School" therefore connotes the quainter aspects of humble village life. The tradition of Scottish folk-scenes in fiction originated in Galt's *Annals of the Parish* and continued through the novels of George MacDonald, with a pictorial counterpart in the paintings of David Wilkie. It could easily have developed into drab portrayal of poverty and Calvinistic narrowness, a northern equivalent of Hardy's Wessex; and Stevenson indeed provides a few glimpses of the grim side of Scottish peasant life. But in general he cast his charming glamour over his native country, and it was transmitted to the Kailyard writers through one of his most ardent devotees, James Matthew Barrie.

Barrie was the son of a handloom weaver in the village of Kirriemuir, but with the Scottish passion for education his family was able to find enough money to see him through Edinburgh University. When he went to London to work as a journalist he soon began to write fiction. His first book, *Better Dead* (1887), was a mediocre imitation of Stevenson's "Suicide Club," and his next, *When a Man's Single*, attempted to weave a romance out of his experiences in journalism. His success began when he turned his nostalgic recollections of his home village into fictional sketches, *Auld Licht Idylls* and *A Window in Thrums*. Many modern readers are embarrassed by the sentimental portrayal of his uncomplaining mother as Jess in the latter book, but the combination of broad dialect and whimsical humor proved irresistibly attractive to a wide public. He used the same setting for a full-fledged romantic novel, *The Little Minister*, in 1891, with the delightful if improbable theme of a love affair between a solemn, inhibited cleric and a wayward gypsy lass who turns out to be a fashionable young lady in disguise. Stevenson's technique of the onlooker-narrator is ingeniously handled, the story being told by the village schoolmaster, who is concealing the secret that he is the little minister's real father; and there are undeveloped psychological implications in the minister's attitude toward his overpossessive mother.

Barrie's fame set the pattern for the whole Kailyard school, in which the oddities of village character are displayed with drollery and affection that partly disguise the undertone of moralizing. His books and Ian Maclaren's, however, are usually composed of loosely linked sketches that do not coalesce into a novel. Apart from *The Little Minister*, Barrie's only novels are *Sentimental Tommy* (1896) and its sequel, *Tommy and Grizel*. Here he made a desperate effort to achieve psychological realism, using an amalgam of his own character and Stevenson's to create Tommy Sandys, who is gifted with creative genius but who lives so vividly in the world of his imagination that he cannot adjust himself to reality. The first volume, dealing with Tommy's boyhood, contains some of Barrie's best humor and insight, and the second one builds up a strong contrast between Tommy's emotional instability and the quiet fortitude of the girl who loves him. Barrie admired Meredith as warmly as Stevenson, and the evils of sentimentalism are castigated in this pair of stories with all Meredith's vindictiveness. Yet with a touch of self-analysis Barrie recognized that this was his own besetting vice, and the paradoxical outcome is a sentimental exposure of a sentimentalist. The unexpected violence of the last scene, when Tommy is accidentally hanged by his overcoat, suggests by its ambiguous mixture of grotesque absurdity and Hardian ironic chance that Barrie was trying to symbolize the destructive contradictions in his own nature.

His greatest fame was still to come, but it was not in the novel. When *The Little Minister* was dramatized its success on the stage turned him to playwriting, and his subsequent career was divided between plays and stories for children. In *Peter Pan* the theme of *Sentimental Tommy* — the boy who cannot grow up — received more satisfactory expression in pure fantasy than had been possible in the guise of realism.

It is significant that the three most gifted in this generation of romantic authors — Stevenson, Kipling, and Barrie — wrote so few novels and achieved such imperfect success, as contrasted with their mastery of short stories, juvenile tales, or plays. They provide the final negative proof that the main stream of the novel has always been essentially realistic.

This fact is relevant to the consideration of an important new author who appeared upon the scene in 1895, and who seems hard to classify because he wrote about exotic settings and perilous adventures that would be appropriate for Kipling, and yet he was a faithful adherent of Henry James. The explanation is that for Joseph Conrad the Malayan islands and the hardy life of seamen were not fascinating because they fulfilled daydreams that were beyond his actual scope; on the contrary, they had been the everyday reality of his life for so many years that they were as familiar to him as a London drawing room was to James or a Dorsetshire village to Hardy. And yet an underlying hint of the romantic idealization still lingered, because Conrad had originally been drawn to elect the seafaring life by a strange enchantment that overcame all commonsense obstacles.

Teodor Jozef Konrad Korzeniowski was born in southeastern Poland, the most landlocked region of Europe. His parents were of the landowning class, his father being an amateur author who translated works of Shakespeare and Hugo into Polish. Accused of conspiring against the Russian government that ruled their country, the family was banished to a town in the heart of Russia when the little boy was five years old. His mother died in exile; Joseph spent several years in reading omnivorously and nursing his ailing father, thus acquiring a melancholy outlook and a susceptibility to nervous disorders. When his father was allowed to return to Poland to die, the boy was orphaned before his twelfth birthday. He attended school in Cracow; but his imagination had been inflamed by reading translations of Marryat and Fenimore Cooper, and he determined to be a sailor. Having learned fluent French, but no English, he went to Marseilles when he was seventeen and made voyages in French trading ships, including two to the Caribbean, on one of which he took part in the secret delivery of munitions for a Central American revolution. This led him into a more extensive venture of smuggling weapons for the Carlist insurrection in Spain, and during the same time he had a love affair with a seductive and mysterious woman in Marseilles.

The simultaneous collapse of his gun-running and his love-making (including a wound in a duel with an American rival) impelled him to leave France for England, where, at the age of twenty, and knowing no more than a few words of the language, he shipped before the mast on a coastwise vessel. "My first English reading," he said subsequently, "was the *Standard* newspaper; and my first acquaintance by the ear with it was in the speech of fishermen, shipwrights, and sailors of the East Coast. . . . I've never opened an English grammar in my life." Nevertheless, two years later he was able to pass the first examination for officers of the merchant service, and became third mate of a clipper ship on the Australia run. Within another six years he had his captain's papers and his British citizenship.

The world-wide range of British shipping kept him mainly in remote areas — the China Sea, the Indian Ocean, the Malay Archipelago. The normal isolation of a captain from his crew was intensified by his alien distinction of manner and his literary interests; he spent countless hours in his cabin reading French and English books; and after he picked up a tropical fever during a trip up the Congo into the mysterious heart of Africa, he worked intermittently on a novel, which occupied him for five years. When declining health forced him ashore, he submitted the manuscript to a publisher.

Almayer's Folly was derived from the personality of a Dutch planter in Indonesia, even the name being changed only slightly from its original form. Conrad's observation of the scene and the characters, white and native alike, had been acute and yet fragmentary, since he saw them in a series of glimpses as his ship came and went; his sensitive and imaginative mind expanded these impressions into a work of art that was not encumbered with too much factual detail.

A second novel, *An Outcast of the Islands*, also dealt with the degeneration of a white man in the tropical solitude of

Borneo. Then Conrad turned to the subject that he knew best, the life of a crew on a sailing ship, and produced one of his most powerful books, *The Nigger of the "Narcissus."* There is virtually no plot or action; it is purely a psychological study of a voyage home from Bombay, during which a dying Negro tyrannizes over his shipmates. Conrad gives realistic details of life in the fo'c'sle and describes the moods of the sea with poetic power; but these elements are overshadowed by the superstitions of the sailors and the sense of doom as Wait gradually weakens, until the total effect becomes a sort of allegory of death.

Conrad knew by this time that he would never be well enough to return to the sea. He settled in a secluded village in Kent and applied himself to writing for a living. Though his mind was full of vivid recollections from his nomadic career, the task of putting them into words was excruciatingly difficult. He thought first in Polish, then translated mentally into French, and thus arrived at the English words he needed. Patient revision was required for polishing every sentence to the precision and melody that his taste demanded. It is amazing that there are so few traces of foreign idiom: the intangible sense of strangeness comes rather from the fact that his prose is consistently more perfect than is customary in fiction in English.

From his early reading in picturesque and sensational fiction — Scott, Dickens, Hugo, even Miss Braddon — he had absorbed the habit of heightening the emotional effect of his stories by atmospheric description. With maturity he had transferred his devotion to the French realists, especially Flaubert and Maupassant. His primary concern, however, was not in creating the illusion of external reality so much as in examining the inner complexities of character. His advice to a novice writer was, "Try and make it a novel of *analysis* on the basis of some strong situation."

This analytical subtlety accounts for the slow growth of Conrad's reputation. The settings of his novels aroused expectation of stirring action, and so readers were nonplussed by the meticulous dissection of mental states. Strict realists, on the other hand, were deterred by the poetic overtones and the implications of symbolism. Only a small band of perceptive critics recognized him as an artist of major rank.

A totally different reception was accorded to another author whose first book also came out in 1895. Herbert George Wells was nine years junior to Conrad, and was as essentially English as the older man was alien. His parentage was like Dickens's, not only in social status but in financial incompetence. His father, originally a gardener, found seasonal employment as a professional cricket player, but was constantly in debt with his china-and-glassware shop; when an injury put an end to his cricketing, Mrs. Wells became housekeeper to a rich lady by whom she had been employed as a maid before her marriage, and young Bertie, at thirteen, was apprenticed to a draper.

Thus, like Dickens, he acquired both a sympathetic intimacy with shabby poverty and a burning determination to escape from it. His escape route, however, was not through journalism but through the newer channel of science. When he was sixteen he rebelled against the intolerable dullness of the drapery business and found employment as assistant master in a local school, where he had an opportunity to take science courses in the evening under an extension program. Within a year he won a scholarship at the Normal College of Science in London.

As a student of biology under Huxley and of astronomy under Norman Lockyer, he became an evangelist of scientific progress; and as a leader in the debating society he picked up radical political ideas. He founded and edited a college magazine, for which he wrote copiously. While earning a B.Sc. degree at London University he spent several years as a teacher in private schools, published a two-volume textbook on biology, and collaborated in one on physiology. Illness, however, forced him to give up teaching, and at the age of twenty-eight, inspired by reading Barrie's novel about journalism, *When a Man's Single*, he began to earn his living with stories and articles in magazines. In 1895 he published no fewer than four books. One was a collection of satirical essays, but the other three were in a genre almost new to English literature — scientific fantasy.

His predecessor obviously was Jules Verne, a Frenchman who had won world-wide fame with a series of exciting adventure-stories about future inventions, beginning with *Five Weeks in a Balloon* (1862). Wells, however, as a trained scientist, was able to make his stories more ingenious and convincing, while his active social consciousness rendered him aware of the implications for human welfare or misery in researches that as yet were little known outside of the laboratories.

His first book of fiction, *The Time Machine*, describes a contrivance based on the theory that time is the fourth dimension. Investigators are carried forward to the year 802,701, when the process of natural selection has produced such perfect adaptation to environment that the human race has separated into two species, a hypercivilized type descended from the leisure class, and a bestial type, descended from the workers, who live underground and eat the elegant, ineffectual "Eloi." Traveling a million years further into the future the explorers find evolution in its final reversal, with giant crustaceans as the highest form of life. Immediately after this book came *The Wonderful Visit*, in which an angel is shot down by an ornithological parson and is puzzled by "the littleness, the narrow horizons, of ordinary people's lives." The final book of that year, *The Stolen Bacillus*, is a collection of short stories.

Next year came *The Island of Dr. Moreau*, a gruesome story of a surgeon who operates on dogs and pigs and transforms them into human beings. Wells then departed for the first time from scientific fantasy in *The Wheels of Chance*, a farcical, episodic yarn about a draper's assistant on his summer vacation, interesting both for its autobiographical glimpses and for its portrayal of a meek character who dramatizes himself in daydreams. *The Invisible Man* (1897) returns to science with a psychological study of a physicist who discovers the secret of invisibility. *The War of the Worlds*, probably the most gripping of this series, describes an invasion by space-ships from Mars, with a tremendous eyewitness report of the evacuation of London. *When the Sleeper Wakes* (1899) uses the Rip Van Winkle theme for a forecast of the world two hundred years in the future, a time of mechanized efficiency and political dictatorship, when capital and labor fight a war to the death with airplanes.

These early works of Wells are in the category of Stevensonian romance. The imaginative escape into the future is equivalent to Kipling's and Haggard's excursions into Asia and Africa and the historical novelists' idealizing of the past. The intensity of suspense and the solving of scientific riddles resemble the Sherlock Holmes stories. There is an element of terror, notably

in *The Island of Dr. Moreau,* that harks back to the Gothic romances, recalling the Rosicrucian stories, *Frankenstein,* and Bulwer-Lytton's experiments with the supernatural. Wells's
stories appealed particularly to men and boys, by the combination of exciting adventure with technological detail. Coming
at a time when education was spreading rapidly and scientific research was invading the newspapers, his books had an
incalculable influence by casting an imaginative glamour over
the new knowledge, just as Haggard and Kipling were enthralling other youths with the vision of imperialism.

Wells's prodigious output and cocksure assertiveness were
soon rivaled by Arnold Bennett, who was eight months younger
and who came from somewhat higher social origins, his father
being a solicitor in the Staffordshire pottery town of Hanley,
the same that Moore had selected for *A Mummer's Wife* as the
ugliest town in England. But whereas Wells began his work in
fiction with romantic fantasy, Bennett set out to be an unsparing
realist.

His education was strictly practical, and his reading of fiction
seems to have been confined to the sensational tales of Ouida.
After leaving school he spent several years in law offices, first
under his father and then in London; but while still in the "Five
Towns" he had contributed to a local newspaper, and at the age
of twenty-five he began to write profusely for London periodicals. He applied himself to remedying the deficiencies of his
education by reading Jane Austen and especially the Continental
realists, Turgeniev, the Goncourts, Maupassant. He gave up
his clerkship to become sub-editor of a women's magazine,
and in 1896 was promoted to the editor's chair. In the same
year he wrote his first novel, though it was not published until
two years later.

A Man from the North is largely autobiographical, telling
about an ambitious young fellow who invades London with the
determination of becoming a great author, only to "arrive ultimately at disillusion and a desolating suburban domesticity."
The meticulously careful style and the insistent note of disenchantment show Bennett's subservience to Flaubert. As soon
as he finished writing this novel he started another; but its
completion was delayed for six years while he earned money
with book reviewing, theatrical criticism, playwriting, and a

practical handbook on *Journalism for Women*. This miscellaneous work endowed him with fluency and keen observation of detail.

In 1898, the year of *A Man from the North*, another first novel appeared and attracted just as little attention. This was entitled *Jocelyn;* and the author, who had previously issued a volume of short stories, *From the Four Winds*, lurked modestly behind the pen name of "John Sinjohn." John Galsworthy was within three months of Bennett in age, and also was the son of an attorney; but here the resemblance ended. The Galsworthys were of Devonshire yeoman stock, but the future novelist's grandfather had migrated to London, where the family prospered financially and socially. The young John received the exclusive education of Harrow and Oxford, but distinguished himself only in athletics. He was called to the bar when he was twenty-three, though with little intention of practicing the profession, since he had sufficient income for a life of elegant leisure. Apparently he was a typical representative of the upper-middle class — handsome, well dressed, formally restrained in manner. His literary taste seemed to be confined to the fox-hunting, horse-racing novels of Whyte-Melville. One person, however, the handsome and sensitive young wife of a cousin, felt convinced that he possessed innate talents; and after he had frittered away three or four years in world travel and social pastimes, she told him firmly that he ought to become a writer.

The short stories in Galsworthy's first volume were inept imitations of Kipling; the brief novel *Jocelyn* shows him attempting something like James's analysis of motives. Encouraged by his friend Conrad (whom he had met during one of his long voyages, while Conrad was still a ship's officer) he then read Turgeniev and Maupassant, who revealed to him that fiction could be a rigorous art, with shapeliness and economy. His second novel, *Villa Rubein* (1900), showed these new influences in its improved proportion and atmosphere.

His deepening perceptiveness was not due solely to study of superior models. From his cousin Ada he received more than literary counsel. Her marriage was loveless, and John Galsworthy's sympathy for her unhappiness developed into devoted love. The situation was a hopeless impasse, for not only did the *mores* of their social group oppose divorce, but since the only legal ground for it was adultery, any move to seek one would have precipitated a scandal exposing their families to humiliation. They resigned themselves to a wretched existence of clandestine meetings. Hence his first two novels both deal with frustrated love affairs: in *Jocelyn*, a girl is in love with a married man, whose wife commits suicide; in *Villa Rubein* a wealthy family refuses to accept an improvident painter as suitor for their daughter.

Another new novelist appearing at this juncture was William Somerset Maugham, whose first book came out in 1897 when he was only twenty-three. His background was much like Galsworthy's; but instead of portraying his own comfortable bourgeois class he drew upon his impressions while a medical interne at St. Thomas's Hospital to describe London slumdwellers in the tradition of Gissing. Several other authors, notably Israel Zangwill (*The Children of the Ghetto*, 1892) and Arthur Morrison (*A Child of the Jago*, 1896), were writing realistically about what Morrison termed "mean streets"; but Maugham's *Liza of Lambeth* was closer to the naturalistic tradition, since his clinical training equipped him with the impassive precision that had been claimed by Zola. He proceeded immediately to write a long novel which displayed his own early life with a few changes of details; but it proved so unsatisfactory that it remained unpublished when he turned to lighter fiction and plays.

The whole brigade of competent new novelists were reaching their full powers as the twentieth century dawned. In 1900 Conrad's *Lord Jim* established his characteristic subject matter and method. It deals with a young ship's officer who fails in his duty in a moment of panic the first time he encounters a crisis, and then spends years in regaining his self-respect in obscurity among Malayan natives until at last he redeems himself by facing death unflinchingly. The story combines the Far Eastern life depicted in Conrad's first two novels with the accurate shipboard atmosphere of *The Nigger of the "Narcissus."* The last section, however, reverses his original theme: instead of degenerating in a primitive tropical village, this European achieves integrity there.

The structure is open to objection: the break in the middle is too drastic, and the later part is less powerful than the beginning. An illusion of both unity and plausibility, however, is supplied by skillful use of the Stevensonian onlooker point of view. The narrative is told mainly by a philosophical-minded officer named Marlow with an active curiosity about other people's character and motives. In a sense this diminishes plausibility, for the precise diction and elaborate sentences, to say nothing of the length of the story, are not consistent with the supposed oral discourse of a nonliterary sailor. This doubt, however, must be weighed against the reader's increased sense of participation, as the facts are gradually pieced together, with many departures from strict time sequence. Jim is first seen as a mysterious figure holding inferior jobs in Bombay, Calcutta, and Penang, and disappearing from each for no apparent reason. When Marlow discovers that Jim always fled to evade contact with anyone who knew about his disgrace, he digs out the evidence about the disaster to the pilgrim ship *Patna* and the desertion of its officers. Jim's final years among the Malays are then reconstructed.

As well as disregarding chronological order, this method has the unusual effect of keeping the central figure at a remote distance. Marlow can only guess at Jim's inner compulsions and conflicts; and yet somehow the fragmentary evidence adds up to a convincing picture of a distraught man who wins our respect as he attains self-mastery.

Conrad's impressionistic method was particularly well suited to work in the intermediate category, longer than short stories and briefer than novels. Three of his best achievements are in this form: "Typhoon" reproduces in words the exact sensations of a seaman in a hurricane, "Youth" records the reactions of a novice sailor when he first visits Asia, and "Heart of Darkness" conveys the brooding atmosphere of terror that Conrad felt during his voyage up the Congo. The two last-named are narrated by Marlow, who thus emerges more distinctly as Conrad's *alter ego*, a quiet bystander whose faintly cynical tone fails to disguise his sympathy for the absurd yet tragic dilemmas of human beings when their idealistic impulses collide with the stubborn realities of existence.

At this time, too, Conrad wrote three novels in collaboration with a younger and more self-confident author, Ford Madox Hueffer, an experience that gave him a wider technical range. He then produced his longest and most ambitious book, *Nos-*

tromo (1904). As usual, it was based on personal recollection, but this time he went back thirty years to his first days at sea. During his gun-running escapade he heard a tale about the theft of a boatload of silver bullion; and at the same time he stored up impressions of the Caribbean coast of Central America. Thus provided with the climax and the setting for his novel, Conrad borrowed his main character from the same epoch: "Nostromo," the tough, venturesome cargadore, is a portrait of a Corsican first mate who initiated the neophyte into sea life on his first long voyage. The heroine of the story was based upon a girl for whom Conrad had felt an adolescent passion before leaving Poland.

These materials were expanded into a magnificent panorama. Conrad created a full geography and history for his fictitious republic of Costaguena. Its local intrigues and revolutions, and its involvement with international finance through an English mining company, are displayed by means of a huge cast of characters, Latinos ranging in rank from generals to peons, and aliens from the efficient mine manager to the questionable French adventurer Decoud. Isolated between the mountains and the sea, these people face a variety of moral crises and spiritual ordeals. Once again Conrad, the exile from his homeland, is studying the psychology of displaced persons who have to rely on their own inner fortitude. The book becomes a microcosm of modern civilization with its inextricable mixture of idealism and brutality, of noble gestures and base expedients. The wide scope does not make for easy reading; but the total effect is a memorable fable of man's struggle to maintain his human identity against the blank indifference of nature.

The new century witnessed the artistic maturing of H. G. Wells also. The comic portrayal of a shabby-genteel youth, which had figured in his slight tale, *The Wheels of Chance*, was resumed in *Love and Mr. Lewisham* (1900). This time it was Wells's years of schoolteaching that provided the material for the absurd yet appealing story. The theme is like that in Bennett's *Man from the North*, for Lewisham gives up his pretentious ambitions for fame in science and leadership in social reform, to take on dull family responsibilities; but instead of Bennett's solemn Flaubertian mood, Wells writes in the hearty humorous vein of Dickens. After publishing two more of his scientific romances (*The First Men in the Moon* and *The Food of the Gods*) and one symbolic fantasy (*The Sea Lady*), he returned to autobiographic comedy in *Kipps* (1905), again with a draper's assistant as hero. This time the young man suddenly acquires wealth and is faced with the problem of adjusting himself to a higher social sphere, where he gets into such ludicrous plights that he is glad to revert to his former shabby obscurity.

Though *Kipps* established Wells in the central tradition of the English novel, and though by this time he was friendly with James, Conrad, Bennett, and Hueffer, all advocates of artistic technique in fiction, he had no patience with "a petty word-mongering"; and except for *Love and Mr. Lewisham*, his novels were not carefully planned in advance. His fecund inventiveness and opinionated digressions rendered him heedless of sound structure and immaculate style. On the other hand, while he was equally friendly with Gissing, and *Kipps* deals with Gissing's urban shopkeeping milieu, Wells's superabundant vitality and his affection for his characters produce an effect utterly unlike the older author's low-spirited passivity.

Meanwhile Bennett brought out his second novel, *Anna of the Five Towns*, in 1902. As the title indicates, it is set in the ganglion of industrial communities in which he had grown up, and thus he came to be considered as the first English regional novelist not associated with a rural area. A somber picture of a girl's slow revolt against a miserly father, in an atmosphere of strict Methodist revivalism, and her sacrifice of love in favor of a prosperous husband, it depicts the pottery business with photographic accuracy.

Bennett, however, was frankly interested in making money and acquiring the luxuries that it could buy; and he found out that grim realism appealed to a very limited readership. He turned to humorous melodrama with *The Grand Babylon Hotel*, a lively story of international intrigue set in the resplendent surroundings of a luxury hotel (still the influence of *New Arabian Nights*). This was followed by *The Gates of Wrath* and other literate thrillers, which he could toss off in a few weeks each.

What is perhaps the most important novel of the decade appeared in 1903, but it was not by any of the generation of writers who were coming into their fame; instead, it was the work of an author who had recently died and who was old enough to be their father. Indeed, *The Way of All Flesh* had been written long before (1872–84), but Samuel Butler withheld it from publication in his lifetime because it dealt so intimately and so scathingly with his own family and upbringing.

Butler was one of the most original and belligerent thinkers of the nineteenth century. The son of a canon and grandson of a bishop, he was destined for the clergy, but soon after leaving Cambridge he developed religious doubts and decided that he wanted to be a painter. From 1859 to 1864 he was a sheep-farmer in New Zealand, where he proved so unexpectedly competent that he doubled the investment he had borrowed from his father, and was able to go home to England with enough capital to have an adequate income. A confirmed bachelor, he occupied rooms in the heart of London and divided his time between painting pictures, composing music, and writing books.

He first attracted attention in 1872 with *Erewhon, or Over the Range,* a work of semi-fiction that cannot be counted as a novel, since plot and characterization are subordinated to a satire upon modern civilization in the guise of a visit to an innocent Utopia in the New Zealand wilderness. Except for a sequel to *Erewhon,* Butler published no other fictitious narrative during the remaining thirty years of his life, but issued a series of learned and pugnacious books, most of which he financed himself, on such diverse subjects as the miracles of Jesus, Shakespeare's sonnets, Italian scenery, the theory of evolution (he believed that development was determined by unconscious memory and not by natural selection), and the authorship of the Homeric poems (he believed that the *Odyssey* was written by Nausicaä).

As might be expected, the sole novel by this eccentric author is as unorthodox as his other work. At a time when serious novelists were accepting James's condemnation of the omniscient author, Butler's book was dominated by his opinions and prejudices. When other novelists were attentive to form and structure, Butler's book sprawled over several generations and suffered a major fracture halfway through. When other novelists were depending upon accumulation of detail and imitation of colloquial speech to produce the illusion of reality, Butler often contented himself with bald summary of both scene and conversation. Nevertheless, *The Way of All Flesh* exerted a tremendous influence upon most of these more skillful technicians.

Though the book belonged to the old-fashioned genre of *David Copperfield* and *Pendennis* — a *Bildungsroman* based upon the author's own experience — Butler was anything but traditional in his attitude toward his material. He began writing the story almost a decade before the angry young rebels, Gissing and Moore, launched their campaign to make English fiction tell the truth about human behavior. But whereas their method was to outrage respectable readers with accounts of gross sensuality and sordid poverty, Butler carried the assault into the citadel of entrenched respectability by insisting that the self-righteous Philistines were themselves cruel, greedy, stupid, and hypocritical, and, above all, that the most cherished stronghold of Victorian morality — the family — was a machine of sadistic tyranny that perpetuated these evils from one generation to the next. As a scientific rationalist, Butler subjected the sentimental sanctions of the home and parental love and filial duty to a chilly anthropological scrutiny; and as an evolutionist he traced the ancestry of his central character to show how the dominant patterns of conduct emerged. The demolition of domestic harmony was all the more thorough by being reinforced by Butler's antipathy to Christian faith in general and the Church of England in particular. His vengeful sense of outrage prevented his book from being an impartial array of evidence and gave it a demonic energy that no reader could ignore.

In a strict sense he cannot be accused of auctorial commentary, for the story is told by an onlooker-narrator; but this fictitious character is obviously the author's mouthpiece. By an ingenious device, Butler divided his own personality into two segments. His youthful self is Ernest Pontifex, a meek, idealistic boy who finally achieves freedom from his oppressive family; but his mature self, at the age when he wrote the book, is Ernest's godfather and confidant, Mr. Overton, a worldly-wise author who builds the story out of family letters and interviews as well as recounting scenes he actually witnessed. Overton's attitude of aloof amusement and his indulgence in sarcasm and mocking understatement give the book its flavor. As in *Ere-whon*, the narrator's ostensible approval of contemporary habits and moral standards startles the reader into recognizing their inherent evils, somewhat as in the writings of Swift.

Because Butler's theory of evolution followed Lamarck rather than Darwin, his novel is of the realistic and not of the natural-istic school. Instead of being a helpless victim of heredity and environment, the apparently passive Ernest has latent will power that rescues him when he seems to be confronted with disaster. Some readers object to this transformation in his character which enables him to make a rational adjustment to life after years of inertia; but Butler's defense would be that this was what happened to himself. Ernest's career is identical with Butler's own, up to the middle of the story; but there it diverges abruptly. The turning point in Ernest's life is not emigration to a colony but sentence to a term in prison; and his subsequent business venture as an old-clothes dealer, and his marriage to a drunken ex-prostitute, have no parallel in Butler's life, but read like a parody of Gissing's most sordid episodes, with the difference that Ernest is released when his wife's husband turns up, and is thus able to settle down as a complacent bachelor. Butler's only actual emotional involve-ment was with a fellow-painter, Elizabeth Savage, an intelligent but crippled woman, to whose devotion he did not warmly respond. In the novel she figures as Ernest's Aunt Alethea, to whom Overton maintains a gentle Platonic attachment.

The younger novelists, who had been inching toward open flouting of Victorian taboos and rituals, were enraptured by this sardonic testimony from inside the sanctum. Butler helped them to realize the value of examining character in the context of family traits and social pressures. Galsworthy, in particular, who was also a rebel within the pale of social orthodoxy, began to speak out more clearly; even the title of his next novel, *The Island Pharisees* (1904), proclaims his indictment of English smugness. Though he rewrote it twice, it remained an awkward and colorless story, with virtually no action and too much didac-tic analysis of the caste system.

Soon after this book was published, the nine years' torture of Galsworthy's love affair culminated: his father's death ab-solved him from what he regarded as his imperative duty to the feelings of his family, and so he and Ada took the overt steps that led to her divorce, after which they were married. The emotional release produced a maturing of his literary power. His next novel dealt with a situation virtually identical with his own, and he handled it with a blend of pity, tolerance, and social awareness. One dominant force in the problem having been the solidarity of the family unit, he began by creating a large, firmly knit family modeled upon his own. Several years previously he had published a short story, "The Salvation of a Forsyte," and from it he developed the Forsyte clan, all of whom are strongly individual and yet are marked both physically and temperamentally with identical traits.

The rise of this family had been due to hardheaded business enterprise; therefore their standards were all identified with material possessions, a fact that Galsworthy emphasized by naming his book *The Man of Property*. Not only the particular instance, but the whole moral and emotional impasse between the sexes, in his view, centered in the legal and social axiom that women were chattels under the absolute control of their husbands. Soames Forsyte regards his pretty wife merely as the most conspicuous among the evidences of his prosperity. The structure of the novel ironically illustrates the theme: Soames decides to build a handsome house to signalize his increasing wealth, and thus his wife encounters an unconventional young architect who becomes her lover. Galsworthy, like Meredith, was determined to make his readers face the full enormity of this domestic tyranny; and the feelings of many were outraged by the climactic scene when, after the lover's death in a traffic accident, Soames grimly reasserts his marital rights. Most readers found that their conventional moral criteria were brought into painful conflict with their emotional sympathies.

Nevertheless, Galsworthy was too honest to present the story in melodramatic terms of good and evil. Bosinney, the lover, though he is the surrogate of the author, is not idealized as a chivalric rescuer of an imprisoned lady. Soames is allowed to feel inarticulate love for his wife, though it is dominated by his worldly principles. And Irene never usurps too much admiration as the victimized wife, for the simple reason that her inner reactions are not revealed at all. The villain of the story is no single person, nor is it the blind cruelty of chance, as in

Hardy; rather it is the stupid pressure of social environment, embodied in the whole self-satisfied, respectable, and often richly comic tribe of the Forsytes.

The publication of *The Man of Property* in 1906 brought Galsworthy his first fame. He followed it promptly with other novels analyzing various upper levels of English society. *The Country House* deals with the landed gentry, whose traditional rules of behavior are as inhibiting as the financial practicality and bourgeois propriety of the Forsytes. Reversing the situation of the previous book, this one tells of a husband who carries on an affair with a disreputable woman and is then taken back by his wife, who still loves him. *Fraternity*, centering upon the literary intelligentsia, again concerns a temporary infidelity: this time the husband deserts his home in favor of a pretty model, through whose love he might have achieved artistic fulfillment; but he abandons her because her lack of refinement jars upon his fastidious sensibility. The title is sarcastic, for the story insists that the idea of any real understanding between upper and lower classes is fantastically visionary. The last novel of this group, *The Patrician* (1911), turns to the aristocracy and presents the parallel dilemmas of a young nobleman and his sister: he falls in love with a clergyman's wife, and cannot decide whether to sacrifice his public career by incurring a scandal; the sister relinquishes a suitor who is a radical agitator, and accepts without love a socially suitable husband.

In this series of novels, as in his plays, which were even more successful during the same years, Galsworthy wrote, as befitted his subject matter, with urbane and mildly ironic realism. But under the calm, gentlemanly surface it is easy to perceive his almost unendurable pity for the people who are caught in the trap of rigid conventions, and his hopelessness as to any solution. As he saw it, the cultivated classes of England were doomed to sterile unhappiness by their tradition-bound and materialistic principles. None of his books has a dramatically tragic ending, but all are as depressing as Gissing's in their depiction of normal emotions thwarted by social environment.

Arnold Bennett had continued intermittently with serious novels of social purpose. Between 1903 and 1908 he published half-a-dozen stories in his vein of quick-moving melodrama and two sheer farces, the second of which, *Buried Alive*, has a perennial appeal through its theme of a famous painter's escape from his identity; the corpse of his valet, mistaken for his, receives a state funeral while the artist finds happiness and a good-humored wife in lower-middle-class obscurity. The three serious novels of these years, interspersed among the comic and sensational tales, resemble Galsworthy's in dealing with extramarital love affairs. In *Leonora* the sensitive wife of a rich but unscrupulous businessman falls in love at the age of forty with one of his competitors, but is constrained by her responsibility to her selfish daughters, and is rewarded with her admirer's hand after her husband commits suicide. *Sacred and Profane Love* is the self-told story of a sensual girl whose reading of erotic literature encourages her to become promiscuous in sex relations. *Whom God Hath Joined* concerns two divorce cases, its chief theme being the misery that is inflicted upon innocent people by the publicity and prejudice resulting even from being a witness in the divorce court.

Though these books showed some insight into the characters of women, they did not forecast the masterpiece that Bennett was able to write in his fortieth year. By this time he had acquired enough wealth, fame, and experience to be able to undertake the great realistic novel that he had always dreamed of writing. The theme for it occurred to him when he saw the patrons in a Paris restaurant sneering at a grotesque, shabby old woman, and realized that she had once been "young, slim, perhaps beautiful." Taking Maupassant's *Une Vie* as a model, he determined to tell the full truth about such a woman in "a heart-rending novel," and then thought that he might excel Maupassant by giving the interwoven histories of two sisters. Calling it *The Old Wives' Tale,* to emphasize that its theme was the tragedy of growing old, he portrayed the daughters of a draper in one of the Five Towns. One of them remains at home, marries an assistant in the shop, and controls the business and her husband with an iron hand. The other, eager for experience, goes off to Paris with a worthless adventurer, and when he deserts her she makes a life for herself as proprietor of a *pension.* The book is so long and detailed that it succeeds in giving the illusion of covering half a century without undue condensation. Nor is it devoid of exciting episodes: in Bursley these range from the shooting of an escaped elephant to a wife murder; in France from a public guillotining to the siege of Paris in the Franco-Prussian War. But the total effect is the accumulation of everyday events that makes up the passage of time. Even the siege is handled (as Thackeray handled the Battle of Waterloo in *Vanity Fair*) by showing the petty inconveniences in Sophia's catering for her boarders. Like *The Man of Property*, the study of the principal characters brings out their family likeness; both sisters are obstinate and competent, and when, old and decrepit, they are finally reunited in their girlhood home, the effect is not so much the pathos of age and weakness as the triumph of the indomitable will to live.

For this reason *The Old Wives' Tale*, for all the drabness of its settings, is never depressing. The author's zest for commonplace people and objects infects the reader. Bennett describes the interior of a tasteless parlor with the loving accuracy that an aesthete would lavish upon a scene of exquisite beauty. The irony of his phrases fails to disguise his affection for the way of life that he describes. He is neither an enlightened intellectual scorning these Philistines for their crass materialism nor a social rebel deploring their shackles. Instead, he is one of themselves, who has had the luck to get on in the world by exercising the same traits of resilience and self-reliance.

In his next novel, *Clayhanger*, Bennett again assembled masses of trivial details to establish the environment, spending almost a year in verifying minutiae before he began to write. This time his central figure is a young man, and one who conspicuously lacks force of character. As in *The Way of All Flesh*, the family background is an essential element. Darius Clayhanger, after a miserable workhouse childhood, has struggled so desperately to establish a printing business that he forces his son to help him in it instead of letting him study architecture. Humiliated by his lack of social graces and ready money, Edwin hates his father and his surroundings but cannot summon up enough spirit for revolt. Through more affluent neighbors he meets a young woman of somber and passionate vitality, Hilda Lessways, who fascinates him even while she infuriates him with insults. At the end of the book, giving no reason, she breaks her engagement to him in favor of another man. To outward seeming, Edwin is an awkward lout doomed to mediocrity in a life of dull routine; but by this time the reader has reluctantly come to sympathize with him enough to share his annoyance at Hilda's rudeness and treachery.

Bennett then proceeded with another book, *Hilda Lessways*, in which her early life is set forth, after which her encounters with Edwin are narrated over again, from her point of view. Now that we understand the crises that have rendered her inwardly insecure and externally savage, we realize how much everyone's judgment of others is conditioned by limitations of knowledge and perception. The retelling of the episodes, instead of being monotonous, provides depth of significance by demonstrating the relativity of our impressions.

Finally, in a third volume, *These Twain*, the couple are shown ten years later, after they eventually marry. No other love story was ever told so unromantically. We fully understand the defects of both — her vile temper and his stupid stubbornness — and yet we have enough tolerance or even affection for them to feel gratified when they blunder and quarrel their way to a sort of adjustment.

The publication of the *Clayhanger* trilogy was spread over six years (1910–15), and as usual Bennett was concurrently writing lighter fiction. One of these other books, *The Card*, and its sequel, *The Regent*, form a sort of comic antithesis to *Clayhanger*. Denry Machin is as quick-witted as Edwin Clayhanger is obtuse, and he is not handicapped by any ethical scruples. From his school days onward he cheats at every opportunity, employs his glib tongue in any shady transaction that turns up, and by sheer effrontery becomes the youngest mayor his town ever elected. In *The Regent* he outgrows the Five Towns and gains further wealth as a theatrical magnate in London.

In a sense Clayhanger and Machin are both projections of Bennett himself. Clayhanger represents what he would have been if he had not fled from his dim work in his father's office; Machin is a caricature of what he actually became — a sophisticated man of the world, getting rich by giving the gullible public what it wants, and yet retaining his North Country accent and his naïve delight in his self-made success. In both books the identification is close enough to win the reader's adherence; just as we forgive Clayhanger's passivity and selfishness, so also we feel guilty satisfaction in Machin's triumphs, even while aware that we ought not to condone his dishonesty.

Wells, during the same years, went through a comparable development toward becoming a recorder of contemporary social pressures. He wrote two further comic novels about the lower-middle-class environment of his youth. *Tono-Bungay* is a satiric account of how a young man with scientific leanings becomes involved with his unprincipled uncle in manufacturing a worthless patent medicine, which makes them rich through spectacular advertising. *The History of Mr. Polly* has the same theme as Bennett's *Buried Alive*, but the central character is lower in the social scale, being a middle-aged shopkeeper who is driven to such desperation by business difficulties and an overbearing wife that he makes a futile effort to kill himself. When he later succeeds in escaping from his troubles, he settles down blissfully with the plump landlady of an inn, just as Bennett's Priam Farll settled down with the plump proprietress of a tobacconist shop.

Wells's activity in Socialist politics, however, was making him increasingly aware of desperate problems that were close to the deceptively serene surface of current life. Actually, his anxiety had been implicit in his scientific romances, and it became obvious in *The War in the Air* (1908), a frighteningly accurate prophecy of the holocaust that came a few years later. The comic novels, too, implied dissatisfaction with the existing order of things: Kipps's disillusionment with his wealth, George Ponderevo's discovery of the jungle tactics of big business in the marketing of Tono-Bungay, Mr. Polly's inability to earn a living and his placid surrender of matrimonial responsibility, all point toward cracks in the social fabric. But at this point Wells undertook a more systematic survey of the whole structure, dividing it into its main categories and dissecting each with impartial sociological curiosity.

Since the changing status of women was one of the key issues, he began with a study of relations between the sexes. Although happily married to an understanding wife, Wells had begun to indulge in erotic adventures that supplied an authentic note to his portrayal of sexually rebellious women. *Ann Veronica* (1909) incurred condemnation as immoral because it depicted an attractive girl who, after living alone and trying vainly to make a career in business, takes a mate without the formality of marriage. The next book in this group, entitled explicitly *Marriage*, repeats the situation of the Lydgates in *Middlemarch:* a man is obliged to give up scientific research and go into business to satisfy the demands of an extravagant wife. In *The Passionate Friends* a woman tries to solve the old dilemma of love *vs.* material advantage by marrying the prosperous suitor and then having relations with the other. *The Wife of Sir Isaac Harman* admits a modicum of comedy in depicting a lady of rank and fashion who alleviates the dull conventional routine by taking part in the campaign for women's suffrage and by encouraging a susceptible author to fall in love with her.

Alongside of these four studies of love and marriage, Wells published two on the more intractable subject of political ideas. *The New Machiavelli* is the autobiography of a politician who plays a central role in public life until his career is ruined when he deserts his wife for a mistress. The book contains satiric portraits of prominent figures of the time, including some of Wells's former associates in the Fabian Society. After this ferocious exposure of incompetence in government, he offered a constructive proposal in *The Research Magnificent,* in which an idealist undertakes to make himself into a selfless and fearless leader who will help to create a World State, but loses his life in a strike riot before he has a chance to put his theories into practice.

By the time *The Research Magnificent* was printed, Europe was in the agony of the First World War, and the society that Wells was so exhaustively analyzing faced a crisis from which it never recovered. The didactic purpose of his six novels thus took on greater significance, just as his scientific fantasies did. His condemnation of society was based on a rationalist's impatience with inconsistency and inefficiency. In years when the English regarded themselves as the most prosperous and the best-governed people in the world, he proclaimed that their culture was doomed because of mismanagement and outworn conventions. In spite of the sometimes tedious exposition of ideas, there is enough vigor of characterization and naturalness of dialogue to give the group of novels a permanent value as a panorama of English life on the eve of catastrophe.

While Wells, Bennett, and Galsworthy occupied the spotlight

of topical relevance, Conrad remained in semi-obscurity. Nor could his slow, painstaking method compete with their fecundity. After the monumental achievement of *Nostromo* he published only two novels in ten years, and in both he tried to get as far away as possible from seafaring adventures in remote regions. *The Secret Agent* and *Under Western Eyes* deal with eastern European revolutionary intrigues like those that had overshadowed his childhood, and in both he probes the inner motives and the ethical conflicts of the plotters. Then in 1914, with *Chance*, he produced one of his finest and most complex novels. The narrator again is the ubiquitous Marlow, and the story is told with elaborate indirection. Beginning at a late stage, the situation is unraveled backward, some of the evidence being transmitted through three or four intermediaries. Out of this tissue of rumors and memories emerges the appealing and tragic figure of Flora de Barral, whose girlhood was wrecked by her father's financial swindling, and whose marriage is ruined by his hatred for her generous husband. Conrad is back in the cabin of a ship, where he feels most at home, and at the same time he is dealing with the cultivated, international type of people whose obscure reactions he intuitively understands.

This book was followed the next year by *Victory*, another masterpiece. Here Conrad returns to his earliest setting, the Malay Archipelago, and to the figure of the lonely white man who has fled from civilization. Axel Heyst, however, is no degenerate planter, but a scholarly recluse whose aristocratic father taught him to shun his fellow men. When an impulse of kindliness prompts him to shelter a persecuted girl, he precipitates an irruption of greed and revenge that destroys everyone concerned, in a climax of murder and suicide reminiscent of Jacobean tragedy. Yet, strangely, the violence and horror contribute to the atmosphere of serenity. The novel's title announces its theme: when Heyst discovers the folly of trying to live without normal human contacts, his innate nobility comes to the surface, though at the cost of his own life and Lena's, since she dies willingly in her love and gratitude to him. By this sacrificial devotion the forces of evil are nullified.

In spite of the accurate local color, *Victory* has a pervasive allegorical quality. Heyst and Lena are Adam and Eve in their island paradise, until her innocent transgression brings evil and death in the guise of the mysterious Mr. Jones, who is depicted in the traditional satanic terms. The overtone of symbolism that haunted Conrad's previous novels here becomes almost too explicit. This fact serves to bring out the essential difference between his work and that of his contemporaries. Wells, Bennett, and Galsworthy were using the tools of realism to represent individual characters beset by the muddled stresses of contemporary society. Conrad, by dealing with people in isolation, was able to offer them as archetypal figures of eternal human impulses. Here his aristocratic heritage and his stoic idealism could be embodied in acts of gallant though often useless self-immolation.

In their own day these four novelists did not stand out with the distinction they later acquired. Never had there been a larger number of competent writers of fiction in England or a wider public for their work. The older romance-spinners — Doyle, Haggard, Anthony Hope — were in full career, and had been joined by new recruits like Maurice Hewlett and Marjorie Bowen. Even such veterans as Miss Braddon and Ouida were still in the field. Eden Philpotts and other regional novelists carried on Hardy's kind of rural tragedy. There was a reversion to the manner of Dickens in the long, rambling novels of William de Morgan, who did not begin to write until he was sixty-seven. In the main current of social analysis were a number of earnest writers, such as Gilbert Cannan, J. D. Beresford, and May Sinclair, who now are scarcely remembered. On the other hand, time has brought recognition to one unpretentious writer, while the renown of better-known rivals has been fading. This is Edward Morgan Forster, who wrote four quiet, sensitive novels between 1905 and 1910. In the tradition of James, he dealt with the elusive misunderstandings and adjustments experienced by ordinary people. Two of the books, *Where Angels Fear to Tread* and *A Room with a View,* have the special Jamesian theme of international differences, showing English people baffled by the extroverted Italian temperament. In *The Longest Journey* and *Howards End* he deals with the English social environment that Galsworthy also was examining, but his attitude is more aloof and his sympathy more diffused.

Several younger novelists showed promise of carrying on the established techniques with distinction. Compton Mackenzie displayed a flair for comedy and what seemed to be daring impropriety in *Carnival* (1912), dealing with the theatrical world to which his parents belonged, and *Sinister Street* (1913), based on his experiences at St. Paul's School and Oxford. A more serious ethical outlook was manifested by Hugh Walpole in *The Prelude to Adventure* and *Fortitude*. Both Mackenzie and Walpole wrote numerous novels through many subsequent years, winning knighthoods as reward for their popular appeal; but neither proved to possess the depth of understanding or the artistic integrity essential for creating great fiction.

In the Edwardian decade the English novel was in the closing phase of an epoch that had lasted for a century. The triumvirate of Wells, Bennett, and Galsworthy, by combining intellectual seriousness with easy readability, temporarily restored the prestige that it had enjoyed in mid-Victorian days. In fact they reproduced with uncanny parallelism the individual traits of the three major figures in the earlier era. Wells resembled Dickens in his impoverished origin, his tireless gusto, and his antagonism toward established institutions. Even some literary devices, such as animistic metaphors endowing everyday objects with traits of living creatures, are shared by the two authors; and both equally disregarded regularity of structure. Galsworthy is akin to Thackeray in his Cambridge education, his ironic tone of disillusionment toward the upper-class society in which he moved, and the excessive sympathy for simple goodness that underlay his gentlemanly poise. Like Thackeray, too, he created his best novels out of his own unhappy experience in loving another man's wife. Bennett is comparable to Trollope as the prolific professional writer who gratified the public by the accuracy with which he reproduced the familiar details of their everyday surroundings. Just as Trollope forfeited critical respect by his *Autobiography* in which he boasted of his daily schedule and gave a financial report of his earnings, so Bennett revealed his businesslike procedures in a book entitled *The Truth About an Author*.

The prevalent sociological mood of the time, which in the political realm was adumbrating the Welfare State in Lloyd George's insurance project, impelled the representative novelists to use their books for a study of the interrelationship of human beings in the complex structure of modern urban society. This tidy rapport between subject matter and literary medium was about to be shattered by profound changes in both components. The apparently rigid pattern of the social system melted into chaotic confusion, while at the same time the novelists' focus of interest was shifted by a new scientific development that displaced the Spencerian social analysis of the late nineteenth century.

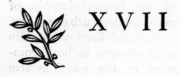

XVII

Exploring the Psyche

(since 1915)

FROM THE MIDDLE of the nineteenth century onward, the strongest influence upon the novel was exerted by science. First the evolutionary biologists implanted the idea that man must be regarded as a specially developed genus of animal, and therefore in fiction the naturalists interpreted human behavior on the basis of primitive instincts. Then the social scientists emphasized the structure of society and the psychological importance of environment, and therefore the later realists examined man in his familial and cultural groups. By the end of the century a new branch of science focused attention on the individual, when Sigmund Freud developed his methods of revealing the unconscious springs of action.

This problem had always been of paramount importance to novelists. From Richardson onward, they had tried to find a convincing way to display a character's inner reactions as well as his overt conduct. Most of them were hampered by the assumption that "thought" was always rational, and could be conveyed in logical predications. Hence came the implausible formality of passages enclosed in quotation marks and labeled, "he said to himself." When Dickens occasionally departed from this convention, as in the dreams and hallucinations of Sikes and Fagin, Jonas Chuzzlewit and Tigg, he was accused of being melodramatic and fantastic. Meredith merely succeeded in baffling his readers when he recorded the disjunctive mental processes of characters in *The Egoist* and *One of Our Conquerors*. But as the news from Freud's clinic came to public attention in the early years of the twentieth century, some novelists realized that this might provide the tools they had been seeking. The naturalists were vindicated so far as their concentration upon irrational motives went, but their narrative method, with its scientific logic, was obviated by the new attention to dreams and uncontrolled reverie.

The novelist who marks the transition from naturalism to psychoanalysis is David Herbert Lawrence. He is also typical of a significant social readjustment by being from a humbler class than any English novelist since Bunyan. The son of a coalminer, he took advantage of the new educational opportunities provided by scholarships, and, like Wells, was able to attend a teacher-training college. Had he been twenty years older he might have followed Wells's pattern by becoming a radical social theorist, except that, originating at the bottom of the class structure, he felt fierce contempt for caste distinctions instead of the gnawing anxiety about them that bedeviled all middle-class novelists, whether those on the lower rung, like Dickens and Wells, or those higher up, like Thackeray and Galsworthy. Besides, unlike Wells, he was inherently a poet, and so when he took to writing fiction he was absorbed in the emotional and imaginative element of the individual. When he came to London as a schoolmaster, in 1908, at the age of twenty-three, he brought the manuscript of a novel, *The White Peacock,* on which he had been working for several years, and it was published in 1911. Told by an onlooker-narrator, it centers upon the gradual breakdown of a farmer's son after the girl he loves has rejected him in favor of a richer suitor. Lawrence at this time admired the work of George Eliot, and the chief distinction of his book is the use of English rural scenery to heighten the emotional atmosphere, though his poetic rhythms and images produce a more opulent effect than did her pedestrian style. Some of the characters were based upon Lawrence's family and friends, but he disguised them by raising their social status, and thereby sacrificed plausibility, for their conversation is stilted and their behavior sometimes inconsistent. The later chapters are weakened by overcondensation of events covering a number of years. Nevertheless, in displaying a man's disintegration resulting from subservience to a selfish woman, the book established Lawrence's principal theme.

The originality of style in *The White Peacock*, and Lawrence's personal charm, brought him friends among the young writers in London, and when illness compelled him to give up teaching they helped him to earn a meager income by writing. His second novel, *The Trespasser*, is inferior to his first, the descriptive passages being turgidly overwritten. Again the theme is a woman's destructive rejection of her lover, and the erotic element pervades the book.

At this juncture Lawrence's own emotional life underwent a change. Hitherto he had been dominated by a possessive mother, who regarded herself as more genteel than her coal-mining neighbors and had insisted on her son's getting a good education. His devotion to her had caused a breach with a girl who attracted him and who had helped him to develop his literary talent; and Mrs. Lawrence's death, just at the time his first novel came out, plunged him into despair. A year later, however, he fell in love with the wife of one of his former professors, four years older than he, and the mother of several children. Together they went to the Continent to meet her family, who were of the German nobility, and wandered there for a year, during which he finished revising a novel that dealt directly with his own early life. The decisive break with his past enabled him to look at it with understanding and detachment.

The title, *Sons and Lovers*, clearly states the book's psychological theme. The technique is more strictly realistic than in his first two novels, presenting the coal-mining village of his childhood as objectively as Bennett depicted Hanley. Paul Morel's drunken but likable father and his stubborn mother are portraits of Lawrence's parents. The mother's control over the sex life of her sons drives the elder to involvement with a mistress and then to physical breakdown and death. The younger son, Paul, loves Miriam Leivers, a strong-minded girl who tries vainly to break his bondage to his mother. After separating from Miriam, Paul has an affair with a married woman, and this time Mrs. Morel reasserts her power through a prolonged illness, which brings Paul back to her and leaves him hopeless when she dies.

The literal accuracy of the autobiographic record is open to question; the woman who was the original of Miriam later published a book which gave a different impression of her relations with Lawrence. But in all essentials he had interpreted his own experience in terms of the Oedipus complex, though as yet he knew about Freud only at second hand. The hatred of the sons for their father, and his frustrated sense of inferiority, which drives him to violence and drink, help to make *Sons and Lovers* the first significant novel of twentieth-century psychological analysis, though in its formal structure and realistic detail it is still in the nineteenth-century tradition. Lawrence was not concerned with his characters in their context of society or with their moral or political ideas; he concentrated upon their most intimate emotional relationships and their sensuous responses to physical surroundings.

It remained for another novelist to evolve a technique that could render this sort of material with more immediacy. James Joyce was almost four years older than Lawrence, but his first novel did not appear until 1916, three years after *Sons and Lovers*. Born in Dublin, the son of a Roman Catholic family that had some pretensions to gentility but was steadily growing poorer, Joyce, like Lawrence, acquired contempt for his feckless father and was pushed onward by a devoted mother, who hoped that he would become a priest. At a Jesuit school and college he received a thorough training in the classical and modern languages; but he rejected the tenets of his family's faith and made up his mind to be an author.

Again like Lawrence, he was immune from the ideological controversies of his time. During his adolescence Dublin was seething with the Irish literary revival and the nationalistic ambitions that accompanied it, but he was scornful of all this commotion. He went to Paris at the age of twenty with a vague intention of studying medicine, but after some aimless months of semi-starvation he was recalled to Dublin by his mother's fatal illness. He spent a year in desultory efforts to find employment as a teacher, and then left Ireland permanently, accompanied by a pretty girl who was willing to share his hardships without the formality of marriage. In Trieste and Rome he worked for a while as a bank clerk, but mainly earned a meager living by giving lessons in English. Beginning, as Lawrence did, with poetry, he published a slim volume of fragile lyrics in 1907. He also wrote a group of short stories which was first accepted for publication as early as 1906, but which differed so radically from the accepted standards and gave such a candid picture of his home city that eight years elapsed before it was printed, under the title *Dubliners*. Lacking formal plot structure, these character sketches seemed fragmentary by contrast with the commercial short story, but they skillfully re-created the atmosphere of Joyce's youthful environment and showed sensitive insight into the feelings of obscure people.

In his first novel, on which he worked for ten years, he recorded his own early life as openly as Lawrence did in *Sons and Lovers*. A gigantic early draft was entitled *Stephen Hero*, but the final and greatly shortened version was given the ambiguous title of *A Portrait of the Artist as a Young Man*, which can mean either a study of a typical specimen of the artistic temperament or (in the art gallery sense) a self-portrait. The central theme had been used in countless *Bildungsromane* — a boy's discovery of the realities of life and his revolt against inhibiting surroundings, but Joyce gave it new vitality by his mode of presentation.

The whole story is kept strictly within the consciousness of the central character, and yet it does not use the formal autobiographical technique. Instead, written in the third person, it begins with the disjointed impressions of a child's earliest memories, expressed in baby-talk, and proceeds through a sequence of episodes in which the boy's comprehension gradually matures. The style keeps pace with the changes in age. While Stephen Dedalus is a small schoolboy, the diction is trite and slangy; when he is a poetry-loving undergraduate it becomes erudite and ornately melodious.

Since the reader remains confined within Stephen's reactions to his experiences while they are happening, there can be no analysis or explanation, none of the usual transitional statements as to when and where the events occur. This all has to be inferred from the impressions that Stephen receives, and these in turn are often a mixture of his responses to external stimuli and his recollections of past experiences that are occupying his mind simultaneously. It is entirely by the selection and arrangement of the episodes that the author suggests their significance.

The importance of the occurrences is wholly subjective, for Stephen's external life is ordinary enough. The scenes that are presented at full length include a Christmas dinner that is ruined by a family political argument, a school football game, a sermon on sin preached by the college chaplain, a day at the beach when Stephen watches a girl wading in the sea. Out of these and other everyday incidents the reader has to construct the growth of Stephen's personality — his revulsion from Irish nationalist big-otry, his lively imagination, his temporary burst of religious ardor, his discovery of sexual instincts. The only scene of dramatic tension is the climax, which by coincidence resembles that of *Sons and Lovers:* Stephen's mother begs him to resume his orthodox faith, and in his refusal he makes the break with the past which frees him for his artistic career.

In concentrating upon one character's responses to ordinary ex-periences, Joyce was following the practice of Henry James's later novels; and for the special technique of displaying the process of "free association" there were also some precedents. Joyce had found this device of "interior monologue" in a French novel of 1887, *Les Lauriers sont coupés,* by Édouard Dujardin. During the ten years' gestation of the *Portrait of the Artist,* Marcel Proust in Paris was at work on a vaster fictionized tran-script of his accumulated memories, of which the first volume, *Du Côté de chez Swann,* came out in 1913, and which grew into the immense *roman fleuve, À la Récherche du temps perdu.*

Joyce finished his novel in Trieste in 1914, but before it found a publisher an English woman, Dorothy M. Richardson, attracted critical attention by using interior monologue exclu-sively throughout a novel entitled *Pointed Roofs* (1915). The book recorded nothing but the thoughts and impressions passing through the mind of a young woman named Miriam. The trivial events of daily life, her opinions of the books she reads and the music she hears, are set down with apparently no selectivity whatsoever, the effect of uncontrolled reverie being achieved mainly by the use of brief declarative sentences or disjointed phrases. A fellow-novelist, May Sinclair, in a review of Dorothy

Richardson's work, borrowed a phrase from William James's psychology and labeled the technique "the stream of consciousness."

From the beginning Miss Richardson had planned that the record of Miriam's feelings should continue through many volumes, under the general title of *Pilgrimage;* and she reached a total of twelve, which were subsequently combined under that name. Though some of her literary contemporaries, interested in technical experimentation, praised her work highly, it never attracted many readers, for the simple reason that she was all too successful in producing the illusion of actuality. The interminable amassing of familiar details, without action or climax or even variation in pace and tone, is intolerably tedious. Proust and Joyce wrote fascinating books out of their own impressions because they possessed superlatively interesting minds; Miss Richardson's Miriam is merely an ordinary woman afflicted with a compulsion for total recall. *Pilgrimage* proves that psychological introspection loses aesthetic justification if it is wedded to the realists' objective of photographic accuracy.

The simplest way to prove this point is to compare Miss Richardson's work with that of another woman, Virginia Woolf, whose first novel, *The Voyage Out,* appeared in the same year as *Pointed Roofs.* Mrs. Woolf also was writing about the intimate sensations of a cultivated woman; but she was gifted with the interesting mind that Miss Richardson lacked. The daughter of Leslie Stephen, a distinguished man of letters, and wife of Leonard Woolf, a publisher and critic, she was from childhood onward in the very center of the vital intellectual life of England. Her critical essays are among the most perceptive of modern literary studies. *The Voyage Out,* combining factual narrative with symbolism, has much in common with the work of her friend E. M. Forster. The heroine sets out on a voyage across the Atlantic which is also an exploration of her own nature, and which proves to be the last experience of her life. Mrs. Woolf's second novel, *Night and Day* (1919), was a drawing-room comedy. In the tradition of Jane Austen, Thackeray, Meredith, and James, she was writing about refined and intelligent people whose emotions are controlled by inherited patterns of conduct, and therefore she did not offer the erotic revelations and the stormy agonies of Lawrence and Joyce. Nevertheless, she shared their determination to find out what goes on within the individual. The older authors also began to move in this direction. Somerset Maugham, who had been writing clever popular fiction and plays for nearly twenty years, in 1917 reverted to the naturalistic mode and produced a masterpiece, *Of Human Bondage,* a reworking of the autobiographical novel that he had written seventeen years before, and which he now brought even closer to the events of his early life. A portrait of a crippled, unhappy boy in revolt against restrictive elders, it has obvious affinities with *Sons and Lovers* and *A Portrait of the Artist;* but Maugham's tone is closer to *The Way of All Flesh.* His account of Philip Carey's student days at Heidelberg, in Montmartre, and in a London hospital, is grimly candid, but the misanthropic mood becomes oppressive and the happy ending is not altogether consistent. Almost equally powerful was a subsequent novel by Maugham, *The Moon and Sixpence* (1919), which was based on the career of the French painter Paul Gauguin, though the nationality was changed to English. It is a somber version of the theme that Bennett and Wells treated humorously in *Buried Alive* and *Mr. Polly* — a middle-aged man's flight from dull respectability to unconventional freedom, in this case on a South Sea island.

By this time, Britain had been engulfed in the First World War, which produced an incalculable change in the whole way of life so rapidly that the novelists could not keep up with it. The military side of the war was ignored in fiction, and the diplomatic side was reflected merely in a shift of sensational mystery stories from the overworked theme of crime detection to the newer one of international intrigue, exploited by such journeyman authors as John Buchan and E. Phillips Oppenheim. Even the impact of war conditions on everyday life was too confusing for any novelist except H. G. Wells, who had enough adaptability and self-confidence to undertake it promptly.

In an eccentric book entitled *Boon,* which he published anonymously in 1915, Wells reasserted his doctrine of social insurgence in fiction, chiefly through an impudent burlesque of the psychological subtleties of Henry James. It was a release of his accumulated contempt for the hypocrisy and frigid gentility that he saw in conventional English life and in the novelists who depicted it. In the light of this iconoclastic attack upon literary timidity, when the international crisis exploded Wells could feel but little hesitation in coming to grips with it. After one final effort to recapture the prewar tone of his lower-class comedy, in *Bealby*, he faced the current mood of the nation in 1916 with *Mr. Britling Sees It Through*. This was not one of his best books, but it attracted immense notice, not only because it was the first attempt to deal seriously with its subject, but also because Wells's reputation as a radical antagonist of the British governmental system lent authority to the earnest patriotism that he conveyed through the mask of an average citizen, whose very name implied his status, since "Britling" must mean "a little Briton." The book restored Wells to the good graces of respectable people, who had been alienated by *Ann Veronica* and his other subversions of conventional morality, and it did much to win sympathy for the British cause in the United States.

One of the notable features of *Mr. Britling* was the avowal that Wells, heretofore an outspoken rationalist, accepted the necessity of God in the scheme of things. Another was his assertion that better education was the only hope for saving civilization from disaster. With characteristic impetuosity he went on to expand these two ideas in his next novels. *The Soul of a Bishop*, depicting the administration of the Church of England, was the vehicle for his theories about religion, and *Joan and Peter* was intended to expound the advantages of progressive coeducation, though this theme was almost crowded out by discussion of how the war was changing the behavior of young people. Reverting to the religious *motif* in *The Undying Fire* (1918), he achieved a *tour de force* by retelling the Book of Job in modern terms.

Regarded as works of art, these novels are defective because they are dominated by the author's didactic purpose. And yet his inherent story-telling gift saves them from tedium. Just when the reader is on the verge of exasperated rebellion against a prolonged lecture, Wells inserts a shrewd characterization, an exciting episode, or a passage of jolly humor. Both *The Soul of a Bishop* and *The Undying Fire* are cast almost totally in dialogue, and therefore they are readily comparable with the polemical plays that Bernard Shaw was writing at the same epoch, such as *Heartbreak House*, which possess similar faults and merits. *Joan and Peter* is formless and infested with irrelevances, but it has immense vitality and charm.

The basic difference between Wells and Bennett was accentuated as time went on. An acute observer of external phenomena and individual behavior, Bennett was little concerned with ideology. Possessing by this time all the wealth he had ever dreamed of, including a yacht and other luxuries, he had no reason for discontent with the existing social system. The war entered merely incidentally into two novels of 1918 — *The Pretty Lady*, which deals mainly with prostitution, and in which a leading character is killed in an air raid on London, and *The Roll Call*, which traces the career of Hilda Lessways' son up to the point when it is interrupted by the war and his enlistment in the army. The immediate postwar period supplied themes for Bennett's novels in the early twenties — the financial problems of depression and profiteering in *Mr. Prohack*, the breaking-down of moral controls in *Lillian*, the ruthless exercise of power by administrators during crisis in *Lord Raingo*. In the midst of these stories, which were topical rather than permanent in their significance, Bennett produced one totally different novel, *Riceyman Steps* (1923). Shorter than his other realistic works, it gives a picture of life in a shabby quarter of London and is confined almost wholly to three characters, a miserly old couple and their illiterate servant girl, who are portrayed with humor and sympathy.

Galsworthy, too, refrained from writing directly about the war; but it heightened his awareness that the ample Victorian way of life was ended forever. Even ten years after *The Man of Property* the Forsyte family continued to haunt his imagination, for he had created them on a scale that transcended the boundaries of a single novel. A short story in 1917, "Indian Summer of a Forsyte," proved how easily he could resuscitate them, and soon afterwards he resumed the chronicle of Soames Forsyte and his problems in a full-length novel, *In Chancery*, which came out in 1920. This was followed the next year by *To Let*, constituting, with *The Man of Property*, a trilogy that was then reissued in one volume as *The Forsyte Saga*, which took a place alongside Bennett's *Clayhanger Family* as an almost Balzacian scrutiny of English life when the solid nineteenth century was giving place to the modern era of flux. Ten years have elapsed between *The Man of Property* and *In Chancery*; Soames gives up his dogged efforts to force his wife to return to him, and marries a young Frenchwoman, while (still following the pattern of Galsworthy's own love affair) the errant Irene marries one of his Forsyte cousins. To emphasize the *Saga's* implications as a history of social change, the volume ends with the pageantry of Queen Victoria's funeral in 1901. The action of *To Let* occurs twenty years later, and the postwar hysterical tension of London society sets the tone for a modern Romeo-and-Juliet situation: Soames's daughter and Irene's son fall in love with each other before discovering the closely guarded secret of the family scandal. The young man then breaks their engagement, and the disillusioned girl marries another man without loving him.

The war was even more completely ignored by Conrad. Racked with physical pain, he withdrew farther from the world of contemporary actuality. The allegorical overtones perceptible in *Victory* become bafflingly pervasive in *The Shadow Line* (1917). The memories of his early voyage to the Orient, as used originally in "Youth," and the theme of seamen's superstitions, as in *The Nigger of the "Narcissus,"* combine to produce an indefinable atmosphere of psychological dread. For his next book he went even deeper into his past; *The Arrow of Gold*, which treats of an idealistic young man's infatuation with a lovely woman in the midst of Carlist plotting, is believed to be an almost literal record of his boyish escapades in Marseilles. The same theme of an unsuspecting man in the toils of a clever woman occurs also in *The Rescue* (1920), but this novel belongs with his first Malayan stories, and the hero, Tom Lingard, had appeared as a character in *Almayer's Folly*. The book had been started at that time, but proved so difficult for Conrad to develop that he rewrote it at intervals over twenty-five years. The portrayal of women was always his greatest trouble. Whether an ignorant girl like Lena in *Victory* or a sophisticated enchantress like Doña Rita in *The Arrow of Gold* and Mrs. Travers in *The Rescue*, his heroines are always seen at a distance, through their disturbing effect upon puzzled men. It is this feature of his work, as much as the exotic settings and the ethical ideals, that makes it seem romantic in an era of realistic fiction that claimed to tell the unpalatable truth about women.

For many years Conrad had been reading for a historical novel on the epic scale, dealing with the Napoleonic period. A by-product of it, *The Rover*, was begun as a short story and grew into a brief novel of adventure, published in 1923. The principal character, a patriotic pirate, is a sort of older version of Nostromo. The larger work, entitled *Suspense,* was unfinished when Conrad died in 1924.

While these senior novelists were relatively unaffected by the war because their literary attitudes had been formed before it broke out, the most important younger ones also remained detached from it, for physical and psychological causes. D. H. Lawrence had outraged conventional people by his elopement with Mrs. Weekley. Upon her divorce they were married, three weeks before the outbreak of war, but thereupon the antagonism took a new direction because of her German origin, especially when her brother became one of the most noted German flying aces. Lawrence's passionate humanitarian sympathy prompted him to condemnation of all war. In poverty and ostracism, and anxious over Lawrence's tubercular symptoms, the couple lived obscurely in various parts of England during the war, and in the midst of it Lawrence published a novel that provoked further animosity.

Entitled *The Rainbow,* it is a rhapsodical book, sprawling over many years and sultry with sexual passion. Beginning in something of the realistic tone of *Sons and Lovers,* it develops into a sort of allegory. It contains some of Lawrence's most sympathetic insight and some of his most beautiful poetic phrasing and rhythm; but the characters are so ravaged with psychopathic conflicts that normal readers find them hard to believe in. Lawrence was becoming obsessed with the idea of the antagonism between the sexes and the admixture of love with hate. Every man, in his view, has an ambivalent feeling toward women, needing them for the gratifiction of his lust and yet loathing them for their power over him. *The Rainbow* takes place mainly in the English countryside, which is depicted with the lyrical sense of natural processes that had distinguished *The White Peacock.* A large farming family is introduced, and then attention is focused upon one of the brothers, an awkward fellow who falls in love with a Polish refugee, widow of a revolutionist. This mixture of bloods is perpetuated through subsequent generations, as the widow's daughter grows up and becomes emotionally involved with her English step-kin, and in turn this girl's daughter, Ursula, engages in an even more passionate affair with a Polish cousin. In each generation the woman is the more dynamic partner in the relationship.

When Ursula finally rejects her inadequate lover, her emotional crises are conveyed in a series of prose-poems, through which Lawrence seeks to suggest a mystical theory that sexual gratification has to be transmuted into some sort of spiritual union. He is transferring into an entirely emotional realm the theme that Meredith had expounded in terms of woman's need for intellectual independence.

When published in 1915, *The Rainbow* was assailed in the press for indecency and was suppressed. The outcry was directed against the frank description of physical intimacies and particularly a Lesbian episode that occurs at one stage of Ursula's search for a solution to her sexual agonies. Defiantly Lawrence went on to write a sequel, *Women in Love,* which was even more explicit in its erotic scenes. Ursula now finds a satisfactory partner in Philip Birkin, who represents Lawrence's own conception of sex; and their love story is contrasted with two others, one of which fails because it is confined to immediate gratification of desire, and the other because the woman is the dominant personality. When no publisher would incur the risk of bringing the book out, it was privately printed in 1920, and provoked a new wave of censure for containing recognizable and mainly unflattering portraits of some of Lawrence's friends.

By this time the Lawrences were living in Italy, and his impressions of the Mediterranean landscape are to be found in his next novel, *The Lost Girl* (1920), couched in his most charming vein of poetic description. Otherwise the book is undistinguished, and it suffers from diffuseness of scene, as it ranges from a draper's shop in a mining town through a student nurse's hospital experience to her life in Italy as the wife of an actor. She is a feminine counterpart of the young men in the realistic novels of Bennett, Wells, and Maugham, and the sexual element was so much less offensive than in Lawrence's preceding books that this one was awarded a major British prize as the best novel of the year.

James Joyce spent the war years in Zurich, totally absorbed in a huge work of fiction. *A Portrait of the Artist,* after being serialized in a London *avant-garde* magazine, was published in New York in 1916, and attracted only a handful of readers. Undeterred by obscurity and penury, Joyce was already deep in the new book, which had been simmering in his mind for years, and which was vastly more experimental and cryptic.

It would be misleading to call it a sequel to the *Portrait*, though Stephen Dedalus figures in it prominently. The intention is now much more than a transcript of the author's past experiences. Even in the earlier book Stephen had been endued with a symbolic aura through his unusual surname, suggesting the mythical artificer who daringly invented wings. Now a different side of Joyce's personality was to be affiliated with Greek legend: he was no longer seen as an ambitious creator spurning the limitations of earth, but as a confused youth in quest of his spiritual identity. The book was a retelling of the *Odyssey*, with Stephen in the role of Telemachus. Joyce, alienated from his parents and an exile from his homeland, could doubly identify himself with the young man searching for his missing father. To replace the wily Ulysses and the faithful Penelope, Joyce invented a naïve, good-natured Irish Jew, Leopold Bloom, and his sexually promiscuous wife, Molly.

This ironic diminution of stature for the characters of the ancient epic is extended to place and time also: instead of covering the Mediterranean world in eight years, the gargantuan novel traverses the shabby streets of Dublin within a span of eighteen hours. In spite of Joyce's prolonged sojourn on the Continent, his imagination remained rigidly confined to the city of his boyhood, which since 1904 he had seen on only two or three brief visits. His immunity to later impressions may be attributed partly to failing eyesight, which dimmed the world in which he moved and invested his early memories with preternatural clarity. But also he was held to the past by psychological bonds that were only strengthened by his repudiation of his origins. He despised Dublin for its provincial narrowness, its religious obscurantism, and its nonrecognition of his own literary talent, and yet he knew and loved it with unshakable devotion.

The action of *Ulysses* is precisely dated on June 16, 1904 (four months before Joyce took his permanent departure from Ireland). It is an ordinary day in the life of Bloom, a rather incompetent advertising-solicitor for a newspaper. Ostensibly in pursuit of business, he rambles about Dublin, talks with friends, eats lunch in a public house, visits the library, drops into bars for drinks, attends a funeral, wanders into a hospital when a baby is being born, and ends at night in a brothel. At intervals he encounters Stephen Dedalus, and the two feel obscurely drawn to one another because Bloom has never ceased to grieve for his son who died in infancy and Stephen unconsciously needs fatherly protection. Their meeting, however, does not provide any dramatic climax, for they drift apart as casually as they came together.

The book is crowded with topographical details of Dublin streets, shops, taverns, and suburbs, and with glimpses of real denizens; and as these are all mentioned in the allusive manner of familiar conversation, the reader acquires simultaneously an illusion of intimate identification and a frustrating sense of remoteness. This, however, is the least crucial of several reasons why the book is difficult to read. A second reason is the complete adoption of the stream-of-consciousness technique, which had been tentatively tried in *A Portrait of the Artist*. A transition from that book is supplied by the opening chapters, which record Stephen's impressions; but the focus soon shifts to Bloom, and the concluding chapter shifts again to Bloom's wife. To sustain the irrational effect of free association, Joyce employed fragmentary phrases, telescoped words, erratic punctuation, phonetic spelling, onomatopoeic syllables, and other devices. The ending, which reproduces Molly's jumbled reverie as she drops off to sleep, consists of forty-five pages without punctuation of any sort.

These artifices, seriously though they thwarted readers who were accustomed to formal syntax, could be accounted for on the basis of realism — a medium for more exact imitation of experience. Another source of difficulty, however, arose from Joyce's enormous and pedantic learning. At first most readers assumed that the title of the book, *Ulysses,* was merely a sarcastic metaphor for Bloom's explorations. Joyce had to drop hints to his friends before scholars realized that the eighteen hours of Bloom's day parallel the structure of the *Odyssey* with incredible ingenuity. The principal episodes and characters recur in proper sequence. Antinous is a bumptious medical student who bullies Stephen, Nausicaä is a lame girl who attracts Bloom's roving fancy, Polyphemus is a drunk citizen who hurls a biscuit-tin when enraged, Nestor is the pompous headmaster of a school where Stephen is temporarily teaching. Ulysses' visit to the underworld is transformed to a drive to the cemetery, the Wandering Rocks are the dangers of street traffic, the Sirens are barmaids, Circe's palace is the brothel where men are bestialized.

Nor is this the full extent of the structural elaboration. Each episode is dominated by a particular color, symbolizes an organ of the human anatomy, and deals with a specific art or science. When these are synthesized, the sum total of the book becomes a complete symbol of man's body and an epitome of man's knowledge. And as the artistic equivalent of these thematic components, each episode is presented in a different stylistic manner. The newspaper office scene introduces all the formal devices of medieval rhetoric; the Sirens scene imitates innumerable musical effects; Bloom's flirtation is narrated in the clichés of cheap sentimental fiction; the maternity ward scene, by parodying the style of typical authors through the past five hundred years, implies the development of the embryo and the infant's heritage of accumulated culture.

All this exhibition of virtuosity can be appreciated only by the rare reader with scholarly equipment and mental agility equivalent to Joyce's own. His pleasure in writing the book, which sustained him through years of indigence, was certainly, in part, his supreme egotism and his mischievous delight in dazzling readers with his superior knowledge. But even a moderately literate person, unwilling to go to the trouble of consulting the handbooks that are now available to guide him through the maze of Joyce's Dublin and the deeper labyrinth of his scholarly allusions and symbolic parallels, can appreciate how the comic effect is intensified by the old mock-heroic device of describing trivial occurrences in epic terms.

Ulysses is one of the great comic novels. It captures the eccentricities of Irish character, the picturesque exaggerations of Irish speech. Joyce's musical talent equipped him with an unerring ear for every inflection of the brogue, which his phonetic devices reproduce on paper. The rowdy mischances and ludicrous misunderstandings are often sheer farce. And in the tradition of comic realism *Ulysses* follows Le Sage and Fielding in its blunt reporting of ugliness, filth, and depravity.

And yet *Ulysses* is a very serious novel, too. The narrative is carefully planned to include the basic events of human experience — birth, lovemaking, death. It probes deeply into the relationship of husband and wife, of father and son. The theme of remorse is woven all through it. Basically, as an allegory of life, it presents Bloom as the eternal average man, as was Ulysses among the monumental Homeric heroes. Bloom stands midway between the instinctive, sensual nature of his wife and the intellectual pride and creative imagination of Stephen. At first we are repelled by Bloom's ineptitude and self-pity; gradually we begin to admire his unselfish kindliness and gentle humility. Some critics have gone so far as to assert that this petty businessman, like the plowman in Langland's medieval vision, develops into a Christ figure.

When *Ulysses* was published in Paris in 1922 it attracted a full measure of the attention that had been withheld from Joyce for twenty years. His fellow-authors were immensely impressed by his stream-of-consciousness technique; but many of them, including Shaw, Wells, Forster, and even Lawrence, were disquieted by the obscenity they found in the book, and the general public was more violently disgusted by this quality. *Ulysses* was banned by censorship in Britain and the United States, and ten years were to elapse before a noteworthy court decision legalized an American edition.

Among the writers who were fascinated by Joyce's experimental method the most distinguished was Virginia Woolf, and in her subsequent novels she adopted a modified version of the stream of consciousness, without Joyce's more flamboyant vagaries. *Jacob's Room* (1922) is a character study of a young man from childhood through his studies at Cambridge and research in the British Museum, his involvement with a London prostitute, and his archeological trip to Athens, ending with his death in action in the war. Reversing Joyce's formula, Mrs. Woolf depicts her young scholar through other people's impressions of him, and the series of random glimpses slowly combines into a convincing portrait. Her next book, *Mrs. Dalloway*, is reminiscent of *Ulysses* in dealing with a single day, as a well-bred English lady moves through the insignificant routine of getting ready for a party. The unifying thread is her sensitive and only half-conscious perception of what goes on around her; but intermittently the author moves away from Mrs. Dalloway to show how some of these simultaneous episodes weave into a pattern that is relevant to her. The other principal character, a shell-shocked veteran, is unknown to her until his suicide is mentioned at her party by a fashionable doctor, who, in his turn, is unaware of being the cause of the deranged man's death. The author is not merely indicating the endless variety of daily incident surrounding any individual; she means to convey that Mrs. Dalloway's inexplicable interest in the dead man is an intuitive recognition that he is her surrogate, for she too has been in a state of neurotic tension all day because an abortive love affair of her youth has suddenly become vivid through the return of her old admirer, and she recognizes her suppressed suicidal impulse in the stranger's act.

In *To the Lighthouse* (1927) Mrs. Woolf moved closer to overt use of symbolism, in a story wherein time and physical objects seem more important than living beings. The first part describes a summer holiday in the Hebrides and a small boy's disappointment when an excursion to the lighthouse is canceled because of stormy weather. Part II, entitled "Time Passes," records the slow disintegration of the deserted house. In the final part a young man, who had been the unhappy little boy, eventually visits the lighthouse and finds the experience meaningless. Out of this uneventful narrative Mrs. Woolf evokes suggestions that make one feel on the verge of comprehending the elusive meaning of life. The distinctive quality of her novels resides in the impression that she and her characters alike are the highly sophisticated product of modern culture, impeccable in taste, hypersensitive to every sensation, and yet dejectedly seeking some remedy for their isolation and spiritual *malaise*, much as Matthew Arnold had uttered his emotional dilemma in poetry two generations before. Indeed, the poetic element is conspicuous in Mrs. Woolf's writing, though, unlike Lawrence and Joyce, she published no verse. The beautiful precision of her phrases, the pattern of rhythm and recurrence, and the abundance of metaphors render her descriptive passages peculiarly charming. The mingling of past and present in each moment's consciousness is more important for her than the logical progression of cause and effect. She sees each personality in the context of all existence since the beginning, every moment as the focus of eternal forces. Each of her novels records a character's preparation for the inner realization of truth that comes only from a constant unspoken search for meaning and identification. The serene, wise Mrs. Ramsay, in *To the Lighthouse*, is the fullest embodiment of Virginia Woolf's elegant and essentially feminine ideal.

One effect of the First World War was a shortage of notable English novelists in the generation that followed. A large proportion of the country's ablest young men lost their lives; and among the survivors those of imaginative temperament were the most likely to have suffered a paralyzing loss of the creative urge. Among the masculine writers who were of military age in 1914, the only outstanding figures in the next decade were Lawrence and Joyce, whose physical disabilities, as well as their abhorrence of war, absolved them from military service. For this reason the older novelists continued to dominate the scene during the twenties.

Arnold Bennett tried to revive the massive realism of *The Old Wives' Tale* and *Clayhanger* in *Imperial Palace* (1930), which centers in a huge London hotel — a theme that had first attracted him in the earliest of his melodramatic novels. He now linked this setting with a psychological study of the aggressive capitalist who owns it and of his involvement with two women; but the reader's interest is distracted by the eighty-two other characters and by innumerable details of hotel operation, the fullest expression of Bennett's genius for finding romantic excitement in the routines of modern business. The effort of collecting authentic information and then writing this monstrous book was disastrous to Bennett's health and he died two years later.

H. G. Wells was made of tougher fiber. The outcome of the war disillusioned him as to the easy remedies for ignorance and injustice that he had embraced in his confident socialistic days, and he dedicated himself to reshaping the fundamental thinking of mankind. As a first step he wrote his *Outline of History* (1920), a compendious survey which sold in gigantic numbers. A decade later he synthesized the other principal fields of modern knowledge in *The Science of Life* and *The Work, Wealth, and Happiness of Mankind*. Naturally, a new urgency invaded his novels, making the didactic purpose more dominant than ever. In *Men Like Gods* (1923) he reverted to the scientific forecasting of the future which had won his original fame; but in place of thrilling adventures and technical marvels he now offered an ambitious program for the intellectual evolution of the race, much as Shaw had done two years before in *Back to Methuselah*. *The Secret Places of the Heart* (also 1923) insists that sexual indulgence is a necessary concomitant of the good life. *Christina Alberta's Father* is ostensibly a return to Wells's former mood of warm-hearted lower-class comedy; but its fantastic central situation (based on the current vogue of spiritualism) carries allegorical implications about the predicament of modern society. Wells then determined to attempt a complete synopsis of the contemporary mind in a single novel, *The World of William Clissold* (1926), which extended to two volumes and covered so many ideas and social phenomena that it sometimes seems to abandon any narrative structure. The autobiographic form reinforces its plausibility, and as usual Wells is expert in depicting his hero's relations with various women. But Wells was so stubbornly opposed to the Jamesian type of fiction that he labored to counteract what he considered the mistaken assumption of recent novelists "that people's lives and actions are never determined by political and social conditions, but only by personal reactions." Clissold is so obviously a composite figure embodying the major forces of modern English society that the book survives less as a novel than as a vivid sociological survey.

During the remaining twenty years of his life Wells published not only a monumental and revealing autobiography and a variety of controversial treatises but also a score of novels. None of them added significantly to his literary stature, though each provided glimpses of the skill and insight that had informed his best work. *The Shape of Things to Come* (1933) attracted the widest attention with its uncomfortably convincing forecast of a devastating world war. When Wells died in 1946, shortly after the end of the war that largely fulfilled his direst prophecies, the novel of social propaganda apparently died with him.

The novel of impartial social analysis had already reached the end of an epoch, for its last major exponent, Galsworthy, died in 1933. His final decade was devoted to the Forsyte family, which he carried through two further trilogies. *The White Monkey, The Silver Spoon,* and *Swan Song* were combined into *A Modern Comedy* (1928). Remoter connections of the family serve as central figures in the third trilogy, *End of the Chapter,* and a set of detached episodes appears in a volume of short stories, *On Forsyte 'Change* (1930). The verisimilitude provided by the family theme was strengthened by numerous details about current events, since each novel dealt with the year immediately preceding its publication. Galsworthy by this time had gained international recognition as the chief chronicler of the essentially English way of life, and he was as acutely aware as Wells that this social fabric was on the brink of drastic change. The artistic power of the series of novels diminished as the author obviously manipulated his stories to illustrate assorted phenomena of the breakdown. The real climax of the Forsyte story had occurred at the end of *A Modern Comedy*, with the death of Soames Forsyte, the most remarkable feature being the gradual transformation of this originally unsympathetic personality into an almost heroic figure. Not since Trollope's portrayal of Plantagenet Palliser in his parliamentary series had an English novelist lived so intimately for a generation with one of his characters and slowly gained a tolerant understanding of him. The painful maturing of Soames's daughter Fleur helps to make the second trilogy appealing.

One other author of the old school of social analysis contributed his last and perhaps his best work. After *Howards End* E. M. Forster did not publish another novel for fourteen years, and then brought out *A Passage to India* in 1924. He still allowed priority to individual feelings and moral decisions rather than to social pressures; but he showed clear awareness of the new type of adjustment that was becoming crucial in place of the rivalries and ambitions of the self-contained class system that provided the material for Galsworthy. In his study of a cultivated English-woman's experiences in India, Forster subtly but kindly probes the intricacies of emotional and cultural differences.

A more remarkable writer who attracted attention in the same year was Ford Madox Ford. Under his prewar name of Hueffer he had collaborated with Conrad in three novels and had been well known in literary circles as critic, essayist, and editor rather than as the author of a string of historical romances. Like Conrad and Forster, he regarded Henry James as the ideal novelist, and held to high standards not only of psychological truth but also of structural organization. Though over forty when the war broke out, he went into the army and served at the front, thus being one of the few English novelists to combine mature literary skill with first-hand knowledge of the fighting. *The Good Soldier*, which was published about the time he joined his regiment, is a profounder psychological study than any of his previous fiction; but in spite of its title it has nothing to do with the war, being a Jamesian study of English country-house society, with subtle analysis of marital infidelity and moral disintegration.

Though now often termed Ford's masterpiece, *The Good Soldier* received little notice in the distracted days of 1915. A similar environment is used in *Some Do Not* (1924), but this novel leads up to the outbreak of the war, and the central character, Christopher Tietjens, proved to be so distinctive a personality that Ford carried him through three further novels, *No More Parades, A Man Could Stand Up,* and *Last Post.* The second and third of the series give a vivid picture of the war years, both in the front-line trenches and at headquarters. The final volume brings Tietjens back to the sexual and social disturbances of postwar London. The whole tetralogy, subsequently combined under the title *Parade's End,* forms a sort of disillusioned, postwar sequel to *Mr. Britling Sees It Through,* showing how a kindly, scholarly, awkward Englishman endured the horrors of trench warfare and the betrayal of family loyalty. Like Galsworthy, Ford was fully aware that he was chronicling the end of an epoch.

The war's aftermath of social and psychological dislocation, however, found its most appropriate expression, not in Ford's aloof veracity or Galsworthy's anxiety or Wells's iconoclasm, but in a mood of cynical comedy that was best voiced by Aldous Huxley. Among his literary contemporaries only Virginia Woolf had anything like a comparable heritage of eminence and brains. His brother became one of the leading biologists of the era; their father was a prominent literary man; their grandfather was the redoubtable scientist who led the battle on behalf of the Darwinian hypothesis. Mrs. Humphry Ward was their aunt, Matthew Arnold their great-uncle. Aldous Huxley was twenty at the outbreak of the war, but bad eyesight debarred him from the armed forces, and after graduation from Oxford he joined the circle of London intelligentsia. The satiric novel of ideas, in the tradition of Peacock, had recently been revived by Norman Douglas in *South Wind* (1917), an almost plotless record of the glittering talk among a group of rich British and American expatriates living on Capri. His prevalent tone was persistently frivolous; Aldous Huxley injected a touch of bitterness in *Crome Yellow, Antic Hay,* and *Those Barren Leaves,* published between 1921 and 1925. Whereas Douglas's inversions of conventional morality existed merely for the pleasure of paradox, Huxley was a cryptomoralist, flouting respectability out of angry contempt for a generation that had abandoned ethical values. Many of his characters were readily recognized as unflattering portraits of well-known contemporaries.

These three novels are alike in their loose narrative line and their interludes of fantastic farce, as well as their urbane, scholarly style. In his next one, *Point Counter Point* (1928), Huxley undertook an elaborate structural experiment, partly suggested by André Gide's book, *Les Faux-monnayeurs*. Trying to approximate the musical device of counterpoint, Huxley shifts abruptly back and forth among several narrative strands to produce the illusion of seeing several aspects of experience simultaneously. One of the characters, a novelist, expresses the author's conception that

> the essence of the new way of looking is multiplicity. Multiplicity of eyes and multiplicity of aspects seen. For instance, one person interprets events in terms of bishops, another in terms of the price of flannel camisoles. . . . And then there's the biologist, the chemist, the physicist, the historian. Each sees, professionally, a different aspect of the event, a different layer of reality. What I want to do is to look with all those eyes at once.

This juxtaposing technique gives the book a sort of scientific precision, as though the author is examining an assortment of specimens representing different ideas and ways of life, while the reader is left to draw his own inferences. The only character toward whom Huxley shows a gleam of cordiality is Mark Rampion, a dynamic, peasant-born painter who is modeled upon D. H. Lawrence. The integrity of Rampion and his aristocratic wife contrasts with the maladjusted intellectualism of all the others, who exemplify the current fads of the artistic and fashionable *mondes*. Interminably they discuss their ideas and analyze their emotions, but none can achieve the balance of "blood, brain, and spirit" that makes wholeness. The novel's uncoordinated structure conveys its principal idea: modern society is fragmented into individuals without common beliefs or duties to hold them together, and so each follows his own desires without regard for anyone else. And the hopelessness of present-day life is implied by the absence of any general climax to knot the separate strands with the old Dickensian dexterity.

Brave New World (1932) is a sardonic inversion of Wells's forecasts of the future; using similar materials, Huxley paints an appalling picture of a totalitarian and mechanized civilization, worshiping Karl Marx and Henry Ford, from which the only escape is flight to the primitive conditions surviving in an Indian reservation.

This revulsion against the hypercivilized modern environment is conveyed directly in *Eyeless in Gaza* (1936), of which the title indicates the pervasive sense of frustration by quoting from Milton's bitter complaint of the fettered Samson. In this book Huxley tries his juxtaposing technique in terms of time rather than of persons; the episodes follow the associative process in the memory of the central character, jumping backward and forward through a thirty-year period. This not only brings out the hidden links of cause and effect but also intensifies the irony that is Huxley's habitual note. The falsity of brittle sophisticates and the repulsiveness of sexuality are still his main themes, but he evinces an incipient interest in politics and also begins to suggest a positive mystical creed as an alternative to materialism.

His only subsequent novel of much importance is *After Many a Summer Dies the Swan* (1939), which intrigued American readers by its repugnant representation of life and celebrities in Southern California, where by that time he had established his home. His comic talent remains efficacious, but his detestation of vulgar crudity and cultivated depravity here impels him to a degree of caricature that precludes the illusion of reality. Thereafter his writing has been mainly devoted to criticism, biography, and theorizing.

In comparison with Huxley's unorthodox brilliance, the other new novelists of the twenties seemed to cling cautiously to established standards. After the decimating effect of the war it is not surprising that some of the most accomplished of them were women, such as Rose Macaulay (*Potterism*, 1920, *Dangerous Ages*, 1921, *Told by an Idiot*, 1923), Rebecca West (*The Judge*, 1922), Storm Jameson (*The Pitiful Wife*, 1923), and Margaret Kennedy (*The Constant Nymph*, 1924). These women wrote about contemporary life, and particularly about sex, with an honesty and technical virtuosity that had not been available for their less emancipated predecessors; but still they contributed nothing essentially fresh. The few new masculine novelists of the decade were even more conspicuously traditionalists. J. B. Priestley was hailed as a successor to Dickens because of the hearty humor and the proletarian sympathy of *The Good Companions* (1929) and *Angel Pavement* (1930).

Charles Morgan, in *Portrait in a Mirror* (1929) and *The Fountain* (1932), displayed a restrained delicacy of touch that harked back to French rather than to English antecedents.

The realistic social novel being in a static interlude, there was an opportunity for a more symbolic technique to emerge. A symptom of this trend can be seen in the temporary and post-humous fame of Mary Webb, who evoked an imaginative aura of poetic imagery and feeling from the landscapes and folk customs of her native Shropshire in *Gone to Earth* (1917) and *Precious Bane* (1924). After she died, worn out with poverty and hard work, in 1927, her stories were highly lauded; but a sentimental strain diminishes their power. Vastly more original were the books of two men who ignored the realistic assumptions so thoroughly that their books proved baffling to average readers. Neither was very young when the war began, and both turned belatedly to fiction to embody mature views evolved through experience in other media.

John Cowper Powys had begun giving university extension lectures on English fiction early in the century, and was known as a critic and poet before he published his first novel, *Wood and Stone*, in 1915. The setting in Wessex, the perpetual linking of the characters with the natural scenery, and the archaic formality of style are reminiscent of Hardy; the difference resides in Powys's spiritually affirmative outlook. He cites Nietzsche in claiming that he is trying to answer the question of "the reconciliation between the Will to Power and the Will to Love." Believing in the unity of all existence, he depicts the struggle of good and evil without glossing over depravity and cruelty, but injecting a note of mystical exaltation.

Similar themes and characters appear in *Ducdame* (1925) which is immensely long and fantastically elaborate. It centers in the decadence of an ancient county family, the hero being "a megalomaniac subjectivist." Powys invokes all the Gothic horrors: the action opens by moonlight at midnight in a grave-yard; the local vicar practices black magic; the hero's mon-strously deformed bastard is hidden by gypsies. Grotesque characters recall the gargoyles of a medieval church.

Powys began to win reluctant approval from critics with *Wolf Solent* (1928), which deals with one year in the life of a man of creative gifts who is frustrated by lack of outlets for his artistic talent. As usual, the scene is Dorsetshire; and in spite of the precise descriptive detail, an impression of symbolism is conveyed by the exaggeration of character traits and the poetic imagery. In *A Glastonbury Romance* (1933) Powys postulated correspondences between solar activity and the human mind, and throughout he insists that a common consciousness links man with animals, reptiles, trees, fungus, even stones. The ancient identification of Glastonbury with the Grail legend endows it with a spiritual atmosphere that facilitates intercourse with the unseen. There is Rabelaisian humor in the book, especially in some of the peasant characters; and there is his customary Gothic terror in the diabolic possession that afflicts Mr. Evans, a mild scholar who seeks to exorcise his fits of sadism by enacting the role of the crucified Christ in a passion play. Other characters are susceptible to mystical visions or are gifted with miraculous healing power. The book could degenerate into a tissue of superstitious moonshine, but the stately rhythms of Powys's prose and his wealth of learned allusion lend it a sort of hypnotic spell.

Jobber Skald (1935) differs only in having a larger infusion of comedy; and *Maiden Castle* (1937) is equally full of earth-mystics, Platonists, and worshipers of pagan gods. *Morwyn, or The Vengeance of God* is a fantasy of a descent into hell, which is inhabited solely by sadists — the Marquis de Sade himself, Torquemada, Calvin, and Nero — with Socrates and Rabelais as visitors from paradise. The theme is a fanatical attack on vivisection. Powys's interest in Celtic tradition then led him toward historical fiction, with *Owen Glendower, Porius, Atlantis,* and *The Brazen Head.*

Using an oversimplified cliché, we may say that Powys is ultra-romantic in his emphasis upon intuition, introspection, and the supernatural. With equal justice the opposite label of ultra-classical can be applied to the other nonconforming novelist of the period, Wyndham Lewis, who was a master of satire and insisted upon rational thinking, explicit statement, and observation of external phenomena. Twelve years younger than Powys, he first became known as leader of the "Vorticist" school of painting, a faction of futurist experimentalists. In 1914–15 he produced two issues of *Blast*, a journal dedicated to demolishing all the prudery and materialism of the Victorian era. His violent controversial tactics and headstrong disregard of caution won him leadership among the radicals in the arts; but as an extreme individualist he was a heretic to all organized groups. Widely informed in many cultures, he wrote volumes of literary criticism and of speculative thought concurrently with his fiction. The hero of his first novel, *Tarr* (1918), is largely a self-portrait, an artist whose paintings and aesthetic theories are the only meaningful element in his life. The Latin Quarter of Paris is depicted with an odd mixture of realism and exaggeration that is a verbal equivalent for the vivid distortions of reality in Lewis's paintings; and the effect is enhanced by irregular syntax and eccentric choice of words. The psychotic intensity of effect is reminiscent of Dostoievski. Ten years later Lewis revised *Tarr* extensively, making the style more orthodox but sacrificing some of the imaginative impact.

In 1928, the year of this revision, he published his second long fiction, *The Childermass*, which is his equivalent to Powys's *Morwyn*. Taking place in a concentration camp outside heaven, it consists of metaphysical arguments between the souls of the newly dead and a fantastic bailiff who is to select them for annihilation or eternal bliss. Lewis's profound theories about space-time, which he had recently expounded in *Time and Western Man*, are set forth in amazing colloquial conversations, including a parody of Joyce's later style. Lewis intended *The Childermass* to be the first volume of a tetralogy; but he suspended it in favor of other works. *The Apes of God* is a gargantuan satire upon the London intellectual clique that centered in Bloomsbury. In *The Revenge for Love* (1937), an exciting anti-communist adventure story, Lewis reverted to a more coherent form of the novel, and the characters become reasonably like real people instead of being automata illustrating the author's views. Finally, near the end of his life, he resumed the *Childermass* project after a quarter-century break, and published in 1955 a second installment, consisting of *Monstre Gai* and *Malign Fiesta*.

Lewis has something in common with Huxley in his loathing for the poses and inconsistencies of modern intellectuals. He is akin to Lawrence in his doctrine that the creative artist is the only man who lives a full and true life, and to Joyce in his dislocations of formal prose. Yet he despised all these contemporaries equally. Believing in the pre-eminence of mind, he had no use for Lawrence's *mystique* of sex or for Joyce's concentration upon the irrational stream of consciousness. His revolution was not merely, however, against his Freudian contemporaries. Essentially he was assailing the bourgeois spirit that had dominated the English novel since Richardson — the sentimentalism, the commonplace details, the complacent moralizing. In opposition to this cozy domesticity Lewis sought to set forth the stark truth about existence in the harsh light of reason. His egomania prevented him from creating characters who sustain objective individuality, and his ferocious cynicism made his fiction aggressively didactic. Nevertheless his novels are so original and authentic that they rank among the major books of his generation.

The mythopoeic genius of Lewis and Powys, their vatic concern with eternal verities, their rhythmic prose and metaphoric language, align them with Lawrence, Joyce, and even Virginia Woolf in transcending the conventional barrier between prose and poetry. Whereas previous writers had failed in attempts to write novels in verse, these in their various ways succeeded in endowing prose fiction with essential poetic qualities. As in the other arts, photographic fidelity to nature gave way to symbolic interpretation.

In Lawrence's later works the poetry was painfully at war with the homiletics. In search of a climate beneficial for his tuberculosis, and of some mode of consciousness free from modern tensions, the Lawrences ranged restlessly from the Mediterranean to Ceylon, Australia, and Mexico, until they found the best conditions in the New Mexican desert. The settings of his novels record the stages of the pilgrimage. *Aaron's Rod* (1922), which is partly autobiographical in its portrayal of a mine-worker with musical gifts, is a loosely constructed story that moves from England to Florence. Aaron Sisson deserts the wife whom he loves, because he feels instinctively that she is engulfing him; and he eventually finds a man friend, Rawdon Lilly, who becomes the *persona* of Lawrence in the later part of the book, struggling to redeem Aaron by his gospel of the "power motive . . . Not intellectual power. Not mental power. Not conscious will-power. Not even wisdom. But dark, living, fructifying power."

The self-portraiture is even more faithful in his Australian novel, *Kangaroo* (1923), in which the hero is a bearded English author, disillusioned by wartime persecution, who seeks isolation in Australia but becomes involved in fascist and socialist organizations. The subsequent riots and violence are uncomfortably prescient of the disturbances that were soon to beset the world. Lawrence's obsession with power weighs heavily on the book, and the hero's soliloquies reiterate his doctrine that "the only thing one can stick to is one's own isolate being, and the God in whom it is rooted. And the only thing to look to is the God who fulfils one from the dark."

Another novel with an Australian setting, *The Boy in the Bush*, is Lawrence's rewriting of a manuscript by a woman whom he met there. Then his visit to Mexico produced the most horrifying of his novels on the theme of power, *The Plumed Serpent* (1926). The ancient Aztec cults satisfied his craving for a primitive frame of reference posited upon the elemental instincts. A cultivated Irish widow marries an Indian general who participates in a revolution dedicated to ousting Christianity from the country in favor of the old gods, and democracy in favor of a fascist dictatorship. Lawrence's descriptive power is at its apex in his representation of the brilliant, crude colors of the Mexican scene, the filth and terror, the ferocity and bloodshed of a bullfight and of a bandit foray. The leader of the revolution indulges in mystical exercises reminiscent of Eastern yogi, and the three principal characters go through a ritual of initiation as reincarnations of the Aztec gods.

Lawrence's favorable portrayal of autocratic leaders in *Kangaroo* and *The Plumed Serpent* seems to reflect his own ambition to initiate a movement toward a Utopia of emotionally liberated souls. His declining health, and the failure of his admirers to join him in an *avant-garde* colony in Taos, put an end to this phase. He began to realize that social revolution entailed militancy, whereas his dream was for a sensitive and tender understanding between individuals. Therefore *The Plumed Serpent* marks the close of his glorification of power, and his next novel concentrated upon his other persistent theme, sex. In *Lady Chatterley's Lover* (1928) he reiterated his lifelong concern over the sexual dilemma — man's physical need for woman and his equally compulsive need for spiritual independence from her. With this he merged his theory that men of the people are superior to the effete products of culture because they follow the normal human impulses without perversion or shame. He returned to the English rural setting of his early novels and told the story of an aristocratic woman who is driven to seek sexual gratification surreptitiously because her husband is paralyzed by wartime injuries. After an unsatisfactory affair with a young playwright, she discovers the beauty and joy of honest passion with a virile gamekeeper. It is true that Mellors has obtained an education for himself, but he is essentially a representative of the lowest social class, as Lawrence idealized it, sensitively loving the beauty of nature and frankly obeying his primitive instincts.

Lawrence considered this to be the most effective manifesto of his doctrines, and he wrote the whole book three times, achieving a unity and a sense of inevitable destiny that contrasted with the lax structure of most of his novels. The original draft, which was printed in 1944 as *The First Lady Chatterley*, is shallower and emotionally less tense than the final rewriting. The explicit record of sexual intercourse places the book in the tradition of naturalism; but Lawrence endued it with his idealistic mission of rescuing the physical function of sex from infamy by depicting it as beautiful. Because he flagrantly employed vulgar words that are seldom seen in print, and because his familiar geographical and social details were less efficient than the exotic environments of his preceding novels in veiling the lewdness of the events, he incurred the old accusation of immorality, and for the second time one of his books was legally suppressed as obscene. Until 1959 the editions available in the United States were a censored version made after the author's death. His only subsequent novel, *The Virgin and the Gypsy*, which has a similar theme, was unfinished when he died in 1930, and was printed from his manuscript draft.

While Lawrence was waging his campaigns for curing the modern spiritual malady, Virginia Woolf remained a detached onlooker, apparently concerned with literary artistry more than with panaceas. Her later fiction falls into two categories. Seeking fresh techniques, she experimented with fantasy in a

couple of books, which are charming but not altogether acceptable as serious works of art. *Orlando* (1928) embodies her
interest in the phenomenon of time: the central character is
modeled upon her friend and fellow-novelist, Victoria Sack-
ville-West, and the setting is Knole, the ancestral mansion of
the Sackvilles, but the story ranges through three centuries,
with Orlando not only surviving down the generations but
changing sex in the process. *Flush* (1933) is less ambitious, and
harks back to the device of *Pompey the Little* by centering
the story upon a lap-dog — in this instance the pet of Elizabeth
Barrett Browning.

More realistic in material and more effective in their analysis
of personality are Mrs. Woolf's other novels, which exemplify the theory that she expressed in an essay on "Modern
Fiction":

> Life is . . . a luminous halo, a semi-transparent envelope sur-
> rounding us from the beginning of consciousness to the end.
> Is it not the task of the novelists to convey this varying, this
> unknown and uncircumscribed spirit? . . . Let us record the
> atoms as they fall upon the mind in the order in which they
> fall, let us trace the pattern, however disconnected and incoherent
> in appearances, which each sight or incident scores upon the con-
> sciousness.

The Waves (1931) abandons plot structure in favor of a
group of character studies of six friends, as revealed in
monologues that they utter at various intervals through their
lives. The story of their relationship transpires through their
separate rememberings, attention being thus deflected away
from the interplay of external events and toward the revelation
of personality. Nevertheless, the total effect is not so much
the differentiation among the characters as their resemblance:
their lives are so intertwined that they seem to have no existence except as parts of a single continuum. The idea that
experience is a rhythmic pattern in the sea of time, symbolized
by the title, is elaborated by a series of prose poems about the
ocean, marking the divisions of the story.

The title of *The Years* (1937) indicates a similar preoccupation with time, and the absence of plot is even more conspicuous. Dealing with a large family throughout the preceding
half century, it records their varied experiences simply for the

sake of recording them, without developing any significant interrelationship. With readers accustomed to the convention that a novelist selects his material so as to construct a chain of causes and effects, *The Years* leaves a peculiar effect of incompleteness.

While there is little that can be termed doctrinaire in Mrs. Woolf's novels, they convey an affirmative attitude. The author loved life and admired the indomitable impulse that defies despair, even though many of her sensitive characters suffer from neurotic anxiety. Therefore a tragic irony attends the close of her life. Like her circle of intellectual friends, she was morally committed to pacifism, and the tension and brutality of the Second World War proved more than her sympathetic nature could endure. In 1941, convinced that she was on the verge of a mental collapse that would render her a responsibility to others in a time of crisis, she drowned herself.

The other member of the trio that took the lead in experiments with psychological exploration, James Joyce, had died in Zurich two months earlier. For seventeen years after the publication of *Ulysses* he had lived in Paris, subsidized by admirers of his work, and occasionally releasing fragments of the gigantic project upon which he was engaged. These glimpses of his "work in progress" were elucidated in 1929 in a book of essays by some of his disciples — a unique instance of a critical volume antedating the book that it discusses. The reading public was thus forewarned that the new work would surpass *Ulysses* in experimental novelty further than *Ulysses* had surpassed previous fiction. Even with so much indoctrination, when *Finnegans Wake* was eventually published in 1939 most people found it incomprehensible.

The title, to begin with, has no recognizable relationship with the book, being the name of a popular comic song about an Irish hod-carrier who came back to life while his friends were drinking around his corpse. The novel itself seemed to deal with a Dublin tavern-keeper named Humphrey Chimpden Earwicker. *Ulysses* had presented the uncontrolled impressions in several minds during one day, ending with an incoherent reverie as Molly Bloom fell asleep. *Finnegans Wake* picks up at this stage and confines itself to the dreams passing through a single mind during one night. In order to suggest the elusive and symbolic impression of dreams, Joyce created a new vocabulary in which multiple meanings are attached to a single word by distortion of spelling and by grafting of syllables. Often it is necessary to read a passage aloud if one is to obtain even a tentative conception of its significance. The beauty of rhythms and the haunting overtones of imagery lend poetic charm as a substitute for rational communication. Scenes and action occasionally emerge for a moment with preternatural vividness before wavering and fading into the continuous flux. No progressive narration is discernible; in fact, the first page begins in the middle of a sentence and the last page ends with the first half of the same sentence.

Some patient analysts claim to have identified the main facts of Earwicker's daytime life that are grotesquely implied in his dreams. Like Bloom, he is fat and middle-aged, and has failed in business ventures. His wife is younger than he. They have a teen-age daughter and twin sons. His dreams reveal hints of suppressed sexual disturbances — discontent that his wife is getting old, incestuous feelings toward his daughter and homosexual impulses toward one of the boys. But the book is not confined to Earwicker's past and present life; it represents him as an epitome of the whole past of the human race, in accordance with Jung's psychological theory of the collective unconscious. Earwicker's personal anxieties expand into vast generalizations by linking themselves with everything that he has ever read or heard. Sometimes he is Tristram, or Adam, or Jonathan Swift, or Oliver Cromwell, or Napoleon, or Humpty Dumpty, or Finnegan the hod-carrier. The initials of his name reappear in symbolic abstractions: Howth Castle and Environs (the local Dublin landscape, which in turn becomes symbolic of the male and female principles), Haveth Childers Everywhere, and particularly Here Comes Everybody. Joyce was strongly influenced by the doctrine of the eighteenth-century Italian philosopher, Giovanni Battista Vico, that all aspects of history move through a fixed cycle of phases — the divine, the heroic, and the human — which is the substance of all mythologies. This historical synopsis detracts from psychological plausibility: Earwicker's mediocre education could not have provided him with the foreign words and esoteric allusions that complicate his dreams. Individual psychology in this book becomes merely a vehicle for universal revelation. Earwicker in his dream embodies all facets of human existence — life and death, youth and old age, masculinity and femininity; and at the same time these various antitheses appear to represent the two sides of the dreamer's own nature, perpetually in conflict. The novel may be said to have a happy ending in that Earwicker's feelings of frustration and guilt seem to have been resolved during the night, and he wakes in a mood of serenity, — or, in mythological terms, the archetypal theme of the Fall (Adam, Humpty Dumpty, Finnegan tumbling off his ladder) has led to redemption and resurrection (Finnegan's return from death).

The unique characteristics of *Finnegans Wake* have been linked to three personal attributes of Joyce: his profession as a teacher of languages, which enabled him to pun inexhaustibly in a score of tongues; his musical proficiency, which made the sound of words more important to him than the sense; and his increasing blindness which substituted his ears for his eyes. But it was also a planned technical *tour de force*, culmination of a lifetime's experiments. Probably it will seldom be read for aesthetic enjoyment, but will stand as a landmark representing the furthest conceivable limit of the effort to remodel syntax and vocabulary into a medium for indicating unconscious processes.

It was inevitable that the novelists who absorbed Freudian psychoanalysis into the texture of fiction should draw mainly upon their personal lives. Not being professional clinicians, they lacked case histories that could be developed with the fullness and plausibility that a novel demands, and so they had no recourse but to project their own yearnings and antagonisms into the characters they invented. In the last analysis, the novels of Lawrence, Joyce, and Virginia Woolf are read as uninhibited revelations of remarkable personalities.

It is too early to decide whether the next generation of novelists, who emerged in the thirties, will survive as permanent figures in the history of English fiction. At least it can be asserted that none of them are as openly experimental as their seniors. All have been satisfied with the established forms of the novel. The cleverest of them, Evelyn Waugh, followed Huxley's example in writing contemptuous satire about sophisticated people. The son and brother of authors, Waugh began novel-writing at twenty-five, in 1928, with *Decline and Fall*. In this and in *Vile Bodies* (1930) the futility of postwar English society is pitilessly ridiculed through characters that are fantastic caricatures rather than believable human beings. His next novels, *Black Mischief, A Handful of Dust*, and *Scoop*, drew upon his travels in Africa for derisive portrayals of both European and native characters in farcical situations. By this time Waugh had been converted to the Roman Catholic faith; and, again like Huxley, he let an earnest concern with spiritual realities glimmer through the frivolous surface of his stories. When he joined the army in 1939 he was at work on a more serious novel, which he never finished. *Put Out More Flags*, written in the midst of the war, is a rather ineffectual mixture of satiric burlesque and grave social criticism. In *Brideshead Revisited* (1945) Waugh finally wrote a thoroughly serious novel about religion, though with distressing intrusions of sentimentality, snobbery, and vulgar ostentation. The religious theme reappears in *Men at Arms* (1952) and *Officers and Gentlemen* (1955), the first volumes of a projected trilogy depicting the war in a disillusioned light. The perfection of Waugh's prose is admired by many critics who dislike his opinions or his impudent manner, especially his trick of trying to shock the reader by inserting episodes of horrible physical suffering in a comic context.

There is some tendency to associate Waugh with Graham Greene, on the basis that both are converts to Catholicism. In *The Man Within* (1929) Greene began a series of suspense stories which combine thrilling plots of crime and international intrigue with a somber search for the meaning of existence. The author's unhappy boyhood, when he had been sometimes on the verge of suicide, sets the tone for all his fiction. In the earlier novels the hero is driven into adventure by a sense of frustration and boredom with the trivialities of everyday routine. The bitterness and tension of the decade before the Second World War, its anticipation of disaster and its irrational hopes, are embodied in Greene's taut stories, some of which have cosmopolitan settings — Stockholm, Middle Europe, Mexico, West Africa. These places are not made exotically charming, but remain as squalid as the English underworld of his other books. Throughout his work escape and betrayal are the recurrent situations, but the pervasive sense of terror does not spring from mere danger but from the author's conviction that failure and cruelty and ugliness are the normal attributes of life. In some books, which he labeled "entertainments," such as *A Gun for Sale*, *The Confidential Agent*, and *The Ministry of Fear*, the element of excitement predominates; but even these contain psychological and ideological analysis that links them with his graver novels, *England Made Me* (1935), *Brighton Rock* (1938), *The Power and the Glory* (1940), *The Heart of the Matter* (1945), and *The End of the Affair* (1951). Gradually the harried intensity of the previous books gave way to a tone of subdued understatement and the religious preoccupation became dominant. The poetic style and technical skill in all his work indicates the literary influences that shaped him: first Stevenson, then Conrad, ultimately Henry James. The concern with spiritual redemption in his later novels shows affinities with recent French Catholic writers, François Mauriac and Charles Peguy.

Another significant novelist, Joyce Cary, was fifteen years older than Waugh and Greene, but he took so much longer to master the craft of fiction that his first novel appeared several years later than theirs, and another decade elapsed before he won any degree of recognition. He, too, used African settings in several books, but with deeper understanding and sympathy, for he had spent seven years as a colonial administrator in Nigeria, which provided material for his early novels, between 1932 and 1939, *Aissa Saved*, *An American Visitor*, *The African Witch*, and *Mr. Johnson*. He then turned his attention to his Anglo-Irish childhood in *Castle Corner* and *A House of Children*, before gaining fame with a trilogy (1941–44) about a painter, Gully Jimson — *Herself Surprised*, *To Be a Pilgrim*, and *The Horse's Mouth*. Having been an art student in his youth, Cary was exceptionally successful in depicting the artist's creative compulsion. The technical virtuosity of the trilogy resides in the changes in point of view: each volume is narrated by a different participant in the events, and their utterly unlike personalities are conveyed not only by their outlook and manner but by their views of one another, so that the reader ends with a complex perception of the relativity of human judgment.

The method is used again in a subsequent trilogy (1952–55), dealing with English politics and consisting of *Prisoner of Grace, Except the Lord*, and *Not Honour More*. At the time of his death in 1957 Cary was finishing *The Captive and the Free*, which was to be the first volume of a trilogy on religious sectarianism.

Cary was primarily concerned with the problem of human freedom and the price it demands. Each of his trilogies contrasts an extroverted man of creative power with one who is conventional and inhibited, while between then stands an impulsive, fervent woman. The author tends to sympathize most with simple people — children, African natives, the political agitator Chester Nimmo, the slum evangelist Walter Preedy — though he is scrupulously just toward his more complicated intellectuals. Never satisfied that he had fully learned the demanding art of the novel, Cary subjected each of his manuscripts to a rigorous discipline of condensation, with the result that the tempo seems uncomfortably fast and there is not enough differentiation between major elements and incidental details.

Resembling their existentialist French contemporaries, Cary and Greene and Waugh are alike in their quest for basic moral values in a world that has lost all established sanctions. Most of the other novelists of their generation confine themselves to recording the phenomena of the scene without suggesting ultimate meanings.

Elizabeth Bowen writes with delicacy of perception and visual exactitude reminiscent of Virginia Woolf. She uses a minimum of plot and seldom creates memorable characters; her skill is in showing the relationship of the individual with his environment, and the behavior of cultivated people under the threat of destruction that overhangs their social system.

Ivy Compton-Burnett, on the other hand, being an older author whose fame came late in life, ignores the contemporary predicament, to create a late-Victorian atmosphere of solid prosperity and family complications. Consisting almost wholly of conversation, which is couched in artificially formal terms, her books present characters that are predominantly vicious and contemptible. Her material is reminiscent of Jane Austen but her outlook is more like Samuel Butler's. She shocks the reader by introducing melodramatic climaxes of forgery, murder, suicide, or incest into the placid household routine; but even more horrifying is the fact that the crimes and perversions go unpunished. The innocent characters (usually children or servants) are always defeated; the hypocrites, tyrants, and sadists remain smugly triumphant.

C. P. Snow draws upon his own distinguished career in science and government service, which has earned him a knighthood, to write a long series of solid, meticulous novels that carry a single character through the bureaucratic mazes of modern universities, scientific research, and public administration.

The young novelists of the fifties seem no more venturesome in their techniques or attitudes. Those who have aroused most discussion — Kingsley Amis, John Braine, and John Wain — portray the new Welfare State with something like the lower-middle-class facetiousness of Wells's *Kipps*. Writers who take a more fastidious intellectual pose, such as L. P. Hartley, Angus Wilson, and Iris Murdoch, walk in the footprints of Huxley or Virginia Woolf. In the vitiating aftermath of the Second World War, the English novel appears deficient in momentum.

Nevertheless, a final backward glance over almost four hundred years of English fiction suggests no probability that the novel is moribund. Through all vicissitudes of romanticism and realism, in the work of competent journeymen as well as in that of creative geniuses, a self-perpetuating vitality has never lapsed. From the time when Lyly and Sidney established one pole of the novel, the Nashe and Deloney the other, the inherent qualities of the whole genre have preserved it as the sole adequate vehicle for the complex, pragmatic, fluctuating milieu of the modern world.

BIBLIOGRAPHY

General

(a) Bibliographies

Esdaile, A. J. K. *A List of English Tales and Prose Romances Printed before 1740*. London, 1912.

Block, A. *The English Novel, 1740–1850: A Catalogue*. London, 1939.

Summers, Montague. *A Gothic Bibliography*. London, 1941.

Hankin, L. J. "Problems and Digressions in the Victorian Novel." *Bulletin of Bibliography*, xvii–xx (1945–50), *passim*.

Sadleir, Michael. *XIX Century Fiction: A Bibliographical Record*. 2 vols. Berkeley, Calif., 1951.

LeClaire, Lucien. *A General Analytical Bibliography of the Regional Novelists of the British Isles, 1800–1950*. Clermont-Ferrand, 1953.

(b) Histories

Baker, E. A. *A History of the English Novel*. 10 vols. London, 1924–39.

Heidler, J. B. *The History, from 1700, of English Criticism of Prose Fiction*. Urbana, Ill., 1928.

Leavis, Q. D. *Fiction and the Reading Public*. London, 1932.

Verschoyle, Derek (ed.). *The English Novelists*. London, 1936.

Taylor, J. T. *Early Opposition to the English Novel: The Popular Reaction from 1760 to 1830*. New York, 1943.

MacCarthy, B. G. *Women Writers: Their Contribution to the English Novel, 1621–1744*. Cork, 1944.

———. *The Later Women Novelists, 1744–1818*. Cork, 1947.

Simon, Irène. *Formes du roman Anglais de Dickens à Joyce*. Liége, 1951.

Rathburn, R. C., and Martin Steinmann (eds.). *From Jane Austen to Joseph Conrad*. Minneapolis, Minn., 1958.

(c) Criticism

Lubbock, Percy. *The Craft of Fiction*. London, 1921.

Forster, E. M. *Aspects of the Novel*. Cambridge, 1927.

495

Muir, Edwin. *The Structure of the Novel.* London, 1928.

Daiches, David. *The Novel and the Modern World.* Chicago, 1940.

Pritchett, V. S. *The Living Novel.* London, 1946.

Leavis, F. R. *The Great Tradition.* London, 1948.

Brown, E. K. *Rhythm in the Novel.* Toronto, 1950.

Mendilow, A. A. *Time and the Novel.* London, 1952.

Van Ghent, Dorothy. *The English Novel: Form and Function.* New York, 1953.

Schorer, Mark (ed.). *Society and Self in the Novel.* New York, 1955.

Praz, Mario. *The Hero in Eclipse in Victorian Fiction.* Trans. A. Davidson. London, 1956.

Zabel, M. D. *Craft and Character: Texts, Method, and Vocation in Modern Fiction.* New York, 1957.

Kennedy, Margaret. *The Outlaws on Parnassus.* London, 1958.

O'Connor, Frank. *The Mirror in the Roadway: A Study of the Modern Novel.* New York, 1958.

Tillyard, E. M. W. *The Epic Strain in the English Novel.* London, 1958.

Allott, Miriam. *Novelists on the Novel.* New York, 1959.

(d) Studies of Themes and Topics

Scarborough, Dorothy. *The Supernatural in Modern English Fiction.* New York, 1917.

Russell, F. T. *Satire in the Victorian Novel.* New York, 1920.

Speare, M. E. *The Political Novel.* New York, 1924.

Horner, J. M. *The English Women Novelists and their Connection with the Feminist Movement (1688–1797).* Northampton, Mass., 1929–30.

Thomson, H. D. *Masters of Mystery: A Study of the Detective Novel.* London, 1931.

Baker, J. E. *The Novel and the Oxford Movement.* Princeton, 1932.

Shepperson, A. B. *The Novel in Motley: A History of the Burlesque Novel in English.* Cambridge, Mass., 1936.

Utter, R. P., and G. P. Needham. *Pamela's Daughters.* New York, 1936.

Marriott, Sir John. *English History in English Fiction.* London, 1940.

Bentley, Phyllis. *The English Regional Novel.* London, 1941.

Gove, P. B. *The Imaginary Voyage in Prose Fiction.* New York, 1941.

Bailey, J. O. *Pilgrims through Space and Time: Trends and Patterns in Scientific Utopian Fiction.* New York, 1943.

Parkinson, C. N. *Portsmouth Point: The British Navy in Fiction.* Liverpool, 1948.

Howe, Susanne. *Novels of Empire.* New York, 1950.

LeClaire, Lucien. *Le Roman regionaliste dans les Îles Britanniques, 1800–1950.* Clermont-Ferrand, 1953.
Proctor, M. R. *The English University Novel.* Berkeley, Calif., 1957.
Murch, A. E. *The Development of the Detective Novel.* London, 1958.
Flanagan, Thomas. *The Irish Novelists, 1800–1850.* New York, 1959.

Chapter I

General. Jusserand, J. J. *The English Novel in the Time of Shakespeare.* Trans. E. Lee. London, 1890.
Chandler, F. W. *The Literature of Roguery.* 2 vols. Boston, 1907.
Woolf, S. L. *The Greek Romances in Elizabethan Prose Fiction.* New York, 1912.
Pruvost, René. *Matteo Bandello and Elizabethan Fiction.* Paris, 1937.
Gascoigne. Bradner, Leicester. "The First English Novel: A Study of George Gascoigne's *Adventures of Master F.J.*" *PMLA*, xlv (1930), 543–52.
Prouty, C. T. *Gascoigne: Elizabethan Courtier, Soldier, and Poet.* New York, 1942.
Grange. Rollins, H. E. "John Grange's *The Golden Aphroditis.*" *Harvard Studies in Philology and Literature*, xvi (1934), 177–88.
Prouty, C. T. "Elizabethan Fiction: Whetstone's *Rinaldo and Giletta* and Grange's *The Golden Aphroditis.*" *Studies in Honor of A.H.R. Fairchild.* Columbia, Mo., 1946.
Lyly. Wilson, J. D. *John Lyly.* London, 1905.
Feuillerat, Albert. *John Lyly: Contribution à l'histoire de la renaissance en Angleterre.* Cambridge, 1910.
Sidney. Wallace, M. W. *The Life of Sir Philip Sidney.* Cambridge, 1915.
Zandvoort, R. W. *Sidney's "Arcadia": A Comparison between the Two Versions.* Amsterdam, 1929.
Goldman, M. S. *Sir Philip Sidney and the "Arcadia."* Urbana, Ill., 1934.
Myrick, K. O. *Sir Philip Sidney as a Literary Craftsman.* Cambridge, Mass., 1935.
Bill, A. H. *Astrophel, or the Life and Death of the Renowned Sir Philip Sidney.* New York, 1937.
Rowe, K. T. *Romantic Love and Parental Authority in Sidney's "Arcadia."* Ann Arbor, Mich., 1947.
Greene. Jordan, J. C. *Robert Greene.* Cambridge, 1915.
Pruvost, René. *Greene et ses romans.* Paris, 1938.

Lodge.   Paradise, N. B. *Thomas Lodge: The History of an Elizabethan Man of Letters.* New Haven, Conn., 1931.
Tenney, E. A. *Thomas Lodge.* Ithaca, N.Y., 1935.

Jest Books.   Wilson, F. P. "The English Jestbooks of the Sixteenth and Early Seventeenth Centuries." *Huntington Library Quarterly,* ii (1939), 121–58.

Nashe.   Bowers, F. T. "Thomas Nashe and the Picaresque Novel." *Studies in Honor of John Calvin Metcalf.* Charlottesville, Va., 1941.
Latham, A. M. C. "Satire on Literary Themes and Modes in *The Unfortunate Traveler.*" *Essays and Studies,* n.s. i (1948), 85–100.

Deloney.   Chevalley, Abel. *Thomas Deloney: Le Roman des métiers au temps de Shakespeare.* Paris, 1926.
Powys, Llewellyn. "Thomas Deloney." *Virginia Quarterly Review,* ix (1933), 578–94.

Chapter II

General.   Morgan, C. E. *The Rise of the Novel of Manners.* New York, 1911.
Rolfe, F. P. "On the Bibliography of Seventeenth-Century Prose Fiction." *PMLA,* xlix (1934), 1071–86.

Character Writers.   Boyce, Benjamin. *The Theophrastian Character in England to 1642.* Cambridge, Mass., 1947.

Heroic Romances.   Haviland, T. P. *The "Roman de Longue Haleine" on English Soil.* Philadelphia, Pa., 1931.

Bunyan.   Brown, John. *John Bunyan: His Life, Times, and Work.* Rev. by F. M. Harrison. London, 1928.
Tindall, W. Y. *John Bunyan, Mechanick Preacher.* New York, 1934.
Talon, H. A. *Bunyan: L'homme et l'oeuvre.* Paris, 1948 (Engl. trans. by B. Wall, 1951).
Harding, M. E. *Journey into Self.* New York, 1956.

Behn.   Platt, H. G. "Astrea and Celadon: An Untouched Portrait of Aphra Behn." *PMLA,* xlix (1934), 544–59.
Woodcock, George. *The Incomparable Aphra.* London, 1948.
Hahn, Emily. *Aphra Behn.* London, 1951.

Chapter III

General.   Tieje, A. J. *The Theory of Characterization in Prose Fiction Prior to 1740.* Minneapolis, Minn., 1916.

Brown. Boyce, Benjamin. *Tom Brown of Facetious Memory.* Cambridge, Mass., 1939.

Ward. Troyer, H. W. *Ned Ward of Grub Street.* Cambridge, Mass., 1946.

Manley. Anderson, P. B. "Delariviere Manley's Prose Fiction." *Philological Quarterly,* xiii (1934), 168–88.

——. "Mistress Delariviere Manley's Biography." *Modern Philology,* xxxiii (1936), 261–78.

Needham, G. B. "Mary de la Riviere Manley, Tory Defender." *Huntington Library Quarterly,* xii (1949), 253–88.

——. "Mrs. Manley, an Eighteenth-Century Wife of Bath." *Ibid.,* xiv (1951), 259–84.

Defoe. Healey, G. H. (ed.). *The Letters of Daniel Defoe.* Oxford, 1955.

Dottin, Paul. *Daniel Defoe et ses romans.* 3 vols. Paris, 1924. Engl. trans. of vol. i by Louise Ragan as *The Life and Strange and Surprising Adventures of Daniel Defoe.* New York, 1929.

Secord, A. W. *Studies in the Narrative Method of Daniel Defoe.* Urbana, Ill., 1924.

Stamm, R. G. "Daniel Defoe: An Artist in the Puritan Tradition." *Philological Quarterly,* xv (1936), 225–46.

Sutherland, James. *Defoe.* London, 1938.

Moore, J. R. *Daniel Defoe, Citizen of the Modern World.* Chicago, 1958.

Swift. Ball, F. E. (ed.). *The Correspondence of Jonathan Swift.* 6 vols. London, 1910–14.

Eddy, W. A. *"Gulliver's Travels": A Critical Study.* Princeton, N.J., 1923.

Quintana, Ricardo. *The Mind and Art of Jonathan Swift.* New York, 1936.

Ross, J. F. *Swift and Defoe: A Study in Relationship.* Berkeley, Calif., 1941.

Case, A. E. *Four Essays on "Gulliver's Travels."* Princeton, N.J., 1945.

Williams, Sir H. *The Text of "Gulliver's Travels."* Cambridge, 1952.

Murry, J. M. *Swift: A Critical Biography.* London, 1954.

Ewald, W. B. *The Masks of Swift.* Oxford, 1954.

Haywood. Whicher, G. F. *The Life and Romances of Mrs. Eliza Haywood.* New York, 1915.

Aubin. McBurney, W. H. "Mrs. Penelope Aubin and the Early Eighteenth-Century Novel in England." *Huntington Library Quarterly,* xx (1957), 245–67.

Davys. McBurney, W. H. "Mrs. Mary Davys, Forerunner of Fielding." *PMLA,* lxxiv (1959), 348–55.

Chapter IV

General. Foster, J. R. "The Abbé Prévost and the English Novel." *PMLA*, xlii (1927), 443–64.

Singer, G. F. *The Epistolary Novel.* Philadelphia, Pa., 1933.

Slagle, K. C. *The English Country Squire as Depicted in English Prose Fiction from 1740 to 1800.* Philadelphia, Pa., 1938.

Van Tieghem, P. "Le Roman sentimental en Europe de Richardson à Rousseau." *Revue de Littérature Comparée*, xx (1940), 129–51.

McKillop, A. D. *The Early Masters of English Fiction.* Lawrence, Kans., 1956.

Watt, Ian. *The Rise of the Novel: Studies in Defoe, Richardson, and Fielding.* Berkeley, Calif., 1957.

Richardson. Barbauld, A. L. (ed.). *The Correspondence of Samuel Richardson.* 6 vols. London, 1804.

McKillop, A. D. *Samuel Richardson, Printer and Novelist.* Chapel Hill, N.C., 1936.

Sale, W. M. *Samuel Richardson, Master Printer.* Ithaca, N.Y., 1950.

Daiches, David. "Samuel Richardson." *Literary Essays.* Edinburgh, 1956.

Fielding. Cross, W. L. *The History of Henry Fielding.* 3 vols. New Haven, Conn., 1918.

Blanchard, F. T. *Fielding the Novelist.* New Haven, Conn., 1926.

Thornbury, E. M. *Henry Fielding's Theory of the Comic Prose Epic.* Madison, Wis., 1931.

Bissell, F. O. *Fielding's Theory of the Novel.* Ithaca, N.Y., 1933.

Irwin, W. R. *The Making of "Jonathan Wild."* New York, 1941.

Dudden, F. H. *Fielding: His Life, Works, and Times.* 2 vols. Oxford, 1952.

Smollett. Noyes, E. S. (ed.). *The Letters of Tobias Smollett.* Cambridge, Mass., 1926.

Buck, H. S. *A Study in Smollett, Chiefly "Peregrine Pickle."* New Haven, Conn., 1925.

Martz, L. L. *The Later Career of Tobias Smollett.* New Haven, Conn., 1942.

Kahrl, G. M. *Tobias Smollett, Traveler-Novelist.* Chicago, 1945.

Boege, F. W. *Smollett's Reputation as a Novelist.* Princeton, N.J., 1947.

Knapp, L. M. *Tobias Smollett, Doctor of Men and Manners.* Princeton, N.J., 1949.

Brander, L. R. M. *Smollett.* London, 1951.

Lennox. Small, M. R. *Charlotte Ramsay Lennox: An Eighteenth-Century Lady of Letters.* New Haven, Conn., 1935.

S. Scott. Crittenden, W. M. *The Life and Writings of Mrs. Sarah Scott, Novelist.* Philadelphia, Pa., 1932.

Chapter V

General. Conant, M. P. *The Oriental Tale in England in the Eighteenth Century.* New York, 1908.

Black, F. G. *The Epistolary Novel in the Late Eighteenth Century.* Eugene, Ore., 1940.

Shebbeare. Foster, J. L. "Smollett's Pamphleteering Foe Shebbeare." *PMLA,* lvii (1942), 1053–1100.

Johnson. Hill, G. B. (ed.). *The Letters of Samuel Johnson.* 2 vols. Oxford, 1892.

Jenkins, H. D. "Some Aspects of the Background of *Rasselas.*" *Studies in English in Honor of R. D. O'Leary.* Lawrence, Kan., 1940.

Tillotson, Geoffrey. "*Rasselas* and the Persian Tales." *Essays in Criticism and Research.* Cambridge, 1942.

Krutch, Joseph Wood. *Samuel Johnson.* New York, 1944.

Lascelles, Mary. "*Rasselas* Reconsidered." *Essays and Studies,* n.s., iv (1951)

Moore, R. E. "Johnson on Fielding and Richardson." *PMLA,* lxvi (1951), 162–81.

Kolb, G. J. "The Structure of *Rasselas.*" *Ibid,* lxvi (1951), 698–717.

Layburn, E. D. "No Romantick Absurdities or Incredible Fictions." *Ibid.,* lxx (1955), 1059–67.

Whitley, Alvin. "The Comedy of *Rasselas.*" *ELH,* xxiii (1956), 48–70.

Sterne. Curtis, L. P. (ed.). *The Letters of Laurence Sterne.* Oxford, 1935.

Cross, W. L. *The Life and Times of Laurence Sterne.* 3rd ed., New Haven, Conn., 1929.

Curtis, L. P. *The Politicks of Laurence Sterne.* London, 1929.

Hartley, Lodwick. *This is Lorence: A Narrative of the Reverend Laurence Sterne.* Chapel Hill, N.C., 1943.

Dilworth, E. N. *The Unsentimental Journey of Laurence Sterne.* New York, 1948.

Traugott, John. *Tristram Shandy's World.* Berkeley, Calif., 1955.

Shaw, M. R. B. *Laurence Sterne: The Making of a Humorist.* London, 1957.

Connely, Willard. *Laurence Sterne as Yorick.* London, 1958.

Howes, A. B. *Yorick and the Critics: Sterne's Reputation in England, 1760–1868.* New Haven, Conn., 1958.

Walpole.   Lewis, W. S. (ed.). *The Correspondence of Horace Walpole.* — vols. New Haven, Conn., 1937–.
Mehrotra, K. K. *Horace Walpole and the English Novel.* Oxford, 1934.
Ketton-Cremer, R. W. *Horace Walpole: A Biography.* Rev. ed., London, 1946.

Brooke.   Scurr, H. M. *Henry Brooke.* Minneapolis, Minn., 1927.

Goldsmith.   Balderston, K. C. (ed.). *The Collected Letters of Oliver Goldsmith.* Cambridge, 1928.
Freeman, William. *Oliver Goldsmith.* London, 1951.
Wardle, R. M. *Oliver Goldsmith.* Lawrence, Kans., 1957.

Mackenzie.   Thompson, H. W. *A Scottish Man of Feeling.* New York, 1931.

Graves.   Hill, C. J. *The Literary Career of Richard Graves.* Northampton, Mass., 1935.

Chapter VI

General.   Howe, Susanne. *Wilhelm Meister and his English Kinsmen.* New York, 1930.
Tomkins, J. M. S. *The Popular Novel in England, 1770–1800.* London, 1932.
Wright, W. F. *Sensibility in English Prose Fiction, 1760–1814.* Urbana, Ill., 1937.
Blakey, Dorothy. *The Minerva Press, 1790–1820.* London, 1939.
Gallaway, W. F. "The Conservative Attitude Toward Fiction, 1770–1830." *PMLA,* lv (1940), 1041–59.
Foster, J. R. *A History of the Pre-Romantic Novel in England.* New York, 1949.

Novels of Doctrine.   Gregory, Allene. *The French Revolution and the English Novel.* New York, 1915.
Proper, C. B. A. *Social Elements in English Prose Fiction between 1770 and 1832.* Amsterdam, 1929.
Whitney, Lois. *Primitivism and the Idea of Progress in English Popular Literature in the Eighteenth Century.* Baltimore, Md., 1934.
Heilman, R. B. *America in English Fiction, 1760–1800.* Baton Rouge, La., 1937.

Gothic Romances.   Birkhead, Edith. *The Tale of Terror.* London, 1921.
Railo, Eino. *The Haunted Castle.* London, 1927.
Summers, Montague. *The Gothic Quest.* London, 1938.
Varma, D. P. *The Gothic Flame.* London, 1957.

Burney. Barrett, Charlotte (ed.). *The Diary and Letters of Fanny Burney.* London, 1904–05.

Hale, W. T. *Mme. d'Arblay's Place in the Development of the English Novel.* Bloomington, Ind., 1916.

Tourtellot, A. B. *Be Loved No More: The Life and Environment of Fanny Burney.* New York, 1938.

Hahn, Emily. *A Degree of Prudery.* London, 1951.

Hemlow, Joyce. *The History of Fanny Burney.* Oxford, 1958.

Holcroft. Colby, Elbridge. "Thomas Holcroft, Man of Letters." *South Atlantic Quarterly,* xxii (1923), 53–70.

Stallbaumer, V. R. "Thomas Holcroft, a Satirist in the Stream of Sentimentalism." *ELH,* iii (1936), 31–62.

Bage. Grabo, C. H. "Robert Bage, a Forgotten Novelist." *Midwest Quarterly,* v (1917), 201–26.

Sutherland, J. H. "Robert Bage, Novelist of Ideas." *Philological Quarterly,* xxxvi (1957), 211–20.

Beckford. Oliver, J. W. *The Life of William Beckford.* London, 1932.

Chapman, Guy. *Beckford.* London, 1937.

Brockman, H. A. N. *The Caliph of Fonthill.* London, 1956.

Day. Gignilliat, G. W. *The Author of "Sandford and Merton."* New York, 1932.

Scott, Sir H. W. *The Exemplary Mr. Day.* London, 1935.

Wollstonecraft. James, H. R. *Mary Wollstonecraft: A Sketch.* London, 1932.

Wardle, R. M. *Mary Wollstonecraft.* Lawrence, Kans., 1952.

Smith. Hilbish, F. M. A. *Charlotte Smith, Poet and Novelist.* Philadelphia, Pa., 1941.

Radcliffe. McIntyre, Clara F. *Ann Radcliffe in Relation to her Time.* New Haven, Conn., 1920.

Grant, Aline. *Ann Radcliffe.* London, 1952.

Godwin. Brown, F. K. *The Life of William Godwin.* New York, 1926.

Woodcock, George. *William Godwin: A Biographical Study.* London, 1946.

Fleisher, David. *William Godwin: A Study in Liberalism.* London, 1951.

Grylls, R. G. *William Godwin and his World.* London, 1953.

Inchbald. Littlewood, S. R. *Elizabeth Inchbald and her Circle.* London, 1921.

McKee, William. *Elizabeth Inchbald, Novelist.* Washington, D.C., 1935.

Chapter VII

General. Rogers, W. H. "The Reaction against Melodramatic Sentimentality in the English Novel, 1796–1830." *PMLA*, xlix (1934), 98–112.

Opie. Macgregor, M. E. *Amelia Anderson Opie, Worldling and Friend.* Northampton, Mass., 1932–33.

Menzies-Wilson, Jacobine, and Helen Lloyd. *Amelia: The Story of a Plain Friend.* London, 1937.

Edgeworth. Hare, A. J. C. *The Life and Letters of Maria Edgeworth.* 2 vols. London, 1894.

Clarke, I. C. *Maria Edgeworth.* London, 1950.

Newby, P. H. *Maria Edgeworth.* London, 1950.

Inglis-Jones, Elisabeth. *The Great Maria.* London, 1959.

Owenson. Stevenson, Lionel. *The Wild Irish Girl.* London, 1936.

Maturin. Idman, Niilo. *Charles Robert Maturin: His Life and Works.* London, 1923.

Scholten, William. *Charles Robert Maturin, the Terror Novelist.* Amsterdam, 1933.

Piper, H. W., and A. N. Jeffares. "Maturin the Innovator." *Huntington Library Quarterly*, xxi (1958), 261–84.

Austen. Austen-Leigh, William and R. A. *Jane Austen: Her Life and Letters.* London, 1913.

Austen-Leigh, M. A. *Personal Aspects of Jane Austen.* London, 1920.

Johnson, R. B. *Jane Austen: Her Life, her Work, her Family, and her Critics.* London, 1930.

Cecil, Lord David. *Jane Austen.* Cambridge, 1935.

Jenkins, Elizabeth. *Jane Austen: A Biography.* London, 1938.

Lascelles, Mary. *Jane Austen and her Art.* Rev. ed., Oxford, 1941.

Chapman, R. W. *Jane Austen: Facts and Problems.* Oxford, 1948.

Kennedy, Margaret. *Jane Austen.* London, 1950.

Mudrick, Marvin. *Jane Austen: Irony as Defense and Discovery.* Princeton, N.J., 1952.

Wright, A. H. *Jane Austen's Novels: A Study in Structure.* London, 1953.

Scott. Grierson, H. J. C. (ed.). *The Letters of Sir Walter Scott.* 12 vols. London, 1932–37.

Lockhart, J. G. *The Life of Sir Walter Scott.* 7 vols. Edinburgh, 1837–38.

Buchan, John. *Sir Walter Scott.* London, 1932.

Hillhouse, J. T. *The Waverley Novels and their Critics.* Minneapolis, Minn., 1836.

Landis, P. N. "The Waverley Novels, or a Hundred Years After." *PMLA* lii (1937), 461–73.

Grierson, H. J. C. *Sir Walter Scott, Bart.* London, 1938.

Fiske, C. F. *Epic Suggestion in the Imagery of the Waverley Novels.* New Haven, Conn., 1940.

Pope-Hennessy, Una. *Sir Walter Scott.* London, 1948.

Pearson, Hesketh. *Walter Scott: His Life and Personality.* London, 1954.

Daiches, David. "Scott's Achievement as a Novelist." *Literary Essays.* Edinburgh, 1956.

Chapter VIII

Shelley. Jones, F. L. (ed.). *The Letters of Mary Wollstonecraft Shelley.* 2 vols. Norman, Okla., 1944.

Grylls, R. G. *Mary Shelley: A Biography.* London, 1938.

Spark, Muriel. *Child of Light: A Reassessment of Mary Wollstone-craft Shelley.* London, 1951.

Nitchie, Elizabeth. *Mary Shelley, Author of "Frankenstein."* New Brunswick, N.J., 1953.

Hope. Baumgarten, Sandor. *La Crépuscule néoclassique: Thomas Hope.* Paris, 1958.

Peacock. Freeman, A. M. *Thomas Love Peacock: A Critical Study.* London, 1911.

Van Doren, Carl. *The Life of Thomas Love Peacock.* New York, 1911.

Priestley, J. B. *Thomas Love Peacock.* London, 1927.

Mayoux, J. J. *Un Épicurean anglais: Thomas Love Peacock.* Paris, 1933.

Brett-Smith, H. F. B., and C. E. Jones. "Biographical Introduction." *The Works of Thomas Love Peacock.* Vol. I. London, 1934.

Campbell, O. W. *Peacock.* London, 1953.

Ferrier. Doyle, J. A. (ed.). *Memoir and Correspondence of Susan Ferrier.* London, 1898.

Grant, Aline. *Susan Ferrier of Edinburgh: A Biography.* Denver, Col., 1957.

Galt. Gordon, R. K. *John Galt.* Toronto, 1920.

Aberdein, J. W. *John Galt.* Oxford, 1936.

Lyell, F. H. *A Study of the Novels of John Galt.* Princeton, N.J., 1942.

Lockhart. Lang, Andrew. *Life of John Gibson Lockhart.* 2 vols. London, 1897.

Macbeth, Gilbert. *John Gibson Lockhart: A Critical Study.* Urbana, Ill., 1935.

Lochhead, Marion. *John Gibson Lockhart.* London, 1954.

Carleton. O'Donoghue, D. J. *The Life of William Carleton.* 2 vols. London, 1896.

Kiely, Benedict. *Poor Scholar: A Study of the Works and Days of William Carleton.* London, 1947.

Mitford. Roberts, W. J. *Mary Russell Mitford: The Tragedy of a Bluestocking.* London, 1913.

Astin, Marjorie. *Mary Russell Mitford: Her Circle and her Books.* London, 1930.

Watson, V. G. *Mary Russell Mitford.* London, 1949.

Hook. Brightfield, M. F. *Theodore Hook and his Novels.* Cambridge, Mass., 1928.

Fashionable Novels. Rosa, M. W. *The Silver Fork School.* New York, 1936.

Schubel, Friedrich. *Die "Fashionable Novels."* Upsala, 1952.

Disraeli. Monypenny, W. F., and G. E. Buckle. *The Life of Benjamin Disraeli, Earl of Beaconsfield.* Rev. ed. 2 vols. London, 1929.

Forbes-Boyd, Eric. "Disraeli the Novelist." *Essays and Studies,* n.s., iii (1950), 100–17.

Holloway, John. "Disraeli's 'View of Life' in the Novels." *Essays in Criticism,* ii (1952), 413–33.

Masefield, Muriel. *Peacocks and Primroses: A Study of Disraeli's Novels.* London, 1953.

Bulwer-Lytton. Lytton, Earl of. *The Life of Edward Bulwer, First Lord Lytton.* 2 vols. London, 1913.

Sadleir, Michael. *Edward and Rosina, 1803–1836.* London, 1931.

Watts, H. H. "Lytton's Theories of Prose Fiction." *PMLA,* l (1935), 274–89.

Lytton, Earl of. *Bulwer-Lytton.* London, 1948.

Dahl, Curtis. "Bulwer-Lytton and the School of Catastrophe." *Philological Quarterly,* xxxii (1953), 428–42.

Chapter IX

Marryat. Lloyd, Christopher. *Captain Marryat and the Old Navy.* London, 1939.

Warner, Oliver. *Captain Marryat: A Rediscovery.* London, 1953.

James. Ellis, S. M. *The Solitary Horseman.* London, 1927.

Ainsworth. Ellis, S. M. *William Harrison Ainsworth and his Friends.* 2 vols. London, 1911.

Blessington. Sadleir, Michael. *Blessington-D'Orsay: A Masquerade.* London, 1933.

Surtees. Cuming, E. D. *Robert Smith Surtees, Creator of Jorrocks.* London, 1924.

Watson, Frederick. *Robert Smith Surtees: A Critical Study.* London, 1933.

Cooper, Leonard. *R. S. Surtees.* London, 1952.

Dickens. Dexter, Walter (ed.). *The Letters of Charles Dickens.* 3 vols. London, 1938.

Forster, John. *Life of Charles Dickens.* Rev. by J. W. T. Ley. London, 1928.

House, Humphry. *The Dickens World.* London, 1941.

Johnson, Edgar. *Charles Dickens: His Tragedy and Triumph.* 2 vols. New York, 1952.

Nisbet, A. B. *Dickens and Ellen Ternan.* Berkeley, Calif., 1952.

Monod, Sylvère. *Dickens romancier.* Paris, 1953.

Ford, G. H. *Dickens and his Readers.* Princeton, N.J., 1955.

Butt, John, and Kathleen Tillotson. *Dickens at Work.* London, 1957.

Fielding, K. J. *Charles Dickens: A Critical Introduction.* London, 1958.

Miller, J. H. *Charles Dickens: The World of his Novels.* Cambridge, Mass., 1958.

Engel, Monroe. *The Maturity of Dickens.* Cambridge, Mass., 1959.

Mrs. Trollope. Trollope, F. E. *Frances Trollope: Her Life and Literary Work.* 2 vols. London, 1895.

Bigland, Elizabeth. *The Indomitable Mrs. Trollope.* London, 1953.

Lever. Stevenson, Lionel. *Doctor Quicksilver.* London, 1939.

Chapter X

General. Cecil, Lord David. *Early Victorian Novelists.* London, 1934.

Tillotson, Kathleen. *Novels of the Eighteen-Forties.* Oxford, 1954.

Thomson, Patricia. *The Victorian Heroine.* London, 1957.

Thackeray. Ray, G. N. (ed.). *The Letters and Private Papers of William Makepeace Thackeray.* 4 vols. Cambridge, Mass., 1945–46.

Dodds, J. W. *Thackeray: A Critical Portrait.* New York, 1941.

Stevenson, Lionel. *The Showman of Vanity Fair.* New York, 1947.

Greig, J. Y. T. *Thackeray: A Reconsideration.* Oxford, 1950.

Ennis, Lambert. *Thackeray: The Sentimental Cynic.* Evanston, Ill., 1951.

Tillotson, Geoffrey. *Thackeray the Novelist.* Cambridge, 1954.

Ray, G. N. *The Buried Life.* London, 1952.

Ray, G. N. *Thackeray:* (i) *The Uses of Adversity.* New York, 1955. (ii) *The Age of Wisdom.* New York, 1958.

Brontës. Gaskell, E. C. *The Life of Charlotte Brontë.* 2 vols. London, 1857.

Shorter, C. K. *The Brontës: Life and Letters.* 2 vols. London, 1908.

Ratchford, F. E. *The Brontës' Web of Childhood.* New York, 1941.

Bentley, Phyllis. *The Brontës.* London, 1947.

Hanson, Laurence and E. M. *The Four Brontës.* London, 1949.

Lane, Margaret. *The Brontë Story.* London, 1953.

Visick, Mary. *The Genesis of "Wuthering Heights."* Hong Kong, 1958.

Hopkins, A. B. *The Father of the Brontës.* Baltimore, Md., 1958.

Paden, W. D. *An Investigation of Gondal.* New York, 1958.

Stanford, Derek, and Muriel Spark. *Anne Brontë.* London, 1959.

Gerin, Winifred. *Anne Brontë.* London, 1959.

Gaskell. Whitefield, A. S. *Mrs. Gaskell: Her Life and Work.* London, 1929.

Sanders, G. D. *Elizabeth Gaskell.* New Haven, Conn., 1929.

Haldane, E. S. *Mrs. Gaskell and her Friends.* London, 1931.

ffrench, Yvonne. *Mrs. Gaskell.* London, 1949.

Rubenius, Aina. *The Woman Question in Mrs. Gaskell's Life and Works.* Cambridge, Mass., 1951.

Hopkins, A. B. *Elizabeth Gaskell: Her Life and Work.* London, 1952.

Kingsley. Kingsley, F. E. (ed.). *Charles Kingsley: His Letters and Memories of his Life.* 2 vols. London, 1877.

Thorp, M. F. *Charles Kingsley, 1818–1875.* Princeton, N.J., 1937.

Kendall, Guy. *Charles Kingsley and his Ideas.* London, 1947.

Pope-Hennessy. Una. *Canon Charles Kingsley.* London, 1948.

Chapter XI

General. Dalziel, Margaret. *Popular Fiction a Hundred Years Ago.* London, 1957.

Borrow. Knapp, W. I. *The Life, Writings, and Correspondence of George Borrow.* London, 1899.

Tilford, J. E. "The Critical Approach to *Lavengro–Romany Rye.*" *Studies in Philology,* xlvi (1949), 79–96.

———. "The Formal Artistry of *Lavengro–Romany Rye.*" *PMLA,* lxiv (1949), 369–84.

Armstrong, Martin. *George Borrow.* London, 1950.

Vesey-Fitzgerald, Brian. *Gypsy Borrow.* London, 1953.

Yonge. Coleridge, Christabel. *Charlotte Mary Yonge: Her Life and Letters.* London, 1903.

Battiscome, Georgina. *Charlotte Mary Yonge: The Story of an Uneventful Life.* London, 1943.

Mare, Margaret, and A. C. Percival. *Victorian Best-Seller: The World of Charlotte Yonge.* London, 1948.

Whyte-Melville. Fortescue, Sir John. "George Whyte-Melville." *The Eighteen-Sixties*, ed. John Drinkwater. Cambridge, 1932.

Chapter XII

General. Stang, Richard. *The Theory of the Novel in England, 1850–1870.* New York, 1959.

Trollope. Booth, B. A. (ed.). *The Letters of Anthony Trollope.* New York, 1951.

Sadleir, Michael. *Trollope: A Commentary.* Rev. ed., London, 1945.

Stebbins, L. P. and R. P. *The Trollopes: The Chronicle of a Writing Family.* New York, 1945.

Gerould, W. G. and J. T. *A Guide to Trollope.* Princeton, N.J., 1948.

Brown, B. C. *Anthony Trollope.* London, 1950.

Cockshutt, A. O. J. *Anthony Trollope: A Critical Study.* London, 1955.

Booth, B. A. *Anthony Trollope: Aspects of his Life and Art.* Bloomington, Ind., 1958.

Sensation Novels. Phillips, W. C. *Dickens, Reade, and Collins, Sensation Novelists.* New York, 1919.

Collins. Robinson, Kenneth. *Wilkie Collins: A Biography.* London, 1951.

Ashley, R. P. *Wilkie Collins.* London, 1952.

Davis, N. P. *The Life of Wilkie Collins.* Urbana, Ill., 1956.

Reade. Elwin, Malcolm. *Charles Reade.* London, 1931.

Turner, A. M. *The Making of "The Cloister and the Hearth."* Chicago, 1938.

Rives, Léonie. *Charles Reade: sa vie, ses romans.* Toulouse, 1940.

Sutcliffe, E. G. "Psychological Presentation in Reade's Novels." *Studies in Philology*, xxxviii (1941), 521–42.

———. "Fact, Realism, and Morality in Reade's Fiction." *Ibid.*, xli (1944), 582–98.

———. "Unique and Repeated Situations and Themes in Reade's Fiction." *PMLA*, lx (1945), 221–30.

Burns, Wayne. "Pre-Raphaelitism in Reade's Early Fiction." *Ibid.*, lx (1945), 1149–64.

Burns, Wayne. "The Sheffield Flood: A Critical Study of Reade's Fiction." *Ibid.*, lxiii (1948), 686–95.

Hughes. Mack, E. C., and W. H. G. Armytage. *Thomas Hughes: The Life of the Author of "Tom Brown's School Days."* London, 1953.

Lawrence. Fleming, G. H. *George Alfred Lawrence and the Victorian Sensation Novel.* Tucson, Ariz., 1952.

Eliot. Haight, G. S. (ed.). *The George Eliot Letters.* 7 vols. New Haven, Conn., 1954–56.

Cross, J. W. *George Eliot's Life as Related in her Letters and Journals.* 3 vols. Edinburgh, 1885.

Williams, B. C. *George Eliot.* New York, 1936.

Haight, G. S. *George Eliot and John Chapman.* New Haven, Conn., 1940.

Bennett, Joan. *George Eliot: Her Mind and Art.* London, 1948.

Hanson, L. and E. M. *Marian Evans and George Eliot.* London, 1952.

Hardy, Barbara. *The Novels of George Eliot.* London, 1959.

Thale, Jerome. *The Novels of George Eliot.* New York, 1959.

Stump, Reva. *Movement and Vision in George Eliot's Novels.* Seattle, Wash., 1959.

Meredith. Meredith, W. M. (ed.). *The Letters of George Meredith.* 2 vols. London, 1912.

Beach, J. W. *The Comic Spirit in George Meredith.* New York, 1911.

Able, A. H. *George Meredith and Thomas Love Peacock: A Study in Literary Influence.* Philadelphia, Pa., 1933.

Sassoon, Siegfried. *Meredith.* London, 1948.

Stevenson, Lionel. *The Ordeal of George Meredith.* New York, 1953.

Wright, W. F. *Art and Substance in George Meredith.* Lincoln, Nebr., 1953.

Chapter XIII

H. Kingsley. Ellis, S. M. *Henry Kingsley, 1830–1876.* London, 1931.

Wolff, R. L. "Henry Kingsley." *Harvard Library Bulletin*, xiii (1959), 195–226.

Ouida. ffrench, Yvonne. *Ouida: A Study in Ostentation.* London, 1938.

Bigland, Elizabeth. *Ouida, the Passionate Victorian.* London, 1950.

Stirling, Monica. *The Fine and the Wicked: The Life and Times of Ouida.* London, 1957.

MacDonald. MacDonald, Greville. *George MacDonald and his Wife.* London, 1924.

Blackmore. Dunn, W. H. *R. D. Blackmore: the Author of "Lorna Doone."* New York, 1956.

LeFanu. Browne, Nelson. *Sheridan Lefanu.* London, 1951.

Chapter XIV

General. Cazamian, M. L. *Le Roman et les idées en Angleterre.* (i) *L'Influence de la science, 1860–1890.* Strasbourg, 1923.

Henkin, L. J. *Darwinism in the English Novel, 1860–1910.* New York, 1940.

Phelps, Gilbert. *The Russian Novel in English Fiction.* London, 1956.

Hardy. Beach, J. W. *The Technique of Thomas Hardy.* Chicago, 1922.

Hardy, F. E. *The Early Life of Thomas Hardy.* London, 1928.

——. *The Later Years of Thomas Hardy.* London, 1930.

Weber, C. J. *Hardy of Wessex.* New York, 1940.

Cecil, Lord David. *Hardy the Novelist.* London, 1943.

Webster, H. C. *On a Darkling Plain: The Art and Thought of Thomas Hardy.* Chicago, 1947.

Guerard, A. J. *Hardy: The Novels and Stories.* Cambridge, Mass., 1949.

Hardy, Evelyn. *Thomas Hardy.* London, 1953.

Black. Reid, T. W. *William Black, Novelist.* London, 1902.

Besant. Boege, F. W. "Sir Walter Besant, Novelist." *Nineteenth-Century Fiction,* x (1956), 248–80; xi (1956), 32–60.

Mallock. Adams, A. B. *The Novels of William Hurrell Mallock.* Orono, Me., 1934.

James. Lubbock, Percy (ed.). *The Letters of Henry James.* 2 vols. London, 1920.

Beach, J. W. *The Method of Henry James.* New Haven, Conn., 1918.

Brooks, Van Wyck. *The Pilgrimage of Henry James.* New York, 1925.

Matthiessen, F. O. *Henry James: The Major Phase.* New York, 1944.

Stevenson, Elizabeth. *The Crooked Corridor: A Study of Henry James.* New York, 1949.

Dupee, F. W. *Henry James.* New York, 1951.

Edel, Leon. *Henry James: The Untried Years, 1843–1870.* Philadelphia, Pa., 1953.

Anderson, Quentin. *The American Henry James.* New Brunswick, N.J., 1957.

Chapter XV

General. Cazamian, M. L. *Le Roman et les idées en Angleterre.* (ii) *L'Anti-intellectualisme et l'estheticisme, 1880–1900.* Paris, 1935. (iii) *Les Doctrines d'action et l'aventure, 1880–1914.* Paris, 1955.

Frierson, W. C. *The English Novel in Transition, 1885–1940.* Norman, Okla., 1942.

Shorthouse. Shorthouse, S. (ed.). *The Life, Letters, and Literary Remains of J. H. Shorthouse.* 2 vols. London, 1905.

Polak, M. *The Historical, Philosophical, and Religious Aspects of "John Inglesant."* Purmerend, Holland, 1933.

Fleming, W. K. "Some Truths about *John Inglesant.*" *Quarterly Review,* ccxlv (1925), 130–48.

Bishop, Morchard. "*John Inglesant* and its Author." *Essays by Divers Hands,* xxix (1958), 73–86.

Hale White. Stone, W. H. *Religion and Art of William Hale White.* Stanford, Calif., 1954.

Maclean, C. M. *Mark Rutherford.* London, 1955.

Stock, Irvin. *William Hale White (Mark Rutherford): A Critical Study.* New York, 1956.

Gissing. Gissing, Algernon and Ellen (eds.). *Letters of George Gissing to Members of his Family.* London, 1927.

Yates, May. *George Gissing: An Appreciation.* Manchester, 1922.

Gapp, S. V. *George Gissing, Classicist.* Philadelphia, Pa., 1936.

Donnelly, M. C. *George Gissing, Grave Comedian.* Cambridge, Mass., 1954.

Roberts, Morley. *The Private Life of Henry Maitland.* Ed. by Morchard Bishop. London, 1958.

Moore. Freeman, John. *A Portrait of George Moore in a Study of his Work.* London, 1922.

Morgan, Charles. *Epitaph on George Moore.* London, 1935.

Hone, Joseph. *The Life of George Moore.* London, 1936.

Brown, M. J. *George Moore: A Reconsideration.* Seattle, Wash., 1955.

Schreiner. Cronwright-Schreiner, S. G. (ed.). *The Letters of Olive Schreiner.* London, 1924.

———. *The Life of Olive Schreiner.* London, 1924.

Buchanan-Gould, Vera. *Not Without Honour: The Life and Writings of Olive Schreiner.* London, 1949.

Stevenson. Balfour, Graham. *The Life of Robert Louis Stevenson.* 2 vols. London, 1901.

Cooper, Lettice. *Robert Louis Stevenson.* London, 1947.

Daiches, David. *Robert Louis Stevenson.* New York, 1947.

Hinkley, L. L. *The Stevensons: Louis and Fanny.* New York, 1950.

Furnas, J. C. *Voyage to Windward: The Life of Robert Louis Stevenson.* New York, 1951.

Haggard. Haggard, L. R. *The Cloak that I Left: A Biography of the Author Henry Rider Haggard.* London, 1951.

Quiller-Couch. Brittain, Fred. *Arthur Quiller-Couch: A Biographical Study of "Q."* Cambridge, 1947.

Doyle. Pearson, Hesketh. *Conan Doyle: His Life and Art.* London, 1943.

Doyle, A. C. *The True Conan Doyle.* London, 1945.

Carr, J. D. *The Life of Sir Arthur Conan Doyle.* London, 1948.

Kipling. Chevrillon, André. *Rudyard Kipling.* Paris, 1936.

Shanks, Edward. *Rudyard Kipling: A Study in Literature and Political Ideas.* London, 1940.

Brown, C. H. *Rudyard Kipling: A New Appreciation.* London, 1945.

Croft-Cooke, Rupert. *Rudyard Kipling.* London, 1948.

Escarpit, Robert. *Rudyard Kipling: Servitude et grandeurs impériales.* Paris, 1955.

Carrington, Charles. *Rudyard Kipling: His Life and Work.* London, 1955.

Tompkins, J. M. S. *The Art of Rudyard Kipling.* London, 1959.

Ward. Walters, J. S. *Mrs. Humphry Ward: Her Work and Influence.* London, 1912.

Trevelyan, J. P. *The Life of Mrs. Humphry Ward.* London, 1923.

Chapter XVI

Hope. Mallet, Sir Charles. *Anthony Hope and his Books.* London, 1935.

Putt, S. G. "The Prisoner of *The Prisoner of Zenda*: Anthony Hope and the Novel of Society." *Essays in Criticism,* vi (1956), 38–59.

Corelli. Bullock, George. *Marie Corelli: The Life and Death of a Best-Seller.* London, 1940.

Bigland, Elizabeth. *Marie Corelli: The Woman and the Legend.* London, 1953.

Du Maurier. Du Maurier, Daphne (ed.). *The Young George Du Maurier: A Selection of his Letters, 1860–67.* London, 1951.

Wood, T. M. *George Du Maurier*. London, 1913.

Whiteley, D. P. *Du Maurier: His Life and Work*. London, 1948.

Kailyard School. Blake, George. *Barrie and the Kailyard School*. London, 1951.

Barrie. Meynell, Viola (ed.). *Letters of J. M. Barrie*. London, 1942.

Mackail, Denis. *The Story of J. M. B.: A Biography*. London, 1941.

Conrad. Crankshaw, Edward. *Joseph Conrad: Some Aspects of the Art of the Novel*. London, 1936.

Gordan, J. D. *Joseph Conrad: The Making of a Novelist*. Cambridge, Mass., 1940.

Wright, W. F. *Romance and Tragedy in Joseph Conrad*. Lincoln, Nebr., 1949.

Jean-Aubry, Gerard. *The Sea Dreamer: A Definitive Biography of Joseph Conrad*. Trans. Helen Sebba. London, 1957.

Curle, Richard. *Joseph Conrad and his Characters*. London, 1957.

Haugh, R. F. *Joseph Conrad: Discovery in Design*. Norman, Okla., 1957.

Moser, Thomas. *Joseph Conrad: Achievement and Decline*. Cambridge, Mass., 1957.

Allen, Jerry. *The Thunder and the Sunshine: A Biography of Joseph Conrad*. New York, 1958.

Guerard, A. J. *Conrad the Novelist*. Cambridge, Mass., 1958.

Baines, Jocelyn. *Joseph Conrad*. London, 1959.

Wells. West, Geoffrey. *H. G. Wells*. London, 1930.

Nicholson, Norman. *H. G. Wells*. London, 1950.

Brome, Vincent. *H. G. Wells: A Biography*. London, 1951.

Bennett. *The Journal of Arnold Bennett*. 3 vols. London, 1932–33.

West, Geoffrey. *The Problem of Arnold Bennett*. London, 1932.

Simons, J. B. *Arnold Bennett and his Novels: A Critical Study*. Oxford, 1936.

Lafourcade, Georges. *Arnold Bennett: A Study*. London, 1939.

Allen, Walter. *Arnold Bennett*. London, 1949.

Pound, Reginald. *Arnold Bennett: A Biography*. London, 1952.

Hall, James. *Arnold Bennett: Primitivism and Taste*. Seattle, Wash., 1959.

Galsworthy. Schalit, L. M. *John Galsworthy: A Survey*. London, 1929.

Croman, Natalie. *John Galsworthy: A Study in Continuity and Contrast*. Cambridge, Mass., 1933.

Guyot, Edouard. *John Galsworthy, le romancier*. Paris, 1933.

Marrot, H. V. *The Life and Letters of John Galsworthy*. London, 1935.

Mottram, R. H. *For Some we Loved: An Intimate Portrait of Ada and John Galsworthy.* London, 1956.
Maugham. McIver, C. S. *William Somerset Maugham: A Study of Technique and Literary Sources.* Philadelphia, Pa., 1936.
Cordell, R. A. *W. Somerset Maugham.* New York, 1937.
Jensen, Helmut. *William Somerset Maugham: Some Aspects of the Man and his Work.* Oslo, 1957.
Pfeiffer, K. G. *W. Somerset Maugham: A Candid Portrait.* New York, 1958.
Butler. Jones, H. F. *Samuel Butler: A Memoir.* 2 vols. London, 1919.
Stillman, C. G. *Samuel Butler: A Mid-Victorian Modern.* New York, 1932.
Fort, J. B. *Samuel Butler.* 2 vols. Bordeaux, 1934–35.
Rattray, R. F. *Samuel Butler: A Chronicle and an Introduction.* London, 1935.
Muggeridge, Malcolm. *The Earnest Atheist: A Study of Samuel Butler.* London, 1936.
Cole, G. D. H. *Samuel Butler and "The Way of All Flesh."* London, 1947.
Furbank, P. N. *Samuel Butler.* Cambridge, 1948.
Henderson, Philip. *Samuel Butler: The Incarnate Bachelor.* London, 1953.
Forster. Macaulay, Rose. *The Writings of E. M. Forster.* London, 1938.
Trilling, Lionel. *E. M. Forster.* Norfolk, Conn., 1943.
Warner, Rex. *E. M. Forster.* Rev. ed., London, 1954.
McConkey, James. *The Novels of E. M. Forster.* Ithaca, N.Y., 1957.
Walpole. Hart-Davis, Rupert. *Hugh Walpole.* London, 1952.

Chapter XVII

General. Jameson, Storm. *The Georgian Novel and Mr. Robinson.* London, 1929.
Beach, J. W. *The Twentieth-Century Novel: Studies in Technique.* New York, 1932.
Humphrey, Robert. *Stream of Consciousness in the Modern Novel.* Berkeley, Calif., 1954.
Friedman, M. J. *Stream of Consciousness: A Study in Literary Method.* New Haven, Conn., 1955.
Edel, Leon. *The Psychological Novel, 1900–1950.* Philadelphia, Pa., 1955.

Gerber, Richard. *Utopian Fantasy: A Study of English Utopian Fiction since the End of the Nineteenth Century.* London, 1955.

O'Faolain, Sean. *The Vanishing Hero: Studies in Novelists of the Twenties.* London, 1956.

McCormick, John. *Catastrophe and Imagination: An Interpretation of the Recent English and American Novel.* London, 1957.

Lawrence. Huxley, Aldous (ed.). *The Letters of D. H. Lawrence.* London, 1932.

Gregory, Horace. *D. H. Lawrence, Pilgrim of the Apocalypse.* New York, 1933.

Tyndall, W. Y. *D. H. Lawrence and Susan his Cow.* New York, 1939.

Moore, H. T. *The Life and Works of D. H. Lawrence.* New York, 1951.

——. *The Intelligent Heart: The Story of D. H. Lawrence.* New York, 1955.

Leavis, F. R. *D. H. Lawrence, Novelist.* London, 1955.

Freeman, Mary. *D. H. Lawrence: A Basic Study of his Ideas.* Gainesville, Fla., 1955.

Spilka, Mark. *The Love Ethic of D. H. Lawrence.* Bloomington, Ind., 1955.

Hough, Graham. *The Dark Sun: A Study of D. H. Lawrence.* London, 1956.

Nehls, Edward (ed.). *D. H. Lawrence: A Composite Biography.* 3 vols. Madison, Wis., 1957–59.

Joyce. Gilbert, Stuart (ed.). *The Letters of James Joyce.* New York, 1957.

——. *James Joyce's "Ulysses": A Study.* New York, 1941.

Gorman, Herbert. *James Joyce.* New York, 1940.

Levin, Harry. *James Joyce: A Critical Introduction.* New York, 1941.

Campbell, Joseph, and H. M. Robinson. *A Skeleton Key to "Finnegans Wake."* New York, 1944.

Kain, R. M. *Fabulous Voyager: James Joyce's "Ulysses."* Chicago, 1947.

Jones, W. P. *James Joyce and the Common Reader.* Norman, Okla., 1955.

Kenner, Hugh. *Dublin's Joyce.* Bloomington, Ind., 1956.

Magalaner, Marvin, and R. M. Kain. *Joyce: The Man, the Work, the Reputation.* New York, 1956.

Hutchins, Patricia. *James Joyce's World.* London, 1957.

Schutte, W. M. *Joyce and Shakespeare: A Study in the Meaning of "Ulysses."* New Haven, Conn., 1957.

Ellmann, Richard. *James Joyce.* New York, 1959.

Woolf. Forster, E. M. *Virginia Woolf.* Cambridge, 1942.

Daiches, David. *Virginia Woolf.* New York, 1942.

Bennett, Joan. *Virginia Woolf: Her Art as a Novelist.* London, 1945.

Chambers, R. L. *The Novels of Virginia Woolf.* Edinburgh, 1947.

Blackstone, Bernard. *Virginia Woolf: A Commentary.* London, 1949.

Hafley, J. R. *The Glass Roof: Virginia Woolf as a Novelist.* Berkeley, Calif., 1954.

Pippett. Aileen. *The Moth and the Star: A Biography of Virginia Woolf.* Boston, 1955.

Ford. Golding, Douglas. *The Last Pre-Raphaelite.* London, 1948.

Young, Kenneth. *Ford Madox Ford.* London, 1956.

Huxley. Henderson, Alexander. *Aldous Huxley.* London, 1935.

Jouguelet, Pierre. *Aldous Huxley.* Paris, 1948.

Brooke, Jocelyn. *Aldous Huxley.* London, 1952.

Atkins, John. *Aldous Huxley: A Literary Study.* London, 1956.

Morgan. Duffin, H. C. *The Novels and Plays of Charles Morgan.* London, 1959.

Lewis. Porteous, W. G. *Wyndham Lewis: A Discursive Exposition.* London, 1932.

Grigson, Geoffrey. *A Master of our Time: A Study of Wyndham Lewis.* London, 1951.

Kenner, Hugh. *Wyndham Lewis.* Norfolk, Conn., 1954.

Wagner, G. A. *Wyndham Lewis: A Portrait of the Artist as the Enemy.* New Haven, Conn., 1957.

Waugh. Hollis, Christopher. *Evelyn Waugh.* London, 1954.

De Vitis, A. A. *Roman Holiday: The Catholic Novels of Evelyn Waugh.* New York, 1956.

Stopp, F. J. *Evelyn Waugh: Portrait of an Artist.* Boston, 1958.

Greene. Madaule, Jacques. *Graham Greene.* Paris, 1949.

Allott, Kenneth, and Miriam Farris. *The Art of Graham Greene.* London, 1955.

Wyndham, Francis. *Graham Greene.* London, 1955.

Atkins, John. *Graham Greene.* London, 1957.

Cary. Allen, Walter. *Joyce Cary.* London, 1953.

Wright, Andrew. *Joyce Cary: A Preface to his Novels.* London, 1958.

Compton-Burnett. Johnson, P. H. *I. Compton-Burnett.* London, 1951.

Liddell, Robert. *The Novels of I. Compton-Burnett.* London, 1955.

Bowen. Brooke, Jocelyn. *Elizabeth Bowen.* London, 1952.

CHRONOLOGICAL SUMMARY

This list is confined to works of fiction and principally to full-length novels. Authors are listed in order of year of birth. Prolific authors are represented by only their significant and characteristic works. For novels that came out serially, the dates of serial issue are followed by the year of publication in volume form if it differs from that of the final installment.

Barnabe RICH, 1540–1617. *Don Simonides*, 1581–84; *Brusanus, Prince of Hungaria*, 1592.

Thomas DELONEY, 1543–1600? *Jack of Newbury*, 1597; *The Gentle Craft*, 1598; *Thomas of Reading*, 1600.

Anthony MUNDAY, 1553–1633. *Zelauto*, 1580.

John LYLY, 1554–1606. *Euphues*, 1578; *Euphues and his England*, 1580.

Sir Philip SIDNEY, 1554–1586. *The Countess of Pembroke's Arcadia*, 1590.

Thomas LODGE, 1557–1625. *Forbonius and Prisceria*, 1584; *Rosalynde*, 1590; *A Margarite of America*, 1596.

Robert GREENE, 1558–1592. *Mamillia*, 1583; *Gwydonius*, 1584; *Arbasto*, 1584; *Pandosto*, 1588; *Menaphon*, 1589.

Thomas NASHE, 1567–1601. *The Unfortunate Traveller*, 1594.

Emanuel FORDE, dates unknown. *Parismus*, 1598; *Ornatus and Artesia*, 1600?

Richard BRATHWAIT, 1588–1673. *Panthalia*, 1659.

Roger BOYLE, Lord Broghill, 1621–1679. *Parthenissa*, 1654–69, 1676.

Nathaniel INGELO, 1621–1683. *Bentivolio and Urania*, 1660–64.

Robert BOYLE, 1627–1691. *Theodora and Didymus*, 1687.

John BULTEEL, dates unknown. *Birinthia*, 1664.

John CROWNE, dates unknown. *Pandion and Amphigenia*, 1665.

John BUNYAN, 1628–1688. *The Pilgrim's Progress*, 1678–84; *The Life and Death of Mr. Badman*, 1680; *The Holy War*, 1682.

518

George MACKENZIE, 1636–1691. *Aretina,* 1660.

Richard HEAD, 1637–1686? *The English Rogue,* 1665–71.

Aphra BEHN, 1640–1689. *Love-letters between a Nobleman and his Sister,* 1684; *Three Histories (Oroonoko, The Fair Jilt, Agnes de Castro),* 1688; *The Lucky Mistake,* 1689; *The History of the Nun,* 1689.

Daniel DEFOE, 1660–1731. *Robinson Crusoe,* 1719; *Memoirs of a Cavalier,* 1720; *Captain Singleton,* 1720; *A Journal of the Plague Year,* 1722; *Moll Flanders,* 1722; *Colonel Jacque,* 1722; *The Fortunate Mistress (Roxana),* 1724.

Jonathan SWIFT, 1667–1745. *Gulliver's Travels,* 1726.

William CONGREVE, 1670–1729. *Incognita,* 1692.

Mary Delarivière MANLEY, 1672–1724. *Letters Written by Mrs. Manley,* 1696 (reissued as *A Stage Coach Journey to Exeter,* 1725); *The Secret History of Queen Zarah,* 1705; *The New Atalantis,* 1709; *Memoirs of Europe towards the Close of the Eighth Century,* 1710; *The Adventures of Rivella,* 1714.

Elizabeth ROWE, 1674–1737. *Letters Moral and Entertaining,* 1729–33.

Mary DAVYS, 1674–1732. *The Reformed Coquet,* 1724; *The Accomplished Rake,* 1727.

Jane BARKER, 1675–1743. *Love Intrigues,* 1713; *Exilius,* 1715; *A Patchwork Screen for the Ladies,* 1723; *The Lining of the Patchwork Screen,* 1726.

Penelope AUBIN, 1685–1731. *Madam de Beaumont,* 1721; *The Count de Vinevil,* 1721; *Lucinda,* 1722; *The Noble Slaves,* 1722; *The Lady Lucy,* 1726; *The Young Count Albertus,* 1728.

Samuel RICHARDSON, 1689–1761. *Pamela,* 1740–41; *Clarissa,* 1747–48; *Sir Charles Grandison,* 1753–54.

Thomas AMORY, 1691–1788. *John Buncle,* 1756–66.

John LELAND, 1691–1766. *Longsword,* 1762.

Eliza HAYWOOD, 1693–1756. *Love in Excess,* 1719; *Idalia,* 1723; *Lasselia,* 1723; *Memoirs of a Certain Island Adjacent to Utopia,* 1725; *The Mercenary Lover,* 1726; *The Court of Caramania,* 1727; *Anti-Pamela,* 1741; *The Fortunate Foundlings,* 1744; *The History of Miss Betsy Thoughtless,* 1751; *The History of Jenny and Jemmy Jessamy,* 1753.

Arabella PLANTIN, dates unknown. *The Ingrateful,* 1727; *Love Led Astray,* 1727.

Elizabeth BOYD, dates unknown. *The Happy Unfortunate,* 1732 (reissued as *The Female Page,* 1737).

Robert PALTOCK, 1697–1767. *Peter Wilkins,* 1751.

Henry BROOKE, 1703–1783. *The Fool of Quality,* 1765–70; *Juliet Grenville,* 1773.

Henry FIELDING, 1707–1754. *An Apology for the Life of Mrs. Shamela Andrews*, 1741; *Joseph Andrews*, 1742; *Jonathan Wild the Great*, 1743; *Tom Jones*, 1749; *Amelia*, 1751.

Samuel JOHNSON, 1709–1784. *Rasselas*, 1759.

John CLELAND, 1709–1789. *Fanny Hill*, 1748–49; *Memoirs of a Coxcomb*, 1751.

John SHEBBEARE, 1709–1788. *The Marriage Act*, 1754; *Lydia*, 1755.

Sarah FIELDING, 1710–1768. *David Simple*, 1744–53; *The Lives of Cleopatra and Octavia*, 1757; *The Countess of Dellwyn*, 1759; *The History of Ophelia*, 1760.

Laurence STERNE, 1713–1768. *Tristram Shandy*, 1760–67.

John HAWKESWORTH, 1715–1773. *Almoran and Hamet*, 1761.

Richard GRAVES, 1715–1804. *The Spiritual Quixote*, 1773.

John HILL, 1716–1775. *The Adventures of Mr. Loveill*, 1750; *The Adventures of George Edwards*, 1751.

Horace WALPOLE, 1717–1797. *The Castle of Otranto*, 1764.

Charles JOHNSTONE, 1719–1800? *Chrysal*, 1760–65.

Elizabeth GRIFFITH, 1720–1793. *Genuine Letters between Henry and Frances*, 1757; *The Delicate Distress*, 1769; *Lady Barton*, 1771; *Juliana Harley*, 1776.

Charlotte Ramsay LENNOX, 1720–1804. *The Life of Harriot Stuart*, 1750; *The Female Quixote*, 1752; *Henrietta*, 1758; *Sophia*, 1760–61; *Euphemia*, 1790.

Tobias SMOLLETT, 1721–1771. *Roderick Random*, 1748; *Peregrine Pickle*, 1751; *Ferdinand, Count Fathom*, 1753; *Sir Launcelot Greaves*, 1760–61, 1762; *The Expedition of Humphry Clinker*, 1771.

Sarah SCOTT, 1723–1795. *The History of Cornelia*, 1750; *Agreeable Ugliness*, 1754; *Millenium Hall*, 1762; *Sir George Ellison*, 1766.

Frances BROOKE, 1724–1789. *Lady Julia Mandeville*, 1763; *Emily Montague*, 1769; *The Excursion*, 1777.

Frances SHERIDAN, 1724–1766. *Sidney Bidulph*, 1761; *Nourjahad*, 1766.

Robert BAGE, 1728–1801. *Mount Henneth*, 1781; *Barham Downs*, 1784; *The Fair Syrian*, 1787; *James Wallace*, 1788; *Man as He Is*, 1792; *Hermsprong*, 1796.

Francis COVENTRY, 1728–1759? *The History of Pompey the Little*, 1751.

Clara REEVE, 1729–1807. *The Champion of Virtue*, 1777 (reissued as *The Old English Baron*, 1778); *The Two Mentors*, 1783; *The Exiles*, 1788; *The School for Widows*, 1791; *Sir Roger de Clarendon*, 1793; *Destination*, 1799.

John MOORE, 1729–1802. *Zeluco*, 1786; *Edward*, 1796; *Mordaunt*, 1800.

Oliver GOLDSMITH, 1730–1774. *The Vicar of Wakefield*, 1766.

John LANGHORNE, 1735–1779. *Solyman and Almena*, 1762.

Hugh KELLY, 1739–1777. *Louisa Mildmay*, 1767.

Henry MACKENZIE, 1745–1831. *The Man of Feeling*, 1771; *The Man of the World*, 1773; *Julia de Roubigné*, 1777.

Thomas HOLCROFT, 1745–1809. *Alwyn*, 1780; *Anna St. Ives*, 1792; *Hugh Trevor*, 1794–97; *Bryan Perdue*, 1805.

Thomas DAY, 1748–1789. *Sandford and Merton*, 1783–89; *The Story of Little Jack*, 1788.

Charlotte SMITH, 1749–1806. *Emmeline*, 1788; *Ethelinde*, 1789; *Celestina*, 1791; *Desmond*, 1792; *The Old Manor House*, 1793; *The Banished Man*, 1794; *Montalbert*, 1795; *Marchmont*, 1796; *The Young Philosopher*, 1798.

Sophia LEE, 1750–1824. *The Recess*, 1785.

Fanny BURNEY, 1752–1840. *Evelina*, 1778; *Cecilia*, 1782; *Camilla*, 1796; *The Wanderer*, 1814.

Elizabeth INCHBALD, 1753–1821. *A Simple Story*, 1791; *Nature and Art*, 1796.

William GODWIN, 1756–1836. *Caleb Williams*, 1794; *St. Leon*, 1799; *Fleetwood*, 1805; *Mandeville*, 1817; *Cloudesley*, 1830; *Deloraine*, 1833.

Mary WOLLSTONECRAFT, 1759–1797. *Mary*, 1788; *The Wrongs of Women*, 1798.

William BECKFORD, 1760–1844. *Vathek*, 1786.

Ann RADCLIFFE, 1764–1823. *The Castles of Athlin and Dunbayne*, 1789; *A Sicilian Romance*, 1790; *The Romance of the Forest*, 1791; *The Mysteries of Udolpho*, 1794; *The Italian*, 1797.

Regina Maria ROCHE, 1764–1845. *The Children of the Abbey*, 1796; *Clermont*, 1798.

Robert Plumer WARD, 1765–1846. *Tremaine*, 1825; *De Vere*, 1827; *De Clifford*, 1841.

Maria EDGEWORTH, 1767–1849. *Castle Rackrent*, 1800; *Belinda*, 1801; *Leonora*, 1806; *Tales of Fashionable Life*, 1809–12; *Patronage*, 1814; *Harrington* and *Ormond*, 1817; *Helen*, 1834.

Amelia OPIE, 1769–1853. *The Father and Daughter*, 1801; *Adeline Mowbray*, 1804; *Temper*, 1812; *Tales of Real Life*, 1813; *Valentine's Eve*, 1816; *Tales of the Heart*, 1820; *Madeline*, 1822.

James HOGG, 1770–1835. *The Confessions of a Justified Sinner*, 1824.

Thomas HOPE, 1770–1831. *Anastasius*, 1819.

Sir Walter SCOTT, 1771–1832. *Waverley*, 1814; *Guy Mannering*, 1815; *The Antiquary*, 1816; *Tales of my Landlord (The Black Dwarf* and *Old Mortality)*, 1817; *Rob Roy*, 1817; *Tales of My Landlord*, 2nd series *(The Heart of Midlothian)*, 1818; 3rd series *(The Bride of Lammermoor* and *A Legend of Montrose)*, 1819; *Ivanhoe*, 1820; *The Monastery*, 1820; *The Abbot*, 1820; *Kenilworth*, 1821; *The Pirate*,

1822; *The Fortunes of Nigel*, 1822; *Peveril of the Peak*, 1822; *Quentin Durward*, 1823; *St. Ronan's Well*, 1824; *Redgauntlet*, 1824; *Tales of the Crusaders (The Betrothed* and *The Talisman)*, 1825; *Woodstock*, 1826; *Chronicles of the Canongate (The Highland Widow, The Two Drovers*, and *The Surgeon's Daughter)*, 1827; 2nd series *(The Fair Maid of Perth)*, 1828; *Anne of Geierstein*, 1829; *Tales of My Land-lord*, 4th series *(Count Robert of Paris* and *Castle Dangerous)*, 1832.

Pierce EGAN, 1772–1849. *Life in London (Tom and Jerry)*, 1821–24; *The Life of an Actor*, 1824–25; *Finish to the Adventures of Tom, Jerry, and Logic*, 1828.

Jane AUSTEN, 1775–1817. *Sense and Sensibility*, 1811; *Pride and Prejudice*, 1813; *Mansfield Park*, 1814; *Emma*, 1816; *Northanger Abbey* and *Persuasion*, 1818.

Matthew Gregory LEWIS, 1775–1818. *The Monk*, 1796.

Lady Charlotte BURY, 1775–1861. *Self Indulgence*, 1812; *Flirtation*, 1827; *A Marriage in High Life*, 1828; *The Separation*, 1830; *The Divorced*, 1837; *Love*, 1837; *The History of a Flirt*, 1840; *The Lady of Fashion*, 1856.

Sydney OWENSON, later Lady Morgan, 1776–1859. *St. Clair*, 1803; *The Novice of St. Dominick*, 1805; *The Wild Irish Girl*, 1806; *Woman, or Ida of Athens*, 1809; *The Missionary*, 1811; *O'Donnel*, 1814; *Florence Macarthy*, 1818; *The O'Briens and the O'Flahertys*, 1827; *The Princess*, 1835.

Jane PORTER, 1776–1850. *Thaddeus of Warsaw*, 1803; *The Scottish Chiefs*, 1810.

Mary BRUNTON, 1778–1818. *Self Control*, 1811; *Discipline*, 1814.

John GALT, 1779–1839. *The Ayrshire Legatees*, 1820–21; *Annals of the Parish*, 1821; *Sir Andrew Wylie*, 1822; *The Provost*, 1822; *The Entail*, 1823; *Ringan Gilhaize*, 1823; *The Spaewife*, 1823; *Rothelan*, 1824; *The Last of the Lairds*, 1826; *Lawrie Todd*, 1830; *Bogle Corbet*, 1831.

Horace SMITH, 1779–1849. *Brambletye House*, 1826; *Reuben Apsley*, 1827; *Zillah*, 1828; *The New Forest*, 1829; *Walter Colyton*, 1830; *Arthur Arundel*, 1844.

Anna Maria PORTER, 1780–1832. *The Lake of Killarney*, 1804; *The Hungarian Brothers*, 1807; *Don Sebastian*, 1809.

Charles Robert MATURIN, 1780–1824. *Fatal Revenge*, 1807; *The Wild Irish Boy*, 1808; *The Milesian Chief*, 1812; *Women, or Pour et Contre*, 1818; *Melmoth the Wanderer*, 1820; *The Albigenses*, 1824.

George CROLY, 1780–1860. *Salathiel*, 1828.

James Justinian MORIER, 1780–1849. *Hajji Baba of Ispahan*, 1824; *Hajji Baba in England*, 1828; *Zohrab the Hostage*, 1832; *Ayesha, the Maid of Kars*, 1834.

Frances TROLLOPE, 1780–1863. *The Refugee in America*, 1832;

Jonathan Jefferson Whitlaw, 1836; *The Vicar of Wrexhill*, 1837; *The Widow Barnaby*, 1839; *Michael Armstrong, the Factory Boy*, 1840; *The Widow Married*, 1840; *The Barnabys in America*, 1843; *Jessie Phillips*, 1843; *Petticoat Government*, 1850.

Charlotte DACRE ("Rosa Matilda"), 1782–1840? *Zafloya*, 1806; *The Libertine*, 1807.

Susan Edmonstone FERRIER, 1782–1854. *Marriage*, 1818; *The Inheritance*, 1824; *Destiny*, 1831.

Thomas Love PEACOCK, 1785–1866. *Headlong Hall*, 1816; *Melincourt*, 1817; *Nightmare Abbey*, 1818; *Maid Marian*, 1822; *The Misfortunes of Elphin*, 1829; *Crotchet Castle*, 1831; *Gryll Grange*, 1860, 1861.

Lady Caroline LAMB, 1785–1828. *Glenarvon*, 1816; *Graham Hamilton*, 1822; *Ada Reis*, 1823.

Mary Russell MITFORD, 1787–1855. *Our Village*, 1824–32.

Theodore HOOK, 1788–1841. *Sayings and Doings*, 1824–28; *Maxwell*, 1830; *The Parson's Daughter*, 1833; *Gilbert Gurney*, 1834–35, 1836; *Jack Brag*, 1837; *Fathers and Sons*, 1840–41, 1842.

Thomas HAMILTON, 1789–1842. *Cyril Thornton*, 1827.

Michael SCOTT, 1789–1835. *Tom Cringle's Log*, 1829–33, 1842; *The Cruise of the Midge*, 1834–35, 1836.

Countess of BLESSINGTON, 1789–1849. *The Repealers*, 1833; *The Two Friends*, 1835; *The Victims of Society*, 1837; *The Governess*, 1839.

Frederick MARRYAT, 1792–1848. *The Naval Officer (Frank Mildmay)*, 1829; *The King's Own*, 1830; *Newton Forster*, 1832; *Peter Simple*, 1832–33, 1834; *Jacob Faithful*, 1833–34; *Japhet in Search of a Father*, 1834–36; *Mr. Midshipman Easy*, 1836; *Snarley-Yow*, 1836–37; *The Phantom Ship*, 1837, 1839; *Masterman Ready*, 1841–42; *The Children of the New Forest*, 1847.

William CARLETON, 1794–1869. *Traits and Stories of the Irish Peasantry*, 1830–33; *Fardorougha the Miser*, 1837–38, 1839; *Valentine McClutchy, the Irish Agent*, 1845; *The Black Prophet*, 1846, 1847; *The Emigrants of Ahadarra*, 1848; *The Tithe Proctor*, 1849; *Willy Reilly and his Dear Cooleen Bawn*, 1850, 1855.

John Gibson LOCKHART, 1794–1854. *Valerius*, 1821; *Adam Blair*, 1822; *Reginald Dalton*, 1823; *Matthew Wald*, 1824.

Edward HOWARD, ?–1841. *Rattlin the Reefer*, 1836; *The Old Commodore*, 1837; *Outward Bound*, 1838; *Jack Ashore*, 1840.

Frederick CHAMIER, 1796–1870. *The Life of a Sailor*, 1832; *Ben Brace*, 1836; *The Spitfire*, 1840; *Tom Bowling*, 1841.

George Robert GLEIG, 1796–1888. *The Subaltern*, 1825; *The Chelsea Pensioners*, 1829; *Allan Breck*, 1834; *The Hussar*, 1837.

Michael BANIM, 1796–1874, and John BANIM, 1798–1842. *Tales of the O'Hara Family*, 1825–26; *The Boyne Water* (J.B.), 1826; *The Croppy*, 1828; *The Anglo-Irish of the Nineteenth Century*, 1828.

Samuel LOVER, 1797–1868. *Rory O'More*, 1837; *Handy Andy*, 1842.

Mary Wollstonecraft SHELLEY, 1797–1851. *Frankenstein*, 1818; *Valperga*, 1823; *The Last Man*, 1826; *Lodore*, 1835.

Earl of MULGRAVE, later Marquess of Normanby, 1797–1863. *Matilda*, 1825; *Yes and No*, 1828; *The Contrast*, 1832.

Catherine G. F. GORE, 1799–1861. *Women as They Are*, 1830; *Mothers and Daughters*, 1831; *Cecil*, 1841; *Cecil a Peer*, 1841.

Thomas Henry LISTER, 1800–1842. *Granby*, 1826; *Herbert Lacy*, 1828; *Arlington*, 1832.

John Henry NEWMAN, 1801–1890. *Loss and Gain*, 1848; *Callista*, 1856.

George Payne Rainsford JAMES, 1801–1860. *Richelieu*, 1829; *Darnley*, 1830; *De L'Orme*, 1830; *Philip Augustus*, 1831; *Henry Masterton*, 1832; *Mary of Burgundy*, 1833; *The Huguenot*, 1839.

Harriet MARTINEAU, 1802–1876. *Illustrations of Political Economy*, 1832–34; *Poor Laws and Paupers Illustrated*, 1833–34; *Deerbrook*, 1839; *The Hour and the Man*, 1841.

Edward BULWER-LYTTON, later Lord Lytton, 1802–1873. *Falkland*, 1827; *Pelham*, 1828; *The Disowned*, 1828; *Devereux*, 1829; *Paul Clifford*, 1830; *Eugene Aram*, 1832; *Godolphin*, 1833; *The Last Days of Pompeii*, 1834; *Rienzi*, 1835; *Ernest Maltravers*, 1837; *Alice*, 1838; *Night and Morning*, 1841; *Zanoni*, 1842; *The Last of the Barons*, 1843; *Lucretia*, 1846; *Harold*, 1848; *The Caxtons*, 1848–49; *My Novel*, 1850–53; *What Will He Do with It?*, 1857–59; *A Strange Story*, 1861–62; *The Coming Race*, 1871; *The Parisians*, 1872–74; *Kenelm Chillingly*, 1873.

Gerald GRIFFIN, 1803–1840. *Tales of the Munster Festivals*, 1827; *The Collegians*, 1829.

Robert Smith SURTEES, 1803–1864. *Jorrocks' Jaunts and Jollities*, 1831–34, 1838; *Handley Cross*, 1843; *Hillingdon Hall*, 1845; *Hawbuck Grange*, 1846–47; *Mr. Sponge's Sporting Tour*, 1853; *Ask Mamma*, 1858; *Plain or Ringlets?*, 1860; *Mr. Romford's Hounds*, 1865.

George BORROW, 1803–1881. *Lavengro*, 1851; *The Romany Rye*, 1857.

Benjamin DISRAELI, later Earl of Beaconsfield, 1804–1881. *Vivian Grey*, 1826–27; *The Young Duke*, 1831; *Contarini Fleming*, 1832; *The Wondrous Tale of Alroy*, 1833; *Henrietta Temple*, 1837; *Venetia*, 1837; *Coningsby*, 1844; *Sybil*, 1845; *Tancred*, 1847; *Lothair*, 1870; *Endymion*, 1880.

William Harrison AINSWORTH, 1805–1882. *Sir John Chiverton* (with J. P. Aston), 1826; *Rookwood*, 1834; *Crichton*, 1837; *Jack*

Sheppard, 1839–40; *The Tower of London*, 1840; *Guy Fawkes*, 1840–41; *Old St. Paul's*, 1841; *Windsor Castle*, 1842–43; *Saint James's*, 1844; *The Lancashire Witches*, 1848, 1849; *The Star Chamber*, 1853, 1854.

Charles LEVER, 1806–1872. *Harry Lorrequer*, 1837–40; *Charles O'Malley*, 1840–41; *Jack Hinton, the Guardsman*, 1842, 1843; *Tom Burke of "Ours,"* 1844; *The O'Donoghue*, 1845; *The Knight of Gwynne*, 1846–47; *Roland Cashel*, 1848–49; *The Daltons*, 1851–52; *The Dodd Family Abroad*, 1852–54; *The Martins of Cro' Martin*, 1854–56; *Davenport Dunn*, 1857–59; *One of Them*, 1859–61; *A Day's Ride: A Life's Romance*, 1860–61, 1863; *Barrington*, 1862–63; *Luttrell of Arran*, 1863–65.

Samuel WARREN, 1807–1877. *Passages from the Diary of a Late Physician*, 1830–37; *Ten Thousand a Year*, 1839–41.

Henry COCKTON, 1807–1853. *Valentine Vox, the Ventriloquist*, 1840; *Sylvester Sound, the Somnambulist*, 1844.

Elizabeth Cleghorn GASKELL, 1810–1865. *Mary Barton*, 1848; *Cranford*, 1851–53; *Ruth*, 1853; *North and South*, 1854–55; *Sylvia's Lovers*, 1863; *Wives and Daughters*, 1864–66.

William Makepeace THACKERAY, 1811–1863. *Barry Lyndon*, 1844, 1856; *Vanity Fair*, 1847–48; *Pendennis*, 1848–50; *Henry Esmond*, 1852; *The Newcomes*, 1853–55; *The Virginians*, 1857–59; *Lovel the Widower*, 1860, 1861; *The Adventures of Philip*, 1861–62; *Denis Duval*, 1864.

Charles DICKENS, 1812–1870. *The Pickwick Papers*, 1836–37; *Oliver Twist*, 1837–39; *Nicholas Nickleby*, 1838–39; *The Old Curiosity Shop*, 1840–41; *Barnaby Rudge*, 1841; *Martin Chuzzlewit*, 1843–44; *Dombey and Son*, 1846–48; *David Copperfield*, 1849–50; *Bleak House*, 1852–53; *Hard Times*, 1854; *Little Dorrit*, 1855–57; *A Tale of Two Cities*, 1859; *Great Expectations*, 1860–61; *Our Mutual Friend*, 1864–65; *The Mystery of Edwin Drood*, 1870.

William Johnson NEALE, 1812–1893. *Cavendish*, 1831; *The Port Admiral*, 1833; *The Flying Dutchman*, 1839; *The Naval Surgeon*, 1841.

G. W. M. REYNOLDS, 1814–1879. *Mysteries of London*, 1847; *The Mysteries of the Court of London*, 1849–56; *Joseph Wilmot*, 1854; *Wagner, the Wehr-Wolf*, 1857.

Charles READE, 1814–1884. *Peg Woffington*, 1853; *Christie Johnstone*, 1853; *It Is Never Too Late to Mend*, 1856; *White Lies*, 1857; *Love Me Little, Love Me Long*, 1859; *The Cloister and the Hearth*, 1861; *Hard Cash*, 1863; *Griffith Gaunt*, 1866; *Foul Play*, 1868; *Put Yourself in His Place*, 1869–70; *A Terrible Temptation*, 1870–71; *A Woman Hater*, 1877; *A Perilous Secret*, 1884.

Mrs. Henry WOOD, 1814–1887. *Danesbury House*, 1860; *East Lynne*, 1860–61; *Mrs. Halliburton's Troubles*, 1862; *The Channings*,

1862; *The Shadow of Ashlydyat*, 1861–63; *Verner's Pride*, 1863;. *Roland Yorke*, 1869.

J. Sheridan LE FANU, 1814–1873. *The Cock and Anchor*, 1845; *The House by the Church-Yard*, 1863; *Wylder's Hand*, 1864; *Uncle Silas*, 1864; *Guy Deverell*, 1865; *The Wyvern Mystery*, 1869; *In a Glass Darkly*, 1872.

Anthony TROLLOPE, 1815–1882. *The Macdermots of Ballycloran,.* 1847; *The Kellys and the O'Kellys*, 1848; *La Vendée*, 1850; *The Warden*, 1855; *Barchester Towers*, 1857; *The Three Clerks*, 1858;. *Doctor Thorne*, 1858; *The Bertrams*, 1859; *Castle Richmond*, 1860;. *Framley Parsonage*, 1860–61; *Orley Farm*, 1861–62; *Rachel Ray*, 1863;. *The Small House at Allington*, 1862–64; *Can You Forgive Her?*, 1864– 65; *Miss Mackenzie*, 1865; *The Belton Estate*, 1865–66; *Nina Balatka,.* 1866–67; *The Last Chronicle of Barset*, 1866–67; *The Claverings,.* 1866–67; *Linda Tressel*, 1867–68; *Phineas Finn*, 1867–69; *He Knew He Was Right*, 1868–69; *The Vicar of Bullhampton*, 1869–70; *Sir Harry Hotspur of Humblethwaite*, 1870–71; *Ralph the Heir*, 1870–71; *The Eustace Diamonds*, 1871–73; *Phineas Redux*, 1873–74; *The Way We Live Now*, 1874–75; *The Prime Minister*, 1875–76; *The American Senator*, 1876–77; *Is He Popenjoy?*, 1877–78; *John Caldigate*, 1878– 79; *The Duke's Children*, 1879–80; *Dr. Wortle's School*, 1880, 1881; *Ayala's Angel*, 1881; *Marian Fay*, 1881–82; *Mr. Scarborough's Family,.* 1883.

Albert SMITH, 1816–1860. *The Adventures of Mr. Ledbury*, 1844; *The Fortunes of the Scattergood Family*, 1845; *Christopher Tadpole,.* 1848.

Charlotte BRONTË, 1816–1855. *Jane Eyre*, 1847; *Shirley*, 1849; *Villette*, 1853; *The Professor*, 1857.

Emily BRONTË, 1818–1848. *Wuthering Heights*, 1847.

James Anthony FROUDE, 1818–1894. *Shadows of the Clouds*, 1847; *The Nemesis of Faith*, 1849.

Francis Edward SMEDLEY, 1818–1864. *Frank Fairlegh*, 1846–47, 1850; *Lewis Arundel*, 1852; *Harry Coverdale's Courtship*, 1855.

Charles KINGSLEY, 1819–1875. *Yeast*, 1848, 1850; *Alton Locke*, 1850; *Hypatia*, 1853; *Westward Ho!*, 1855; *Two Years Ago*, 1857; *Hereward the Wake*, 1865, 1866.

George ELIOT, 1819–1880. *Scenes of Clerical Life*, 1857, 1858; *Adam Bede*, 1859; *The Mill on the Floss*, 1860; *Silas Marner*, 1861; *Romola*, 1862–63; *Felix Holt the Radical*, 1866; *Middlemarch*, 1871–72; *Daniel Deronda*, 1876.

Anne BRONTË, 1820–1849. *Agnes Grey*, 1847; *The Tenant of Wildfell Hall*, 1848.

G. J. WHYTE-MELVILLE, 1821–1878. *Captain Digby Grand*, 1851– 52, 1853; *Tilbury Nego*, 1854; *General Bounce*, 1854, 1855; *Kate*

Coventry, 1856; *Holmby House*, 1859–60; *Market Harborough*, 1861; *The Queen's Maries*, 1862; *The Gladiators*, 1863; *Sarchedon*, 1871; *Katerfelto*, 1875.

James GRANT, 1822–1887. *The Romance of War*, 1846–47; *The Scottish Cavalier*, 1850; *Jane Seton*, 1853; *Bothwell*, 1854; *Philip Rollo*, 1854; *Frank Hilton*, 1855; *Harry Ogilvie*, 1856; *The Phantom Regiment*, 1856; *Hollywood Hall*, 1859; *First Love and Last Love*, 1868.

Eliza Lynn LINTON, 1822–1898. *Lizzie Norton of Greyrigg*, 1866; *Joshua Davidson*, 1872; *Patricia Kemball*, 1874; *The Atonement of Leam Dundas*, 1875–76, 1877; *Christopher Kirkland*, 1885.

Thomas HUGHES, 1822–1896. *Tom Brown's School Days*, 1857; *Tom Brown at Oxford*, 1859–61.

Charlotte M. YONGE, 1823–1901. *The Heir of Redclyffe*, 1853; *Heartsease*, 1854; *The Lances of Lynwood*, 1855; *The Daisy Chain*, 1856; *Dynevor Terrace*, 1857; *The Trial*, 1864; *The Clever Woman of the Family*, 1865; *The Dove in the Eagle's Nest*, 1866; *The Pillars of the House*, 1873.

Wilkie COLLINS, 1824–1889. *Antonina*, 1850; *Basil*, 1852; *Hide and Seek*, 1854; *The Dead Secret*, 1857; *The Woman in White*, 1859–60; *No Name*, 1862–63; *Armadale*, 1864–66; *The Moonstone*, 1868; *Man and Wife*, 1870; *Poor Miss Finch*, 1871–72; *The New Magdalen*, 1872–73; *Heart and Science*, 1882–83.

George MACDONALD, 1824–1905. *Phantastes*, 1858; *David Elginbrod*, 1863; *Alec Forbes of Howglen*, 1865; *Annals of a Quiet Neighborhood*, 1866, 1867; *Robert Falconer*, 1867, 1868; *Malcolm*, 1875; *The Marquis of Lossie*, 1877; *Sir Gibbie*, 1879; *Lilith*, 1895.

R. D. BLACKMORE, 1825–1900. *Clara Vaughan*, 1864; *Cradock Nowell*, 1865–66; *Lorna Doone*, 1869; *The Maid of Sker*, 1871–72; *Alice Lorraine*, 1874–75; *Cripps the Carrier*, 1876; *Springhaven*, 1886–87.

Dinah Maria MULOCK, later Mrs. Craik, 1826–1887. *John Halifax, Gentleman*, 1856; *A Life for a Life*, 1859; *A Noble Life*, 1866; *Hannah*, 1872.

Cuthbert BEDE, 1827–1889. *The Adventures of Mr. Verdant Green*, 1853–57.

George Alfred LAWRENCE, 1827–1876. *Guy Livingstone*, 1857; *Sword and Gown*, 1859; *Barren Honor*, 1861–62; *Brakespeare*, 1868.

Margaret O. W. OLIPHANT, 1828–1897. *Margaret Maitland*, 1849; *Katie Stewart*, 1853; *The Rector and the Doctor's Family*, 1861–62, 1863; *Salem Chapel*, 1862–63; *The Perpetual Curate*, 1863–64; *Miss Marjoribanks*, 1865–66; *Phoebe Junior*, 1876; *A Beleaguered City*, 1880; *A Little Pilgrim of the Unseen*, 1882; *The Land of Darkness*, 1888.

George MEREDITH, 1828–1909. *The Shaving of Shagpat,* 1856; *Farina,* 1857; *The Ordeal of Richard Feverel,* 1859; *Evan Harrington,* 1860, 1861; *Emilia in England,* 1864 (reissued as *Sandra Belloni,* 1887); *Rhoda Fleming,* 1865; *Vittoria,* 1866–67; *Harry Richmond,* 1870–71; *Beauchamp's Career,* 1874–75, 1876; *The Egoist,* 1879; *The Tragic Comedians,* 1880–81; *Diana of the Crossways,* 1884, 1885; *One of Our Conquerors,* 1891; *Lord Ormont and His Aminta,* 1894; *The Amazing Marriage,* 1895.

Henry KINGSLEY, 1830–1876. *Geoffrey Hamlyn,* 1859; *Ravenshoe,* 1861–62; *Austin Elliott,* 1863; *The Hillyars and the Burtons,* 1863–65; *Silcote of Silcotes,* 1866–67; *Mademoiselle Mathilde,* 1867–68.

James PAYN, 1830–1898. *Lost Sir Massingberd,* 1864; *Carlyon's Year,* 1868; *By Proxy,* 1878; *The Talk of the Town,* 1885.

Frederic William FARRAR, 1831–1903. *Eric, or Little by Little,* 1858; *Julian Home,* 1859; *St. Winifred's,* 1862.

William Hale WHITE, 1831–1913. *The Autobiography of Mark Rutherford,* 1881; *Mark Rutherford's Deliverance,* 1885; *The Revolution in Tanner's Lane,* 1887; *Catharine Furze,* 1893.

Joseph Henry SHORTHOUSE, 1834–1903. *John Inglesant,* 1880; *The Little Schoolmaster Mark,* 1883–84; *Sir Percival,* 1886; *The Countess Eve,* 1888.

George DU MAURIER, 1834–1896. *Peter Ibbetson,* 1891, 1892; *Trilby,* 1894; *The Martian,* 1896–97.

Samuel BUTLER, 1835–1902. *Erewhon,* 1872; *Erewhon Revisited,* 1901; *The Way of All Flesh,* 1903.

Walter BESANT, 1836–1901, and James RICE, 1843–1882. *Ready-Money Mortiboy,* 1872; *The Golden Butterfly,* 1876; *The Chaplain of the Fleet,* 1881. (By Besant alone) *All Sorts and Conditions of Men,* 1882; *Dorothy Forster,* 1884; *Children of Gibeon,* 1886; *The World Went Very Well Then,* 1887; *Armorel of Lyonesse,* 1890; *Beyond the Dreams of Avarice,* 1895.

Mary Elizabeth BRADDON, 1837–1915. *Lady Audley's Secret,* 1862; *Aurora Floyd,* 1863; *John Marchmont's Legacy,* 1863; *Dead Men's Shoes,* 1876; *Vixen,* 1879; *London Pride,* 1896.

OUIDA, 1839–1908. *Granville de Vigne,* 1861–63 (in book form as *Held in Bondage*); *Strathmore,* 1863–65; *Chandos,* 1866; *Under Two Flags,* 1867; *Pascarel,* 1873; *Signa,* 1875; *Moths,* 1880; *In Maremma,* 1882; *Othmar,* 1885.

Walter PATER, 1839–1894. *Marius the Epicurean,* 1885.

Thomas HARDY, 1840–1928. *Desperate Remedies,* 1871; *Under the Greenwood Tree,* 1872; *A Pair of Blue Eyes,* 1872–73; *Far from the Madding Crowd,* 1874; *The Hand of Ethelberta,* 1875–76; *The Return of the Native,* 1878; *The Trumpet-Major,* 1880; *A Laodicean,* 1880–81; *Two on a Tower,* 1882; *The Mayor of Casterbridge,* 1886; *The*

Woodlanders, 1886–87; *Tess of the d'Urbervilles*, 1891; *The Well-Beloved*, 1892, 1897. *Jude the Obscure*, 1894–95.

Rhoda BROUGHTON, 1840–1920. *Not Wisely, but too Well*, 1867; *Cometh up as a Flower*, 1867; *Red as a Rose Is She*, 1869–70; *Belinda*, 1883–84.

William BLACK, 1841–1898. *Kilmeny*, 1870; *A Daughter of Heth*, 1871; *The Strange Adventures of a Phaeton*, 1872; *A Princess of Thule*, 1873; *Madcap Violet*, 1876; *Macleod of Dare*, 1878.

Henry JAMES, 1843–1916. *Roderick Hudson*, 1876; *The American*, 1877; *The Europeans*, 1878; *Daisy Miller*, 1879; *Washington Square*, 1881; *The Portrait of a Lady*, 1881; *The Bostonians*, 1886; *The Princess Casamassima*, 1886; *The Tragic Muse*, 1890; *The Spoils of Poynton*, 1897; *The Wings of the Dove*, 1902; *The Ambassadors*, 1903; *The Golden Bowl*, 1904.

W. H. MALLOCK, 1849–1923. *The New Republic*, 1877; *The New Paul and Virginia*, 1878; *A Romance of the Nineteenth Century*, 1881.

Robert Louis STEVENSON, 1850–1894. *New Arabian Nights*, 1878–82; *Treasure Island*, 1881–82, 1883; *The Black Arrow*, 1883, 1888; *Prince Otto*, 1885; *The Strange Case of Dr. Jekyll and Mr. Hyde*, 1886; *Kidnapped*, 1886; *The Master of Ballantrae*, 1888–89; *Catriona*, 1892–93; *Weir of Hermiston*, 1896; *St. Ives* (completed by A. T. Quiller-Couch), 1896–97.

Mrs. Humphry WARD, 1851–1920. *Miss Bretherton*, 1884; *Robert Elsmere*, 1888; *The History of David Grieve*, 1892; *Marcella*, 1894; *Sir George Tressady*, 1895–96; *Helbeck of Bannisdale*, 1898; *Eleanor*, 1900; *Lady Rose's Daughter*, 1902–03; *The Marriage of William Ashe*, 1904–05; *Fenwick's Career*, 1906; *The Case of Richard Meynell*, 1911.

Hall CAINE, 1853–1931. *The Shadow of a Crime*, 1885; *The Deemster*, 1887; *A Son of Hagar*, 1887; *The Bondman*, 1890; *The Manxman*, 1894; *The Christian*, 1897; *The Eternal City*, 1901; *The Prodigal Son*, 1904; *The Woman Thou Gavest Me*, 1913.

Oscar WILDE, 1854–1900. *The Picture of Dorian Gray*, 1890, 1891.

Marie CORELLI, 1855–1924. *A Romance of Two Worlds*, 1886; *Vendetta*, 1886; *Thelma*, 1887; *Ardath*, 1889; *Wormwood*, 1890; *The Soul of Lilith*, 1892; *Barabbas*, 1893; *The Sorrows of Satan*, 1895; *The Master Christian*, 1900; *Temporal Power*, 1902; *God's Good Man*, 1904; *Holy Orders*, 1908; *The Life Everlasting*, 1911.

Olive SCHREINER, 1855–1920. *The Story of an African Farm*, 1883; *Dreams*, 1891; *Trooper Peter Halket of Mashonaland*, 1897.

Stanley J. WEYMAN, 1855–1928. *The House of the Wolf*, 1883, 1890; *A Gentleman of France*, 1893; *Under the Red Robe*, 1894; *The Red Cockade*, 1895; *Shrewsbury*, 1898; *The Long Night*, 1903; *Chippinge*, 1906.

Henry Rider HAGGARD, 1856–1925. *Dawn*, 1884; *The Witch's*

Head, 1884; *King Solomon's Mines*, 1885; *She*, 1886–87; *Allan Quater-main*, 1887; *Colonel Quaritch*, *V. C.*, 1888; *Cleopatra*, 1889; *The World's Desire* (with Andrew Lang), 1890; *Eric Brighteyes*, 1891; *Nada the Lily*, 1892; *Montezuma's Daughter*, 1893; *Ayesha*, 1905.

George Bernard SHAW, 1856–1950. *An Unsocial Socialist*, 1884, 1887; *Cashel Byron's Profession*, 1885–86; *The Irrational Knot*, 1885–87, 1905; *Love among the Artists*, 1887–88, 1900.

George GISSING, 1857–1903. *Workers in the Dawn*, 1880; *The Unclassed*, 1884; *Demos*, 1886; *Isabel Clarendon*, 1886; *Thyrza*, 1887; *A Life's Morning*, 1888; *The Nether World*, 1889; *The Emancipated*, 1890; *New Grub Street*, 1891; *Born in Exile*, 1892; *Denzil Quarrier*, 1892; *The Odd Women*, 1893; *In the Year of Jubilee*, 1894; *Eve's Ransom*, 1895; *The Paying Guest*, 1895; *Sleeping Fires*, 1895; *The Whirlpool*, 1897; *The Town Traveller*, 1898; *Veranilda*, 1904.

George MOORE, 1857–1933. *A Modern Lover*, 1883 (rewritten as *Lewis Seymour and Some Women*, 1917); *A Mummer's Wife*, 1885; *A Drama in Muslin*, 1886 (rewritten as *Muslin*, 1915); *A Mere Acci-dent*, 1887; *Spring Days*, 1888; *Mike Fletcher*, 1889; *Vain Fortune*, 1890; *Esther Waters*, 1894; *Evelyn Innes*, 1898; *Sister Teresa*, 1901; *The Lake*, 1905; *The Brook Kerith*, 1916; *Ulick and Soracha*, 1926.

Joseph CONRAD, 1857–1924. *Almayer's Folly*, 1895; *An Outcast of the Islands*, 1896; *The Nigger of the "Narcissus,"* 1897; *Lord Jim*, 1900; *The Inheritors* (with F. M. Hueffer), 1901; *Youth*, 1902; *Ty-phoon*, 1903; *Romance* (with F. M. Hueffer), 1903; *Nostromo*, 1904; *The Secret Agent*, 1907; *Under Western Eyes*, 1911; *Chance*, 1914; *Victory*, 1915; *The Shadow-Line*, 1917; *The Arrow of Gold*, 1919; *The Rescue*, 1920; *The Rover*, 1923; *Suspense*, 1925.

A. Conan DOYLE, 1859–1930. *A Study in Scarlet*, 1887; *Micah Clarke*, 1889; *The Sign of Four*, 1890; *The White Company*, 1891; *The Adventures of Sherlock Holmes*, 1891–92; *The Memoirs of Sherlock Holmes*, 1892–93, 1894; *Rodney Stone*, 1896; *The Hound of the Baskervilles*, 1901–02; *Sir Nigel*, 1905–06; *The Lost World*, 1912; *The Poison Belt*, 1913; *The Valley of Fear*, 1914–15.

J. M. BARRIE, 1860–1937. *Better Dead*, 1888; *When a Man's Single*, 1888; *The Little Minister*, 1891; *Sentimental Tommy*, 1896; *Tommy and Grizel*, 1900.

Maurice HEWLETT, 1861–1923. *The Forest Lovers*, 1898; *Richard Yea-and-Nay*, 1900; *The Queen's Quair*, 1904; *The Fool Errant*, 1905; *The Stooping Lady*, 1907; *Halfway House*, 1908; *Open Country*, 1909; *Rest Harrow*, 1910.

A. T. QUILLER-COUCH, 1863–1944. *Dead Man's Rock*, 1887; *The Astonishing History of Troy Town*, 1888; *The Splendid Spur*, 1889; *The Blue Pavilions*, 1892; *The Ship of Stars*, 1899; *Hetty Wesley*, 1903.

Anthony HOPE, 1863–1933. *A Man of Mark,* 1890; *Father Stafford,* 1891; *The Dolly Dialogues,* 1894; *The Prisoner of Zenda,* 1894; *The God in the Car,* 1894; *Rupert of Hentzau,* 1898; *The King's Mirror,* 1899; *Quisanté,* 1900; *Tristram of Blent,* 1901; *Sophie of Kravonia,* 1906.

Rudyard KIPLING, 1865–1936. *Plain Tales from the Hills,* 1888; *Soldiers Three,* 1888; *The Light that Failed,* 1891; *The Naulahka* (with Wolcott Balestier), 1892; *Captains Courageous,* 1897; *Stalky & Co.,* 1899; *Kim,* 1901.

H. G. WELLS, 1866–1946. *The Time Machine,* 1895; *The Wonderful Visit,* 1895; *The Island of Dr. Moreau,* 1896; *The Wheels of Chance,* 1896; *The Invisible Man,* 1897; *The War of the Worlds,* 1898; *When the Sleeper Wakes,* 1899; *Love and Mr. Lewisham,* 1900; *The First Men in the Moon,* 1901; *The Sea Lady,* 1902; *The Food of the Gods,* 1904; *Kipps,* 1905; *A Modern Utopia,* 1905; *In the Days of the Comet,* 1906; *The War in the Air,* 1908; *Tono-Bungay,* 1909; *Ann Veronica,* 1909; *The History of Mr. Polly,* 1910; *The New Machiavelli,* 1911; *Marriage,* 1912; *The Passionate Friends,* 1913; *The World Set Free,* 1914; *The Wife of Sir Isaac Harman,* 1914; *Bealby,* 1914–15; *The Research Magnificent,* 1915; *Mr. Britling Sees It Through,* 1916; *The Soul of a Bishop,* 1917; *Joan and Peter,* 1918; *The Undying Fire,* 1919; *The Secret Places of the Heart,* 1922; *Men Like Gods,* 1923; *The Dream,* 1924; *Christina Alberta's Father,* 1925; *The World of William Clissold,* 1926; *Meanwhile,* 1926; *Mr. Blettsworthy on Rampole Island,* 1928; *The Autocracy of Mr. Parham,* 1930; *The Shape of Things to Come,* 1933; *The Bulpington of Blup,* 1933; *The Croquet Player,* 1937; *Star-Begotten,* 1937; *Brynhild,* 1937.

Arnold BENNETT, 1866–1931. *A Man from the North,* 1898; *Anna of the Five Towns,* 1902; *The Grand Babylon Hotel,* 1902; *The Gates of Wrath,* 1903; *Leonora,* 1903; *A Great Man,* 1904; *Teresa of Watling Street,* 1904; *Sacred and Profane Love,* 1905; *The Loot of Cities,* 1905; *Hugo,* 1906; *Whom God Hath Joined,* 1906; *The Ghost,* 1907; *The City of Pleasure,* 1907; *Buried Alive,* 1908; *The Old Wives' Tale,* 1908; *The Glimpse,* 1909; *Helen with the High Hand,* 1910; *Clayhanger,* 1910; *The Card,* 1911; *Hilda Lessways,* 1911; *The Regent,* 1913; *The Price of Love,* 1914; *These Twain,* 1915; *The Lion's Share,* 1916; *The Pretty Lady,* 1918; *The Roll Call,* 1918; *Lilian,* 1922; *Mr. Prohack,* 1922; *Riceyman Steps,* 1923; *Lord Raingo,* 1926; *Imperial Palace,* 1930; *Venus Rising from the Sea,* 1931.

John GALSWORTHY, 1867–1933. *Jocelyn,* 1898; *Villa Rubein,* 1900; *The Island Pharisees,* 1904; *The Man of Property,* 1906; *The Country House,* 1907; *Fraternity,* 1908; *The Patrician,* 1911; *The Dark Flower,* 1913; *The Freelands,* 1915; *Beyond,* 1917; *Saint's Progress,* 1919; *In Chancery,* 1920; *To Let,* 1921; *The White Monkey,* 1924; *The Silver*

Spoon, 1926; *Swan Song*, 1928; *Maid in Waiting*, 1931; *Flowering Wilderness*, 1932; *Over the River*, 1933.

Norman DOUGLAS, 1868–1952. *South Wind*, 1917.

Algernon BLACKWOOD, 1869–1951. *John Silence*, 1908; *The Human Chord*, 1910; *The Centaur*, 1911; *The Wave*, 1916; *Julius Le Vallon*, 1916; *The Promise of Air*, 1918; *The Garden of Survival*, 1918.

John Cowper POWYS, 1872–   . *Wood and Stone*, 1915; *Ducdame*, 1925; *Wolf Solent*, 1929; *A Glastonbury Romance*, 1932; *Jobber Skald*, 1935; *Maiden Castle*, 1936; *Morwyn*, 1937; *Owen Glendower*, 1941; *Porius*, 1952; *The Brazen Head*, 1956.

Dorothy M. RICHARDSON, 1873–1951. *Pointed Roofs*, 1915; *Backwater*, 1916; *Honeycomb*, 1917; *The Tunnel*, 1919; *Interim*, 1919.

Ford Madox HUEFFER, later Ford, 1873–1939. *The Fifth Queen*, 1905; *Privy Seal*, 1907; *The Fifth Queen Crowned*, 1908; *Ladies Whose Bright Eyes*, 1911; *The Good Soldier*, 1915; *Some Do Not*, 1924; *No More Parades*, 1925; *A Man Could Stand Up*, 1926; *Last Post*, 1928. (See also Conrad.)

W. Somerset MAUGHAM, 1874–   . *Liza of Lambeth*, 1897; *Of Human Bondage*, 1915; *The Moon and Sixpence*, 1919; *The Razor's Edge*, 1944.

Gilbert Keith CHESTERTON, 1874–1936. *The Napoleon of Notting Hill*, 1904; *The Club of Queer Trades*, 1905; *The Man Who Was Thursday*, 1908; *The Ball and the Cross*, 1909; *The Flying Inn*, 1914; *Manalive*, 1915; *The Man Who Knew Too Much*, 1922.

E. M. FORSTER, 1879–   . *Where Angels Fear to Tread*, 1905; *The Longest Journey*, 1907; *A Room with a View*, 1908; *Howards End*, 1910; *A Passage to India*, 1924.

Rose MACAULAY, 1881–1958. *Potterism*, 1920; *Dangerous Ages*, 1921; *Told by an Idiot*, 1923; *Orphan Island*, 1924; *Keeping up Appearances*, 1928; *Staying with Relations*, 1930; *The Towers of Trebizond*, 1956.

James JOYCE, 1882–1941. *A Portrait of the Artist as a Young Man*, 1915, 1916; *Ulysses*, 1922; *Finnegans Wake*, 1939.

Virginia WOOLF, 1882–1941. *The Voyage Out*, 1915; *Night and Day*, 1919; *Jacob's Room*, 1922; *Mrs. Dalloway*, 1925; *To the Lighthouse*, 1927; *Orlando*, 1928; *The Waves*, 1931; *Flush*, 1933; *The Years*, 1937.

Compton MACKENZIE, 1883–   . *Carnival*, 1912; *Sinister Street*, 1913–14; *Guy and Pauline*, 1915; *Sylvia Scarlett*, 1918; *The Altar Steps*, 1922; *The Parson's Progress*, 1923; *The Heavenly Ladder*, 1924; *The Four Winds of Love: The East Wind*, 1937; *The South Wind*, 1937; *The West Wind*, 1940; *West and North*, 1940; *The North Wind*, 1944–45; *Whisky Galore*, 1947.

Mary WEBB, 1883–1927. *The Golden Arrow*, 1916; *Gone to Earth*,

1917; *The House in Dormer Forest*, 1920; *Precious Bane*, 1924.

Hugh WALPOLE, 1884–1941. *Mr. Perrin and Mr. Traill*, 1911; *Fortitude*, 1913; *The Duchess of Wrexe*, 1914; *The Dark Forest*, 1916; *The Secret City*, 1919; *Jeremy*, 1919; *The Captives*, 1920; *The Cathedral*, 1922; *The Old Ladies*, 1924; *Portrait of a Man with Red Hair*, 1925; *Harmer John*, 1926; *Wintersmoon*, 1928; *Hans Frost*, 1929; *Rogue Herries*, 1930; *Judith Paris*, 1931; *The Fortress*, 1932; *Vanessa*, 1933; *The Inquisitor*, 1935; *The Bright Pavilions*, 1940.

Wyndham LEWIS, 1884–1957. *Tarr*, 1917, 1918; *The Childermass*, 1928; *The Apes of God*, 1930; *Snooty Baronet*, 1932; *The Revenge for Love*, 1937; *The Vulgar Streak*, 1941; *Monstre Gai* and *Malign Fiesta*, 1955.

D. H. LAWRENCE, 1885–1930. *The White Peacock*, 1911; *The Trespasser*, 1912; *Sons and Lovers*, 1913; *The Rainbow*, 1915; *The Lost Girl*, 1920; *Women in Love*, 1921; *Aaron's Rod*, 1922; *Kangaroo*, 1923; *The Boy in the Bush* (with M. L. Skinner), 1924; *The Plumed Serpent*, 1926; *Lady Chatterley's Lover*, 1928; *The Virgin and the Gypsy*, 1930.

IVY COMPTON-BURNETT. *Pastors and Masters*, 1925; *Brothers and Sisters*, 1929; *Men and Wives*, 1931; *More Women than Men*, 1933; *A House and its Head*, 1935; *Daughters and Sons*, 1937; *A Family and a Fortune*, 1939; *Parents and Children*, 1941; *Elders and Betters*, 1944; *Manservant and Maidservant*, 1947; *Darkness and Day*, 1951.

Joyce CARY, 1888–1957. *Aissa Saved*, 1932; *An American Visitor*, 1933; *The African Witch*, 1936; *Castle Corner*, 1938; *Mister Johnson*, 1939; *Charley Is My Darling*, 1940; *A House of Children*, 1941; *Herself Surprised*, 1941; *To Be a Pilgrim*, 1942; *The Horse's Mouth*, 1944; *The Moonlight*, 1946; *A Fearful Joy*, 1949; *Prisoner of Grace*, 1952; *Except the Lord*, 1953; *Not Honour More*, 1955; *The Captive and the Free*, 1958.

Rebecca WEST, 1892–   . *The Return of the Soldier*, 1918; *The Judge*, 1922; *Harriet Hume*, 1929.

Aldous HUXLEY, 1894–   . *Crome Yellow*, 1921; *Antic Hay*, 1923; *Point Counter Point*, 1928; *Brave New World*, 1932; *Eyeless in Gaza*, 1936; *After Many a Summer Dies the Swan*, 1939; *Time Must Have a Stop*, 1945.

J. B. PRIESTLEY, 1894–   . *The Good Companions*, 1929; *Angel Pavement*, 1930; *Faraway*, 1932; *Wonder Hero*, 1933; *They Walk in the City*, 1936.

Charles MORGAN, 1894–1958. *The Gunroom*, 1919; *Portrait in a Mirror*, 1929; *The Fountain*, 1932; *Sparkenbroke*, 1936; *The Voyage*, 1940; *The Empty Room*, 1941; *The River Line*, 1949.

Margaret KENNEDY, 1896–   . *The Constant Nymph*, 1924; *Red Sky at Morning*, 1927; *The Fool of the Family*, 1930; *Return I Dare*

Not, 1931; *A Long Time Ago*, 1932; *Together and Apart*, 1936; *The Feast*, 1950; *Lucy Carmichael*, 1951; *Troy Chimneys*, 1953; *Act of God*, 1955.

Storm JAMESON, 1897–   . *The Pitiful Wife*, 1923; *The Lovely Ship*, 1927; *The Voyage Home*, 1930; *A Richer Dust*, 1931; *Company Parade*, 1934; *Love in Winter*, 1935; *None Go Back*, 1936; *The Moon Is Making*, 1937; *The Captain's Wife*, 1939.

Elizabeth BOWEN, 1899–   . *The Hotel*, 1927; *The Last September*, 1929; *Friends and Relations*, 1931; *The House in Paris*, 1935; *The Death of the Heart*, 1938; *The Heat of the Day*, 1949.

Evelyn WAUGH, 1903–   . *Decline and Fall*, 1928; *Vile Bodies*, 1930; *Black Mischief*, 1932; *A Handful of Dust*, 1934; *Scoop*, 1938; *Put Out More Flags*, 1942; *Brideshead Revisited*, 1945; *The Loved One*, 1948; *Men at Arms*, 1952; *Officers and Gentlemen*, 1955; *The Ordeal of Gilbert Pinfold*, 1958.

Graham GREENE, 1904–   . *The Man Within*, 1929; *The Name of Action*, 1930; *England Made Me*, 1935; *Brighton Rock*, 1938; *The Power and the Glory*, 1940; *The Heart of the Matter*, 1948; *The End of the Affair*, 1951; *The Quiet American*, 1956.

INDEX

Index